Marion Foucher · Annie Dumont · Lukas Werther
Doris Wollenberg (eds)

Inland Harbours in Central Europe: Nodes between Northern Europe and the Mediterranean Sea

RGZM – TAGUNGEN
Band 38

zugleich

INTERDISZIPLINÄRE FORSCHUNGEN
zu den Häfen von der Römischen Kaiserzeit bis zum Mittelalter in Europa
Band 6

Herausgegeben von Claus von Carnap-Bornheim, Falko Daim, Peter Ettel und Ursula Warnke

DFG Deutsche Forschungsgemeinschaft

Römisch-Germanisches Zentralmuseum
Leibniz-Forschungsinstitut für Archäologie
RGZM

SPP 1630 HÄFEN

Römisch-Germanisches Zentralmuseum
Leibniz-Forschungsinstitut für Archäologie

Marion Foucher · Annie Dumont · Lukas Werther
Doris Wollenberg (eds)

INLAND HARBOURS IN CENTRAL EUROPE: NODES BETWEEN NORTHERN EUROPE AND THE MEDITERRANEAN SEA

International conference, 1-2 december 2016,
Maison des Sciences de l'Homme (MSH) de Dijon
within the framework of the Special Research Programme
(DFG-SPP 1630) »Harbours from the Roman Period to the Middle Ages«

Verlag des Römisch-Germanischen Zentralmuseums Mainz 2019

The conference was funded by:
Deutsche Forschungsgemeinschaft; Jena University; Université de Bourgogne (BQR); UMR 6298-ARTEHIS; Institut national de recherches archéologiques préventives (Inrap); Ministère de la Culture: Direction régionale de l'archéologie en Bourgogne-Franche-Comté

DFG Deutsche Forschungsgemeinschaft

UMR 6298 ARTEHIS Archéologie Terre Histoire Sociétés

Liberté • Égalité • Fraternité
République Française

Friedrich-Schiller-Universität Jena

Ministère Culture Communication

Institut national de recherches archéologiques préventives
Inrap

Direction régionale des affaires culturelles Bourgogne Franche-Comté

uB Université de Bourgogne

Maison des Sciences de l'Homme de Dijon

drassm

Redaktion: Annie Dumont (Ministère de la Culture, DRASSM + ARTEHIS UMR 6298), Marion Foucher (Université de Bourgogne Franche-Comté + ARTEHIS UMR 6298), Lukas Werther (Tübingen University; Jena University), Doris Wollenberg, Anne Jerosch , Nina Korbel (Jena University); Claudia Nickel, Marie Reiter (RGZM)
Translations and Language Editing: Carmela Chateau-Smith, Marion Foucher, Nina Korbel, Lukas Werther, Doris Wollenberg
Umschlaggestaltung: Claudia Nickel (RGZM)

Bibliografische Information der Deutschen Nationalbibliothek

Die Deutsche Nationalbibliothek verzeichnet diese Publikation in der Deutschen Nationalbibliografie: Detaillierte bibliografische Daten sind im Internet über **http://dnb.d-nb.de** abrufbar.

ISBN 978-3-88467-318-8
ISSN 1862-4812

Druck: johnen-druck GmbH & Co. KG, Bernkastel-Kues
Printed in Germany.

CONTENTS

Inland Harbours: Middle Ages

PREAMBLE

The Priority Programme 1630 »Harbours from the Roman Period to the Middle Ages« funded by the German Research Foundation (Deutsche Forschungsgemeinschaft) in the years 2011-2018 has made it its priority to unite and connect multidimensional approaches to harbour research within the vast area from the North Atlantic to the Mediterranean. Modern approaches of the last three to four decades have particularly shown how the integration of historical, archaeological, geophysical and geoarchaeological sources and methods have stimulated harbour research – and how crucial it is to offer a framework for international discussion and scientific exchange. The conference hold in Dijon in the framework of the Priority Programme significantly contributes to this approach, especially to the French-German research network, which is illustrated by this conference volume. Our thanks go especially to Marion Foucher, Annie Dumont, Lukas Werther and Doris Wollenberg, who were responsible for both organizing the conference and for the editorial responsibilities of this volume. Moreover, our thanks go to the editorial team of the RGZM in Mainz.

The initiators of the SPP 1630 »Harbours from the Roman Period to the Middle Ages«
Claus von Carnap-Bornheim
Falko Daim
Peter Ettel
Ursula Warnke

ANNIE DUMONT · MARION FOUCHER · LUKAS WERTHER · DORIS WOLLENBERG

INLAND HARBOURS IN CENTRAL EUROPE: NODES BETWEEN NORTHERN EUROPE AND THE MEDITERRANEAN SEA – AN INTRODUCTION

While organizing the conference »Inland Harbours in Central Europe: Nodes between Northern Europe and the Mediterranean Sea« in December 2016 in Dijon, an exhaustive presentation of research on European inland harbours from Antiquity to the Middle Ages as a whole has never been aimed. The major aim of the conference was to establish a dialogue between archaeologists who are currently dealing with harbours in several countries of Northern and Central Europe: Scandinavia, Hungaria, Czech Republic, Belgium, Germany, Swiss and France. Compared to the maritime perspective, well studied in the last years by both archaeologists and historians [1], inland navigation and harbours have received significantly less attention. The 20 articles published in this volume in a more or less chronological order (amongst the 27 talks on the conference) focus on this rather neglected topic [2]. However, they inherit the archaeological research tradition of the so-called Waterfront Archaeology, which started in the early 1970s and focused on large urban centers of Northern Europe such as London [3].

The general urban expansion and intense river engineering (banks and channels) as well as the dynamic development of rescue archaeology, have led to a significant number of larger harbour excavations in contemporary city centers. This is represented exemplarily by Lyon, where the construction of an underground car park on the Saône riverbanks (Parc Saint Georges) revealed 16 antique, medieval and modern wrecks. These boats landed alongside a harbour settlement which developed from the 1st century AD until the 19th century AD [4]. In Germany, excavations of the Donaumarkt in Regensburg revealed the comparably complex organization of a waterfront settlement area during the Middle Ages: all along the banks of the Danube, the space was not only occupied by several scattered harbour zones, but also by canals which have been used either for water mills or as a safe passage for boats. Our knowledge of smaller watercourses did also benefit from large-scale excavations, which is illustrated by the River Schwarzach, where bank arrangements and mills from the 9th century AD have been revealed during construction works at the High Speed Railway line between Munich and Nuremberg. Last but not least, the successive and repeated archaeological interventions in the city of Nantes did step by step provide data for a deeper understanding and reconstruction of the natural and artificial evolution in this upstream zone of the Loire Estuary.

Also beyond transformations linked to urban development, many rivers have been deeply modified along with their courses since centuries. This applies above all for the major navigable rivers, such as the Rhine or the Seine. Their riverbeds have subsequently been canalised, straightened and intensively dredged in order to adapt their watercourses to the evolution of shipping and trade. Even recently, such hydro-engineering as well as extensive sand extraction, which still affect active as well as abandoned channels on a large scale, have hardly ever been followed by systematic archaeological observations. As a result of these modifications, many banks and water courses are affected by escalating erosion. In the Loire, heritage preservation is particularly concerned by this effect, since the archaeological remains are cleared by the channel migration and deepening, thus exposed to short-term erosion and destruction. The deepening of the estuary by

Fig. 1 Participants of the conference.

dredging downstream led to a lower water level in the riverbed upstream of Nantes, so that archaeological remains such as wooden parts of fisheries, mills, dykes and wrecks emerge during low water and are fully exposed to degradation.

Improvements for navigation did also implicate the destruction of many islands, as they were often considered as obstacles for a safe passage and a free fairway. Considering the high density of harbour installations on some of the preserved islands (e.g. in urban areas), we can barely imagine the number of harbours, port settlements and wrecks that disappeared during this process.

If objects are found and reported during construction works, it is usually hard – but not impossible – to connect it to specific sites and to interpret it in the framework of regional navigation. Concerning this difficulty, the new examination of a big anchor dredged in the Seine Estuary years ago and the contribution of recent research on a regional scale, shedding light on local and regional navigation during Antiquity, is particularly interesting. The anchor, dated to the first centuries AD, may be related to the contemporaneous quay wall excavated in Aizier. Moreover, according to the anchor size, it is likely that this harbour was accessible for sea-going vessels of big tonnage from the Atlantic Ocean.

Lakes are less impacted by big hydro-engineering projects and bank modifications, but inland navigation has nevertheless been rather neglected since research hitherto focused mainly on pre- and protohistoric pile-dwelling sites, recently inscribed on the UNESCO's World Heritage List. Nevertheless, lakes are well known for their strategic position in economic networks of Antiquity as well as of the Middle Ages, offering favourable connections between the fluvio-lacustrine and the terrestrial transportation. Two articles dealing with French and Swiss lakes in this volume underline the high potential of lakes for the research of inland navigation by revealing their great density of harbours and bank settlements. The excavations of the Antique port of Lousonna on the Lake Geneva caused by the construction of the International Olympic Committee (IOC) are one of the few examples of rescue archaeology for historical periods in a lacustrine context.

During the last years, the study of inland harbours and navigation did benefit from multidisciplinary research programmes[5] as well as several PhD theses[6]. Additionally, geoarchaeological projects enlightened the complexity of fluvial and lacustrine environments having been exposed to climatic as well as anthropogenic impacts[7]. Despite the specific research areas and research foci, the available resources, methods and tools as well as the individual preservation conditions determine the quantity and quality of available data, resulting in a very heterogeneous overall picture. Therefore, it is particularly important to integrate methods and sources beyond archaeology (texts, images, maps, sediments), as it is a common feature of all the articles presented in this volume.

Furthermore, the analysis of harbours in fluvial and lacustrine environments implicate another challenge for archaeologists, as archaeological finds and features are often preserved partially under water and partially on land. Even terrestrial operations and surveys often need specific arrangements under humid environmental conditions, such as the use of waterproof caissons or constant dewatering by pumping. Furthermore, the relative scarcity of underwater archaeology in European rivers and the inherent difficulties linked to their organisation explain the few number of articles dealing with underwater excavations in rivers (Clain and Charente). This lack has to be underlined regarding the proven high archaeological potential of active riverbeds and the subsequent loss of archaeological sources due to more than 150 years of river engineering and construction works, as well as to instability due to climate change and natural river dynamics.

A major research question and the main issue for most of the authors are the identification and localization of harbours. The individual criteria are however varied, among others depending on the local conditions. The long-term evolution of the landscape shaped by continuous hydrological and climatological variability (e. g. sea-level changes, the high lateral dynamic of watercourses during the Little Ice Age) has sometimes deeply transformed the floodplain, resulting in profound changes of occupation conditions[8]. Since bank-lines migrated through times, many ancient harbours are not spatially connected to the current riverbed and bank-line anymore. Former riverine settlements and harbour installations, *de facto* abandoned, have either been silted-up (migration of the active channel away from the site) or exposed to strong erosion (migration of the active channel towards the site). These processes explain the relative scarcity of Roman and Medieval harbour-related remains, for example, in the Seine Estuary. For the Medieval period, the archaeological remains hardly correspond to half of the harbours documented by historical sources and are mainly located in areas which have been less affected by the contemporary evolution of the floodplain. Not only at the River Seine, but all the harbours located in river mouth positions did suffer from a constant process of silting. This is also documented in Narbonne, where the harbour moved towards deeper water step by step, or in Rezé, where the harbour has been obstructed by sand deposits since the 2nd century AD and abandoned after the 3rd century AD. Similar processes have been observed in other riverine areas further upstream as well. In Mikulčice, sand deposits and the meandering channels of the Morava have subsequently buried or eroded medieval fluvial infrastructure.

It has also to be pointed to the fact that archaeological remains of inland harbours are often meagre and sometimes even non-existent. Therefore, several authors offer a critical discussion of shape, nature and archaeological visibility of fluvial harbours. Taking written sources as well as Late Medieval and Early Modern iconography, wrecks and cargo discoveries into consideration, it seems to be quite common that port activities have been carried out at simple landing places with no substantial infrastructure (e. g. beaches, shores). Furthermore, a significant gap does exist between historical mentions and archaeological discoveries of inland harbours. Both traditions enlighten past navigation in different facets, but they are hardly matching. Each set of sources is conditioned by its own nature and has its specific informative value: archaeological remains could often give accurate information about the location, duration, nature and infrastructure as well as the general importance of the adjacent settlement(s). Written sources, on the other hand, could often give accurate information about the chronology, political, economic or social context of a harbour. If this kind of sources does not suffer from the issues of preservation already mentioned about archaeological remains, it, however, refers to specific infrastructures as well as to, sometimes, topography and natural condition or even to rights, with no precise location (Middle Ages).

Furthermore, a harbour may have fulfilled multiple functions, which are sometimes hard to identify and to separate. This is even harder for sites used over a long period. All the sources agree on the multi-functionality of most of the harbours, being fortifications, water-exploitation infrastructure, bank arrangements,

Fig. 2 Conference logo, underlining the French-German starting point and focus. – (Drawing Marcel Treffort).

craft areas and protection against floods or erosion as well.
The perception of this riverine and harbour-related environment, the effects of fluvial and anthropogenic modifications (e.g. floods), and therefore the way societies reacted and interacted, evolved through times.

It is sometimes fruitful to use means and sources to identify harbours, which go beyond the harbour itself. In addition to navigation, every river did attract riverine activities that might have been in competition for water access, power/energy or cleanliness[9]. The number of records documenting such conflicts in medieval and modern archives may not only give clues for the identification of harbour settlements, but it also sheds light on local, regional and supraregional river management. Often it is not possible to understand the harbour phenomenon without a wider context: therefore, possible obstacles for navigation (e.g. mills, fisheries, bridges, fords, dams, sluices) have been included in a database on French rivers. From the very beginning, many examples demonstrate the variety of solutions which have been found to combine different ways to use the water. On the Rivers Spree and Havel, sluices and bypass canals have been built to make navigation compatible with the exploitation of water mills. The combination of mill, dam and canal built during the 13th-14th century AD did persist until the Modern period. Already in the 9th century AD mills have been built on the Schwarzach River at some distance from the active channel and supplied with water by bypass canals. Thanks to this spatial organisation and occupation pattern, the riverbanks remained free for harbour constructions, particularly useful in this area for iron ore transhipment.
The Schwarzach example with the exploitation of a small watercourse for mills as well as harbours raises the question of the hierarchy of the fluvial hydro-system and the spatial distribution of riverine activities. River sections of every size have had a role in the complex networks of exchange and communication. A long-durée point of view underlines this complexity, by revealing the plasticity of a system based on and affected by continuous environmental and socio-economical changes. The analysis of the spatial distribution of riverine activities, including not only navigation but also competing forms of use, have been tested in a theoretical approach by using the Strahler rank in a case study. This classification system considers every river section in relation to its position within the whole network and allows for a spatial analysis based on very heterogeneous and scattered data. Its use at a European scale would, therefore, be promising[10].

Another common ground of several studies concerns the location of multifunctional harbours at confluences. Regensburg, at the confluence of the Rivers Danube, Naab and Regen or the Antique urban area of Vieux-Poitiers at the confluence of the rivers Clain and Vienne, highlight such strategical locations. These confluence harbours do often also correspond with places of power, either capitals of provinces during the Roman period, or political as well as religious centres in the Middle Ages. The interplay of harbour settlements and town infrastructure, such as the town walls of Nantes, Regensburg or Frankfurt, is, therefore, another lead to follow. Sometimes the water itself has been part of the defence system, e.g. in the 9th-10th century AD fortified central place of Mikulčice in the Morava floodplain. Beyond the strong

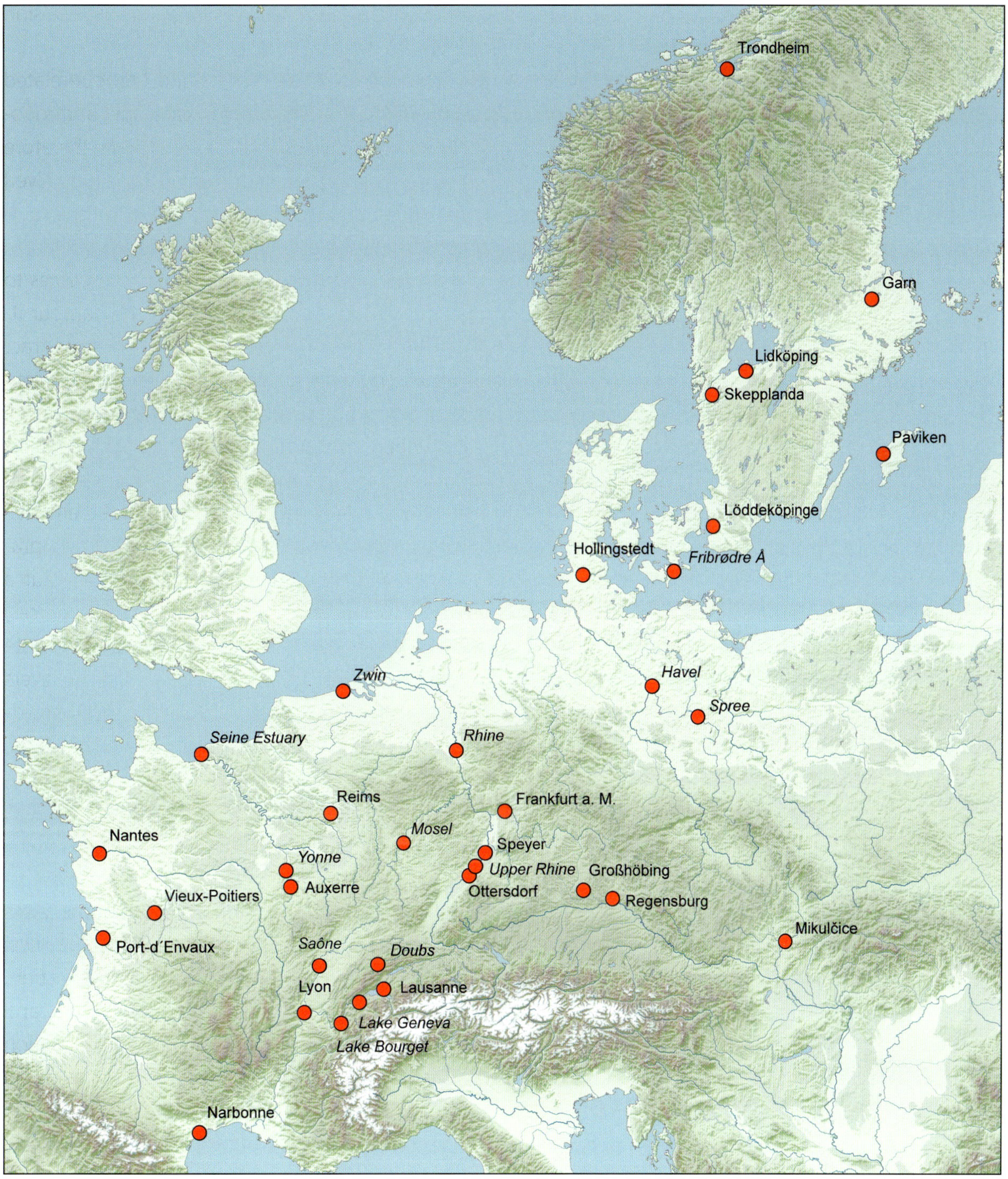

Fig. 3 Map of major sites discussed in the volume. – (L. Werther, using a template of Th. Schmidts; graphics K. Hölzl, RGZM).

and obvious link between urban centres and harbours, the correlation between harbours, settlements and toll facilities (or other rights) has still to be questioned in greater detail, at least for the Medieval and Early Modern period.

The importance of some harbours is particularly striking considering the huge amount of work which has been invested to construct them. Sometimes harbours are located in positions with a weaker water flow, for example, a smaller tributary or, as in Rezé, a secondary channel [11]. Elsewhere, if the natural preconditions have been less favourable, societies have decided to dig canals or to re-arrange river channels. In Narbonne, at the crossroad of maritime and terrestrial routes, monumental works aimed at the canalisation of the River Aude in order to create transhipment areas. In Nantes, the construction of the Saint Felix Canal may already have taken place in the Early Middle Ages, but archaeological proof is still missing. In the Central Middle Ages, many navigable canals have been dug all over Europe. In Regensburg, one of these canals has been used before the 11th - 12th century AD at the Donaumarkt, a second canal did exist in Stadtamhof at the Northern bank of the Danube in the 12th century AD. This canal may have been a consequence of the construction of the first stone bridge since the piles of the bridge have created swirls highly dangerous for navigation. This is a vivid example for the fact that construction and evolution of harbours did not only depend on environmental conditions, but also on anthropogenic transformations.

From Antiquity until the Modern period, wood has been the main material for inland harbour construction. From vertical stakes to planks, from wooden caissons made of beams to terrace support, timber dominates the range of construction techniques used to arrange, strengthen and protect riverbanks. Thousands of stakes and sheet piles have been used in jetties or pontoons like in Narbonne. Beyond the topic of harbours and navigation as well as details of construction techniques, dendrological studies of well-preserved wood samples could reveal hitherto unknown information on ancient forest exploitation. Nevertheless, the wooden material is fragile. Each time a site is exposed to erosion and aerobic conditions, not only a part of the wood but also a part of the archive which could tell us an environmental, as well as an economic story, is irreversibly lost. Since wood as an archaeological source is not an endless and always available resource, developing research programmes and recommendations on a European scale for sample preservation as well as databanks for future research becomes more and more urgent.
Furthermore, the rivers themselves have been a very common means of transport for timber – which could be found later on far from the river, like in the wooden frameworks of churches and houses of the Yonne Valley. These remains – fragile as well – offer new insight in wood transportation on the Yonne River and all the production line from specialised harbours, to squaring areas and building sites.
Finally, wood is also the main material for building boats which navigated inland waterways. Nevertheless, compared to the numerous proof for trade and exchange of goods in written and archaeological sources, the number of inland vessels from Antiquity as well as from the Middle Ages which have been preserved and/or studied appears particularly small, if logboats are excluded[12]. Many of the wrecks have been destroyed by dredging without any archaeological surveillance and documentation on-site. Additionally, the complexity of the preservation process makes the systematic study of wrecks a tricky task, limiting the number of remains which have been studied in detail.
As most of the wrecks are lacking any archaeological context, it is often quite difficult to interpret them and to embed them in the wider framework of harbours and navigation. The three wrecks of Port d'Envaux-Le Prioutè in the Charente River do perfectly illustrate this: they are dated to a period (7th - 8th century AD) for which we do not have any other information concerning trade and settlements in the surrounding area[13]. Furthermore, in this specific fluvial context, cargo is hardly ever preserved, depriving us of any information concerning the actual use for trade (local or long distance, small or large scale) or other riverine activities (e. g. fishing, passenger transportation).
Finally, we have to keep in mind that navigation was usually a seasonal or at least periodical activity. Harbours have therefore also been temporary shelters, which have been used while waiting for the right season or better conditions for navigation. The Saône River, for example, was only navigable six months per year until the construction of dams (1880), excluding foggy and icy days as well as periods of floods and shallow water.

Apart from distinct cargo, relatively few artefacts could enlighten and give proof for harbour activity. Even for finds from harbour-related areas which do clearly suggest distant origins, it is often not possible to distinguish artefacts directly resulting from harbour activities[14] and discharge of riverine inhabitants without any direct relation to the harbour. In Antiquity as well as in the Middle Ages (and still nowadays) riverbanks have been a widely used location to get rid of rubbish, sometimes connected to the intention of levelling the banks at the same time.

Finally, we would like to end this introduction with a statement made by S. Bütow in his article: »Research has to go on!« – and it has to go on in a multidisciplinary framework. The crucial need for research which crosses the boundaries of disciplines and sources is underlined by the French harbour database: only 7 % of the registered harbour sites are documented by archaeological and written sources at the same time, the remaining 93 % are only documented in one of both groups of sources. The high potential of a multidisciplinary and multinational dialogue, which was one of the aims of this conference, becomes obvious looking at this example. Neither the multidisciplinary nor the multinational approach is always easy. One of the challenges has been the heterogeneous mother tongues and research terminologies. Our decision to publish all the articles in English pursued the objective to allow easy access for a wider audience. Nevertheless, none of us and none of the authors is a native speaker and we did not have sufficient resources for a full professional language editing, so we apologise for any mistakes.

Notes

1) e.g. Tranchant 2018. – Lebecq/Béthouart/Verslype 2010. – Sanchez/Jézégou 2016.

2) Seven articles are nevertheless dealing with harbours at river estuaries and therefore interfaces between river and sea: in France, Narbonne, Nantes, Rezé, le Prioutė, the Seine Estuary, in Scandinavia, the inland Viking harbours, in Belgium harbours on the Zwin connected to the North Sea.

3) Milne/Hobley 1981.

4) Ayala 2013.

5) e.g. SPP 1630 Häfen, PCR (Common Research Programme) »Les cours d'eau de Bourgogne-Franche-Comté. Patrimoine immergé et évolution des hydrosystèmes sur la longue durée« (ARTEHIS-Université de Bourgogne Franche-Comté).

6) e.g. Bütow 2015. – Mouchard 2008. – Kröger 2014. – Wunschel 2017. Several other PhD theses will soon be finished, among them D. Wollenberg, I. Niessen and C. Haase.

7) e.g. Leitholdt 2014. – Steinmann 2015.

8) e.g. Franconi 2016. – Steinmann 2015.

9) Fournier/Lavaud 2012.

10) Preiser-Kapeller/Werther 2018.

11) Nevertheless, at the river Rhine most of the Roman harbours have been located at the cut bar with the strongest current, see Gerlach/Meurers-Balke 2014.

12) e.g. Kröger 2018.

13) Dumont/Mariotti 2013.

14) e.g. Bonnamour 2000.

References

Ayala 2013: G. Ayala (ed.), Lyon, Saint-Georges. Archéologie, environnement et histoire d'un espace fluvial en bord de Saône. Documents d'Archéologie Française 10 (Paris 2013).

Bonnamour 2000: L. Bonnamour, Archéologie de la Saône. 150 ans de recherches (Paris 2000).

Bütow 2015: S. Bütow, Straßen im Fluss. Schifffahrt, Flussnutzung und der lange Wandel der Verkehrsinfrastruktur in der Mark Brandenburg und der Niederlausitz vom 13. bis zum 16. Jahrhundert. Studien zur brandenburgischen und vergleichenden Landesgeschichte 18 (Berlin 2015).

Dumont/Mariotti 2013: A. Dumont / J.-F. Mariotti (eds), Archéologie et histoire du fleuve Charente. Taillebourg – Port d'Envaux: une zone portuaire du haut Moyen Âge sur le fleuve Charente (Dijon 2013).

Fournier/Lavaud 2012: P. Fournier / S. Lavaud, Eaux et conflits dans l'Europe médiévale et moderne. Flaran 32 (Toulouse 2012).

Franconi 2016: T. V. Franconi, Climatic influences on riverine transport on the Roman Rhine. In: Ch. Schäfer (ed.), Connecting the Ancient world. Mediterranean shipping, maritime networks and their impact. Pharos 38 (Rahden/Westf. 2016) 27-44.

Gerlach/Meurers-Balke 2014: R. Gerlach / J. Meurers-Balke, Wo wurden römische Häfen am Niederrhein angelegt? Die Beispiele Colonia Ulpia Traiana (Xanten) und Burginatium (Kaikar). In: H. Kennecke (ed.), Der Rhein als europäische Verkehrsachse. Die Römerzeit. Bonner Beiträge zur vor- und frühgeschichtlichen Archäologie 16 (Bonn 2014) 199-208.

Kröger 2014: L. Kröger, Fähren an Main und Neckar. Eine archäologische und historisch-geographische Entwicklungsanalyse mittelalterlicher und frühneuzeitlicher Verkehrsinfrastruktur [diss. Univ. Bamberg 2014].

2018: L. Kröger, Within the network of fluvial ports. In: L. Werther / H. Müller / M. Foucher (eds), European Harbour Data Repository, Vol. 01 (Jena 2018). DOI: 10.22032/dbt.35240 (pdf), 10.22032/dbt.35241 (csv), 10.22032/dbt.35242 (excel).

Lebecq/Béthouart/Verslype 2010: S. Lebecq / B. Béthouart / L. Verslype, Quentovic, environnement, archéologie, histoire (Lille 2010).

Leitholdt 2014: E. Leitholdt, Der Karlsgraben. Überwindung der Europäischen Hauptwasserscheide auf dem Wasserweg. Rekonstruktion der Kanalanlage und deren Sedimentationsgeschichte vom Frühmittelalter bis heute [diss. Univ. Leipzig 2014].

Milne/Hobley 1981: G. Milne / B. Hobley (eds), Waterfront archaeology in Britain and northern Europe: a review of current research in waterfront archaeology in six European countries. First International Conference on Waterfront Archaeology in North European Towns, London 1979 (London 1981).

Mouchard 2008: J. Mouchard, Les sites portuaires gallo-romains et médiévaux de l'estuaire de la Seine [diss. Univ. Rouen 2008].

Preiser-Kapeller/Werther 2018: J. Preiser-Kapeller / L. Werther, Connecting Harbours. A Comparison of Traffic Networks across Ancient and Medieval Europe. In: C. von Carnap-Bornheim / F. Daim / P. Ettel / U. Warnke (eds), Harbours as Objects of Interdisciplinary Research – Archaeology + History + Geosciences. RGZM – Tagungen 34 = Interdisziplinäre Forschungen zu den Häfen von der Römischen Kaiserzeit bis zum Mittelalter in Europa 5 (Mainz 2018) 7-31.

Sanchez/Jézégou 2016: C. Sanchez / M.-P. Jézégou, Les ports dans l'espace Méditerranéen antique. Narbonne et les systèmes portuaires fluvio-lagunaires. Archéologique de Narbonnaise, Supplément 44 (Montpellier 2016).

Steinmann 2015: R. Steinmann, L'influence climatique et anthropique sur trois cours d'eau bourguignons: géoarchéologie de sites de franchissement sur la Loire, la Saône et le Doubs au cours de l'Holocène [diss. Univ. Bourgogne 2015].

Tranchant 2018: M. Tranchant, Les ports maritimes de la France atlantique (XIe-XVe siècle). I: Tableau géohistorique (Rennes 2018).

Wunschel 2017: A. Wunschel, Von Karlburg nach Salz – Interdisziplinäre Studien zu den Wasserwegen Mittelmain und Fränkische Saale im Früh- und Hochmittelalter [diss. Univ. Jena 2017].

INLAND HARBOURS: DIACHRONIC APPROACHES

MARION FOUCHER · ANNIE DUMONT · LUKAS WERTHER
HARTMUT MÜLLER · PETER ETTEL*

INLAND HARBOURS: PRELIMINARY RESULTS AND PERSPECTIVES FOR THE FRENCH SECTION OF THE PROJECT »INLAND HARBOURS IN CENTRAL EUROPE«

A harbour, whatever the dating, size or river system, is first and foremost an interface between land and water, a hub between hinterland and waterways. Its extent, its organisation and the complexity of its infrastructures are significant indicators of the links that exist between settlements and navigation. Harbour structure and evolution can therefore be used to interpret the complex interplay between human agents and landscape[1]. At a larger scale, especially significant for river systems, each harbour is a node in a complex network, and has played a crucial role in exchanges, whether economic or of ideas, and in the transportation of people and goods[2]. The Priority Program (SPP) 1630, funded by the Deutsche Forschungsgemeinschaft (DFG), was developed from this perspective. It aims to analyse navigation in Europe through case studies and specific topics, spanning time (Roman conquest to the Late Middle Ages) and space (European mainland)[3]. To unite these diverse approaches and to answer broader-based questions, one of the applications in SPP 1630 is the systematic collection of harbour and navigation data in a shared database[4]. The Dijon workshop on »Inland Harbours in Central Europe« provided an opportunity to present the work carried out during 2016 in France, as part of the sub-project »Studies on Inland Harbours in Central Europe as Hubs for European Communication Networks«[5].

In this paper, we present the data collection strategy, with a precise description of the French database content, underlining the limitations of the database and the pitfalls encountered. Although data collection is still ongoing, the French data collected so far can already be used for several types of analysis. Furthermore, this section of the database provides an opportunity to propose solutions to deal with heterogeneous data on historic navigation and river occupation.

DATA COLLECTION PROCESS: TOPICS AND SOURCES

The French database is also an integral part of the HArbour Research Environment »HARE«, which aims to gather evidence for harbours and navigation in the entire European mainland[6]. The cornerstone of this cross-topic, cross-discipline, cross-period and cross-project approach is the development of a shared research environment about harbours, vessels, and navigation. Based on more than 20 projects in the SPP, the framework of the common HARE database has been developed to bring together all the information relevant to the many different sites, topics, and approaches involved. The database also imposes on every contributor the same set of concepts, language, and keywords[7].

Harbour, navigation, and other river uses

In order to obtain a broad panorama of the past uses of French rivers, we selected a set of topics linked to riverine navigation, over a long period, from the Roman conquest (1st century BC) to the Late Middle Ages (15th century AD). Data collection thus extends to harbour structures themselves, but also includes evidence of mooring places without any artificial installations (temporary or provisional use, etc.). As a port is not limited only to its bank arrangement, the database may also include information about port activities, navigation and trade, with archaeological or historical evidence of infrastructures like *horrea*, salt stores, and warehouses, and written evidence of navigation-related professions. Especially relevant for Medieval times, tolls linked to exchange of goods or travel by people also provide significant clues about harbours and navigational networks. The variety of aspects considered when characterising harbour activities may help to situate each site within a complex system and identify its structural evolution over time. Additionally, the information gathered is broader than the navigation theme. As rivers are regarded as complex spatial entities, with numerous possibilities for exploitation[8], data collection also includes infrastructures in competition with navigation on rivers. These possible obstacles include mills, fisheries, dams, and river-crossing infrastructures, such as bridges and fords.

As an exhaustive inventory was not possible within the timeframe of the SPP, we organised two prospecting scales. After a general overview of the entire territory, data collection focused mainly on three rivers in the east of France, the Saône, the Doubs, and the Moselle, which are connected to the north-eastern watershed, the core of the European project[9].

A dialogue between archaeology and history: the sources

In the current context of multidisciplinary approaches, developed as a concept in historical network analysis[10], the harbour topic draws upon both historical and archaeological sources. We reviewed many published studies, and included grey literature in our review, with a much more complete compilation for the areas of the Saône, Doubs, and Moselle.

Archaeological data from national heritage records were also obtained from the »Carte Archéologique Nationale« (PATRIARCHE) and the »base Architecture Mérimée«[11], both databases developed by the French Ministry of Culture. The aim of the PATRIARCHE database is to identify archaeological potential by recording all discoveries and excavations. Spatial accuracy and content description may vary considerably from one entry to another, depending on the author, the date of the archaeological discovery, and the type of investigation. The database nevertheless contains a significant amount of data about river uses, obtained through rescue archaeology, which is well developed in France, and through numerous underwater surveys. For the Saône, Doubs, and French Moselle, raw data from archaeological reports complete the collection. The MERIMEE national database, specialising in built heritage, was mainly used to obtain information about built entities, including bridges, warehouses, and salt stores.

Data from archives and published historical sources are rather more patchy, as they were collected by team members during specific research projects. Documents related to lands management, as conflicts, and tax sources, as well as cartularies, provide more useful information about tolls, river crossing, and exploitation structures (mills, fisheries, etc.), than about harbours themselves. Sources from Antiquity and the Early Middle Ages have also provided evidence for travel, exchanges of goods, and navigation, with descriptions of territories, political events, and history. Despite the variety of sources considered, or perhaps because of that very plethora, the French database currently provides only a scattered survey. Given the timeframe of the project[12], choices had to be made, and many references are clearly missing yet.

Content

To avoid compatibility issues between the many researchers involved in the project, and to ensure future open access, the HARE team chose to use the widely available Excel software[13]. Each site corresponds to a row in an Excel sheet, where different sets of information are recorded, each with its own critical indicators, linked to accuracy, origin, and quality:

- the location (country, city, coordinates);
- the hydrological and topographical position;
- the description of the harbour or river-linked site, including elements about infrastructures, activities, exchanges of goods, and the hierarchy within the river network and on land;
- information about chronology expressed as centuries and periods;
- information about the author of the dataset as well as the sources and literature references used and cited.

The current state of data collection includes 1,790 places linked to river uses. Within this total, harbours represent 56 % of the data. The other main category of sites recorded is that of potential navigation obstacles (29 %), mainly divided into river crossings (17 %), and river exploitation structures, such as mills or fisheries (7 %). There is less information about vessels (9 %)[14], evidence of navigable waterways (5 %), and canals (1 %). Harbour information is intended to be representative of the historical river landscape, while other types of river uses, arrangements, and infrastructures were not the main focus of the survey.

STRENGTHS AND LIMITATIONS OF THE FRENCH DATABASE

»The need for larger and more integrated geospatial data and analyses cross-cuts virtually all of our goals and aspirations as a science. These require us to produce data and results that are scientific (testable, replicable), authentic (a faithful representation of the archaeological record and the human past), and ethical (protects cultural resources).« [15]

The database framework and data entry process seek to respect these prerequisites. Sources used to document each dataset are fully recorded. Their accuracy, nature, and quality are systematically documented. Each dataset has one (or several) author(s), clearly identified, responsible for data collection, literature review, and data integration in conformity with database architecture and framework. The expertise of each author in a given field ensures the quality of the data collected. Data collection is thus an integral part of each research project, with clearly identified spatial, chronological, and thematic boundaries. Critical examination of content nevertheless remains necessary, to assess data origin, quality, and distribution, before further exploitation.

Advantages of a multidisciplinary survey

As previously stated, the data integration process is the result of a multidisciplinary survey, combining historical and archaeological records. The distribution pattern of data sources highlights the interest of cross-referencing information from different disciplines and sources: quantifying the origin of the used sources reveals a comparable distribution pattern between sites documented only by archaeological sources (37 %) or only by historical sources (40 %). Sites with both archaeological and historical data are so far in a minority (7 %). Each type of source has its limits: for example, the input of archaeological records is de facto limited by the preservation of remains, as most of the navigable French rivers have been dredged to improve navigation.

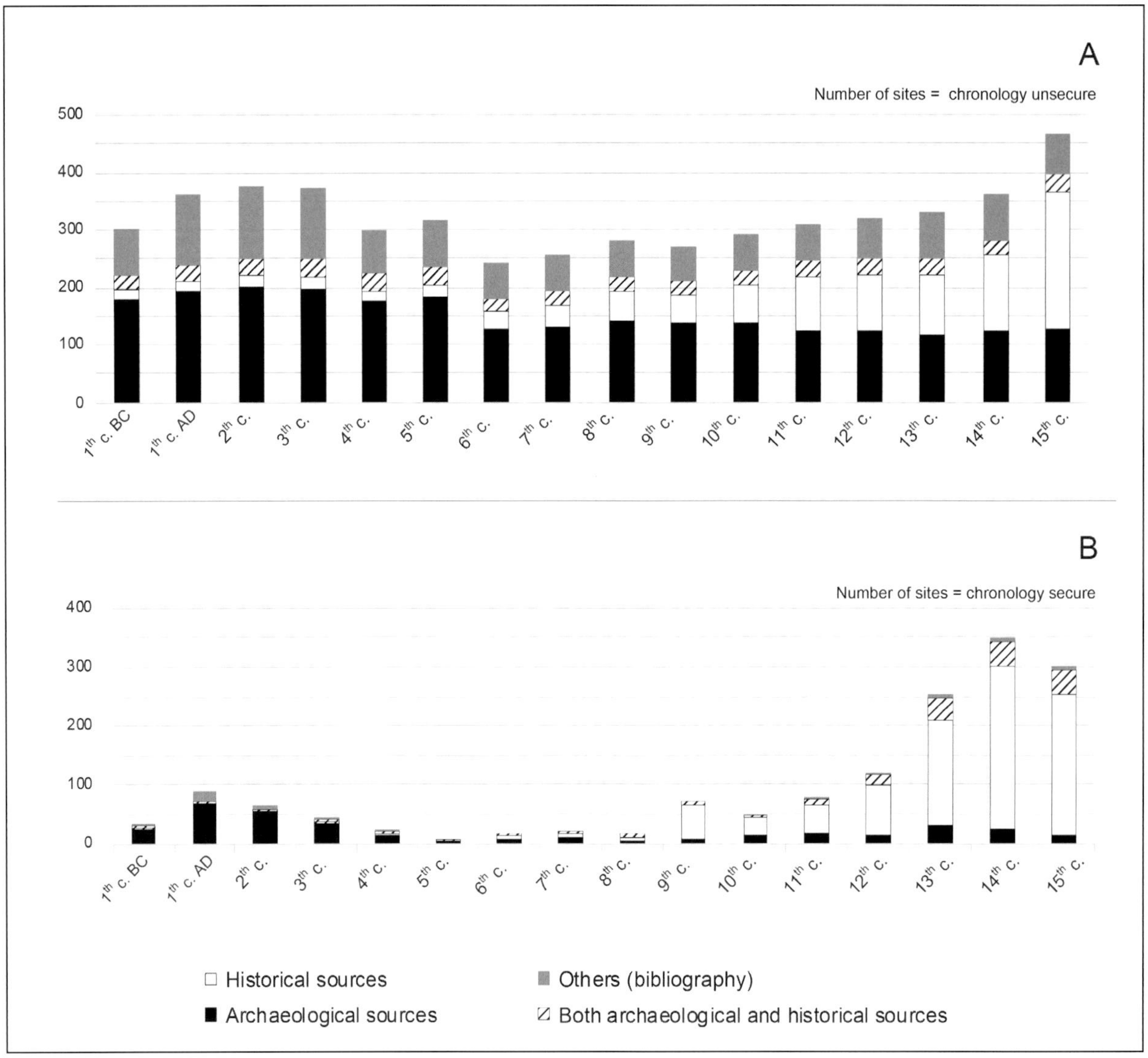

Fig. 1 Sources distribution over time. Sources distribution for **A**: sites with uncertain chronological evidence and for **B**: sites with reliable chronological evidence. – (M. Foucher [database status: 03/2018]).

Combining archaeological and historical approaches therefore seems crucial to fill the gaps that exist in every set of sources, in order to obtain a more reliable overview of historical navigation.
Nevertheless, an investigation of the source distribution patterns over time reveals great heterogeneity in representativeness, century by century (**fig. 1**). The same analysis was carried out for sites with uncertain (**fig. 1A**) and reliable (**fig. 1B**) chronological evidence. Although similar trends are visible, they are much more pronounced for well-dated sites. The Gallo-Roman period is characterised by an over-representation of archaeological data. The lower graph (**fig. 1B**) shows the finer temporal resolution for the 1st and 2nd centuries AD, with many sites dated by archaeology, dendrochronology, and radiocarbon dating, while later centuries benefit from the increasing availability of historical documents. The second peak, from the 13th to the 15th centuries AD, results partly from the enormous increase in document production at the end of the Middle Ages, but also from discrete historical records, with little indication of duration. These graphs highlight as well a major gap in the chronological distribution between the 5th and 6th centuries AD (between Late Antiquity and the Early Middle Ages). After further investigation of the data, this gap appears to be linked to a less precise chronological identification, by period alone, in publications. The artefact thus cre-

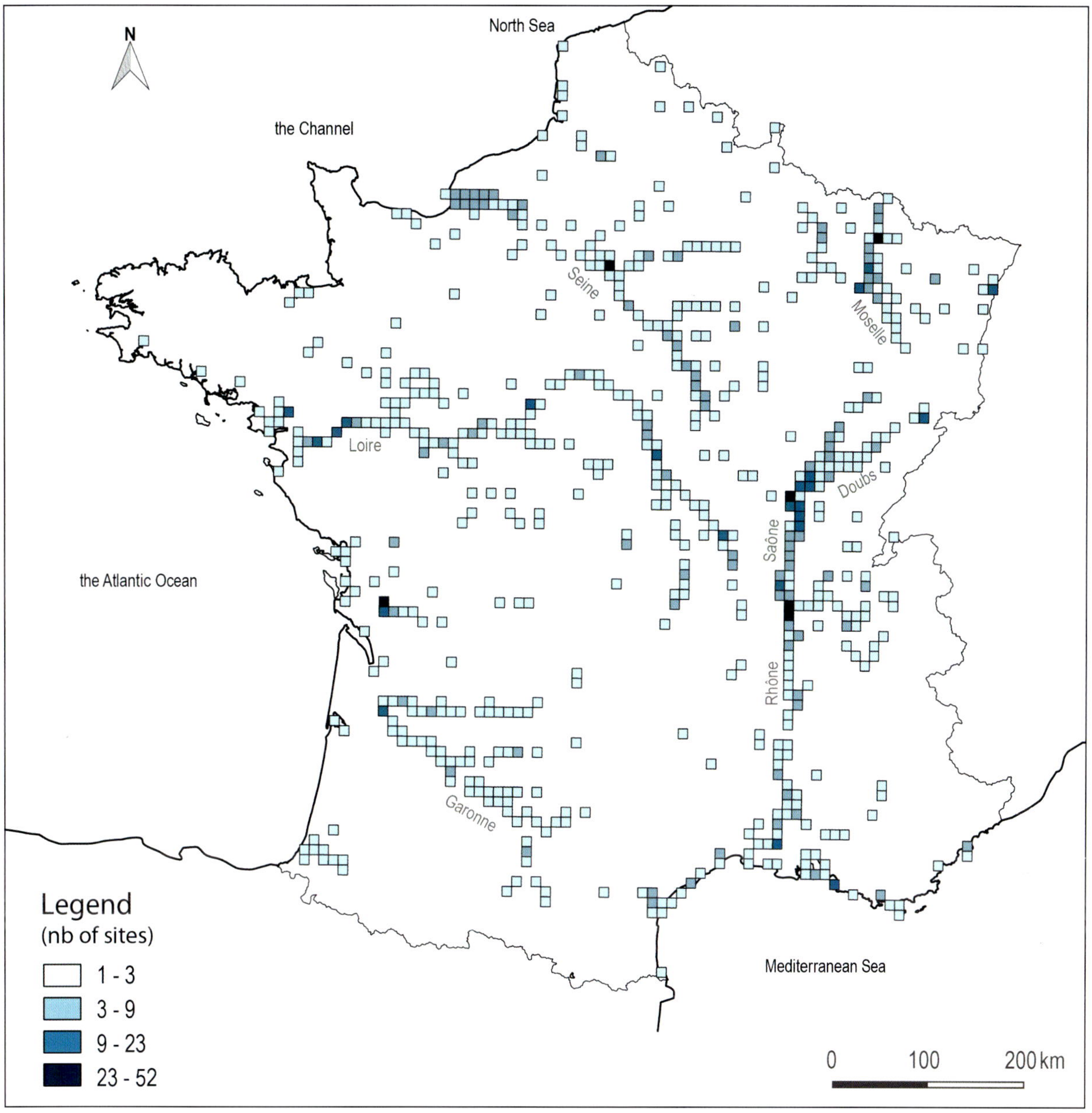

Fig. 2 Density map of riverine sites linked to either navigation or other activities. Only the rivers broached by the survey appear. – (M. Foucher [database status: 03/2018]).

ated may lead to analytical bias. As the information linked to harbours, their activities, their infrastructures, and their rank, depends a great deal on the sources used, the nature of data and its quality are therefore not homogeneous, and follow the rhythms of source distribution. Caution must consequently prevail when using the data, including taking these over-representations and chronological artefacts into account.

Limitations and pitfalls of spatial distribution

The French database cannot give an exact picture of historical inland navigation, because of the limited timeframe allocated to the study. At the national scale, a density map of recorded sites mainly reflects the state of progress, and the focus on the Saône, Doubs, and Moselle Rivers (**fig. 2**). However, areas of high density also highlight the research dynamism of some places. Some rivers – or river sections – are well documented, at least for a specific period or topic. This is the case in Lyon (dép. Rhône/F), for example, notably in the confluence area (Saône/Rhône), with its rich archaeological potential brought to light through urban development (rescue archaeology). This area has also attracted clusters of archaeologists and researchers, deeply interested in alluvial contexts[16]. Elsewhere, detailed studies and long-term projects have provided precise overviews of more limited areas. One such study, of water tolls between the 12th and 15th centuries AD[17], has brought to light detailed information about harbour distribution throughout the Garonne catchment. However, this information only covers harbours linked to toll records, during those specific centuries. By contrast, such well-documented areas underline the lack of information about other sites, particularly for the navigable sections of a river.

Ultimately, even for well-documented areas, a simple harbour distribution map cannot fully reflect past navigation history, since a general harbour map does not differentiate between local access to water bodies and harbours of supra-regional scale, with no notion of hierarchy.

HARBOURS IN RIVERINE LANDSCAPES: PRELIMINARY RESULTS FROM A HETEROGENEOUS DATASET

Since macro-scale distribution is obviously patchy, it is clearly necessary »to verify and restrict content spatially and temporally«, as recommended by Roosen and Curtis[18], before collecting data, and before all further analysis. Topics should also be restricted, and data quality (classification, chronology, interpretation, etc.) must always be kept in mind[19]. Considering these restrictions, we have tested methods of analysis for such heterogeneous material, in order to recontextualise it.

Strahler rank and competition phenomena on rivers

Many different types of constructions, such as bridges, fords, fisheries, and mills, tend to cluster on rivers, and may compete with river navigability. Historical sources often reveal how the coexistence of these activities on rivers can be a key issue, bringing different scales of interests into competition, therefore often implying power struggles[20]. This competition phenomenon, through the solutions found, can be the indicator of territorial structuring. For example, the existence – or absence – of a strong centralised power, or more likely shared initiatives[21], would affect the activities promoted, at a local scale (e. g. mills), or at a larger scale (navigation). To contribute to the analysis of such phenomena, we focused on the distribution of activities along the waterways studied, using the information in the database about navigation and about these other types of river exploitation.

In this analysis, we have tried to identify the distribution of activities according to the river type. A vision of a river as a whole cannot integrate linear waterway evolution, network complexity, or relationships within the river basin. To go beyond this vision, and for a more in-depth study, we then used the method of stream classification developed by Horton, Schumm, and Strahler since the mid-20th century AD[22]. This well-established and uncomplicated classification scheme – Strahler rank or order – aims to assess each river's size and complexity by considering the catchment as a tree structure, with tributaries and confluences[23]. This method ranks the sections of a river, based on their location within the network, and on its complexity. From source to estuary, each confluence marks the end of a section, and the section closest to the source is

Fig. 3 Strahler classification system: following this classification system, a river section needs a section of equal rank to increase its value of one. Consequently, if a river section of rank 2 joins another tributary of rank 2, the following section becomes rank 3; but if it joins a rank 1, it remains at rank 2. – (M. Foucher, after Strahler 1957).

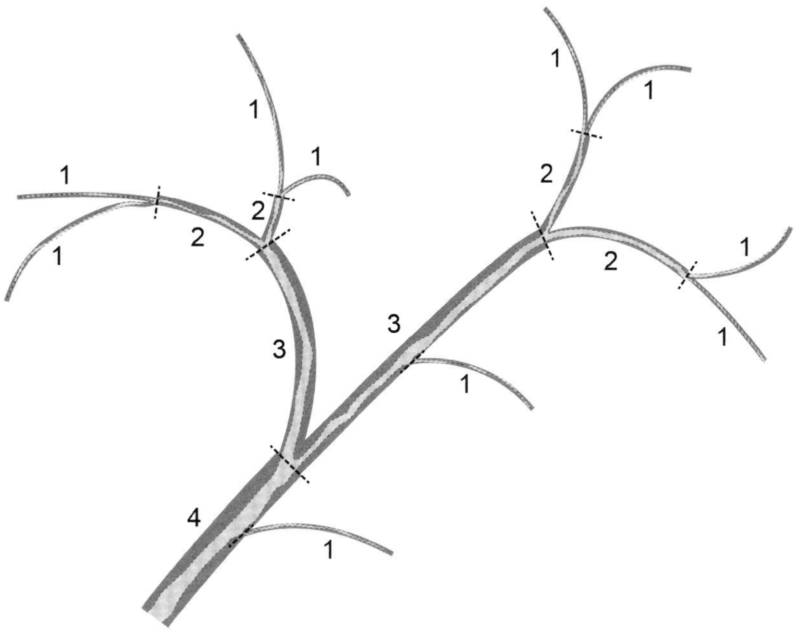

Fig. 4 Comparison between the distribution of French rivers sections and sites by ranks of Strahler. – (M. Foucher [database status: 03/2018]).

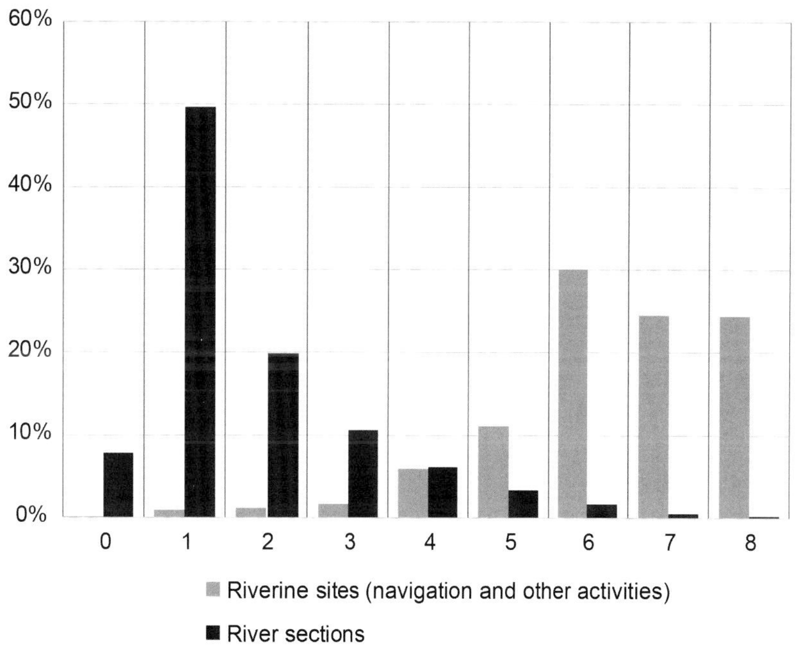

ranked 1. The rank increases by an increment of one when two sections of equal rank meet at a confluence (**fig. 3**). Rank 8 is the highest in the French river network.

Here, this stream classification system is used to analyse the theoretical distribution of navigation and river-linked activities, in relation to river section rank. To test this approach, we used the Strahler rank information, obtained from the open-source river database of the European Environment Agency (EEA), which covers the entire European river network[24]. This database is particularly well adapted for historical approaches, as it does not include modern and contemporary artificial channels, which could increase a river's rank by connecting two catchments, thus misrepresenting the past river network[25]. Nevertheless, applying the junction-by-proximity process using GIS software is not easy, as river geometries in the EEA database are not entirely consistent with those in the French database. There is also a problem with the somewhat fuzzy identification of historical places, which may disrupt the attribution process, particularly because of the

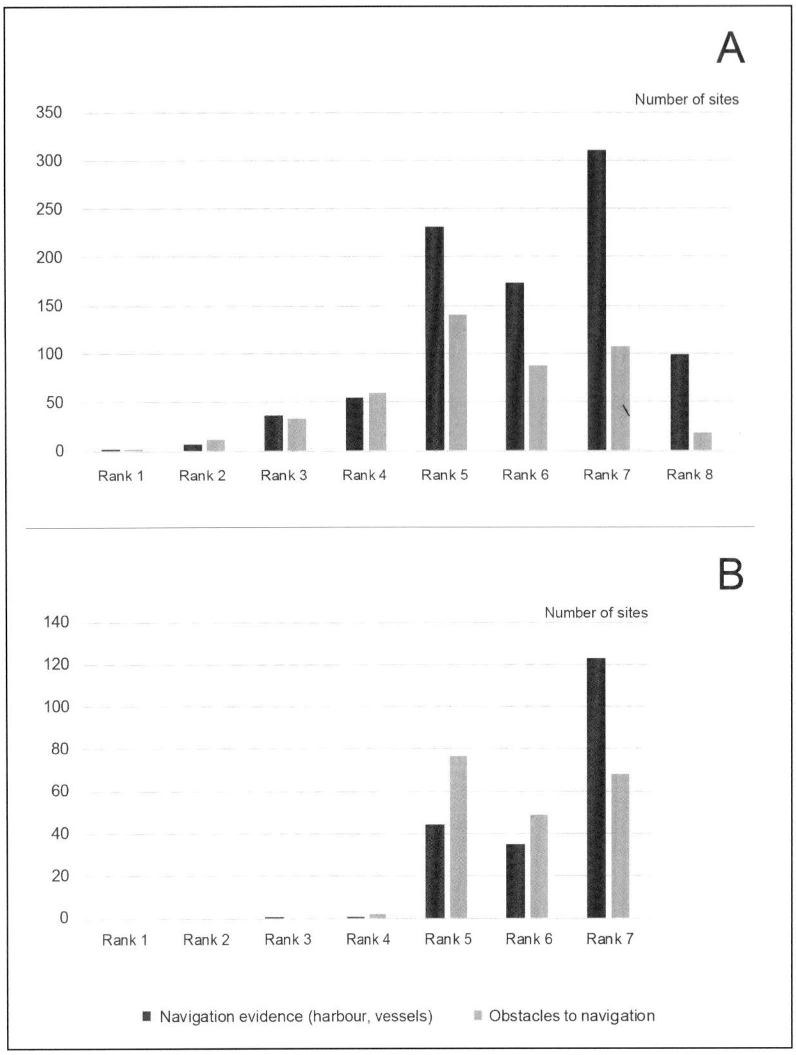

Fig. 5 Comparison between the distribution of navigation evidence and other river uses (potential obstacles) by ranks of Strahler. – **A** the French territory. – **B** focus on the Rivers Saône, Doubs and Moselle. – (M. Foucher [database status: 03/2018]).

numerous small tributaries of lower rank. Such very small tributaries cover the whole of France, but are not navigable. For now, the most reliable method is to trust in the expertise of each contributor to the database, as a certain degree of interpretation is necessary to link historical places correctly to their relevant Strahler number.

This test has been carried out on the French database for harbours, vessels, and other river uses[26]. The first result shows that the Strahler ranking for most French river sections is from 1 to 4, although historical sites are predominantly located on the larger sections with Strahler ranking from 5 to 8 (**fig. 4**)[27]. Considering navigation and the distribution of other forms of use (**fig. 5A**), the abrupt drop at rank 8 may be explained by the relative paucity of sections above rank 7 within the French river network, where the only rank 8 sections are the Rhône from its confluence with the Saône, and the Loire after Angers. As the principal focus for the database, navigation, benefited from an exhaustive survey, the scarcity of evidence for navigation on lower-ranked river sections may be considered significant. In sections of higher rank (5-7), there is considerable evidence for navigation, with some evidence for obstacles to navigation, suggesting high competition potential. This observation is in accordance with Rossiaud's remarks about the multiplication of riverine infrastructures during the feudal period, temporarily detrimental to navigation, particularly for smaller rivers[28].

This preliminary analysis underlines the need for a more exhaustive survey of all riverine activities, for the whole of France. Since all types of river-linked remains for the Saône, Doubs, and Moselle Rivers were ex-

Fig. 6 Rhythms in harbour installation: these graphs present **A**: quantity of harbours that disappeared per century (%), and **B**: quantity of new harbours per century (%). – (M. Foucher [database status: 03/2018]).

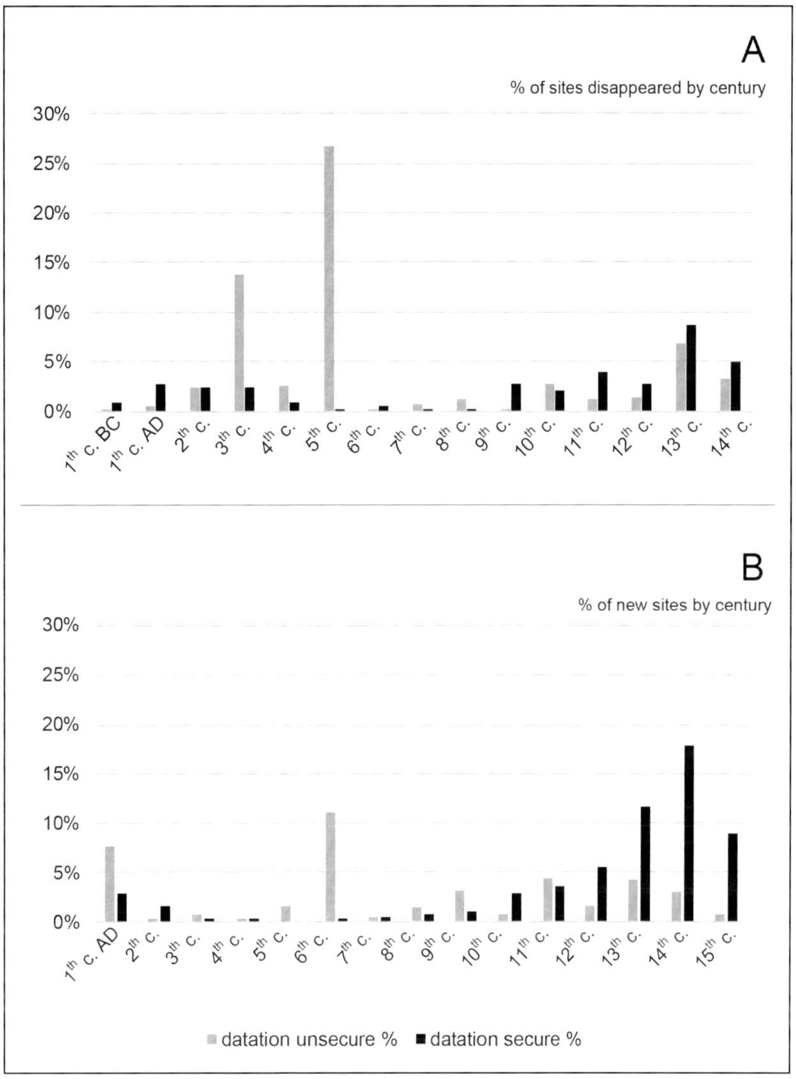

haustively recorded in the database[29], a more detailed picture of riverine activities and potential competition emerges (**fig. 5B**). Although the majority of the evidence is yet again found in the higher ranks (5-7), data about navigation and navigation obstacles are still not evenly distributed. However, in sections of ranks 5 and 6, local riverine exploitation (obstacles) is preponderant. Navigation is the dominant activity only in the downstream part of the network. Downstream, where there is higher connectivity, economic activities are clustered around hubs of regional and supraregional influence (e. g. Lyon, Metz – dép. Moselle / F). This insight into the theoretical distribution of harbours within the entire river network, and their connectivity as hubs, should now be combined with other network analysis systems. The method developed by Preiser-Kapeller and Werther does not consider the location of a harbour within the river network, as we did, but rather its relative position within the harbour network[30]. As this method does not include maritime routes, harbours located downstream appear to be among the weakest »hubs of connectivity«. Nevertheless, the two methods do agree on the high connectivity potential of central nodes, such as Lyon. The next logical step is to focus on the chronological distribution of sites in Strahler's theoretical river network, in order to assess the evolution of river uses, and to compare the results with the chronological patterns of betweenness centrality nodes.

We are very much aware that our overview of river uses needs to be improved, both in data representativeness, and in the method itself. The potential of the tool seems nevertheless promising for other topics, such as the evolution of the relationship between societies and rivers from Antiquity to the Late Middle Ages, or in order to highlight the archaeological potential[31] in such a changing landscape.

Harbour rhythms

These investigations of harbours and river exploitation must be set within the broader panorama of each period's political, social, and economic context. The shifting nature of waterways also makes it necessary to take account of climatic changes, and alluvial dynamics. In archaeological reports and geomorphological studies, many authors mention the disappearance of sites and the abandonment of the riverbanks. All such studies relate this phenomenon to climatic degradation periods, often with an increased frequency and intensity of floods[32]. We sought to identify the potential echo of such rhythms in riverbank occupation, by considering harbour installation and abandonment or natural destruction.

To estimate harbour disappearance, we have quantified the number of sites in each century that no longer exist in the following century (**fig. 6A**). To estimate the appearance of new harbours, we have quantified the number of sites for each century that did not exist during the previous century (**fig. 6B**). The two graphs show an unequal distribution of data along the timeline. Drawing on expertise regarding the distribution of sources within the database, it seems clear that some peaks are artefacts related to sources distribution. The chronology-depending hiatus between Late Antiquity and the Early Middle Ages – many harbours are classified either as »Antique« or as »Medieval« – explains the peak for poorly dated harbours in the 5th century AD, with a corresponding peak for new harbours in the 6th century AD. For both datasets, the increase of harbour disappearance/appearance during later centuries seems to result mainly from the number of one-off mentions (e.g. toll records) that are characteristic for data from this period. These sources do not give information about the duration of site exploitation, thus creating an artefact in this analysis. Nevertheless, some of the variations between these peaks may highlight finer patterns in harbour settlement and riverbank occupation.

The Gallo-Roman period is initially characterised by new settlements in the 1st century AD, echoing territory structuration after the Roman conquest (**fig. 6**). The same tendency is observed for the construction of bridges on French rivers[33]. These harbours have been used throughout the Gallo-Roman period until they start to disappear in the 2nd century AD, a phenomenon peaking in the 3rd century AD. Regarding the drop in the number of new harbours since the 2nd century AD, this phenomenon does not appear to correspond to the replacement of disused harbours. Field studies within the Rhine Basin and the Lyon peninsula underline the impact of climate degradation on riverine settlements during Roman Antiquity[34]. Many sites were abandoned or moved after successive floods or river migration, such as Ehl (2nd century AD), Horburg (late 2nd/early 3rd century AD), and Oedenburg (4th century AD). In other places, the organisation of the towns had to be adapted, with anti-flood measures (Lyon and Strasbourg), shifting infrastructures, and the end of some activities (Cologne and Voorburg). In Lyon[35], at the confluence between the Saône and the Rhône, the distribution of river-linked infrastructures underlines the reaction of the community to riverine evolution: while harbour settlements and navigation are still clustered on the banks of the Saône, infrastructures built to fight floods and river migration or to stabilise the ground, mainly cluster on the lands between the Rhône and the Saône.

During the Central Middle Ages, harbour construction/destruction rhythms do not follow this pattern. The phenomena of appearance and disappearance are both well represented, with two higher peaks around the 9th and 11th centuries AD. This seems to be a period of change in riverine occupation, with the abandonment of some harbours, and the creation of new settlements. The peaks during the Carolingian and

Romanesque periods may echo the dynamics of economic development and territorial structuration linked to different political contexts[36]. From that perspective, the significant increase in references to tolls from the 11th century AD onwards seems to be characteristic for the break-up of the territory around little power nodes, after the progressive erosion of great domains[37]. It is still necessary to test whether these new tolls correspond – or not – to a real change in harbour settlements. The vast increase in the number of harbours after the 13th century AD, together with the increase in historical records, may well coincide with the development of large-scale trade[38].

CONCLUSION

This survey of French inland navigation and harbours has highlighted the wealth of archaeological data already discovered, and the complementarity with historical records. Although the database is not yet complete, we have already been able to demonstrate the potential of quantitative analysis for the exploration of these newly compiled data. Other approaches may require a firmer basis, and perhaps deeper reflexion regarding potential database queries at different spatial scales. One major result is the need for a critical approach with this dataset: without considering the quality and origin of the data, collection strategies, and the limitations that can lead to analytical bias, it would be hazardous to propose sound hypotheses, as Roosen and Curtis have previously demonstrated in their review of well-known studies of plague dispersion[39].

To continue this survey, two main axes should be developed, one linked to chronology, the other to the topic itself. The preliminary boundary, at the end of the 15th century AD, was imposed by the existing framework of the project. Yet, a better understanding of river uses and historical navigation would benefit from a broader time-scale, extended up to the Industrial Era. Not only was the legislative framework greatly altered after the French Revolution, but river management was even more profoundly modified. During the 19th century AD, almost all the main navigable waterways were reorganised, and split into artificial canals dug in order to improve navigation. These extensive works have permanently modified the uses of the fluvial area.

A broader perspective seems fundamental for a more accurate understanding of the phenomenon, in particular from the European perspective targeted by the harbour SPP. Inland navigation must be set within a more complex system, including land structuring[40] and, more importantly, maritime harbours and navigation, topics that have been extensively explored, in new ways, over the past few years[41]. To understand the phenomenon of navigation, the relationships between inland harbours and maritime and estuarine ports are of primordial importance. The development of towns such as Lyon, far inland, is directly related to their maritime connections.

Finally, as shown by both archives and national archaeological survey records, harbour activities and the commercial importance of waterways are not always synonymous with clear and substantial remains. Isolated wrecks, toll records, offloading and river-crossing sites, together with evidence of large-scale trade, can all provide clues for a more complete overview of navigation and river exploitation over time.

Notes

*) Acknowledgements to C. Chateau Smith for her expertise on translation.

1) e.g. Le Jan 2005, 7. – Dumont/Mariotti 2013.

2) e.g. Adams/Laurence 2001. – Schmidts 2011. – Preiser-Kapeller/Werther 2018.

3) www.spp-haefen.de/en/home/

4) Engel et al. 2018.

5) www.spp-haefen.de/en/projects/binnenhaefen-im-fraenkisch-deutschen-reich/

6) Werther et al. 2018.

7) Engel et al. 2017; 2018. – Werther et al. 2018. – Engel/Werther 2017.

8) e.g. Wilson 2012, 5. – Billot 1978.

9) Preiser-Kapeller/Werther 2018. – Werther/Kröger 2017.

10) e.g. Collar et al. 2014.

11) Base Architecture Mérimée 1995.

12) A period of about eight months was allotted to data collection.

13) Werther et al. 2018. – Engel et al. 2018. – Werther/Müller/Foucher 2018.

14) Vessels and wrecks are part of another project within the Harbour SPP (Kröger 2018).

15) McCoy 2017, 74.

16) Franc 2016, 13.

17) Higounet 1978.

18) Roosen/Curtis 2018, 108.

19) See also Wilson 2014. – Cooper/Green 2015.

20) e.g. Billot 1978. – Quantin 1885. – Bauchet 2000. – Fournier/Lavaud 2012.

21) Fournier/Lavaud 2012, 16-18.

22) Horton 1945. – Schumm 1956. – Strahler 1957.

23) e.g. Pierson et al. 2008, 3. – Vogt et al. 2007, 48-49.

24) European Environment Agency 2012.

25) We would like to thank R. Steinmann for his advice on this topic.

26) This did not include sites with uncertain location, whether according to author comments in the datasets, or to location issues (e.g. for confluence sites where it is still impossible to choose the correct river section).

27) The survey mainly focused on navigable river sections. Therefore, the distribution of other river uses is less reliable.

28) Rossiaud 2005, 13.

29) All excavations and survey reports for discoveries along these three rivers were exhaustively recorded in the database.

30) Preiser-Kapeller/Werther 2018.

31) Steinmann 2015, 352-358.

32) e.g. Bravard/Vérot-Bourrély/Franc 1997. – Cremonini/Labate/Curina 2013. – Steinmann 2015, 315. 324. – Franc 2016, 164-168.

33) e.g. Barruol/Fiches/Garmy 2011.

34) Franconi 2016. – Bravard/Vérot-Bourrély/Franc 1997. – Ayala 2011.

35) See also the evolution of the northern district of Lyon, around the banks of the Saône in Vaise (Franc 2016, 166).

36) e.g. Devroey 2006.

37) Dubois 1976. – Rossiaud 2005, 12-13.

38) Dubois 1976.

39) Roosen/Curtis 2018.

40) Territory analyses would undoubtedly benefit from the interplay with other large-scale projects dealing with land structuring, such as, for the Middle Ages, cartularies and normative sources (e.g. Chartae Galliae 2012).

41) e.g. Tranchant 2018. – Lebecq/Béthouart/Verslype 2010. – Sanchez/Jézégou 2016.

References

Adams/Laurence 2001: C. Adams / R. Laurence (eds), Travel and geography in the Roman Empire (London, New York 2001).

Ayala 2011: G. Ayala, Aménagements de berge et activités portuaires à Lugdunum: les apports de la fouille du parc Saint-Georges. In: G. Boetto / P. Pomey / A. Tchernia (eds), Batellerie gallo-romaine. Pratiques régionales et influences maritimes méditerranéennes. Bibliothèque d'Archéologie Méditerranéenne et Africaine 9 (Paris 2011) 77-87.

Barruol/Fiches/Garmy 2011: G. Barruol / J.-L. Fiches / P. Garmy, Les ponts routiers en Gaule romaine. Revue Archéologique de Narbonnaise 41 (Montpellier 2011).

Base Architecture Mérimée 1995: Base Architecture Mérimée, base de données sur le patrimoine architectural français. http://www2.culture.gouv.fr/culture/inventai/patrimoine/ (14.12.2018).

Bauchet 2000: O. Bauchet, Les moulins de la Marne. In: L. Bonnamour, Archéologie de la Saône. 150 ans de recherches (Paris 2000) 127-131.

Billot 1978: C. Billot Chartres et la navigation sur l'Eure à la fin du Moyen Âge. Annales de Bretagne et des Pays de l'Ouest 85/2, 1978, 245-259.

Bravard/Vérot-Bourrély/Franc 1997: J.-P. Bravard / A. Vérot-Bourrély / O. Franc, Paléodynamique du site fluvial de Lyon depuis le

Tardiglaciaire. In: J.-P. Bravard / M. Prestreau (eds), Dynamique du paysage: Entretiens de géoarchéologie. Documents d'Archéologie en Rhône-Alpes 15 (Lyon 1997) 177-202.

Chartae Galliae 2012: Chartae Galliae. Base de données des actes relatifs à la France jusqu'à la fin du XIIIe siècle, portée par la plateforme TELMA (CNRS-IRHT). www.cn-telma.fr/chartae-galliae/index/ (14.12.2018).

Collar et al. 2014: A. Collar / T. Brughmans / F. Coward / C. Lemercier, Analyser les réseaux du passé en archéologie et en histoire. Les Nouvelles de l'Archéologie 135, 2014, 9-13.

Cooper/Green 2015: A. Cooper / C. Green, Embracing the complexities of »big data« in archaeology: the case of the English Landscape and Identities project. Journal of Archaeological Method and Theory 23/1, 2015, 271-304.

Cremonini/Labate/Curina 2013: S. Cremonini / D. Labate / R. Curina, The Late Antiquity environmental crisis in Emilia region (Po river plain, Northern Italy): Geoarchaeological evidence and paleoclimatic considerations. Quaternary International 316, 2013, 162-178.

Devroey 2006: J.-P. Devroey, Économie et société rurales du Haut Moyen Âge occidental: lecture dynamique des sources, compréhension dynamique de la société. Bulletin de la Classe des Lettres de l'Académie Royale de Belgique 17, 2006, 77-99.

Dubois 1976: H. Dubois, Les foires de Chalon et le commerce dans la vallée de la Saône à la fin du Moyen Âge (vers 1280-vers 1430) (Paris 1976).

Dumont/Mariotti 2013: A. Dumont / J.-F. Mariotti (eds), Archéologie et histoire du fleuve Charente. Taillebourg – Port d'Envaux: une zone portuaire du haut Moyen Âge sur le fleuve Charente (Dijon 2013).

Engel/Werther 2017: T. Engel / L. Werther, Harbour Terminology for Data Integration in HARE (Harbour Research Environment), Version 1.0. http://haefen.i3mainz.hs-mainz.de/resources/vendor/HARE_Terminology%20for%20Harbour%20Data%20entry.pdf (25.7.2019).

Engel et al. 2017: T. Engel / L. Werther / M. Foucher / S. Steppan, Short Introduction and Guideline for Harbour Data Entry in HARE. http://haefen.i3mainz.hs-mainz.de/resources/vendor/HARE%20Data%20Entry%20Short%20Introduction%20and%20Guideline.pdf (25.7.2019).

2018: T. Engel / A. Kunz / H. Müller / L. Werther, Towards a Virtual Research Environment for Ancient Harbour Data. In: C. von Carnap-Bornheim / F. Daim / P. Ettel / U. Warnke (eds), Harbours as Objects of Interdisciplinary Research – Archaeology + History + Geosciences. RGZM – Tagungen 34 = Interdisziplinäre Forschungen zu den Häfen von der Römischen Kaiserzeit bis zum Mittelalter in Europa 5 (Mainz 2018) 59-69.

European Environment Agency 2012: European Environment Agency, EEA Catchments and Rivers Network System ECRINS v1.1. Rationales, building and improving for widening uses to Water Accounts and WISE applications (Copenhagen 2012). www.eea.europa.eu/data-and-maps (21.11.2018).

Fournier/Lavaud 2012: P. Fournier / S. Lavaud, Eaux et conflits dans l'Europe médiévale et moderne. Flaran 32 (Toulouse 2012).

Franc 2016: O. Franc (ed.), Histoire des paysages et des sociétés en bord de Saône depuis la dernière glaciation, Lyon-Vaise. Documents d'Archéologie en Rhône-Alpes 44 (Lyon 2016).

Franconi 2016: T. V. Franconi, Climatic influences on riverine transport on the Roman Rhine. In: Ch. Schäfer (ed.), Connecting the Ancient world. Mediterranean shipping, maritime networks and their impact. Pharos 38 (Rahden/Westf. 2016) 27-44.

Higounet 1978: C. Higounet, Géographie des péages de la Garonne et de ses affluents au Moyen Âge. Journal des Savants 1978, 105-130.

Horton 1945: R. E. Horton, Erosional development of streams and their drainage basins; hydrophysical approach to quantitative morphology. Bulletin of the Geological Society of America 56, 1945, 275-370.

Kröger 2018: L. Kröger, Within the network of fluvial ports. In: L. Werther / H. Müller / M. Foucher (eds), European Harbour Data Repository, Vol. 01 (Jena 2018). DOI: 10.22032/dbt.35240 (pdf), 10.22032/dbt.35241 (csv), 10.22032/dbt.35242 (excel).

Lebecq/Béthouart/Verslype 2010: S. Lebecq / B. Béthouart / L. Verslype, Quentovic, environnement, archéologie, histoire (Lille 2010).

Le Jan 2005: R. Le Jan, Avant-propos. In: Ports maritimes et ports fluviaux au Moyen Âge. XXXVe congrès de la SHMES (La Rochelle, 5 et 6 juin 2004). Série Histoire Ancienne et Médiévale 81 (Paris 2005) 7-8.

McCoy 2017: M. D. McCoy, Geospatial Big Data and archaeology: Prospects and problems too great to ignore. Journal of Archaeological Science 84, 2017, 74-94.

Pierson et al. 2008: S. M. Pierson / B. J. Rosenbaum / L. D. McKay / T. G. Dewald, Strahler stream order and Strahler calculator values in NHDPlus [unpubl. SOSC technical paper, 2008].

Preiser-Kapeller/Werther 2018: J. Preiser-Kapeller / L. Werther, Connecting Harbours. A Comparison of Traffic Networks across Ancient and Medieval Europe. In: C. von Carnap-Bornheim / F. Daim / P. Ettel / U. Warnke (eds), Harbours as Objects of Interdisciplinary Research – Archaeology + History + Geosciences. RGZM – Tagungen 34 = Interdisziplinäre Forschungen zu den Häfen von der Römischen Kaiserzeit bis zum Mittelalter in Europa 5 (Mainz 2018) 7-31.

Quantin 1885: M. Quantin, Histoire de la rivière d'Yonne. Bulletin de la Société des Sciences Historiques et Naturelles de l'Yonne 39/1, 1885, 349-498.

Roosen/Curtis 2018: J. Roosen / D. R. Curtis, Dangers of noncritical use of historical plague data. Emerging Infectious Diseases 24/1, 2018, 103-110.

Rossiaud 2005: J. Rossiaud, Les ports fluviaux au Moyen Âge (France, Italie). In: Ports maritimes et ports fluviaux au Moyen Âge. XXXVe congrès de la SHMES (La Rochelle, 5 et 6 juin 2004). Série Histoire Ancienne et Médiévale 81 (Paris 2005) 9-19.

Sanchez/Jézégou 2016: C. Sanchez / M.-P. Jézégou, Les ports dans l'espace Méditerranéen antique. Narbonne et les systèmes portuaires fluvio-lagunaires. Revue Archéologique de Narbonnaise, Supplément 44 (Montpellier 2016).

Schmidts 2011: Th. Schmidts, Akteure und Organisation der Handelsschifffahrt in den nordwestlichen Provinzen des Römischen Reiches. Monographien des RGZM 97 (Mainz 2011).

Schumm 1956: S. A. Schumm, Evolution of drainage systems and slopes in badlands at Perth Amboy, New Jersey. Bulletin of the Geological Society of America 67, 1956, 597-646.

Steinmann 2015: R. Steinmann, L'influence climatique et anthropique sur trois cours d'eaux bourguignons: géoarchéologie de sites de franchissement sur la Loire, la Saône et le Doubs au cours de l'Holocène [diss. Univ. Bourgogne 2015].

Strahler 1957: A. N. Strahler, Quantitative analysis of watershed geomorphology. American Geophysical Union Transactions 38/6, 1957, 913-920.

Tranchant 2018: M. Tranchant, Les ports maritimes de la France atlantique (XIe-XVe siècle). I: Tableau géohistorique (Rennes 2018).

Vogt et al. 2007: J. Vogt / P. Soille / A. de Jager / E. Rimavičiūtė / W. Mehl / S. Foisneau / K. Bódis / J. Dusart / M. L. Paracchini / P. Haastrup / C. Bamps, A pan-European River and Catchment Database. Reference Report of the Joint Research Centre of The European Commission (Luxembourg 2007).

Werther/Kröger 2017: L. Werther / L. Kröger, Medieval inland navigation and the shifting fluvial landscape between Rhine and Danube (Germany). European Journal of Postclassical Archaeologies 7, 2017, 65-96.

Werther/Müller/Foucher 2018: L. Werther / H. Müller / M. Foucher (eds), European Harbour Data Repository. www.db-thueringen.de/receive/dbt_mods_00035239 (14.12.2018).

Werther et al. 2018: L. Werther / M. Foucher / S. Steppan / H. Müller, HArbour Research Environment (HARE), Conference River valleys, river vessels, river harbours – Records from Antiquities and Medieval times, Jena, 2018, poster. DOI: 10.13140/RG.2.2.21261.03047.

Wilson 2012: A. Wilson, Water, power and culture in the Roman and Byzantine worlds: an introduction. Water History 4/1, 2012, 1-9.

2014: A. Wilson, Quantifying roman economic performance by means of proxies: pitfalls and potential. In: F. De Callataÿ (ed.), Quantifying the Greco-Roman economy and beyond (Edipuglia 2014) 147-167.

Summary

Inland harbours, essential links between the Mediterranean and Northern Europe, are the object of the Priority Program Studies of inland harbours in Central Europe as hubs for European communication networks, funded by the Deutsche Forschungsgemeinschaft (DFG). Since 2016, the project has also focused on the French inland river network, in association with the Friedrich-Schiller-University Jena (Germany) and the University of Burgundy (Dijon, France).
Inland harbours can be perceived as multifaceted phenomena, based on comparative, diachronic, multidisciplinary analyses. The modes of harbour installation and the socio-economic processes are examined here, together with the management of waterways and the conditions for navigability, from the 1st century BC to the 15th century AD. The French GIS dataset was compiled to fit the existing database structure, which already contains data for Germany, Benelux, and Northern Italy. Although data distribution for France is still patchy, at this state of the project, our dataset can already be useful for many spatial and/or quantitative analyses. This paper therefore proposes, first, a critical overview of the database, and then a discussion of the type of analyses that can accommodate heterogeneous data. Various methods, including network analysis (Strahler order), and pattern analysis (focusing on the rhythm of appearance and abandonment of harbours), are used to examine the harbour phenomenon within the broader context of historical river uses, competing riverine activities, and reaction to climatic changes.

Résumé

Relais essentiels dans la communication entre Méditerranée et Europe du Nord, les ports des eaux intérieures (rivières et lacs) sont l'objet depuis plusieurs années du programme de recherche « Studies of inland harbours in Central Europe as hubs for European communication networks », financé par la Fondation Allemande pour la Recherche (DFG). En 2016, un nouveau volet, mené en collaboration entre l'Université Friedrich Schiller (Iéna, Allemagne) et l'Université de Bourgogne (Dijon, France), a été consacré à l'ensemble des eaux intérieures du territoire français.
Sur la longue période envisagée, du 1er siècle avant notre ère à la fin du Moyen Âge, le projet s'intéresse aux modalités d'installation des ports, aux fonctionnements socio-économiques sous-jacents, à la gestion des cours d'eau et aux conditions de navigabilité. La compréhension de ces lieux, en tant que phénomènes complexes, se fonde ici sur une vaste analyse comparative, diachronique et pluridisciplinaire des sources relatives aux ports fluviaux et lacustres français. Intégrées à une base de données initiée dans le premier volet du projet sur l'Allemagne, le Benelux et l'Italie du Nord, ces données permettront d'envisager toute une variété d'analyses spatiales et/ou quantitatives. En l'état actuel du projet, les données sont encore très hétérogènes. Après une description critique de la base et de son contenu, cet article est l'occasion de tester différentes méthodes adaptées à des données disparates. L'utilisation de méthodes d'analyse des réseaux fluviaux (rang de Strahler) et la prise en compte des rythmes d'apparition/disparition des ports permettent de replacer le phénomène port dans le contexte plus large de l'exploitation des rivières, des questions de compétition sur cet espace stratégique, et de réactions aux évolutions du milieu naturel.

JIMMY MOUCHARD*

PORT ARCHAEOLOGY IN THE SEINE ESTUARY (FROM ANTIQUITY TO THE MODERN ERA)

The main objective of the research project – doctoral thesis which began in 2003 and to which we have devoted numerous years of archival research – was to take stock of the documentary information concerning the confirmed and supposed ancient and medieval ports of the Seine estuary between Honfleur (dép. Calvados/F) and Caudebec-en-Caux (dép. Seine-Maritime/F). Once the list of 52 paleoports had been compiled, the potential port sites that were still accessible had to be identified. A regressive method and a considerable prospecting effort with surface surveys enabled us to document and inventory the port sites and installations still preserved in the field. Most of these sites were from the Modern or Contemporary periods. Based on these younger sites it also became possible to target those that seemed most likely to be of Roman and/or medieval origin and to set up a campaign of geophysical prospection, microtopographical evaluation and archaeological excavation. The southern bank of the Seine River, which has been less affected by industrialization in the 19th and 20th century AD, provides many opportunities for exploration. Therefore, most of the archaeological operations has been carried out on the southern bank.

DESERTED AND FOSSILIZED PALEOPORT IN AN ESTUARY THAT WAS CHANGING CONTINUALLY THROUGHOUT THE 19TH AND 20TH CENTURY AD

This research to detect paleoports in an estuarial environment was accompanied by certain difficulties. The archaeological features were often destroyed by unprecedented construction works in the 19th and 20th century AD with the channeling of the Seine and the establishment of industrial (petrochemical and refinery) facilities. The maximized utilization of natural resources and raw materials (aggregate mining) have been numerous unfavourable filters for the archaeological sources. These had to be removed if there should be any hope of returning to a state that would approximate the morphology that the Seine had taken by the end of the Modern period.

Between 1848 and 2008 AD, the estuary was subject of five large periods of work, which included dredging and diking operations related to canalizing and deepening the river. This radical transformation of the major and minor riverbeds led to a change of the once natural estuary with multiple river arms to an artificially reshaped estuary with a single canalized channel (**fig. 1**). This transformation was also intended to counter or even eliminate the tidal bore, a wave which is also known as a »riptide« or »swell«. It occurs if tides have a greater coefficient than 100. Within a short time, the water flows back up into the wide and shallow mouth of the estuary. The shallowness and the sudden narrowing of the riverbed upstream of Quillebeuf-sur-Seine (dép. Eure/F), coupled with the confrontation between the rising sea and the drain of the river, accentuate the spread of the tidal bore (from 25 to 40 km/h and up to 2 m high). Observed since Medieval times, the tidal bore has destroyed many anchored and docked boats and even existing riverbank constructions. To reduce or abolish the periodic erosion caused by this phenomenon, diking the Seine became a priority in

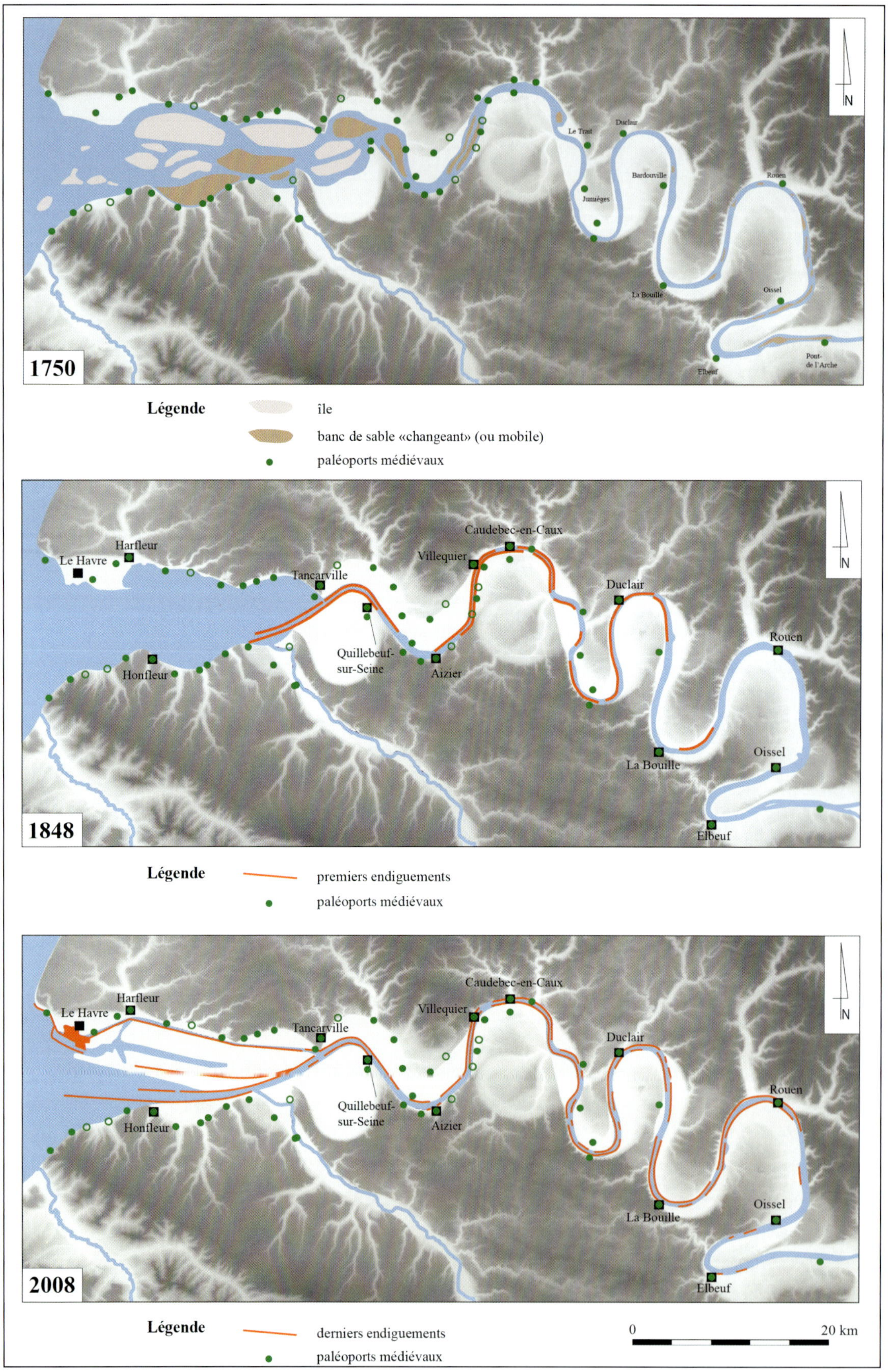

Fig. 1 Development of the course of the Seine since the 18th century AD and the locations of identified antique and medieval paleoports. – (Mouchard 2012).

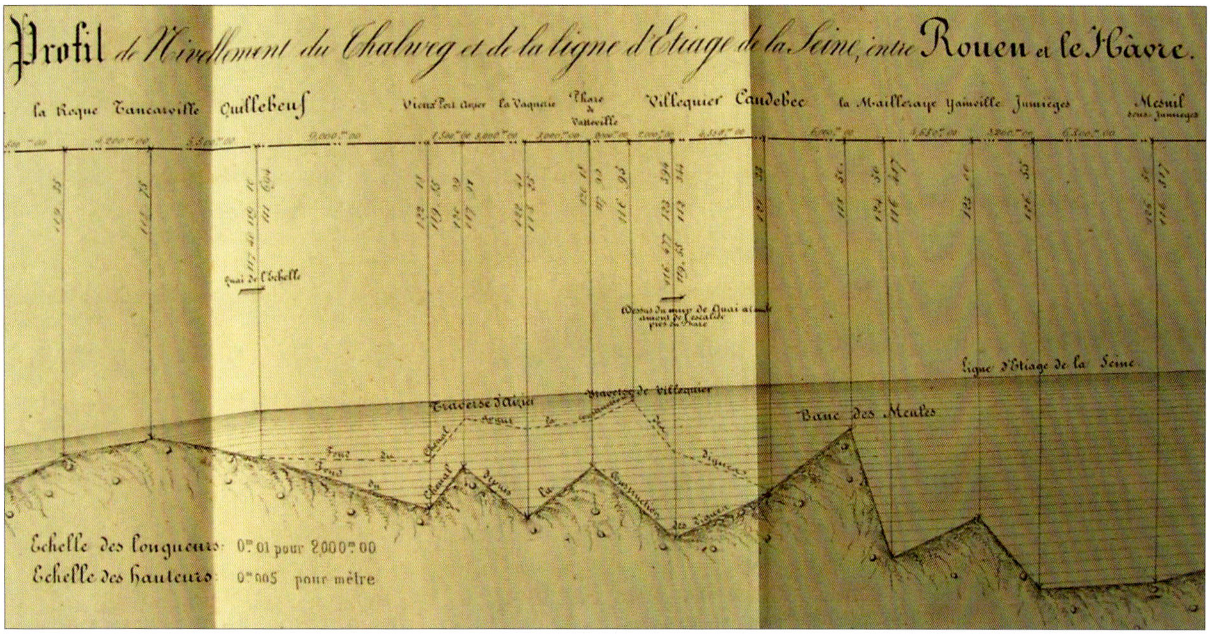

Fig. 2 The shoal or »traverse« of Aizier (dép. Eure/F) before the dyking of the Seine, from a profile created during research of the two dyking projects in Seine-Maritime, by Doyat, 16th July 1850. – (Seine-Maritime Departmental Archives, BSE 484).

1848 AD. But it took more than one century (until 1961 AD) to stop the erosion completely and to construct a new dyke in the downstream estuary.

From the middle of the 19th century AD onwards, almost all natural islands, riverbanks and weirs, which caused numerous shipwrecks since the Middle Ages, were completely destroyed, such as the banks of sediment or »traverses« of Aizier (dép. Eure/F) and Villequier (former dép. Seine-Maritime/F). This was sometimes done at great cost and many dredges were damaged in the process. Not only in the Middle Ages, but still in the 19th century AD, these sedimentary deposits were considerable obstacles for navigation and caused wreckage: between 1842 and 1847 AD, 184 ships stranded on the Villequier »traverse«, and between Aizier and Villequier 105 ships were »lost« from 1830 to 1852 AD. This place was called the »boat cemetery« by sailors. In 1861 AD, Charles Darcel has indicated that:

»... on the Villequier traverse (a moving ridge of silty sand that stretches out, traversing the Seine), the Seine had attained a breadth that was no less than 1,500 m and was scarcely 40 cm deep at low tide. In this period, the largest vessels sailing to Rouen were of a capacity of hardly more than 300 casks and could only pass through the shoals of Aizier during high waters of the spring tides. Further, this traverse had become famous by the numerous shipwrecks: Atthis location, the riptide overturned the vessels that ventured here by misfortune or imprudence and moved them into the mud that finally covered them. Soon the masts could no longer be seen over the sandbanks« [1].

The archives of the Ponts-et-Chaussées [Civil Engineering] and the Port Autonome [Autonomous Port] of Rouen (dép. Seine-Maritime/F) also provide us with a great deal of information concerning the working conditions in 1861 AD and the repercussions of the dredging and diking activities on the ancient historical installations, as well as the historical course of the Seine (**fig. 2**). The engineers left a series of documents including profile drawings, detailed plans, bathymetric charts, land surveys, proposals and reports which enable us to evaluate and appreciate the number of navigational structures having been removed, such as the Aizier »traverse« (which might have been used to ford the river in ancient times) or the permanent fishing weirs of »Roule« in Vatteville-la-Rue (dép. Seine-Maritime/F). Concerning the work related to the improvement of the channel and the dredging in 1922/1923 AD between river kilometres 214,250 and 215,450, it was noted that:

»... this work is complete. Contractors were required to take on additional expenses as a result of the presence of 340 posts, which were approximately 2 m long and had a diameter of 0.15-0.30 m. These posts were joined together along with rubble stones, they belonged to former fisheries... Pulling out the posts and removing the rubble stone was a lengthy and difficult task, and since this work had not been planned, an additional price schedule had to be determined in order to pay the contractors... As a result, two prices were proposed: 25 francs per post for the removal of posts and 30 francs per cubic metre of dredged rubble stone...«[2].

The discovery of a rare Roman iron anchor from northern Gaul resulted precisely from these dredging operations in the meander of Aizier.

As part of the review of the documentation, cartographical materials from the Modern period, which are mainly located in departmental and national archives, were also consulted and provided an opportunity to use the regressive method to reconstruct the historical geography of the estuary from the mid-17th to the 19th century AD. In this period, the configuration and layout of the estuary was similar to the appearance which is recorded in the Napoleonic cadastre, still replete with numerous channels and lined with shoals and islands.

Based on a decade of research, we were able to establish a corpus of 52 supposed ancient and medieval port sites (**fig. 3**). It should nevertheless be noted that due to manifold geomorphological and anthropogenic filters (briefly described above), only about half of these paleoports have been preserved and are still accessible. Among these, several ports were selected to serve as »laboratory sites« for archaeological surveys and analyses. In the next two sections of this article, an overview of several examples of Roman and medieval sites will be presented; these sites have retained their natural form of access (inlet, cove, bay...) or did contain remains of port facilities and equipment.

ROMAN PORT SITES: THE EXAMPLE OF AIZIER

Situated on low terraces, the village of Aizier had long suffered from the consequences of the meandering riverbed before it was canalized in the mid-19th century AD. Flooding and riverbank overflow had the effect of speeding up the silting process and the filling rate between the foot of the hillside and the recent dykes. This new terrain was built up on the floodplain and covered almost all ancient port sites. Still saturated with water and very unstable, this terrain demanded both an archaeological methodology suited to humid environments and specific safety measures to secure the levels during excavation. Most of our knowledge of Aizier comes from a research programme that began in 2003 and was augmented by two survey campaigns in 2005 and 2006. The surveys were followed by an excavation programme from 2009 to 2013.

The researches on Aizier, located on the southern bank between Rouen and Le Havre (dép. Seine-Maritime/F), aimed to highlight the port and the fluvial-maritime development of this nautical area from Antiquity to the present day[3]. The excavation campaign was completed in September 2013, and some of its preliminary findings can now be brought forward.

Situated within the ancient province of Gallia Lugdunensis, this port had a favourable location within the topography of the estuary: it was close to Lillebonne (Juliobona), the main settlement of the Calates on the opposite bank, and connected to overland roads from Brionne (Breviodurum) and Lisieux (Noviomagus, main settlement of the Lexovii on the southern bank). Even if the main ancient sources do not refer to Aizier, they do mention a significant port and trade activity in this region. As Strabo wrote in the 1st century AD:

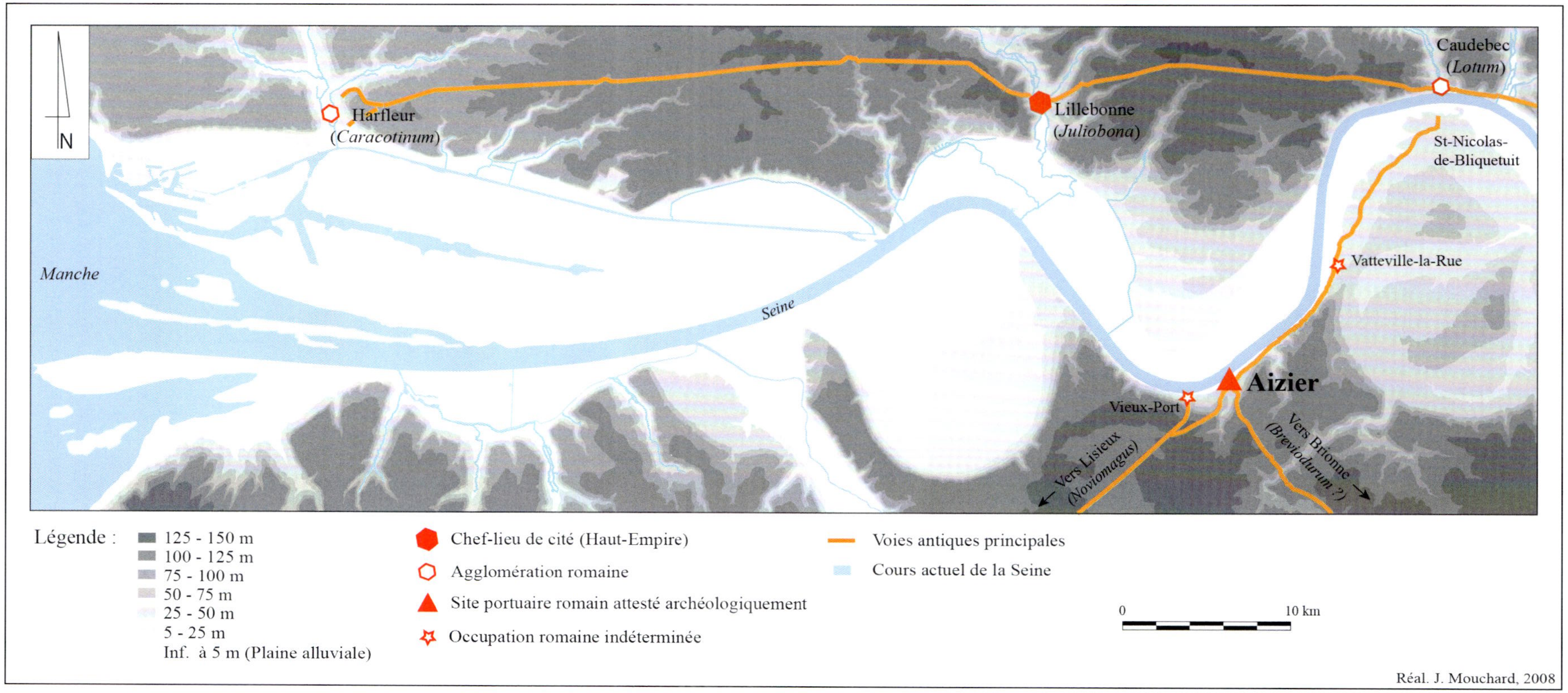

Fig. 3 Paleotopography of the Roman towns and the main roads in the Seine estuary. – (Mouchard 2008).

Fig. 4 The port of Aizier (dép. Eure/F) with the Roman port terrace and its northern facing, constructed in the 2nd century AD. – (Mouchard 2013).

»…the Rhodanus [Rhône] is succeeded by the Arar [Saône], and by the Dubis [Doubs] (which empties into the Arar); then the traffic goes by land as far as the Sequana [Seine] River; and thence it begins its voyage down to the ocean, and to the Lexobii and Caleti«[4].

One of the parcels investigated between 2006 and 2013 has already made it possible to shed light on a set of harbour terraces, observed for nearly 25 m long from east to west, for 13.40 m from north to south, for about 335 m² of artificial bank attributed to the Roman period[5]. At least two main monumental features emerge from the mound of flint limestone masonry work, providing an excellent insight into the development of the installations (lines of quays) developed during the 2st and 3nd century AD.

The first stone feature, which is partially covered by the later terrace, resembles a quay line set slightly farther back by several metres, and in direct contact with the *substratum* (limestone). It consists of a strong facing made of squared slabs assembled with dry-mounted butt joints (**fig. 4**) and holding back dense rubble fill topped with a ground level of compacted limestone.

The second stone feature extends further to the north. It has a large limestone facing assembled with butt joints, it is fully covered by blocks of a different petrographic nature. These blocks are not particularly squared-off and are located close to the riprap (**fig. 5**). This monumental facing is placed directly on the *substratum* (at approximately 1.98 m NGF [General Levelling of France]) and has no specific foundation. It appears preserved best at around 1.4 m height, and it is better preserved in the east in particular. This facing is placed to the rear with perpendicular walls (stiffeners), thus partitioning off some rubble stones in flint and some blocks of limestone scattered about in a jumble. Even if the upper covering of the second Roman terrace was partially salvaged in more recent periods, the few remaining pieces of paving still

Fig. 5 The port of Aizier (dép. Eure/F) with the addition of a new northern facing and the reconstruction of a larger port terrace during the 3rd century AD. – (Mouchard 2013).

in place allow to reconstruct the original floor. It should also be noted that the southern part of the last terrace still has vestiges of two Roman wells. One of them can be reached by stairs cutting the rubble fill of the terrace.

Furthermore, this group of ancient platforms is overlaid with thick, successive deposits of river sediments, which have filled in the gaps and irregularities of the rubble stone terrace, which was partially destroyed and then renewed after having been abandoned. In some sections, the grey deposited sand contains pieces of driftwood (sometimes remnants of naval architecture), and even some medieval dug structures. Increasingly numerous towards the west, these ones are signs for the reoccupation of the riverbank before the sector has been modified completely in the Modern era and a new quay line was installed.

This coordinated research effort, which involved several campaigns under difficult conditions, gave us a compelling perspective on the architectural and morphological characteristics of the roman transhipment facility that had long been thought to have been located there. As these multiple constructions and arrangements correspond to different conditions, serval way of landing or docking for varied hull draft were then possible. In this respect, let us add that a re-examination of the 2.2 m long iron anchor mentioned above, which was discovered during the previous dredging operations several dozens of metres from this site is interesting: this artefact can now be dated to the period between the 1st and the 3rd century AD. It is also clear that it was used on a vessel of relatively considerable tonnage, which was most likely seagoing[6]. Although it is too early to answer the question of the type of goods that passed through the port, at this stage, Aizier is the only site in the downstream section of the Seine estuary that has yielded remains of roman port constructions. Furthermore, these constructions shave characteristics of maritime architecture.

MEDIEVAL PORT SITES AND THEIR GEO-TOPOGRAPHICAL ORIGINS

Within our research of the Roman infrastructure, we were also able to expand our understanding of the Medieval period. We did not only find evidence of dense port settlements dating from the 13th to the 16th century AD (approximately 40 sites), but it was also possible to identify different types of paleoports[7]. The bulk of this research is based not on detecting possible vestigial infrastructure, but instead on locating places where natural and topographical features favoured the establishment of port activities. The variety of topographical conditions is reflected in the terminology in written sources (bay [baie], cove [anse], inlet [crique], haven [havre], pool [fosse] and so on). The vocabulary and the terms actually used between the Medieval and the Modern era are perfect indicators for the port characteristics in regard of the places chosen. This first step in discovering sites that are naturally favourable for all kinds of port activity is to gain expertise concerning topography. In the end, this research shows that the Seine estuary, with its specific topographical, hydrological and geomorphological features, was a favourable environment for the development of ports. The port sites could be divided into two types: those in deep water and those that take advantage of beaches and alluvial fills.

First, ports which made use of eroded areas in deep water are predominant. From these open and hollow settings, several categories of sites emerge: inlets, coves, pools, harbours [rades] and other gulfs that take advantage of the topographical irregularities and inlets along the riverbank. This array of recesses along the shore can correspond to different situations that are transverse to the course of the river to a greater or lesser degree or stretch longitudinally to the bank.

One of the most significant sites is the »fosse« or stream pool of Leure (dép. Seine-Maritime/F) which stretched along the former course of the Seine like a canal in the 12th century AD. Parallel to the river course for a length of nearly 1.5 km, it served as an outer harbour for the fortified town of Harfleur (dép. Seine-Maritime/F), providing an exceptional place for high tonnage vessels to dock. This situation is documented by accounts of the heavy rain and flooding of 1407 AD, when 52 vessels were trapped in the »fosse de Leure«[8]. The site vanished during the Modern era, due to the development of the town of Le Havre, and to the multiplication of many phenomena of aggradation and silting at the Lézarde River outlet as well.

Further, the port »inlets [criques]«, such as those at Graville, Tancarville and even Vatteville-la-Rue (all dép. Seine-Maritime/F) are well documented. In the Middle Ages, the first was situated at the mouth of the Seine, on the northern bank near the »fosse de Leure«. Known as the »crique de Graville« in 1372 AD, it could correspond to the »*Giraldi fossa*« mentioned in 855 AD or even to the »crique Le Brasseur«, which survived until the 16th century AD[9]. Connected to the numerous channels/estuarine inlets arriving from the ocean and penetrating into the floodplain, it was located at the foot of the medieval Mallet's castle. This is quite typical, and several other estuary inlets did also have well-established links to fortifications. According to Le Maho, »the part of the motte that passed forward out of the terrace was surrounded by ponds that fed a neighbouring spring and overflowed into a natural inlet, the ›Fosse-de-Graville‹«[10]. As the »crique de Vatteville« has already been extensively described[11], the Tancarville inlet, which sometimes is referred to as an »hable« or haven, deserves to be discussed briefly. Mentioned as early as 1114, the port of Tancarville was frequently referred to in connection with the transport of goods and building materials via its »hable«[12] (haven) and its »cais« (quays), especially between the 15th and 18th century AD[13]. It consists of a semi-circular, concave port basin located at the confluence of a small waterway that emptied into the Seine. It was surmounted by one of the largest fortresses of the lower Seine area. In a map from 1717 AD, the Tancarville haven is still surrounded by water and, like Graville and Vatteville, it has the shape of a horn (**fig. 6a**). The site was gradually silted up during the 18th century AD and its fate was sealed by the dyking operations and the inevitable filling-in with alluvial sediments at the foot of the castle. This is indicated in a

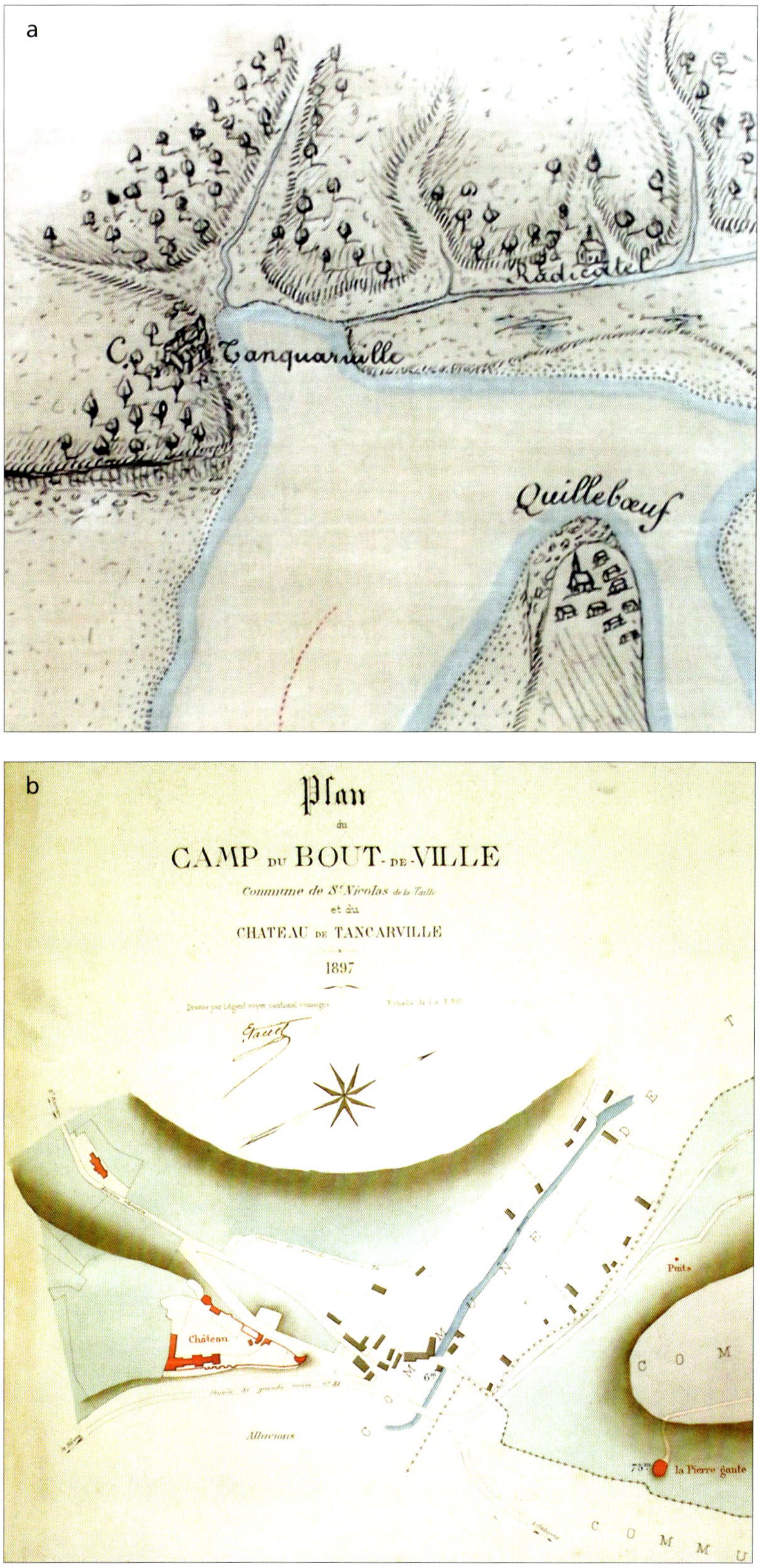

Fig. 6 Tancarville (dép. Seine-Maritime/F): **a** the inlet or haven, according to the »Map of the Seine River as would be expected, with its deeps and shallows, in the month of November 1717, and the Canal to the south«. – **b** the haven filled in with alluvial sediments, map of the Bout-de-ville encampment, the village of Saint-Nicolas-de-la-Taille and of the castle of Tancarville, 1897. – (a 1st map, plate XIX, École Nationale des Ponts et Chaussées, uncatalogued; b Seine-Maritime Departmental Archives, 6FI 36 Fi 3).

map from 1897 AD preserved in the departmental archives (**fig. 6b**), which also shows the outlet of the river that drove the watermill of the »hable« during the Middle Ages[14]. The shape of the former haven remains clearly visible today in the semi-circular shape of the settlement and land parcels.

The second category of medieval paleoports developed on sedimentary deposits. These types of ports have been documented on the left riverbank, between Fatouville-Grestain (dép. Eure/F) and Saint-Nicolas-de-Bliquetuit (dép. Seine-Maritime/F). Several terms in the written sources refer to the specific topographical configuration of this category, for example, »grève« or »strand« and »perrey« or »shingle beach«, such as the »perrey de Leure« near the »fosse« mentioned earlier. Geographers and cartographers indicate that »grève« is a very old word. Its meaning is connected to the notion of a shallow shore that slopes gently to the water's edge; its shallowness facilitates the landing of boats and thus makes the installation of port facilities such as quays, pontoons, piers and docks optional. Isolated today in the dry land, the paleoport of Berville (dép. Eure/F) was once characterised by a landing site called the »perrey« of the river. It was also associated with the term »posée« or place for boats to anchor [15]. We also have to mention the medieval »perrey« of Quillebeuf located close to the »rue aux Bœufs« [16], the point of departure for ferries leaving for Tancarville on the opposite bank. Now covered by reeds and grasses, this ancient perré or shore for beaching vessels is largely unknown and awaiting a field study.
From this common point, the meanders of the Seine with the convex areas provide many possible locations for port installations (silting and alluvial deposits). In the Middle Ages and even in the Modern era, these new sites were modified so that they were more or less perpendicular to the line of the riverbank. This is demonstrated by some port dykes that were usually unsinkable, and intended to ensure the connection between the two riverbanks. Such sites included Petiville (dép. Seine-Maritime/F) positioned on the diagonal facing the port of »Courval« (Trouville-la-Haule, dép. Eure/F) and Saint-Nicolas-de-Bliquetuit, which faces Caudebec (Caudebec-en-Caux). This sort of »port and passage« arrangement can be found throughout the estuary since 1137 AD documented by the Calde Becci »*Passagium portus*« [17]; it seems to have remained functional until the 19th century AD. The Saint Nicolas dyke was built on an accumulation of alluvial sediments. This caused recurrent problems in the Modern era, and more filling material often had to be added for mainting the dyke. Thus, several inspections were organized in 1535-1536 AD to promote and make plans for the maintenance and repair of the dyke [18]. The successful petition for repairing the port and passage dyke of the Seine River suggests that repairs were carried out in 1661 and 1689 AD. This involved work similar to overland roads which were covered with successive loads of stone in order to improve the flow of pedestrians, carts and animal traffic on the sodden, swampy terrain. The dyke in Moulineaux (dép. Seine-Maritime/F), which followed the course of the Seine up to the gates of the town of Rouen, had the same characteristics, since it crossed the marsh: »Beneath the castle of Moulineaux [which is where] the dyke began that closely crossed the Seine, and is still there, by which all merchants and merchandise, wagons, carts and carriages travel to the bank of the Seine and are loaded onto vessels and boats and cross the aforesaid river« [19].

CONCLUSION

The historical and geoarchaeological research of the Seine estuary has enlightened many new port sites. They are conveyed in the medieval and modern vocabulary, which does not refer to men-made structures and port installations but to the topography and the natural conditions. This topographical knowledge is crucial to avoid potential pitfalls for prospection and surface surveys. In the 19th and 20th century AD, the search for vestiges of ancient port activities was skewed and misdirected as a result of distorted definitions of ports and their components. In general, efforts were focused exclusively on trying to find evidence of port facilities, particularly quays and their rings of mooring.
The second crucial point, which must be taken into account, is that only half of all the identified historical sites can still be studied archaeologically; most of them are located on the southern riverbank, which has

been less affected by the radical modern transformations and the loss of archaeological sources. In the end, studying an estuary paleoport at least in the Seine Valley leads us to reflect on three potential configurations, which can appear in numerous combinations: sites that make use of recesses in the shoreline and take advantage of the deep water, sites that develop on alluvial deposits, and sites with solid harbour constructions. Inlets, havens, dykes, quays and ancient medieval port terraces are usually silted up today. Nevertheless, even if we managed to highlight in this study some types of antique and medieval ports typical for the Seine estuary, one has to keep in mind the difficulties of archaeological researches in such environments and all adapted methods they may require[20].

Notes

*) Translation by J. Holland, J. Mouchard and M. Foucher.

1) Seine-Maritime Departmental Archives, 3 S, Darcel (Ch.), 1861. »Amélioration de la Seine Maritime, prolongement de l'endiguement vers la mer, enquête de 1860«, report by M. Darcel (Ch.), Rouen, 5-6.

2) Seine-Maritime Departmental Archives, 3 S 213: Dragages, 1922-1923.

3) Arthuis et al. 2010. – Arthuis/Guitton/Mouchard 2010. – Mouchard 2013.

4) Strab. IV, 1, 14; after Jones 1923, 211 bk. IV § 1.14.

5) Mouchard 2011; 2013.

6) Mouchard/Sadania 2012.

7) Mouchard in print.

8) Mollat 1952, 6.

9) Chazelas 1977, 238. – Martin 1917, 5.

10) Le Maho 1976, 109.

11) Mouchard in print.

12) Seine-Maritime Departmental Archives, 1 ER 222.

13) Seine-Maritime Departmental Archives, 1 ER 122. – Seine-Maritime Departmental Archives, 1 ER 84-F° 201 v.

14) Seine-Maritime Departmental Archives, 1 ER 11: On 22 May 1496, the accounts of Tancarville indicate: »Item, tous batteaux prostrez, qui adhesent dedans le hable du moulin dudit lieu, pour chascun battel, on doibt quatre deniers… [Item: all unfit boats that are at rest in the haven of the mill at the aforesaid place, for each of these is owed four pieces of silver…]«.

15) Seine-Maritime Departmental Archives, 1 ER 286.

16) Seine-Maritime Departmental Archives, 1 ER 10.

17) Lot 1913, 121.

18) Seine-Maritime Departmental Archives, 16 H 128-16 H 130.

19) Robillard de Beaurepaire 1856, 172: »Soubz le chastel de Moulineaux [où] commençait la chaussée qui s'en aloit à travers des prez en Seine, et encore y est, par laquelle touz marchanz et toutes marchandises, charriots, charrettes et voitures alouent jusque sur le bord de la Seine et illec chargeoient en Fleites et bateaux et traversoient ladite rivière«.

20) Appropriate logistics (power shovels, power pumps, thermal core drillers and so on), strong focus on security, and safe methods of sampling and data collection.

Source

Jones 1923: The Geography of Strabo, vol. II, translated by H. L. Jones. The Loeb Classical Library 50 (London 1923).

References

Arthuis/Guitton/Mouchard 2010: R. Arthuis / D. Guitton / J. Mouchard, D'un estuaire à l'autre: Géoarchéologie comparée des ports antiques d'Aizier (Seine) et de Rezé (Loire). Archéopages 30, 2010, 26-35.

Arthuis et al. 2010: R. Arthuis / D. Guitton / M. Monteil / J. Mouchard / O. de Perreti, Archéologie portuaire estuarienne entre Loire et Seine: principaux résultats et questions d'ordre méthodologique. L'exemple des sites antiques d'Aizier (Eure) et de Rezé (Loire-Atlantique). In: L. Hugot / L. Tranoy (eds), Actes de la Journée d'études sur les structures portuaires de l'arc atlantique dans l'Antiquité (bilan et perspectives de recherches), La Rochelle 2008. Aquitania, Supplément 18 (Bordeaux 2010) 61-82.

Chazelas 1977: A. Chazelas, Documents relatifs au clos des galées et aux armées de mer du roi de France de 1293 à 1418 (Paris 1977).

Le Maho 1976: J. Le Maho, L'apparition des seigneuries châtelaines dans le Grand-Caux à l'époque ducale. Archéologie Médiévale 6, 1976, 5-148.

Lot 1913: F. Lot, Études critiques sur l'abbaye de Saint-Wandrille (Paris 1913).

Martin 1917: A. Martin, IVe Centenaire du Havre, origines du XIIe au XVIe siècle (Le Havre 1917).

Mollat 1952: M. Mollat, Le commerce maritime normand à la fin du Moyen Âge. Études d'histoire économique et sociale (Paris 1952).

Mouchard 2008: J. Mouchard, Les sites portuaires gallo-romains et médiévaux de l'estuaire de la Seine [diss. Univ. Rouen 2008].

2011: J. Mouchard, Aizier (Eure), géoarchéologie d'un paléoport estuarien. In: Journées Archéologiques de Haute-Normandie, Harfleur, 23-25 Avril 2010 (2011), 201-218.

2013: J. Mouchard, Le port romain d'Aizier (Eure): principaux résultats de la campagne 2011. In: Journées Archéologiques de Haute-Normandie, Rouen, 11-13 mai 2012 (2013), 93-102.

in print: J. Mouchard, Archéologie portuaire estuarienne entre Loire et Seine: possibilités et limites (approche diachronique). In: Actes de la Table ronde internationale organisée à Namur en 2012, Les fleuve, les hommes: Spécificités et variabilités des études en milieu fluvial (in print) 104-122.

Mouchard/Sadania 2012: J. Mouchard / M. Sadania, L'ancre à jas mobile d'Aizier. Cahiers d'Archéologie Subaquatique 19, 2012, 37-47.

Robillard de Beaurepaire 1856: Ch. Robillard de Beaurepaire, De la Vicomté de l'eau de Rouen et de ses Coutumes au XIIIe et au XIVe siècle (Evreux 1856).

Summary

This article discusses research from 2003 to 2013 with the aim of detecting, studying and obtaining a better understanding of the Roman and medieval port sites of the Seine River estuary. After some trial and error (2003-2005), it has been possible to apply a method of gathering and recording data in a riverine environment that has too often been considered hostile for archaeological research. We had surmised, incorrectly and for a long time, that these ancient ports had been destroyed during the 20th century AD by the establishment of numerous industrial facilities, by the operation of aggregate mining facilities, and, especially, by the significant dredging and dyking operations from the 19th century AD onwards. The present diachronic research effort has enabled us to establish an inventory of 52 potential antique and medieval port sites; we have also highlighted sites that are truly lost and inaccessible, threatened by erosion and/or destruction, and sites that have been preserved and allow for further analyses. Finally, the different archaeological campaigns on several of these sites enlighten some of their morphological and architectural features, thus contributing to the gradual development of a typological catalogue of the »paleoports« constructed in the estuary during the last two millennia.

Résumé

Cet article fait état d'une recherche effectuée entre 2003 et 2013, ayant pour objectifs de détecter, étudier et mieux caractériser les sites portuaires romains, médiévaux et post-médiévaux établis dans l'estuaire de la Seine. Après de nombreux tâtonnements (2003-2005), il a été possible d'appliquer une méthode d'acquisition et d'enregistrement des données dans un espace nautique trop souvent considéré comme hostile par les archéologues. Pendant longtemps, nous pensions que ces anciens ports avaient été éradiqués par la mise en place – au cours du 20e siècle apr. J.-C. – de réserves naturelles, par la présence d'une forte industrialisation, par l'exploitation de sites d'extraction de granulats, et surtout, par les importants travaux de dragages et d'endiguements opérés depuis le 19e siècle apr. J.-C. Cette recherche diachronique a permis d'arrêter l'inventaire à cinquante-deux sites potentiels, principalement médiévaux, tout en soulignant les sites réellement condamnés et inaccessibles, les sites menacés d'érosion et/ou de destruction ainsi que les sites préservés et en attente d'étude. Enfin, les différentes campagnes de prospections et de fouilles réalisées sur certains d'entre eux renseignent désormais sur quelques aspects morphologiques et architecturaux, favorisant l'émergence progressive d'un catalogue typologique des paléo-ports installés dans cet estuaire sur les deux derniers millénaires.

RÉMY ARTHUIS · FRÉDÉRIC MERCIER · ÉRIC ARMYNOT DU CHÂTELET
AXELLE GANNE · EVELYNE GOUBERT*

NANTES AND THE LOIRE: A COMPLEX HISTORY AT THE CROSSROADS BETWEEN HUMANITIES AND EARTH SCIENCE

The town of Nantes (dép. Loire-Atlantique/F) developed at the confluence of the Erdre and the Loire Rivers, a strategic choice of location. The relationship between the city and the rivers therefore merits investigation, from the earliest agglomeration in Antiquity to the Medieval, Modern, and Contemporary periods. The position of the city is clearly linked to the traffic on the river, controlling as it does the head of the estuary, at the point of transhipment between fluvial and maritime navigation. Since its earliest days, Nantes probably played the strategic role it continues to play in the management of all forms of transport. Not only river and maritime transport, but also terrestrial traffic, via a network of roads that converge towards the river crossing, materialized by a line of bridges attested in the archives since at least the 9th century AD.
Even though the geographic context was probably decisive in the choice of location for the city, as historians have long emphasized[1], this hypothesis has yet to be confirmed by scientific evidence. Among the research objectives for the Loire River studies, the primary goal is to identify and locate the initial river crossing, at the time of the earliest agglomeration. The oldest traces so far known are dated around 30-40 AD. Another major goal is to identify the location of the city's ports prior to the 13th century AD.
The initial goal was to understand the evolution of the river on the outskirts of Nantes, in order to identify any traces of earlier Loire landscapes (islands, channels, marshes, etc.). Such traces could help to identify sites suited to the establishment of a river crossing and a harbour. Beyond this structural theme, studies have also focused more broadly on the search for proven or potential traces of human activities directly linked to the Loire River, such as boundary walls, canals, mills, and fisheries[2] (**fig. 1**).

TRACING THE EVOLUTION OF THE RIVER AND ITS LANDSCAPE FROM THE MODERN PERIOD, THROUGH THE MIDDLE AGES, BACK TO ANTIQUITY

In 1968, the first geological maps of the lower Loire Valley were published, providing an »autopsy« of alluvial filling. The analysis of biological and archaeological remains therein would bring the opening sequences of the river's evolution to light[3]. Very quickly, these initial observations of alluvial content, correlated with historical evidences, unambiguously indicated that the lower part of the Loire, between Ponts-de-Cé (dép. Maine et Loire/F) and the estuary, had transported a great deal of sand since the 16th century AD[4]. These sediment dynamics are the result of soil erosion in the Loire catchment area, due to human activity, no doubt accentuated by the worsening climate of the Little Ice Age. Together, these two factors led to famine, a major catalyst of the French Revolution. The abundant bedload of sand was also the result of the acceleration of alluvial transfer following the narrowing of the Loire riverbed by the establishment of levees during the Middle Ages. Many accretions were thus formed[5], and then reinforced and stabilised by riparian farmers seeking to extend their land. It worth pointing out that, in the 17th century AD, one of the rights of the Lords of Ancenis (dép. Loire-Atlantique/F) was the right of extension into the River Loire, and that of

Fig. 1 Reprint of the Map of Nantes showing growth and changes that have occurred since 1757 AD, Paris, Le Rouge, 1766. – (Reprinted by Nantes City Library, 1991, Inv. 1Fi 40).

planting the islands, shores, mounds and humps[6]. These sediment dynamics, coupled with the desire by riparian farmers to seize new lands, led to the accretion and consolidation of islands in the river. This situation evolved gradually, with 22 islands visible in the Loire riverbed between Saint-Florent-le-Vieil (dép. Maine et Loire/F) and Champtoceaux (dép. Maine et Loire/F) in 1666 AD, then 17 in 1765 AD, 13 in 1811 AD, 10 in 1851 AD, and only 8 in 1973 AD[7].

Fig. 2 The Gué aux Moines (monks' ford) fishery, at Saint-Florent-le-Vieil Abbey, built in the late 10th century AD, and maintained until the beginning of the 13th century AD. – (Photo D. Fillon, Inrap, 2009).

For the Medieval period, the numerous archaeological sites discovered in the active channel of the Loire River, upstream of Nantes, provide the best information about the way the river functioned. These sites, previously covered with sand accumulated during the Modern period, became visible in the main channel after it deepened, due to intensive dredging, aggregate extraction, and the narrowing of the channel, as dikes and groynes were installed along the riverbanks. The remains of fisheries, mills, and shipwrecks have been identified, dating from the 9th to the 15th century AD. Chronological analyses of the Gué aux Moines (monks' ford) fishery show that such structures, if well-maintained, could serve for several generations, even centuries (**fig. 2**)[8]. Many such installations along the Loire Valley operated during the same period and were located at similar altitudes, indicating that the river flow has changed little over time. It was also during this period that canals intended for navigation were dug along the hillsides, to serve towns and villages in the Loire Valley that were isolated from the river to some extent by marshy flood zones[9]. The presence of such structures, particularly sensitive to fluvial changes, especially those likely to increase the alluvial load transported, which silted up the river mouth in the Modern period, thus also indicates a certain hydrological tranquillity. It is therefore likely that the Lower Loire landscape at the beginning of the Middle Ages was not that different from the one of the 16th century AD, although channel avulsion may have occurred and temporary islands may have appeared and disappeared as the river flooded its banks.
Few archaeological traces have been identified for periods prior to the Middle Ages, with the notable exception of the ancient port of Saint-Lupien at Rezé (dép. Loire-Atlantique/F), and some isolated shipwrecks. The evolution of the course of the Lower Loire and its islands can therefore only be understood by observation and analysis of the alluvium transported to Nantes, which is around 30 m thick today[10]. An analysis of this fossil alluvium shows that sediment accumulation was mainly due to a rise in sea level, a consequence of the global warming that transformed the climate from glacial to temperate. St. Nazaire (dép. Loire-Atlantique/F) was originally at a distance of 100 km from the ocean. In only 15,000 years, the rapid rise in sea level moved the shoreline to its present level. This strong dynamic allowed the ocean to enter the Loire Valley as far as Nantes and even beyond, some 7,500 years ago. The valley at Nantes was at that time a ria, composed of a vast mud floodplain colonized by vegetation, through which flowed tidal channels. This mud, from 10 to 15 m thick, sealed off the valley floor and erased the previous Loire River network. About 4,500 years ago, at the end of the Neolithic period, as the rise in sea level slowed down, the ocean gradually withdrew from

the valley. In its place was a conquering river, transporting sand, and incising channels in the mud of the estuary and the ocean. This process formed the hydrographic network that can be seen today, beginning with the creation of the Madeleine and Pirmil branches of the Loire. This means that the Prairie aux Ducs island, separating these two branches, and occupying a predominant place in the valley today, has been in existence for 4,500 years, alongside the island of Grande Biesse, which is even older, formed as it was from a rocky outcrop.

The considerable mass of sediments accumulated in the valley reactivated the fault scarp of the Sillon de Bretagne. This caused a relative tilt of the alluvial plain, resulting in the southward migration of the Pirmil channel and, to a lesser extent, that of the Madeleine channel. The Madeleine and Mauves plains north of the valley were spared by the active river channels, and continued to function as somewhat marshy floodplains 4,500 years later. This migration is the least well-known aspect of the river's history, yet it involved a third of the surface of the floodplain. The lateral displacement of these branches of the Loire caused erosion and aggradation, actions conducive both to the formation of islands and to their disappearance. Recent research has shown that two islands, Chevaliers and Vertais, located in the zone affected by the migration of the Pirmil branch, were already in place at the end of Protohistory. Does this mean that the migration to the south occurred earlier, and that for about 2,500 years, the main channels of the Loire have been in their current location? This debate has not yet been resolved (**fig. 3**).

THE FLUVIAL COMPONENTS OF THE LOIRE LANDSCAPE BETWEEN THE ANCIENT CITIES OF CONDEVICNUM (NANTES) AND RATIATUM (REZÉ)

The oldest elements of the Loire landscape around Nantes are the island of Grande Biesse, that of Prairie aux Ducs, the floodplains of Madeleine and Mauves, and the Rezé marsh, located downstream from the confluence with the Sèvre Nantaise. These features appeared 4,500 years ago, in the Late Neolithic, when the Loire Valley near Nantes, a true ria dominated by marine influences, gradually gave way to a conquering river that incised the Pirmil and Madeleine branches. Later, during the southward migration of the Pirmil branch, at least two islands developed (recognised by radiocarbon dating), during the end of Protohistory, around 2,500 years ago: the islands of Chevaliers and Vertais[11].

Paleogeography thus makes it possible to form some impression of the ancient Loire landscape at a time when two ancient cities were founded, Condevicnum (Nantes) and Ratiatum (Rezé), one on each side of the river.

The position of the island of Chevaliers, at the entrance to the ancient port of Saint-Lupien in Rezé, provides information about the branch of the Loire River on which the quays lay. It was a secondary branch, separated from the main channels, which may explain why it silted up rapidly at the end of Antiquity, leading to the abandonment of the port[12].

The presence of Vertais near the island of Grande Biesse and the Madeleine plain indicates that the geological foundation of the medieval line of bridges, recorded in the archives since the 9th century AD, was in place before Antiquity. The layout of the islands south of Nantes was therefore already suitable for a river crossing. This geographic particularity probably influenced the choice of location for the two cities and for the route between the ancient provinces of Gallia Aquitania to the south, and Gallia Lugdunensis to the north. This hypothesis, based on geological and environmental data, has not yet been validated by structural archaeological observations.

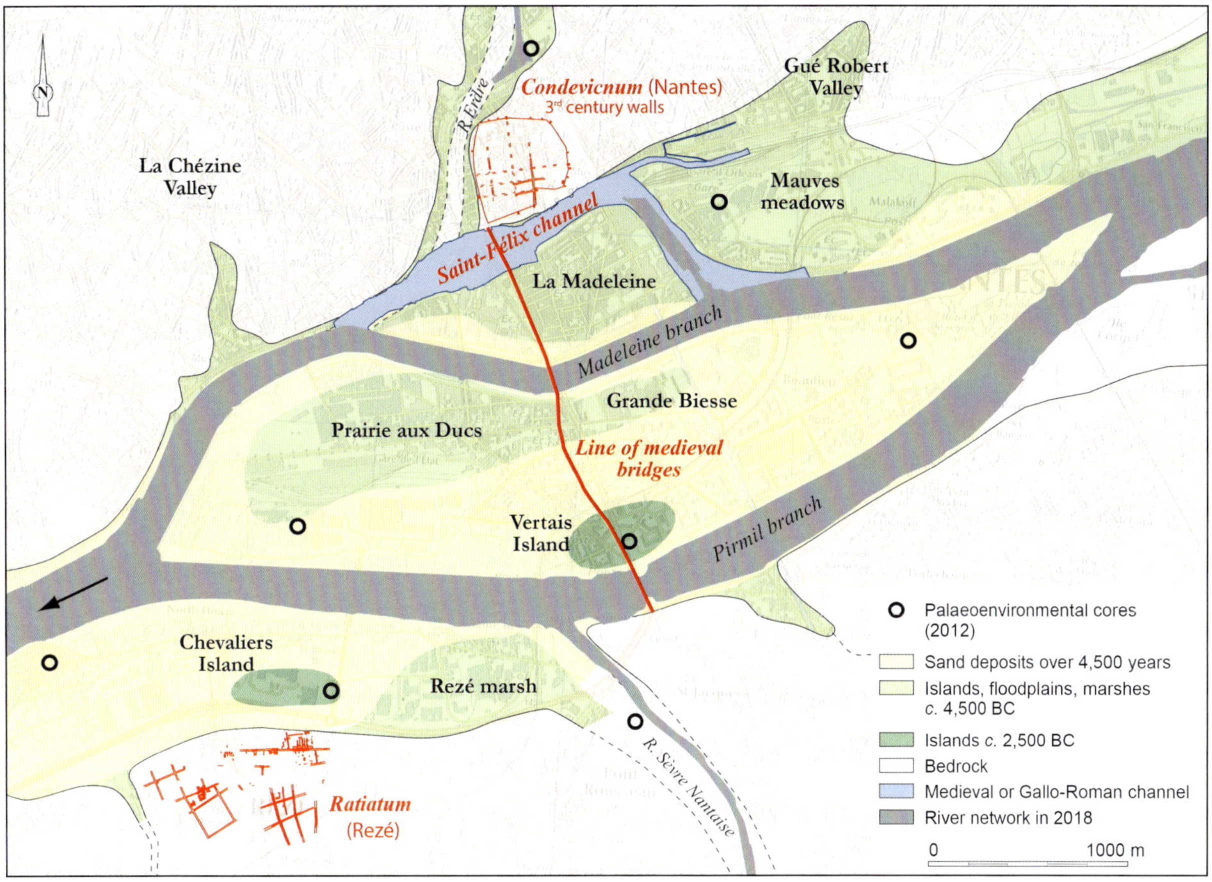

Fig. 3 The fluvial and archaeological components of the Loire Valley near Nantes. – (R. Arthuis / H. Hostein, Inrap, 2017).

THE RELATIONSHIP BETWEEN THE CITY AND THE RIVER: CANAL AND PORTS

Recent studies show that, at the end of Protohistory, the city of Nantes was bounded by a vast floodplain and marshes, replaced today by the meadows of Madeleine and Mauves. The nearest channel, the Madeleine branch of the Loire River, was a kilometre away. At the beginning of the 4th century AD, the ancient walled city was therefore not on the Loire, but on the banks of the Erdre River, which was better suited to the creation of a port. The Saint-Félix channel ran parallel to the southern ramparts of the ancient city. Had it been in existence at that time, the channel would have linked the city to the Loire, and a tidal river port could have been installed there. The history of this channel is therefore essential for the relationship between the city of Nantes and the Loire River. What has recent research revealed about it?

The question of the origin of this channel, natural or artificial, which still ran past the Île Feydeau in the early 20th century AD, has been debated by historians since Dubuisson-Aubenay who visited Brittany in 1636 AD. He mused about the singularity of its layout, physically interwoven with the city in Antiquity, and in the Middle Ages[13]. There is an unusual adaptation of the morphology to the southern town boundaries, following exactly the contours of the first fortification of Nantes (3th-4th century AD). Dubuisson-Aubenay was the first to formulate the hypothesis of a canal, attributed to Felix, bishop of Nantes in the 6th century AD. He drew upon a poem by Fortunatus, bishop of Poitiers, a contemporary of Felix, who glorified the monumental hydraulic work of his friend in Nantes, without, however, specifying the exact place and the real nature of the work. The attribution of the creation of a canal to bishop Félix by historians relies exclusively on this

text. It has been part of local toponymy from the middle of the 18th century AD, with the designation Saint-Félix Canal for the channel that ran alongside the Roman and medieval ramparts.
In 2011, two rescue operations were conducted by Nantes Metropole (Carré-Feydeau) and by the Inrap (Bouffay-Feydeau). They provided the opportunity to verify this hypothesis. This research project followed on from several previous paleo-environmental studies[14].
The results of this investigation were unequivocal: the Saint-Félix channel was a canal. This characterization is based on geological analysis, showing it to be a morphological anomaly in the Loire River network. In comparison with the Madeleine and Pirmil branches, both of which are more than 200 m wide, with channels that have moved 10 m vertically, and more than 500 m laterally, the Saint-Félix channel never measured more than 100 m wide, with a maximum depth of 4 m. The course of the Saint-Félix channel remained unchanged until the 1930s AD, when it was filled in. The Madeleine and Pirmil branches, with a geological footprint dating back 4,500 years, were marked by lateral movements powered by water and sand transport. In contrast, the geometry and layout of the Saint-Félix channel remained stable over time. This stability shows that water flow alone could never have provided the power necessary to dig out such a channel, which must, therefore, have resulted from human intervention.
Consequently, a canal must have flowed along the base of the medieval walls, and possibly even along the Roman city wall. This canal, because of its position and size, must have contributed both to the defence of the city, and to the economic vitality of its port.
Archaeological excavation of the Saint-Félix canal, however, did not make it possible to specify when it was first dug, as repeated dredging over time not only cleaned the channel, but also eradicated the oldest remains, whether structural (docks or pontoons), sedimentary, or more mobile (no traces of wrecks). The only certainty is that the canal was dug out before the 13th century AD, when its presence can be identified by references in historical texts to the ports of Maillard and Pierre de France. It must have been created at the end of the Iron Age or at the beginning of Antiquity, for reasons of compatibility in water level between the canal and the Loire River. The historical origin of the channel is therefore certain. It remains essential to identify more precisely when the canal was built. The presence of a canal would affect the city in many fundamental ways, whether for the transport of goods and men, for the flow of water necessary for the economy (hydropower, and water for tanneries), or for defence, acting as a moat at the base of the ramparts.
Several important periods in the history of the city may be considered as politically and economically favourable for the creation of such a unique and ambitious hydraulic structure, which would govern the economy and defence of the city for many centuries. Several hypotheses will be proposed here, none as yet validated by archaeological observations, regarding the political and historical moments most opportune for the digging of the canal.

THE CREATION OF THE CITY

The first city, which started to develop around 50 AD, or probably even at the beginning of the 1st century AD, was bound to the north and west by the course of the Erdre, probably with some development on the right bank. To the east, the limits of the agglomeration were not determined by a natural feature, but by the establishment of necropolises along the roads leading to the city, which is known at that time to mark the division between world of the dead and the living[15].
In contrast, nothing is known about the city's southern limits. What landscape could be found on the right bank of the Loire River at the beginning of our era, when the confluence town of Condevicnum was still being built? What was the influence of this new agglomeration, which seems to have been well structured

by its network of roads and its residential areas, especially south of the city, where the presence of a port is attested by epigraphy (*vicus portensis*)? Where was the contact zone between the city and the river, and where was the port located? Many questions about the geography of this first agglomeration of the Upper Empire still remain unanswered, but two hypotheses can be proposed:

1. South of the town, the Madeleine branch defined the right bank of the river, along a course similar to today's one. Between this branch of the Loire and the centre of the agglomeration, where the bedrock rises a few metres near the current Place du Bouffay, there is a great deal of space. The landscape was a more or less marshy alluvial plain, probably already partially cleaned, backfilled, and urbanized, near a possible port site located on the north bank of the Madeleine channel. It is surprising, however, that so far no ancient remains have been found during the many refurbishments.
2. The second hypothesis is that of the creation of a protected port area integrated directly into the new agglomeration of Condevicnum. North of the alluvial plain, close to the centre of the town built on bedrock, this port area would have been protected from river floods by a diversion channel (the Saint-Félix canal). This hypothesis is conceivable within a political framework of the reasoned and organized creation of an agglomeration, where economic activity depended greatly on the efficiency of its port installation.

THE WALLED CITY AT THE END OF ANTIQUITY (4TH CENTURY AD)

At the end of the 3rd or at the very beginning of the 4th century AD, the construction of a defensive wall profoundly modified the morphology of the city, and probably also its modes of operation, whether military, economic, logistic or social. The new city was thus a quadrilateral nearly 1,700 m long, enclosing a limited urban zone of 18 ha, which was nevertheless one of the largest of the newly fortified western city-state capitals[16].

The hypothesis that the Saint-Félix canal could have been dug as part of the major works related to the construction of the city wall is very attractive. The city wall and the ancient Saint-Félix channel form a single homogeneous whole, both from the point of view of their spatial implantation and from that of their functional relationship. The channel delimits, protects, and serves the entire southern edge of the city, including two points – one to the west and one to the east – where the seats of the county, ducal and episcopal power would be established during the Early Middle Ages.

THE CHRISTIAN CITY OF THE EARLY MIDDLE AGES

In the 5th - 6th century AD, the city is still enclosed behind its *castrum* wall. Once again, it underwent several metamorphoses, in particular with the establishment of several ecclesiastical poles that would continue to develop over the centuries, within and outside the walls. Amongst them, are the great funerary basilicas of St. Donatien to the east, and St. Similien to the north[17].

After a short period of political stability under Frankish tutelage, the Namnetes territory again came under threat from invasions by Brittany. The indigence of the secular power at the time opened the way for the only power able to organize and defend the city: that of the clergy and especially the bishop, who was at that time the main initiator and promoter of urban development.

Among the bishops who succeeded one another in Nantes during this period, Félix is certainly the one whose texts have preserved the best evidence of the political action that he carried out during the second half of the 6th century AD. The two written sources that provide information about the life of this man are, in fact, very contradictory. The unflattering writings of his colleague and rival, Gregory of Tours, are opposed by the poetic and particularly laudatory testimonies of his friend, Venantius Fortunatus, who was, at that time, bishop of Poitiers. Félix was praised for the quality of his undertakings, sometimes described in detail, such as those related to the completion of his cathedral, but sometimes less precise, as with all the major works relating to the port and hydraulic infrastructure that Fortunatus attributed to him for the site of Nantes. Fortunatus' text clearly evokes work diverting »old rivers« to new paths, building dykes or filling in valleys that turned into »fertile ground« [18]. This enumeration of colossal works takes on an almost biblical dimension here, conferring on their author and creator a power of almost divine order since he was able to control and master the forces of nature. If the style of the text and its succession of superlatives leave little doubt regarding the benevolence felt by the author with regard to Felix, nothing calls into doubt, however, the very real nature of these undertakings. Locating the site of the infrastructure on the basis of this panegyric alone, however, remains a delicate exercise. Are these developments related to the Loire River and its floodplain meadows, Mauves and Madeleine? Do they refer, in particular, to the possible creation of the Saint-Félix Canal, or even to restructuring the lower valley of the Erdre, such as the area around the Barbin crossing? To date, neither historical sources nor archaeological data have provided a clear answer to these questions.

At the end of the 10th century AD, the fortifications in place had scarcely been modified since Antiquity, and the enclosed area had remained the same. The fortified settlements created at the end of the Early Middle Ages correspond to internal enclosures determining two rival urban poles within the city, that of the temporal power of the count, and that of the spiritual power of the bishop [19]. Associated with these two territories were the county palace, Bouffay Castle, to the south-east of the *castrum*, at the end of the line of bridges, while on the site of the current castle, to the south-west, lay the episcopal palace of the bishop. Both palaces were built on the edge of the channel, which acted as a moat. Although a moat may have been built during this period, it is unlikely, as no mention of digging works can be found in the text of the Nantes chronicle (an 11th century AD narrative recounting the history of the County of Nantes between the 6th and 11th centuries AD).

When the new city wall, the Reunion wall, was erected a little later in the early 13th century AD, it surrounded an area of 26 ha, incorporating suburbs west of the city, including the parish of St. Nicholas, as it crossed the Erdre. The power of the duke was then definitively imposed over that of the bishop, resulting in the building of the Chastel de la Tour Neuve (New Tower Castle) on the most strategic site in the city, that of the castle today [20]. Trade was booming, benefitting from new infrastructures directly integrated into the urban defensive system, such as the ports that developed on the southern side. Port Maillard was located on the Saint-Félix canal, which had already been installed, and which was called the north branch of the Loire at that time (**fig. 4**).

THE SOUTHERN ENTRANCE TO THE CITY, WHERE THE LINE OF BRIDGES ENDED AT THE SAINT-FÉLIX CANAL

The line of bridges is mentioned in archives from the 9th century AD onwards, yet geological clues suggest that it may well have been the site of a much more ancient Loire River crossing. Similarly, the Saint-Félix canal is only attested from the 13th century AD onwards, yet the way it is interwoven into the urban fabric strongly suggests that it may have been dug in Antiquity. The recent archaeological operations carried out on the southern fringe of the city have made possible the study of these two monumental structuring developments of the town of Nantes at their point of intersection. Here, the road from the south over the line of bridges cuts across the Saint-Félix canal.

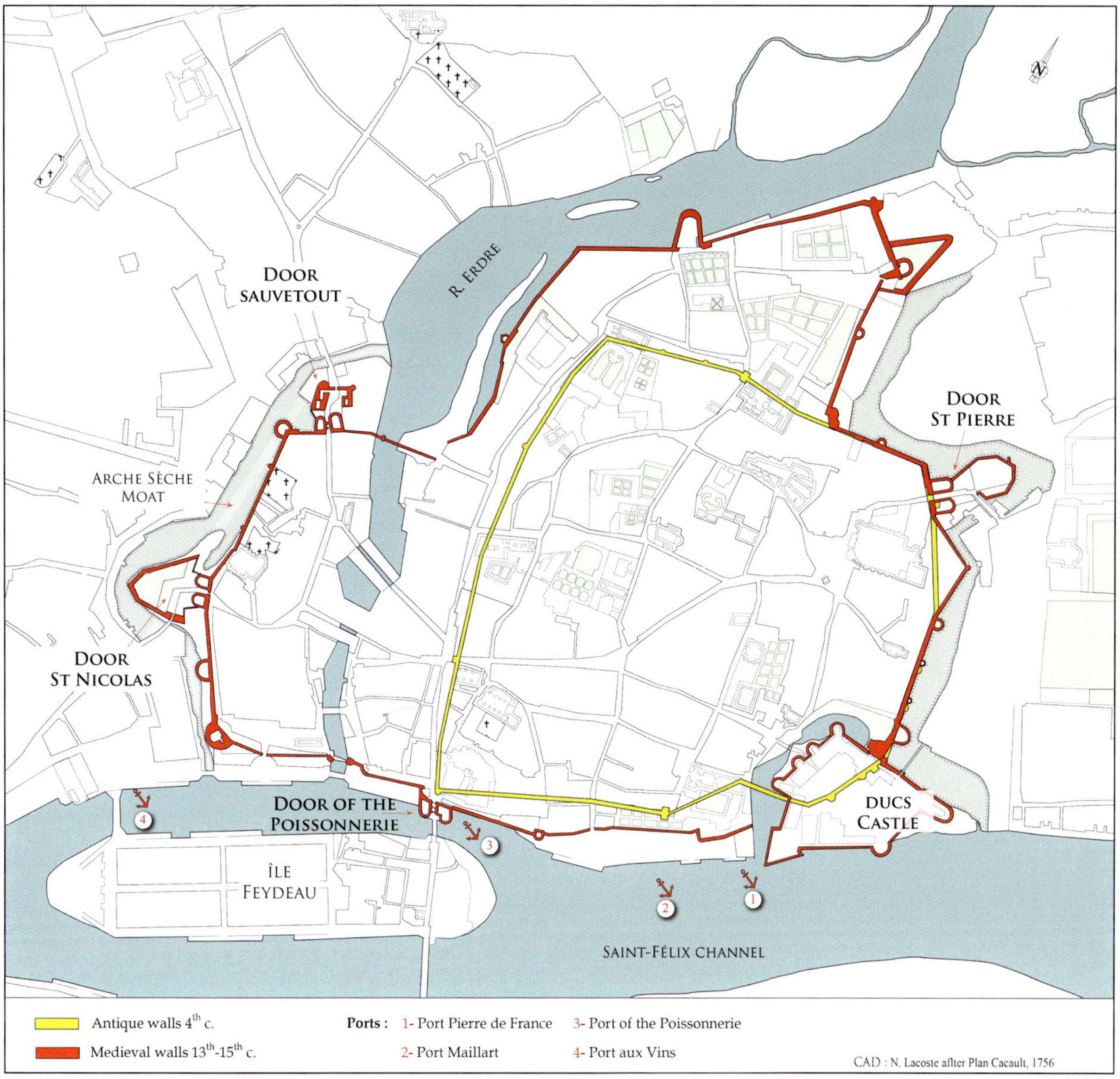

Fig. 4 The location of the ports of the fortified city of Nantes between the 13th and 15th century AD. – (N. Lacoste, Archaeological Mission of Nantes Métropole, based on the map by Cacault 1756).

At this site, in the 1930s AD, before the canal was filled in, there were two bridges, one on either side of the islet of Saulzaie, in the middle of the canal. The island of Saulzaie became the Île Feydeau, when it was extended to the west in the mid-18th century AD.

Recent archaeological data show that this islet, built on embankments placed on the flat bottom of the canal, must be artificial. It may have been built in the 13th century AD[21]. Archival documents (texts, maps and drawings) and recent archaeological observations, together with the position of the islet to the right of the Poissonnerie city gate, indicate that this structure was fortified and used as the final defensive bastion of the line of bridges crossing the Loire River. This bastion was separated from the city gates by a moat (Poissonnerie channel) dug partly from the bedrock, which was still crossed by a drawbridge during the 15th century AD. This same defensive system can be found to the south, at the other end of the line of bridges, with the installation in the 14th century AD of the fortress of Pirmil. Located on an islet separated from the shore by a moat dug from the rock, this fortification can be seen in 17th century AD maps and was represented in many ancient engravings (**fig. 5**).

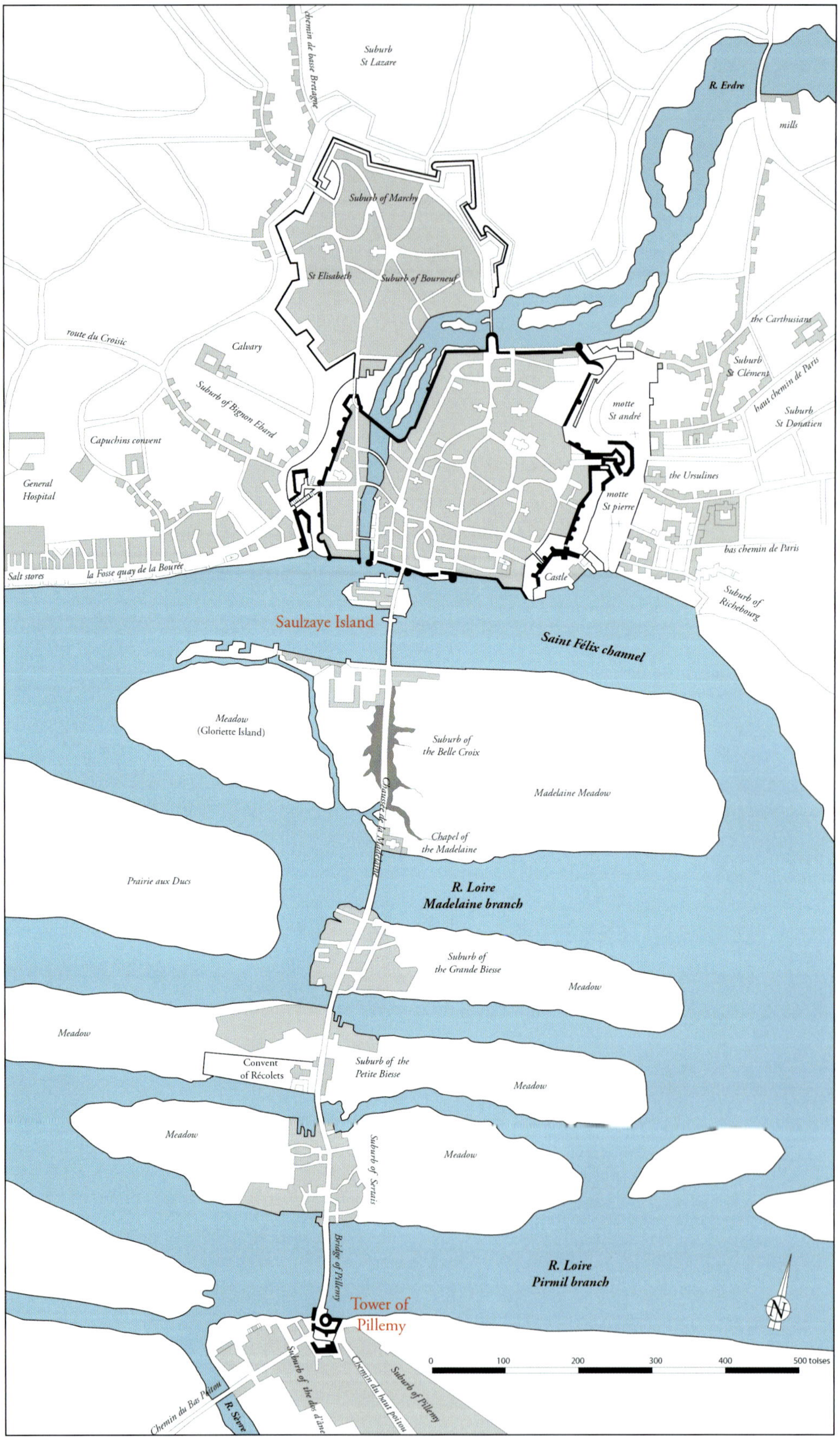

Fig. 5 The fortified island of Saulzaie and the fortress of Pirmil on either side of the medieval line of bridges (Nantes in 1716 AD, based on the map with legends by Nicolas de Fer, AMN [1Fi 587]). – (Graphic J. Martineau, Inrap, 2006).

Fig. 6 The filling-in of the Saint-Félix canal in 1937 AD. – (Nantes Municipal Archives, Inv. 26Fi1447).

These new observations show that those undoubtedly ancient structures, the canal and the line of bridges, evolved continuously, adapting to the needs of local inhabitants and to the constraints imposed by the river. The image of the canal that can be seen in early 20th century AD photographs probably differs very much from the original state of the structure. Its proportions, which seem oversized today, are in fact the result of a series of modifications that occurred over several centuries, or even millennia.

CONCLUSION

In Nantes, research into the evolution of the river has shown that the components of the Loire landscape (alluvial plains, islands, and major channels) at the scale of the Loire Valley have evolved little, as geographic entities, from the end of the Protohistory to the Modern period. The establishment of a network of channels during the middle of the Medieval period transformed sites previously connected to land into islands. The line of medieval bridges in Nantes was therefore based on a string of islands that had developed much earlier. The medieval bridges may therefore replace an ancient crossing that may well have led to the initial implantation of two cities, Condevicnum (Nantes) and Ratiatum (Rezé), on opposite sides of the Loire. This hypothesis has, however, not yet been validated by archaeological observations.
On the outskirts of the city of Nantes, environmental research into the evolution of the river together with archaeological research on sites in the historic southern districts (Bouffay-Feydeau neighbourhoods) reveal the complex relationships and permanent interactions that the city has maintained with its natural environment, and with the Loire River in particular. The physical link between the city and the river was materialized by the Saint-Félix canal, although it is still not known whether this canal was dug during Antiquity or in the

Middle Ages. The port activity of the city must have been organized around this structure. Port activity is partially documented, but only for the period after the 13th century AD.
How have communities adapted to the constraints of their natural environment? How have they changed the contours of their environment to adapt it to their economic, strategic, and political needs? This is the history that archaeology attempts to trace through the opportunities for observation offered by urban developments. Metamorphosis affects everything: the river itself has incessantly changed shape over the centuries, at the heart of the Nantes landscape, because of changes in climate or through the intentions of its residents. The river was brought into the centre of the city by an artificial channel in early historic times, thus contributing to its prosperity. Later, in the mid-20th century AD, for reasons of insalubrity, after the Saint-Félix channel was filled in, the river was excluded from the city, putting an end to an economic, military, and industrial adventure that has ultimately left few material traces (**fig. 6**).

Notes

*) Translation by C. Chateau Smith and M. Foucher.

1) Bois 1977.

2) This article is based on the results of the Collaborative Research Project entitled »River Archaeology and Holocene Environments of the Loire Valley and its Tributaries in the Nantes Region«. Since 2011, this project has brought together the skills of geographers, geologists, environmentalists, archaeologists and historians from the Universities of Nantes, South Brittany, Rennes, and Lille, and from the Inrap, the BRGM and Nantes Métropole. This research is primarily based on an environmental study of the Loire, particularly through the analysis of nine sediment cores and on the results of rescue and programmed archaeology.

3) Ottmann/Alix/Limasset 1968.

4) Ménanteau 1973.

5) Dion 1961.

6) »droit d'accroissement dans la rivière de Loire, et planter les isles, greves, butes et buteaux«. Loire-Atlantique Departmental Archives, 1938, Table of Sentences of the 16th volume, July 16th, 1681, fol. 13.

7) Ménanteau 1973.

8) Viau/Guitton 2015. – Fillon 2015.

9) Arthuis/Miejac/Nauleau 2015.

10) Visset et al. 2001. – Armynot du Chatelet et al. 2015. – Arthuis/Nauleau 2007. – Arthuis et al. 2015.

11) Armynot du Chatelet et al. 2015.

12) Arthuis et al. 2010.

13) Monteil/Santro 2011.

14) Mercier/Arthuis/Le Boulaire 2014. – Mercier/Arthuis 2017. – Arthuis/Nauleau 2007. – Arthuis et al. 2015.

15) Lacoste 2014.

16) Monteil 2008.

17) Monteil 2008.

18) Venance Fortunat 1887.

19) Laurens-Berge 2015.

20) Laurens-Berge 2015.

21) Mercier/Arthuis/Le Boulaire 2014.

Source

Venance Fortunat 1887: Venance Fortunat, Poésies mêlées, Livre III, translation by Charles Nisard (Paris 1887).

References

Armynot du Chatelet et al. 2015: E. Armynot du Chatelet / M. Delaine / A. Ganne / E. Goubert / V. Le Cadre, Le programme »paléoenvironnement« sur la fenêtre de Nantes et Rezé. In: R. Arthuis / M. Monteil (eds), Rapport de projet de recherche européen »archéologie fluviale et environnements holocènes des vallées de la Loire et ses affluents en Pays nantais« [unpubl. report of the European research project »archéologie fluviale et environnements holocènes des vallées de la Loire et ses affluents en Pays nantais«, Archives scientifiques du Service Régional de l'Archéologie des Pays de la Loire 2015] 46-107.

Arthuis/Nauleau 2007: R. Arthuis / J.-F. Nauleau, La Loire à Nantes: bilan sédimentaire; conséquences géomorphologiques et archéologiques. Préliminaires à l'étude du paysage. In: A. de Saulce (ed.), Rapport d'activité du Projet Collectif de Recherche »Des Pont-de-Cé à l'Estuaire, interactions Homme/Milieu de la Loire et ses affluents« [unpubl. report of the collective research project

»Des Pont-de-Cé à l'Estuaire, interactions Homme/Milieu de la Loire et ses affluents«, Service Régional de l'Archéologie des Pays de la Loire 2007].

Arthuis/Miejac/Nauleau 2015: R. Arthuis / E. Miejac / J.-F. Nauleau, La navigation fluviale: une affaire de canal? La »boire Torse«, exemple d'un canal creusé au Moyen Âge entre Ingrandes et Anetz. In: R. Arthuis / M. Monteil (eds), Archéologie et géoarchéologie de la Basse-Loire entre Nantes (Loire-Atlantique) et Montjean-sur-Loire (Maine-et-Loire). Approches nouvelles et premiers résultats (Rennes 2015) 149-171.

Arthuis et al. 2010: R. Arthuis / D. Guitton / M. Monteil / J. Mouchard / O. de Perreti, Archéologie portuaire estuarienne entre Loire et Seine: principaux résultats et questions d'ordre méthodologique. L'exemple des sites antiques d'Aizier (Eure) et de Rezé (Loire-Atlantique). In: L. Hugot / L. Tranoy (eds), Actes de la Journée d'études sur les structures portuaires de l'arc atlantique dans l'Antiquité (bilan et perspectives de recherches), La Rochelle 2008. Aquitania, Supplément 18 (Bordeaux 2010) 61-82.

2015: R. Arthuis / J.-F. Nauleau / E. Goubert / D. Barbier-Pain / V. Baudouin, Reconstitution paléogéographique de la vallée de la Loire à Nantes depuis 8000 ans. In: R. Arthuis / M. Monteil (eds), Archéologie et géoarchéologie de la Basse-Loire entre Nantes (Loire-Atlantique) et Montjean-sur-Loire (Maine-et-Loire). Approches nouvelles et premiers résultats (Rennes 2015) 23-43.

Bois 1977: P. Bois, Histoire de Nantes. Univers de la France et des Pays Francophones 39 (Toulouse 1977).

Dion 1961: R. Dion, Histoire des Levées de la Loire (Paris 1961).

Fillon 2015: D. Fillon, Des pêcheries dans le fleuve à Saint-Florent-le-Vieil (Maine-et-Loire): premier bilan. In: R. Arthuis / M. Monteil (eds), Archéologie et géoarchéologie de la Basse-Loire entre Nantes (Loire-Atlantique) et Montjean-sur-Loire (Maine-et-Loire). Approches nouvelles et premiers résultats (Rennes 2015) 107-139.

Lacoste 2014: N. Lacoste, Rue Auvours, une nécropole à crémations du Haut-Empire [unpubl. report, Direction du Patrimoine et de l'Archéologie-Nantes 2014].

Laurens-Berge 2015: M. Laurens-Berge, 2, rue Portail/5, rue Ogée, Empire [unpubl. report, Service Régional de l'Archéologie, DRAC Pays-de-Loire, Nantes 2015].

Ménanteau 1973: L. Ménanteau, Le lit de la Loire entre Saint-Florent-le-Vieil et Champtoceaux: essai de géographie holocène [diss. Univ. Nantes 1973].

Mercier/Arthuis 2017: F. Mercier / R. Arthuis, Nantes et la Loire. La Loire et ses Terroirs, Numéro Spécial Géoarchéologie Fluviale 2017, 60-65.

Mercier/Arthuis/Le Boulaire 2014: F. Mercier / R. Arthuis / C. Le Boulaire, D'île en île, de Saulzaie à Feydeau... par le canal Saint-Félix, opération Neptune, Carré-Feydeau [unpubl. report, Mission archéologique de Nantes Métropole, Archives scientifiques du Service Régional de l'Archéologie des Pays de la Loire et de l'Inrap, Nantes 2014].

Monteil 2008: M. Monteil, Les édifices des premiers temps chrétiens (IVe-VIIe s. de n.è.) à Nantes (Loire-Atlantique). In: Nantes religieuse, de l'Antiquité à nos jours. Actes du colloque de l'Université de Nantes, 20-21 octobre 2006 (Nantes 2008) 15-60.

Monteil/Santrot 2011: M. Monteil / J. Santrot, La naissance de l'archéologie régionale dans l'Ouest armoricain: une enquête à développer. Annales de Bretagne et des Pays de l'Ouest 118/3, 2011, 9-32.

Ottmann/Alix/Limasset 1968: F. Ottmann / Y. Alix / O. Limasset, Sur le »lit ancien« de la Loire dans son cours inférieur. Bulletin du BRGM 1/2, 1968, 27-56.

Viau/Guitton 2015: Y. Viau / V. Guitton, Vestige de meunerie hydraulique du haut Moyen Âge (VIIe-Xe s.) au Marillais (Maine-et-Loire). In: R. Arthuis / M. Monteil (eds), Archéologie et géoarchéologie de la Basse-Loire entre Nantes (Loire-Atlantique) et Montjean-sur-Loire (Maine-et-Loire). Approches nouvelles et premiers résultats (Rennes 2015) 45-105.

Visset et al. 2001: L. Visset / G. Hauray / L. Charriau / N. Rouzeau, Paléoenvironnement urbain: histoire du comblement des vallées de la métropole nantaise, du Tardiglaciaire à la fin de l'Holocène. Annales de Bretagne et des Pays de l'Ouest 108/1, 2001, 147-165.

Summary

The city of Nantes developed at the confluence of the Erdre and the Loire, a strategic choice of location. The relationship between the city and the river therefore merits investigation, from the earliest agglomeration in Antiquity to Contemporary period. The aim of current research is to understand the evolution of the river around the city in order to identify any residual elements of earlier Loire landscapes, and to evaluate which sites would have been suitable for a river crossing prior to the 9th century AD, and for a port prior to the 13th century AD.

It is now proved that upstream and around Nantes, the components of the Loire landscape at the scale of the Loire Valley (alluvial plains, islands, and channels) have evolved little, as geographic entities, from the end of Protohistory to the Modern period. Nevertheless, the network of channels that developed in the middle of the Medieval period transformed sites previously connected to land into islands. The line of medieval bridges in Nantes was therefore based on a chain of islands that developed much earlier. This suggests that it replaced an ancient crossing probably related to the implantation on either side of the Loire of the cities of Condevicnum (Nantes) and Ratiatum (Rezé). Archaeological observations have not yet confirmed this hypothesis.

In the immediate vicinity of Nantes, research has revealed the complex relationship and permanent interactions between the city and the river over time. The physical link between them was materialized by a channel called »Canal Saint-Félix«. New data has confirmed the artificial nature of this channel, which must therefore have been a canal. Its dating, either Medieval or Antique, remains uncertain, since repeated dredging has eradicated the oldest traces. It is

clear that the canal was built before the 13th century AD, as historical mentions of the ports of Maillard and Pierre de France attests to its existence, and after the end of the Iron Age or at the beginning of Antiquity, for reasons of water-level compatibility between the canal and the river. More precise information about its creation is essential, as this link was vital to the city, for the transportation of goods and men, the transport of water necessary for the economy and for its defence, by acting as a moat at the foot of the city wall. Several periods in the history of the city can be considered as politically and economically favourable to the creation of such a singularly ambitious hydraulic structure. The canal was dug either during the creation of the agglomeration in the 1st century AD of our era or during the installation of the castrum at the beginning of the 4th century AD. The canal may also have been developed under the leadership of bishop Felix in the 6th century AD, according to his contemporaries, as he undertook a great deal of hydraulic work on the river network around Nantes. Finally, the canal might have been built during the construction of Bouffay Castle, at the end of the 10th century AD.
The line of bridges can still be seen in ancient documents but, in the 1930s, the canal was filled in. Recent archaeological discoveries have identified a defensive bastion where the islet of Saulzaie lay, in the middle of the canal, at the end of the line of bridges crossing the Loire. Such finds show that these two features are the result of a series of developments that occurred over several centuries, or even millennia. Such transformations responded to evolutions in the economic and defensive needs of the city, which should be better understood after future rescue excavation campaigns.

Résumé

La ville de Nantes s'est développée à la confluence de l'Erdre et la Loire, une implantation qui ne doit rien au hasard. Elle soulève la question de la relation entretenue entre la ville et le fleuve depuis la genèse de l'agglomération antique jusqu'à la période contemporaine. L'objectif des recherches actuelles est de comprendre l'évolution du fleuve aux abords de la ville afin d'identifier les éléments résiduels des paysages ligériens anciens et d'évaluer ainsi les sites potentiels pour l'aménagement d'un franchissement avant le 9e siècle apr. J.-C. ou d'un port avant le 13e siècle apr. J.-C.
Il est désormais avéré qu'en amont et au droit de la ville, les composantes du paysage ligérien à l'échelle de la vallée de la Loire, à savoir les plaines alluviales, les îles et les chenaux principaux ont, en tant qu'entités géographiques, au final assez peu évolué entre la fin de la Protohistoire et l'époque moderne, même si la mise en place d'un réseau de canaux au milieu du Moyen Âge a transformé des espaces jusqu'alors reliés à la terre, en îles. La ligne de ponts médiévale à Nantes repose donc sur un chapelet d'îles dont la mise en place est beaucoup plus ancienne, ce qui laisse supposer qu'elle se substitue à un franchissement antique qui n'est sans doute pas étranger à l'implantation, de part et d'autre de la Loire, des cités de Condevicnum (Nantes) et Ratiatum (Rezé). Cette hypothèse n'est cependant toujours pas validée par des observations archéologiques.
Aux abords immédiats de la ville de Nantes, les recherches révèlent les relations complexes et les interactions permanentes entretenues entre la ville et le fleuve. Le lien physique entre ces deux entités est matérialisé par un chenal dit « canal Saint-Félix ». Des données récentes confirment la nature artificielle de ce chenal qui est donc bien un canal. Sa datation, médiévale ou antique, reste incertaine, les nombreux curages successifs de l'ouvrage ayant fait disparaître les témoignages plus anciens. Seule certitude, ce canal est antérieur au 13e siècle apr. J.-C., période à laquelle les mentions des Port Maillard et Port Pierre de France attestent de son fonctionnement, et postérieur à la fin de l'Âge du Fer ou le début de l'Antiquité pour des raisons de compatibilité de niveau d'eau entre le canal et la Loire. Il paraît cependant primordial de connaître précisément la date de création du canal, tant il conditionne le fonctionnement même de la ville, que ce soit pour le transport des marchandises et des hommes, l'acheminement de l'eau nécessaire à l'économie ou encore sur le plan défensif en faisant office de douve au pied de l'enceinte urbaine.
Plusieurs « temps forts » dans l'histoire de la ville peuvent être considérés comme « favorables », sur les plans politique et économique, à la création d'un ouvrage hydraulique aussi singulier et ambitieux. Le canal a pu être creusé lors de la création de l'agglomération au 1er siècle de notre ère ou lors de l'installation du castrum au début du 4e siècle apr. J.-C. Le canal pourrait aussi avoir été conçu sous l'impulsion de l'évêque Félix au 6e siècle apr. J.-C. lequel, selon ses contemporains, aurait entrepris de nombreux travaux hydrauliques sur le réseau fluvial nantais, ou bien encore avoir été aménagé lors de la création du château du Bouffay à la fin du 10e siècle apr. J.-C.
Les découvertes archéologiques récentes, notamment celle d'un bastion défensif en lieu et place de l'îlot de la Saulzaie, situé au milieu du canal et au débouché de la ligne de ponts qui traverse la Loire, montrent que le canal, avant son comblement dans les années 1930, et la ligne de ponts, telle qu'elle est figurée dans les documents anciens, sont le résultat d'une suite d'aménagements étalés sur plusieurs siècles, voire plusieurs millénaires. Ces transformations répondent aux évolutions des besoins économiques et défensifs de la ville, qu'il nous faudra comprendre grâce aux fouilles préventives à venir.

LARS KRÖGER

THE DEVELOPMENT OF PRE-INDUSTRIAL SHIP CONSTRUCTION AT THE RIVER RHINE

The central European landmass is dominated by its rivers. Small rivers with a high current enable the use of mills whereas large, slow running rivers are suited for shipping and transportation. Fluid waterbodies attracted settlements based on their ability to gather aliments and water, provide security and spatial structure, and communication along their banks. Over the centuries, this led to an unparalleled dense cultural landscape in valleys. The most important river in Central Europe, at least from a German perspective, is the River Rhine.

The Rhine, originally an alpine river, flows from Switzerland through Lake Constance, France, and Germany, and has its delta in the Netherlands. The Rhine remains one of the most frequented rivers in the world and has probably been so since Antiquity. This analysis focuses on the section from the Rhine Falls near Schaffhausen, until the North Sea. The Alpine Rhine and the Lake Constance are excluded due to the fact that no direct shipping connection was possible because the Rhine Fall was impassable.

Fluvial geomorphology is relevant for the analysis of shipping at the Rhine. The High Rhine, between Lake Constance and Basel (canton of Basel-Stadt/CH), is characterized by high current and several cataracts, making navigation difficult. The Upper Rhine until Bingen (Rhineland-Palatinate/D) is flowing in the wide Upper Rhine Plain. Before the straightening of the stream, this section was represented by several oxbow lakes, meanders, islands, and swamp areas. With the entry of the Rhine into the Mittelgebirge, a landscape dominated by hills and highland of moderate altitude, the river is again forced into a gorge, with several cataracts causing trouble for navigators. The hill land ends at Bonn (North Rhine-Westphalia/D), where the Rhine enters a plain area, called the Lower Rhine, until the Dutch border, where it starts to split in several streams: the Waal, Rijn, and Ijssel (**fig. 1**)[1].

Not surprisingly for a major river like the Rhine, populations at its banks have been documented for every period. During prehistory, communication had a central role[2]. Unexpectedly at the same time, prehistoric vessels are missing from our records[3]. With the spread of the Roman Empire to the north, the Rhine gained major importance, being used to support the

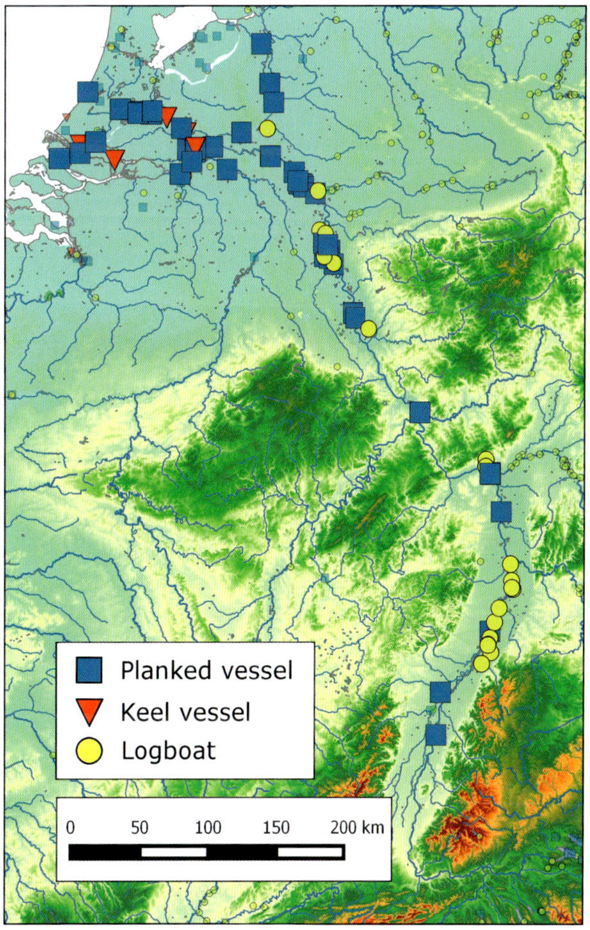

Fig. 1 Overview of vessels found in the Rhine area. – (Mapping L. Kröger 2018; map data SRTM-GDEM © NASA 2009, CCM River and Catchment Database © European Commission 2007).

troops and the fast-growing urban areas. In connection with the Saône/Rhône River system, the Rhine was the main transportation route for heavy goods from the south to the north, avoiding transportation through the Strait of Gibraltar and the Atlantic. The importance of the river for the Roman economy has been well-discussed[4]. It should be mentioned that Roman shipping was centrally organized and various specialized professions developed[5]. The Rhine was also part of the Limes system, which was used to control and protect the borders of the Roman Empire[6].

During Medieval times, the political system changed from a centrally organized, strong kingdom to a realm divided into smaller lordships. This is best reflected in the growth of toll stations along the Rhine[7]. During this period, the king was officially in charge of the river, but the reality reflects the diverse interests of the high nobility[8]. The maintenance of the river was a significant problem, with mobile riverbanks and cataracts. In post-medieval time a lot of efforts were undertaken by channelling and destructing barriers to improve the shipping conditions[9]. These actions changed the river drastically, providing room for larger ships, without the need for locks on the major parts of the river. With the development of the railway system, shipping on most rivers lost its importance[10]. This has not been the case for the Rhine where river-based transportation remained important. Despite that, shipping has lost its almost monopoly position in the 19th century AD[11], the foundation for the origin of the politically used myth for the »German« »father Rhine« was laid at the same time. In the context of competition and rivalry about the dominance at the river and several transitions of power between Germany and France, a strong nationalism was formed and created the image of the Rhine as the most German of all rivers. The Rhine remains a dominant point of identification in western Germany[12].

ROMAN BOAT CONSTRUCTION

The Roman Empire introduced a quantum leap in boat-building technology to the north. It is assumed that the knowledge of planked vessels was present north of the Alps before the spread of the Roman Empire. Despite this, no planked vessels are known from northern European rivers. The first exclusively inland vessels were probably built at the Rhône, represented by boats like Arles-Rhône 3 (dép. Bouches du Rhône/F)[13] or Lyon, Place Tolozan (dép. Rhône/F)[14]. Arles-Rhône 3 was built by forming a rectangular cross section with minor L-shaped transition planks connected to a framing system via iron nails. This system continued to be used until the Middle Ages. The connection technique of the Lyon find, with mortise-and-tenon joints, is strongly influenced by Mediterranean building techniques used for sailing ships. This technique was mostly used for vessels close to the Roman Legion, and disappears completely with the decline of the Roman Empire in northern Europe. A parallel development is visible at the northern Adria and neighbouring regions. The technique to connect planks with stitches or clamps is represented in several finds, such as Laibach (Ljubljana/SLO)[15] and Sinja Gorica (Osrednjeslovenska/SLO)[16] – both at the River Ljubljanica in Slovenia – or the Stella 1 (prov. di Udine/I)[17] from northern Italy, all dating to the 1st century AD. This technique had no further impact north of the Alps[18].

Not surprisingly, inland and maritime environments are not fully independent operation areas. River mouth, delta areas, and coastal regions are the operation areas of maritime-fluvial vessels – smaller boats fit for sailing with a keel but also a minor draught for river use. The presumably oldest vessel in the Rhine River system is a boat from Vechten (prov. Utrecht/NL), at the River Waal, dating into the first quarter of the 1st century AD. It features a sailing mast and a clearly distinct edge at the keel, but at the same time fit for rowing by 18-20 persons. The wreck can be interpreted as a vessel used by the military, similar to those known from Mainz (Rhineland-Palatinate/D) and other regions north of the Alps[19]. Several vessels from Mainz are

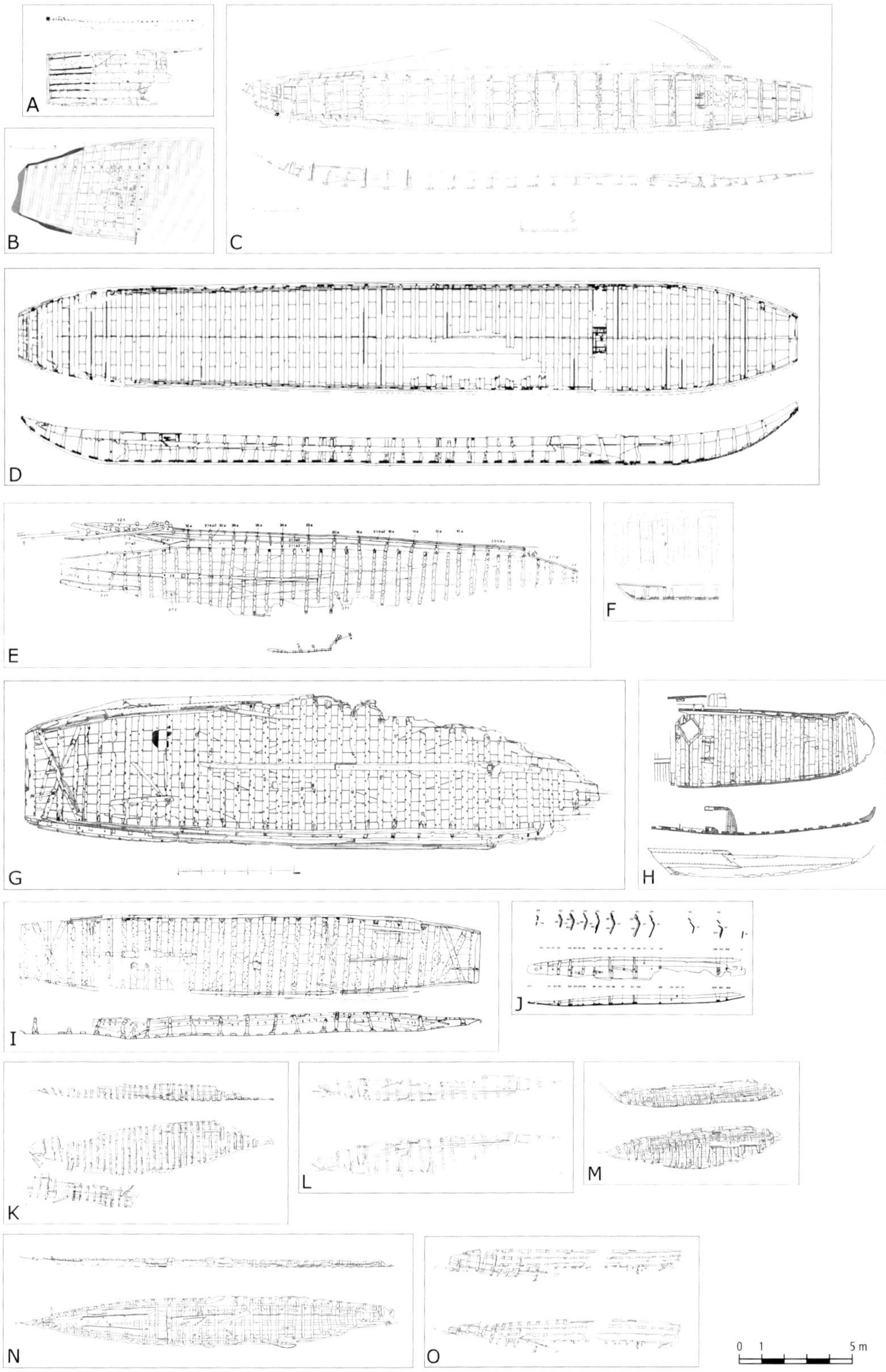

Fig. 2 Roman vessels found in the Rhine area: **A** Xanten-Wardt (around 100 AD). – **B** De Meern 4 (around 100 AD). – **C** De Meern 1 (after 148 AD). – **D** Zwammerdam 4 (after 98 AD). – **E** Zwammerdam 2 (2nd half of the 2nd century AD). – **F** Druten, hypothetical reconstruction (late 2nd - 3rd century AD). – **G** Woerden 7 (around 162 AD). – **H** Woerden 1 (around 185 AD). – **I** Zwammerdam 6 (2nd half of the 2nd century AD). – **J** Zwammerdam 3 (2nd half of the 2nd century AD). – **K** Mainz 3 (end of 3rd century AD). – **L** Mainz 2 (after 287 AD). – **M** Mainz 1 (around 376 AD). – **N** Mainz 5 (around 390 AD). – **O** Mainz 4 (after 393 AD). – (Compilation of drawings by L. Kröger 2018 after Peiß 2012, 328; Heeringen et al. 2007, 9; Jansma/Morel 2007, leaflet 1; Bockius 2002a, 42; de Weerd 1988, pl. B; Lehmann 1978, 266; Vos/Morel/Hazenberg 2011, 106; Haalebos 1996, 483; de Weerd 1988, 70 pl. A; Bockius 2006, addenda).

the last known representatives of this type, dating to the beginning and end of the 4th century AD[20]. These rowing vessels had high flexibility in the way they have been used and navigated. One of their main duties was to show the presence of the Roman army in certain regions, and being quickly deployed to engage in encounters with hostile groups[21]. At the same time, they were able to transport or convoy goods. The inclusion of rowing devices made them adaptable and allowed transport with or against the current at any time. Simultaneously, the presence of mast steps proves that sails could be used to support the 18-24 rowers. The need for manpower to operate this sort of boat made them relatively uneconomic for mass transportation. While the handling of this kind of vessel shows a longer tradition, the construction technique evolved from a Mediterranean influence towards northern European craftsmanship[22].

In Mainz, another novel vessel type is found at the Rhine; a flat-bottomed vessel with a rectangular cross-section. These typically large vessels were not prepared for rowing but could be navigated by punting, howling or sailing. The main duty for such vessels was the transport of bulk cargo. Early examples can be seen in the 1st century AD vessels of Mainz 6 and 7[23], Cologne-Alter Markt 1 (North Rhine-Westphalia/D)[24], Xanten-Wardt (North Rhine-Westphalia/D)[25], Zwammerdam 4 (prov. South Holland/NL)[26], and Kapel-Avezaath (prov. Gelderland/NL)[27]. From the 2nd century AD, several vessels from the Netherlands like De Meern[28], Woerden (prov. Utrecht/NL)[29], Zwammerdam 4 (prov. South Holland/NL)[30], and Druten (prov. Gelderland/NL) have been reported (**fig. 2**)[31]. These vessels share several similarities, such as a general systematic framing and planking system, propulsion technique and rectangular cross-section, but differ in their construction details and generic features. These differences can be the centre point for further questions. As an example, the size of the vessels can be taken into consideration. The Xanten-Wardt vessel, built around 95 AD, is constructed in the typical way, but has a diameter of only 2.6m, obviously smaller than other vessels of this kind found at the Rhine. This raises the question of why? An explanation could be found in the early dating of the find and the later change to larger boats. Another plausible explanation could be an alternative use. The vessel was found in the vicinity of the important Roman town of Colonia Ulpia Traiana (North Rhine-Westphalia/D). To cross the river, a ferry service could have been installed. The unusual dense framing pattern could improve the stability if heavy waggons have been loaded on board. Iron bands between the planks at the bottom of the preserved bow could protect the integrity of the hull and keep the caulking material in position, even if the vessel was frequently landed on the riverbanks[32]. In addition, the different construction details on vessels from the same region and timeframe raise questions. The well-preserved vessels 2 and 6 from Zwammerdam and the vessel 7 from Woerden[33] all date to the second half of the 2nd century AD. While Zwammerdam 6 and Woerden 7 show the same building technique, Zwammerdam 2 differs in many aspects; starting with a more narrow bow and stern construction, without intersecting enhancements, as well as small square-shaped frames. Whereas for the framing system of Zwammerdam 6 and Woerden 7 rectangular and larger frames have been used, again with another nailing system of two rows[34]. The question is, why do we see such differences? A possible reason could be the different building place of Zwammerdam 2. Boats are moveable objects. Woerden 7 and probably Zwammerdam 6 have been built in the Delta region, whereas Zwammerdam 2 was not, and has been moved there during its services. A dendrochronological analysis with provenance determination could support or disprove such an idea. Although we are aware of several finds from the Roman time, many questions remain unanswered.

MEDIEVAL BOAT CONSTRUCTION

While a larger number of Roman vessels of the 1st until the 4th century AD have been excavated along the riverbanks of the Rhine, we see a dramatic decline of known vessels in the 5th-8th century AD, whereas nu-

Fig. 3 Representation of dated vessels at the Rhine River. – (Graph L. Kröger 2018).

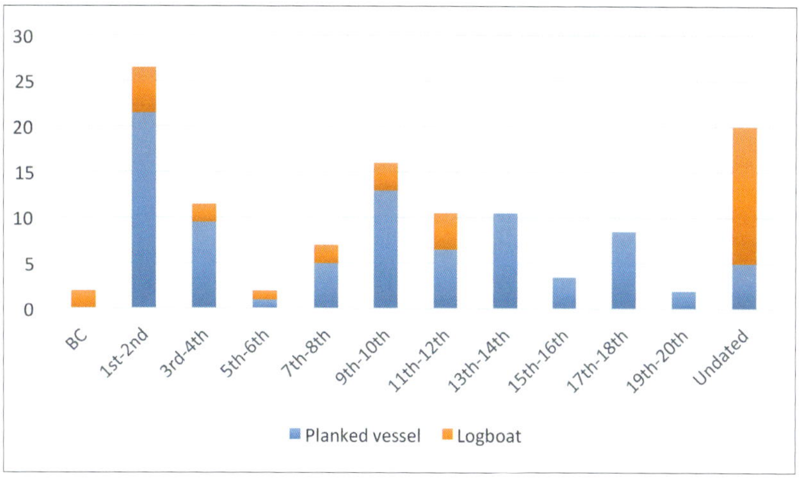

merous finds of the 9th - 10th century AD are well-known again (**figs 3-4**). The dating of several of these vessels is not 100 % secured, for instance in the case of the finds from Katwijk (prov. South Holland / NL)[35] and Gimbsheim (Rhineland-Palatinate / D)[36]. Some have been found in fragments only, like Mainz S8 (Rhineland-Palatinate / D)[37] and Dorestadt (prov. Utrecht / NL)[38], or not fully excavated, like Vleuten 1 (prov. Utrecht / NL)[39] and Lüttingen (North Rhine-Westphalia / D)[40]. Parts of vessels are regularly found in the Rhine delta in the Netherlands in paleo-river channels. Due to their often bad state of preservation, they have usually limited potential to inform about boat construction. Most of these finds are just broken pieces or reused planks, and have never been properly published, making analysis impossible[41]. This makes an interpretation of the shift of technology from the Roman to early Medieval times difficult.

In Germany, several well-preserved vessels exist. However, these have been unknown to the research community so far, despite having been excavated in the 1970s. During a large research excavation at the Motte-castle Haus Meer, near Düsseldorf (North Rhine-Westphalia / D), four boats were found. All boats were disposed or reused after their active use on the river. By ^{14}C-analysis, boat 3 was dated to around 1180 AD. Similar dates can be applied to boats 1, 2 and 4 based on the archaeological record. Except for boat 2, all boats are built from a single log, with added frames or later repairs. Boat 1 was 6.5 m long. Large parts of the assumed bow are missing. During its use as a vessel, the log cracked in the stern part and had to be fixed with moss caulking and sintels. At least six floor timbers have been added, likely to strengthen the construction. If the drawings are trustworthy, the oak trunk had no knotholes but was twisted. Boat 3 was similar; also being made of a knothole free oak and with a remaining length of 6.5 m. Larger cracks have also been repaired with sintels and caulking. Several frames were sued to support one of the side-walls. Numerous other floor timbers or frames were lost; their former existence is only indicated by holes drilled into the floor. One piece of wood was cut out of the floor and replaced, as well as a piece of wood added to the sidewall, probably to strengthen this side. A 1.25 m long paddle with a transverse grip at the end was found next to the boat laid. Boat 4 (**fig. 4**), with a remaining 11.5 m, is the longest of the four vessels. The inside is covered with frames and floor timbers connected by wooden nails, except for one section where no components have been installed. This could suggest that these timbers have been added at a later event to straighten the vessel. The presence of sintels and caulking support the thesis of later repairs. While the boats 1, 3, and 4 are quite similar, boat 2 – with a length of 3.65 m – is smaller and lacks internal wooden constructional elements. The published drawings suggest a round shaped cross-section[42]. Vessels of this form and size are known to have been used along the River Main, a tributary to the Rhine, as floating devices for ferry constructions[43]. We cannot exclude this possibility in the case of logboat number 2.

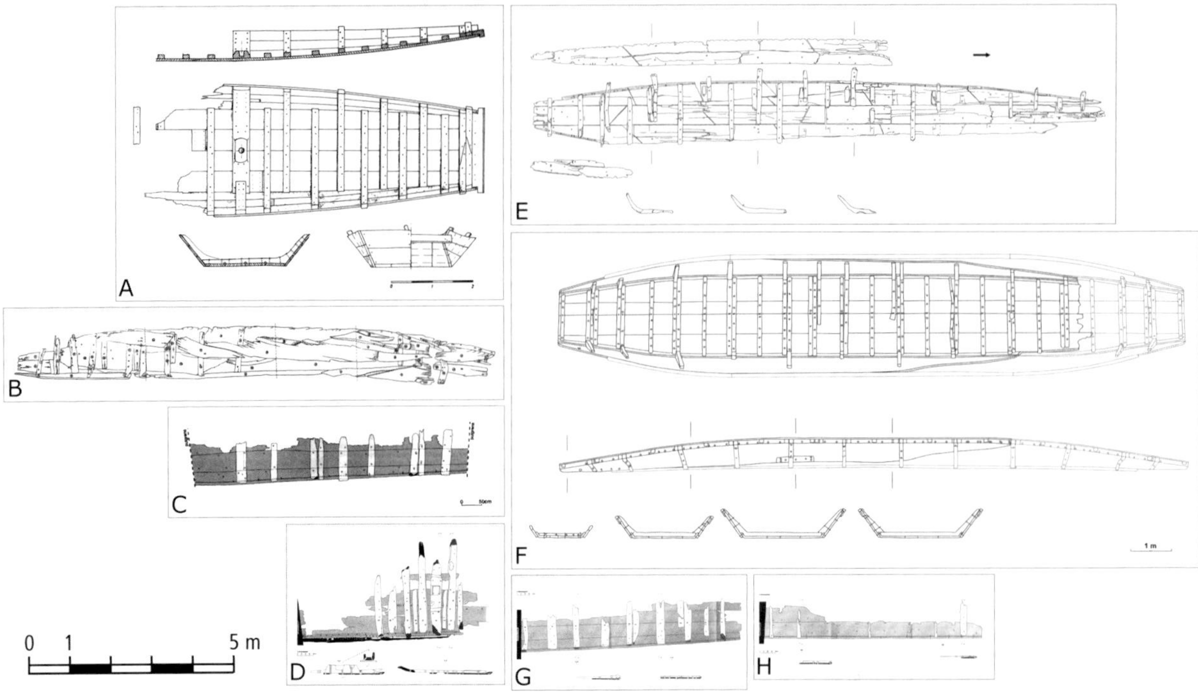

Fig. 4 Medieval vessels found in the Rhine area: **A** Krefeld-Gellep I (assumed around 1300 AD). – **B** Haus Meer 4 (2nd half of the 12th century AD). – **C** Tiel I (around 990 AD). – **D** Deventer-Ijsselstraat II (after 1047 AD). – **E** Kalkar-Niedermörmter (after 802 AD). – **F** Krefeld-Gellep III (assumed 8th century AD). – **G** Deventer-Ijsselstraat I (after 990 AD). – **H** Deventer-Ijsselstraat III (after 913 AD). – (Compilation of drawings by L. Kröger 2018 after Dammann 1974, 10 [adjusted by L. Kröger 2018]; Janssen/Janssen/Knörzer 1999, pl. 4; Vlierman 2002, 130; 1996, addendum 11; Kröger 2017b, 310-311; Vlierman 1996, addenda 10 and 12).

The vessels from Haus Meer show us that people in the 12th century AD made a lot of effort to repair and maintain smaller boats. The paddle that was found shows how these vessels were propelled. The use of such boats is normally associated with regional transportation or fishing. Medieval logboats could carry up to three tons. Therefore, they might also have been used for long-distance trade[44]. The use of logboats was common in Central Europe until Modern times, but always dependent on the supply of high-quality trunks, which became increasingly difficult to source. Already in the mid of the 14th century AD, the supply with suitable oaks at the River Main was problematic[45]. Only if the resources are available, like at Alpine lakes, logboats had many advantages over planked vessels, such as being easy to build and maintain. In addition, the missing of an inner structure benefits the life period and operation (e. g. of fishing nets).

A different medieval building technique can be seen in the vessels from Krefeld and Kalkar-Niedermörmter. Both sites are located at the Lower Rhine in the surroundings of the town of Duisburg (North Rhine-Westphalia/D). In Krefeld-Gellep, three vessels have been found during dredging work, as well as one vessel in Kalkar-Niedermörmter. All boats are not well-published or have only recently been reported. Therefore, they are mostly unknown to the wider research community. The vessels Krefeld-Gellep III and Kalkar-Niedermörmter show almost the same construction layout, which is similar to the Roman vessels Zwammerdam 6 and Woerden 7. Krefeld-Gellep III and Kalkar-Niedermörmter were built around 800 AD and were 15.2 m respectively 13.8 m long (**fig. 4**). Three or four bottom planks and one side plank form both hull layouts. The outer bottom planks consist of a slight L-shaped cross-section. These features connect the bottom and sidewall planks and give the general construction stability. The whole structure is strengthened via a pair of alternating frames followed by one bottom frame. This very regular pattern can be changed by later additions, such as those seen in Krefeld-Gellep III. Both vessels have an open bow and stern ending, supported only by a light bottom frame. Other possible features are lost or, in the case of Kalkar-Niedermörmter, only preserved in the remaining holes in the sidewalls. Their use cannot be determinate at the moment but could be connected to the installation of a rudder. In contrast to the Roman vessels, all fastenings have been made of wooden nails rather than iron. The only use of iron was for sintels at Krefeld-Gellep III. For Kalkar-Niedermörmter, the loading capacity was about 4.4 tons, having a draught of 35 cm. For Krefeld-Gellep III, the loading capacity was almost seven tons, having a draught of 45 cm. The bigger construction and higher loading capacity perhaps made a mast step inevitable for Krefeld-Gellep III, even though it was a relatively small one. Because of its loss, it is unclear what the mast bank would look like. A mast of such a vessel could be used primarily for towing the vessel against the current if punting is not possible. In the region of the Lower Rhine, sailing was also possible under favorable right conditions. A model test in an artificial towing tank showed that even with low sidewalls or an open bow construction, the risk of water coming into the boat was not present[46]. If both vessels can be addressed as a product of the same boat workshop or represent a very homogeny, regional building tradition cannot be claimed. The absence of iron nails and the outwards facing sidewalls seem to be a characteristic for early medieval inland vessels, as several boats of this time from various regions show[47].

Fig. 5 Mast-step and assumed mast-bank supporter of Krefeld-Gellep I. – (Photos by W. Lahn 1972 © German Maritime Museum).

For Krefeld-Gellep I, although initially seeming similar to Krefeld-Gellep III and Kalkar-Niedermörmter, upon closer inspection a different construction is visible[48]. The frame system was reconstructed in a regular pattern, without floor timbers. The opposite frames are not grouped in pairs. Four bottom planks form the floor construction but without L-shaped cross-sections. The sidewalls consist of three planks connected using the carvel technique. The cross-section is the same as the already presented boats. The bow form, like the other two ships, is formed in a trapezoid. A single wooden constructive element supports the tip of the bow. A striking difference from other already presented vessels is the massive mast step, also functioning as a frame. Compared to Krefeld-Gellep III, the mast step is much more stable and has a larger diameter. A documented metal object could have been part of a mast-bank support, as is known from other Roman finds[49] (**fig. 5**). The length of the vessel of Krefeld-Gellep I is estimated with 14.5 m and a loading capacity of five to seven tons[50]. It is unclear if these calculations are correct due to a questionable reconstruction. Similar to the other Rhine vessels, sintels and calking material are visible on the photographs, without any further information available. Following this description, iron nails have been used sporadically. Wooden nails have been used to make the majority of fastenings, but it is unclear why these kinds of nails were used. Boat dating is a major problem and in this case was only based on ceramics of the 13th and 14th century AD found in the surroundings. The construction could support a dating after early Medieval times, based on the available data. However, a connection to later post-medieval construction is more plausible due to its design.

For the Medieval period, iconographic sources play an important role. They help us to understand missing parts and handling situations. At the same time, they are often accompanied by descriptive text. In the 1970s, much focus was given to medieval inland vessel names and types. Especially D. Ellmers, founding

Fig. 6 Collection of different ship types on the Rhine in front of the Cologne harbour. – (Picture detail of A. Woensam's townscape of Cologne from 1531 © German Maritime Museum).

director of the German Maritime Museum, made significant efforts in this regard[51]. One of the central sources of Ellmers was a town scape of Cologne by A. Woensam, from 1531 (**fig. 6**). This woodcut shows the complete town, with its harbour situation in the foreground. Based on this source and the descriptive part, Ellmers tried to define a vessel type called Oberländer[52]. He claims a building tradition developed from the logboat to a divided logboat, to vessels fit for heavy load, as depicted on the Woensam woodcut. To support his theory, Ellmers discusses Krefeld-Gellep II as a representative of this type[53]. This vessel was dated by Ellmers around 1000 AD, but in fact was dendrochronologically dated around 1200 AD[54], and could be used for various purposes. Ellmers suggested a fishing vessel, but it might also have been used as a floater for a ship mill. In the end, Ellmers postulated evolutionary theory from logboats to the Oberländer type was correctly neglected and seen as a focus in a wrong direction[55]. Nevertheless, a systematic analysis of existing iconographic sources for inland vessels is missing. It could help to improve our knowledge about constructions, ship parts, and day-to-day practices not preserved in the archaeological record.

POST-MEDIEVAL BOAT CONSTRUCTION

The importance of iconographic sources increased rapidly during the 16th century AD. Vessels are shown as a decorative framework, as well as in detailed depictions. Descriptively written sources present an almost complete image of the transportation systems, regulations, and people involved in navigation. A glimpse into the available sources is provided in A. Fimpeler's compendium on navigation on the lower Rhine[56]. This book describes the most important aspects of ship usage in this area. Archaeological sources are given less attention; even so, the author mentions the important finds in her working area[57]. Again, several of the excavated vessels have not been properly published[58]. The case of a vessel from the estimated 19th century AD, found in 1978 AD at Düsseldorf (North Rhine-Westphalia/D), Mönchenwerth, shows the archaeological »behavior« for a long time, concerning post-medieval objects. The ship had a remaining length of 35 m and width of 6 m and was in an excellent state of preservation. About 80 % of the ship are preserved, and only the stern was destroyed (**fig. 7**). Nevertheless, the whole ship was demolished by purpose and is

Fig. 7 Overview photos of an estimated vessel from the 19th century AD found at Düsseldorf, Mönchenwerth. – (Jaeger 1979, 81-82).

therefore lost forever[59]. It is difficult to say how many vessels were lost in this way, but it is likely to have been many[60].

A boat similar in design to the medieval boats was found at Kessel, in the Maas, north of 's-Hertogenbosch (prov. North Brabant/NL). Despite the fact that this vessel from the first half of the 16th century AD[61] was not found in the Rhine, but in the close periphery, it is still an object that shows some medieval-like construction features. The reconstructed vessel is 12.5 m long. The bow and stern are supposed to look the same. Even if this could be discussed due to the bad preservation, an alternating system of frames is still visible, but without floor timbers. The floor is built from several smaller strakes without an L-shaped side. The sidewall is built by two strakes, connected in the clinker technique[62] (**fig. 8**).

A comparison to other 16th and early 17th century AD vessels is difficult, as comparable vessels are only known from Cologne (Poller Wiesen) and Mainz (Fort Malakoff), further south of the Rhine. The vessels from Cologne were found during construction works and were heavily damaged. Both had been turned upside down and used as parts of a bank reinforcement. Furthermore, only the bow or stern section is preserved but without the floor part. At least for vessel 1 from Cologne, the bow narrows to a tipped end. The sidewalls are made of three clinkered strakes, fastened with iron nails. Sintels, caulking woods, and caulking material are preserved and were used to seal the gaps. Several cracks have been repaired using the same technique. The excavator describes the vessel as an Aak, a type used mostly in the lower Rhine regions. However, as described above, such denominations are highly problematic, especially if the vessel is not

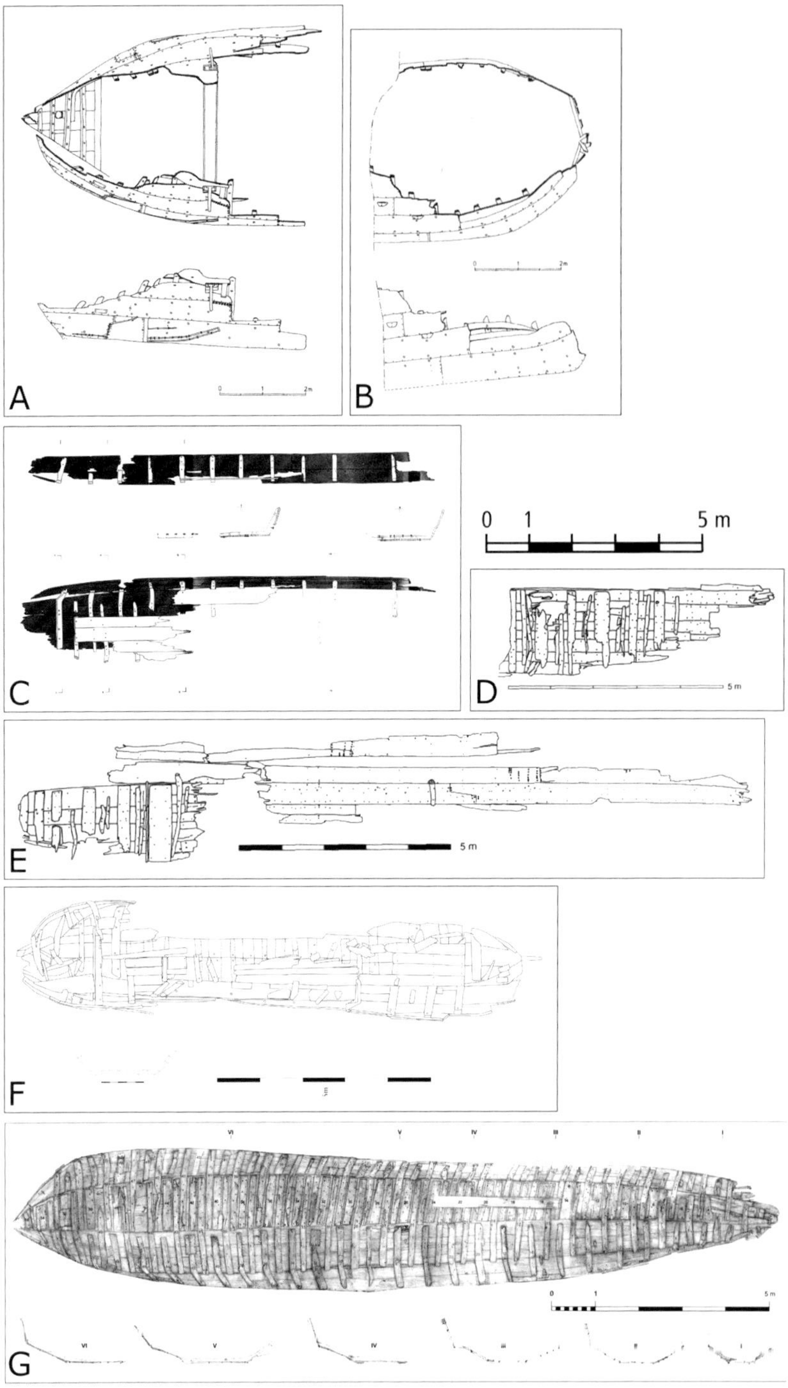

Fig. 8 Post-medieval vessels found in the Rhine area: **A** Cologne, Poller Wiesen 1 (around 1530 AD). – **B** Cologne, Poller Wiesen 2 (around 1590 AD). – **C** Kessel (around 1535 AD). – **D** Mainz, Fort Malakoff 1 (around 1575 AD). – **E** Mainz, Fort Malakoff 2 (around 1625 AD). – **F** Zutphena (after 1647 AD). – **G** Düsseldorf, Kaiserswerth (around 1700 AD). – (Compilation of drawings by L. Kröger 2018 after Trier 2005, 175-176; Vliemann 1996, addendum 3; Höckmann 2000, 68; Fermin 2015, 40; Schletter 2012, addendum 1).

well preserved. Both vessels have been dated via dendrochronology, vessel 1 around 1530 AD, and vessel 2 around 1590 AD. The planks of a third (destroyed) vessel have been dated around 1525 AD[63] (**fig. 8**).
The two fragments of vessels found in Mainz at the Malakoff fortification are only represented by their floor planks and a few floor timbers. The possibilities for reliable statements are therefore limited. The preserved parts of 17 m/6 m show an unsystematic construction pattern which suggests a framing pattern of two frames and one floor timber. The planks have been sawn. The moss for caulking is held in position by sintels, but not by caulking woods. Höckmann suggests that the caulking was put between the strakes during the building process and not hammered in the gaps afterward. To fasten the construction, wooden and iron

nails have been used. How the propulsion of both vessels was managed cannot be determined. Iconographic sources of this time at least suggest a mast for towing and sailing vessels of this size[64] (**fig. 8**).

A vessel found at Düsseldorf, Kaiserswerth, is in a far better state of preservation. With a length of 18m, the ship is almost complete. Stratigraphic layers date the vessel around 1700 AD. The systematic hull constructions of half-frames, hard chines, and floor timbers are visible, as well as constructive details, including a ruder post, a thwart for the mast bank with a mast step and a post for a windlass. The mast itself is lost, but it can be assumed that it was used for towing. The whole construction is made of oak, except for several later repairs made out of softwood. Again, moss was used for caulking together with sintels. In contrast to the medieval vessels, the find from Kaiserswerth shows a double kinked cross-section, meaning that one plank at a flat angle is attached to the bottom planks and a further strake is added in an almost vertical direction connected to the first one. This gives the ship a more rounded shape than the boxlike cross sections in Roman and Medieval times and improves the capsizing abilities. The complete building process can be retracted and is accessible for detailed cross-border research thanks to an unusually good publication[65].

OVERVIEW / CONCLUSION

Compared to other European rivers, a large number of vessels have been found, documented, and published in the last 50 years along the Rhine. The presented boats and ships demonstrate the many variations possible in ship construction. It should be noted that the boats described here probably only represent a small proportion of the whole diversity of boat types, especially because Woensam's town scape shows a great number of designs and functions at one spot within a short period. General developments in ship construction at the River Rhine can be seen in the archaeological record. One gets the impression that transportation habits and resource management have a more sustainable impact on hull design than technical development finding their way to the ships yards. Furthermore, the names used for vessels develop as slowly as the construction methods. The way a vessel is denominated can differ not only in dissimilar regions but also in the linguistic usage of one single person[66]. Future work addressing the Rhine's vessels from a techno-historical perspective should focus on publishing any unpublished or preliminary published vessels. Detailed studies on certain construction criteria are needed to fully understand the main principals of the building processes and handling practices. Furthermore, local heritage managers should be supported to preserve (or at least document) as many archaeological finds as possible. Only then does the step from collecting data to understanding the historical reality become possible.

Notes

1) Rahe/Stieghorst/Weber 2011.
2) Nessel/Uhnér 2018.
3) A hollowed-out wooden trunk has been found 1978 in Mannheim (Baden-Württemberg/D). ^{14}C-analysis dates this object around 3,500 BC. Due to an unsymmetrical shape and a remaining branch an interpretation as a logboat is questioned (Hirte 1987, catalogue IX 412). A second logboat dating to the 2nd century BC was found in Empel (prov. North Brabant/NL) at the Maas. The published information does not allow any further interpretation (Lanting 1997/1998, 636). Also, in the tributaries only a few prehistoric logboats are known (Kröger 2018b).
4) Du Plat Taylor/Cleere 1978. – Kennecke 2014.
5) Schmidts 2011.
6) Eger 2018.
7) Pfeiffer 1997.
8) Fimpeler-Philippen 2008, 125ff. – von Plessen 2016, 103ff.
9) Spies 1992.
10) Custodis 1990.
11) Rahe/Stieghorst/Weber 2011, 68ff.
12) Rahe/Stieghorst/Weber 2011, 253ff.

13) Marlier 2014.

14) Rieth 2011.

15) Boetto/Rousse 2011.

16) Erič et al. 2014.

17) Castro/Capulli 2016.

18) The chosen technique example to connect bottom planks is of course only one of the features that form a vessel, even thought it is an important one and the foundation of other constructive structures. To get in a detailed analysis of the development of flat-bottomed vessels all over Europe is not the goal of the article. For further information, the 2003 published article of R. Bockius on Roman vessels is highly recommended (Bockius 2003).

19) Bockius 2002b; 2002c.

20) Bockius 2006, 208ff.

21) Bockius 2006, 208ff.

22) Bockius 2007, 64ff.

23) Bockius 2003, 471ff.

24) Hermanns/Höpken 2014, 148ff.

25) Obladen-Kauder 2008.

26) de Weerd 1988.

27) Brouwers/Jansma/Manders 2013, 26. – Lehmann 1990, 79ff.

28) Jansma/Morel 2007. – Brouwers/Jansma/Manders 2013, 22-23. – van Holk 2006.

29) Vorst 2005. – Haalebos 1996. – Brouwers/Jansma/Manders 2013, 23-24. – Vos/Morel/Hazenberg 2011.

30) de Weerd 1988.

31) Lehmann 1990.

32) Obladen-Kauder 1995, 86ff.

33) The distance between both finding spots is about 10km.

34) de Weerd 1988. – Vos/Morel/Hazenberg 2011.

35) van de Moortel 2011, 78.

36) Höckmann 1994, 109ff. – Kröger 2014, 95.

37) Bockius 2006, 10ff. 189ff.

38) Vlierman 2002, 139.

39) Manders 2017.

40) Hinz 1962, 235ff.

41) See for example the collected vessels in Vlierman 2002, van de Moortel 2011 and Brouwers/Jansma/Manders 2015. The same must be said about the vessel from Wörth am Rhein at the Upper Rhine region published only in short reports. Only some sketches of the flat-bottomed vessel build around 1265 AD are available so far (Billig 2006; 2008). The vessels still wait in detail research.

42) Janssen/Janssen/Knörzer 1999, 58ff.

43) Kröger 2017a; 2018a.

44) Kröger in print, 180.

45) Kröger 2017a, 96.

46) The publishing of the results of the towing test is planned by the author in the year 2018 together with an analysis of different propulsion techniques used in pre-industrial times.

47) Kröger 2017b; 2014.

48) Unfortunately, parts of the documentation seem to be lost. The comparison of remaining drawings and photographs with two published reconstructions from the 1970s show a general accuracy, but cannot be confirmed for all details. Basis for this article is the drawing by W. Lahn from 1972 and a reconstruction based on this drawing by G. Salemke from 1974 (Dammann 1974, 10).

49) de Weerd 1988, 149. 152.

50) Dammann 1974.

51) Ellmers 1978; 1991; 2002; 2004.

52) Oberländer can be translated as an object coming from the upper regions in comparison to vessels from the low lands (Niederländer). Ellmers 2002, 59.

53) Ellmers 1996, 58.

54) Veltman 2011, 9.

55) Hakelberg 2003, 135ff. 143.

56) Fimpeler-Philippen 2008.

57) Fimpeler-Philippen 2008, 34ff.

58) This must be said for the three vessels from Koblenz-Ehrenbreitstein (Rhineland-Palatinate/D), dated into the 17th century AD (Fehr 2000 and Bode/Nießen 2007/2008), the vessel from Grave (prov. North Brabant/NL), also dated into the 17th century AD (Waldus/van Breda 2011, 17) and the vessel from Düsseldorf (North Rhine-Westphalia/D), Rheinufer Tunnel dated after 1792 AD (Lommerzheim/Oesterwind 2004, 146-147). The vessel Büderich Kanal near Xanten was found in the 19th century AD and is lost (Böcking 1980, 340).

59) Jaeger 1979.

60) Another vessel from the 19th century AD appears every now and then at Kleve near the German and Dutch border. The vessel »De Hoop« was built around 1875 AD and destroyed due to an explosion 1895 AD. This ship has also never been documented (www.schanz2.de/schenkenschanz/wrack01.html).

61) It was dated via radiocarbon analysis between 1510 and 1560.

62) Vlierman 1996, 19ff.

63) Trier 2005/2006.

64) Höckmann 1999; 2000.

65) Schletter 2012.

66) Kröger 2018a, 410. – Arneth 1972, 110-111. 227ff. Here in a text written 1541 the same vessel is named as a »schellich« and later again as an »achen«.

References

Billig 2006: M. Billig, Das Schiffswrack von Wörth am Rhein. Bericht zur Ausbildung zum Archäologischen Forschungstaucher (Freiburg i. Br. 2006).

2008: M. Billig, Ein spätmittelalterliches Schiffswrack im Rathjensee bei Wörth am Rhein. Archäologie in Deutschland 2008/2, 47-48.

Böcking 1980: W. Böcking, Die Geschichte der Rheinschiffahrt. Schiffe auf dem Rhein in drei Jahrtausenden (Moers 1980).

Bockius 2002a: R. Bockius, Die Schiffe von Zwammerdam. In: A. W. Mees / B. Pferdehirt (eds), Römerzeitliche Schiffsfunde in der Datenbank »Navis I«. Kataloge vor- und frühgeschichtlicher Altertümer 29 (Mainz 2002) 40-49.

2002b: R. Bockius, Das Wrack von Vechten. In: A. W. Mees / B. Pferdehirt (eds), Römerzeitliche Schiffsfunde in der Datenbank »Navis I«. Kataloge vor- und frühgeschichtlicher Altertümer 29 (Mainz 2002) 60-62.

2002c: R. Bockius, Die römerzeitlichen Schiffsfunde von Oberstimm (Bayern). Monographien des RGZM 50 (Mainz 2002).

2003: R. Bockius, Antike Prahme. Monumentale Zeugnisse keltisch-römischer Binnenschiffahrt aus der Zeit vom 2. Jh. v. Chr. bis ins 3. Jh. n. Chr. Jahrbuch des RGZM 47, 2003, 439-493.

2006: R. Bockius, Die spätrömischen Schiffswracks aus Mainz. Schiffsarchäologisch-technikgeschichtliche Untersuchung spätantiker Schiffsfunde vom nördlichen Oberrhein. Monographien des RGZM 67 (Mainz 2006).

2007: R. Bockius, Schifffahrt und Schiffbau in der Antike (Stuttgart 2007).

Boetto/Rousse 2011: G. Boetto / C. Rousse, Le chaland de Lipe (Ljubljana, Slovénie) et la tradition de construction »sur sole« de l'Europe sud-orientale. Quelles influences méditerranéennes? In: G. Boetto / P. Pomey / A. Tchernia (eds), Batellerie gallo-romaine. Pratiques régionales et influences maritimes méditerranéennes. Bibliothèque d'Archéologie Méditerranéenne et Africaine 9 (Paris 2011) 179-191.

Bode/Nießen 2007/2008: G. Bode / E. Nießen, Ehrenbreitsteiner Schiff. Beiträge zur Rheinkunde 59/60, 2007/2008, 79-93.

Brouwers/Jansma/Manders 2013: W. Brouwers / E. Jansma / M. R. Manders, Romeinse scheepsresten in Nederland. Archeobrief Jaargang 17/4, 2013, 13-27.

2015: W. Brouwers / E. Jansma / M. R. Manders, Middeleeuwse scheepsresten in Nederland. De vroege middeleeuwen 500-1050. Archeobrief 19/3, 2015, 6-24.

Castro/Capulli 2016: F. Castro / M. Capulli, A Preliminary report of recording the Stella 1 Roman River Barge, Italy. The International Journal of Nautical Archaeology 45/1, 2016, 29-41.

Custodis 1990: P.-G. Custodis, Die Frühzeit der Eisenbahn am Mittelrhein. Beiträge zur Rheinkunde 42, 1990, 40-51.

Dammann 1974: W. Dammann, Rheinschiffe aus Krefeld und Zwammerdam. Das Logbuch 1, 1974, 4-10.

Eger 2018: Ch. Eger, Handel, Logistik und Transport am römischen Niederrhein. Eine Einführung. In: Ch. Eger (ed.), Warenwege – Warenflüsse. Handel, Logistik und Transport am römischen Niederrhein [exhibition catalogue]. Xantener Berichte 32 (Mainz 2018) XV-XXXI.

Ellmers 1978: D. Ellmers, Ein Nachen mit Streichruder aus der Lippe bei Hünxe. Bonner Jahrbücher 178, 1978, 43-51.

1991: D. Ellmers, Schiffsarchäologie am Rhein. In: U. Löber / B. Schmutzler (eds), 2000 Jahre Rheinschiffahrt [exhibition catalogue]. Veröffentlichungen des Landesmuseums Koblenz: Reihe B, Einzelveröffentlichungen 40 (Koblenz 1991) 29-47.

1996: D. Ellmers, Celtic Plank Boats and Ships, 500 BC 55-AD 1000. In: R. Gardiner (ed.), The earliest ships. The evolution of boats into ships (London 1996) 52-71.

2002: D. Ellmers, Baumschiff und Oberländer – Archäologie, Ikonografie und Typenbezeichnungen einer mittelalterlichen Binnenschiffsfamilie. In: K. Elmshäuser (ed.), Häfen, Schiffe, Wasserwege. Zur Schiffahrt des Mittelalters. Schriften des Deutschen Schiffahrtsmuseums 58 (Hamburg 2002) 97-106.

2004: D. Ellmers, Kahn, Prahm und andere flachbodige Schiffstypen. Ein Beitrag zur Wörter-und-Sachen-Forschung. In: K. Brandt / H. J. Kühn (eds), Der Prahm aus dem Hafen von Haithabu. Beiträge zu antiken und mittelalterlichen Flachbodenschiffen. Schriften des Archäologischen Landesmuseums, Ergänzungsreihe 2 (Neumünster 2004) 55-69.

Fehr 2000: A. Fehr, Funde von Flussschiffen des späten 17. Jahrhunderts in Koblenz-Ehrenbreitstein. Beiträge zur Rheinkunde 52, 2000, 7-18.

Du Plat Taylor/Cleere 1978: J. Du Plat Taylor / H. Cleere (eds), Roman shipping and trade. Britain and the Rhine provinces. Council for British Archaelogy: Research Report 24 (London 1978).

Erič et al. 2014: M. Erič / A. Gaspari / K. Čufar / F. Solina / T. Verbič, Early Roman barge from the Ljubljanica River at Sinja Gorica. Arheološki Vestnik 65, 2014, 187-254.

Fimpeler-Philippen 2008: A. Fimpeler-Philippen, Die Schifffahrt und ihre Fahrzeuge auf dem Niederrhein vom späten Mittelalter bis ins 18. Jahrhundert. Studien zur Düsseldorfer Wirtschaftsgeschichte 5 = Veröffentlichungen aus dem Stadtarchiv Düsseldorf 19 (Düsseldorf 2008).

Haalebos 1996: J. K. Haalebos, Ein römisches Getreideschiff in Woerden (NL). Jahrbuch des RGZM 43, 1996, 475-509.

Hakelberg 2003: D. Hakelberg, Das Kippenhorn bei Immenstaad. Archäologische Untersuchungen zu Schiffahrt und Holzschiffbau am Bodensee vor 1900. Materialhefte zur Archäologie in Baden-Württemberg 56 (Stuttgart 2003).

Heeringen et al. 2007: R. M. van Heeringen / T. de Groot / J.-M. A. W. Morel / E. Jansma / F. Dallmeijer / D. J. Huisman / A. Smit / K. Linthout, Romeins schip in Utrechtse bodem. Vitruvius 1, 2007, 6-13.

Hermanns/Höpken 2014: M. H. Hermanns / C. Höpken, Zur Schiffbarkeit des Kölner Hafens. Wrackteile römischer Flachbodenschiffe in der Rinne zwischen Stadt und Rheininsel. In: Kennecke 2014, 145-174.

Hinz 1962: H. Hinz, Einige niederrheinische Fundstellen mit mittelalterlicher Keramik. Bonner Jahrbücher 162, 1962, 231-259.

Hirte 1987: C. Hirte, Zur Archäologie monoxyler Wasserfahrzeuge im nördlichen Mitteleuropa. Eine Studie zur Repräsentativität der Quellen in chorologischer, chronologischer und konzeptioneller Hinsicht (Kiel 1987).

Höckmann 1994: O. Höckmann, Post-Roman Timbers and a Floating Mill from the Upper Rhine. In: C. Westerdahl (ed.), Crossroads in ancient shipbuilding. Proceedings of the Sixth International Symposium on Boat and Ship Archaeology, Roskilde, 1991. ISBSA 6. Oxbow Monograph 40 (Oxford 1994) 105-116.

1999: O. Höckmann, Früh-neuzeitliche Schiffsfunde von der Baustelle »Malakoff-Zentrum« in Mainz. Mainzer Archäologische Zeitschrift 5/6, 1999, 293-318.

2000: O. Höckmann, Post-Medieval Rhine Vessels from Mainz, Germany. In: J. Litwin (ed.), Down the River to the Sea. Eighth International Symposium on Boat and Ship Archaeology, Gdańsk 1997 (Gdańsk 2000) 67-70.

van Holk 2006: A. F. L. van Holk, A Roman barge with an artefactual inventory from De Meern (the Netherlands). In: L. K. Blue / F. M. Hocker / A. Englert (eds), Connected by the sea. Proceedings of the Tenth International Symposium on Boat and Ship Archaeology, Roskilde 2003 (Oxford 2006) 295-299.

Jansma/Morel 2007: E. Jansma / J.-M. A. W. Morel, Een Romeinse Rijnaak, gevonden in Utrecht-De Meern. Resultaten van het onderzoek naar de platbodem »De Meern 1«. Rapportage Archeologische Monumentenzorg 144 (Amersfoort 2007).

Jaeger 1979: W. Jaeger, Die Aak von Mönchenwerth und die Bedeutung ihres Verlustes für die Technikgeschichte. Das Logbuch 15/3, 1979, 81-86.

Janssen/Janssen/Knörzer 1999: W. Janssen / B. Janssen / K.-H. Knörzer, Die frühmittelalterliche Niederungsburg bei Haus Meer, Kreis Neuss. Archäologische und naturwissenschaftliche Untersuchungen. Rheinische Ausgrabungen 46 (Köln 1999).

Kennecke 2014: H. Kennecke (ed.), Der Rhein als europäische Verkehrsachse. Die Römerzeit 16 (Bonn 2014).

Kröger 2014: L. Kröger, Früh- und hochmittelalterliche Binnenschiffe in Mitteleuropa. Ein Überblick zum aktuellen Stand der Forschung. Přehled Výzkumů 55, 2014, 91-123.

2017a: L. Kröger, Crossing the river. Ferries as part of the maritime landscape of the River Main (Germany). In: J. Gawronski / A. F. L. van Holk / J. Schokkenbroek (eds), Ships and maritime landscapes. Proceedings of the Thirteenth International Symposium on Boat and Ship Archaeology, Amsterdam 2012. ISBSA 13 (Eelde 2017) 95-101.

2017b: L. Kröger, Two »New« Early Medieval Inland Vessels in the River Rhine in Germany. In: J. Litwin (ed.), Baltic and beyond. Change and continuity in shipbuilding. Proceedings of the Fourteenth International Symposium on Boat and Ship Archaeology Gdańsk 2015. ISBSA 14 (Gdańsk 2017) 307-314.

2018a: L. Kröger, Ferry Stations as Small Harbours. The Role of River Crossings in the Workaday Life at Southern German Rivers. In: C. von Carnap-Bornheim / F. Daim / P. Ettel / U. Warnke (eds), Harbours as Objects of Interdisciplinary Research – Archaeology + History + Geosciences. RGZM – Tagungen 34 = Interdisziplinäre Forschungen zu den Häfen von der Römischen Kaiserzeit bis zum Mittelalter in Europa 5 (Mainz 2018) 403-414.

2018b: L. Kröger, Within the network of fluvial ports. In: L. Werther / H. Müller / M. Foucher (eds), European Harbour Data Repository, Vol. 01 (Jena 2018). DOI: 10.22032/dbt.35240 (pdf), 10.22032/dbt.35241 (csv), 10.22032/dbt.35242 (excel).

in print: L. Kröger, Fähren an Main und Neckar. Eine archäologische und historisch-geographische Entwicklungsanalyse mittelalterlicher und frühneuzeitlicher Verkehrsinfrastruktur [PhD thesis Univ. Bamberg 2016]. Monographien des RGZM 145 (in print).

Lanting 1997/1998: J. N. Lanting, Dates for origin and diffusion of the European Logboats. Palaeohistoria 39/40, 1997/1998, 627-650.

Lehmann 1978: L. T. Lehmann, The flat-bottomed Roman boat from Druten, Netherlands. The International Journal of Nautical Archaeology 7/4, 1978, 259-267.

1990: L. T. Lehmann, The Romano-Celtic boats from Druten and Kapel-Avezaath. In: S. McGrail (ed.), Maritime Celts, Frisians, and Saxons. Papers presented to a conference at Oxford in November 1988 (London 1990) 77-81.

Lommerzheim/Oesterwind 2004: R. Lommerzheim / B. Oesterwind, Rheinzeiten. Archäologische Entdeckungen am Düsseldorfer Rheinufer (Düsseldorf 2004).

Manders 2017: M. R. Manders, A coincidence? Two medieval boats (Vleuten 1 and 2) found during the construction of a housing development at Leidsche Rijn (the Netherlands). In: J. Gawronski / A. F. L. van Holk / J. Schokkenbroek (eds), Ships and maritime landscapes. Proceedings of the Thirteenth International Symposium on Boat and Ship Archaeology, Amsterdam 2012. ISBSA 13 (Eelde 2017) 466-471.

Marlier 2014: S. Marlier (ed.), Arles-Rhône 3. Un chaland gallo-romain du 1er siècle après Jésus-Christ. Archaeonautica 18 (Paris 2014).

van de Moortel 2011: A. van de Moortel, Medieval boats and ships of Germany, the Low Countries, and northeast France. Archaeological evidence for shipbuilding traditions, shipbuilding resources, trade, and communication. In: F. Bittmann / J. Ey / M. Karle et al. (eds), Flüsse als Kommunikations- und Handelswege. Siedlungs- und Küstenforschung im südlichen Nordseegebiet 34 (Rahden/Westf. 2011) 67-104.

Nessel/Uhnér 2018: B. Nessel / C. Uhnér, Spezialisierte Transporteure in der Bronzezeit? Überlegungen zu Natur und Organisation von Nah- und Ferntransporten in Europa nördlich des Balkan-Gebirges. In: B. Nessel / D. Neumann / M. Bartelheim (eds), Bronzezeitlicher Transport. Akteure, Mittel und Wege. Ressourcenkulturen 8 (Tübingen 2018) 59-75.

Obladen-Kauder 1995: J. Obladen-Kauder, Bodendenkmalpflege am Beispiel der niederrheinischen Kiesgruben. Aspekte rezenter fluvialer Archäologie. In: D. Planck (ed.), Archäologie unter Wasser. Forschungen und Berichte zur Unterwasserarchäologie zwischen Alpenrand-Seen und Nordmeer. Archäologische Informationen aus Baden-Württemberg 33 (Stuttgart 1995) 85-91.

2008: J. Obladen-Kauder, Spuren römischer Lastschifffahrt am Unteren Niederrhein. In: M. Müller (ed.), Colonia Ulpia Traiana. Xanten und sein Umland in römischer Zeit (Mainz 2008) 507-523.

Peiß 2012: A. Peiß, From Excavation to Presentation. 17 Years Work on a Roman Barge from Xanten-Wardt. In: K. Strætkvern / E. Williams (eds), Proceedings of the 11th ICOM-CC Group on Wet Organic Archaeological Materials Conference. Greenville 2010 (Greenville 2012) 327-336.

Pfeiffer 1997: F. Pfeiffer, Rheinische Transitzölle im Mittelalter (Oldenburg 1997).

von Plessen 2016: M.-L. von Plessen, Der Rhein. Eine europäische Flussbiografie (München 2016).

Rahe/Stieghorts/Weber 2011: J. Rahe / M. Stieghorst / U. Weber (eds), Handbuch Rhein (Darmstadt 2011).

Rieth 2011: É. Rieth, L'épave du chaland gallo-romain de la place Tolozan a Lyon. Approche d'une tradition régionale de construction »sur sole« en relation avec l'architecture navale maritime méditerranéenne. In: G. Boetto / P. Pomey / A. Tchernia (eds), Batellerie gallo-romaine. Pratiques régionales et influences maritimes méditerranéennes. Bibliothèque d'Archéologie Méditerranéenne et Africaine 9 (Paris 2011) 63-72.

Schletter 2012: H.-P. Schletter, Der Kaiserswerther Nachen. Ein archäologischer Beitrag zur Rheinschifffahrt der Frühen Neuzeit. Deutsches Schiffahrtsarchiv 35, 2012, 13-72.

Schmidts 2011: Th. Schmidts, Akteure und Organisation der Handelsschifffahrt in den nordwestlichen Provinzen des Römischen Reiches. Monographien des RGZM 97 (Mainz 2011).

Spies 1992: G. Spies, Technik der Steingewinnung und der Flußschiffahrt im Harzvorland in früher Neuzeit (Braunschweig 1992).

Trier 2005/2006: M. Trier, Mitteralterlicher Hochwasserschutz in Köln. »... mit gwaltigen Unkosten (gleich zu ersehen) gelecht und angerichtet ...«. Skyllis 7/1-2, 2005/2006, 172-185.

Veltman 2011: R. Veltman, Erweiterte Einbäume aus Krefeld und Arnheim. Analyse zweier mittelalterlicher Schiffsfunde vom Niederrhein [unpubl. B.A. thesis, Univ. Münster 2011].

Vlierman 1996: K. Vlierman, Kleine bootjes en middeleeuws scheepshout met constructiedetails. Scheeparcheologie II 404 (Lelystad 1996).

2002: K. Vlierman, Scheeps- en stadsarcheologie. De betekenis van scheeps(hout)vondsten in Nederlandse middeleeuwse steden. In: H. Sarfatij / P. J. Woltering / D. P. Hallewas et al. (eds), Middeleeuwse toestanden. Archeologie, geschiedenis en monumentenzorg: aangeboden aan Herbert Sarfatij bij zijn 65e verjaardag (Hilversum 2002) 119-148.

Vorst 2005: Y. Vorst, De constructie en herkomst van de Romeinse platbodem »Woerden 7«. Een studie van jaarringpatronen en bewerkingssporen (Amsterdam 2005).

Vos/Morel/Hazenberg 2011: W. K. Vos / J. Morel / T. Hazenberg, The Woerden 7. An oar-powered Roman barge built in the Netherlands. Archäologisches Korrespondenzblatt 41, 2011, 101-118.

Waldus/van Breda 2011: W. B. Waldus / W. van Breda, Archaeological research in the Lower Rhine – theory and practice. Archäologische Untersuchungen im Niederrheingebiet – Theorie und Praxis. In: F. Bittmann / J. Ey / M. Karle et al. (eds), Flüsse als Kommunikations- und Handelswege. Siedlungs- und Küstenforschung im südlichen Nordseegebiet 34 (Rahden/Westf. 2011) 13-21.

de Weerd 1988: M. D. de Weerd, Schepen voor Zwammerdam. Bouwwijze en herkomst van enkele vaartuigtypen in West- en Middeneuropa uit de Romeinse tijd en de Middeleeuwen in archeologisch perspectief (Amsterdam 1988).

Summary

Over the centuries the Rhine was one of the most important axes for communication in Central Europe. Transported goods, as well as vessels used for their shipping, are documented since Roman Antiquity. Relatively many boats dating to the Roman period are known from the archaeological context. However, only a few medieval vessels have been found yet. Furthermore, the quality of publications is often not optimal. A similar situation can be seen for objects from post-medieval time. It should be noted that, together with changes concerning construction principles, a size reduction of the boats from Antiquity to the Medieval periods is traceable. This paper provides an overview of the sometimes scattered published finds, as well as a general idea of construction trends at the Rhine to a wider audience.

Zusammenfassung

Der Rhein stellte über Jahrhunderte eine der bedeutendsten Kommunikationsachsen in Mitteleuropa dar. Seit der römischen Antike sind nicht nur Transportgüter, sondern auch die für den Verkehr genutzten Fahrzeuge nachweisbar. Aus römischer Zeit stehen verhältnismäßig viele Boote aus dem archäologischen Kontext der Forschung zur Verfügung. Hingegen konnten bislang deutlich weniger mittelalterliche Fahrzeuge aufgefunden werden, die zudem häufig schlecht publiziert vorliegen. Eine ähnliche Situation ist für die frühe Neuzeit zu konstatieren. Dabei ist festzustellen, dass neben der Veränderung bestimmter Bauprinzipien besonders eine Reduktion der Fahrzeuggrößen von der Antike zum Mittelalter bemerkbar ist. Der vorliegende Beitrag hat das Ziel, die z. T. sehr verstreut publizierten Funde in einer Zusammenschau vorzustellen und grobe Entwicklungslinien innerhalb der Bootsbautechnik am Rhein einem weiteren Interessentenkreis aufzuzeigen.

INLAND HARBOURS: ANTIQUITY

CORINNE SANCHEZ · MARIE-PIERRE JÉZÉGOU · JULIEN CAVERO
CAMILLE FAISSE · VIVIEN MATHÉ · CLÉMENT FLAUX
ADRIEN CAMUS · GUILLAUME BRUNIAUX

THE ANCIENT PORT OF NARBONNE: FIVE CENTURIES OF FLUVIO-LAGOONAL DEVELOPMENT

When Strabo wrote about the *emporium* of Narbonne (dép. Aude/F), he specified that the city was situated behind the Narbonitis (IV, 1, 6), which corresponds to the lagoons, and that the River Aude was navigable upstream of the city for a short distance (IV, 1, 14). With these words, the ancient author highlighted the importance of the river and the lagoon. This »favourable situation«, as described by Diodorus of Sicily (V, 38), facilitated the development of port activities in this fluvio-lagoonal area, enabling Narbonne to become a hub for the Mediterranean, as well as for Atlantic trade. It was here, at the intersection of sea and land routes, on the Gallic isthmus between the Mediterranean and the Atlantic, facing a sheltered lagoon into which a navigable river flowed, that the first Roman colony outside of Italy was founded as of 118 BC (**fig. 1**). The sustainment of harbour activities then depended on paleoenvironmental and economic changes. In order to identify the complex evolutions of the Narbonne port system in Antiquity, a collaborative research project[1] led by an interdisciplinary team of geographers, historians, archaeologists and paleoenvironmentalists has been underway since 2010. Paleogeographic studies offer an initial view of the modifications of the coastline around the Bages and Sigean Lagoons[2]. Data from these studies are

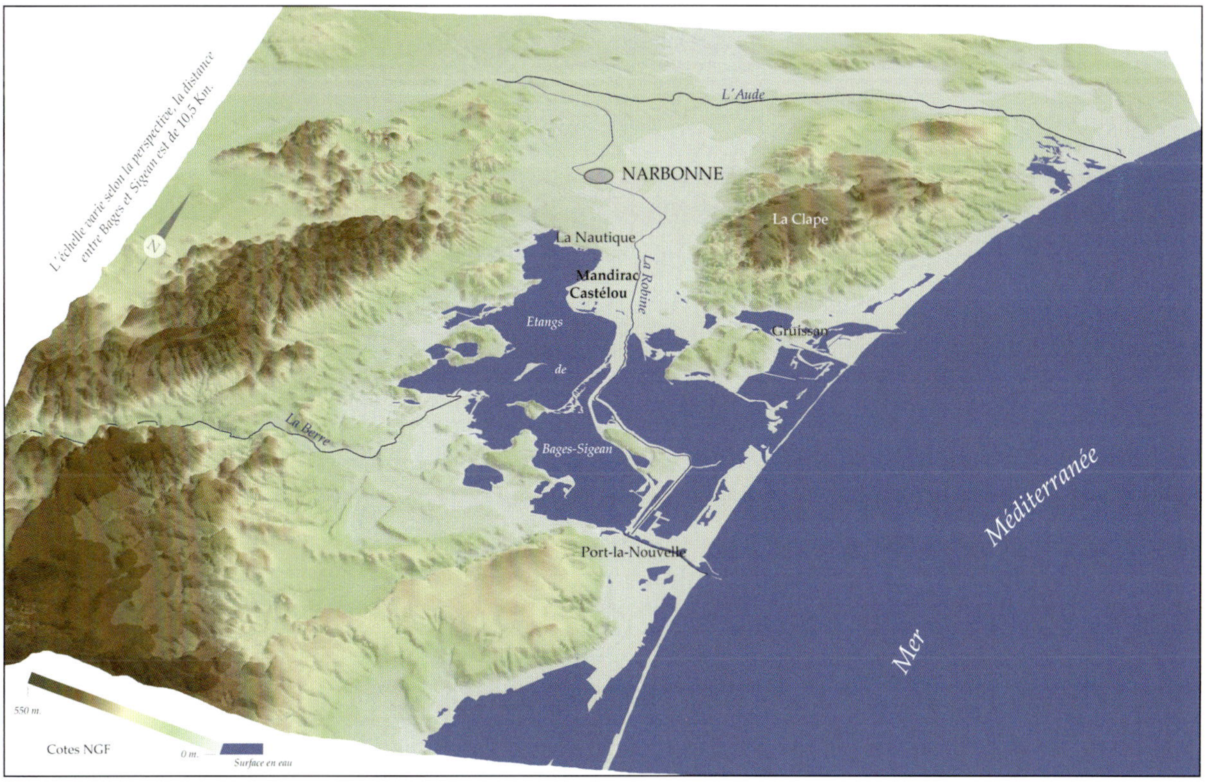

Fig. 1 DTM of the Narbonne region and localization of the Le Castélou/Mandirac site. – (J. Cavero 2010).

combined in a GIS (Geographic Information System) with data from geophysical surveys and archaeological investigations to better understand the difficulties of maintaining the port areas over the long term. The shifting of the river is a recurring problem in tracing the history of Narbonne: although the Aude now flows north of the city, in Antiquity a southern branch connected it to the Bages and Sigean lagoons. Recent excavations conducted in the sectors of Le Castélou and Mandirac, south of Narbonne, revealed that the river mouth in the lagoons had undergone monumental work to channel the watercourse and create unloading areas. The resources expended attest to a strong determination by the public powers to ensure the smooth functioning of economic activities.

PALEOGEOGRAPHY

Founded on an ancient alluvial terrace of the Aude, Narbonne overlooks, from its promontory, a lagoonal landscape dotted with islands, already described by ancient geographers and historians. Strabo placed the city behind a lagoon and the river mouth of the Atax (the Aude River)[3]. Pomponius Mela specified that the Atax emptied into a vast lake called Rubresus, which is a narrow passage connected to the sea, and Pliny the Elder indicated that the city was located at a distance of 18 km from the sea. In the absence of direct contact with the sea, the ancient Narbonne port system was built around the lagoons and the river, which both facilitated and restricted access to it.

All that remains of the ancient Lake Rubresus today is a group of disconnected lagoons. Although in the Bages-Sigean Lagoon, the islands of l'Aute and Planasse have retained their insularity, this is not true for Roc de Conilhac, southeast of the Mandirac-Castélou plain, or the islands of Saint-Martin and Sainte-Lucie, now connected to the barrier beach. The modification of this environment, subject to the fluctuations of the Aude, which now flows north of the city and the Massif de La Clape, was one of the main reasons for installations in the lagoons.

Although the exact topography of the lagoons in Antiquity remains difficult to trace, it was necessarily situated somewhere between the overly vast Rubresus and the current configuration. Ancient maps reveal the modifications that have occurred over the past few centuries and illustrate the extreme mobility of these lagoonal environments.

La Nautique appears to be the only sector that did not experience any major transformations of its shore until recent times. At this site, remains have been uncovered that attest to the existence of a pier operating for a short time between 30 BC and 70 AD. The early abandonment of the pier raises many questions. The most likely hypothesis is that the La Nautique port was close to the river mouth and abandoned when the river was channeled southeast to the Mandirac-Castélou sector at a distance of 1.5 km. We are particularly interested in this latter site because it relates directly to our questions concerning watercourses.

The Mandirac-Castélou coast was much more clearly defined at the end of the 18th century AD (**fig. 2**). It was bordered to the south by the Gulf of Tournebelle – an evocative name deriving from Torne veles (»turn the sails«) in the Occitan language – to the east by a canal, the Robine, and to the west by the island of Mandirac, as attested in a 9th century AD charter. The northern shore was called the coast of Demi-Vaillant and ended with an inlet penetrating the land, just south of the domain of Montfort.

This topography and toponymy quickly evolved: by 1852 AD, the sedimentation of the Gulf of Tournebelle had reached the island of Mandirac, of which only the southern tip, the point of the Îlette, remained. In 1901 AD, the inlet of Montfort had become entirely sanded up. The silting of the Gulf was almost complete and the point of the Îlette – in geographical and toponymic terms – had disappeared. In 1952 AD, the silting of this area had progressed: to the west, with the advancement of the coast of Demi-Vaillant, no longer

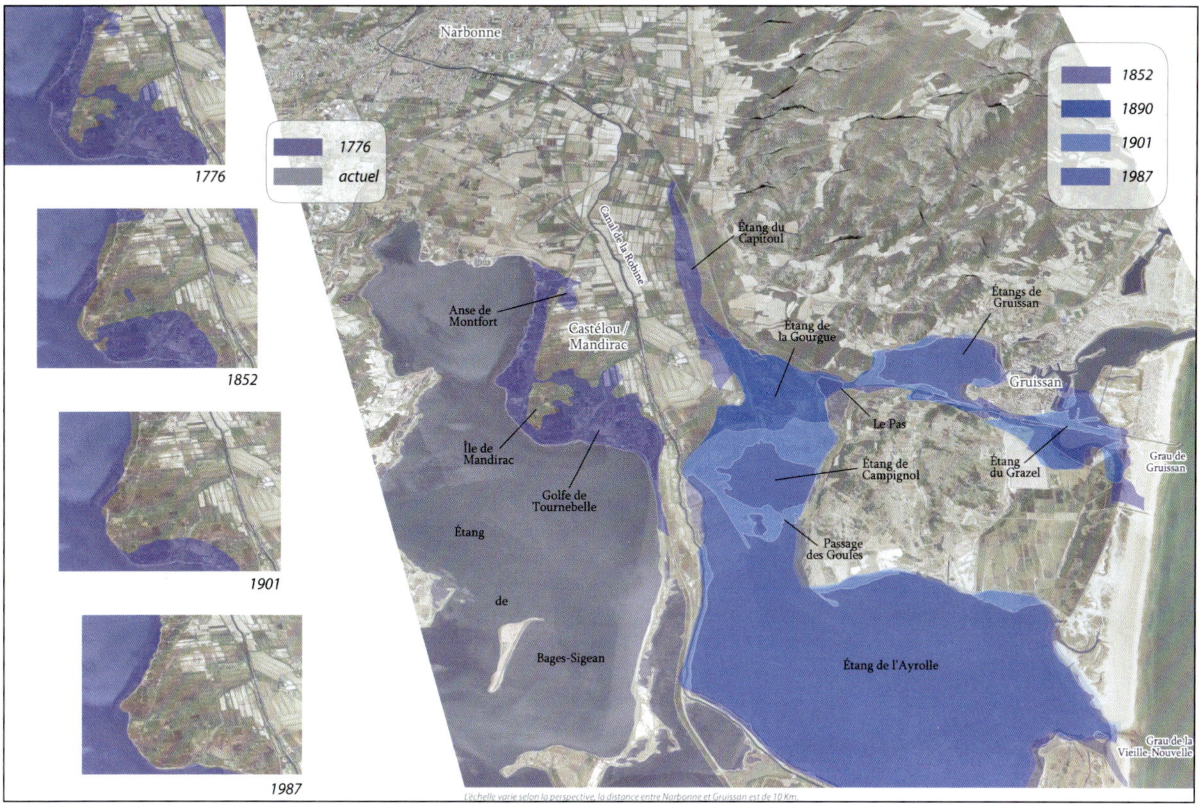

Fig. 2 Narbonne lagoons paleogeography, particularly the area of Le Castélou. – (J. Cavero 2010).

known by that name, and to the south with the sanding up of the Gulf of Tournebelle, which would be complete by the end of the 20th century AD.

These are the shifting natural areas in which the current research focuses. The history of the river, the ancient installations of the Mandirac-Castélou plain and establishment of the various sites around the lagoons are all reminders of this evolution. The geographic conditions are therefore significant: an alluvial plain, where a navigable river flows, providing access to one of the major trade routes of Gaul, is a particularly attractive environment for the settling of merchants and a community.

GEOMORPHOLOGICAL DATA

Although geomorphological research covering a long time scale has been conducted[4], other studies focus on specific historical periods, linked to archaeological remains[5]. Today, the Aude flows 6 km north of Narbonne and discharges at Fleury d'Aude (dép. Aude/F). The northern branch, attested in the Middle Ages, has probably always been active. The Robine canal, a 17th century AD construction, roughly corresponds to the former path of the southern branch of the Aude. It passes through Narbonne and the Bages and Sigean Lagoons, ending in Port-la-Nouvelle (dép. Aude/F). The southern branch, linked to human constructions, has benefited from many observations in the plain of the Aude, archaeological rescue operations in urban areas and excavations at the ancient ports on the shore of the lagoons. Although this division into two branches is the legacy of a complex history, it certainly reflects a configuration close to that in Antiquity: two watercourses seem to have been coexisting, one north of the La Clape Massif, and the other to the south, toward the lagoons. It is not possible today to decide which was the main course.

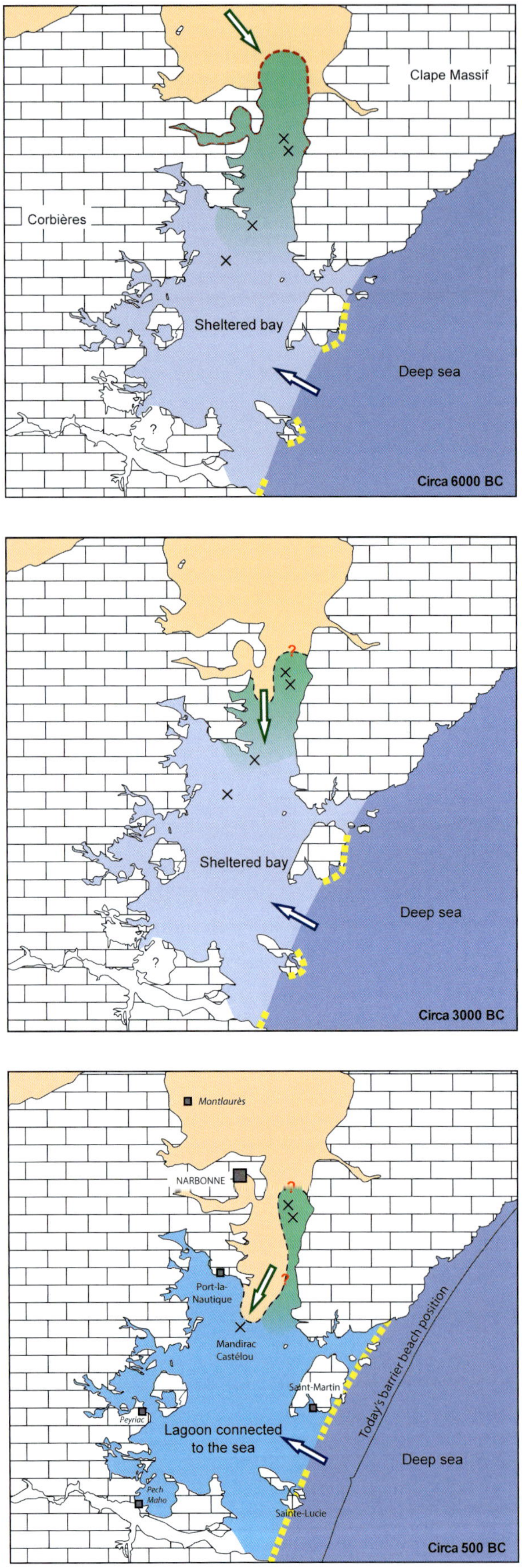

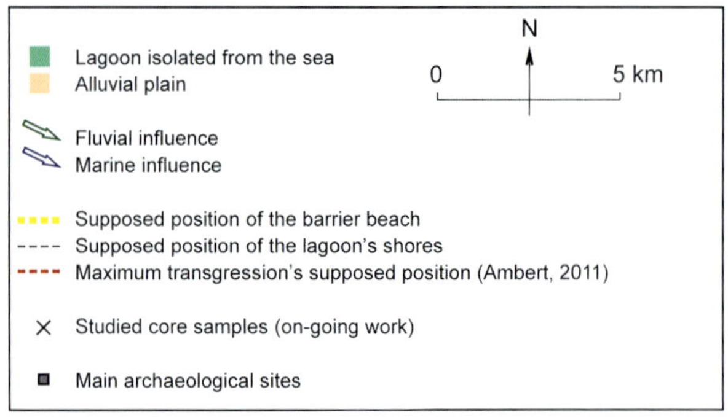

Fig. 3 Lagoon evolution south of Narbonne. – (T. Salel 2012).

The question of lagoon depth and the passage of the river are of vital importance to establishing the port areas. A branch of the Aude discharged into the lagoons in Antiquity. Easy access to the port was required to maintain economic activity, which relied on the smooth functioning of port areas. Although there was a port in the city, outer harbours also existed close by or at the river mouth in the lagoon, with sites at Port-la-Nautique, Le Castélou, and Mandirac. During the early period of the Roman settlement, the lagoon was sufficiently deep, but it is very likely that the acceleration of the silting process quickly became a public concern.

The boundaries and the depth of the lagoon in Antiquity have to be defined more clearly yet. Two corings carried out 3.5 km southeast of Narbonne show that an euryhaline lagoon existed from the 3rd millennium BC and continued to exist after the 1st century AD, with a water column of about 1 m during the Roman era[6]. Further south, in the Le Castélou and Mandirac sectors, paleogeographic approaches have highlighted the speed and extent of shore modifications[7]. The lagoon formed a vast expanse corresponding to a basin covering more than 60 km^2. However, the northern boundary in the low area between the plateau of the Quatourze and La Clape is not known. The silting process, which accelerated in recent periods, is caused by alluvial deposits from the Aude and the Berre (**fig. 3**)[8].

In the 2nd century BC, the depth of the lagoon at Le Castélou can be estimated at approximately 5 m[9]. The silting of the lagoon appears to have been rapid, on the scale of Antiquity: about 1 m of sediment was deposited between the 2nd century BC levels and remains from Port-la-Nautique traffic dating to the 1st century AD [10]. The depth of the lagoon west of Port-la-Nautique has been estimated at -2.2 m in the middle of the 1st century AD, compared with -3.2 m (NGF, the vertical datum for France) in the 2nd century BC [11]. The problem, shared by other ports such as Ostia (Latium/I), was therefore silting and the need for a series of installations to maintain adequate draft depth for ship access. The question of the river mouth is a central one. Although the channeled part of the river could be maintained, its outlet into the lagoon was a difficult area to manage. Today, the research program into the ancient ports of Narbonne is providing new data on the evolution of the river and the lagoon and the harbour installations that were constructed there.

THE CONSTRUCTION OF THE RIVER MOUTH

A clear understanding of the operation of the port of Narbonne is based on research of the river mouth. Geophysical surveys were an essential prerequisite to this research covering a vast area [12]. The methods implemented were systematically adapted to the context [13]. The marshy sector of Mandirac and Le Castélou provides essential data on the mouth of the Aude River, a fluvial artery that changed course over time. Excavations have confirmed the construction of two parallel jetties in a wetland environment, flanking the 50 m wide and approximately 3.5-4 m deep river (**fig. 4**) [14]. Between 15 and 25 m wide, the jetties were paved at the end of the 1st century AD using several cubic metres of materials and thousands of wooden piles to reinforce the banks. The two roadways on each side of the river featured symmetrical profiles and large rockfill structures stabilized by a network of stakes. The river depth was evaluated by sediment corings to be 3.5 m. A third construction completed the installations: an alignment of stones approximately 800 m long, identified through geophysical surveys and staking. The purpose of this breakwater was to reduce wave action to protect the vulnerable area in the curve of the roadway between Mandirac and Le Castélou. Rockfill structures on the lagoon side compensate the absence of this construction further north: wooden caissons filled with rocks, placed to interrupt the flow of sand and prevent the construction from being undermined. These 7 m wide wooden caissons form an underpinning supporting platform to stabilize this structure.

It was also necessary to extend these constructions periodically afterward to bypass the sanded-up area and preserve enough depth for ships to reach the river mouth. The endpoint in the lagoon was located at Petit-Castélou through staking, penetration tests and geophysical surveys. The river mouth presents the same configuration as that of the current-day Aude: the eastern jetty is about 50 m longer [15]. Although the constructions discovered there are equally monumental, due to the instability of the terrain and a high water discharge rate, it was not possible to carry out research any further. It should nevertheless be envisioned that the extremities of these jetties were equipped with a signaling system, possibly beacons or lighthouses.

Constructions of this size channeling rivers have been uncovered anywhere else in the Roman world. However, these works had impact on the development of the lagoon, especially the acceleration of its silting, judging from the sedimentation rate. These public constructions underscore the determination to control a shifting environment and ensure the stability and sustainability of these exchanges and trade places. The archaeological data provides detailed information on the environment and offers chronological references for the geomorphological observations. The water column between the two roadways has been evaluated to be 3.5 m, making them accessible to ships with deep draughts [16]. They also served as quays to unload and transfer goods to small boats or carts for transport to the city. All ships did not, in fact, sail up the river to the city, so some products were transferred to lighter boats to be transhipped to an urban port that remains to be identified. Storage areas were required for this handling. A building 7.60 m wide and at least 18 m long was discovered on one of the quays of Le Castélou. It was most certainly a warehouse and also

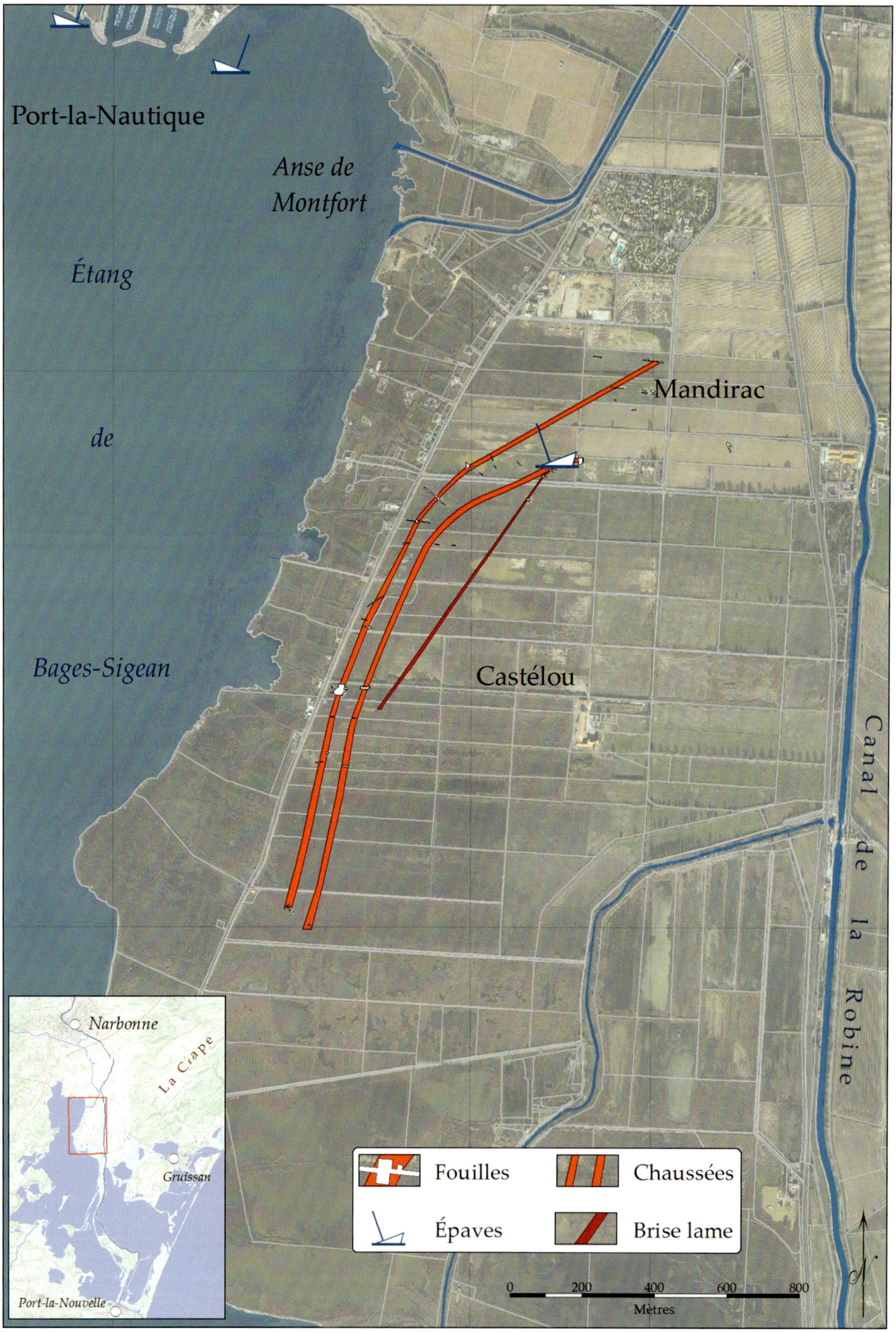

Fig. 4 The two parallel jetties and the breakwater discovered on the banks of the Bages and Sigean Lagoons (Narbonne). These two jetties were used to channel the river. – (Aerodata background map, J. Cavero 2010).

played an administrative role for the verification of goods. From the 4th century AD on, new constructions were required to reinforce this river mouth, weakened by an impetuous river. Extending for 1.9 km, these quays seem to disappear toward the northeast in Mandirac. The geophysical surveys have not identified any continuation of the constructions, which implies that only the river mouth required major work.

MANAGEMENT OF FLUVIO-LAGOONAL DYNAMICS

The results of excavations over the roughly 2 km that were explored attest to the complex evolution of this area, due to the instability of the wetlands and to constraints imposed by the river and the lagoon. These quays and dikes – by definition linear structures stretching over long distances – had to encounter (and resist) considerable pressures, as well as stress specific to certain spots (curves, narrowings, etc.). Construction methods were therefore adapted to the risks and are not homogenous throughout the studied length, as observed in 2013 on the left bank in Mandirac: numerous structural changes over a 100 m length were identified. Excavations enabled a scenario to be proposed regarding the overall evolution of the constructions and their environment in an area where the river was restricted. In the Mandirac sector, located in the northern extension of Le Castélou, the two roadways parted from each other, forming a bottleneck. This narrowing was certainly intentional. Narrowing the river's flow section increases the velocity of the current and creates a sediment-flushing effect. This sector constituted a weak point, especially since it coincides with a change in direction of the watercourse. To the east, a breakwater formed by piles of blocks protected the eastern jetty from the undermining effects of the concentrated wave action in the bends. This configuration made Mandirac a sector, where the jetties were subjected to high hydraulic pressure and would sometimes break, usually close to or at a narrowing point[17]. There was, therefore, a constant need for repairs, sometimes urgently, as evidenced by their late state, which is also the most monumental, in every sense of the word.
The Mandirac excavations also provided important chronological elements to understand the evolution of this river mouth between the 1st and 5th century AD. The first »major« river installations can be situated in the second half of the 1st century AD. This observation does not exclude earlier traffic in the area as evidenced by certain elements: excavations have revealed the occupation of a sandy island close to the river, to the west, in the 1st century BC. It attests to a specific installation for the handling of marine products as well as a complex topography, with emerged areas in the lagoon. This level seems to continue more sparsely to the east, as shown by the same sandy layers with anthropic traces under the first wooden installations. A levee formed by sand deposits between the river and the lagoon has been recognized over a length of at least 500 m and was occupied from the end of the 1st century BC. An early phase, when blocks from large buildings were reused, demonstrates the need to reinforce the Mandirac area right from the beginning because the narrowing of the river mouth was subject of significant pressure. Repairs were frequently carried out during the early Roman Empire and show how difficult it was keeping the watercourse in its bed. The left bank was raised in Late Antiquity, through the addition of a very large number of blocks and a wreck dating to the end of the 4th century or beginning of the 5th century AD (**fig. 5**). This riverboat, which still contained part of its cargo, attests the destruction or at least the rupture of the former states and the emergency repair of the bank. It can, therefore, be said that the dike broke and, at the same time, a sudden (and/or catastrophic) event damaged a boat, which was then used to fill a breach area and raise the dike. Hundreds of fragments of blocks cover the wreck, which is held beneath two alignments of boulders from dismantled monuments. The presence of these architectural elements highlights the urban transformation in the 4th or 5th century AD, at a time, when maintaining the trade areas was a priority.

Fig. 5 Mandirac. Overview of facilities on the left bank. In the background, the Bages/Sigean Lagoon. In the foreground, the wreck incorporated into the dike. – (Photo taken to the southwest in 2013 by C. Durand, CNRS/CCJ).

TOWARD THE CITY

Through geophysical surveys, the path of a diked, paleochannel of the Aude has now been established from the river mouth in the Bages-Sigean Lagoon along a distance of 1.9km towards the north. This has been confirmed by archaeological excavations and sediment corings[18]. Geographically, the paths of paleochannels heading north to Narbonne remain unknown and are currently the subject of a PhD thesis[19]. In 2015 and 2016, apparent electrical conductivity maps (electromagnetic surveys) and electrical resistivity sections were established from the paleoriver mouth to the foot of the city of Narbonne[20], following the modern-day path of the Robine canal, which at least partially coincides with the former course of the Aude. Contrasts in conductivity and resistivity of the subsoil, observed in plan or cross-section views, reveal the presence of conductivity/resistivity anomalies. However, there is no direct correlation between an archaeological or sedimentary structure and the anomaly which can be caused by other factors, such as the presence of groundwater of varying salinity. Therefore, electrical resistivity contrasts must be explored through archaeological or sedimentological surveys.

Among the sectors explored, the Craboules/Craboulette area, located about 4km north of the paleoriver mouth of the Aude (**fig. 6**), was analyzed in detail, comparing geophysical and coring data. By combining electromagnetic surveys and electrical resistivity sections, a higher conductivity anomaly has been identified, which could indicate a paleochannel (**fig. 6**). The location of the core drilling transect was determined through the interdisciplinary collaboration of geophysicists, geomorphologists, and archaeologists. 14 core drillings[21] were carried out along a profile perpendicular to the recent axis of the Robine canal. This profile intersected with the north-south axis of the paleochannel detected by the electrical conductivity map and confirmed by the resistivity section 1. A depth between 5 and 10m below the surface was attained. **Figure 6** reproduces the geophysical surveys carried out in 2015: an electrical conductivity map and two electrical resistivity sections[22]. The conductivity map shows anomaly P1, having the highest conductivity (greater than 70 mS/m), whose meandering path could indicate a 46m wide, north-south oriented paleochannel. Resistivity sections 1 and 2 were produced perpendicularly to this last paleochannel. Section 1 appears to confirm the presence of a channel, also of higher conductivity, narrower (28m) than on the conductivity map and with a depth of 4.2m. However, the channel does not appear in section 2, possibly due to a draining effect from the proximity of the Robine canal (N5).

The results from this coring transect have enabled the reconstruction of the morpho-sedimentary history, as following:

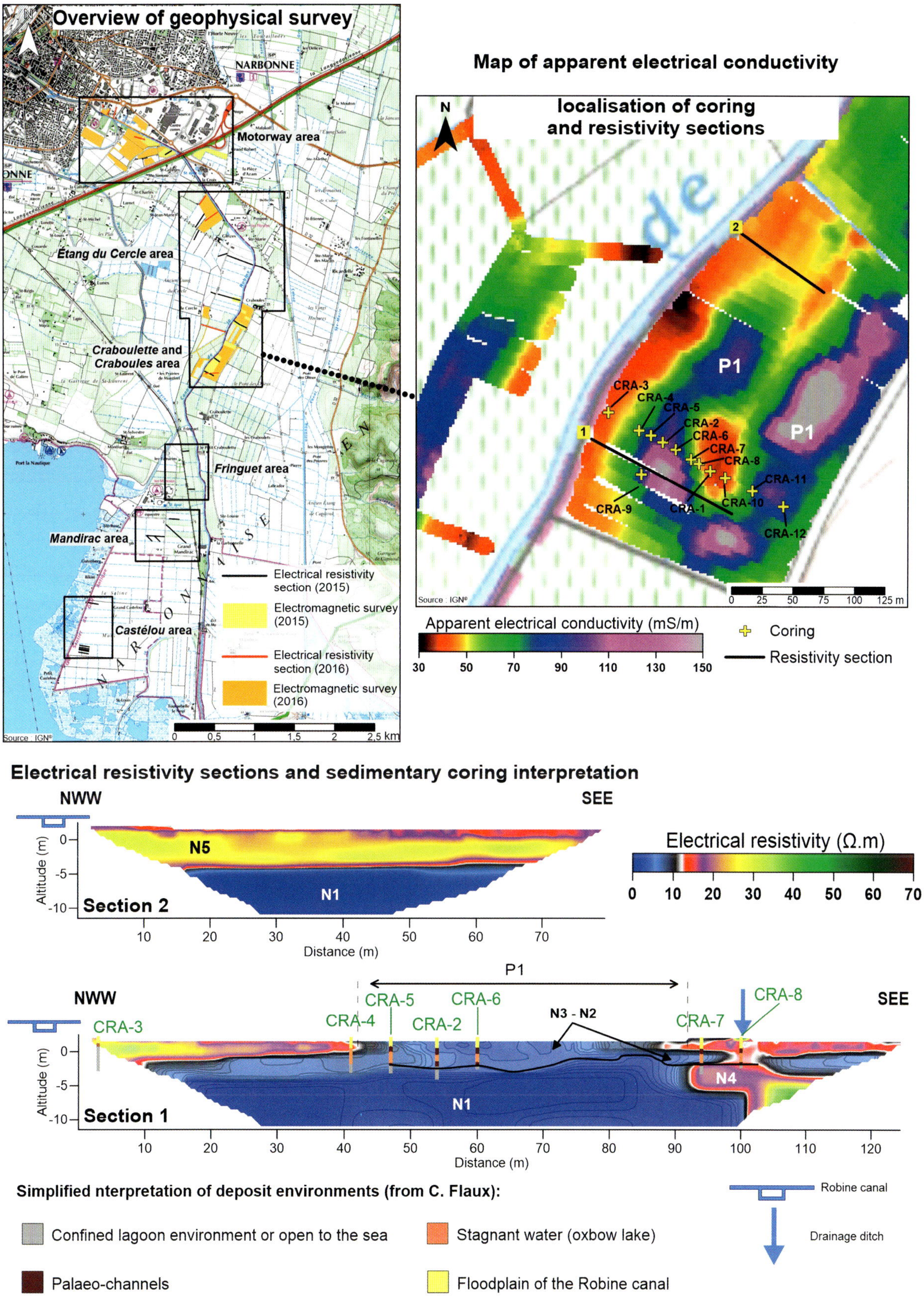

Fig. 6 Locations of the various geophysical survey areas, from the ancient course of the Aude channeling (Castélou-Mandirac) to the city of Narbonne. Apparent electrical conductivity map showing the P1 anomaly corresponding to a paleochannel structure. Resistivity sections carried out perpendicular to the P1 anomaly. – (G. Bruniaux / V. Mathé / A. Camus 2015).

1. Sedimentation in a partially confined lagoonal environment (from -9 to approx. -4.5 m beneath the surface).
2. Sedimentation in a lagoonal environment exposed to open marine conditions.
3. Establishment of the Aude River mouth in the Bages-Sigean Lagoon, reflecting the progradation of the delta. The sandy gravel channel-bottom deposit is situated between -4.5 and -3.6 m and is well defined over a width of approximately 75 m.
4. Diffluence of the channel and partial silting of the oxbow lake.
5. Establishment of a second paleochannel at the location, where the first one was filling up, probably related to a water level rise of the Aude. The medium to coarse sand deposit at the bottom of this channel is situated between -2.75 and -1.6 m and is well defined over a width of approximately 60 m.
6. New diffluence and floodplain deposit, apparently related to the activity of the Robine canal. Cultivation of the sector.

Of course, this reconstruction applies locally. As a complement to the PhDs being prepared by Tiphaine Salel[23] and Camille Faïsse[24], which examine the paleogeography of the Aude delta during the Holocene, the sedimentological data from the Craboulette area contribute new insight to the understanding of delta evolution of the Aude. By comparing the corings with electrical section 1, an interpretation can be given concerning the identified resistivity anomalies. Accordingly, the base of sections 1 and 2 is characterized by a highly conductive environment (N1), which corresponds to a lagoonal environment. The successive paleochannels are associated with the higher conductivity anomalies (N3-N2). The hypothetical path of the base of the first channel is proposed (black line).

However, the non-detection of any port structures using geophysical methods does not allow these paleochannels to be directly attributed to the Roman period.

Geophysical surveys were continued up north to the boundary of the Narbonne agglomeration. Several electrical anomalies, similar to P1 (detected in the Craboulette area), were detected in the Étang du Cercle and motorway areas. They may correspond to paleochannels. However, these ones are not associated with anomalies in the electrical conductivity maps and sections that could be assimilated with port structures (dikes, banks, etc.). Interpreting the geophysical data is therefore complex and does not enable, for the moment, a clear identification of the paleocourse or courses of the Aude in Antiquity. Geophysical surveys could be pursued using magnetic methods (in particular in the motorway area), in order to detect magnetic anomalies related to the shifting of the old course of the Aude, as for the Mandirac area[25]. Identifying the shifting of the river could help to focus research on those areas corresponding to the oldest channels.

Upstream, the city recently benefited from geomorphological observations on the banks of the Robine canal during rescue excavations carried out by O. Ginouvez at the 14 Quai d'Alsace[26]. The question of the passage of the river is a fundamental one: for P. Ambert[27], P. Verdeil[28] and S. Rescanières[29], the Aude did not pass through Narbonne and the course has been dug in the terrace at the time of the Roman settlement. Although these conclusions were drawn based on a series of corings, the stratigraphic observations made at Quai d'Alsace revealed the passage of the river in the 3rd century BC, which moved west in the 1st century AD[30]. It is therefore established that a »paleo-Robine« passed through Narbonne in Antiquity, but was modified during the Roman era. The bank installations and the warehouses bordering the river[31] confirm its navigability up to the city and very certainly the existence of a river port.

CONCLUSION

The questions raised by research on the ancient ports of Narbonne, in particular the natural constraints of alluvial plains, fluvial risk and the impact of anthropization, necessitated an interdisciplinary approach: this is an area, where human-environment interaction plays a significant role. This research investigating the path of the river is an example for an interdisciplinary and methodological approach in these specific environments. Geophysical surveys, excavations, and paleoenvironmental studies have been mutually enriching and contributing to the understanding of these complex installations. Understanding how the river, the lagoon and the impact of human structures interact requires a close collaboration.

The main purpose of the construction of the river mouth was to obtain an adequate depth for ship access. However, the river and the lagoon generate sedimentation that had to be controlled. The sanding up of river mouths and the silting of the lagoons was a continuous process that required constant extension work towards deeper waters. When the Romans undertook this work at Mandirac and Le Castélou, they were surrounded by water: the river discharged into a shallow lagoon. They relied on natural jetties that they reinforced with a wooden pile system. Backfill was then added to raise the structure above the water. The result was effective containment, reducing the shifting of the river and enabling its maintenance, particularly dredging. These dikes were adapted into quays and roadways attaining an average width of 17 m and extending along 1.9 km. Spaces for circulation and warehouses were built to allow the handling of certain goods. The right bank is a full-fledged communication route that could be used as a towpath and a land route to the city. It is, therefore, possible to reconstruct an area of intense activity, where many flat-bottomed boats were used to directly unload large vessels, towed boats and transfers of products to carts or warehouses.

Although recent research has revealed the major role of the Aude River mouth south of Narbonne, particularly in the Le Castélou and Mandirac area, during the Roman era, one question remains unanswered: where did the Aude flow after the 5th century AD? The abandonment of this branch is evidenced by the deterioration of the left bank dike associated with massive silting, whereas the port activity of Narbonne remains attested until the Middle Ages.

Notes

1) Collaborative research project on the ancient ports of Narbonne, coordinated by C. Sanchez, CNRS and M.-P. Jézégou, DRASSM. Since 2010, this project has been a partnership between the Occitanie Region, the CNRS, Université Montpellier 3, the French Ministry of Culture (DRAC and DRASSM) and the cities of Narbonne and Gruissan. It falls under thematic axis 3 of the scientific program of Labex ARCHIMEDE, program IA-ANR-11-LABX-0032-01.

2) Cavero 2010.

3) Not including the Rhône, the ancient Atax of the Romans was the largest river of the French Mediterranean coastline, due to the area of its basin (5,160 km^2) and its length (223 km).

4) Verdeil 1970. – Ambert 1998; 2000. – Dolez et al. 2015.

5) Geomorphological observations have been made during university research conducted by S. Rescanières at Montlaurès, by C. Faïsse and C. Flaux at excavations of the antique ports and by T. Salel on the low plain of the Aude. See also Sanchez et al. 2014 and Faïsse et al. 2018.

6) Salel 2012, 198.

7) Cavero 2010.

8) Falguéra et al. 2000. – Ambert et al. 1993, 130.

9) Salel 2012, 47.

10) ANTÉAS 2012, 208.

11) Falguéra et al. 2000, 18.

12) Mathé et al. 2016.

13) A long-term collaboration based on the complementarity of the geophysical surveys and the excavations, leading to conclusive results.

14) Sanchez et al. 2016, 132.

15) Mathé et al. 2016.

16) Mathé et al. 2016. – Faïsse et al. 2018.

17) Lino/Mériaux/Royet 2000, 52.

18) Mathé et al. 2016. – Faïsse et al. 2018.

19) Guillaume Bruniaux, Reconstitution paléogéographique et prospection archéologique en zone littorale par approches géophysiques multi-méthodes et multi-échelles [Paleogeographic reconstruction and archeological surveys of shorelines employing multi-method and multi-scale geophysical approaches], under the supervision of V. Mathé, Université de la Rochelle.

20) The areas designated as Craboules and Craboulette, Étang du Cercle and the motorway.

21) Core drilling was performed using a percussion corer (Cobra TT or similar) from the UMR 5140's sedimentology laboratory.

22) Bruniaux et al. 2015.

23) Tiphaine Salel: Paléo-géographie des paysages fluvio-lagunaires de la basse vallée de l'Aude à l'Holocène: (Région de Narbonne, France) [Paleogeography of fluvio-lagoonal landscapes in the low valley of the Aude during the Holocene: Narbonne region, France], under the supervision of David Lefèvre and Hélène Bruneton, Université Montpellier 3.

24) Camille Faïsse: Les ports antiques de Narbonne: approche géo-archéologique [The ancient ports of Narbonne: a geo-archaeological approach], under the supervision of David Lefèvre, Université Montpellier 3.

25) Mathé et al. 2016.

26) Ginouvez et al. 2016. – Ollivier 2016.

27) Ambert 2000.

28) Verdeil 1967.

29) Rescanières 2002.

30) Ginouvez et al. 2016.

31) Ginouvez/Labarussiat/Pomaredes 1992. – Falguéra et al. 2000.

References

Ambert 1998: P. Ambert, Le cadre géographique et géologique de Narbonne antique. In: C. Gabriel (ed.), L'Homme préhistorique et la mer. Actes du 120e congrès national des sociétés historiques et scientifiques, Aix-en-Provence 1995 (Paris 1998) 93-105.

2000: P. Ambert, Narbonne antique et ses ports, géomorphologie et archéologie, certitudes et hypothèses. Revue Archéologique de Narbonnaise 33, 2000, 295-307.

Ambert et al. 1993: P. Ambert / J. André / P. Guenet / G. Jalut / S. Leroy, Principaux résultats concernant l'évolution des paléoenvironnements holocènes de la basse vallée de l'Aude. Bulletin Scientifique Régional de la région Languedoc-Roussillon 1993 (1994), 25-27.

ANTEAS 2012: Association Narbonnaise de Travaux et d'Études d'Archéologie Subaquatique en Narbonnais 1987-2012, 25 ans d'archéologie subaquatique en Narbonnais (Saint Pierre La Mer 2012).

Bruniaux et al. 2015: G. Bruniaux / V. Mathé / A. Camus / C. Faïsse, Résultats des prospections géophysiques effectuées pour la recherche du paléo-chenal de l'Aude du Grand-Castélou à Narbonne [rapport d'étude, CNRS UMR 7266 – Université la Rochelle 2015].

Cavero 2010: J. Cavero, Paléogéographie des étangs narbonnais d'après les sources cartographiques anciennes. Géocarrefour 85/1, 2010, 29-40.

Dolez et al. 2015: L. Dolez / T. Salel / H. Bruneton / G. Colpo / B. Devillers / D. Lefèvre / S. D. Muller / C. Sanchez, Holocene palaeoenvironments of the Bages-Sigean Lagoon (France). Geobios 48, 2015, 297-308.

Faïsse et al. 2018: C. Faïsse / V. Mathé / G. Bruniaux / J. Labussière / J. Cavero / M.-P. Jézégou / D. Lefèvre / C. Sanchez, Palaeoenvironmental and archaeological records for the reconstruction of the ancient landscape of the Roman harbour of Narbonne (Aude, France). Quaternary International 463, 2018, 124-139.

Falguéra et al. 2000: J.-M. Falguéra / F. Falguéra / M. Guy / A. Marsal, Narbonne: cadre naturel et ports à l'époque romaine. In: C. Morhange (ed.), Ports antiques et paléoenvironnements littoraux. Méditerranée 94 (Aix-en-Provence 2000) 15-24.

Ginouvez/Labarussiat/Pomaredes 1992: O. Ginouvez / C. Labarussiat / H. Pomaredes, Saint-Loup: Un paysage fluvial aux portes de Narbonne (étude d'impact archéologique). Archéologie en Languedoc 16, 1992, 95-107.

Ginouvez et al. 2016: O. Ginouvez / C. Jorda / S. Martin avec la collaboration de V. Canut, Saint-Loup: La question du port urbain et de la Robine antique: l'apport du 14 quai d'Alsace à Narbonne. In: C. Sanchez / M.-P. Jézégou (eds), Les ports dans l'espace Méditerranéen antique. Narbonne et les systèmes portuaires fluvio-lagunaires. Actes du colloque de Montpellier des 22-24 mai 2014. Revue Archéologique de Narbonnaise, Supplément 44 (Montpellier 2016) 123-135.

Lino/Mériaux/Royet 2000: M. Lino / P. Mériaux / P. Royet, Méthodologie de diagnostic des digues. Appliquée aux levées de la Loire moyenne (Paris 2000).

Mathé et al. 2016: V. Mathé / C. Sanchez / G. Bruniaux / A. Camus / J. Cavero / C. Faïsse / M.-P. Jézégou / J. Labussière / F. Lévêque, Prospections géophysiques multi-méthodes de structures portuaires antiques à Narbonne (Aude, France). ArchéoSciences 40, 2016, 47-63.

Ollivier 2016: J. Ollivier, Artisanat et commerce en bordure du canal de la Robine: 19-20 quai d'Alsace à Narbonne, In: C. Sanchez / M.-P. Jézégou (eds), Les ports dans l'espace Méditerranéen antique. Narbonne et les systèmes portuaires fluvio-lagunaires. Actes du colloque de Montpellier des 22-24 mai 2014. Revue Archéologique de Narbonnaise, Supplément 44 (Montpellier 2016) 109-122.

Rescanières 2002: S. Rescanières, Essai sur le cadre géographique antique du Narbonnais. In: E. Dellong (ed.), Narbonne et le Narbonnais. Carte archéologique de la Gaule 11, 1 (Paris 2002) 44-50.

Salel 2012: T. Salel, Paléoenvironnements holocènes de la basse vallée de l'Aude. Stratigraphie et paléoécologie des paysages lagunaires de Narbonne [mémoire de Master 2, Univ. Montpellier III, 2012].

Sanchez et al. 2014: C. Sanchez / C. Faïsse / M.-P. Jézégou / V. Mathé, Le système portuaire de Narbonne antique: approche géoarchéologique. In: L. Mercuri / R. Gonsalez Villaescusa / F. Bertoncello (eds), Implantations humaines en milieu littoral méditerranéen: facteurs d'installation et processus d'appropriation de l'espace (Préhistoire, Antiquité, Moyen Âge). Actes des XXXIVe rencontres internationales d'archéologie et d'histoire d'Antibes (Antibes 2014) 125-136.

2016: C. Sanchez / J. Labussière / M.-P. Jézégou / V. Mathé / J. Cavero, Les fouilles de l'embouchure du fleuve antique dans les étangs narbonnais. In: C. Sanchez / M.-P. Jézégou (eds), Les ports dans l'espace Méditerranéen antique. Narbonne et les systèmes portuaires fluvio-lagunaires. Actes du colloque de Montpellier des 22-24 mai 2014. Revue Archéologique de Narbonnaise, Supplément 44 (Montpellier 2016) 59-69.

Verdeil 1967: P. Verdeil, Essai de paléo-hydrographie de l'Aude. Bulletin de la Société d'Études Scientifiques de l'Aude XLVII, 1967, 66-105.

1970: P. Verdeil, Données nouvelles sur le Quaternaire de la basse vallée de l'Aude. Bulletin de la Société Géologique de France S7-XII/3, 1970, 413-425.

Summary

In 118 BC, Narbonne, the first Roman colony outside Italy, was founded in Gaul at the base of the isthmus between the Aude and Garonne, at the crossroads of sea and land routes connecting the Mediterranean with the Atlantic. From high on a promontory, the city overlooks a sheltered lagoon through which flows a navigable river. The continuing existence of this river route is linked to paleoenvironmental and economic changes. Since 2010, a Collective Research Project with a team of geographers, historians, archaeologists, and paleoenvironmentalists, has sought to unravel the complex evolution of the ancient Narbonne port system.
Paleogeographic studies have provided the first information about long-term shoreline evolution around the Bages and Sigean Lagoons. These studies, coupled with geophysical surveys, and archaeological excavations, have been integrated into a Geographic Information System. Around Castelou and Mandirac, south of Narbonne, recent excavations have shown that the lake mouths must have undergone major work to channel the river and to construct unloading zones. The main purpose of canalizing the mouth of the river was to provide sufficient water depth for boats. However, the lagoons have continually been subjected to processes of silting up and clogging that have required work to extend them to deeper waters.

Résumé

En 118 BC, Narbonne, première colonie romaine hors d'Italie, est fondée au carrefour de voies maritimes et terrestres et au départ de l'isthme gaulois (l'axe Aude/Garonne), qui reliait la Méditerranée à l'Atlantique. La ville domine de son promontoire une lagune abritée dans laquelle se jette un fleuve navigable. Or, le maintien de cette voie fluviale dépend des changements paléoenvironnementaux et économiques. C'est afin de cerner les évolutions complexes du système portuaire de Narbonne antique qu'un Projet Collectif de Recherche est mené depuis 2010 par une équipe pluridisciplinaire constituée de géographes, d'historiens, d'archéologues et de paléoenvironnementalistes. Les études paléogéographiques offrent un premier aperçu des évolutions du littoral autour des étangs de Bages et Sigean sur le temps long. Elles sont couplées au sein d'un SIG avec les prospections géophysiques et les recherches archéologiques.
Les fouilles récentes menées dans le secteur du Castélou et de Mandirac, au sud de Narbonne, ont montré que l'embouchure dans les étangs avait dû faire l'objet de travaux monumentaux pour canaliser le cours d'eau et développer des espaces de déchargements. La canalisation de l'embouchure du fleuve a eu pour principal objectif d'obtenir une profondeur d'eau suffisante pour les bateaux. Cependant l'ensablement des embouchures et le colmatage des étangs ont été des processus continus qui ont demandé des travaux d'extension vers des eaux plus profondes.

SÉBASTIEN NIELOUD-MULLER

PORT STRUCTURES ON THE LAKES IN THE TERRITORY OF THE ALLOBROGES

Besides Geneva, no urban harbour planning is known in the city (*civitas*) of the Allobroges. In the areas outside Annecy (dép. Haute-Savoie/F) and Aix-les-Bains (dép. Savoie/F) research did not reveal significant remains of ports. They could either have been destroyed or are still hidden by successive sediment fillings. However, there are some lacustrine sites from the Roman period that were interpreted as port structures[1]. The presentation of these little-known sites and the careful review of the available documentation allows a debate on various issues, especially concerning their chronology and function.

This contribution limits itself to the presentation of different sites from the end of the 2nd century BC to the 4th century AD which are located on the antique territory of the Allobroges (**fig. 1**). After general considerations about research activities conducted during the past few decades in the large Savoyard lakes, the two sites of Lake Geneva and the two sites of Lake Bourget will be reviewed. Finally, linking those sites together will suggest new research perspectives.

MANY DISCOVERIES IN A FAVOURABLE SCIENTIFIC CONTEXT

The first lake dwellings were discovered in the middle of the 19th century AD, but there was no census of the findings and many objects have disappeared. After that, there were only a few known finds from the Roman period in the Savoyard lakes. The attention was mainly focused on the discoveries of beautiful objects from the Bronze Age, and there is no clearly identified Roman site in the first lakeside site inventories.

After a long time of disinterest, lacustrine archaeology emerged in the second half of the 20th century AD. The invention of the self-contained diving system (scuba set), along with the definition of a specific method of intervention, encouraged underwater investigations. The first extensive research followed, while prospecting intensified. During one of the surveys, a Roman pottery workshop has been found in Lake Bourget (Conjux IV site, dép. Savoie/F)[2]. This was the only site of the Roman period having been recorded in 1976 in the general inventory of the known lakeside deposits in the French alpine lakes[3].

In this favourable context, the Centre National de Recherches Archéologiques Subaquatiques (CNRAS)[4] was founded in 1980. In this institution, André Marguet launched the archaeological mapping of the

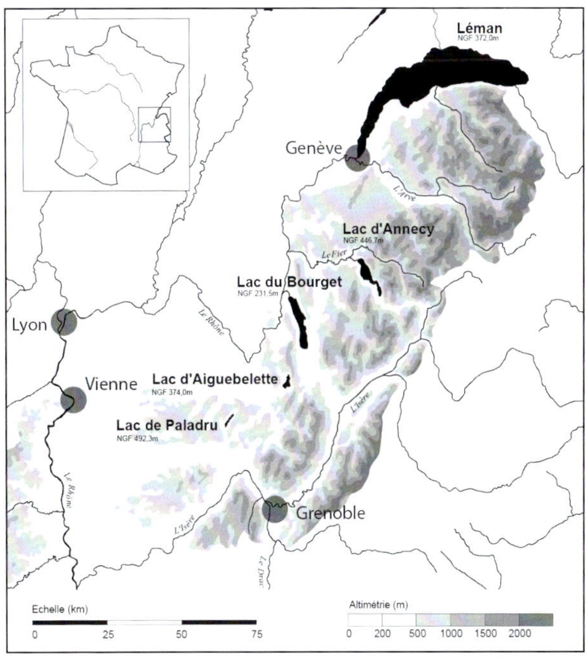

Fig. 1 Location of the main towns and large lakes of the Allobroges' territory. – (A. Marguet / P.-J. Rey).

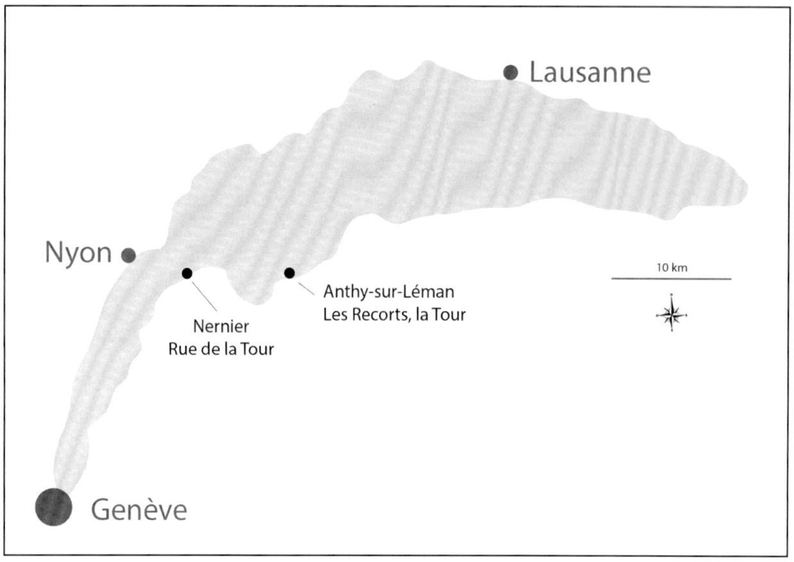

Fig. 2 Outline of Lake Geneva with locations of the two sites mentioned in the text. – (S. Nieloud-Muller).

underwater lacustrine sites in the Savoyard lakes[5]. During the seven campaigns that were conducted for a systematic inventory (1995-2001), all the near-shore areas (beines) have been prospected by diving. The lacustrine archaeological remains were mapped and each zone was carefully scoured on the surface levels. The location of all the apparent wooden piles was recorded, and the surface artefacts were extracted along with some wooden piles for dendrochronological and radiocarbon dating[6].
These research activities have provided documentation for a good number of important sites, especially from periods without sufficient documentation. For the Roman period, 15 lakeside sites are known now, which remain to be studied[7]. To date, one of the Lake Bourget sites is undergoing further investigation (since 2009)[8]. A first synthesis on antique lacustrine sites of the Lake Aiguebelette has also been compiled[9].

SHORE SITES FROM THE ROMAN PERIOD

Lake sites from Lake Geneva

The two sites at Lake Geneva, Nernier and Anthy-sur-Léman (dép. Haute-Savoie/F) (**fig. 2**), are located on the French lakeshore. The first site is located at the very end of the Small Lake.

Nernier – Rue de la Tour

The Roman site in Nernier is situated near the Rue de la Tour (**fig. 3**). It was discovered in 1995 during the first underwater survey for the inventory of the Savoyard sub-lacustrine sites[10]. In 1996, the site itself was surveyed, and some wooden piles[11]. Xavier Coquoz subsequently led some further investigations and published them[12].
The site is located on the lake floor approximately 50 m from the modern shore. Twelve wooden piles have been found at a depth of 1.5-1.6 m. Eleven of them are organised in a semi-circle, 12 m in diameter. The last wooden pile is situated between the structure and the shore, approximately 5 m toward the shore.
The wooden piles have been cut from entire tree trunks. They have a polygonal or quadrangular section measuring between 20 and 30 cm. Two piles have been extracted and confirmed as oak (*Quercus* sp.). The

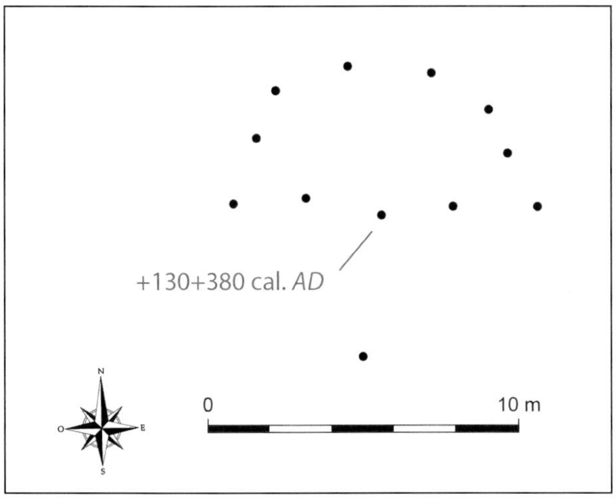

Fig. 3 Map of the site in Nernier (Haute-Savoie), Rue de la Tour (based on Coquoz 1999, pl. XXVII fig. 81 and Coquoz 2000, 33 fig. 7), with the radiocarbon dating of a pile (according to the report Archéolabs ARC 96/R843C).

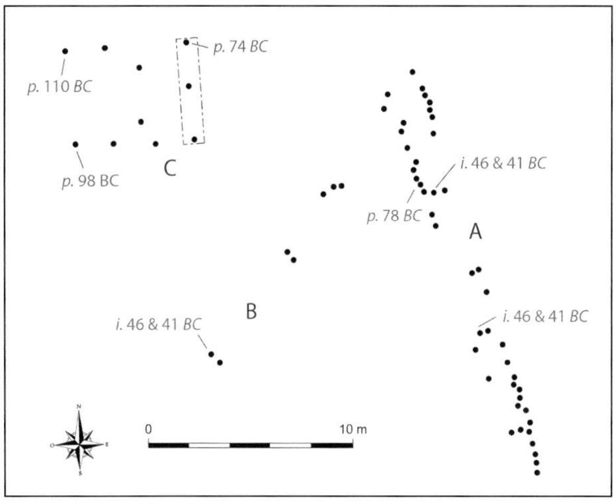

Fig. 4 Map of the site in Anthy-sur-Léman (Haute-Savoie), Les Recorts, La Tour. i. = inter; p. = post (based on A. Marguet' drawing in Coquoz/Marguet 2003, 53 fig. 1 and Coquoz/Marguet 2003, 111 fig. 58), with the dendrochronological dating (according to the report Archéolabs ARC 98/R1895D/2). – **A** pier; **B** boom; **C** landing stage.

dendrochronological analysis permitted to establish a 77 years sequence, but unfortunately dating it was not possible[13]. Nevertheless, a radiocarbon sample of one of the piles has been dated between 130 and 380 AD (1770±40 BP) and therefore the classification as Roman is verified[14].
Regarding the function of the site, it has been suggested that the piles are remains of a pier or a landing stage. A different interpretation see the structure as linked to a villa located nearby, a lighthouse, or a cult place. However, it has been underlined that without further excavation, it is impossible to come to a final conclusion.

Anthy-sur-Léman – Les Recorts/La Tour

The site of Les Recorts and La Tour (**fig. 4**) has been located in 1996 during the second inventory survey that took place in Lake Geneva[15]. This lacustrine site is well-known to the lake users and has been reported by a few authors at the beginning of the 20th century AD. The remains have been interpreted as a lake dwelling. In 1997, the visible wooden piles were mapped and some samples were extracted[16]. The last intervention on the site took place in autumn 1998. All data was included in Xavier Coquoz's work[17].
The first identified structures are located on the near-shore area approximately 40 m from the modern shore. The remains cover an area of 300 m², with a depth of 2.2-2.8 m. The spatial pattern of the 62 wooden piles show three different groups, separated from each other. In the east, 45 piles are aligned perpendicular to the shore, in some sections arranged in a double row (**fig. 4A**). Further west, seven piles are more or less aligned (**fig. 4B**). In the northwest, parallel to the shore and a bit secluded, ten more piles are arranged in a regular rectangle of 6 m × 4.7 m (**fig. 4C**).
All wooden structures of this site look like vertical piles, having diameters from 6 to 24 cm. No horizontal timber has been identified. Six oak piles have been sampled and two more have been extracted whole. These piles were made of split trunks and their ends had been sharpened to help driving them into the sediments. One of the piles showed traces of an square mortise (4 cm section and a depth of 7 cm) in the part that was buried, indicating a secondary use.

Among the eight extracted wooden piles, seven allowed to constitute a tree-ring series of 106 years, dated between 158 and 53 BC[18]. The felling of the piles of structure A and B have been dated from 46 to 41 BC and after 78 BC, and the piles from structures C, after 110 BC, 98 BC, and 74 BC.
Further artefacts are limited to a few iron nails, a net weight made of stone, and six coins dating from the Augustean period[19].
Based on these data, it was suggested to interpret the site as a port structure, that consisted of a pier (A), a boom (B) and a landing stage (C). For structure C, a cultic function may also be considered.

Bourget Lake

Two other Roman sites are located in the northern part of Lake Bourget (**fig. 5**), one in Chindrieux and the second in Conjux (dép. Savoie/F).

Chindrieux – Châtillon Port 1 (Châtillon II)

In autumn 1993, Raymond Castel and his team decided to survey the lake shore around the »rock« of Châtillon in the northern part of Lake Bourget (**fig. 6**). Some fishermen and divers had reported several wooden piles nearby. The survey allowed to identify wooden structures right at the foot of a limestone cliff that reaches out into the floodplain[20].
The entire structure consists of 134 wooden piles. 130 of them are aligned in a shore-parallel row, which is 77.8 m long and approximately 20-25 m away from the cliff. Between the cliff and the line of wooden piles, four other isolated piles were detected.
All the wooden piles show nearly the same cylindrical shapes and are roughly squared at the base. They are pushed down an average 70 cm into the sediment. 26 piles have been extracted. They were mainly made of oak (*Quercus* sp.), except one made of elm (*Ulmus*) and one made of alder (*Alnus*).
Out of the oak piles, 17 have been chosen for tree-ring dating. Results show that wood cutting can be dated around 286/287 AD. Two of the wooden piles that were located between the alignment and the cliff are dated to the Bronze Age (cut in 1065 BC)[21].
A small number of ceramics and architectural terracottas that were found relates to the structure and its surrounding.

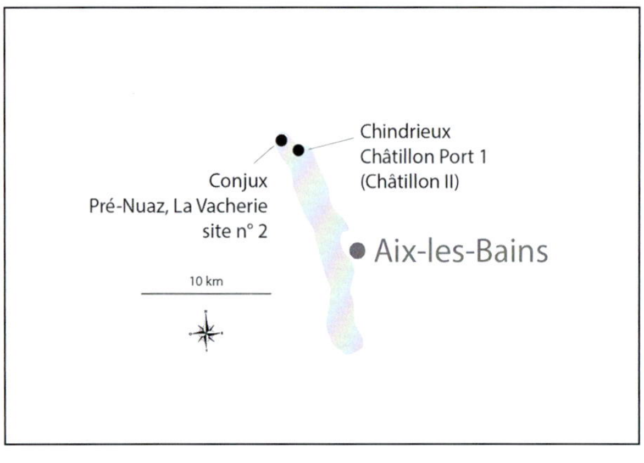

Fig. 5 Outline of Lake Bourget with locations of the two sites mentioned in the text. – (S. Nieloud-Muller).

The function of this site is not clear, as the elevation of the wooden piles cannot be surveyed and the limited range of artefacts does not allow for an interpretation. It was suggested that it could have been a modest fishing harbour, but a commercial or a military harbour is also considered[22].

Conjux – Pré-Nuaz/La Vacherie, second site

Not far from Châtillon Port 1 another site has been found (**fig. 7**). It is located near the entrance of the Canal de Savières, the natural exit of the lake that

Fig. 6 Map of the site of Chindrieux (Savoie), Châtillon Port 1 or Châtillon II (according to Castel 2004, 142), with the postponement of the dendrochronological dating (according to the reports Archéolabs ARC 94/R1360D and ARC 97/R1360D/2).

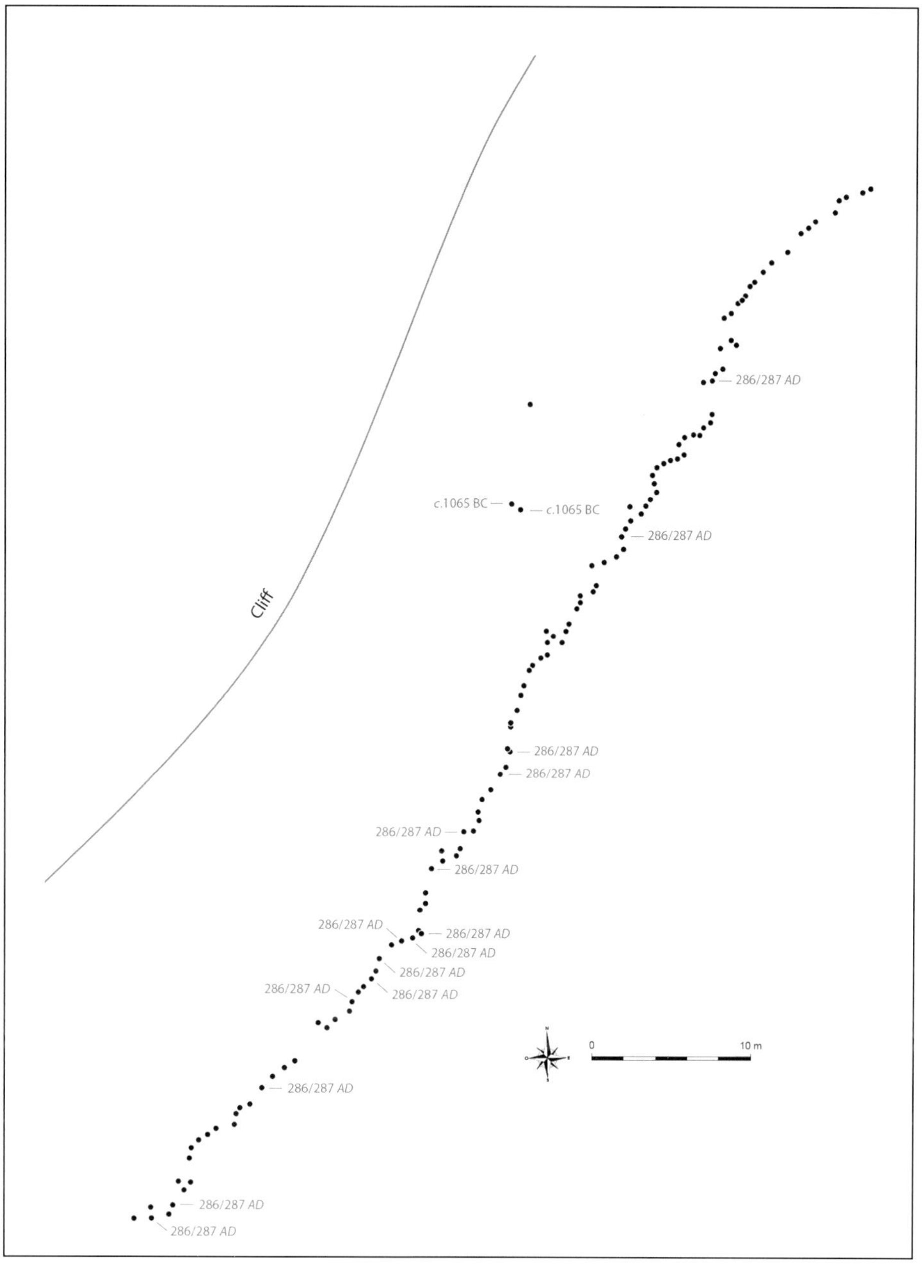

flows straight into the Rhône, on a wide near-shore area where an important number of archaeological sites have been found.

The wooden piles related to the structure were mentioned for the first time during fieldwork in 1999[23]. In 2000, André Marguet and his team surveyed the area and found three different lacustrine sites[24]. Each site was excavated on an area of approximately 10 m² and all the woods and artefacts were removed.

The first site (PNLV 1) was dated to the 2nd century AD based on tree-ring analysis and numismatic evidence. Remains of this lacustrine deposit are now regarded as a lakeside cult place[25]. The second deposit (PNLV 2) was dated to the end of the 2nd century BC based on the tree-rings dating and interpreted as a pontoon landing stage. The third site (PNLV 3) shows alignments slightly parallel to the actual lakeshore. It consists of wooden piles from two periods, the Bronze Age and the Early Middle Ages. It may have been part of bank revetments against the erosive waves. Following these works, further underwater research was conducted on the lakeside sites PNLV 2 and PNLV 3 during the following five years. These investigations gave the op-

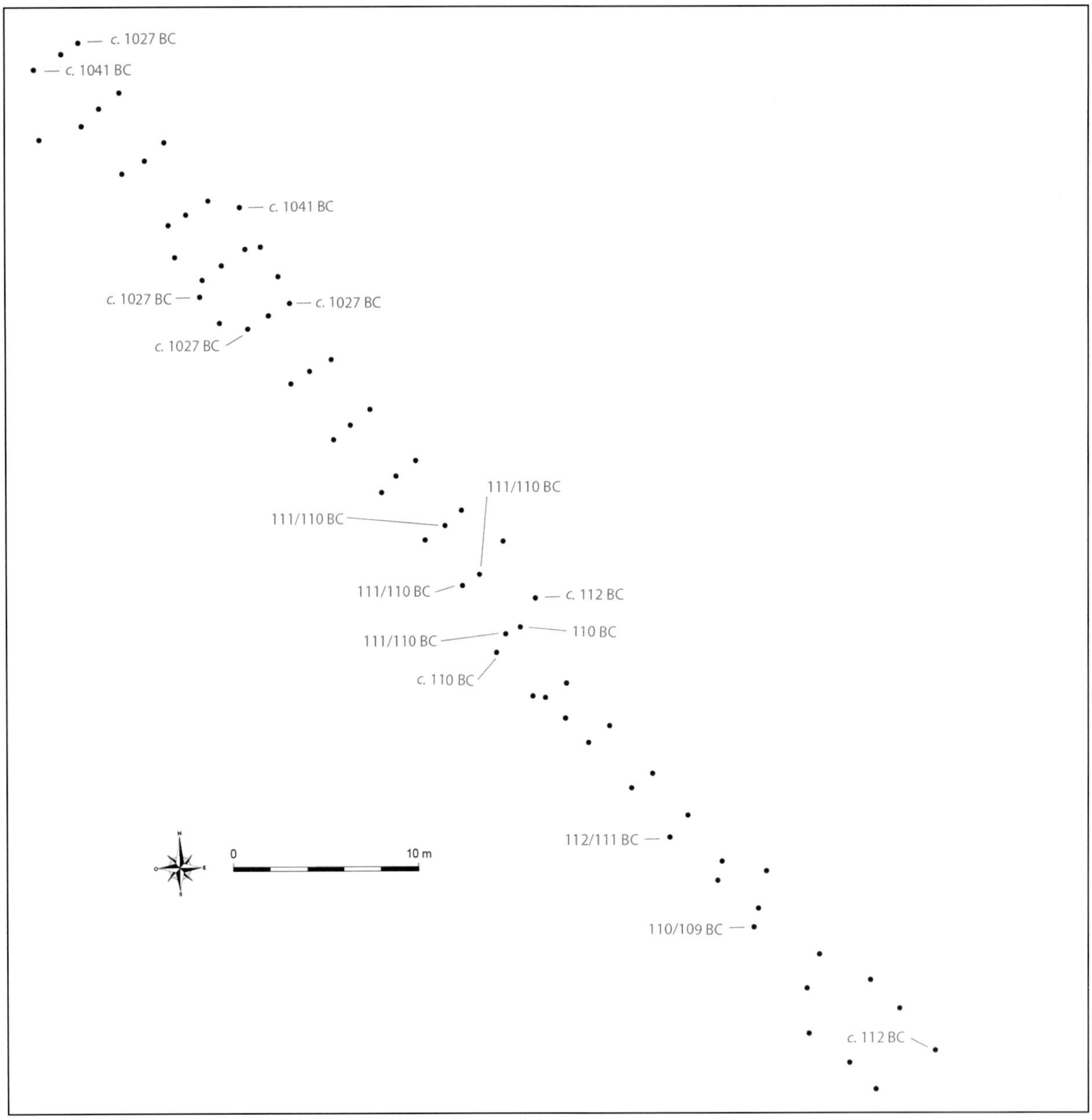

Fig. 7 Map of the site of Conjux (Savoie), Pré-Nuaz, La Vacherie, site no. 2 (after Gassani 2004), with the postponement of the dendrochronological dating (according to the reports Archéolabs ARC 00/R2531D, ARC 03/R2607D/1 and ARC 04/R3065D/1).

portunity to reveal the spatial arrangement of the wooden piles and to extract further piles in order to clarify the chronology[26]. We will take a detailed look at the PNLV 2 site only.

The 67 wooden piles form a structure 72 m in length and 3.5 m in width. Two important areas could be distinguished: in the northwest, there is a regular arrangement consisting of ten lines of three piles each. Some additional wooden piles complete the structure on its side. In the southeast another wooden pile line has been found, which is less regular.

All of the extracted timber consist of big oak piles. They are either circular tree trunks that have been cut or piles cut from large boles (of a diameter of 80 cm). They measured approximately 20 cm in width and 25-30 cm in length. The shaping marks are clearly visible and some of the piles have small vertical mortise lines (around 10 cm under the ground).

16 wooden piles were dated by dendrochronology. They belong to two different sets. The first one, in the northwest, is dated between 1041 and 1027 BC, while the second one in the southeast, is dated between 112 and 109 BC[27].
The discovered artefacts were not substantial, mainly consisting of fragments of ceramics dating to the Early Roman Empire[28]. Besides chronology, this material does not allow to confirm the function of this site. Nevertheless, the planimetry, the length of the structure and the strength of the wooden piles indicate a pontoon or a landing stage.

MATERIAL FOR CONSIDERATION

The data presented here allows for a discussion of the location, the layout, the constitutive elements, the chronology and the function of the discussed sites in the Allobroges territory.
First, it seems that all these sites were situated in strategic places (**figs 1-2. 5**). This is most apparent for the two sites situated in the northern area of Lake Bourget. The first one is located at the outlet of the lake, near the Canal de Savières, linked to the Rhône[29], while the second one is located at the foot of the Châtillon rock, from where the main part of the Haut-Rhône and the whole Lake can be watched over. For the lacustrine sites of Lake Geneva, the site of Nernier is located at the narrow point of the transition between the Petit Lac and the Grand Lac. All these sites are near a border or on a border, first of the province, then of the city.
Regarding their layout, the sites show great variety, which is not surprising, as each site shows an adaptation to technical requirements and topographical constraints. This makes it difficult to define a typology[30]. The elongate structures seem to be the more specific. The site of Conjux shows the typical shape of a pontoon or a wharf. The same conclusions could be drawn for the features number 1 and 2 at the site of Anthy-sur Léman. The wooden pile lines at the site of Châtillon do most likely belong to booms or breakwaters. Concerning the quadrangular feature number 3 in Anthy-sur-Léman and the semi-circular feature in Nernier, it is hard to determine their function.
The use of wood as building material was more widespread than the use of stone, like the small number of documented stones prove. The wooden piles are mostly made of oak (*Quercus* sp.). Usually, only entire trunks were cut and sharpened at the base to simplify driving them into the sediments. In some cases, old trunks may have been re-used. The massive size of the timber points to an interpretation as a substruction for other structures. Mortises on some of the timber in Conjux and Anthy-sur-Léman show that the wooden piles were used, in the first place, to support horizontal constructive elements that have not been found yet or which are not preserved.
Concerning the chronology of the sites, even the precise dendrochronological data does not allow to answer all questions. For Châtillon, all the results are similar and date the installation of these wooden piles in one period. For Conjux, the situation is more complicated. The datings indicate that the site was set up at the end of the 2nd century BC. However, the wooden features from the final Bronze Age in the same structure may point to the reuse of old wood. In Anthy-sur-Léman, construction C could also have been built with re-used wood. The datings document cutting activities after 110 BC, 98 BC, and 74 BC, and from 46 to 41 BC and after 78 BC for the piles of structures A and B. Furthermore, also in Conjux the mortises under the modern sediment level could indicate that the wood was re-used. Therefore, the wooden piles and the arrangement and direction of the mortises have to be located precisely in order to evaluate their function.
The archaeological artefacts add further chronological information. For example, in Conjux, material from the 1st and 2nd centuries AD found around the stakes could be an indication for an extended period of use.

At structure C in Anthy-sur-Léman, six coins from the Augustean period were found, while dendrochronological datings indicate an earlier construction. For the other sites, artefacts are nearly non-existent.
If we keep all this in mind, what can be said about the function of these sites? Today, all of them are isolated and it is not possible to link them to nearby settlements. The layout of the identified structures varies but points to an interpretation as pontoons, landing stages or booms. But even if it is correct and these sites were part of port infrastructures, it is hard to be precise about their function.
However, it is possible to go further if we link these data to the historical events known for the city of the Allobroges[31]. For example, if we focus on the cutting of the wooden piles from Conjux, they date just after the Transalpine conquest (c. 120 BC). The construction was contemporary with the first port of Geneva[32]. The same observation can be drawn for the site of Anthy-sur-Léman, which is located at the border of the city and the province. The datings of structure C cover the period from the Transalpine conquest to Caesar's Gallic War (58-52 BC). Structures A and B on the other hand were contemporary with the foundation of the Latin colony in Vienne (dép. Isère/F) and the Roman colony in Nyon (canton of Vaud/CH) on the shore of Lake Geneva (c. 45 BC). Finally, the datings of Chindrieux can be linked to the 3rd century AD, when towns were fortified and the city of the Allobroges was segmented while Grenoble (dép. Isère/F) and Geneva became cities. Furthermore, Lake Bourget seems to have been the border between these two new independent cities. The contemporaneity between the dates of the sites and historical events, and the absence of ports structures for the *Pax Romana*, suggest a military function for some of these sites.

CONCLUSION AND OUTLOOK

Thanks to the research activities in the Savoyard lakes in the past twenty years, scientific data for the Roman period is now available.
In her publication about the Roman inland harbours, Christina Wawrzinek pointed to a certain disinterest of the scientific community and a lack of research regarding this subject[33]. Her work offers a varied and little-known documentation that can be used for precious syntheses. She collected data on a significant number of sites on rivers, but only a limited number of sites on lakes[34]. With this contribution, we wish to add some little-known or unpublished information.
For each site, we considered the location, layout, wood characteristics, chronology and artefact available. However, it is difficult to know more about the function of these sites by considering only these data. It is by linking them with the geographical and historical events known for the territory of the Allobroges that they make better sense. It seems that some of these sites could have had a military function in large strategic lakes (surveillance, defense, territorial marker, etc.). To understand more, it would be necessary to conduct fresh archaeological research. Another survey would help to discover artefacts to determine their time of construction and period of use. This would also allow for a better understanding of their function. Finally, research would benefit from supra-regional comparisons with other Roman lake sites that have not been studied yet.

Notes

1) At least if one retains a broad definition of »port«, which can have different meanings, it generally refers to any structure present in the interface area between land and water, where people and goods can circulate between a boat and the land (Wawrzinek 2014, 9).
2) Castel 2004, 102-113.
3) Bocquet/Laurent 1976, 141-145.
4) The CNRAS and the DRASM (Direction des Recherches Archéologiques Sous-Marines) would later be merged into the DRASSM

(Département des Recherches Archéologiques Subaquatiques et Sous-Marine).

5) This inventory includes the four northern pre-alpine lakes: Lake Geneva, Lake Bourget, Lake Annecy and Lake Aiguebelette. For a description of the inventory process, its different steps and the results, refer back to the scientific reports of the DRASSM and the Rhône-Alpes area in general.

6) Marguet 2004. This work has been used for the French report of the file for the admission of pile dwellings as World Heritage Sites. Eleven French sites have been classified as World Heritage at the 35th plenary meeting of the UNESCO, the 27th of June 2011.

7) Marguet/Piningre 2013, 21-22.

8) Nieloud-Muller 2015; in print a. – Nieloud-Muller/Marguet in print.

9) Nieloud-Muller in print b.

10) Marguet 1995, 48-52; 1996b.

11) Marguet 1996a, 37-47.

12) Coquoz 1999; 2000, 32.

13) Archeolabs ARC 96/R843D.

14) Archeolabs ARC 96/R843C.

15) Marguet 1996a, 37-47; 1997, 44.

16) Marguet 2001, 128-129.

17) Coquoz 1999; 2000, 31-32.

18) Archeolabs ARC 98/R1895D/2.

19) Michel Amandry study/BnF.

20) Castel 1994; 2004.

21) Archeolabs ARC 94/R1360D and ARC97/R1360D/2.

22) Castel 1994.

23) Gassani 1999.

24) Marguet 2002, 123-124.

25) Nieloud-Muller 2015; in print a. – Nieloud-Muller/Marguet in print.

26) Gassani 2000; 2001; 2002; 2003; 2004.

27) Archeolabs ARC 00/R2531D, ARC 03/R2607D/1 and ARC 04/R3065D/1.

28) Amaury Gilles study/UMR 5140 – ASM.

29) Close to the »Portout« locality.

30) Wawrzinek 2014, 75.

31) Jospin 2002.

32) Bonnet et al. 1989.

33) Wawrzinek 2014, 12.

34) The lakeside sites amount to less than 10 % of the identified sites (Wawrzinek 2014, 166), which is ten proven deposits and ten deposits with a hypothetic harbour function.

References

Bocquet/Laurent 1976: A. Bocquet / R. Laurent, Les stations des lacs alpins. In: A. Bocquet / C. Legrand, Néolithique et âges des Métaux dans les Alpes françaises. IXe congrès de l'Union Internationale des Sciences Préhistoriques et Protohistoriques, livret-guide de l'excursion A9 (Nice 1976) 139-145.

Bonnet et al. 1989: C. Bonnet / G. Zoller / P. Broillet / M.-A. Haldimann / C.-A. Baud / C. Kramar / C. Simon / C. Olive / Y. Billaud, Les premiers ports de Genève. Archéologie Suisse 12/1, 1989, 2-24.

Castel 1994: R. Castel, Le lac du Bourget. La baie de Châtillon. Site de Châtillon II. Aménagement gallo-romain, Rapport déposé à la DRAC Rhône-Alpes [unpubl. excavation report 1994].

2004: R. Castel, Le lac du Bourget. 50 ans de recherches archéologiques. 5000 ans d'histoire (Montmélian 2004).

Coquoz 1999: X. Coquoz, Nernier et Anthy-sur-Léman. Deux sites portuaires antiques immergés dans le Léman [diss. Univ. Genève 1999].

2000: X. Coquoz, La navigation sur le Léman à l'époque gallo-romaine. Kaineus 8, 2000, 28-36.

Coquoz/Marguet 2003: X. Coquoz / A. Marguet, Haute-Savoie, Anthy-sur-Léman, Lac Léman: les Recorts, La Tour. DRASSM. Bilan scientifique 1998, Ministère de la culture et de la communication, 2003, 110-113.

Gassani 1999: J.-P. Gassani, Prospection inventaire subaquatique de la plate-forme immergée au Nord-Ouest du lac du Bourget. Rapport déposé à la DRAC Rhône-Alpes [unpubl. excavation report 1999].

2000: J.-P. Gassani, Prospection inventaire subaquatique de la plate-forme immergée au Nord-Ouest du lac du Bourget. Rapport déposé à la DRAC Rhône-Alpes [unpubl. excavation report 2000].

2001: J.-P. Gassani, Prospection inventaire subaquatique de la plate-forme immergée au Nord-Ouest du lac du Bourget. Rapport déposé à la DRAC Rhône-Alpes [unpubl. excavation report 2001].

2002: J.-P. Gassani, Prospection inventaire subaquatique de la plate-forme immergée au Nord-Ouest du lac du Bourget. Rapport déposé à la DRAC Rhône-Alpes [unpubl. excavation report 2002].

2003: J.-P. Gassani, Prospection inventaire subaquatique de la plate-forme immergée au Nord-Ouest du lac du Bourget. Rapport déposé à la DRAC Rhône-Alpes [unpubl. excavation report 2003].

2004: J.-P. Gassani, Prospection inventaire subaquatique de la plate-forme immergée au Nord-Ouest du lac du Bourget. Rapport déposé à la DRAC Rhône-Alpes [unpubl. excavation report 2004].

Jospin 2002: J.-P. Jospin, Les Allobroges. Gaulois et romains du Rhône aux Alpes. De l'indépendance à la période romaine (4e siècle av. J.-C. - 2e siècle apr. J.-C.) (Gollion 2002).

Marguet 1995: A. Marguet, Arrondissement de Thonon. Prospection subaquatique/inventaire des sites sous-lacustres haut-savoyards. Elaboration de la carte archéologique des gisements lémaniques. Revue Savoisienne 135, 1995, 48-52.

1996a: A. Marguet, Arrondissement de Thonon-les-Bains. Prospection subaquatique/inventaire des sites sous-lacustres haut-savoyards. Elaboration de la carte archéologique des gisements lémaniques. Revue Savoisienne 136, 1996, 37-47.

1996b: A. Marguet, Eléboration de la carte archéologique des gisements lémaniques. Prospection subaquatique/inventaire des sites sous-lacustres hauts-savoyards, Région Rhône-Alpes. DRASSM. Bilan scientifique 1995, Ministère de la Culture et de la Communication, 1996, 199-201.

1997: A. Marguet, Carte archéologique. La rive française du lac Léman, Haute-Savoie. DRASSM. Bilan scientifique 1996, Ministère de la Culture et de la Communication, 1997, 43-48.

2001: A. Marguet, Carte archéologique de la rive française du lac Léman. DRASSM. Bilan scientifique 1997, Ministère de la Culture et de la Communication, 2001, 128-137.

2002: A. Marguet, Elaboration de la carte archéologique des gisements du lac du Bourget (Savoie). DRASSM. Bilan scientifique 2000, Ministère de la culture et de la communication, 2002, 117-137.

2004: A. Marguet, Repères chronologiques des installations littorales savoyardes. In: C. Jourdain-Annequin (ed.), Atlas culturel des Alpes occidentales: de la préhistoire à la fin du Moyen Âge (Paris 2004) 66-69.

Marguet/Piningre 2013: A. Marguet / J.-F. Piningre, Historique de l'archéologie lacustre et la question palafittique. Les Dossiers de l'Archéologie 355, 2013, 14-23.

Nieloud-Muller 2015: S. Nieloud-Muller, Site et dépôts cultuels gallo-romains en contexte lacustre: l'exemple du site de Conjux (lac du Bourget, Savoie). In: A. Dumont / P.-J. Rey (eds), L'homme et son environnement: des lacs, des montagnes et des rivières. Bulles d'archéologie offertes à André Marguet. Revue Archéologique de l'Est, Supplément 40 (Dijon 2015) 209-240.

in print a: S. Nieloud-Muller, Le mobilier archéologique du site cultuel lacustre romain de Conjux (lac du Bourget, Savoie, F). Chronologie, répartition, association et traitement. In: Mobiliers et sanctuaires dans les provinces romaines occidentales (fin Ier siècle av. J.-C. - Ve siècle ap. J-C.). La place de l'artisanat et des productions manufacturées dans les espaces sacrés et dans les pratiques religieuses, Colloque International Instrumentum, Le Mans, 4-6 juin 2015 (in print).

in print b: S. Nieloud-Muller, Le lac d'Aiguebelette à la période romaine. Etat des connaissances. Les Dossiers du Musée Savoisien: Revue numérique [en ligne] (in print).

Nieloud-Muller/Marguet in print: S. Nieloud-Muller / A. Marguet, Apports des observations dendroarchéologiques à la connaissance d'un site lacustre à caractère cultuel (132-186 ap. J.-C. – Conjux, Lac du Bourget, Savoie, FR). In: Sacrée Science! Apports des études environnementales à la connaissance des sanctuaires celtes et romains du Nord-ouest européen, Actes de la table ronde d'Amiens, 6-8 juin 2013, Centre départemental de Ribemont-sur-Ancre, Inrap, Archéosite d'Aubechies et du Cravo (in print).

Wawrzinek 2014: Ch. Wawrzinek, In portum navigare. Römische Häfen an Flüssen und Seen (Berlin 2014).

Summary

Between 1995 and 2001, seven surveys were conducted in the Savoyard lakes (France). This systematic inventory allowed to expand the knowledge about the already known pre- and protohistoric lake dwellings significantly. Furthermore, based on the inventory many lacustrine sites of historical periods including the Roman period have been re-evaluated. In this contribution, we present selected lacustrine sites that could correspond to port structures. We review the documentation available to discuss the location, morphology, chronology and function of these archaeological sites. The contemporaneity between the dates of the sites and historical events suggests a military function for some of these sites.

Résumé

Entre 1995 et 2001, sept campagnes de prospections ont été menées dans les lacs subalpins (France). Cet inventaire systématique a permis de renouveler les connaissances des stations lacustres pré- et protohistoriques connues antérieurement, mais a également livré de nombreux gisements des périodes historiques, notamment de la période romaine. Dans le cadre de cette contribution, nous avons choisi de présenter les gisements pouvant correspondre à des aménagements portuaires. L'examen de la documentation disponible permet d'aborder plusieurs points relatifs à leur environnement, leur morphologie, leur chronologie et leur fonction. La mise en relation de ces données avec les événements historiques connus pour la cité des Allobroges invite à proposer une fonction militaire pour quelques-uns de ces sites.

JIMMY MOUCHARD · DAVID GUITTON*

THE ROMAN PORT OF REZÉ / RATIATUM: 2013-2016 RESEARCH PROGRAMME PRELIMINARY RESULTS

The field phase of this project was carried out by the University of Nantes from 2005 to 2016 with support of the city of Rezé, the Nantes Metropolis, the Inrap (French National Institute for Preventive Archaeological Research), and the CNRS (French National Centre for Scientific Research). Although Rezé (dép. Loire-Atlantique/F) has a long history of research in Ratiatum, since the Roman settlement had already been identified in this location in the 17th century AD, this is not the case of one of its neighbourhoods, Saint-Lupien, located to the north-east of the Roman urban stronghold. Initially, an excavation programme that took place between 1982 and 1985 revealed large structures, which were interpreted as storehouses. The importance of this district thus became apparent, and the interest about the role of Saint-Lupien rose with the revival of the excavation programme in 2005. It served as a workshop and teaching site for the university and its objectives were to finish the work that began 20 years earlier, to establish the link with the former bed of the Loire River (riverbank constructions) and to verify whether it constituted the eastern edge of Roman Ratiatum.

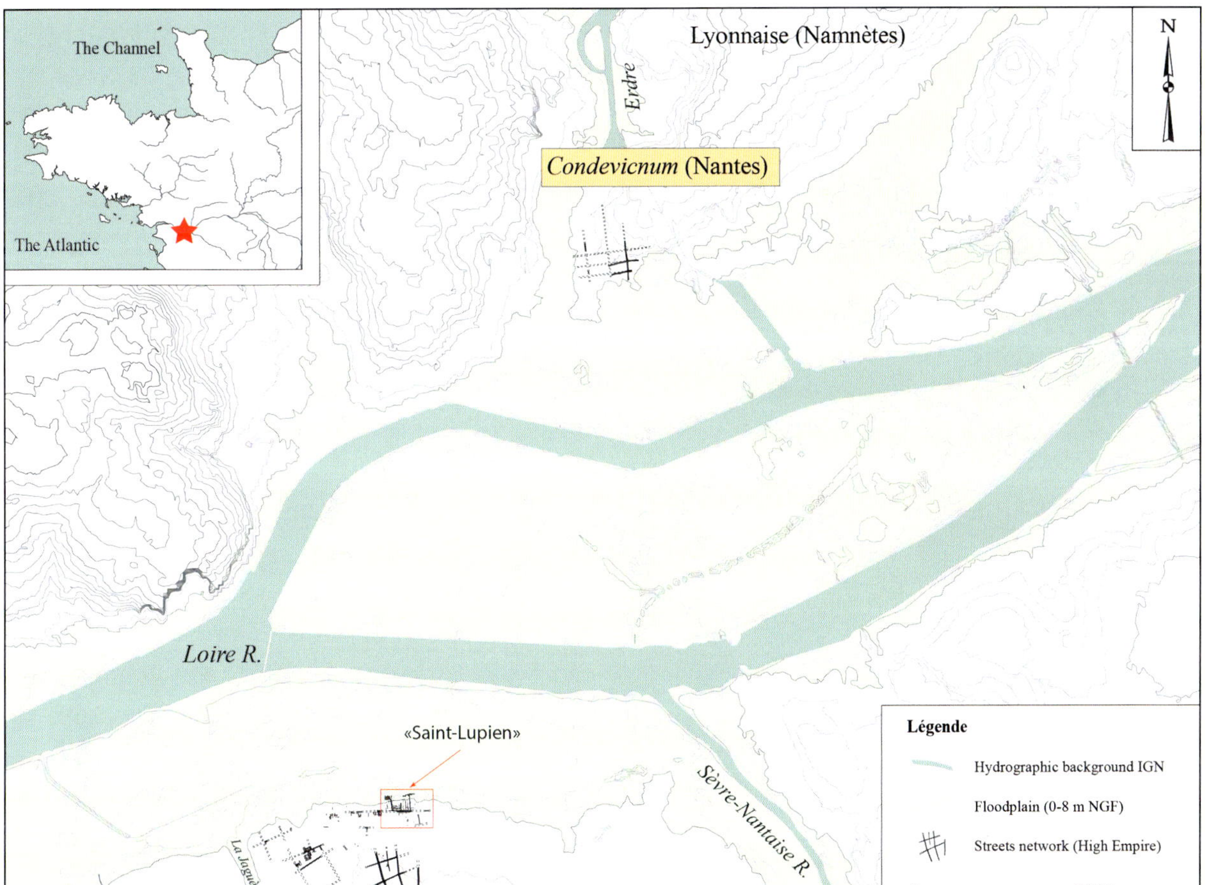

Fig. 1 Location of the Roman town of Ratiatum/Rezé (dép. Loire-Atlantique/F) in the Loire estuary. – (R. Arthuis / M. Monteil / J. Mouchard 2010).

CONTEXT OF THE STUDY AND METHODOLOGICAL ISSUES

Slumbering beneath the present-day city with its 35,000 residents, the Roman settlement of Ratiatum extended for over 40-50 ha, at its height at the beginning of the 2nd century AD. It is approximately 1 km in width and over 300-400 m in length, an area that is doubled by including the peripheral border to the south, which featured artisanal workplaces (ceramic and glass production), quarries where stone were mined, and necropolises. Created on the empty field during the Augustan period, it was located in the north of the province of Aquitania and in the north-west of the territory of the Pictones with the capital Limonum (present-day Poitiers). While Ratiatum was regularly mentioned by ancient authors, in Antiquity as well as at the beginning of the Early Medieval period, Ptolemy clearly indicated that »the Pictones occupy the most northern parts of Aquitania near the sea. Their towns [include]: Ratiatum [Rezé] [... and] Limonum [Poitiers]« [1]. We also recall that the ancient town of Rezé faced another large town: Condevicnum (Nantes, dép. Loire-Atlantique/F), the seat of the Namnetes tribe, located in Gallia Lugdunensis with the Loire as administrative border (**fig. 1**). The case of Rezé and Nantes is thus a perfect example of metropolitan settlements nestled at the base of an estuary, which is a recurring pattern after the Roman conquest.

A series of three programmes were carried out in Saint-Lupien between 2005 and 2016, the first two (2005-2008 and 2009-2012) were focused on the upper part of the district (storehouses and streets) and its lower part (riverbank constructions)[2]. The third and final programme (2013-2016) concentrated exclusively on several sections of the riverbank construction, which are among the best preserved and date to the High Empire. At the end of the twelfth summer of excavation, it has become possible to estimate that the surface of the district was approximately 1.4 ha. To summarize, the upper part of the site appears as somewhat leveled (a consequence of having been planted, tilled, dug up for materials, and exposed to other erosive phenomena). It is very levelled where the slope ends, which does not allow recognizing any stratigraphic connection between the vestiges located in the upper (storehouses) and lower (riverbank constructions) parts of the east of the site. In contrast, the site is much better preserved at the base, at between 0 and 5 m NGF [General Levelling of France] (the alluvial plane).

Fig. 2 Rezé, Saint-Lupien, zone 4, sectors 14 and 15. Excavation and removal of the piles (indicated by the white labels) related to the first Roman riverbank developments. – (Photo J. Mouchard 2013).

From a technical perspective, the excavations, between 2009 and 2016, took place in a sealed and anaerobic environment, since the Loire River currently flows 520 m north of the site (**figs 1-2**). Therefore, the archaeological staff working in Saint-Lupien was split into two teams: one team working in the »dry area« in the upper section (storehouses ...) and one in the »wet« lower section. In fact, the excavation campaigns were accomplished in strict cooperation between the technical and scientific directives required for working in humid environments. Under

Fig. 3 Rezé, Saint-Lupien, zone 4. General view of the site at the beginning of the campaign, on the right the retention pond built to store the water from the pumping. – (Photo J. Mouchard 2014).

these conditions and thanks to the long experience in conducting archaeological work in silted up fluvial environments, during the final years, we decided to schedule the excavation campaigns of eight to twelve weeks involving 50-60 volunteer participants per campaign. To some extent, we copied this from both the Charavines model and the approach used by Eric Verdel and Michel Colardelle on the banks of Lake Paladru (dép. Isère/F)[3].

For the waterside aspect, each excavation campaign required a substantial mechanization phase, proficiency with pumping, and above all, the establishment and upkeep of safety platforms. At the area of the former riverbed, to the right of the identified structures, the banks, which had resulted from the presence of sand from the Loire, were unstable, a condition that prevented any form of archaeological access, whether manual or mechanical. Sheet piling, shored trenches or slurry walls could not be set up because they were too costly. Therefore, additional data was obtained by 47 core drillings, which allowed a better understanding of the ancient river dynamics. Another methodological concern involved the difficulty of ensuring that wood would be preserved in a state of permanent humidity, both during each excavation campaign and from one year to the next. The creation of a large reservoir basin several metres from the excavation allowed to lead the water pumped and back to the site in a controlled manner at the end of each campaign (**fig. 3**). Each day, a watering system (initially planned for all sectors of open excavation in the lower zone), coupled with the use of floorcloths and geotextiles, allowed protecting all the organic remains from lightand high temperature. At the end of the campaign, wood that had not been dismantled or studied was coated with clay and then dumped, which provided a sort of natural protection against xylophagous insects and clandestine prospectors.

In this respect, Saint-Lupien, which is often described as a »laboratory«, has provided an arena for testing material and new tools (drones, photogrammetry, etc.) as well as developing scientific approaches that have only rarely been applied to port archaeology. One of the most relevant is certainly the employment of use-wear analysis: tools marks has been studied occasionally on stones and, in a systematic way, on woods and every architectural remains of oak used during the monumental phase. In connection with entomological studies and other approaches to »wood« as a material, this analysis is used by archaeologists to explore the way natural resources were utilized and which raw materials were propitious for river construction, as well as the quality of materials that were used, and the stages by which work was done at these port construction sites during the Roman period.

Fig. 4 Rezé, Saint-Lupien, zone 4, sector 16. Unbuilt area or mudflat bordering the Roman quay to the west. – (Photo J. Mouchard 2014).

The final programme (2013-2016), which was completely devoted to the excavation of a quay (no. 9) and its neighbouring environment (mudflat). It was accompanied by additional methodological problems. The mudflat approaches from the centre of sector 16 and corresponds to an area that had not been built. This area appeared as a sandy beach, like it still can be found today in the estuary. It gradually silted up during Antiquity. From a paleoenvironmental perspective, this unexpected discovery was a real boon, because it preserved sedimentary archive trapped within a small area. A veritable repository safeguarded the environmental memory of the port site (about 2 m of stratigraphy from the substrate to the last backfilling from Late Antiquity) and provided an unexpected, authentic laboratory of nearly 2,500 m³ of sediment (**fig. 4**). Because of the significant and exceptional archaeological potential of the site for discovering artefacts and ecofacts, we decided, with the accord of our approximately 30 collaborators, to set up a protocol for purposive, considered, and, especially, programmed sampling to be carried out in terms of everyone's scheduled interventions and combined with protocols for recording particular remains[4].

PRELIMINARY RESULTS: A ROMAN PORT DISTRICT ESTABLISHED AT THE ESCARPMENT

The excavations carried out since 2005 have allowed to confirm the existence of riverbank constructions and port structures that became more and more elaborate between the 1st decades AD and the middle of the 2nd century AD.

From these first constructions, relatively simple, only remain variably preserved vestigial points (or tips) of micropiles, some stuck in the sand covering the substratum and, some penetrating both layers (**fig. 5**). At

Fig. 5 Rezé, Saint-Lupien, zone 4, sectors 14 and 15. General view of the survey 3b excavated from the northwest. Sandy sequence sealing piles marked with white labels. – (Favreau 2014).

the scale of the district, these rather lightweight wooden remains appear intermittently, but are distributed along the whole foot of the slope from upstream to downstream. Several hundred samples were taken. A first dendrological analysis carried out by Lydiane Gantier, provided a useful way to describe these deteriorated structures[5]. Observations on a small surface of the spatial distribution of these little posts (or even stakes in some cases) seem to suggest several lines of constructions related to different chronological phases of tree felling. Depending on the varieties that were recorded and geolocated, these lines of constructions could have served to reinforce the riverbanks or to support the pontoon or jetty (research about this is ongoing). Xylophagous analyses proved a taxonomical diversity of the young tree trunks of small diameter and branches, and clearly indicated that the raw materials were obtained relatively local. For the moment, it seems possible to identify at least four construction phases, which correspond to four phases of tree felling between 5 and 70 AD.

These first riverbank constructions would be synchronous with this district's first phase of urbanization, characterised by the establishment of streets and artisanal workshops (little steel industry, probable brickyard), as well as the gradual construction of the first storehouses. This interpretation is based on their classic floor plan in the form of extended rectangles, which is typical for storehouses in the Roman provinces of Gaul. Their construction above plinths made of mica schist, or even of gneiss, points to rising walls made of wood and clay and covered with tiled roofs. Unfortunately, that part of the site including these large buildings was levelled off a lot and poorly preserved. As a result, the interior layout, the type of flooring of the houses as well as the nature of the goods stored here remain unknown.

At the end of the 1st century AD, a vast construction programme was undertaken to reorganize the area entirely. The contour of the riverbanks was completely reworked, accentuated with monumental new bank revetments in the form of great platforms (or terraces), made from wood and stone, sometimes connected with dry masonry embankment walls. These quadrangular platforms jutting into the bed of the former river were built directly on the sand and covered over a few scraps of micropiles that had been cut and destroyed for this purpose during the preliminary work. These constructions provide an irregular (such as having a crenelated design) and diachronic extension, both of which result from the multiple phases of maintenance and restructuring (enlargement or reduction) that took place between the last decade of the 1st century AD and the middle of the 2nd century AD. This high degree of artificial manipulation of the natural environment certainly facilitated mooring of vessels and the loading and unloading of goods. These constructions also provided a monumental facade along the length of the riverbank and offered a solid foundation for buildings in the southern dwelling zone. At the same time, the storehouses were completely reconstructed and enlarged. Covered in granite rubble stone and mortar (with ironwork seals), these storehouses were compatible with the slope and provided a storage surface estimated of more than 3,000 m^2. The last excavation campaigns also revealed service buildings between these buildings and the structures that were in contact with the Loire, comprising a heated room, small thermal baths, and communal latrines. It is quite plausible to suppose that these services were intended for the boatmen and merchants.

The platforms/terraces located in the northern centre of the district have only come down to us in a very levelled-off state. This indicates a notable amount of dismantling and recuperation of materials during the Middle Ages, when the local monastery was built. The situation is very different to the one in the west, where composite platforms/terraces (mainly made from oak and mica schist) are remarkably well preserved thanks to a necropolis from Late Antiquity and the Early Middle Ages, which has protected the Roman remains below.

Of all platforms/terraces, no. 9 is the most typical and best preserved. Both its design and its construction feature fully all advanced Roman engineering and architectural requirements. The identification of the timber frame technique (**fig. 6**) used for the facades/front of these platforms/terraces have revolutionized cur-

Fig. 6 Rezé, Saint-Lupien. View of the north façade of platform/terrace no. 9. – (Mouchard 2011).

rent knowledge about river port construction in Atlantic Europe[6]. The structure is characterised by the use of half-lapped joints with oak ground beams for the first frame of the ongoing platform. Placed at ground level, this frame have needed to be levelled, sometimes on a plinth of mica schist directly on the sand (in the north), sometimes in a trench (in the south). This construction *de facto* provided a disbursement protection against erosion of the sediment at the foot of the slope. On these half-rounds or heartwood beams used as ground beams (varying by platform/terrace), mortise and tenon joints were used for assembling and then raising vertical beams, which were probably joined at the top to a second line of horizontal beams that are missing/not preserved. This construction system of Rezé differs from traditional timber-frame constructions – at least as described by Vitruvius in Antiquity[7] – especially in its use of a stone infill material between each post, established by the raising of slabs of mica schist that were dry-mounted with butt joints. During the construction of the he masonry facades, the interior was also gradually filled with carefully arranged blocks, slabs and scrap cuttings of mica schist. This rubble infill was required for the final form of the platforms/terraces. In some aspects, the remains on the façade of the quay constructions in Rezé are reminiscent of the *opus craticium*, a building technique often associated with timber frame construction (that is to say a composite architecture associating a wooden frame with a raw earth filling, above a masonry foundation of small rubble stones)[8]. Although it does feature several variants, Rezé both in its components and in the choice of materials (for example, the use of stone, rather than something else, as a filler) could rightly be considered the result of a reworked and rethought approach to construction, one that was adapted and adjusted to suit the local situation and the raw materials available there. The base of this timber frame had a protective covering in form of two superimposed lines of large oak plates that were secured with nails to the frame as described above.

In the area studied, the dendrochronological analysis indicates that there was a slight lapse of time – between 88 and 108 AD between the platforms/terraces – regarding the felling dates of the trees used for the timber framing. This consistent gap of about 20 years suggests that the construction moved from the east

to the west or from downhill to uphill. It seems likely that each successive period of tree felling corresponds to a new construction phase of the platform/terrace as a consequence of the continuation of the building programme. The chronology of the development of these riverbank constructions, from their implementation to their abandonment, are becoming clearer. By means of different research approaches, it was possible to show the extent to which these structures were modified and/or reworked over more than half a century. One of the most evident architectural developments is the gradual movement during the 2nd century AD from a composite construction technique using wood and stone to a technique exclusively using stone.
Finally, the unexpected discovery of an unbuilt area considered as a swamp area (mudflat) along the Roman quay, have encouraged us to set up a sampling protocol that have contributed to the paleoenvironmental approach of the port and river shore. This anaerobic environment is a tremendous archive for archaeoscience (in particular zooarchaeology and ichthyological, entomological, paleoparasitological, carpological and geomorphological analysis). As the sedimentary archives are distributed around the riverbank revetments, they provide crucial and previously unexpected information concerning the development and functioning of the port during Antiquity.

CONCLUSION

To sum up, it can be stated that an urban environment adapts to the natural topography of its underlying terrain. In the case of Rezé, we have a perfect example for a town spread out along the former course of the Loire, depending on the river, and completely built at the escarpment and in form of stacked rows of successive platforms/terraces. From the middle of the 2nd century AD, the river zone studied up to the Saint-Lupien neighbourhood underwent a gradual silting process. By the beginning of the 3rd century AD, it led to the reduction and eventually to the complete cessation of the port, artisan and trade activity. Nevertheless, to return to the years of prosperity, the development of the town between 90 and 100 AD indicates a significant financial investment. This involved sorting and selecting raw materials such as wood (very high-quality oak timber), minerals (establishing stone mining quarries), managing and mastering routes and conveyances that brought these materials to the construction sites, and especially using groups of craftsmen who specialized in carpentry, and, more generally, in fluvial and maritime engineering. This project may have involved directly the Senate of the Pictones, because Rezé was the main access point for river and sea trade. However, it is quite likely that local notables, who had made their fortunes from the development of local economy, might have also contributed to this vast project. Evidence of their presence in this town can be found in something that is certainly not a mere coincidence: the contemporaneous construction of *domūs* with centre courtyards, the only ones known to us in any of the secondary cities of the Pays de la Loire and Bretagne regions.

Notes

*) Translation by J. Holland, J. Mouchard and M. Foucher.

1) Ptol. 2, 7; after Berggren/Jones 2002, 97 bk. 2 § 7.

2) For more information about these two programmes, see Arthuis et al. 2010 and Arthuis/Guitton/Mouchard 2010.

3) Colardelle/Verdel 1993.

4) Protocols and aspects of the programme developed in cooperation? with Wetlands & Archeology, the 6th International Conference of the Research Group on History of Wetlands, European Archeological Center of the Mont Beuvray, Glux-en-Glenne (Nièvre). 9-11 November 2017, »Methodology: A Resolutely Interdisciplinary Approach« session, Borvon/Guitton/Mouchard: »The Roman Port Site of Ratiatum (Rezé, Loire-Atlantique): Sampling Policy and Paleoenvironmental Research (2013-2016)«.

5) Gantier 2016, 48-49.

6) For more information about identified architectural principles and the work of Roman carpenters at Saint-Lupien, see Mouchard 2013 and Mouchard/Epaud/Guitton 2016.

7) Rougier-Blanc 2011.

8) Darles/Cabarrou/Viers 2013, 99-116.

Source

Berggren/Jones 2002: Ptolemy's Geography: An Annotated Translation of the Theoretical Chapters, translated by J. Berggren and Alexander Jones (Princeton NJ 2002).

References

Arthuis/Guitton/Mouchard 2010: R. Arthuis / D. Guitton / J. Mouchard, D'un estuaire à l'autre: Géoarchéologie comparée des ports antiques d'Aizier (Seine) et de Rezé (Loire). Archéopages 30, 2010, 26-35.

Arthuis et al. 2010: R. Arthuis / D. Guitton / M. Monteil / J. Mouchard / O. de Perreti, Archéologie portuaire estuarienne entre Loire et Seine: principaux résultats et questions d'ordre méthodologique. L'exemple des sites antiques d'Aizier (Eure) et de Rezé (Loire-Atlantique). In: L. Hugot / L. Tranoy (eds), Actes de la Journée d'études sur les structures portuaires de l'arc atlantique dans l'Antiquité (bilan et perspectives de recherches), La Rochelle 2008. Aquitania, Supplément 18 (Bordeaux 2010) 61-82.

Colardelle/Verdel 1993: M. Colardelle / E. Verdel, Les habitants du lac de Paladru (Isère) dans leur environnement. La formation d'un terroir au XIe siècle. Documents d'Archéologie Française 40 (Paris 1993).

Darles/Cabarrou/Viers 2013: Ch. Darles / M. Cabarrou / C. Viers, L'emploi de l'opus craticium dans le sud-ouest de la Gaule Antique. In: A. Sousa Melo / M. Do Carmo Ribiero (eds), História da construção. Arquiteturas e technicas constructivas (Braga 2013) 99-116.

Gantier 2016: L. Gantier, Étude dendro-archéologique des bois du quartier Saint-Lupien à Rezé (Loire-Atlantique): Des premiers aménagements de berge aux structures monumentales [M.A. thesis Univ. Rennes 2, 2016].

Mouchard 2013: J. Mouchard, Archéologie portuaire: le site de Rezé (Loire-Atlantique) comme récent témoignage d'un quai gallo-romain en fond d'estuaire. In: M.-Y. Daire / C. Dupont / A. Baudry / C. Billard / J.-M. Large / L. Lespez / E. Normand / Ch. Scarre (eds), Anciens peuplements littoraux et relations Homme/Milieu sur les côtesde l'Europe atlantique / Ancient Maritime Communities and the Relationship Between People and Environment Along the European Atlantic Coasts. British Archaeological Reports: International Series 2570 (Oxford 2013) 247-258.

Mouchard/Epaud/Guitton 2016: J. Mouchard / F. Epaud / D. Guitton, with X. Favreau, M. Monteil et M. Yacger, Entre fleuve et océan, les quais à pans de bois du port antique de Rezé/Ratiatum (Loire-Atlantique). In: C. Sanchez / M.-P. Jézegou (eds), Les ports dans l'espace méditerranéen antique. Narbonne et les systèmes portuaires fluvio-lagunaires. Actes du colloque international tenu à Montpellier du 22 au 24 mai 2014. Revue Archéologique de Narbonnaise, Supplément 44 (Montpellier-Lattes 2016) 247-262.

Rougier-Blanc 2011: S. Rougier-Blanc, Le bois et ses usages dans le De architectura de Vitruve. Cahiers des Études Anciennes XLVIII, 2011, 89-117.

Summary

The municipality of Rezé is located at the base of the Loire estuary and on the southern bank of the Loire River, facing the city of Nantes. This populous area, located in the former province of Gallia Aquitania in the territory of the Pictones, occupies a large junction of overland roads, inland waterways and sea-lanes. At its peak at the beginning of the 2nd century AD, it extended along the river over approximately 40-50 ha. Excavations carried out since 2005 in the Saint-Lupien neighbourhood, in the east of Rezé, have confirmed the presence of port structures closely connected with storehouses which had already been identified in the 1980s. After the first phase very rudimentary structures on wooden piles, these riverbank constructions became much more imposing by the end of the 1st century AD. In this period, the whole area underwent a significant reorganisation, which in particular involved the construction of the large storehouses. At present, monumental constructions of nearly 200 m length built directly at the Loire have been discovered and investigated. The constructions identified in Rezé often combine wood and stone and were built using a box-structure technique. The front side was built with timber frames. One of the platforms/terraces, which was completely (21 m on one side) and very well preserved (1.3 m elevation), was extensively excavated between 2013 and 2016. These invaluable remains indicate that the river zone was constantly under construction during the High Roman Empire and that an exceptional level of financial resources was involved in this project.

Résumé

La commune de Rezé est localisée au fond de l'estuaire de la Loire et en rive sud du fleuve, face à la ville de Nantes. L'agglomération – située en province Aquitaine et en territoire picton – occupe un important carrefour de voies terrestres, fluviales et maritimes et se développe le long du fleuve sur environ 40-50 ha à son apogée au début du 2e siècle de notre ère. Les fouilles conduites depuis 2005 dans le quartier de Saint-Lupien, à l'extrémité orientale de la ville, ont permis de confirmer l'existence d'aménagements portuaires en étroite relation avec une série d'entrepôts déjà reconnus dans les années 1980. Relativement modestes dans un premier temps (constructions sur micro-pieux), ces aménagements de berge sont bien plus imposants à partir de la fin du 1er siècle apr. J.-C., époque durant laquelle l'ensemble du quartier fait alors l'objet d'un vaste programme de restructuration, illustré notamment par la reconstruction des grands entrepôts. Pour l'heure, l'ensemble monumental établi au contact de la Loire a été reconnu puis étudié sur plus de 200 m de long. Les ouvrages portuaires identifiés à Rezé associent très souvent le bois et la pierre, respectant le principe de construction en caisson, le tout étant fermé par des façades élevées selon le principe du pan de bois. L'un des quais, de plan complet (21 m de côté) et le mieux conservé (1,30 m d'élévation), a fait l'objet entre 2013 et 2016 d'un démontage exhaustif. Ces précieux témoignages renforcent l'idée d'un chantier portuaire quasi permanent durant le Haut Empire et qui a bénéficié de capacités de financement exceptionnelles.

DAVID GUCKER · ÉMILIE JOUHET · PHILIPPE ROLLET

HARBOUR STRUCTURES AND CRAFT ACTIVITIES ON THE RIGHT BANK OF THE VESLE ON THE FRINGES OF THE ANCIENT CITY OF DUROCORTORUM

EXCAVATIONS OF BOULEVARD HENROT IN REIMS

The dig site of the Boulevard Henrot in Reims (dép. Marne/F), led on an area of 4,000 m², is the first preventive excavation that has offered the opportunity to discover and study the antique right bank of the Vesle River on a length of 50 m [1]. This modest waterway, with an estimated width of 20 m, a flow rate of 3 m³/s and a depth of 1 m, is the western limit of Durocortorum, capital of the Belgic Gaul (**fig. 1**). This location on the old riverbed and the proximity of the phreatic table allowed an excellent conservation of organic materials, including wood, leather, seeds and pollen. The results of the various studies allow to retrace the evolution of a zone located on the fringes of the city, in which different artisanal activities developed, some of which being directly related to the presence of the watercourse.

At the turn of our era, only a few pits testify an anthropogenic activity. From the years 15/20 AD, the first major works in the zone, including the installation of a quay revetment and a dyke, stabilize the right bank of the river while controlling possible flooding (period 1). This area is then connected to the city, since the traces of the first fittings of a street that leads to the quay, are observed. This street, constituting the continuation of a *decumanus* already located in several points towards east, fits perfectly into the road network of the city established from the beginning of the 1st century AD.

Between the last third of the 1st century AD and the beginning or the middle of the 2nd century AD (period 2), we are witnessing an important step in the evolution of this part of the city, which will take a more »urban« character. Major works are undertaken. They will concern both the right bank of the river, with the construction of a new quay revetment ahead of the previous one, and the southern zone, where the spreading of chalk embankments will allow to reclaim the sediments related to the presence of the river. As a result of this work, the street is equipped with a pavement. A building is erected on the street frontage and near the river, while in the southern part of the excavation the first masonry constructions are created.

It is from the beginning or the middle of the 2nd century AD until the end of the 3rd century AD (period 3) that the area is really urbanized: a new construction much more massive replaces the previous quay and the street is equipped with a new roadway, wooden gutters and sidewalks made out of chalk. In the area, thus delimited by the quay and the street, new constructions are established, reserved for craft activities. Quay revetment and gutters located in a humid environment have maintained in a very good state of conservation, while the surface remains (walls, floors, etc.) have undergone a strong anthropogenic or natural erosion.

Although artisanal activities are reduced from the middle of the 3rd century AD (period 4), an imposing building is built in 306/307 AD, whose walls, nearly 1 m wide, have foundations in chalk resting on oak piles. These constructions were destroyed at the turn of the 4th and 5th centuries AD.

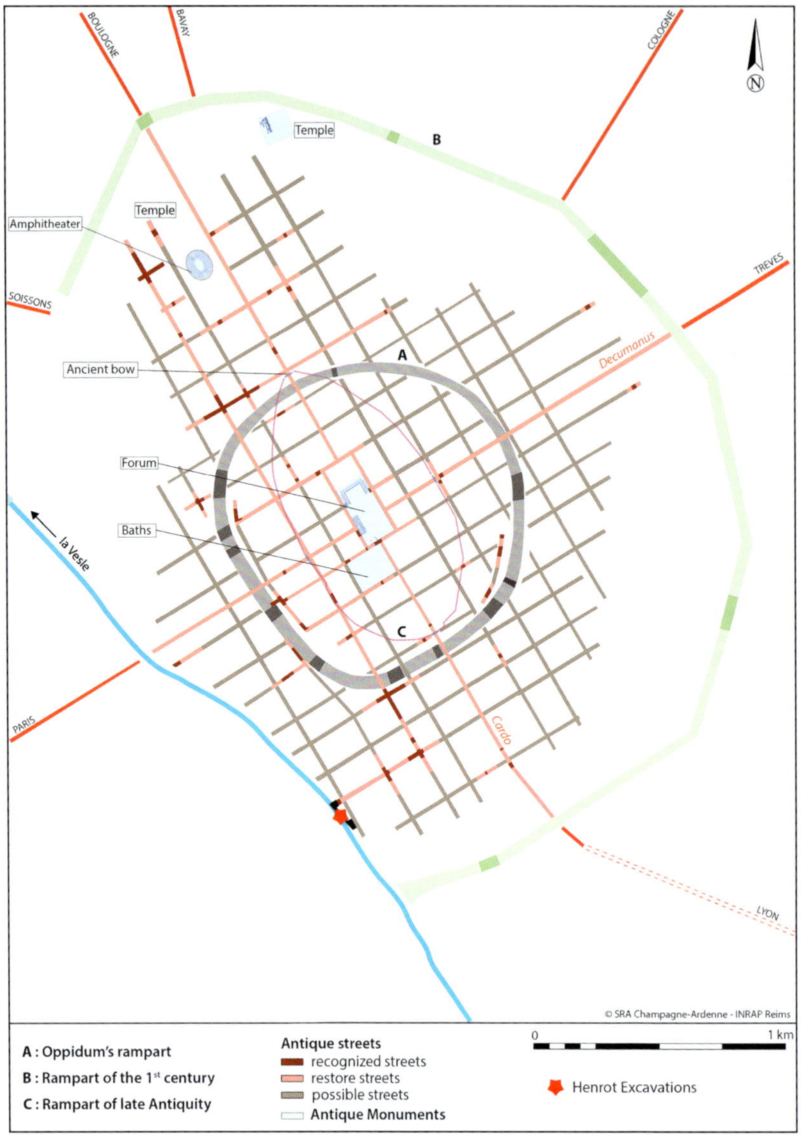

Fig. 1 Location of the excavation of the Boulevard Henrot in Reims on the restored plot of the streets of the ancient city and its enclosures. – (© Inrap).

HARBOUR STRUCTURES OF THE 1ST-3RD CENTURY AD

The first riverbank revetments of the ancient Vesle at the turn of our era

In period 1 (15/20 AD), the first bank facilities on the right side of the river are built. At the north of the dig site, a quay revetment is built, to which a dyke is added, perpendicular to the stream (**fig. 2a**) and in the southern part, embankments are constructed.

The quay Qu.562 was excavated on a length of 13 m. This riverbank stretch, oriented at approximately 20° west, has a slight curve. Its revetment consists of two levels of 3-4.50 m long oak planks, installed edgeways and held in place by piles of 0.06-0.10 m in diameter, in some cases in split wood. On the east side, the planks are doubled by thin joined slats of split oak, 0.10-0.18 m wide and 0.015 m thick, cut from trees more than 100 years old (**fig. 2b**). The assembly was reinforced on the east side by few irregularly spaced piles and a compact infill consisting of clay mixed with chalk rubble.

Along Qu.562, an installation (Ft.561) consisting of four tree trunks was discovered under a thick layer of sand brought by the river. Only one trunk could be excavated along its entire length (**fig. 2c**). The oak trunks

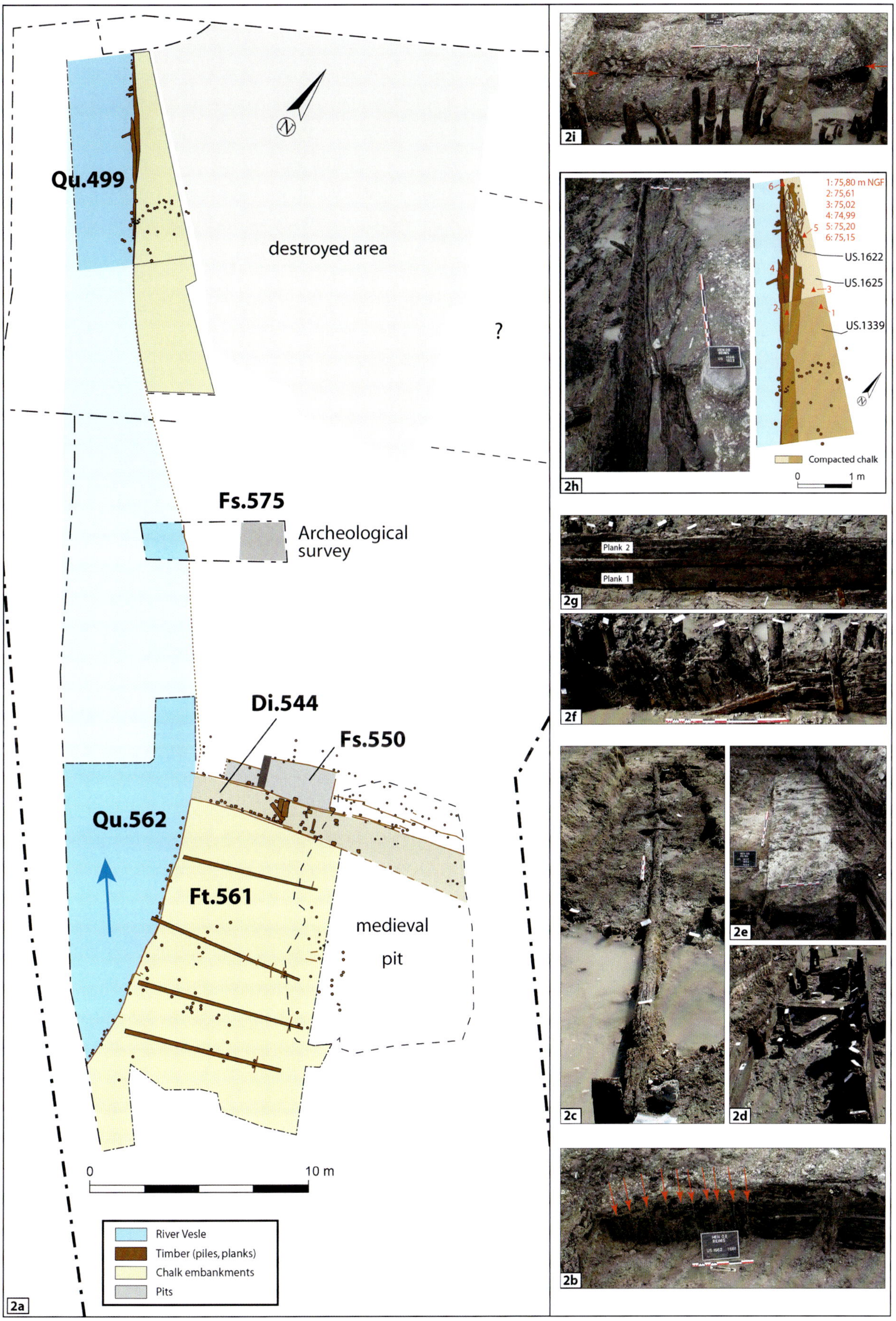

Fig. 2 Plan and views of the quay and the dyke at period 1. – (© Inrap).

were arranged perpendicularly to the river. They are between 6.50 and 8.20 m long with a maximum diameter of 0.12 m. On the side of the quay, these elements are irregularly spaced at distances between 2.20 and 3 m. The trunks were laid parallel to each other, except for the one, which was excavated entirely, whose summit end is off-axis to the south by nearly 1 m. Its base at the quay is held in place by a vertical stake. These logs are also propped, at the other end, by small stakes, pushed in from either side of the trunk. These are positioned above (notches) or below the trunks, or even pass through them by means of a mortise.

North of quay Qu.562 and structure Ft.561, a particular construction was exposed perpendicularly to the river. It is a dyke designed to preserve the area of possible floods. Its remains (Di.544) are characterized by a trench, oriented at 110° west, dug over a width of 1.20 m and a depth of 0.60 m in the sandy layers brought by the river. On both sides of the trench, two revetments of planks held by stakes have been identified over a length of nearly 15 m to the north and 12.80 m to the south. To the west, the southern edge corresponds to the limit of quay Qu.562, while to the northern one extends to the west. In the east, the dyke extends beyond the excavation area (**fig. 2a**). In the area between the two revetments, large squared reused timber elements are installed transversely to maintain the caisson, which is then filled with clay to waterproof the structure (**fig. 2d-e**). The northern revetment is consolidated by 2.40-4.60 m long oak planks arranged on two levels and held in place by stakes. These piles with circular cross-sections, split or squared off, are irregularly distributed on both sides of the planks. The southern revetment consists of thin small planks of split oak nailed on slats that form vertical and horizontal panels laid according to their length and which rest on a line of piles (**fig. 2f**). A series of oak planks, from 2.40 to 5.15 m long, are also laid edgeways on two levels and cover the panels (**fig. 2g**). In the north-western corner of the excavation the Qu.499 quay section, which was partially destroyed during Antiquity and again in the 20th century AD, was discovered on a length of over 10 m and a width of 1 m to the north and 3.30 m to the south. A chalk rubble embankment of 0.40 m thick precedes the setting of the construction. The quay consists of a layer of chalk held in place on the side of the river by a wooden revetment made of planks and stakes oriented at 38° west. The construction of this first quay presents disparate elements. At first, oak planks over 3.50 m long were laid flat on river alluvium. Another series of boards, at least, 5.70 m long, was then put in place edgeways in front of the previous ones, held on the riverside by many stakes irregularly spaced. This »L« revetment serves to maintain chalk embankments which form the circulation area of the quay. A bundle of willow branches that rests on a board in a grey sediment has been observed to the north. These branches are covered by an embankment of chalk including a blocks of stone (**fig. 2h**).

At the end of period 1 (between 15/20 and 65/70 AD), the last works are made on the different quay platforms. To the north, the circulation area of section quay Qu.499 is refitted with chalk. A layer of compacted chalk rubble covers the previous ones and presents a regular surface, sloping towards the edge of the quay where blocks have been observed along the planks (**fig. 2i**). Southward, behind quay section Qu.562, the dyke and the remains which border it on the north (Di.544, Fs.550 and Ft.552) are abandoned, covered by two successive embankments of chalk.

Located near the right bank of the river, in a humid environment, this area, originally dependent on fluctuations in the watercourse and floodable, was therefore the subject of important works during period 2, which allow controlling the bed of the river and its possible floods on the west fringes of the ancient city, now urbanisable. Although these riverbank constructions are in no way comparable with stone structures built along major rivers, they nevertheless show the undeniable interest that has been brought to the »practicability« of this part of the city. The presence of four tree trunks, installed in the angle formed by the quay and the dyke, is the only trace related to an activity probably related to the immediate proximity of the watercourse. This space, of at least 90 m², is similar to a work area for a specific activity; is it rather an area reserved for loading/unloading of materials or goods like a ramp? The abandonment of the dyke

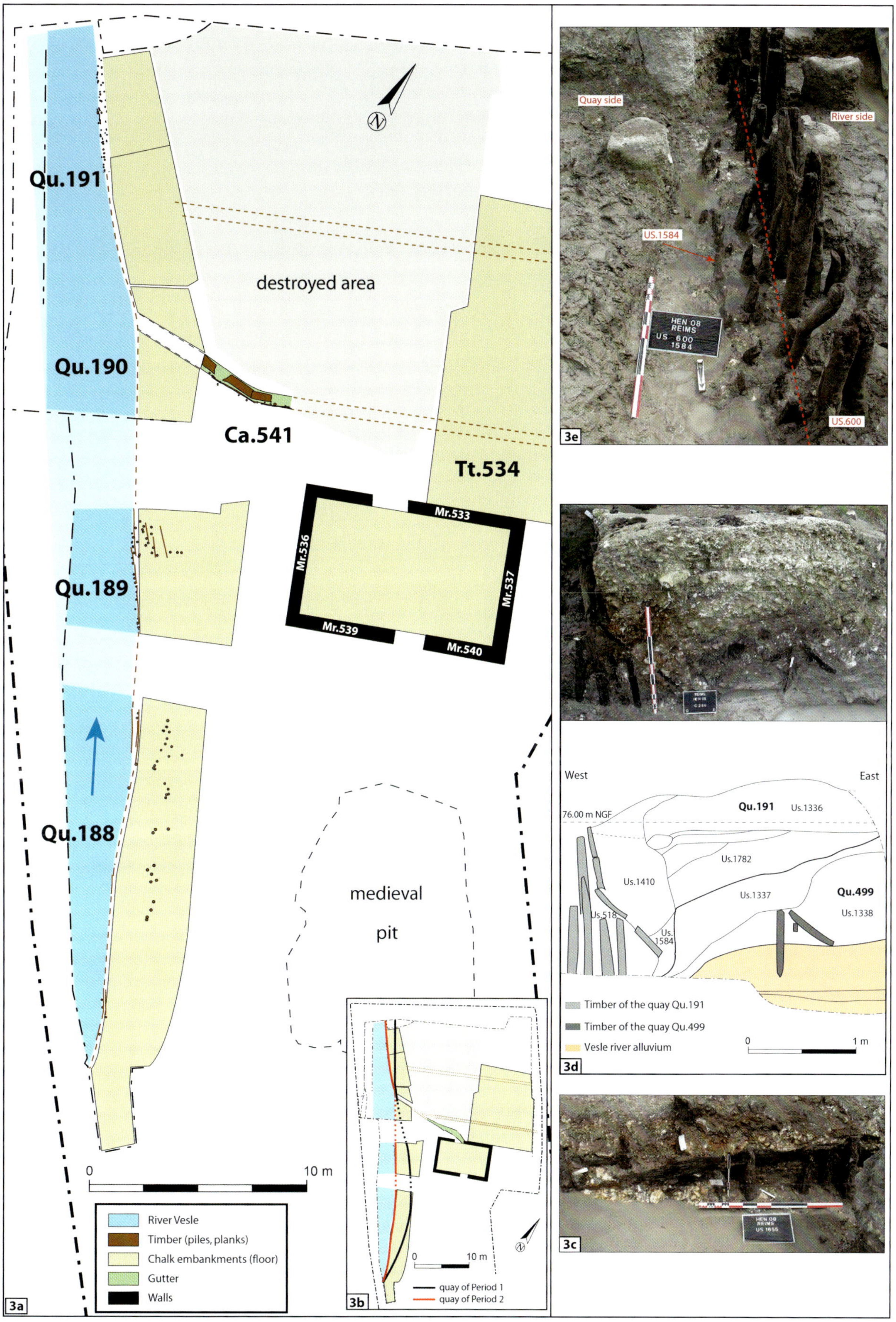

Fig. 3 Plan and views of the quay at period 2. – (© Inrap).

between 15/40 and 45/70 AD marks an important transition in the area. The city is expanding, new districts are built and the urban grid moves towards the river. A wooded gutter is constructed and its orientation fits perfectly with the ancient grid, more precisely with the extension of a *decumanus* already identified several times towards the east[2].

A new quay built at the end of the 1st century AD

At the beginning of period 2 (between 65/90 and 110/160 AD), a new quay is set up (**fig. 3a**). This new revetment built ahead of the previous one, has been identified for a maximum length of 47.70 m. It is located on the western periphery of the excavation, has a relatively linear outline oriented south-east/north-west, but marks a slight inflexion in its central part (**fig. 3b**). Four areas of study were defined: Qu.188 in the south, Qu.189 and Qu.190 in the central part and Qu.191 in the north of the archaeological site. The vestiges of this quay are tenuous and have been discovered only occasionally, because they have been largely destroyed by a more massive construction, which has more or less the same limits. In the south, the first section of the riverbank (Qu.188) rests on the previous quay (Qu.562). It was built at the beginning of the 1st century AD and head northward about 3 m to the west. In this section, remains of the first construction phase have been observed in fragmentary form on a length of 8.60 m to the south and 2.75 m to the north. It retains the same orientation at 30° west and rests on the alluvial sand of the river. At least two levels of oak planks are held by small stakes and a few piles. The stakes have a diameter of 0.05-0.07 m. The boards, which lie underneath those of later constructions, have a poor state of conservation and are between 0.50 and 2.50 m long. This timbering holds a bank of indurated chalk observed on an average thickness of 0.65 m. A line of stakes is at a practically equal distance from the old quay and the new construction and seems to work as a reinforcement of this embankment. The dendrochronological analysis of the stakes and the planks make it possible to date the construction to the end of the 1st century AD. Another plank from a tree felled in 105 AD probably marks a later repair.
In the middle of the quay (Qu.189), here orientated to 36° west, the same mode of construction has been observed. The planks with a length of 0.68-2.06 m are disposed on one level and held in place by about 20 stakes, some of which are split, of 0.04-0.14 m cross-section (**fig. 3c**). This set makes it possible to hold a chalk rubble that reaches 0.60 m high, consisting of small chalk stones mixed with brown silt. This layer is later covered by a new chalk layer associated with a more massive wooden construction of the next quay.
Finally, on the quay area Qu.191, located to the north, this state of construction has been excavated over a length of 5 m. The construction, built at a distance of 1.50 m to the west forward the previous quay (Qu.499), consists of two parallel rows of small stakes spaced about 0.20 m, which determine an orientation at 42° west (**fig. 3d**). These rows ensure the support of small boards that hold an embankment of chalk rubble. These planks, the longest is 3.50 m, are in poor condition and on a single level. They are held by 0.04-0.10 m cross-section stakes, mostly circular, mainly made of oak but also of willow (**fig. 3e**). This installation partially destroy the last occupation layer of the previous quay Qu.499 and a slight recharge of some chalk stones then covers and mingles with this last layer of occupancy. These few blocks probably allow to obtain a plane level and in the continuity of the blockage observed on the quay Qu.189, but with an embankment of less chalk. Taking the subsidence of the boards into account, it is possible to propose a supply of chalk with a thickness of about 0.60 m.
The period 2 is illustrated by the importance of the work that has been undertaken to create new building surface to answer to a major urban expansion and an influx of many inhabitants and/or craftsmen having been attracted by an impressive city. However, the remains of the new quay that we have excavated,

mainly made of oak wood again, are fragmentary. The course of the new revetment is practically linear, substantially rectifies the course of the anterior quay and definitively fixes the limit between the river and the constructed surfaces (**fig. 3b**). Parallel to the construction of the quay revetment, large chalk embankments stabilize the clayey sediments of the watercourse to the north and south-east. This state of construction constitutes a transitional stage of preparation that prefigures a new organization of this district to integrate it into the urban space. In fact, in a large part of the city, the road network is transformed with the installation of a different sewage or rainwater drainage system, the latter being now drained to the river by a new network of wood gutters.

A more massive quay built in the middle of the 2nd century AD

At the beginning of period 3, which covers nearly two centuries (between 110/160 and 280/320 AD), a new quay with a similar outline to the previous one was constructed (**fig. 4a**). This quay is much more massive than the older one and has been excavated in the four study areas already defined before.
The Qu.188 quay portion appears at the southern border of the excavation area on a length of 17 m. It draws a very slight curve, from east to west, and is oriented at 30° west. It consists of sawed planks which are 2.50-3.90 m long and installed edgeways in two to three levels, without particular assembly and held in place by many oak stakes. The piles form a regular sowing and are distributed fairly uniformly with spacings between 0.20 and 0.40 m. They have a cross-section of 0.02-0.13 m in diameter and are invariably split and squared off. A certain number of stakes of an average cross-section of 0.10 m × 0.15 m complete the piling of piles. Two of these quadrangular cross-section stakes were used in replacement. The first, by its large dimensions, probably corresponds to a beam and the second presents four large mortises that cross right through it. The Qu.188 quay revetment is strengthened on the eastern side by compacted chalk rubble. This blocking, 0.65 m thick and in contact with the last level of planks, is cut to its base by a digging along the two levels of planks on a width of 0.84 m. It is filled with sandy silt mixed with chalk rubble. The layer of compacted chalk that forms the platform of the quay is contemporary with the chalk embankments that extend to the east presumably until contact with the front wall (Mr.112). These observations make it possible to reconstruct the top of the quay with a slope of nearly 10 %, oriented from east to west, between the ancient buildings and the Vesle River. Concerning the used wood species, all the samples are oak. The results of the dendrochronological analysis provide felling dates during the second half of the 1st century AD.
In section Qu.189, the construction was excavated on a length of over 6.80 m. The planks, kept on two levels, are arranged in two to three parallel lines oriented at 36° west (**fig. 4b**). They are 1.11-3.10 m long. They are held by stakes, mostly of circular cross-section and 0.04-0.10 m in diameter, and spaced from 0.15 to 0.20 m. Several times, concentrations of many small diameter stakes have been observed. These piles are mainly oak, with some elements in alder. The layout also includes a number of reused oak stakes. A squared pile taken from the centre of the excavated section has two mortises. Two other piles bear the marks of previous use. A squared pile of quadrangular cross-section has a tenon at its summit end and another has a mid-wood assemblage at its summit end. These two elements are timber that may belong to a framework and/or a wood framing structure. Samples taken throughout this section indicate that the large majority of the elements are made of oak. Six of the trees have been felled after the years 123-141 AD. Like the previous section Qu.188, a compacted and smoothed chalk layer, approximately 0.35 m thick, covers the quay and is practically in contact with the quay revetment planks. There, the chalk has undergone erosion, probably due to the fluctuations of the river, which results in the presence of a grey-coloured sediment ob-

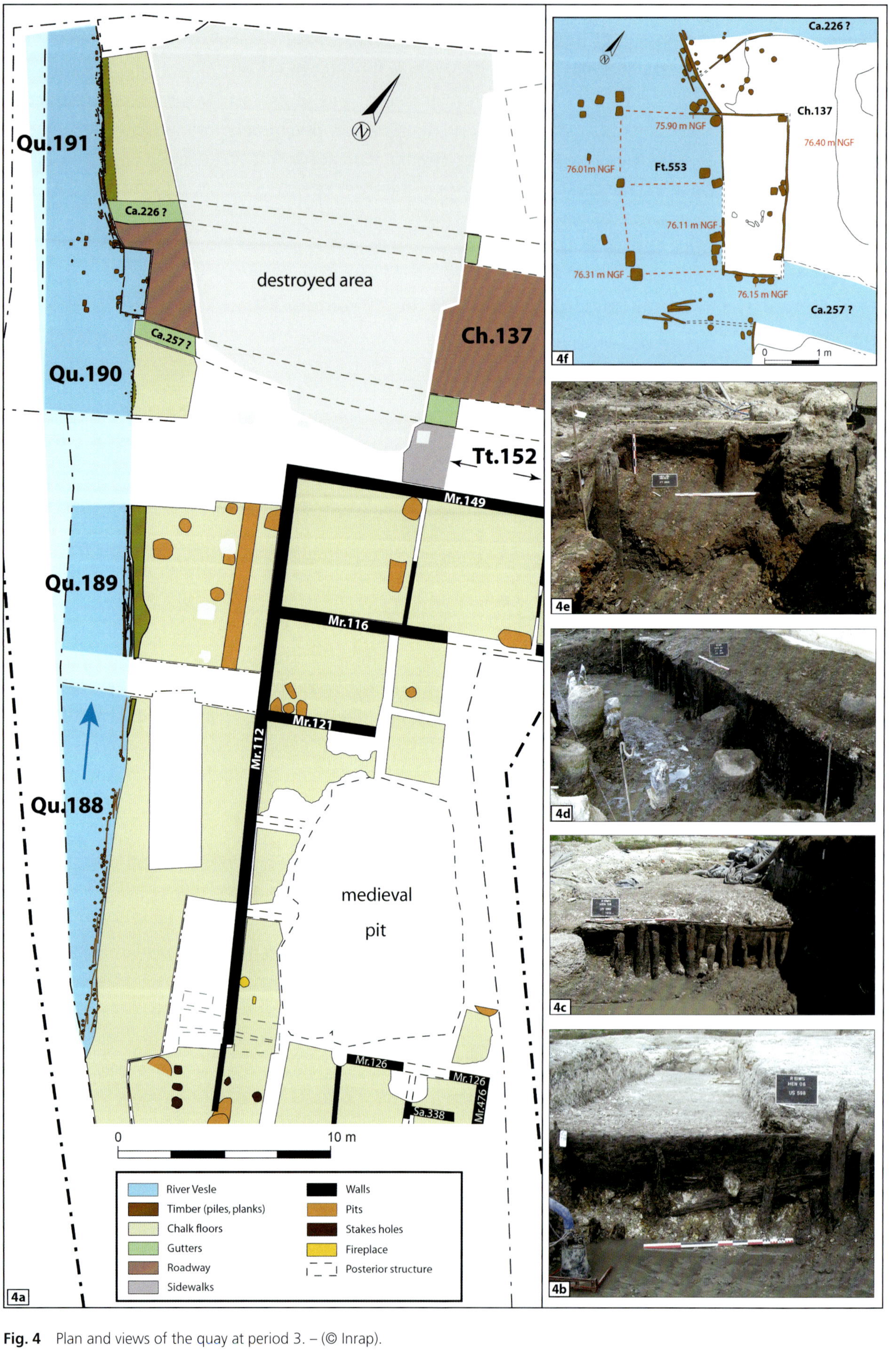

Fig. 4 Plan and views of the quay at period 3. – (© Inrap).

served over a width of 0.55-1.10 m. A layer of fine dark grey sediment with pottery fragments covers the complex and documents the frequentation and use.
The two Qu.190 and Qu.191 sections are located on both sides of the antique street and the archaeological feature Ft.553, which corresponds to a wooden structure built upon the outlet of the street to the river. The quay section Qu.190, excavated on a length of 3.80 m, is straight and oriented at 37° west. This section corresponds to the part of the quay south of the street (Ch.137) and is limited at its northern end by the first state of the gutter (Ca.257). On this section, one level of planks, 1.35-2.35 m long, is held in place by stakes with a circular cross-section of 0.04-0.08 m (**fig. 4c**). All piles and planks support an embankment of compacted chalk, which corresponds to the platform of the quay and has been excavated 3.30 m long and 2.20 m wide. An occupation layer of 0.25 m thickness covers the platform. The pottery analysis[3] of the latter attests that it was deposited between 110/120 and 270/280 AD, which corresponds to the period of use of this structure. Sometimes, a brown silt associated with small blocks of chalk was observed between the planks and the chalk platform, similar to the layer on quay Qu.189.
To the north of the roadway, whose gutter c. 226 marks the limit, the quay section Qu.191 was excavated over a length of 8 m. The construction is linear and oriented at 40° west. This massive work is superimposed on the previous state by advancing very slightly towards the river. It consists of four levels of planks and piles which hold in place a chalk embankment which forms the blocking and platform of the quay (**fig. 4d**). Saw-cut boards, 1.58-5.66 m in length, are arranged on edge, one on top of the other, without any particular layout. The first level of boards is held by small pegs on the riverside and rare stakes on the bank side. It did subside and has a steep inclination. The lack of consistent maintenance on the bank side led the first level of boards to separate from the rest. These planks are held on the riverside by piles of circular section, squared off or split and for some re-used. Stakes are at the base of the layout and hold the first board. A sowing of piles of circular section and 0.04-0.10 m in diameter, regularly distributed, holds the four levels of planks. A number of piles of 0.14-0.28 m cross-section complete this construction. They are spaced by a series of two stakes every metre and correspond, in part, to re-used piles. One of these holding piles, perforated with two large mortises in its upper part, was taken at 1.20 m from the northern limit of the excavation area. It could initially come from the same piece of wood like a pile taken further south on the same quay revetment. Similarly, three piles include a possible groove, the remains of a mortise and a notch. All these different pieces could come from the demolition of a wood framing structure. The analysis of the samples taken from the piles and planks of this revetment specify that they are all made of oak (except of one poplar pile). Furthermore, the planks gave dendrochronological dates of tree having been felled in 124 and 127 AD. Two piles correspond to trees felled after 150 and 169 AD, which points to later maintenance and repair. A re-used pile provided a felling date of 18 AD ± 10.
The top of the quay was observed over a length of 6.50 m and had a maximum width of 3.20 m near the street (Ch.137). The preserved surface of the platform of the quay consists of two successive and massive chalk embankments with a maximum thickness of 0.50 m each. The first embankment levelled the slope at the edge of the river to obtain a level plane and seems directly related to the establishment of the quay. In a second construction phase, this embankment is carved in part to set up revetment boards held in place by the piles on the riverside. This digging, which is 0.64 m wide and up to 0.90 m deep, is filled by sandy silt embankment mixed with chalk blocks, mortar and ceramic sherds and used to wedge the boards and hold the construction in place. The embankment was probably compacted when the four planks were put in place. The second embankment with a slightly curved profile covers the platform of the quay. It reaches a maximum height of 1.30 m above the level of the older platform. This last embankment of chalk serves as a level of circulation on the bank of the river and on its surface a lot of artefacts related to the occupation have been found. This uppermost embankment of chalk, partially eroded, was

probably repaired, because a board of 2.38 m length was added parallel to the level of the main board, which was removed.
Between section Qu.190 and Qu.191, the ancient street was observed on a total width of 6 m. The roadway is 4.50 m wide and bordered by gutters to the north and south (Ca.226 and Ca.257). The proximity of the river offers the opportunity to easily manage the maintenance of the sewage or rainwater drainage network since the gutters spill there. From then on, near the river, the gutters had to be regularly cleaned.
At the edge of the quay, the west end of the street is a quadrangular wooden structure (Ft.553) that extends into the riverbed with a series of large piles. The quadrangular construction is not exactly centred on the roadway but shifted to the south in the immediate vicinity of the Ca.257 gutter (**fig. 4e**). The assemblage draws a rectangle 3 m long and 1.15 m wide to the south and 1.28 m to the north, oriented substantially at 35° west (**fig. 4f**). Planks are placed edgeways on one level and have been severely eroded. The western and eastern planks are held by piles on the east side and the south plank on the south side by four small stakes. In front of this structure and at a distance of 2 m on average towards the west, a series of large piles mark the extension of this construction into the riverbed. Other piles of smaller dimensions seem to complete or strengthen this construction. The analysis of samples taken from the piles and planks specifies that all wooden elements are of oak. Several felling dates give proof that the construction was built in the first half of the 2nd century AD (119 ± 10, 134 ± 10). Furthermore, a stake was made of a tree felled after 151 AD, which points to later maintenance.
In the river, at the edge of each section of the quay, there is a significant accumulation of material consisting essentially of ceramic sherds and animal bones. This layer marks the abandonment of the quay because it was no longer possible to have direct access to the watercourse from the chalk platforms built along the bank. It cannot be excluded that much of this material, at least for sections Qu.190 and Qu.191, comes from ancient street gutters, which have been flowing directly into the watercourse. However, the regularity and the extent of this refilling testify of the will of the residents to take space on the river to avoid the problems of siltation of the riverbank. The collected archaeological artefacts are abundant and date from the first half of the 3rd century AD (215/220-240/245 AD). To the south, in front of the quay section Qu.188, this layer was accumulated over a maximum width of 3 m west of the bank revetment. Beyond ceramics, a lot of bone needles or pins as well as many everyday objects and some rare coins have been found. Wooden objects are also present (probably turned furniture, pawn box) as well as metal objects like fibulas, buttons or gaff, related to the port activity. In front of section Qu.189, a layer of embankment associated with sandy alluvium contains ceramics and animal bones, two fragments of shoes and a bone hinge. To the north, ahead of sections Qu.190 and Qu.191, which also corresponds to a significant accumulation of material, many objects have been found, too. In addition to pottery and faunal remains, 156 objects were collected there, including ornaments, many tools, objects made of bone, wood and leather (400 seals and leather scraps). The wood and leather objects were particularly well preserved in the wet environment and have hitherto not been published for the site of ancient Reims.

CRAFT ACTIVITIES ON THE RIGHT RIVERBANK

A low attendance of the right bank in the 1st century AD

The beginning of period 1 (5 BC to 20 AD) is characterized by only a few vestiges that show a small attendance of the zone. Two pits, a wooden structure and layers of embankments correspond to this period. The pit Fs.567 is rectangular in shape, 3.80 m long, 3.30 m wide and 0.80 m deep. It is revetted by small stakes, maximum 12 cm in diameter, which is hold by wattle work. In the lower filling of the pit, at least 14 still connected skeletons of horses were deposited and covered by a layer of plant debris and bark. A ^{14}C-analysis gives a high probability of dating from 15 BC to 3 AD. This deposit corresponds to an activity of butchering on the outskirts of the ancient city. No trace of meat cutting was observed, but traces of skin and tendon recovery, as well as bone, may be suggested.

At the end of the 1st century AD (period 2), in the northern zone, a quadrangular building with chalk wall foundations was built parallel to the street at a distance of 6 m from the river after the fitting of the new quay. Oriented at 120° west, it is slightly trapezoidal with a length of 10.30 m and a width of 6.35-6.60 m, which represents a total area of 66.50 m² for a usable area of nearly 46 m². Although it was not possible to excavate its entire floor, a fireplace consisting of large fragments of tiles and located in a layer of ashes was documented, which was not contiguous to a wall. It is likely that this building near the river and the street, but away from inhabited areas, is linked to small-scale metalworking activity, which became much more important in the following period. In the south-eastern zone, previously filled in, the constructions point to a more »urban« character. Indeed, a succession of walls over 40 m long, oriented north-south, separates two distinct spaces. To the west, there is a built-up area where the partition walls delimit three rooms and a cellar. The entire building exudes a sense of solidness with walls whose foundations are exclusively made of stone. The entrance to the cellar is located to the west and a ventilation opening is located in the eastern wall. East of the different walls, the area is apparently undeveloped. In this zone, the few remains which have been uncovered in a rather poor state of conservation document the beginning of craft activities that will increase in the following period.

Metallurgic and textile craft during the mid-2nd to late 3rd centuries AD

The period 3 is characterized by vestiges of craft activities. Behind the new quay, the clay sediments are covered with large quantities of chalk which, after being compacted, formed the floor of future constructions. Whether in the north or the south, the buildings did not undergo major transformations during this period. The built-up areas expanded but respected the initial framework.

In the northern zone, the quadrangular building from the previous period is destroyed for a much larger building that includes at least 14 rooms reserved for craft activity. To the north and west, two perpendicular walls constitute its limits while the remains of small partitions made of perishable materials mark the internal division. Although it is difficult to characterize precisely the function of each of the identified rooms and the internal circulations in the building, several vestiges bear witness to an activity centred mainly on small metallurgy. The presence of numerous fireplaces, stones that could have served as anvils, fragments of tuyeres or crucibles, mill scale (metallic dust) collected in the ashy layers and blacksmith tongs in the banks of the river constitutes altogether clear proofs of this activity (**fig. 5**). The metallurgic activity continued throughout the whole period in this area, even if some minor transformations were made in the ground plan. Floors have been retread, but the rooms retained their original function. One problem concerning the production remains, because nothing allows to determine what was manufactured in these workshops. No object, finished or in-process, waste or run-out has been found.

In the southern zone, on the east side, the density of buildings increases during this period and a set of small rooms has been identified. They are separated from each other by partitions in perishable materials, similar to those installed in the building for use in the north. The floors are chalk, perforated with stake holes. One was reinforced by a series of 30 loom weights grouped in the corner of the room. The presence of weaving weights may refer to textile production. Usually, no other remains of textile craft are preserved because of

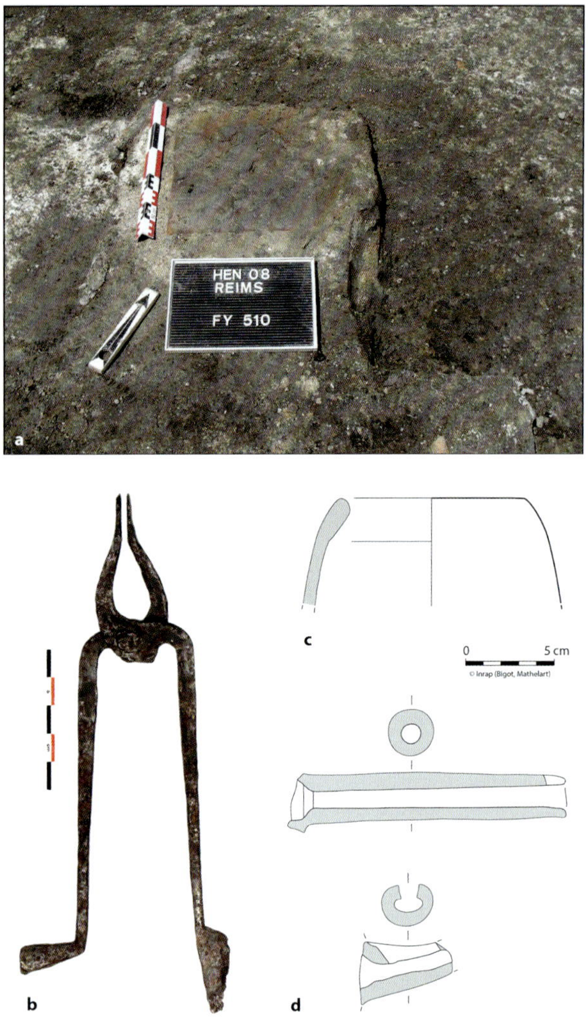

Fig. 5 Remains of the metallurgical activity on the bank of the 2nd and 3rd centuries AD: **a** fireplace. – **b** tongs. – **c** crucible. – **d** tuyere of furnace. – (© Inrap).

the perishable nature of the organic material. In this case, some other elements allow identifying different kinds of textile production such as weaving or spinning. On the one hand, there are hollow structures used as storage pits of smectic clay or »fuller's soil«. On the other hand, there are many craft-related objects from the nearby sediments of the river, such as a carding comb, numerous fragments of brushes to refine the sheets (**fig. 6**), needles made of bone and iron and only one proven fusillium. Furthermore, numerous fragments of Richborough 527 amphoras from Lipari were identified, which served as containers for the transport of alum (these sherds are the most important collection discovered in Reims). The combination of all these elements gives clear proof for an intense textile production with all steps from the preparation of the wool until the manufacture of the fabrics and even the finalization of the clothes. The clay in storage pits, which have hitherto been unpublished in Reims, was used by the fullers to soften the textile fibres of the wool. Although no remains of tanks or vats have been discovered, this work must have been taken place in the immediate vicinity of the excavation area.

Throughout this third period, whose peak is during the first half of the 3rd century AD, this district keeps its focus on craft. Different sorts of activities take place with a certain intensity and bear witness to commercial relations. The presence of amphoras from different countries of the Mediterranean basin has been verified by the study of pottery remains. Within the built-up areas, several archaeological remains give indirect proof for other kinds of commercial exchange between the capital of Belgic Gaul and the provinces of southern Gaul as well as the whole Mediterranean basin. Some of this proof is provided by the wells. As the river had become a dumping area, the inhabitants had to dig wells to get clean water. Among the eleven wells discovered, eight have wood casings of quadrangular cross-section. The other three wells have been cased with re-used barrels, which has not been documented in Reims before. A first study specifies that this barrels contained wine[4]. Their presence is to be attached to the transport of this precious liquid and/or storage in the warehouses of traders. In any case, their re-use indicates that they have become too old to be used in their original function and had to be recycled. Furthermore, trade and import is also enlightened by the study of plant macro-remains[5]. The diversity of species identified is exceptional. Concerning spices, coriander, savoury, fennel and cumin reveal the arrival of species from southeast Asia and Mediterranean Basin. Although, cumin, which is native in Upper Egypt, is hitherto the only reference in northern Gaul. Among the spectrum of fruits, several rare species such as melon, fig, black mulberry, peach or loquat have been found. All these species are first-order references for the north of Gaul, thus confirming the primary place occupied by Reims in the trade networks.

Fig. 6 Remains of the textile processing on the bank of the 2nd and 3rd centuries AD: **a** pit of smectic clay. – **b** weights of weaving. – **c** carding comb. – **d** carding brush. – **e** alum amphora Rich. 527 of Lipari. – (© Inrap).

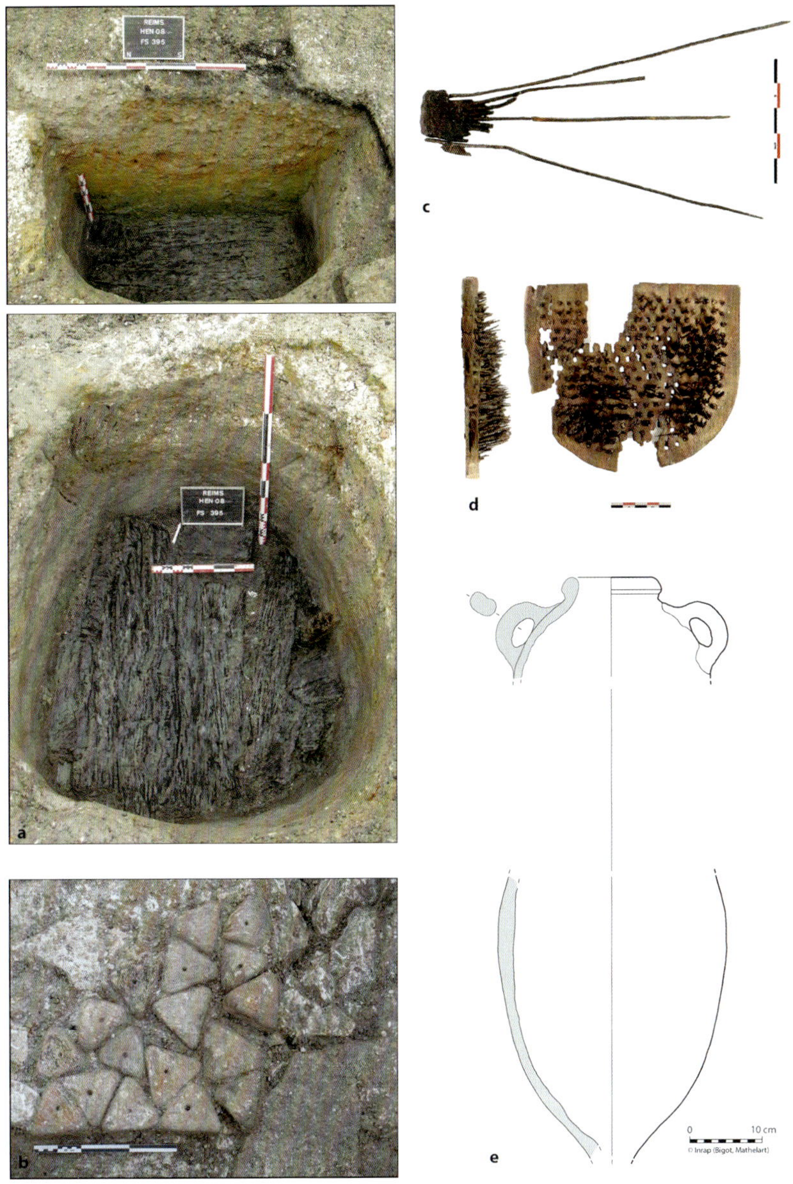

A monumental building of the 4th century AD

At the beginning of the 4th century AD (period 4), a large building was constructed in the excavation area of the Boulevard Henrot. Given the imposing character of this building, it seems clear that access to it from the city and the river is kept. However, due to a poor conservation status, no level of road or quay attached to this period has been uncovered. In addition, the junction between this building and the river is located outside the excavation area.

Three of the walls of the rectangular building were visible in the excavation area. They belong to a building extending 11.50 m from north to south and at least 20 m from east to west, which has, therefore, an internal space of nearly 161.50 m².

The foundations of these walls are composed of a compacted chalk base mixed with calcareous and burrstone stones, 1.10-1.50 m wide and 0.45 m high. This foundation rests on four to five rows of wooden piles hammered, through the clayey and sandy alluvium of an old arm of the Vesle to the geological chalk. These piles are distributed in a relatively regular manner, spaced apart from each other by an average of 0.15 m, forming a mesh of about 16 piles per m². 449 stakes were excavated under two of the three walls and 392 of them were collected, cleaned and inventoried precisely. They have fairly similar characteristics. The quasi-rough logs (part of the trunk with very often still sapwood and sometimes the bark) measure 1.20 m in length on average and the tips have been carved with an axe on four sides. These piles are predominantly of the quadrangular cross-section from 0.08-0.12 m × 0.12-0.15 m, but also oval, square and round. The xylological and dendrochronological analyses carried out by W. Tegel[6] covered 86 stakes. The oak trees started to grow between 230 and 277 AD and have been felled rather young, aged 51 years on average (31-77 years). The 60 samples revealed a period of tree felling between winter 306 and spring 307 AD. This is certainly very close to the moment of their use within the foundations because the study showed that green wood has been manufactured. However, this slight difference in dating between the piles does not correspond to the progress of the construction site since the trunks felled at one gap season are found both in one wall and in the other in a random manner. It rather reveals the existence of a raw material order prior to construction of the building, but shortly before this one.

In the upper part, the remains of portions of substructure and upper part of the walls were excavated. The substructure was 1.10 m wide and built of massive limestone blocks of at least 1 m side length and 0.30 m thickness. Only one of the walls still had an upper part still partially in place. It was 0.98 m wide and consists of a double facing of limestone and internal blocking linked with a rather compact tile mortar.

In the heart of this building, a series of ovens was built along a wall. This battery of fireplaces separated by low walls has been identified on a length of at least 14 m (its western limit is outside the limits of excavation) and 2.30 m width. On a length of 6 m, three soles and two low walls were still in place. One of the soles was almost completely preserved. It is 1.20 m² and built of four terracotta tiles. A fifth slab of the same aspect is placed in the middle of the southern side of the sole, probably at the mouth of the hearth. By extrapolation, it can be deduced that at least seven ovens were located in the uncovered part of the building.

The whole building has characteristics that are not comparable to those of the previous periods. The vestiges of this building are imposing and give an impression of strength and solidity. The dimensions and especially the techniques and materials used for its construction bear witness of significant financial resources. The specific support and foundation technique is generally used for important public buildings in wet or even floodable environments, such as in Arles with about 30,000 piles to stabilize the walls of the circus[7].

It is possible to estimate the number of material that was necessary to build the foundations of this building. At 16 piles per m², at least 1,000 stakes had to be cut from 200 trees to support the four supposed walls of the building. This represents a volume of almost 85 m³ or 80 tons of timber which had to be cut, landed and then transported. On three piles, we were able to observe »X« marks struck with a sharp tool. These marks probably correspond to a counting system carried out in the forest. They were made after the stakes were squared off, but before the cutting of the point since some of these crosses are only partially preserved.

In any case, this building of the beginning of the 4th century AD has a monumental and industrial character. In addition, its location near the Vesle documents the need to have direct access to the river. Indeed, it is located more than 700 m from the city and rather isolated in a zone where the districts have already been abandoned. Was it the intention of being able to draw water at will or to take advantage of the watercourse as a means of transport for the supply of raw materials or the export of a finished product or to use hydraulic power to run a mill? Although there are no clues or related structures to answer the question what was produced or processed here, the presence of at least seven ovens gives proof for intense activity. The current hypothesis is that it was a bakery on an »industrial« scale, perhaps to supply the shops in the centre of the then rapidly changing city. The proximity of the river could have guaranteed the easy transport of grain or flour and also wood for the operation of the ovens from the surrounding countryside.

CONCLUSION: AN ORGANIZED AND SYSTEMATIC CONSTRUCTION

All the work on the different states of the quay required a large and qualified workforce, both for the supply of raw material and the construction itself. During all periods, the same elements were used: piles, small boards and planks. A quick calculation shows that for the construction of 50 m of quay revetment and dyke between 13 and 15 m^3 of oak timber was necessary. Several planks are nearly 6 m long and 0.35-0.45 m wide. It is likely that the trees were therefore chosen specifically to meet a specific need. The dendrochronological analysis indicates that some of the planks were made of trees more than 200 years old and that the large majority of planks has been sawed and not split. Felling and cutting of the branches have obviously been carried out in the forest. Nevertheless, there is no evidence where the logs have been cut, some of which weighed more than two tonnes (6-7 m long and at least 0.60 m in diameter). The transport of these heavy logs over long distances seems unlikely. The use of the River Vesle for floating was limited, because it has a low water level with rarely more than 1 m where »green« oak with a density of eight to ten cannot float easily. It can be assumed that the logs were transported by animals from the forest area where they have been cut to a place where they are debited. This procedure is mentioned several times by Ancient authors and described by D. Mulliez: »Once a tree was felled, it was necessary to guarantee its transport to a place which was accessible to a team of horses or oxen and then to a waterway or the place of further processing and use«[8]. Then it was easier to get the planks to the construction site by transporting them on wagons or on low draught boats.

Notes

1) Rollet 2016.

2) Rollet 2001a; 2001b.

3) Pierre Mathelart, Inrap.

4) Ing (laboratoire Nicolas Garnier).

5) Véronique Zech-Matterne, CNRS and Murielle Boulen, Inrap.

6) Laboratory DendroNet.

7) Allinne 2007.

8) »Une fois l'arbre abattu, il faut notamment en assurer le transport jusqu'en des lieux accessibles aux attelages, jusqu'à un cours d'eau ou jusqu'aux lieux d'utilisation«, Mulliez 1982.

References

Allinne 2007: C. Allinne, Les villes romaines face aux inondations. La place des données archéologiques dans l'étude des risques fluviaux. Géomorphologie: Relief, Processus, Environnement 13/1, 2007, 61-78. DOI: 10.4000/geomorphologie.674.

Mulliez 1982: D. Mulliez, Notes sur le transport du bois. Bulletin de Correspondance Hellénique 106/1, 1982, 107-118.

Rollet 2001a: P. Rollet, Reims (Marne) 37 rue de Venise. Document final de synthèse de fouille archéologique, Afan, SRA Champagne-Ardenne (Châlons-en-Champagne 2001).

2001b: P. Rollet, Reims (Marne) rue de l'Equerre. Bilan Scientifique Régional SRA Champagne-Ardenne (Châlons-en-Champagne 2001).

2016: P. Rollet, Aménagements antiques et médiévaux en bord de Vesle (I^e^-Ve siècle et XIVe-XVe siècle). Rapport de fouilles (Metz 2016).

Summary

The operation of the »Zac du Vieux Port«, led on a surface area of 4,000 m², enabled to discover and study about 50 m long of the antique right bank of the Vesle River. This waterway marks the western boundary of the antique town of Durocortorum, capital of the Belgic Gaul. Thanks to this localisation, added to the phreatic table proximity, organic matters, in particular wood, leather, seeds and pollen, are very well preserved. According to the results of this excavation, evolution of this area can be reconstructed since the beginning of our era until our days. Some equine animal carcass deposits, used to provide some raw material for various craft activities, have been found in a few pits dated to the second part of Augustus reign. About 15/20 AD, the river right bank is stabilised by a wooden construction that controls the waterway and a dyke has been built to preserve the place from possible floods. Quay and dyke are made of oak planks, kept vertical by many oak stakes. A street, running on from a *decumanus*, already detected in several places toward East, comes out on the quay. From the 2nd century AD, the area started to be truly urbanized: a heavier construction, in which oak is still predominant, replaces the quay. This well made work is preserved on about 1.30 m high: planks and stakes keep a thick embankment of chalk that forms a circulation space on the riverbank. In the same time, the street is equipped with a roadway, gutters and pavements. New buildings set up, saved for craft activities. These activities include little metal industry with numerous fireplaces detected on a zone of almost 400 m², textile industry with storage pits for smectic clay, loom wights, and a lot of brushes to refine woollen fabric, but also giblets food and horn transformation, leather work, or bone marrow exploitation. An impressive construction has been built since years 306/307 AD. Its walls are about 1 m of thickness, and the building lays on hundreds of oak stakes stuck in underlying clayey sediments. The building houses an ovens series, separated by low walls. These constructions have been destroyed at the turn of the 4th and 5th centuries AD.

Résumé

À Reims, l'aménagement de la « Zac du Vieux Port » (boulevard Henrot), a été précédé d'une importante fouille archéologique préventive. Au sud-ouest de la ville antique, elle couvre une superficie de 4000 m². Cette opération est la première ayant offert l'opportunité d'étudier, sur près de 50 m de long, la rive droite de la rivière Vesle durant l'Antiquité. Ce cours d'eau, sur lequel s'appuie l'enceinte du Haut-Empire, matérialise, de fait, la limite occidentale de la ville antique de Durocortorum, capitale de la province de Gaule Belgique. Cette localisation sur l'ancien lit de la rivière et la proximité de la nappe phréatique ont permis une excellente préservation des architectures en matériaux périssables. De même, la très bonne conservation des graines et des pollens fournit un matériel de qualité dont l'étude offre une réelle vision de l'alimentation et permet de distinguer la présence de produits importés. Durant la phase 1, les premières traces d'occupation apparaissent dès la seconde partie du règne d'Auguste. Les vestiges se trouvent alors dans une zone humide, occupée par les sédiments liés aux fluctuations de la rivière ou aux paléocours, et donc difficile à urbaniser par rapport au reste de la ville où le toit de la craie se trouve à une altitude bien supérieure à celle de la nappe phréatique. Les lieux sont alors peu fréquentés et seules quelques fosses de rejets artisanaux sont repérées. Vers 15/20 apr. J.-C., les premiers grands travaux vont être réalisés. La rive droite de la rivière est stabilisée par une construction en bois qui permet d'en contrôler le cours et une digue est construite pour préserver le nord de la zone d'éventuelles crues en direction de la ville. Jusque 65/70 apr. J.-C., une chaussée ou, tout au moins, une couche de craie bordée de caniveaux boisés est mise en place. Elle s'intègre parfaitement dans le maillage du réseau de rues installé dans le reste de la cité dès la période augustéenne puisqu'elle constitue le prolongement d'un decumanus déjà repéré en plusieurs points vers l'Est. À la phase 2, entre le dernier tiers du Ier et le début ou le milieu du 2e siècle apr. J.-C., on assiste à une étape importante dans l'évolution de ce secteur de la ville qui va revêtir un caractère plus « urbain ». Des travaux de grande ampleur sont entrepris. Ils vont concerner à la fois la rive droite de la rivière, avec la construction d'un nouveau quai en avant du précédent, et la zone sud où l'épandage de remblais de craie va permettre d'assainir les sédiments liés à la présence du cours d'eau. À la suite de ces travaux, la rue est équipée d'une chaussée. Un bâtiment est installé en façade de rue et à proximité de la rivière, tandis que la partie sud de la fouille voit la création des premières constructions maçonnées. À la phase 3, le quai édifié précédemment est remplacé par une nouvelle construction beaucoup plus massive dans laquelle l'utilisation du bois de chêne est une nouvelle fois privilégiée. De même, la rue est équipée d'une nouvelle bande de roulement, de caniveaux et de trottoirs. En retrait de la rivière et de la rue, de nouvelles constructions sont établies et réservées à des activités artisanales. Ces dernières concernent la petite métallurgie, avec la présence de nombreux foyers et de couches charbonneuses, et l'activité textile avec la découverte de fosses de stockage d'argile smectique, de nombreux pesons de métiers à tisser ainsi qu'une grande quantité de brosses à carder. Enfin, un imposant bâtiment est construit à partir des années 306/307 apr. J.-C. (phase 4). Ses murs, de près d'1 m de largeur, reposent sur des centaines de pieux en chêne enfoncés dans les sédiments argileux sous jacents. Ce bâtiment abrite une série de fours. Aucun indice ne permet de caractériser avec certitude la destination de cet ensemble. Ce bâtiment est détruit au tournant des 4e-5e siècles apr. J.-C.

MORGANE CAYRE

THE ROMAN QUAY OF THE SITE »LES BERTHONS« (NAINTRÉ 86)

The site »Les Berthons« belongs to the ancient urban area of Vieux-Poitiers, in the town of Naintré (dép. Vienne/F). This ancient city is situated on the right bank of the River Clain, approximately 3 km from its confluence with the River Vienne (**fig. 1**), on a site favourable for human settlement[1]. It is, amongst other things, a strategic place for trading, thanks to a direct connection to the Atlantic Ocean via the river basin of the Loire. Indeed, the River Clain flows into the River Vienne, which then joins the River Loire. Its proximity to Poitiers (dép. Vienne/F), Limonum capital of the Pictons, makes it an even more interesting site from a commercial point of view.

The Clain is a river that rises in the north of the department of the Charente before going through Poitiers, bordering the area of Vieux-Poitiers and flowing into the River Vienne. Men have always wanted to make it navigable by trying to channel it, to develop it, but without real success[2]. Today, the presence of manifold construction work has changed the shape of the river, from what it looked like during Antiquity. Therefore, the question of navigation is still unsettled. If navigation did exist between Vieux-Poitiers and Poitiers, it must have been reduced and time-limited, because of the low-water flow of the river[3].

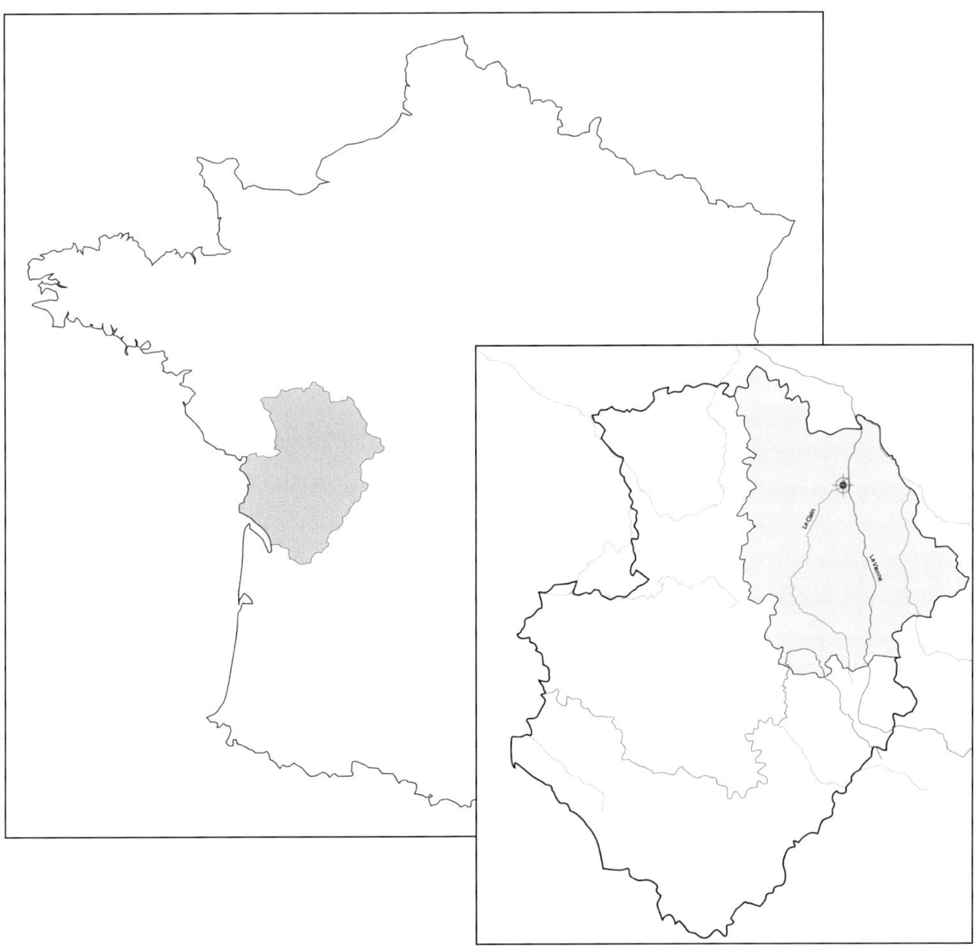

Fig. 1 Localisation of the site. – (CAD M. Cayre).

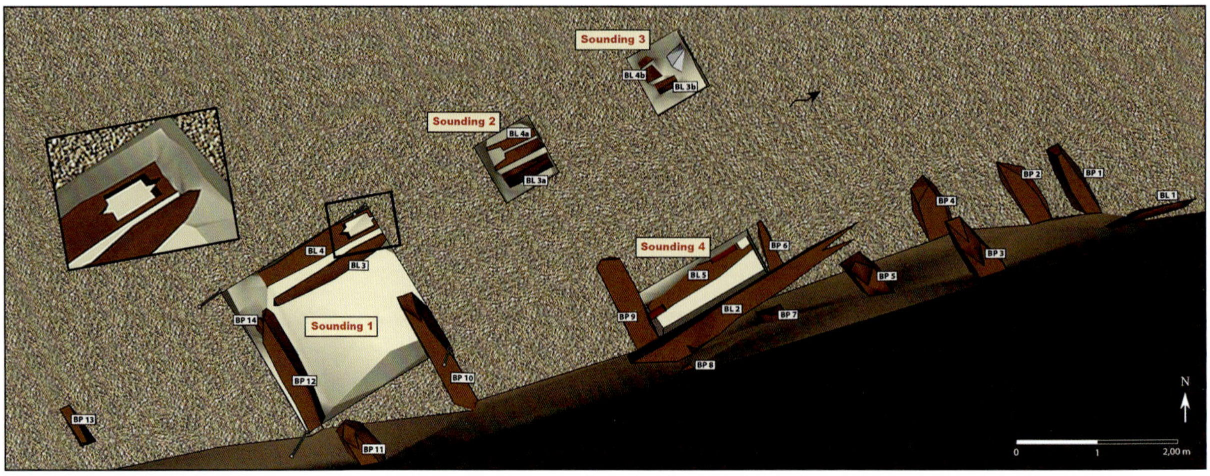

Fig. 2 First sondages in 2013-2014. – (Topography J.-F. Mariotti; CAD M. Cayre).

The ancient urban area of Vieux-Poitiers is known for its remains that extends over approximately 60 ha on the right bank of the Clain. It is crossed, on the west, by the Roman way connecting Poitiers and Tours (dép. Indre-et-Loire/F), which appears on the Peutinger's Table and on the Antonine's route. This road network, coupled with the river system, makes Vieux-Poitiers a possible transhipment area for the shipping of goods.

The knowledge of the urban organisation of the city is largely based on the observation and the interpretation of aerial photos, particularly those taken during aerial prospections led by A. Ollivier. These rectified images enabled the drawing and publishing of the urban area plan in 2000[4]. On this map, at the riverbanks, tracks are identified as a possible harbour zone. In 2012, during a survey in the area, a set of wooden beams has been discovered. These came out of the riverbank at a maximal depth of 1.20 m under the water[5]. Excavations have since followed each year until today.

In 2015, an electromagnetic survey has been carried out on the riverbanks. It has confirmed the presence of numerous structures in the field adjoining the site: routes, big buildings, circular enclosures, housing and manifold other structures. It also confirms the on-site arrival of a route coming from the urban area. This suggests that this site belongs to the urban organisation of Vieux Poitiers. If we keep in mind the possibility of a transhipment point in this area, then the big buildings may as well have been warehouses. Only an excavation of these remains would allow us to know more about them and give a proper interpretation.

PRESENTATION OF THE STRUCTURE

At the time of their discovery, there were 15 beams. 13 were perpendicular to the bank (named BP for »bois perpendiculaire« [perpendicular wood]) while two of them were approximately parallel to it (named BL for »bois longitudinal« [longitudinal wood]). Some barely came out of the sediment while others were situated between 20 and 50 cm above the bottom. These pieces of wood present a similar module, despite of their strong degree of erosion. They are relatively squared sections measuring 30 cm on the side. The visible structure then develops to approximately 10 m in length and 1 m in width from the foot of the bank. We cannot assert that it is the total length. Indeed, upstream, the current bed of the river continues to rise, possibly protecting other beams.

The layout of the wood and the length of the structure are likely to correspond to a quay structure. Moreover, the perpendicular crossing of woods on several levels leads to the consideration of the presence of

Fig. 3 Orthophotography of four caissons during the excavation of 2016. – (Photo and formatting J.-F. Mariotti).

wooden boxes that may have carried a platform over the water along the bank. In order to pursue the investigations, four campaigns of excavation were carried out in the riverbed of the Clain from 2013 to 2016 (**fig. 2**). New excavations are still in progress.

The excavation allowed identifying modifications on some pieces of wood, in particular, an assembly wood with cross-lap wood joint (visible in the junction of wood BP 8 and BL 2). Furthermore, wood BL 4 and BL 5 present, what seem to be holes for anchoring or mortised cross-pieces. Their presence could be explained by the necessity of assembling and holding the woods together by using stakes. Unfortunately, no vertical element was found to support this hypothesis; all holes for anchoring were empty. However, a stake was discovered immediately upstream from wood BP 12. With a diameter of about 30cm, it is preserved to a height of 1.30m. Its bottom end is pointed and has an iron pile shoe that could not have been extracted from the sediment. It has no connections with any of the other observed horizontal wooden elements, nor does it fit into any parts.

The presence of wooden boxes being then confirmed, we could observe different kinds of fillings. Within the wooden boxes, different kinds of fillings have been found. They seem to correspond to the organisation of the caissons in rows, extending from upstream to downstream, parallel to the bank. At the foot of the bank, the sediment is finer. It does mainly consist of alternating layers of gravel mixed with some stones. Both lines of caissons close by (channel side) present a very different alternation in their top part. Indeed, the presence of much more imposing stone blocks can be found here. Below the stones, is a level of encrusted limestone, which was hardly found in the first line of wooden boxes (**fig. 3**). Only under the last level of the horizontal woods, a unit with layers of gravel has been found in the filling of the structure. The whole structure rests directly upon the bedrock in a depth of approximately 2 m.

It is important not to separate the underwater context from the terrestrial one as a quay is made to be the junction between these two elements. This is why, as well as the underwater aspect, terrestrial excavations were undertaken since 2015 (**fig. 4**).

The first sondage has been made as close as possible to the structure discovered in the river, to find its continuation and possibly the connection with the constructions visible in aerial photos further away in the field. The following year, it has been decided to widen the zone of excavation to the continuation of longitudinal woods BL 1 and BL 2. The shoreline having a little recess in the southeast, it seemed to be more likely discovering the continuation of remains. The first archaeological layers were discovered approximately 1.10 m deep under several layers of alluvium. This first level of clay loam with numerous wooden elements (branches, twigs, splinters) also contains some rare blocks of tufa. These blocks are much more numerous in the level just below. This one is characterised by quantities of rubble stones and wooden elements, some of them being crafted (stakes, cut branches, etc.). The border of this layer seems to follow the axis of woods BL 1 and BL 2 more or less (**fig. 4**). It could then be one of the last occupation layers during the period of use of the structure. Deeper, after a succession of layers of loam, clay and gravel, an alignment of stakes had been seen in the continuation of longitudinal woods BL 1 and BL 2. As many as 15 stakes seem to separate the natural substratum on the landward side and the new layers of gravel on the riverside. The first hypothesis assumes that it is a reinforcement of the bank relating to the installation of the structure. Gravel on the riverside are very similar to the fillings of the caissons. However, this resemblance must be interpreted cautiously, as long as no correlation can be proven for sure.

So far, no evidence for a route or for some area arranged for traffic or storage has been discovered around the structure. One can simply observe a rise of the natural level towards the field.

During the various campaigns, 13 pieces of wood were sampled for dendrochronological analysis. The results enabled us to observe two successive phases of occupation.

A FIRST DEVELOPMENT AT THE BEGINNING OF THE 1ST CENTURY AD?

Dendrochronological dating of two stakes suggests a first period of activity at the beginning of the 1st century AD. These stakes are very well preserved. One of them has a complete sapwood that confirms cutting during autumn or winter 15/16 AD. The second gives a little wider set of dates between the years 18 and 22 AD. A third date comes from the stake discovered underwater with the last ring observed dating to the year 20 BC. According to dendrochronological analysis, one would have to add approximately 50 years to it, to be able to estimate a cutting date, which corresponds to cutting in the first half of the 1st century AD.

The ceramic analysis carried out during the various campaigns supports this chronological framework. The material discovered in the layers of the underwater sondage date before the middle of the 1st century AD and perhaps even to the end of the 1st century BC. The material of the more recent layers is well represented with a chronological focus in the years 40-70 AD. Thus, we have to assume that in the period of transition between the 1st century BC and the 1st century AD an alignment of stakes separated the natural substratum from an anthropogenic filling. This could be a means of retaining the bank and stabilizing it. The dating of more stakes would clarify the period of use and maintenance of this alignment and especially possible repairs.

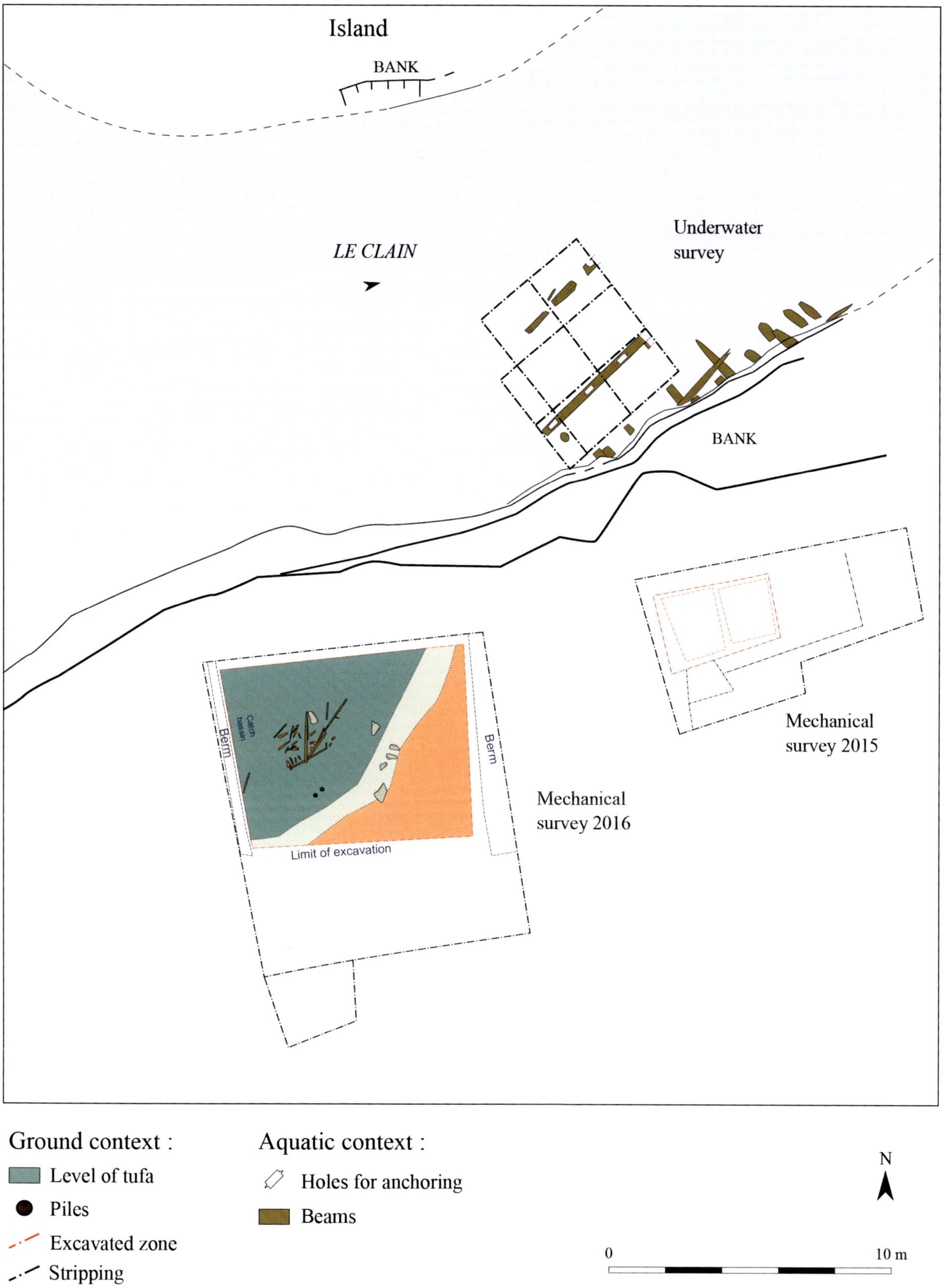

Fig. 4 Plan of the excavation after the campaign of 2016. – (Topography F. Lecendrier / C. Chouzenoux; CAD F. Lecendrier / C. Chouzenoux / M. Cayre).

This alignment would therefore be contemporary with the stake discovered in the river. At the present state of research, it is impossible to say if this isolated one is the only stake in the water, or part of a larger group or construction. The diameter of this stake (30 cm), suggests that it may have been several metres long. However, its upper end was cut already in the ancient period. We can thus imagine that at the end of the first period of use of the whole construction, the stake has been shortened to allow the installation of a new structure. Ceramic elements from the beginning of the 1st century AD and from the 40/70 AD period have been found almost everywhere in the stratigraphy, sometimes mixed with older items. Therefore, it seems possible that during a reorganization in the second period of use, layers were mixed, even inverted in some places. Some blocks of greenstone have been observed at the bottom of the underwater excavations, just before reaching the bedrock. These stones are similar to the bedrock discovered at a deeper level. Therefore, it is possible that the riverbed was deepened and backfilled with compacted sediments, which contained these fragments of bedrock. The vertical stake was put into these sediments. In approximately the upper half of this layer of compacted sediments, a great number of iron nails has been found. The sizes and forms of these nails vary considerably.

The interpretation of this first period of use is still difficult, since so many elements are tenuous, but the hypothesis of mooring pole set up to fix boats seems plausible. The exchange of goods seems to start at the beginning of the 1st century AD. Indeed, the ceramic elements of this time are largely made of fragments of crockery for storage and transport. The scarce presence of the ceramic objects from the beginning of the 1st century AD can be explained by a moderate activity that increased over time. It can also be the result of a posterior reorganization that came to disrupt the layers at the beginning of the 1st century AD. It seems that this structure has been used until the 2nd century AD.

It will be necessary expanding the excavations, to answer the question which type of boats could have moored here. Was it intended for small fishing boats, larger boats, flat-bottomed boats or even boats with a higher draft?

MAJOR CHANGES AT THE BEGINNING OF THE 2ND CENTURY AD

Dendrochronological analyses carried out on 7 of the 21 horizontal woods found underwater, point to an implementation of the structure at the beginning or in the middle of the 2nd century AD. The construction of wooden boxes reflects the desire for a longer-lasting, more stable arrangement. The reuse of old timber could perhaps explain the presence of mortised cross-pieces. At least two large pieces without a clear function within the structure point to the re-use of large-dimension construction timber. The wood BL 4 measures at least 7 m in length with none of its extremities being uncovered yet.

In the 2nd century AD, Poitiers was the capital of Gaul Aquitaine[6]. This new status may have gone hand in hand with an intensification of trade, particularly those passing in transit by the waterway from the Atlantic Arc. If navigation to Poitiers was difficult, it would be very likely that Vieux-Poitiers became a more important transhipment point – reflected by the construction of a more advanced harbour infrastructure.

The ways and means of storage and transportation are well represented in the ceramic material posterior to the year 70 AD discovered in the filling of caissons, as well as in the terrestrial sondage. As for the older period of use, this supports the hypothesis of a transhipment area, which has been used from the beginning of the 1st century AD onwards. It is still too early to compare the ceramic quantities of the various layers and therefore the various periods. Nevertheless, the structure seems to have been in use for more or less two centuries. The end of use and maintenance would then be contemporary with an assumed period of abandonment of the urban area of Vieux-Poitiers and most of the urban areas of the Pictons[7].

The whole structure can be compared with a similar construction discovered in Bordeaux (dép. Gironde/F) on the Garonne River[8]. The modules of woods and caissons are identical at both sites: wood of a square section of 30 cm and wooden boxes with a side length between 1.5 and 2 m.
However, there are still numerous unsettled questions concerning the 2nd century AD development of these arrangements. One of these questions concerns the presence of a possible ramp. During the underwater excavation, an incline of the archaeological layers as well as of the longitudinal woods BL 3 and BL 4 have been observed. This cannot be explained with the subsidence of the ground, on which the structure is located, because the timber parts rest on the bedrock. Could it be a slipway or another installation?

CONCLUSION

Finally, it has to be stated that this site has still not disclosed all of its secrets. However, two main periods of use and construction phases have been identified. A first installation has been made by vertical elements at the beginning of the 1st century AD, completed since the 2nd century AD by a second one of horizontal elements.
Nevertheless, the occupation of the bank does not necessarily require any particular arrangement and it is very likely that it already has been occupied earlier. Furthermore, the end of repair and maintenance of the structure with caissons does not necessarily mean a complete abandonment. Some ceramic elements from the 4th century AD point to a possible continuation of activity, but on a smaller scale. Afterwards, the structure was covered by alluvium and then abandoned.
The continuation of the series of terrestrial as well as underwater excavations will enable us to find out more about this development. Following the observations led on its internal structure, it would be necessary to study its top and frontage external covering, in order to verify the existence of a stonework structure, and a wooden floor. This question could only be resolved by a survey on the banks, as the upper part of the remains within the Clain have been either eroded or destroyed to improve navigation. On the contrary, the alluvial deposits that are composing the current bank may have preserved this part of the structure.
Archaeological research on the River Clain is still at the very beginning, but fieldwork has also started in Poitiers[9] and at the point of the confluence Clain-Vienne[10]. A comparative view on the results will enable us to develop a more detailed idea of the use of this river over time.

Notes

1) de Izarra 1993, 59.
2) de La Marsonnière 1897, 237-258.
3) Bourgeois 2000, 163-194.
4) Bourgeois 2000, 177.
5) Cayre 2012.
6) Gerber 2014, 14-21.
7) Bourgeois 2000, 172-173.
8) Gerber 2006, 67.
9) Survey conducted by C. Gorin.
10) Survey conducted by H. Schillinger.

References

Bourgeois 2000: L. Bourgeois, De Vieux-Poitiers à Châtellerault: Le confluent de la Vienne et du Clain de l'Antiquité au Moyen-Âge. Bulletin de la Société des Antiquaires de l'Ouest, 5e Série, 14, 2000, 163-194.

Cayre 2012: M. Cayre, Rapport de prospection subaquatique. Rivière: Clain et Vienne (Poitiers 2012).

Gerber 2014: F. Gerber, Poitiers antique. 40 ans d'archéologie préventive. Mémoire de Fouilles 2 (Poitiers 2014).

2006: F. Gerber, Chantiers archéologiques »Bourse, Saint Rémi, Jean Jaurès et Gabriel«. Des rivages garonnais de Burdigala au Port de la Mer: étude de 2000 ans de rapports entre Bordeaux et son fleuve: présentation des opérations et synthèse des principaux résultats (Pessac 2006).

de Izarra 1993: F. de Izarra, Le fleuve et les hommes en Gaule romaine (Paris 1993).

de La Marsonnière 1897: J. de La Marsonnière, La navigation du Clain. Bulletin de la Société des Antiquaires de l'Ouest 1897, 237-258.

Summary

The Roman town of Old Poitiers is localised 3 km from the confluence between the Clain and Vienne Rivers, around 25 km north of the nowadays city of Poitiers. Whether the urban network of the Roman town and its theatre are well known since some decades, the remains of a structure that may be the harbour related to the city has only been discovered in 2012. This bank arrangement takes place in the extension of a Roman road, straightly to the Roman town. Geophysical surveys, led in a field next the remains, revealed the plan of many structures. Some of them, which may be interpreted as storage facilities, had already been detected on aerial photographs.
Thanks to an underwater survey, a quay wall has been discovered. The arrangement is made of around 20 horizontal beams (some stuck, some parallel to the bank) that constitute wooden boxes filled up with pebble, stones or blocks. A stakes alignment has been discovered during excavations conducted since 2015. It extends the remains observed underwater and may belong to antique bank arrangements.
Dendrochonological dating indicates an establishment of the structure in the beginning of the 1st century AD, and a functioning until about the beginning of the 2nd century AD. The ceramic studies confirm the chronological framework and reveal the use of amount of storage containers. This last clue reinforces the harbour hypothesis.
The Old Poitiers, located at the confluence of Clain and Vienne, and directly linked to the Loire River and the Atlantic Ocean, is a crossroad of fluvial and terrestrial networks, as the road between Poitiers and Tours. Thanks to its location, the place is an ideal spot of transhipment for the antique capital of Pictons' provisioning.

Résumé

À 3 km de la confluence du Clain et de la Vienne, à environ 25 km au nord-est de la ville de Poitiers, se situe l'agglomération antique de Vieux Poitiers. Si la trame de la ville antique et son théâtre sont connus depuis quelques décennies, c'est en 2012 que sont découverts les vestiges d'une structure pouvant être le port de la ville. Cet aménagement de berge de situe dans le prolongement d'une voie venant tout droit de l'agglomération antique. Dans le champ attenant, une prospection géophysique a révélé le plan de nombreuses structures, notamment ce qui semble être de grands bâtiments pouvant correspondre à des bâtiments de stockage. Ils avaient déjà été en partie repérés lors de prospections aériennes. L'aménagement immergé découvert en 2012 est composé d'une vingtaine de bois horizontaux. Ces madriers d'une section moyenne approchant les 30 cm sont organisés de façon à créer des caissons remplis par des graviers, des pierres et de gros blocs.
Une fouille terrestre menée en parallèle à partir de 2015, a permis de mettre au jour, dans la continuité de l'aménagement repéré dans la rivière, un alignement de pieux servant très certainement à maintenir la berge à l'époque antique. Les datations dendrochronologiques effectuées suggèrent un premier aménagement au début du 1er siècle apr. J.-C., composé des éléments verticaux (terrestres et subaquatiques), puis un deuxième au début du 2e siècle apr. J.-C. constitué de madriers horizontaux. L'étude céramique appuie ces datations et met en évidence la présence de nombreux fragments de récipients de stockage et de transport.
Le Vieux Poitiers, à la confluence du Clain et de la Vienne, est en lien direct avec la Loire et l'océan Atlantique. Il est ainsi un carrefour entre routes fluviales et terrestres, avec notamment la voie reliant Poitiers à Tours. Cela en ferait l'emplacement idéal pour un point de rupture de charge visant à alimenter la capitale des Pictons, Limonum (Poitiers).

ROMAIN GUICHON

LAUSANNE, »OLYMPIC HOUSE«: DISCOVERY OF NEW HARBOUR STRUCTURES IN THE *VICUS* OF LOUSONNA

REGIONAL CONTEXT

Situated on the northern shore of Lake Geneva, the ancient Roman city of Lousonna (Vidy, Lausanne, Kt. Waadt/CH) was part of a wide network connecting southern and northern Europe. The city, pictured on the *Tabula Peutingeriana*, has been long considered as a strategic junction between water and terrestrial transportation: connecting to the alpine roads from Italy, providing access to Southern Gaul via Genava (Geneva/CH) and the Rhône River, and access to the Rhine basin through the overland route to Eburodunum (Yverdon, Kt. Waadt/CH), the Lakes of Neuchâtel and Bienne, and the River Aar (**fig. 1**)[1].

While ancient texts do not explicitly refer to local riverine transport systems, archaeological evidence and epigraphical sources provide information about these activities in the region surrounding Lousonna[2]. The professional corporations (*collegia*) of the boatmen of the Aar River and probably the Thièle River (*nautae aruranci et aramici*) had their headquarters (*schola*) at Aventicum (Avenches, Kt. Waadt/CH), the capital of the Helvetic territory[3]. Archaeological investigations at Lake Morat, situated near Avenches, have revealed evidence of a Roman harbour. At the beginning of the 1st century AD, a trapezoidal pier was constructed on

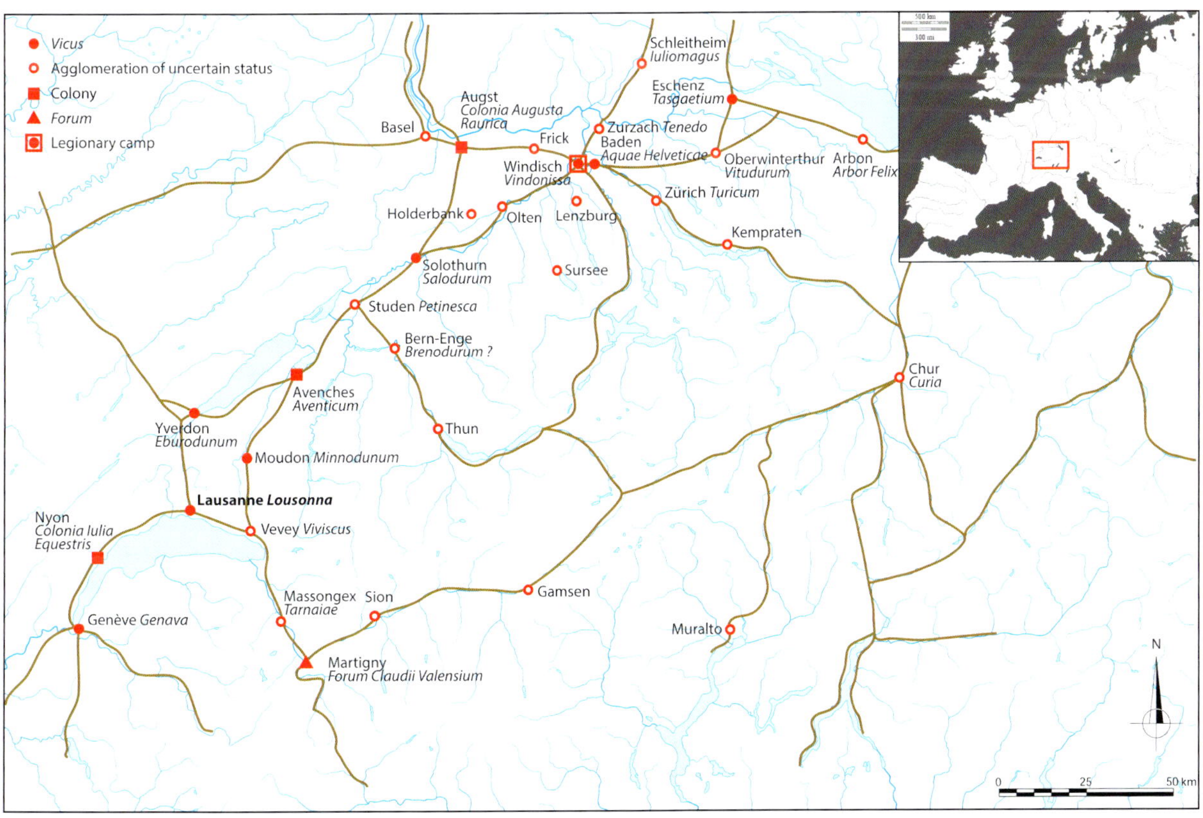

Fig. 1 Lousonna (Vidy, Lausanne): regional situation. – (Cartography Archeodunum SA).

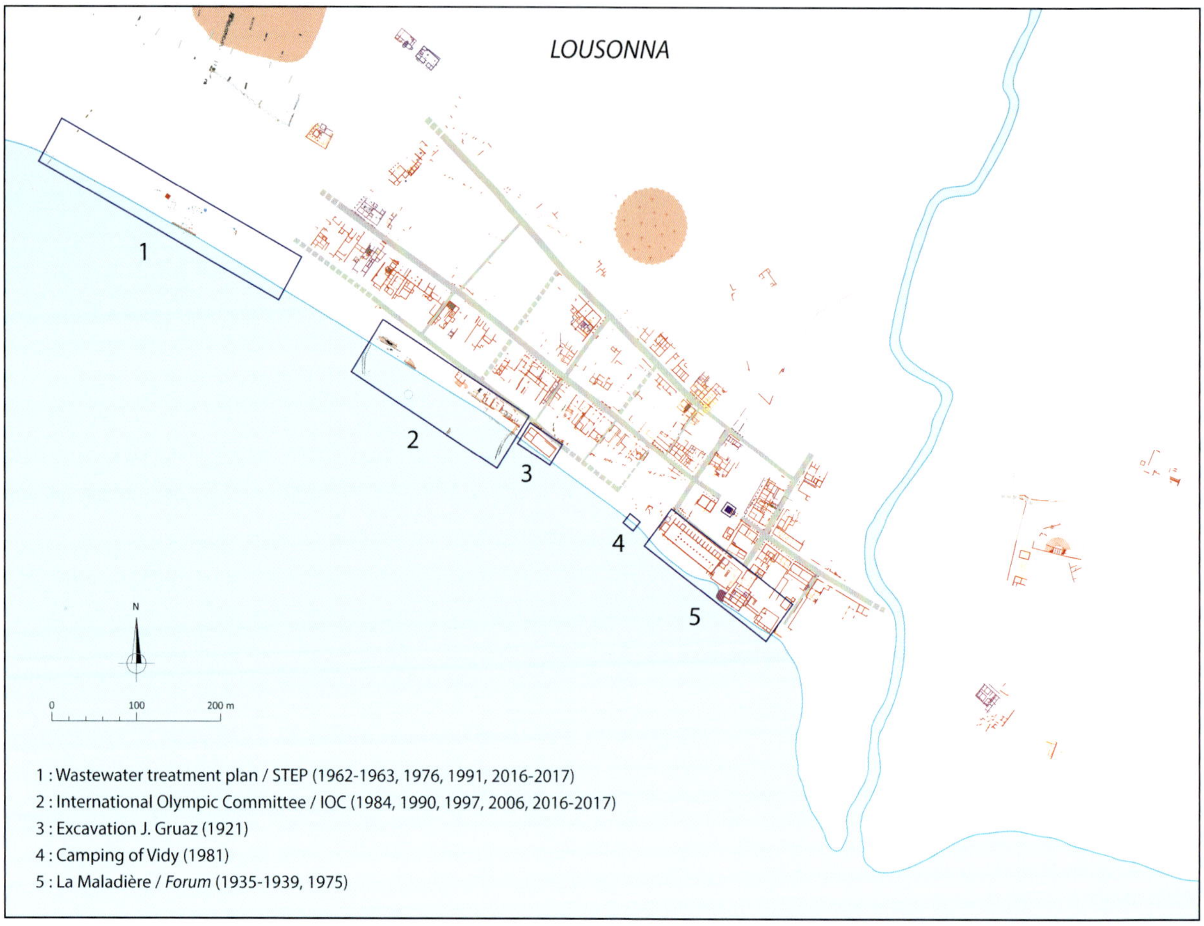

Fig. 2 Lousonna (Vidy, Lausanne): general map of Roman vestiges and location of lake bank arrangements. – (Cartography Archeodunum SA).

the shore and was directly connected to the city by a 1 km long road. During the 2nd century AD, this pier was linked to a *villa suburbana* by an 800 m long navigable canal[4]. An excavation at the terrestrial end of the canal produced various reused ship planks and a column dedicated to Silvanus and Neptune, the tutelary deities of woods and navigation. These finds suggest the presence of a shipbuilding yard in the area[5]. The discovery of three Gallo-Roman barges in Lake of Neuchâtel enables a better understanding of regional transportation methods. Two were found in Yverdon and one in Bevaix; all three are flat-bottomed barges constructed from oak planks nailed to transversal ribs[6]. These shallow draft vessels measuring 10, 20 and 22 m long were capable of transporting loads ranging from seven to ten tonnes.

Situated at the outflow of Lake of Geneva was an important harbour for the Roman city of Genava (Geneva). According to inscriptions, the city housed the headquarters of a boatmen's corporation (*ratiarii superiores*) and a customs office of the Quadragesima Galliarum[7]. The ruins of the harbour at the foot of the Saint-Pierre Hill were partially identified in the early 20th century AD and further explored in the late 1980s in the area under the Rues-Basses[8]. The first phase of construction, dated by dendrochronology between 123 and 105 BC, consists of thousands of wooden piles reinforcing the riverbank, plus those supporting a large angled pier in the middle of the bay. Due to lake level fluctuations, these structures were replaced during the 1st century AD by bankside revetments, several jetties, a building, and storage areas.

HISTORY OF THE RESEARCH ABOUT THE LOUSONNA PORT

The first mention of the Lousonna port occurs in F. Troyon's 1868 »Monuments de l'Antiquité dans l'Europe barbare«, at a time when very little was known about the Roman town: »On croit que l'ancien port était une espèce de rade creusée par la main des hommes, dont il reste à peine quelques traces entre la Chamberonnaz et les Pierrettes, et que cette partie au sud-ouest de la ville était le *ad lacum Losanele* de la carte itinéraire de Théodose«[9]. However, it was not until the beginning of the following century, during excavations carried out in 1921 near the castle of Vidy, that the first archaeological remains of the port area came to light (**fig. 2**). They consisted of a massive 38m × 14m masonry-walled building bordered by a rockfill on the south side. First interpreted as a part of a *villa rustica*, then as a public building, it is today considered as a warehouse with a protective dike[10].

The large excavations led by F. Gilliard in the years 1935-1939 at »La Maladière« revealed other waterfront structures, especially on the southern end of the *forum*, where a large hall or basilica was identified, occupying an area of 69.5m × 17m. The building is divided into two naves by a median row of masonry bases and bordered on the north by 14 small rooms, which are considered to be a market[11]. An inscription discovered in one of these rooms is dedicated to the geniuses of the emperors by the boatmen of Lake of Geneva (*nautae lacu Lemanno*), hence its designation as the »*schola* des bateliers«[12]. Immediately to the east of the basilica, a square space of 22.5m × 23m was first interpreted as a loading square[13]. However, the religious function of this area is also indicated by the presence of three central *aediculae*[14], near which was found a fragment of an altar dedicated to Neptune by the same boatmen's association[15]. The southern wall of this square or sanctuary forms a quay overlooking a masonry ramp perpendicular to the shore. This feature serves a group of buildings that could be used as both warehouses and private dwellings[16]. All these discoveries were immediately identified as the port of Lousonna, but questions remained about the organization and extent of the site. F. Gilliard noted that structures were too small to have been used as a port, as well as the absence of a protective dike[17]. Further surveys in 1975 revealed a massive rockfill wall parallel to the shore nearly 20m south of the basilica, thus providing convincing evidence for a breakwater[18].

Between the years 1984 and 1997, rescue excavations linked to the construction of the International Olympic Committee (IOC) head office revealed several harbour structures nearly 300m west of the *forum*, near the hall/warehouse discovered in 1921 (*supra*). In 1984, a row of massive wooden piles was ripped off by construction machines without archaeological supervision[19]. In 1990, a 20m long stone embankment maintained by a double row of stakes was excavated, as well as another row of piles perpendicular to the shore and the wall of a waterfront building[20]. These various structures have been dated by dendrochronology between the years 20/21 and 73 AD. The stratigraphic sequences of the lakeshore at this site were documented, showing both man-made and natural deposits. The first discoveries from the IOC site were presented in a report, including a summary of archaeological information and hypothesis about the port and shores of Lousonna[21]. Further evidence was found in 1997 at the IOC site by the discovery of a row of another 34 wooden piles, divided into two series respectively dated around the years 56 and 120 AD[22].

Between the years 1962 and 1991, various works executed on the wastewater treatment plant (STEP) also revealed wooden piled banks in the western part of the *vicus*[23]. These finds permitted the hypothesis of a port that extended the length of the *vicus*, about 1km along the Roman lakeshore[24]. In 2006, the construction of a new extension to the IOC headquarters led to a 970m² archaeological excavation located on both the foreshore and the quay. Part of a masonry building was discovered, bordered by rockfill and pile rows extending towards the lake, constructed between the years 22 and 159-160 AD. This intervention also helped to document the abandonment phase of the harbour area during Late Antiquity and its transformation into a cemetery in the Medieval period[25].

EXCAVATIONS AT THE »OLYMPIC HOUSE« SITE (2016-2017)

From February 2016 to April 2017, the construction of the »Olympic House« led to an excavation of 8,000 m² of land for the head office and underground parking[26] (**fig. 3**). In addition to the medieval and modern occupations related to the church and the castle of Vidy, the project directly impacted 200 m linear to the Roman lakeside[27]. The archaeological intervention was carried out in stages, each area being excavated according to the advancement of the construction work. The archaeological information is currently being analyzed, but the first research results have been published as punctual notices and in an article[28]. The precise chronology of the remains has yet to be established and will depend upon the results of the dendrochronological analysis of the wooden pieces. The following section presents the general discoveries from the Roman quay arrangements, with a particular focus on aspects related to harbour activities.

The lake banks are entirely strengthened with rockfill maintained by hundreds of vertical oak piles and posts, behind which occasional preserved horizontal planks or baulks were found. To the northwest, the first quay consisted of two juxtaposed foundations measuring at least 32 m × 8 m, with a right angle return on the east side. The remains of two rows of piles with divergent orientations suggest that the area had been transformed several times. The western section of the quay contained a deposit of around 60 complete amphorae, interpreted as a drainage system installed at the end of the 2nd century AD or the beginning of the 3rd century AD. At least four other similar constructions with amphorae are known in Lousonna[29] and various parallels are attested elsewhere in similar fluvial contexts (Lyon/Lugdunum [F], Mainz/Mogontiacum [D], etc.)[30]. The foundation for this quay may have had a wooden deck and possibly served as a landing stage linked to the pier excavated nearby (*infra*).

About 10 m to the east of the first quay is a second rectangular quay foundation measuring 16 m × 7 m, consisting of two rows of piles parallel to the shore with a right angle return at each end (**fig. 4**). Along the front of the structure, a half-trunk of a resinous tree was preserved behind the wooden piles. Remains of other timbers along the sides indicate that this foundation was a box construction, retaining stones and layers of backfill deposited in the center of the structure. In the earth and stone rubble surface of the foundation, the negative imprints of joists and beams with iron clamps were conserved *in situ*. These elements suggest a wooden plank platform similar to the reconstruction proposed at Vindonissa (Windisch, Kt. Aargau/CH)[31].

To the west of the castle of Vidy, a third quay platform was found and is a continuation of the ruins discovered in 2006. The foundation measures 19 m × 9 m and was constructed of five rows of wooden piles and posts roughly spaced and with stone backfill. The chronology and exact reconstruction of this complex structure have not yet been determined. Behind the quay a semi-excavated building of 4 m × 4 m is located, that housed well-preserved latrines, consisting of dry-stone and compacted earth walls, as well as six peripheral posts, which would have supported a plank floor. The bottom and edges of the pit were lined by vegetable fiber matting nailed to three circular section joists and possibly functioned as a barrier for facilitating emptying the latrines of accumulated material. In the same pit several amphorae, that probably had a secondary purpose as urinals, were found. A 9 m long timber lined drain carried liquid waste and overflow to the lake. The pit was gradually filled by several organic layers and during the last phase of use, a barrel placed in a wooden crate in the center of the space served as a toilet. This construction is comparable to a quadrangular well found near the *forum* of Lousanna[32], as well as various other excavated latrines in the region[33]. To the east of the latrines is a narrow building with at least three small rooms being heated by a hypocaust. This building and the latrines may be part of the same spa complex.

To the east of the quay was a 40 m long piled embankment wall associated with several wood and earth buildings dating from the Augusto-Tiberian period (posts, bottom plates, hearths, etc.). These occupation levels were destroyed in the middle of the 1st century AD by the construction of a large waterfront ware-

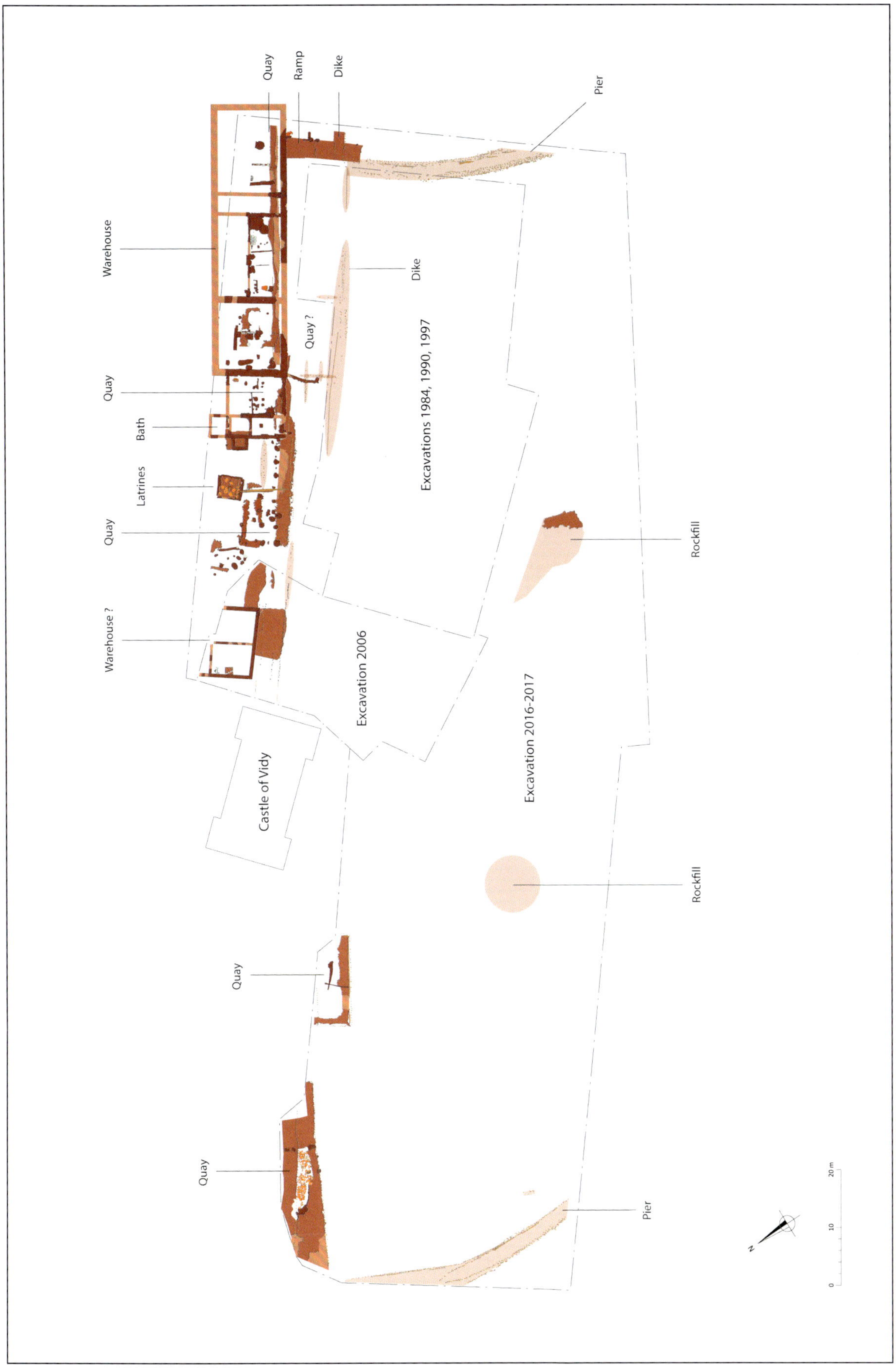

Fig. 3 Lausanne, International Olympic Committee: general map of Roman vestiges. – (Cartography Archeodunum SA).

Fig. 4 Lausanne, »Olympic House«: **a** general view of a quay foundation. – **b** detail of the fastening system. – **c** Windisch/Vindonissa: reconstruction of a wooden platform. – (a-b Photography Archeodunum SA; c Pauli-Gabi 2002, fig. 12).

house or *horreum* occupying at least 43 m × 13.50 m (**fig. 5**). The building is divided into two naves by a middle row of masonry bases, with an internal division wall in the western section delimiting a square space of 13.50 m × 13.50 m. The beaten clay levels below the foundations' height are an indication that a raised plank floor was probably used in this building as protection against humidity. Buried in the southwest corner of the building was a wooden box containing six ceramic and glass vessels, perhaps placed there as a foundation deposit. The warehouse could be accessed from the west via the quay or directly from the lake by a platform or small jetties protected by wooden dikes. To the southeast, the warehouse was also served by a ramp extending into the lake and by a long pier (*infra*). This *horreum* is directly comparable to the »hall« discovered to the east in 1921, as well as being similar to the basilica of the Lousonna *forum*. This type of warehouse with central pillars also appears at other ports, like those at Ratiatum (Rezé, dép. Loire-Atlantique) in France or Aquileia (prov. Udine) in Italy[34].

Two piers were discovered 190 m apart from each other on each edge of the excavation site (**fig. 6**). The two structures, one at the east, the other to the west, are quite similar in size and construction: 42 and 37 m long, with an average width of 3-3.5 m, consisting of wooden pile walls with rock backfill. Both angles towards the east and have longitudinal reinforcing timbers, among which are re-used ship planks. The outer wall of the eastern pier has reinforcement piles while the western pier is protected by a rockfill. Most of the piles are sunk deep into the natural marl; some have a preserved length of up to 3.40 m. The degraded condition of the wood and the collapse of the stone structures hinder a clear reconstruction of the piers, but it is possible that a wooden decking was used.

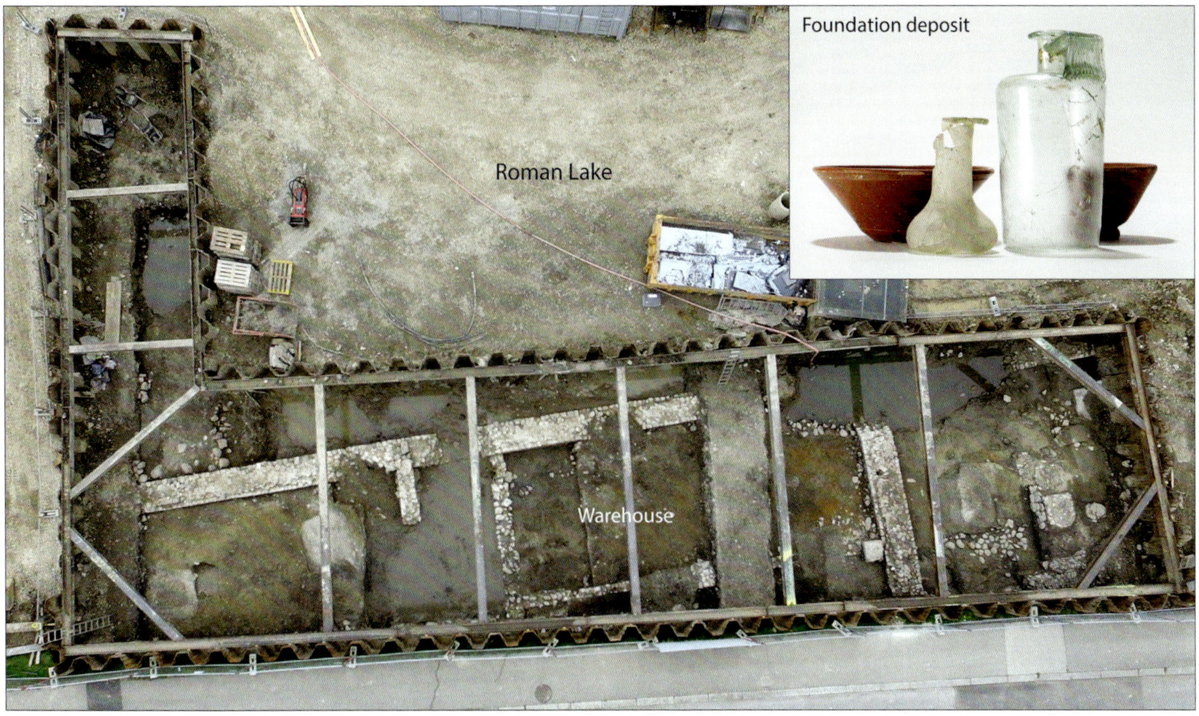

Fig. 5 Lausanne, »Olympic House«: aerial view of the warehouse/*horreum* and detail of the supposed foundation deposit. – (Photography Archeodunum SA, Y. André/MCAH).

According to the recent assessment by C. Wawrzinek, at least eleven river or lakeside harbours are equipped with piers in the Western Roman Provinces, including Avenches and Geneva (*supra*)[35]. Both jetties in Lausanne were built using techniques quite similar to those described by Vitruvius for maritime harbours[36]. These structures enclosed areas protected from the southwest winds and probably served as landing stages during periods of low waters. Before the correction of the Rhône River in the late 19th century AD, Lake of Geneva was subjected to seasonal variations of up to 2 m in the water level – due to the torrential regime of its tributaries – meaning the shore was alternatively dry and inundated[37]. In the bay of Vidy, the average slope of the beach is about 3 %, which means that a one-metre drop of the water level must have exposed the shoreline a further 30 m[38]. The space between the two jetties could have worked as a dry harbour during low tide periods. The occasional presence of a stone and tiles embankment observed on the foreshore testifies to maintenance in this area. During the periods of high tide, the area could have functioned as a navigable port. Two rockfills were discovered about 30-40 m in front of the quays, and are placed equally between the piers, these presumably protected and indicated the navigation channels. The reconstruction of a true enclosed harbour basin is possible if, in the southern terrain, which is outside of the excavation field, the piers would extend or there would be a system of protective dikes.

The Flon River flanks the Vidy site on the eastern side and the Chambronne River on the western side; both contribute to the formation of significant alluvial cones. The piers, dikes, embankments, etc. were certainly placed also to prevent the bay from silting up. However, stratigraphic profiles show that silting was already a problem during the Roman period. To the west of the site, for example, an alternation of man-made embankments and natural sandy deposits was recorded as being 1.20 m high in front of the quay and covered by a layer of the dark earth during the Late Antiquity. This silting phenomenon is observed all over the site, sometimes up to 2 m high. The first geomorphological observations revealed lacustrine peat on these sands, suggesting a slow process, but exceptional events cannot be ruled out. A significant tsunami caused by an immense mountain avalanche on the eastern part of Lake of Geneva in 563 AD (Tauredunum)[39] destroyed

Fig. 6 Lausanne, »Olympic House«: general views of the piers. – (Photography Archeodunum SA).

bridges in Geneva and a 13 m high wave broke along the Lausanne coast[40]. By the end of the 7th century or the beginning of the 8th century AD, the site was reoccupied, with a cemetery surrounded by wooden buildings[41]. All these structures were implanted in the black soil layers deposited on the lacustrine sand previously mentioned. Although the existence of a port is presumed at Vidy during the Early Middle Ages[42], the nature of the settlement discovered at the IOC still needs to be clarified.

RESEARCH PROSPECTS

After a century of intermittent research in Lousonna, the 2016-2017 IOC excavations reopened a new window on the Roman shores at Lausanne-Vidy. The excavation results confirm the presence of harbour structures west of the forum. The presence of a pier and a landing stage further west of the IOC excavation also reinforces the hypothesis of an extension of these arrangements in the western part of the *vicus*. The Roman town was built along a central road, leading some researchers to qualify it as a »street town« but with the recently documented port installations running the length of the site, it could equally be considered as a »port town«. The resumption of the typo-chronological work initiated by S. Berti on the *forum*, IOC and STEP sites is essential for proving this hypothesis.
Regarding the excavations of the »Olympic House« site, the phasing and dating of the vestiges are currently underway. Within the framework of a future excavation report, the material studies should also provide

additional information about the chronology and function of the harbour area. Among the 32,000 pottery sherds excavated, the presence of numerous amphorae provides information about commercial activities at the site. The considerable quantity of building elements and animal bones, plus the small finds in metal and glassware are also to be presented in the report, providing both quantitative and qualitative data[43].
The multitude of wooden artefacts preserved by the high water table is remarkable: the post-excavation inventory includes at least 1,300 piles and posts, plus a hundred various elements (planks, baulks, barrels, etc.). The current study is multidisciplinary and brings together several researchers from different institutions. The dendrochronological analysis of the pieces should eventually constitute an important regional reference for the Roman period[44]. The techno-typological study (working traces, manufacturing techniques, etc.) aims to document the variety of parts used, leading in particular to a plausible architectural reconstruction of the wooden structures[45]. Finally, a dendro-ecological approach is proposed for the site and the *vicus*, with the aim of evaluating the human impact on the surrounding forests (forestry harvesting and practices, environmental usages, access routes, etc.)[46].
The geomorphological study of the site should also eventually make it possible to specify the use dynamics of the harbour area[47]. It will include several stratigraphic profiles documented in each excavated area, as references from the top of the quays to the lower lake levels. Sediment samples and micro-morphological analysis will constitute a complementary data source providing information on sedimentary dynamics specific to fluvio-lacustrine environments. Issues relating to the level of the lake, its seasonal and secular variations, and the processes of silting and the abandon of the Roman structures, are among the topics to be explored. The results of the geological study could be compared to those of the dendrochronological analysis, possibly palynological and carpological, for studying the paleoenvironment of the port of Lousonna.

Notes

1) Flutsch 2010, 78-79. – Abetel 2011.
2) Haldimann 2002.
3) Meylan Krause/Delbarre-Bärtschi 2013.
4) Bonnet 1982. – Castella 2013.
5) Arnold 2009.
6) Arnold 1992; 2013.
7) Haldimann 2002.
8) Bonnet et al. 1989.
9) Troyon 1868, 48: »We believe that the ancient port was a sort of a harbour dug out by hand, of which remains a few traces between Chamberonnaz and the Pierrettes, and that this part to the south west of the town was the *ad lacum Losanele* of Theodosius' travel map«.
10) Gruaz 1921, 247-249. – Kaenel 1977, 24.
11) Gilliard 1943. – Kaenel/Tuor 1978.
12) Collart/Van Berchem 1939: »*Numinibus Aug(ustorum) nautae [lac]u Lemanno qui Leuso[nn]ae consistunt, l(oco) [d(ato)] d(ecreto) d(ecurionum)*«.
13) Gilliard 1947.
14) Bögli/Sitterding 1963, 116-122.
15) Collart/Van Berchem 1941: »*Neptuno, nautae Leuson(enses) ex inpen[sa…]*«.
16) Bögli/Sitterding 1963, 108-115.
17) Gilliard 1947, 198: »Orienté comme il l'était, le petit port était exposé aux vents du sud-ouest et risquait d'être ensablé peu à peu«; »Oriented as it was, the small harbour was exposed to southwest winds and could be gradually silted up«.
18) Kaenel/Klausener/Fehlmann 1980, 138-140.
19) Abetel 1986.
20) Berti/May Castella 1992.
21) Berti 1992.
22) May Castella/Reymond 1998.
23) Interventions in 1962, 1963, 1976 and 1991. Cf. Berti 1992, 13-22.
24) Tarpin et al. 1999, 40: »Le ›port‹ n'était donc sans doute qu'une plage située au fond d'une baie encadrée par les deux deltas«; »The ›port‹ was probably a beach at the bottom of a bay flanked by two deltas«.
25) Henny/Steiner 2007. – Steiner et al. 2008.
26) Archaeological investigations by Archeodunum SA, on mandate of the International Olympic Committee, under the authorization and supervision of the Archéologie cantonale vaudoise.
27) Julita/Guélat 2015. – Guichon et al. 2018.
28) Guichon/Thorimbert/Bohny 2017.

29) Bögli/Sitterding 1963, 135. 149. 154. 184.

30) Arlaud et al. 1998. – Ehmig 2002.

31) Pauli-Gabi 2002.

32) Kaenel/Klausener/Fehlmann 1980, 95-97.

33) Bouet 2009, 106-108: Oberwinterthur, Eschenz, Augst, Besançon, Brumath, Strasbourg, Oberaden, etc.

34) Arthuis et al. 2010; Wawrzinek 2014, pl. 20.

35) Wawrzinek 2014, pl. 4: Chester, Velsen, Xanten, Pommeroeul, Mainz, Straubing, Seeon-Seebruck, Avenches, Genève, Padenghe.

36) Vitr. V, 12.

37) Tarpin et al. 1999, 33-34.

38) Tarpin et al. 1999, 40. Cf. also Gallay/Kaenel 1981 for the relation between the archaeological evidence and the geological situation of Lousonna/Vidy (system of the glaciolacustrine terraces, evolution of the levels of the lake during the Holocene, etc.).

39) Marius d'Avenches, Chroniques, année 563. – Greg. Tur. Franc. IV, 31.

40) Kremer/Simpson/Girardclos 2012.

41) Steiner et al. 2015. – Hervé/Guichon 2017.

42) According to the story of the transport of Saint-Gorgon's relics in 846 AD (Acta Sanctorum Martii, t. II): »Nous sommes arrivés au port qui se trouve à deux milles environ de Lausanne…«; »We arrived at the port wich is about two miles from Lausanne…«. Cf. Steiner et al. 2015, 52.

43) Pottery: Sylvie Barrier (Archeodunum SA, UNIL); metal: Aurélie Crausaz (Archeodunum SA, UNIL); glass: Francesca Pirrami (UNIL).

44) Jean-Pierre Hurni and Bertrand Yerly (Laboratoire Romand de Dendrochronologie).

45) Marc Haller and Anne-Lyse Gentizon Haller (Archéologie Expérimentale et Techniques Anciennes).

46) François Blondel (Université Bourgogne Franche-Comté – Dijon, UMR 6298 ArTéHIS).

47) Michel Guélat (Sediqua Géosciences sàrl).

Sources

Marius d'Avenches, Chroniques: J. Favrod, La Chronique de Marius d'Avenches (455-581). Texte, traduction et commentaire. Cahiers Lausannois d'Histoire Médiévale 4 (Lausanne 1991).

Greg. Tur. Franc.: Gregorii episcopi Turonensis historiarum libri X: Fasc. I, Lib. I-V. Curavit B. Krusch / W. Levison. Monumenta Germaniae historica. Scriptores rerum Merovingicarum 1/2 (Hannoverae 1937).

Vitr.: Vitruve, De l'architecture. Livre V. Traduction C. Saliou. Collection des Universités de France: Serie Latine 393 (Paris 2009).

References

Abetel 1986: E. Abetel, Vidy, Siège du C.I.O. Annuaire de la Société Suisse de Préhistoire et d'Archéologie 69, 1986, 269.

2011: E. Abetel, Ports et relations commerciales sur les cours d'eau en Helvétie. In: R. Bedon (ed.), Macella, tabernae, portus. Les structures matérielles de l'économie en Gaule romaine et dans les régions voisines. Caesarodunum XLIII-XIV (Limoges 2011) 147-178.

Arlaud et al. 1998: C. Arlaud / E. Bertrand / F. Laubenheimer / J.-M. Lurol, Un vide sanitaire rue Chidebert à Lyon. In: F. Laubenheimer (ed.), Les amphores en Gaule. Production et circulation II (Besançon 1998) 193-204.

Arnold 1992: B. Arnold, Batellerie gallo-romaine sur le lac de Neuchâtel 1-2. Archéologie Neuchâteloise 12-13 (Sainte-Blaise 1992).

2009: B. Arnold, A Gallo-Roman naval building yard at Avenches/En Chaplix. In: R. Bockius (ed.), Between the Seas. Transfer and exchange in nautical technology. Proceedings of the eleventh International Symposium on Boat and Ship Archaeology (Mainz 25-29 September 2006). RGZM – Tagungen 3 (Mainz 2009) 167-175.

2013: B. Arnold, Les embarcations gallo-romaines de la région des Trois-Lacs: un missing link entre Méditerranée et mer du Nord. In: Delbarre-Bärtschi/Hataway 2013, 24-37.

Arthuis et al. 2010: R. Arthuis / D. Guitton / M. Monteil / J. Mouchard / O. de Perreti, Archéologie portuaire estuarienne entre Loire et Seine: principaux résultats et questions d'ordre méthodologique. L'exemple des sites antiques d'Aizier (Eure) et de Rezé (Loire-Atlantique). In: L. Hugot / L. Tranoy (eds), Actes de la Journée d'études sur les structures portuaires de l'arc atlantique dans l'Antiquité (bilan et perspectives de recherches), La Rochelle 2008. Aquitania, Supplément 18 (Bordeaux 2010) 61-82.

Berti 1992: S. Berti, Les aménagements riverains et le niveau du lac Léman à l'époque romaine. Les interventions archéologiques du CIO et de la STEP (1990-1991). Rapport de fouille (Lausanne 1992).

Berti/May Castella 1992: S. Berti / C. May Castella, Lausanne VD, Lousonna-Vidy, Comité International Olympique. Annuaire de la Société Suisse de Préhistoire et d'Archéologie 75, 1992, 217.

Bögli/Sitterding 1963: H. Bögli / M. Sitterding, Lousonna. Les fouilles entreprises jusqu'en 1963 dans le vicus romain de Lausanne (Vidy). Revue Historique Vaudoise 71, 1963, 97-186.

Bonnet et al. 1989: Ch. Bonnet / G. Zoller / Ph. Broillet / M.-A. Haldimann / Ch.-A. Baud / Ch. Kramar / Ch. Simon / C. Olive / Y. Billaud, Les premiers ports de Genève. Archéologie Suisse 12, 1989, 2-24.

Bonnet 1982: F. Bonnet, Les ports romains d'Aventicum. Archéologie Suisse 5, 1982, 127-131.

Bouet 2009: A. Bouet, Les latrines dans les provinces gauloises, germaniques et alpines. Gallia, Supplément 59 (Paris 2009).

Castella 2013: D. Castella, Aventicum, côté lac. In: Delbarre-Bärtschi/Hataway 2013, 48-55.

Collart/Van Berchem 1939: P. Collart / D. Van Berchem, Inscriptions de Vidy. Revue Historique Vaudoise 47, 1939, 127-145.

1941: P. Collart / D. Van Berchem, Inscriptions de Vidy (Deuxième série). Revue Historique Vaudoise 49, 1941, 59-65.

Delbarre-Bärtschi/Hataway 2013: S. Delbarre-Bärtschi / N. Hataway (eds), Entre Lacs. Le Pays des Trois-Lacs à l'époque romaine (Avenches 2013).

Ehmig 2002: U. Ehmig, Deux assainissements avec amphores à Mayence (Germanie supérieure). Gallia 59, 2002, 233-251.

Flutsch 2010: L. Flutsch, L'époque romaine ou la Méditerrannée au nord des Alpes (Lausanne 2010).

Gallay/Kaenel 1981: A. Gallay / G. Kaenel, Repères archéologiques pour une histoire des terrasses du Léman. Archives Suisses d'Anthropologie Générale 45, 1981, 129-194.

Gruaz 1921: J. Gruaz, Fouilles d'Allaman et de Vidy (1920-1921). Revue Historique Vaudoise 29, 1921, 240-249.

Gilliard 1943: F. Gilliard, Un quartier de Lousonna à la Maladière (Vidy). Le marché et la grande halle (ou basilique). Revue Historique Vaudoise 51, 1943, 2-12.

1947: F. Gilliard, Un quartier de Lousonna à la Maladière (Vidy). Aux abords du marché – Une place de débarquement. Revue Historique Vaudoise 55, 1947, 192-199.

Guichon/Thorimbert/Bohny 2017: R. Guichon / S. Thorimbert / J. Bohny, Lausanne VD, Vidy, Comité International Olympique. Annuaire d'Archéologie Suisse 100, 2017, 235-236.

Guichon et al. 2018: R. Guichon / S. Barrier / J. Bohny / A. Crausaz / C. Hervé / A. Pignolet / S. Thorimbert, Du nouveau sur les origines et le port de Lousonna. La tranchée SEL et le chantier Maison Olympique. Archéologie vaudoise (AVd). Chroniques 2017, Archéologie cantonale (Lausanne 2018) 54-69.

Haldimann 2002: M.-A. Haldimann, Le commerce. In: L. Flutsch / U. Niffeler / F. Rossi (eds), La Suisse du Paléolithique à l'aube du Moyen-Âge. V: Époque romaine (Bâle 2002) 187-196.

Henny/Steiner 2007: C. Henny / L. Steiner, Lausanne VD, Lousonna-Vidy, Comité International Olympique. Annuaire d'Archéologie Suisse 90, 2007, 168-169.

Hervé/Guichon 2017: C. Hervé / R. Guichon, Lausanne-Lousonna (VD, Suisse): du vicus à la capitale d'évêché. Association Française d'Archéologie Mérovingienne, Bulletin de liaison 41, 2017, 52-54.

Julita/Guélat 2015: B. Julita / M. Guélat, Lausanne Vidy. Nouveau campus CIO. Rapport final de la campagne de sondages archéologiques et suivi sédimentologique (Gollion 2015).

Kaenel 1977: G. Kaenel, Lousonna. La promenade archéologique de Vidy. Guides Archéologiques de la Suisse 9 (Lausanne 1977).

Kaenel/Tuor 1978: G. Kaenel / A. Tuor, Les basiliques romaines de Nyon et Vidy. Archéologie Suisse 1/2, 1978, 79-83.

Kaenel/Klausener/Fehlmann 1980: G. Kaenel / M. Klausener / S. Fehlmann, Nouvelles recherches sur le vicus gallo-romain de Lousonna (Vidy-Lausanne). Lousonna 2 = Cahiers d'Archéologie Romande 18 (Lausanne 1980).

Kremer/Simpson/Girardclos 2012: K. Kremer / G. Simpson / S. Girardclos, Giant Lake Geneva tsunami in 563 AD. Nature Geoscience 5, 2012, 756-757.

May Castella/Reymond 1998: C. May Castella / S. Reymond, Lausanne VD, Lousonna-Vidy, Comité International Olympique. Annuaire de la Société Suisse de Préhistoire et d'Archéologie 81, 1998, 297.

Meylan Krause/Delbarre-Bärtschi 2013: M.-F. Meylan Krause / S. Delbarre-Bärtschi, Commerce et transport de marchandises. In: Delbarre-Bärtschi/Hataway 2013, 38-47.

Pauli-Gabi 2002: T. Pauli-Gabi, Ein Flusshafen in Vindonissa. Gesellschaft Pro Vindonissa, Jahresbericht 2002, 27-36.

Steiner et al. 2008: L. Steiner (dir.) / C. Henny / B. Julita, Lausanne Vidy, CIO, fouilles de 2006. Description des structures romaines (Gollion 2008).

2015: L. Steiner (dir.) / S. Freudiger / A. Gallay / C. Hervé / Y. Mühlemann, Lausanne-Vidy, CIO 2006. Rapport sur les fouilles de la nécropole médiévale (Gollion 2015).

Tarpin et al. 1999: M. Tarpin / S. Berti / M.-A. Haldimann / F. Rossi / L. Steiner, Le bassin lémanique gallo-romain. Gallia 56, 1999, 33-44.

Troyon 1868: F. Troyon, Monuments de l'Antiquité dans l'Europe barbare. Suivis d'une statistique des antiquités de la Suisse occidentale et d'une notice sur les antiquités du canton de Vaud. Société d'Histoire de la Suisse Romande: Mémoires et Documents 25 (Lausanne 1868).

Wawrzinek 2014: Ch. Wawrzinek, In portum navigare. Römische Häfen an Flüssen und Seen (Berlin 2014).

Summary

The ancient Roman city of Lousonna (Vidy, Lausanne), on the northern shore of the Lake Geneva, has been long considered as a strategic crossroad between Italy, Southern Gaul and the Rhine basin. Regional archaeological evidence and epigraphical sources provide information about an important fluvio-lacustrine transport network, notably in Aventicum (Avenches) and Genava (Geneva). At Lousonna, the excavations at the *forum* in 1934-1939 revealed a large hall or basilica, a square and a ramp, interpreted as a port complex led by the boatmen of the Lake Geneva (*nautae lacu Lemanno*). Between the years 1984 and 2006, several excavations at the International Olympic Committee (IOC) head office came to light rows of wooden piles, stone embankments and masonry-walled constructions, immediately to the west of a long *horreum* discovered in 1921. Various works executed on the wastewater treatment plant (STEP) also revealed wooden piled banks in the western part of the *vicus*. From February 2016 to April 2017, the construction of the »Olympic House« led to a new excavation of 8,000 m² on the Roman lakeside. The banks are entirely strengthened with rockfill and hundreds oak piles. Occasional preserved planks or baulks, imprints of beams and iron clamps suggest the reconstruction of wooden plank platforms. A large warehouse is built in the middle of the 1st century AD, bordered on the west side by latrines and a thermal area. Two long piers discovered 190 m apart from each other enclosed an area protected from the southwest winds and probably served as landing stages during periods of low water. The sector is partly abandoned during the Late Antiquity, while the bay silting up already started, then reoccupied by the end of the 7th century or the beginning of the 8th century AD, with a cemetery surrounded by wooden buildings. The multidisciplinary study of the remains is ongoing (structures, ceramic, small finds, wood elements, geomorphology, etc.) and should contribute ultimately to a better knowledge of the Roman shores of Lake Geneva.

Résumé

L'agglomération antique de Lousonna (Vidy, Lausanne) est située sur un carrefour fluvio-terrestre dont on suppose depuis longtemps la vocation portuaire. Idéalement placée sur la rive nord du lac Léman, au débouché de routes alpines vers l'Italie et en amont de la voie du Rhône vers la Gaule méridionale, la ville était également une rupture de charge naturelle vers le bassin du Rhin, par l'intermédiaire d'une voie de portage conduisant à Eburodunum (Yverdon). Les sources épigraphiques et archéologiques régionales permettent de restituer un réseau de transport fluvio-lacustre développé, notamment à partir des villes d'Aventicum (Avenches) et de Genava (Genève) qui abritaient des corporations de bateliers et des infrastructures portuaires. Les fouilles menées à Lousonna depuis près d'un siècle ont également livré des vestiges liés au port ou plus largement à l'aménagement des berges. Dans les années 1934-1939, la fouille du *forum* a révélé en particulier une grande halle ou basilique, une place et une rampe de halage interprétées comme un complexe portuaire contrôlé par les Nautes du Léman (*nautae lacu Lemanno*). Entre 1984 et 2006, plusieurs fouilles réalisées sur le site du Comité International Olympique ont mis en évidence d'autres aménagements riverains (alignements de pieux, enrochements, pontons, constructions maçonnées), dans une zone où avait déjà été repéré un grand *horreum* en 1921. Les recherches archéologiques menées depuis 1962 sur le site de la station d'épuration (STEP) ont montré que les berges étaient également aménagées à l'ouest de la ville.
À l'occasion de nouveaux travaux d'agrandissement du siège du CIO en 2016 et 2017 (construction de la « Maison olympique » et d'un parking souterrain), une intervention archéologique a permis d'explorer le rivage antique sur une surface de 8000 m². Les berges sont entièrement renforcées par des enrochements maintenus par des centaines de pieux en chêne, derrière lesquels sont parfois conservés des planches ou des madriers horizontaux. Des empreintes de poutres et de poteaux internes, avec divers éléments de fixation, suggèrent la restitution de plateformes planchéiées. Un petit bâtiment semi-enterré abrite des latrines probablement liées à un espace thermal et un grand entrepôt à piliers centraux est installé dans le courant du 1er siècle apr. J.-C. sur des aménagements de berge plus anciens. Cet *horreum* était accessible par le quai ou directement depuis le lac au moyen d'appontements secondaires. Deux grandes jetées découvertes à 190 m de distance l'une de l'autre devaient délimiter un bassin de navigation protégé des vents du sud-ouest et fonctionner comme débarcadères en période de basses eaux. Les grèves aménagées par des épandages de pierres et de tuiles pouvaient aussi fonctionner comme un port d'échouage. Le secteur est désaffecté durant l'Antiquité tardive, lorsque les rives du lac étaient déjà en partie ensablées, puis réoccupé à la fin du 7e siècle ou au début du 8e siècle apr. J.-C. sous la forme d'un habitat sur poteaux bordant un cimetière. L'étude pluridisciplinaire de ce gisement est en cours (mobiliers, éléments en bois, géomorphologie, etc.) et devrait à terme contribuer à une meilleure connaissance de l'occupation antique des rives du lac Léman.

MARC GUYON · LAURE MEUNIER

STUDY AND CONSERVATION OF LYON SAINT-GEORGES 4, A FLAT-BOTTOM BOAT FROM THE 2ND CENTURY AD

Several levels of the fossilised right bank of the River Saône located in Lyon (dép. Rhône/F) were excavated between October 2002 and June 2004, and revealed 16 wrecks dated from the 1st century to the 18th century AD (**fig. 1**). The Institute of Preventive Archaeological Research (Inrap), at the request of the Ministry of Culture, carried out the excavation of this harbour site, found on the future Parc Saint-Georges' car park. Grégoire Ayala was the manager of this huge archaeological operation and Marc Guyon was responsible for the study of the wrecks. The operation was conducted in a cofferdam using traditional methods of terrestrial archaeology, on a surface of approximately 4,000 m^2 and a depth of 10 m[1].

Six of the 16 shipwrecks, which were found, were Gallo-Roman wrecks of different length, width and height, in various states of conservation.

Except of wreck LSG5, preserved in an area of less than 10 m length and less than 1 m width, the other wrecks were mainly well preserved. They were between 14.50 and 20 m long and between 3 and 5 m wide (**fig. 2**).

The documentation collected on the wrecks is based on a precise dating techniques and their historical analysis proves that they belong to the same hydrographical system formed by the Rivers Rhône and Saône[2].

The harbour remains discovered from the Gallo-Roman period mainly consist of a wooden wharf. Many shards of amphorae, which may have been most likely thrown overboard during the operations of loading and unloading cargoes, testify to a harbour sector particularly well developed during the 1st - 3rd century AD (**fig. 3**).

Taking the scientific and cultural interest of this whole range of wrecks into account, which documents regional river craft over a long period ranging from Antiquity to Modern times[3], a consequential decision has been taken, on the technical and economic aspects of the conservation project, and for conserving the best preserved and most representative Gallo-Roman wrecks for museum display.

Thus, of these six Gallo-Roman boats, three were chosen (wrecks LSG4 [**fig. 4**], LSG7 and LSG8) and dissected into 22 sections of 2 m length on average. These elements were removed from the excavation site and transported to a temporary storage lake, before being handled by the laboratory ARC-Nucléart in Grenoble, which carried out the conservation and restoration of wreck LSG4 for its display in the Gallo-Roman museum of Lyon-Fourvière.

In 2013, financial conditions allowed the launch of the LSG4 project over a three-year period for raising the wreck, consolidating the wood, restoring and supporting the boat and studying it archaeologically.

CONSERVATION WITH ARCHAEOLOGICAL MONITORING

During the excavation of the Parc Saint-Georges in Lyon from 2003 to 2004, it was not possible to complete the study of the boat, because of the simultaneous discovery of several other shipwrecks, which reduced the time to study each one in-depth.

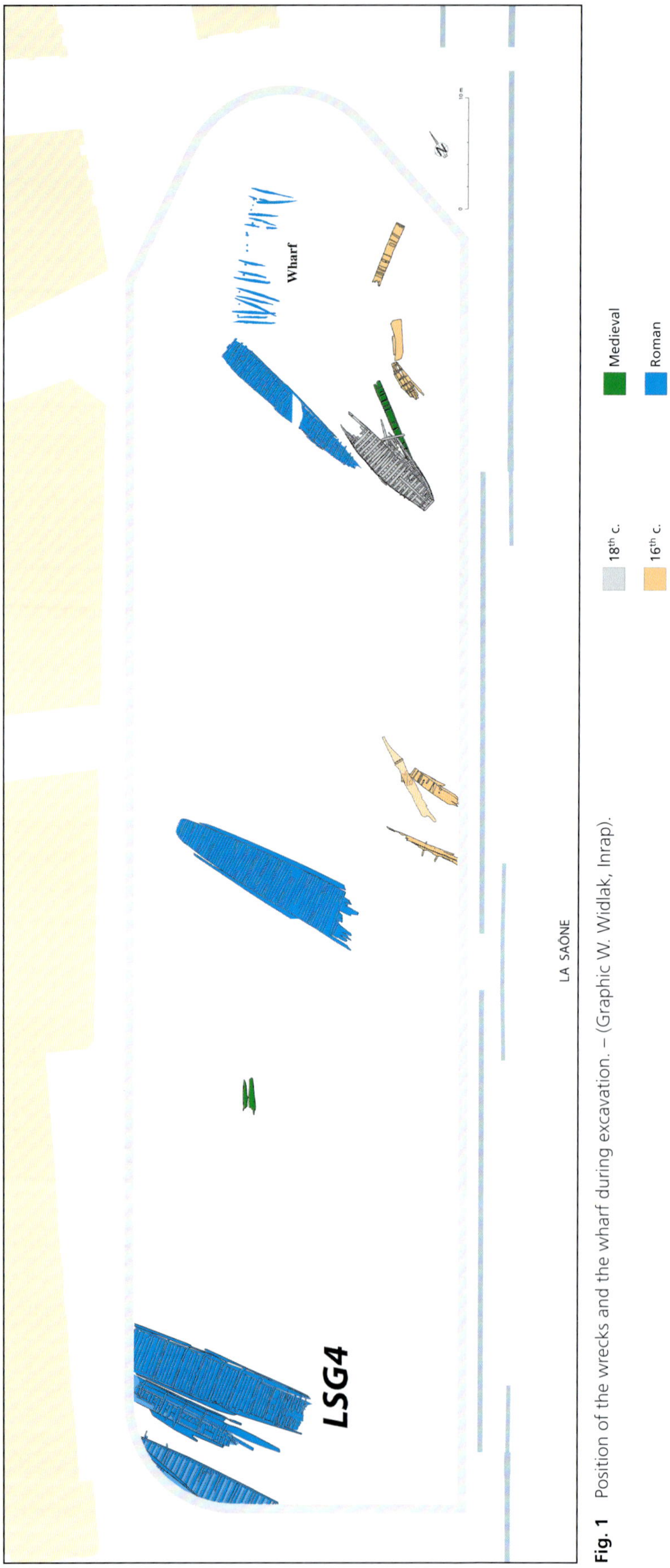

Fig. 1 Position of the wrecks and the wharf during excavation. – (Graphic W. Widlak, Inrap).

Fig. 2 The barge on its metallic frame. – (Photo C. Terpent, ARC-Nucléart).

Fig. 3 Vestiges of 1st century AD wharf. – (Photo Inrap).

Fig. 4 The 2nd century AD LSG4 boat. – (Photo Inrap).

Three of them were studied *in situ* and showed a regional character in their construction[4]. This group of wrecks, using a mixture of Mediterranean and Celtic techniques, enlightens that this exceptional discovery belongs to the »Rhône-Saône group«. It includes shipwrecks from Chalon-sur-Saône[5], discovered during a subaquatic excavation of the antique foundation of the bridge, the Tolozan shipwreck in Lyon[6], discovered during an archaeological excavation of Tolozan square, antique shipwrecks from Arles, mainly Arles Rhône 3[7], and of course the Parc Saint-Georges' shipwrecks. This group highlights the techniques, used over three centuries, on this important fluvial exchange route with the Antique Mediterranean world.

Today, the Lyon Saint-Georges 4 boat has been raised and could be studied in depth. Due to the important rate of pyrite (iron sulphide) in the wood, specific care had to be taken when it arrived at the laboratory ARC-Nucléart in Grenoble. It meant a complete dismantling of the boat, removing every piece of wood, and undoing every assemblage. This step allowed a complete removal of the iron parts (including its nails and corroded parts), but also more widely entailed a removal of every metallic component before consolidation treatment and a curettage of every piece of wood (nearly 1,000) of the shipwreck (**fig. 5**). This was done as a long-term conservation project because iron sulphide contained in archaeological wood can lead to an acidification of the material due to conservation conditions that may be too moist, such as for the Vasa wreck[8]. A very strict control of the air conditioning system during the display of the boat is necessary to avoid or to slow down the development of acidity. This work was not envisaged at first, but it allowed the collection of all the archaeological data in order to understand how the boat had been built and which techniques were used.

It quickly turned out that the archaeological and conservational analyses were complimentary. Due to the fragmentation of the shipwreck, this was a unique opportunity to understand the fabrication; this was impossible with the Arles Rhône 3 shipwreck because it was not completely dismantled. At Lyon Saint-Georges 4, it was possible to have a corresponding investigation, enabling the discovery of new knowledge concerning both shipwrecks, which cannot be obtained after the boat goes on display.

At each step of the conservation treatment, new archaeological data has been recorded for a thorough mapping the wreck. The entire dismantlement allowed an exact observation of the flat-bottom, after having removed numerous frames, which gave a complete vision of the boat. Every plank, on every side, has been sketched (**fig. 6**). These planks also reveal tool marks in the sections of the frames because these surfaces were protected from erosion by the wood. It is also important to understand how the construction was se-

Fig. 5 The nearly 1,000 pieces of the shipwreck are now stored on shelves, waiting for being displayed in the museum. – (Photo L. Meunier, ARC-Nucléart).

quenced, prepared and which tools were used. The tool marks recorded will be compared to the carpenters' tools found during the excavation of Parc Saint-Georges.

In the previous publication of the Parc Saint-Georges of Lyon[9], the caulking technique was defined as a specific design looking like an inverted »V« between the planks of the flat-bottom, oriented with the wide space down, and with a slight protrusion downwards to keep the caulking material in place without any other means to secure it (documented on the LSG3 boat). This profile is preserved only on a few planks of LSG4, because of the problems, which incurred maintaining the caulking system. This protrusion has been removed together with the ancient caulking material. During this operation, the boat was not dismantled, the seals were just purged of the defective caulking material, and so the protrusion disappeared. By recording the sides of the flat-bottom planks with precision, a mapping of caulking maintenance could be carried out.

Lots of round and square dowels were systematically recorded during the ongoing conservation and drawn on a map. They were not easily discernible and several observations at different times during the conservation process have been necessary for finding all of them. They mark the position of the planks during the construction of the boat. The very high number of dowels can also indicate the reuse of some of the planks or repairs.

Moreover, several caulking areas have been identified on the downside of the flat-bottom; they are certainly repairs before launching the boat and were found on defective areas of the wood such as knots. This side of the boat has also been completely recorded. For this operation the planks were turned.

While dismantling the shipwreck, near 25 linear metres of caulking material from the space between the sides and the flat-bottom have been removed. They are made of textile and pitch. These elements will be

Fig. 6 Archaeological data collection. – (Photo C. Terpent, ARC-Nucléart).

compared to similar wrecks known, to study fabrication techniques and to compare them with other wrecks as well as to analyse the way textiles were prepared to be used as caulking material, the volume that was necessary to caulk a boat like this or the reuse of textile in the Roman period in general.
Furthermore, it is planned to analyse the metallic parts of the boat. There are nearly 90 nails per frame, and 20 nails per rib. This important set will permit further investigations on the metallurgy.
Analyses will be conducted on the quality of the material and its structural state, to find out, which alloy was used, how the nails were treated thermically, and how they have been forged. The chemical signature will also be discovered by investigating metallic impurities and inclusions composition to compare them with the signatures of known iron ores.
Of course, archaeodendrometry has been carried out upon every piece of the shipwreck and will bring precious information on wood transformation, tree selection as well as its position within the boat. It will of course also give a precise dating, and perhaps allow us to get information on the various repairs, observed while dismantling the boat.

CONCLUSION

Thanks to ARC-Nucléart's experience in archaeological shipwrecks, samples have been taken in order to perform further analysis after dismantling. Through these analyses we try to know how long this type of boat was used and how it was repaired.

The circumstances of the abandonment of the LSG4 shipwreck have also been re-examined, while the archaeological survey was recorded in detail. The decomposition of the boat was attested before its burial by the state of the wood and the nails which were badly oxydated[10]. The lack of fittings or cargo, which has been found neither inside nor nearby the shipwrecks, and the location in a dead-end Roman paleochannel of the River Saône downstream of Lugdunum, leads to the hypothesis of a boat dump.

Notes

1) Ayala 2013.

2) Guyon/Rieth 2010.

3) Ayala 2013.

4) Guyon/Rieth 2010.

5) Lonchambon 2000.

6) Becker/Rieth 1995.

7) Marlier 2014.

8) Hocker 2006.

9) Guyon/Rieth 2010.

10) Personal conversation with Gilles Chaumat (ARC-Nucléart).

References

Ayala 2013: G. Ayala, Lyon, Saint-Georges. Archéologie, environnement et histoire d'un espace fluvial en bord de Saône. Documents d'Archéologie Française 106 (Paris 2013).

Becker/Rieth 1995: C. Becker / E. Rieth, L'épave gallo-romaine de la place Tolozan à Lyon: un chaland à coque monoxyle-assemblée. In: J. C. Béal, L'arbre et la forêt, le bois dans l'Antiquité. Publications de la Bibliothèque Salomon Reinach 7 (Lyon 1995) 77-91.

Guyon/Rieth 2010: M. Guyon / E. Rieth, Les épaves de Saint-Georges. Lyon – Ier-XVIIIe siècles: Les épaves gallo-romaines. In: E. Rieth (ed.), Les épaves de Saint-Georges. Lyon – Ier-XVIIIe siècles. Analyse architecturale et études complémentaires. Archaeonautica 16 (Paris 2010) 247-248.

Hocker 2006: E. Hocker, From the Micro- to the Macro-: Managing the conservation of the warship, Vasa. Macromolecular Symposia 238/1, 2006, 16-21. DOI: 10.1002/masy.200650603.

Lonchambon 2000: C. Lonchambon, Un bateau monoxyle-assemblé à Chalon-sur-Saône (Ier siècle après J.-C.). In: L. Bonnamour (ed.), Archéologie des fleuves et des rivières (Paris 2000) 174-178.

Marlier 2014: S. Marlier, Arles-Rhône 3, un chaland gallo-romain du Ier s. ap. J.-C. Archaeonautica 18 (Paris 2014).

Summary

The boat called Lyon Saint-Georges 4 (LSG4) belongs to a larger set of 16 shipwrecks of different periods discovered in a rescue excavation during the construction of a car park in Lyon (dép. Rhône/F) on a bank of the Saône in 2003. Three of the six Roman boats were extracted and stored in a lake near Lyon, waiting for project funding. In 2013, the three-year project LSG4 did start to consolidate the waterlogged wood and restore the boat, and carrying out a complete archaeological survey.

The complementarity of the archaeological and the conservational analyses quickly became apparent. Due to the presence of pyrite in the wood, special care was needed from the arrival of the shipwreck at ARC-Nucléart. This meant a total dismantling of the boat, with a removal of the corrosion. A complete archaeological study has been conducted by accessing all pieces to reconstruct the history of the ship, from its construction until its abandonment. The archaeological data, recorded, was not limited to the dismantlement, because new data became available at each step of the conservation process.

Thanks to ARC-Nucléart's experience in archaeological shipwrecks, samples for further analyses were removed during the dismantlement. Among these were caulking textiles, nails and the lead sheet reparations located at the front of the shipwreck. Based on these analyses, it was also possible to assess the lifetime of the boat.
Furthermore, the context of its abandonment has been re-evaluated during the general archaeological investigation. The degradation of the shipwreck before its burial has been proven by the state of the wood and the nails. Neither fittings, nor cargo was found inside or nearby the Roman shipwrecks. Together with their location in a Roman paleo-channel of the Saône, downstream of Lugdunum a boat dump seems possible.

Résumé

Lyon Saint-Georges 4 (LSG4) appartient à un ensemble de 16 épaves de différentes périodes découvertes lors d'une fouille préventive pendant la construction d'un parking souterrain à Lyon (dép. Rhône/F) en rive droite de la Saône en 2003. Trois des six épaves gallo-romaines ont été prélevées et stockées dans un lac près de Lyon, en attente d'un projet et d'un financement. En 2013, le projet LSG4 a commencé pour une durée de trois ans afin de consolider le bois gorgé d'eau, restaurer le bateau et mener une étude archéologique complète.
La complémentarité des approches archéologiques et de restaurations est rapidement apparue. À cause de la présence de pyrite dans le bois, une prise en charge spéciale a été nécessaire dès l'arrivée du bateau à ARC-Nucléart. Cela a signifié un démantèlement complet du bateau, ainsi qu'un retrait des produits de corrosion. À travers l'expertise de tous les éléments du bateau, l'étude archéologique a eu pour but d'en retrouver l'histoire depuis sa construction jusqu'à son abandon. Les données archéologiques enregistrées n'ont pas été limitées au démantèlement, car de nouvelles observations apparaissaient à chaque étape du processus de conservation.
Grace à l'expérience d'ARC-Nucléart, dans le traitement des épaves archéologiques, des prélèvements ont été pratiqués pendant le démantèlement pour des analyses ultérieures. Parmi ceux-ci, des textiles de calfatage, des clous et des réparations en plomb provenant de l'avant du bateau. À partir de ces analyses, il sera possible d'évaluer la durée d'utilisation du bateau.
De plus, le contexte de son abandon a été réexaminé pendant l'étude archéologique générale. La dégradation du chaland avant son enfouissement a été prouvée par l'état du bois et des clous. Ni aménagement, ni cargaison n'ont été trouvés à l'intérieur ou à proximité du groupe d'épaves dont LSG4 fait partie. Ceci joint à leur localisation dans un ancien paléochenal de la Saône à l'époque romaine en aval de l'enceinte gallo-romaine de Lugdunum ouvre la possibilité d'un dépotoir à bateaux.

INLAND HARBOURS: MIDDLE AGES

DORIS WOLLENBERG · IRIS NIESSEN

HOW TO IDENTIFY A HARBOUR IN THE ARCHAEOLOGICAL RECORD IN MEDIEVAL URBAN CONTEXTS?

A CASE STUDY OF REGENSBURG, FRANKFURT/MAIN AND SPEYER

The river system of Rhine and Main has already been navigated in early medieval times by many different groups of users such as merchants, pilgrims, military troops or kings on their itinerary[1]. Charlemagne, for example, put a strong effort into the construction of a navigable canal for crossing the European watershed to connect the river system of Rhine and Main with the river system of the Danube[2]. With regard to the final implementation of Charlemagne's canal project within the Rhine-Main-Danube-Canal of the 19th and 20th century AD[3], the importance for navigation of the three rivers mentioned above is evident for centuries. Nevertheless, clearly identifiable medieval harbour structures on lakes and rivers seem to be rare or at least difficult to detect, although historical sources prove their existence.

WHAT DO WE EXPECT? THE PROBLEM OF THE DEFINITION OF AN INLAND HARBOUR

Maybe we ask the wrong questions if we consider a harbour to be a complex of man-made constructions forming a well-defined harbour-area with a sharp bank line. Quays, piers, steadied landing sites, breakwaters and jetties[4] can be possible features of medieval inland harbours, especially for the High and Late Middle Ages, but they were not always necessarily an inherent part of it.

If we take a look on general modern definitions of the term »harbour«[5], it appears they refer to both maritime harbours and to harbours of modern times and cannot be applied to medieval harbours at rivers and lakes. Apart from that, these definitions usually mention two characteristic points of view: 1. The function of harbours as places of shelter for protecting water vessels of currents and winds. 2. The reference of masonry or wooden building structures such as quay walls, piers, and jetties. In the project »Medieval inland harbours in central Europe«[6], it became more and more obvious that, compared to maritime harbours, inland harbours do not fit a definition that is based on constructive elements only[7]. Thus, to reach a better understanding of how a medieval inland harbour might have looked like, it is necessary to widen our perspective on the functional requirements of medieval inland vessels for landing, loading and unloading. Furthermore, it is necessary to analyse the natural topography of the site as well as the landward topography of the corresponding settlement and especially the landward harbour referred infrastructure such as storehouses, merchants' cellars, tollhouses, fishing huts, combustible respectively hydrophilic crafts, town gates, markets etc. Localizing functional areas of the settlement, therefore, allows the prospection of probable subsequent harbour zones.

WHAT KIND OF ARCHAEOLOGICAL FEATURES DO WE USUALLY CONSIDER TO BE PART OF HARBOUR CONSTRUCTIONS?

The preservation of ancient harbour constructions underlies a bunch of filters that have to be considered while searching for and interpreting their archaeological remains. The main building material for inland harbour constructions in the Middle Ages was wood, which can only be preserved in anaerobic humid conditions. A change of the water level or a shifting of a riverbed, therefore, can be a reason for the natural decomposition of these remains. Additionally, we must keep in mind that if the water level sank, only sub-constructions could have outlasted. Wooden poles are typical archaeological features usually being primarily interpreted as parts of river embankments or harbour structures. They are often cut off or have rotten upper ends, no constructive joints, and are often not datable by dendrochronology because of their small diameter and the use of soft lumber[8]. Since many of these poles are found in muddy sediments or water, they are often not – if identified and recovered at all – documented stratigraphically due to the difficult working conditions or due to discoveries made by dredging tasks. Without secondary criteria, they can be interpreted either as parts of harbour constructions such as jetties or mooring piles, or equally as sub-constructions for buildings, town walls, bridges or working platforms for hydrophilic crafts such as tanning, dying etc.

Masonry or wooden quays and piers constructed with horizontal planks, vertical poles or stone and wooden box constructions filled with sediment[9] can be easily mistaken for river embankments or earthwork for land reclamation. Nevertheless, they indicate a transition zone between water and land. A multifunctional use including navigation seems probable.

Natural landing sites can come along without any archaeological features/additional construction[10] at all, or – if reinforced – can be detected by relics of brushwood or raw logwood, that likewise did not have any constructive elements. The determination as landing site can therefore only be predicted by secondary features.

Regardless of the number and quality of the assumed harbour features, the primary question to be answered is the location of the corresponding historical riverbank. Archaeological features of bank revetments, besides wooden poles or planks, like fascines or wattle work which can be easily mistaken for land boundaries. As a secondary criterion, a slope in the profile of the terrain in combination with characteristic fluvial sediments[11] can support the localization of the former riverbank.

Medieval shipbuilding and harbour installations

Considering a more functional approach, inland harbours compared to maritime harbours may have had other technical requirements caused by a different construction of inland vessels. Their shape and design were perfectly adapted to the conditions of inland navigation. Besides log boats, planked vessels, especially the huge flat-bottomed barges, were constructed to carry a maximum tonnage for a minimum water level, which allowed navigation also on small rivers or during dry seasons. The hulk of these inland vessels, therefore, was flat, had a low draft and a slightly curved bow, allowing ships to land on natural landing sites without any additional constructions[12].

Underwater archaeology in Germany

Two reasons for the current state of research concerning inland harbours in Germany are the structural conditions of heritage conservation and the state of development of underwater archaeology in Germany. In contrast to France and other countries, underwater archaeology is not an inherent element of heritage conservation in Germany[13]. Therefore, a lot of archaeological features underwater, or in the amphibious zone between water and land, are often being destroyed unobserved due to a lack of knowledge about the existence of these monuments, a lack of work routine, special equipment, special skilled archaeologic staff and of course lack of funding. Except for certain areas with a high density of underwater monuments, such as the alpine lakes with its pile dwelling settlements, underwater excavations, surveys or rescue works are often executed by non-archaeological staff such as construction divers, fire brigade divers or amateur archaeologists what demonstrates the provisional character of the state of underwater archaeology in most regions in Germany[14]. Unlike in France, in most parts of Germany there is no budget provided for underwater archaeology, systematic prospection of water bodies and appropriate storage for large amounts of wooden finds or huge wooden objects such as wrecks[15].

The following three case studies present different types of harbour structures from the 9th to the 14th century AD within the particular historical, infrastructural and topographical development of the medieval town and waterfront. Methodological questions concerning the identification and interpretation of archaeological harbour features, inland navigation and the use of rivers and water bodies will be discussed. The three selected sites of Regensburg, Frankfurt on the Main and Speyer give an example of the opportunities and the challenges which urban rescue excavations in the amphibious zone offer for medieval harbour research.

REGENSBURG (BAVARIA / D)

Regensburg is a major medieval town with Roman roots at the River Danube – the main aquatic route between East and West[16]. It had a significant topographical position already since the Roman period. In the year 179 AD a Roman fort[17] was built vis-à-vis of the estuary of the River Regen. Its fortification was still used in the Early Middle Ages when the town became the seat of the Bavarian duke and was raised to the status of an early diocesan town in 739 AD[18] (**fig. 1**). After Charlemagne defeated the Avars, Regensburg became a trading node for long-distance trade between the Slavic East and the Western Empire[19]. For the year 792 AD historical sources describe that the Frankish troops used a pontoon bridge in Regensburg for military operations against the Avars[20]. In 794 AD Charlemagne deposed the duke Tassilo III, Bavaria got integrated into the Frankish kingdom and Regensburg became royal seat and capital of the Eastern Frankish Empire[21]. Due to missionary activities in Bohemia and Moravia[22], Regensburg was also an important sacral centre. The position of Regensburg between the confluences of the River Naab and the River Regen into the Danube surely was another benefit for regional river trade to the northern Bavaria (Upper Palatinate) with its rich iron deposits[23] and the Bavarian forest.

The early medieval harbour of Regensburg is first mentioned by bishop Arbeo of Freising in 770 AD: he describes the harbour as a *portus saluber*, which means good-conditioned or safe[24]. It is unclear though whether the report can be understood literally, or relates to the still existing and surely impressive walls of the Roman fort. Furthermore, the same source mentions a ferry crossing the Danube from a landing stage at the estuary of the River Regen to the harbour of Regensburg at the opposite site (**fig. 1**)[25].

In the 10th century AD, the town expanded and a new town wall was built (**fig. 1**). It left out a broad stretch of the riverbank, which might have been used for inland navigation. From 1135 to 1146 AD the Stone Bridge

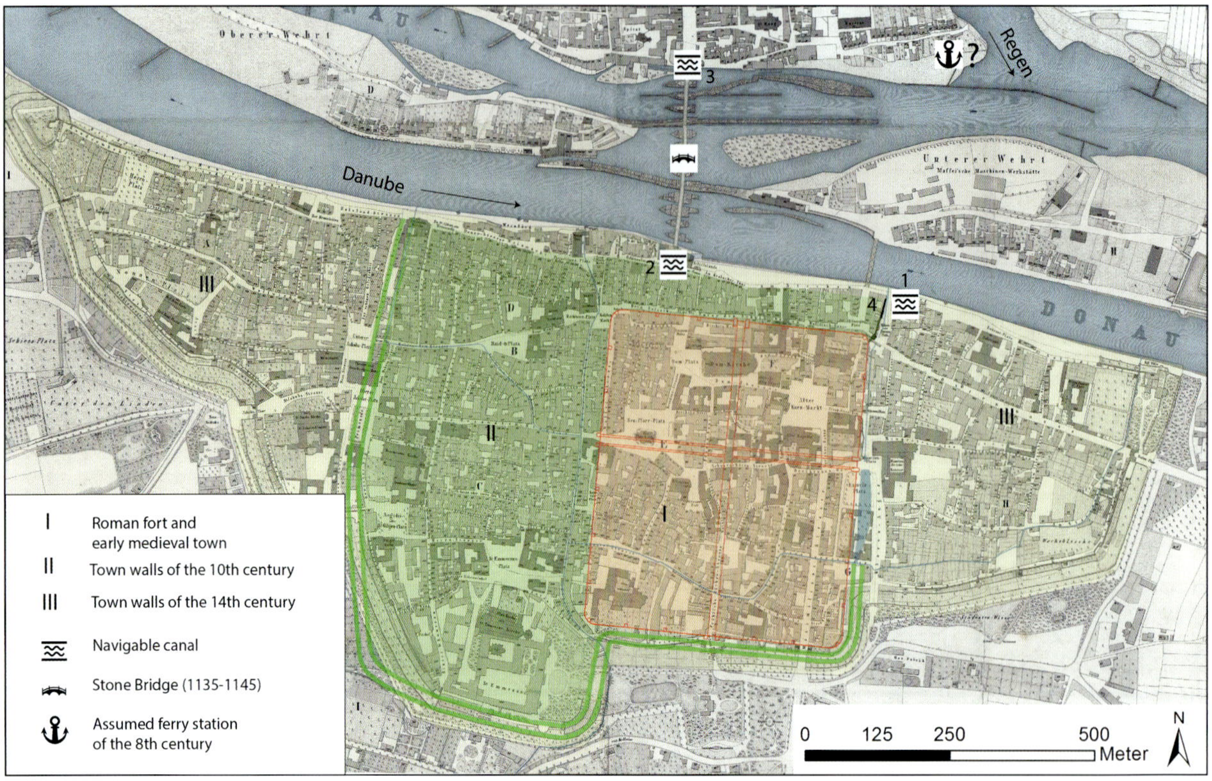

Fig. 1 Regensburg, historical map from 1812 AD with the Roman fort (red), the first urban expansion of the 10th century AD (green) and the second urban expansion of the 14th century AD (yellow). – Important excavation sites: **1** Donaumarkt. – **2** Wiedfang. – **3** Spital of St. Catharine, Stadtamhof. – **4** Donaumarkt, course of the medieval town wall of the late 11th century AD. – (Map R. Röhrl, BLfD; modifications D. Wollenberg / I. Nießen).

(»Steinerne Brücke«) was built, assuring a constant crossing of the Danube regardless of weather conditions or the changing level of the river. Yet for inland navigation, it was an enormous obstacle. The massive bridge pillars had a large impact on the flow dynamic of the Danube. Upstream the bridge, they caused a backwater which was (and still is today) responsible for dangerous vortexes downriver of the bridge[26]. The construction of the Stone Bridge therefore might have led to severe changes in the necessary infrastructure for inland navigation.

Until now archaeology was unable to contribute significantly to our knowledge of the medieval harbour of Regensburg, and even the location of the Roman harbour is unknown[27]. It was not until urban archaeological excavations of the last years[28] that – due to the favourable preservation conditions – profound features of the medieval harbour in the eastern suburb of Regensburg were revealed. The results show the use of canals for inland navigation[29] and demonstrate that Regensburg is an important example for archaeological features of inland harbours.

Canals seem to be a special feature of the medieval harbours in general and as well as in Regensburg[30]. They highlight the importance of inland navigation for the town, since much effort was needed to build and maintain artificial waterways that could have been used as harbours and for many other purposes. In general, canals allowed avoiding dangers like strong currents, vortexes, and obstacles such as fords and bridges[31]. At the same time, canals with adjustable water management were used to assure the water supply for different crafts or mills and could have worked as flood ditches in case of flood events[32]. Remains of different medieval canals have been detected in Regensburg. They ran parallel to the main stream of the Danube and were used for shipping or wood rafting and as a water supply for craft activities. Archaeological remains of these canals have been detected at two sites: the Wiedfang south of the medieval Stone Bridge (1135-1146 AD) already in 1987[33], and lately also the Donaumarkt north-east of the medieval suburb (**fig. 1**).

Regensburg Donaumarkt

From 2009 to 2015, a huge area north-east of the former Roman fort and the early medieval town wall was excavated due to the construction of the Museum of Bavarian History. The excavation of the Donaumarkt[34] (**fig. 1**) was one of the biggest projects of urban archaeology in the last years and revealed manifold remains of the historical riverbank, as well as harbour and canal structures and constructions connected to water exploitation for different purposes.

Archaeological features give proof for a sidearm of the Danube about 12-14 m wide, that ran approximately 20 m south of the modern riverbank, parallel to the main stream of the Danube. This navigable canal was 2-3 m deep and allowed ships to navigate independently and protected from the river current. It is unclear if the sidearm is the result of natural fluvial processes or artificial modifications. The immense width of the side arm speaks compared to other canal structures[35] rather for a natural emergence. Due to its intensive use and modification, the term canal is used consistently hereinafter. Peaty sediments at the bottom indicate stagnant water, which was divided from the main stream. From the south, the canalized Vitusbach, that was part of the town wall's moat, flowed into the canal (**fig. 1**). We have proof for the canal in two sondages located 31 m apart. The total length, as well as the beginning and ending of the canal, are unknown, respectively it is unclear where it branches off and flowed into the Danube again. Concerning its period of use, pottery finds and dendrochronological data prove that it had already been silted during the 11th-12th century AD. Its main period of use, therefore, must have been earlier. ^{14}C-data[36] from the alluvial loams that are cut by the canal indicate that it was formed at the end of the 9th/10th century AD. The silting process with dendrochronological dates from 1078 to 1114 AD happened simultaneously with the extension of the town wall to the north. It was built for closing the distance between the north-eastern corner of the former Roman fort to the Danube in the north. Dendrochronological data indicate two main building phases of the town wall: a southern section built during 1052-1064 AD and a northern section built between 1073/1076 and 1079/1080 AD. The town wall has been investigated for the first time during the excavation of the Donaumarkt. Due to these examinations, we can conclude that with the silting of the canal and the resulting movement of the riverbank to the north an extension of the fortification was needed as well. The fortification can be set in context with the Investiture Controversy and the conflict between Henry IV (king of the Holy Roman Empire since 1056 AD; imperator from 1084 to 1105 AD) and his son Henry V (king since 1106 AD, imperator from 1111 to 1125 AD), in which Henry IV sought refuge at Regensburg. In this case, the function of the town wall as a special protection of the harbour – an area with sensitive infrastructure especially during times of crisis – should be reflected.

Several wooden piles, which were preserved in the humid soil, are part of the river embankment of the 10th/11th century AD together with a wooden tracery and stepping stones[37]. Furthermore, a ditch, 50 cm wide and 80 cm deep, was located at the riverbank: six poles, 23-26 cm wide and up to 60 cm deep, stood closely in the ditch (**fig. 3**). They allow reconstructing a reinforcement of the riverbank with a wooden palisade. Both constructions seem to have been built according to the particular requirements of the urban population, which used this area of the riverbank for different purposes. The provisional, heterogeneous character of these features seems to indicate that they were not a centrally planned construction project. It seems more likely that the individual users took care for the maintenance themselves by means of simple tools.

The most spectacular record of the excavation is a timber house of the late 10th century AD, which was exceptionally well preserved (**fig. 2**). It is located on the southern bank of the above-mentioned canal. The timber house[38] was built as a post construction with slotted upright columns[39] and wall fillings made of round timbers and planks[40]. The ground plot is rectangular and the smaller side of around 3 m faces the water. Dendrochronological analyses date the house back to 985 AD[41]. Shortly after its construction, the

Fig. 2 Regensburg, excavation Donaumarkt 2013: **1** path of wooden planks (dendro: 994 AD). – **2** timber house (dendro: 985 AD). – **3** substructure/pile foundation of the north eastern town wall (dendro: 1073/1076 and 1079/1080 AD). – **4** multi-phase town wall of the late 11th century AD. – **5** moat in front of the town wall with wooden internals (dendro: 1027/1032/1114 AD). – (Photo Archaios GmbH).

building was flooded. As a result, the area in front of the house silted up. For this reason, a path of wooden planks cut in the year 994 AD has been built on the bank. Another corner pole of a second timber house has been dated to the year 999 AD. For the construction of the house, timbers of softwood like white fir, pine and spruce were used. Thanks to the extraordinary preservation of the wood, we cannot only prove the construction of the house, but also document the intensive and dynamic use of the riverbank considering the danger of flooding. The timber house is an excellent example of a landing stage located at the bank of the canal in the late 10th century AD.

Archaeobotanical analyses[42] prove that the bank was in full sunlight, free of tall vegetation and frequently disturbed during the 11th and 12th century AD, which indicates regular human activity. Compressed wood fibres (in fluvial sediments), which remained at the bank after the excoriation of the trunks, indicate the rafting of softwood. Furthermore, a craft area of the 9th-12th century AD is documented at the canal outside the medieval town (*extra muros*) (**fig. 1**). More than 50 kilns have been documented. Their function is not completely cleared yet. However, the situation illustrates the use of the waterfront for combustive handcraft as well. Therefore, for the Early and High Middle Ages, we can prove a large canal with stagnant water, which flowed parallel to the Danube. It was used for floating, probably also for navigation, for the watering of the moat, as well as a water supply for crafts.

With the construction of the late medieval town wall in 1320/1330 AD at the former riverbank (**fig. 1**), the Donaumarkt became part of the nucleated town and the shift of the riverbank ended. The riverbank north of the town wall was reinforced and fixed with a wooden construction that has possibly been pictured in a historical streetscape of Georg Bahre from 1630 AD (**fig. 4**)[43].

Fig. 3 Regensburg, excavation Donaumarkt 2009/2010: **1** alluvial river sediment. – **2** layers of the silted still water/canal. – **3** embankment of a wooden palisade (archaeological record: six poles standing closely in a ditch). – (Photo Archaios GmbH).

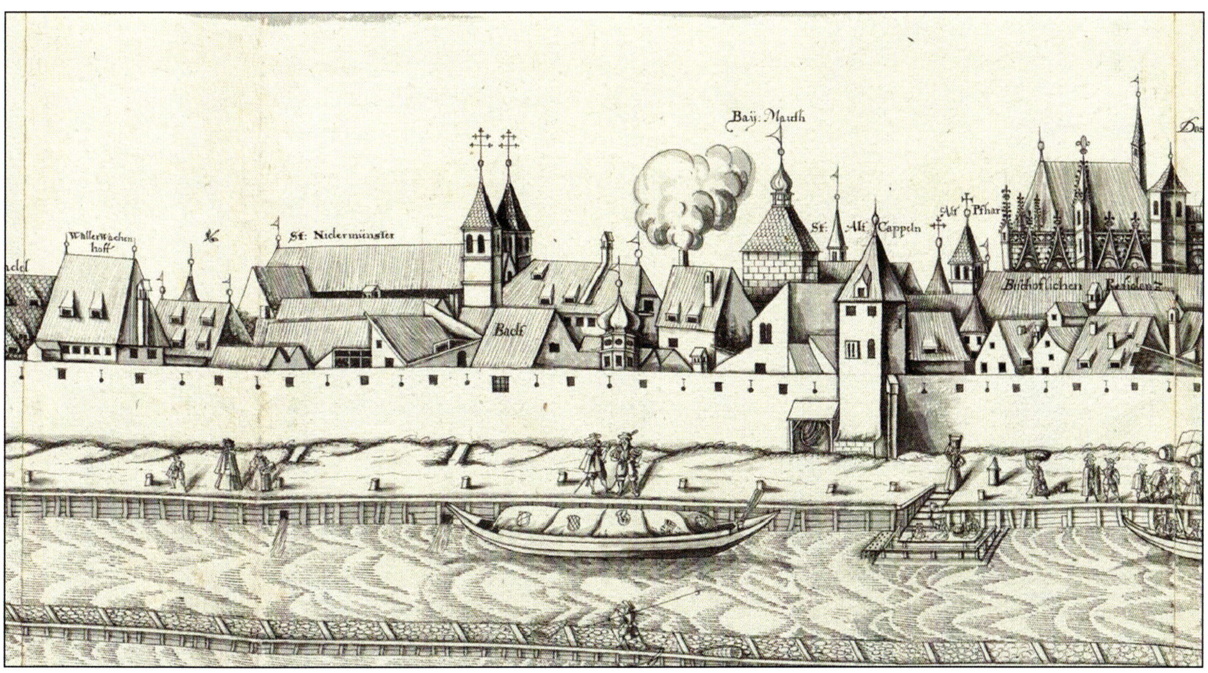

Fig. 4 Detail from the Town Scape of Regensburg from 1630 AD. – (Abriß der Stadt Regensburg östlich und westlich der Steinernen Brücke – BSB Cod. icon. 198, Regensburg, 1630 [BSB-Hss Cod. icon. 198] from the digital collection of the Bavarian State Archive).

Wood rafting in Regensburg

Regarding the importance of Regensburg as a royal, sacral and economic centre, we must assume a very high demand for timber and firewood to run ovens respectively kilns in residential houses, palaces, public baths, as well as forges and manifold workshops[44]. Due to the fact that the tributary Rivers Regen and Naab flowed into the Danube and assured a fluvial connection between Regensburg and the Bavarian Forest, it seems likely that wood might have been floated downstream on these tributaries[45]. For this assumption, we can find proof in historical sources from the 10th century AD[46] to the 19th century AD[47]. A 19th century AD map of Regensburg and its urban hinterland indicates a wood yard east of the mouth of the River Regen at the northern bank of the Danube[48]. Furthermore, the streetscape of Regensburg from 1630 AD[49] pictures a landing site for wood in a defined area of the riverbank west of St. Oswald. The function of this section of the riverbank reflects in the street name »Holzlände« (landing site for wood) until today. This area was also used to store raw wood stockpiled right in front of the town wall. Packages of chipped wood in the sediments of the above-mentioned canal at the Donaumarkt may prove the rafting of wood in Regensburg in the Early Middle Ages. An ongoing master thesis at the University of Heidelberg[50] deals with the question if the wooden finds from Regensburg-Donaumarkt really originate from the Bavarian Forest.

The navigable canal under the Stone Bridge

However, a comparable situation of a canal connected with large amounts of chipped wood[51] could also be found west of the Stone Bridge in the so-called Wiedfang area (**fig. 1**): first hypotheses concerning the localisation of a medieval harbour in this area were discussed already in the late 19th and the early 20th century AD[52]. Like at the Donaumarkt, packages of chipped wood were observed in the soil during construction works[53]. Based on historical records[54] and archaeological excavations[55], L. Dallmeier and M. Hensch have reconstructed a bypass canal, which is supposed to have been used for navigation, probably in order to avoid the dangerous vortexes downstream the Stone Bridge[56] and the current of the main stream of the Danube[57]. Compared to the canal at the Donaumarkt, the reconstructed maximum fairway width is only 3 m west of the Stone Bridge and therefore much narrower, but still navigable[58]. Wooden rafts coming from the Naab, however, would have had to be landed upstream of the Stone Bridge to be disassembled or conveyed – probably at the Wiedfang. This would have required a wider entrance to the riverbank than the current reconstruction suggests. Since the reconstruction of the narrow canal entrance in the west is based only on a 15th century AD townscape of Regensburg, and was never documented archaeologically, it must be taken into account that the situation might have looked differently in the 12th century AD.

With regard to the natural topography indicating a small bay here, a group of historians and chroniclers of the 19th and 20th century AD supposed a harbour basin instead of a canal west of the Stone Bridge. Maybe the hypothesis of a harbour basin and the partly proven canal do not necessarily exclude each other, but might be interpreted as different chronological phases of the waterfront[59]. Respecting the course of the northern town wall in the 10th century AD, the Wiedfang area seems to have been yet in the sphere of influence of floodwaters. The first stone buildings were erected not before 1200 AD[60]. An older harbour basin seems conceivable referring to a shifting of the riverbank documented at the Donaumarkt and does not exclude the existence of a more recent harbour canal.

A canal at Stadtamhof

A similar situation is documented at the opposite site of the stone bridge in Stadtamhof at the northern bank of the Danube (**fig. 1**): until modern times, a bypass canal was used here for driving a mill since 1236/1241 AD[61]. The canal is mentioned along with a jack that pulled ships through the difficult hydrologic situation at the Stone Bridge[62]. At the streetscape of Georg Bahre from 1630 AD, the entrance of the canal seems to have been used for navigating ships in protection against the river current. During a survey in 1999/2000, a bank revetment of 33 wooden poles, stiffened by capping pieces and with iron pile shoes, was documented near this site. Dendrochronological analyses date the poles between 1510 and 1560 AD. A few poles dating to the 18th century AD are interpreted as parts of more recent repairs[63]. The construction of the bank revetment is comparable to the one pictured at the streetscape from 1630 AD. Although the archaeological analysis of Regensburg's waterfront is still work in progress, we can already state that the medieval harbour of Regensburg was not a strictly delimited area. Obviously, the whole waterfront and especially artificial canals have been used as a harbour zone that has been divided into functional areas according to the landward urban topography and the specific needs of its users.

FRANKFURT (HESSE / D)

Location

Due to its favourable topographical and geopolitical location, medieval Frankfurt at the River Main was a town of major importance, thus situated in the centre of East Francia and the Holy Roman Empire and located close to the major confluence of the Rivers Main and Rhine[64]. Like Regensburg, Frankfurt developed on a Roman preceding settlement that was located on a flood-protected elevated terrain west of the so-called Main gorge of the River Main[65]. Politically and geographically, its location can be described as a bottleneck. From early to late medieval times, it was a centre for superregional trade, a residence of kings and a place for imperial assemblies and church synods[66]. Therefore, Frankfurt was a node for terrestrial and fluvial traffic. An evidence of the effort that was put into the construction of river embankments and landing sites in Frankfurt is a 13th-14th century AD quay wall built in stone and wood[67]. It is located in the south of the historic town centre, around 50 m north of the modern riverbank of the Main. Its remains were uncovered during rescue excavations in 2012. The site is located inside the court of the medieval Saalhof that houses the exhibition rooms of the Historical Museum of Frankfurt (**fig. 5**).

Construction and Dating

The quay wall made of stone and wood has been detected on a section of 20 m (**fig. 6**). It runs parallel to the court wall of the so-called Saalhof – a high medieval building complex which will be discussed later on. The strip of ground between the court wall and the front edge of the quay is approximately 2 m wide and stone paved. The front of the quay consists of a limestone wall which is about 1 m high. The top of the wall ends with large horizontal beams, which show constructive joints of different shape and size on the surface. Their particular constructive function is yet unknown, but they remind of timber frame constructions common in house construction[68]. Maybe the quay was roofed like it has been proposed for the quay of San Vincenzo al Volturno (prov. Isernia / I) (8th-13th century AD)[69].

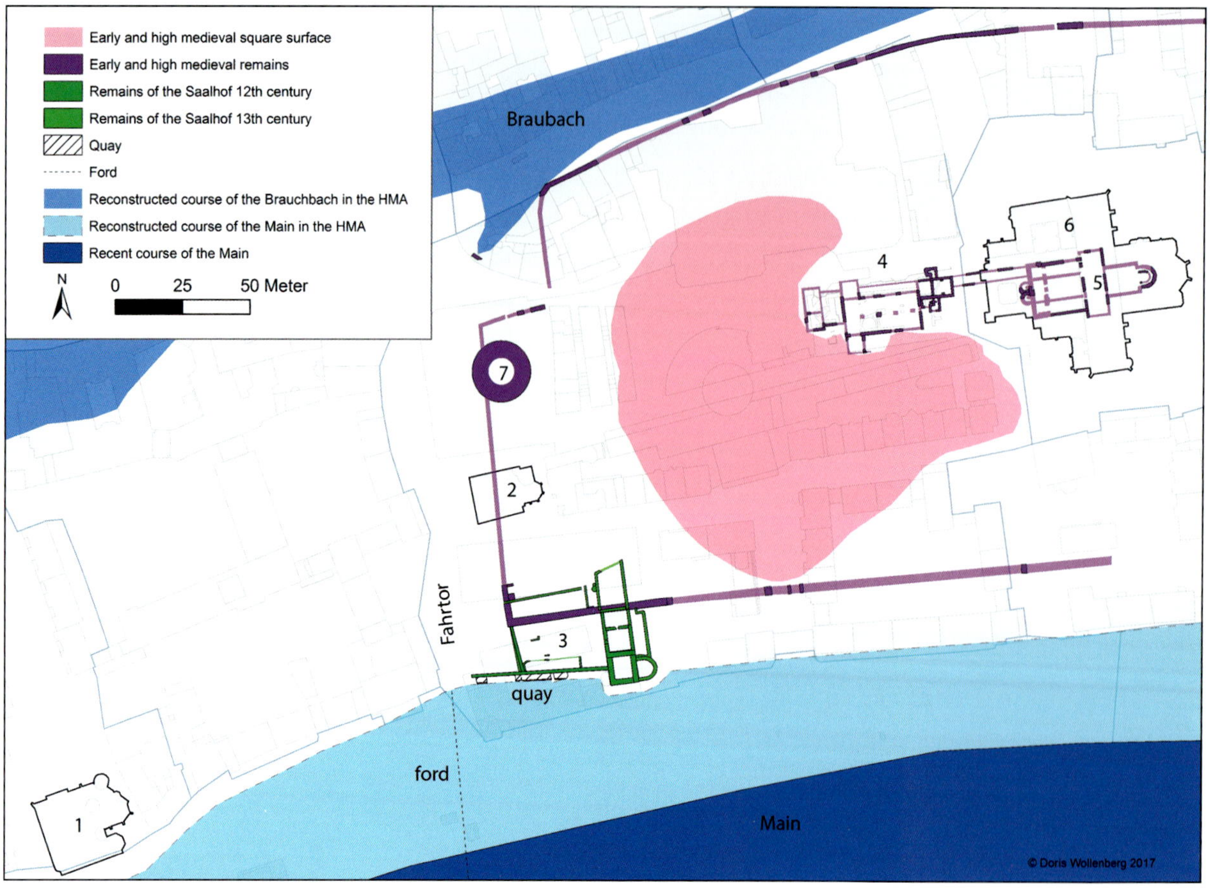

Fig. 5 The quay of Frankfurt on the Main in the context of the medieval topography: **1** St. Leonhard (1219 AD). – **2** St. Nikolai (middle of the 12th century AD). – **3** Saalhof (12th-13th century AD). – **4** Carolingian-Ottonian imperial palace. – **5** St. Salvator (middle of the 9th century AD). – **6** St. Bartholomäus (1239 AD). – **7** foundations of the donjon *terminus ante quem* 13th century AD. – (Basic data: digital field map 2016 © Stadtvermessungsamt der Stadt Frankfurt am Main 2016; rendering of rising masonry walls and excavated foundations after Schalles-Fischer 1969, fig. 3; Wintergerst 2002, plan 19; Hampel 2016, fig. 2; plan of the Saalhof 1978, Archäologisches Museum Frankfurt am Main; Stamm 1967, Annexe 2; the course of the Braubach after Nahrgang 1949, fig. 7; the position of the ford after Fischer 1971, 238. – Cartography D. Wollenberg).

The quay wall in Frankfurt enabled vessels to moor afloat. Based on the height of the quay, also bigger vessels with a draft up to 80cm[70] and even small keelboats were able to land here. Two beams of the quay have been dated dendrochronologically after 1303 and 1314 AD (± 10)[71]. Since these beams have permanently been exposed alternately to water and air, A. Hampel assumed they must have been exchanged regularly and only mark the last period of use or the last period of repairs[72]. Another dendrochronological sample of a timber plank below the pavement may be interpreted as a part of a substruction. Its dating after 1218 AD[73] (without sapwood) marks the earliest possible date for the installation of the quay. Pottery finds on the pavement and in front of the quay wall prove that the quay was abandoned during the 14th century AD.

The arrangement of the joints on both beams seems to follow a regular system, which indicates a constructive function in the context of the quay wall. The huge horizontal beams are connected with each other by scarphs that are fixed with smaller vertical poles. A constructive connection between quay wall and beams could not be recognized. The beams seem to simply lie on the top of the wall. Unfortunately, details of the inner construction of the quay are yet unknown, since no profiles were created during the process of its uncovering[74]. The quay was preserved in situ in the courtyard as a part of the museum's exhibition.

Concerning the substruction, comparisons with other masonry and wooden harbour features and riverbank revetments as well as constructions for land reclamation point to an interpretation as wooden caissons filled

Fig. 6 The high medieval quay of Frankfurt on the Main. – (Photo Denkmalamt Frankfurt am Main 2012).

with deposit sediments and stabilized with vertical poles[75]. If the visible front of the limestone quay wall is either superimposed in front of, or connected with, the assumed wooden box construction cannot be answered, but a constructive connection with the substruction seems plausible.

Function and meaning of the quay in context with the Saalhof

Regarding the small space of only 2 m between the water's edge and the court wall of the Saalhof, it seems improbable that huge amounts of cargo have been unloaded or stored here. The commercial harbour of Frankfurt, therefore, must have been somewhere else. Hence a functional meaning related to the Saalhof should be taken into account: this building complex, consisting of a donjon (1160 AD), a palas, a chapel (*terminus post quem* 1200 AD) and a walled courtyard, was constructed in multiple steps from approximately 1160 AD until the 13th century AD. It was further expanded and renovated in the 13th-14th century AD[76]. The dendrochronological dating of a wooden plank from the substruction of the quay (see above) indicates that the main part of the Saalhof had already been built (donjon, palas, chapel), when the quay wall was installed. Archaeological profiles inside the courtyard indicate that the area was a land tongue of natural alluvial clay deposits, which was not built-up before the 12th century AD[77]. It was encircled by water and extended several metres into the River Main. Massive levelings and sediment fills up to 4 m high were necessary to create a plain and stable building ground[78]. Thus, the Saalhof is located in a part of the town, which once belonged to the former flood plain of the River Main. Therefore, the whole area was at a high risk of being flooded[79]. In this context, the quay wall may have had a double function as a landing site and a bank revetment after land reclamation.

Without any doubt, the view from the opposite side of the riverbank on the entire complex[80] with its three-storied tower and the court wall with arcades must have been impressive[81]. Due to comparisons with similar buildings, it seems likely to interpret the Saalhof as a typical castle of the Staufer period (1138-1254 AD)[82]. A function as an imperial palace is controversial[83]. The building is first mentioned after the Staufer period in 1277 AD as the seat of the *curia regis*[84] and the royal magistrate[85], which suggests an administrative, legal function as well as the revenue of tax and tolls. It might be reasonable that also water tolls were collected at the Saalhof. They are mentioned in Frankfurt for the first time 1157 AD but without referencing the location[86]. For the Saalhof, water toll collection is proved since at least 1456 AD with the erection of a toll tower (»Rententurm«) as an annexe in the west of the courtyard[87].

Because of its location at one of the main roads (»Fahrtor«) leading from the riverside into the town (**fig. 5**), and its topographic position pushed forward into the River Main, the Saalhof, and the quay would have been very suitable for collecting water tolls. At the same time, they offered an appropriate architectural setting for the demonstration of the royal and later civil jurisdiction. A comparison with the royal Staufer palace and the so-called tax castle of Kaiserswerth on the Rhine may support this consideration[88]. In 1174 AD, emperor Frederick I Barbarossa transferred the water toll from Tiel (prov. Gueldre/NL) to Kaiserswerth (North Rhine-Westphalia/D) on the Rhine, and restored and expanded the castle complex[89]. 20 years earlier the same happened in Frankfurt. In 1157 AD, a short period before the construction of the Saalhof and the quay wall, the king abolished all water tolls on the Main: from that time on, water toll collection was restricted to Neustadt (Bavaria/D), Aschaffenburg (Bavaria/D), and Frankfurt[90]. On the one hand, this event demonstrates that the River Main was highly frequented by merchant vessels already in the 12th century AD. On the other hand, the toll abolishment was a facilitation and stimulation of the navigation on the Main. It went hand in hand with the promotion of the city of Frankfurt as a centre of supraregional trade[91] and an extension of the architectural infrastructure including the construction of the harbour and harbour related facilities in the 12th and 13th century AD[92]. The quay of the Saalhof castle was most likely both: a river embankment that was needed after land reclamation and a landing site for ships, although it was surely not the main trading harbour of the town. Due to the spatial proximity to the Saalhof, it seems more probable that this part of the harbour was used for passengers' navigation, most likely for an exclusive circle of people like the magistrate, the castle guards, toll-keeper, the royal court members and their guests. Thus, a representative function can be assumed[93].

SPEYER (RHINELAND-PALATINATE / D)

Regarding the above-mentioned criteria for the identification of harbour constructions in archaeological records, a supposedly medieval quay wall excavated in Speyer[94] on the Rhine in 1987 gives an example for the need of critical analysis of prior field documentation. During construction works for the Historical Museum of the Palatinate, workers discovered a masonry wall and a line of 13 vertical poles in front of it (**figs 7-8**). Rescue excavations were carried out under difficult circumstances. Because of the proximity of the site to the floodplain of the Rhine, the rising groundwater and muddy sediments, the archaeological features have quickly been interpreted as a quay wall of a medieval harbour[95] in a supposed silted river branch of the Rhine[96]. An unlocated harbour in Speyer is mentioned as *navalis portus* in 1084 AD[97]. The fact that the Roman harbour of Speyer is assumed in the same area[98] as the excavation site at the Historical Museum may have had an influence on the interpretation too, as well as historical sources mentioning fishermen in this district and ferry connections nearby crossing the Rhine in the south-east of Speyer[99]. However, after the review of the field documentation, there are several reasons to doubt the interpretation of the wall as a medieval quay[100].

Topography

Fig. 7 The supposed quay wall of Speyer. View from north-east. – (Photo Generaldirektion Kulturelles Erbe Rheinland-Pfalz, Außenstelle Speyer 1987, edited by D. Wollenberg).

Speyer is located on the lower terrace on the western riverbank of the Upper Rhine. Like in Regensburg, the early medieval bishop's town emerged on a Roman preceding settlement[101]. Between the 9th and 12th century AD, Speyer expanded several times and was provided with new town walls (**fig. 9**). Since the 12th century AD, suburbs started developing outside the town walls and, not before the 14th century AD, they were integrated into the town fortification. The archaeological site with the supposed quay wall is located in one of these suburbs called »Fischervorstadt« (=suburb of the fishermen)[102] approximately 230 m south of the Speyer Cathedral (**fig. 9**). The western bank of the Rhine is recently about 670 m away from the site. The excavated wall is located 35 m south of the former Ottonian town wall (1050 AD) and runs parallel to it. Furthermore, the wall is close to the area studied by geoarchaeologists from the University of Heidelberg[103].

Regarding the criteria for interpreting archaeological features as harbour constructions, the primary question to be answered is the location of the Rhine branches in the Middle Ages. Although much has been written about the Rhine in Speyer[104], we still do not know its course in detail for the Middle Ages, since there have been no systematic area-wide geomorphological investigations yet. The hitherto existing reconstructions of the medieval course of the Rhine in Speyer mainly seem to be based on historical maps and townscapes from early modern times, which picture a situation that cannot be attributed necessarily to medieval times[105]. But what maps and historical sources do prove is that the Rhine had many side branches before its regulation in the 19th century AD[106], which could change their courses dramatically as a result of a single flood event[107].

First evidence-based results concerning the historical hydrologic situation in Speyer were achieved lately by the geoarchaeological project »Land unter? – Floods and flood prevention at the Upper Rhine during Early and High Middle Ages« at Heidelberg University[108]. Tomographies and corings point to an older Rhine arm (*terminus ante quem* 1600 AD), which ran significantly further westwards than the modern Rhine and crossed the Domgarten. This Rhine arm is located nearly 200 m from the assumed quay wall. On the other hand, after 1600 AD narrow channels are proved running exactly in the direction of the site at the Historical Museum that is subject of this paper[109].

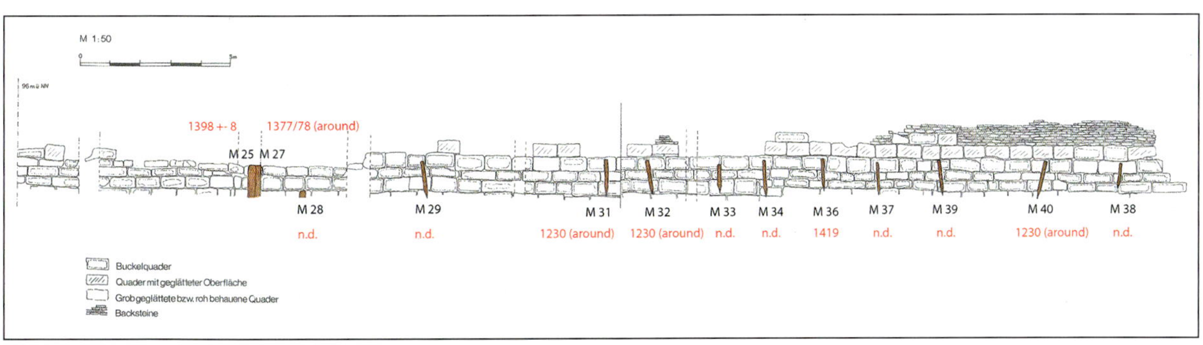

Fig. 8 Technical drawing of the wall and wooden pole from the excavation »Historical Museum« in 1987. – (Generaldirektion Kulturelles Erbe Rheinland-Pfalz, Außenstelle Speyer 1987, edited by D. Wollenberg).

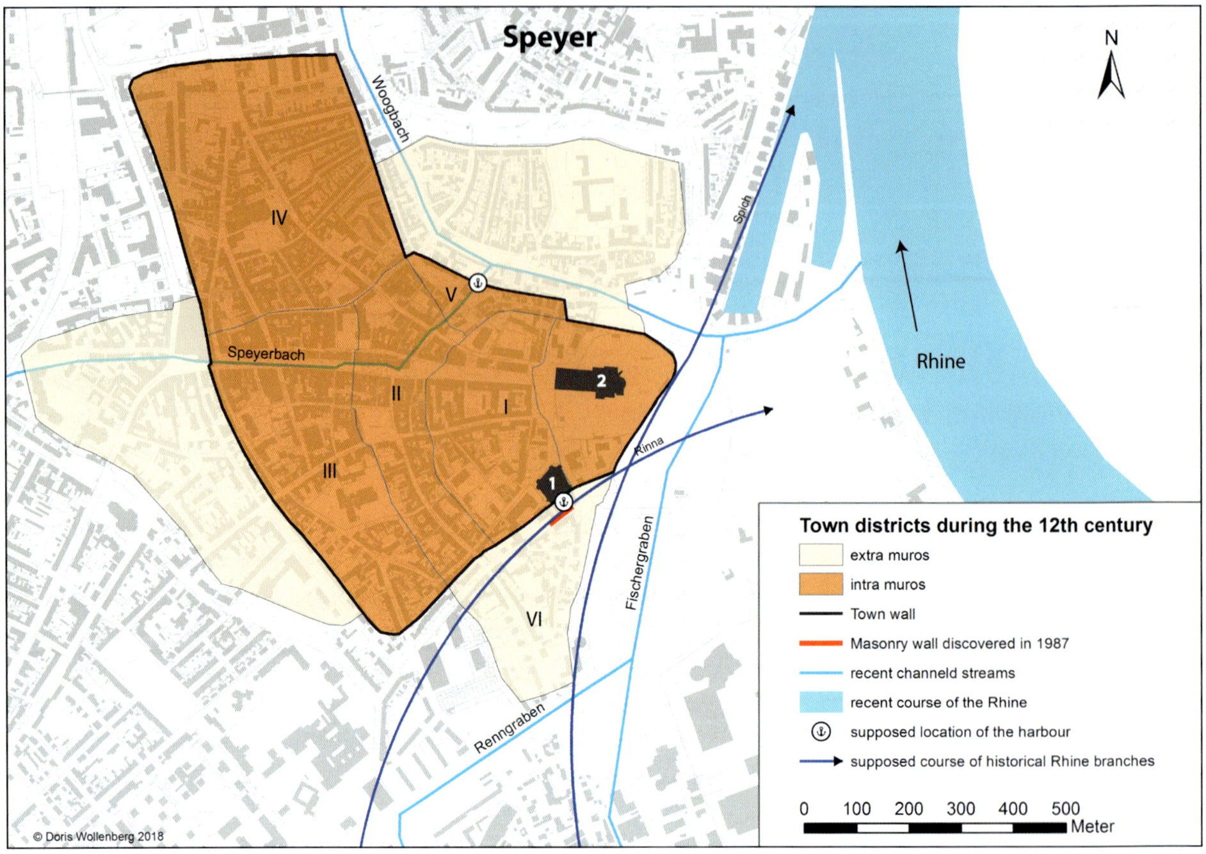

Fig. 9 Map of Speyer: **I** Ottonian *civitas*. – **II** late Ottonian/early Salian merchants' district. – **III** Salian urban expansion. – **IV** late Salian/early Staufer urban expansion. – **V** assumed late medieval harbour and stack (proved by written sources). – **VI** suburban district of the fishermen. – **1** Historical Museum. – **2** Speyer Cathedral. – (Basic data LiKa Speyer: Landesamt für Vermessung und Geobasisinformation Rheinland-Pfalz 2016; R. Engels 2011; 1989a, 489-547; 1989b; R. Müller 1982; Bernhard 2011).

Description of the archaeological features

The wall was documented in a section of 39 m but was uncovered only at its northern surface, since it ran along the excavation boundaries. It was built with different kinds of cut stones, among them bossed sandstones (**figs 7-8**). These cut stones were superimposing a yellow brick wall core. The same bricks were also used to brick up the wall above the five layers of cut stones. A foundation has not been observed. In front of the wall, 13 wooden poles made of oak, fir and alder were documented in an interval of 1.5-2 m. Their upper ends were mostly rotten while their lower ends were sometimes axed-pointed. In some cases, small drill holes at the upper part of the point have been observed. Most of the poles had a rectangular shape, some were round. Their measurements varied between 8-10 cm in diameter respectively 8 cm × 14 cm or 20 cm × 25 cm length of an edge. The longest pole had a preserved length of 1.24 m[110]. Shape, size, and type of wood do not show a regular pattern.

Dating

These poles were interpreted as mooring poles and it was assumed that they have been installed contemporaneously with and as a functional unit of the wall[111]. This assumption must be doubted due to stratigraphic reasons and absolute dating: the poles end above the lower edge of the wall. Since the wall does not show

a foundation[112], its surface must have been visible more or less completely. Therefore, the poles cannot be contemporaneous with the wall because there was no sediment to drive them in in front of the wall. It is much more likely that they have been installed in a more recent stratum which was deposited after the erection of the wall.
Dendrochronological analyses carried out in 1987, dated the poles[113] in a period starting from around 1230 AD until the end of the 14th or the beginning of the 15th century AD. Only five of the 13 poles along the wall were dated at all (**fig. 8**). In the first publication of the site, H.-J. Engels stated that the dendrochronological dates of the poles are homogenous around 1230 AD[114]. This interpretation must be doubted for two reasons: 1. The period of dating is much wider, covering c. 200 years. 2. The oldest dates around 1230 AD are least reliable: they originate from fir tree poles without sapwood and bark and offer not more than a *terminus post quem*. Reliable precise dates with preserved terminal rings originate from pieces dating to the end of the 14th and the beginning of the 15th century AD (M 25 and M 36). If all the poles have been installed at once, which seems probable although not provable, they give a *terminus ante quem* for the construction of the wall before the late 14th/early 15th century AD. Several other poles and wooden planks without spatial reference from the same site are dated predominantly to the 14th-17th century AD[115].
H.-J. Engels has dated the bossed stones of the wall to the 12th and 13th century AD, referring to the dendrochronological data from the poles and to bossed stones as a typical element of castle architecture of the Staufer period (12th-13th century AD). It is true that bossed stones reached their peak of use in this period. But they still appear in the 14th and 15th century AD and are no unique feature of the Staufer architecture at all, especially when used as building material for town walls or contrescarpe walls of the town moat[116], which seems to be the case here[117].

Re-interpretation of the archaeological features

An overlap of the position of the assumed quay wall with a georeferenced 19th century AD map of Speyer shows that the wall follows exactly the course of a moat that had been dug parallel to the medieval town wall in the late 14th century AD[118]. The wall was still intact, though built up supplementary, until the beginning of the 20th century AD: an old photograph from 1905 shows the upper part of the wall in front of the moat[119]. Since there is no evidence for construction phases before the 14th century AD, it seems very likely that the wall is not a quay wall, but a counterscarp that stabilized the outer part of the moat. During the 14th century AD, Speyer was repeatedly under attack: to the year 1375 AD, the construction of a moat is mentioned in written sources when Speyer expected a siege by the count Emich von Leiningen. According to the description, this moat can be located in the area of the archaeological excavation[120]. Only one year later, in 1376 AD, Speyer was again besieged by bishop Adolf von Nassau[121]. The contextualization of the archaeological features with a historic event is surely debatable, but it demonstrates a general phenomenon that we observe in many late medieval towns: urban expansions and the development of weapons and siege technique lead to the construction of new town walls that are adapted to the new weapons technology with secondary obstacles like scarps[122]. In summary, topographical, chronological and functional considerations show that the »quay wall« is in fact a counterscarp of a 14th or 15th century AD fortification of. The analysis of the field documentation does not indicate any late medieval harbour features in this area. Nevertheless, a layer of peat between the town wall and the counterscarp indicates a former water body south of the lower terrace that might have silted up before the wall was constructed. The existence of a pre-14th century AD navigable watercourse in this area, perhaps a side branch of the Rhine, is therefore still possible – but not yet scientifically proved. Nevertheless, for this earlier period the absence of harbour installations does not exclude inland navigation.

CONCLUSION

From our point of view, there are different reasons for the limited archaeological prove of medieval inland harbours in Central Europe. The main point here is that harbours are more than mere mooring facilities. So we have to widen our focus on material remains of all kinds of harbour activities. Archaeological features indicate that medieval inland harbours did not necessarily need solid constructions. It seems like constructive elements were simply not always necessary and boats could be pulled on land also without any additional constructions. Thus, the identification of medieval inland harbours can be difficult if the search is based only on primary harbour features, meaning material remains of constructions in the water or at the riverbank that are related exclusively to navigation.

Identifying archaeological features as remains of inland harbours and identifying harbours without constructive elements, therefore, requires the application of additional criteria. The development of a harbour in medieval urban contexts, which are in the focus of this paper, is usually connected to adjacent settlement structures and the needs of its residents. A structural analysis of the urban topography can be a useful approach for identifying medieval inland harbours or functional harbour zones according to the landward topography of the town. The following set of secondary criteria shall be a first attempt to identify inland harbours in medieval urban contexts more systematically:

1. The localisation of the historic riverbank should be based on multi-disciplinary research with methods and data from geoarchaeology and historical geography.
2. It is crucial to identify the maximum riverine extension of the dwelling zone and building structures of a particular period in order to distinguish harbour features from concurrent building remains of other function (e. g. wooden substructures for buildings on unstable subsoil).
3. Town walls and corresponding moats are spatial markers for the beginning of the dwelling zone that exclude concurrent primary harbour structures. The town wall can be seen as a *signum ante quem* for the localisation of a potential concurrent harbour.
4. Craft areas within the town, especially those with a high demand for water and/or wood (such as tanners, smiths, dyers, shoemakers, pottery workshops, public baths, mills, and so on) are often clustered along the riverbank. They indicate the position of the former riverbank during a certain period and other kinds of water usage that in some cases may have complicated and sometime even excluded navigation.
5. Since harbours seem to have stretched along the whole riverbank, harbour and trade-related waterfront facilities (e. g. cranes, town scales, storehouses, merchants' houses and shipyards) mark different functional zones of a harbour, indicate various harbour activities, and mark different areas of control.

The application of these criteria on our case studies revealed that waterfront constructions were often multifunctional and usually used for navigation, fortification, bank revetment (especially after land reclamation) and water exploitation related to hydrophilic craft at the same time. A comparison with other towns like for example Lübeck (Schleswig-Holstein/D)[123] indicates that from the High and Late Middle Ages on can observe that the multifunctional use of the riverbank decreases in favour of a growing spatial and functional differentiation. This process seems to be linked to the gradual shrinking space between waterfront and town wall. The same applies to masonry harbour constructions such as quays and jetties which correspond to the increasing use of stone as building material in towns, whereas in early and high medieval times, wood appears to be the major building material for inland harbours.

It has to be stressed that especially bank parallel revetments cannot be distinguished clearly from harbour constructions. The decision to spend time and effort on solid bank revetments was therefore not related exclusively to navigation. The necessity for such revetments seems to be caused primarily by people's needs on the landward side of the river respectively of the contemporary settlement. A reliable identification of medieval inland harbours has therefore to be conducted both from the river perspective as well as from the land. Only by considering secondary criteria for harbour activity, the functioning of the harbour or different functional zones of the harbour can be distinguished. Compared to France, the current state of research on medieval inland harbours in Germany reflects a lack of systematic surveys and field work in underwater archaeology as an integral part of heritage conservation[124] and demonstrates that this topic is not fully exploited yet.

Notes

1) Werther/Kröger 2017, 71-74. – Zettler 2000. – Rückert 2004.

2) Werther et al. 2015; 2018.

3) Koch/Leininger 1993.

4) For archaeological evidence of harbours as well as harbour terminology see Werther/Müller/Foucher 2018.

5) Cambridge Dictionary: https://dictionary.cambridge.org/dictionary/english/harbour (11.1.2019). – Oxford Dictionary: https://en.oxforddictionaries.com/definition/harbour (11.1.2019).

6) The project is one of 15 projects of the Priority Program »Harbours of the Roman Period to the Middle Ages« (SPP 1630) funded by the German Research Foundation (Deutsche Forschungsgemeinschaft).

7) Werther/Kröger 2017. – Wunschel et al. 2015; 2018. – Kenecke 2014.

8) This problem occurred during the author's analyses of probable riverine harbour remains that were excavated within smaller rescue excavations at the riverbank of the Danube in Regensburg. See also Blobel in this volume.

9) See Kröger 2018, fig. 1.

10) Wunschel et al. 2018.

11) See for e.g. Heine 2008. – Lang et al. 2003.

12) Ellmers 2004. – Kröger 2014.

13) Obladen-Kauder 2011. – Kramer/Schlichtherle 1995a; 1995b. – Kunow 2011.

14) This statement is explicitly not intended to devaluate the partly very professional work of »amateurs« like e.g. the work of the Bavarian Society for Underwater archaeology (Bayerische Gesellschaft für Unterwasserarchäologie). Rather it should be noted that the outsourcing of underwater archaeological expertise to costless alternatives, respectively the yet missing insourcing of professional underwater archaeology into the responsibilities of national heritage conservation is criticized.

15) Obladen-Kauder 2011.

16) Freund/Hardt/Weigel 2007.

17) Dietz et al. 1979.

18) About the urban development of Regensburg: Boos/Codreanu-Windauer/Wintergerst 1995. – Codreanu-Windauer/Wintergerst 2000. – Codreanu-Windauer et al. 2000. – Dallmeier 2000.

19) Wanderwitz 2006, 46-50. – Hardt 2007.

20) Annales regni Francorum, s.a. 792, p. 178: »... *Pons super navigia flumina transeuntia factus est, anchoris et funibus ita cohaerens, ut iungi et dissolvi possit* ...«.

21) Schmid 1977.

22) Mai 2006.

23) Hensch 2018.

24) Hardt 2007, 109.

25) »*in montem staretur super plantatione vinearum: inter conflenta Donubii et Imbris sitis dinoscitur; ...et urbem avidam, moeniis et turrium constructione muntam. ...et dum portum pervenissent, puppem ingressus, transmissio amnis fluenta, ad portum salubrem plagae urbis*«, Bischof 1953, 74-77. – Ettel/Wunschel 2014, 79-80.

26) Heilmeier 2008, 81.

27) The localization of the Roman harbour not based on reliable archaeological features but singular finds and must be doubted. See Dietz et al. 1979, 69.

28) Codreanu-Windauer/Reuter 2008. – Codreanu-Windauer 2005. – Dallmeier 2009.

29) Bond 2007. – Kalmring/Kröger/Kirchner 2017. – Kröger/Kirchner/Werther 2017.

30) Bond 2007, 153-206. – Werther et al. 2018.

31) Werther et al. 2018, 355-372.

32) Elmshäuser 1992. – Lohrmann 1984.

33) Dallmeier 1988; 2011. – Dallmeier/Hensch 2011.

34) Codreanu-Windauer/Dallmeier 2015a; 2015b; 2014. – Dallmeier/Kirpal 2011.

35) Werther et al. 2018, 355-372.

36) Klaus-Tschira-Archäometrie-Zentrum, sample number 33590, radiocarbon years 1180±21, 1-sigma: 778-886 cal AD, 2-sigma: 773-937 cal AD, Report: R. Friedrich (30.1.2018). – AMS-Labor Erlangen, sample number R-Donaumarkt 01/14-10, Erl-19224, radiocarbon years 1120±30, 1-sigma: 889-977 cal AD, 2-sigma: 857-998 cal AD, Report: A. Scharf (5.5.2014).

37) Dallmeier/Kirpal 2011, 132-134. – Herzig 2012.

38) Nießen/Wollenberg 2019.

39) German term: Schlitzpfosten – author's note.

40) For details of the construction and dendrochronological analyses: Codreanu-Windauer/Herzig 2015.

41) Codreanu-Windauer/Herzig 2015.

42) Report: Rössner 2013.

43) Abriß der Stadt Regensburg.

44) Schmid 2010, 335-337.

45) Wolfsteiner 2006.

46) Wolfsteiner 2006.

47) Wolfsteiner 2006, 85. – Eißing/Dittmar 2011, 139.

48) Urkataster der Stadt Regensburg von 1811.

49) Abriß der Stadt Regensburg 1630.

50) Mario Ranzinger, University of Heidelberg; Title: Timber supply at Regensburg – Provenance analysis using ICP-MS measurements on wooden samples from the excavation at the Danube Market (ongoing master-thesis).

51) Schmetzer 1925, 81.

52) Schmetzer 1925, 81.

53) Schmetzer 1925, 81.

54) Schmetzer 1925, 76. – Schedelsche Weltchronik.

55) Dallmeier 1988; 2011. – Dallmeier/Hensch 2011.

56) Dallmeier/Hensch 2011, 31 fig. 40.

57) The Stone Bridge as one of the »turning points« of the environmental history of Regensburg and its influence on navigation: Knoll 2013, 268-299.

58) Kröger 2013; 2014.

59) Schmetzer 1925.

60) Dallmeier/Hensch 2011, fig. 40.

61) König 2002, 72.

62) König 2002, 69-80.

63) König 2002, 75.

64) Orth 1994, 20-21.

65) Schalles-Fischer 1969, 16 fig. 1.

66) Schalles-Fischer 1969, 85-199. 503 ff. – Orth 1994, 13-25. 28-31.

67) Hampel 2013a; 2013b. – Ehlers 2013.

68) Walbe 1979. – Großmann 1983. – Großmann/Michels 2002, 29-59. – Untermann 2009, 255-267.

69) Luciano 2016, 23.

70) Wunschel et al. 2015.

71) Dendrochronological report by Dr. Thorsten Westphal (2.7.2012). Dendrochronologisches Labor Westphal Frankfurt (DLWF), Marburger Straße 15, 60487 Frankfurt am Main. Labor-Nr. DLWF 6310-6312.

72) Hampel 2013a, 23.

73) Dendrochronological report by Thorsten Westphal (4.9.2017), Dendrochronologisches Labor am Klaus-Tschira-Archäometrie-Zentrum des Curt-Engelhorn-Zentrum Archäometrie gGmbH, D 6,3, 68159 Mannheim, MA 175682, Labor-Nr. MAD 1653.

74) The quay was preserved completely *in situ* for the exhibition in the museum's court.

75) Konstanz: Röber 2000; Dumitrache 1993. – Lübeck: Gläser 2009; Schalies 1992; 2009; 2014. – Schleswig: Müller/Rösch/Schimmer 2014; Rösch 2016; Luciano 2016, 20.

76) Binding 1996, 335-336. 345-436. – Hampel 2016, 126-127. – Stamm 1967, 50-52.

77) Stamm 1967, 17.

78) Stamm 1967, 17-18.

79) Stamm 1967, 18. 29.

80) Werther/Wollenberg in prep.

81) Binding 1996, 338. – Stamm 1967, 29.

82) See Gelnhausen, Kaiserswerth or Seligenstadt; Binding 1996, 262-292. 318-326. 389-396.

83) Binding 1996, 336-337.

84) Royal council. – Zotz 2003, 374-375.

85) German term »Schultheiß« – author's note.

86) Codex Diplomaticus Moenofrancofurtus 15-16.

87) Cilleßen 2017.

88) See Wollenberg et al. 2019.

89) Binding 1996, 319. – Eschbach 1903.

90) Codex Diplomaticus Moenofrancofurtus 15.

91) Fried 1984, 195-239. – Escher/Hirschmann 2005, 200-203. – Fuhrmann 2010, 378-398. – Brübach 1996. – Irsigler 1971; 1996. – Rothmann 1998. – Bönnen 2010.

92) See Wollenberg et al. 2019.

93) See Werther/Wollenberg in prep.

94) H.-J. Engels 1989.

95) Newspaper article from 1987: »Steinerne Zeugen aus dem Mittelalter entdeckt. Dem ersten Yachthafen auf der Spur«. Speyerer Tageblatt 24.9.1987. – H.-J. Engels 1989.

96) Doll 1999, 306.

97) Müller 1994, 63.

98) Wawrzinek 2014, 58-59. 158. 435. – Müller 1994, 19.

99) Doll/Harthausen 1999, 303.

100) A full analysis of the site is part of Doris Wollenberg's ongoing PhD thesis »Medieval Inland Harbours in Central Europe«.

101) Unlike in Regensburg the medieval settlement on the cathedral area of Speyer is spatially orientated on the late antique burgus and not on the Roman fort (10 BC) like it is the case in Regensburg.

102) Later called Marxenvorstadt. This area was integrated into the town walls in the second half of the 14th century AD (after 1365): Müller 1994, 223.

103) See Conijn et al. in this volume.

104) Doll/Harthausen 1999, 304-307. – H.-J. Engels 1989. – R. Engels 1989a; 1989b. – Müller 1994, 64-67.

105) Klipfelsauplan (1547); Ansicht Speyer (1592); Civitas orbis terrarum (1572); Merian (1637).

106) Ebeling 2005.

107) Dambeck 2005.

108) See Conijn et al. in this volume, especially fig. 5. – For the Roman Iron Age see Gerlach/Meuers-Balke/Becker 2007. – Kennecke 2014.

109) See Conjin et al. in this volume, fig. 4 (map showing the situation after 1600).

110) Neyses 1989.

111) H.-J. Engels 1989.

112) Most town walls show only a very shallow foundation. Contrescarpe walls as part of the town moat were usually built without any foundation. Biller 2016, 74.

113) Neyses 1989.

114) H.-J. Engels 1989, 101.

115) Neyses 1989.

116) Biller 2016, 61-65.

117) Müller 1994, 66. 223.

118) Map of Speyer from 1820 AD. Landesamt für Vermessung und Geobasisinformation Rheinland-Pfalz; concerning the dating of the moat Müller 1994, 171.

119) Müller 1994, 204 fig. 143.

120) Müller 1994, 204.

121) Müller 1994, 197.

122) Müller 1994, 197. 203-205. – Biller 2016, 351-356.

123) Schalies 1992; 2009; 2014. – Hammel-Kiesow 2001.

124 Kramer/Schlichtherle 1995a; 1995b, 16. – Obladen-Kauder 2011.

Sources

Codex Diplomaticus Moenofrancofurtus: J. F. Boehmer (ed.), Codex Diplomaticus Moenofrancofurtus. Urkundenbuch der Reichsstadt Frankfurt 1 (Frankfurt a. M. 1836).

Regino Chronik: Reginonis Chronicon ad. a. 792, ed. G. H. Pertz, Monumenta Germaniae historica. Scriptores 1 (Hannoverae 1826) 537-629, hier 561.

Schedelsche Weltchronik: M. Wohlgemut, Regensburg im Jahr 1493. In: Hartmann Schedel, Weltchronik (Nürnberg 1493).

Urkataster der Stadt Regensburg von 1811. Bayerisches Landesvermessungsamt München, Nr. 558/03.

References

Bernhard 2011: H. Bernhard, Steinhäuser und Holzhäuser im hochmittelalterlichen Speyer des 11. und 12. Jahrhunderts. In: L. Heeg (ed.), Die Salier. Macht im Wandel [exhibiton catalogue Speyer] (München 2011) 194-195.

Biller 2016: Th. Biller, Die mittelalterlichen Stadtbefestigungen im deutschsprachigen Raum. Ein Handbuch. 1: Systematischer Teil (Darmstadt 2016).

Binding 1996: G. Binding, Deutsche Königspfalzen. Von Karl dem Grossen bis Friedrich II. (765-1240) (Darmstadt 1996).

Bischof 1953: B. Bischof (ed.), Arbeo, Vita et passio Sancti Haimhrammi Martyris. Leben und Leiden des Hl. Emmeram. Lateinisch-deutsch (München 1953).

Blackmore 1999: L. Blackmore, Commerce and capital: archaeological aspects of London's trade 1100-1700. In: M. Gläser (ed.), Lübecker Kolloquium zur Stadtarchäologie im Hanseraum. II: Der Handel (Lübeck 1999) 37-58.

Bond 2007: J. Bond, Canal Construction in the Early Middle Ages: An Introductory Review. In: J. Blair (ed.), Waterways and canal-building in medieval England (Oxford 2007) 153-206.

Boos/Codreanu-Windauer/Wintergerst 1995: A. Boos / S. Codreanu-Windauer / E. Wintergerst, Regensburg zwischen Antike und Mittelalter. In: M. Angerer / H. Wanderwitz (eds), Regensburg im Mittelalter. 1: Beiträge zur Stadtgeschichte vom frühen Mittelalter bis zum Beginn der Neuzeit (Regensburg 1995) 31-44.

1998: A. Bos / S. Codreanu-Windauer / E. Wintergerst, Regensburg zwischen Antike und Mittelalter. In: M. Angerer / H. Wanderwitz (eds), Regensburg im Mittelalter. 1: Beiträge zur Stadtgeschichte vom frühen Mittelalter bis zum Beginn der Neuzeit (Regensburg [2]1998) 31-44.

Bönnen 2010: G. Bönnen, Rhein-Main-Neckar-Region: Herrschaftsorganisation nach konsensualem Muster. In: B. Schneidmüller / S. Weinfurter / A. Wieczorek (eds), Verwandlungen des Stauferreichs. Drei Innovationsregionen im mittelalterlichen Europa (Darmstadt 2010) 94-111.

Brübach 1996: N. Brübach, Die Entstehung und die Frühzeit der Frankfurter Messen. In: P. Johanek / H. Stoob (eds), Europäische Messen und Märktesysteme in Mittelalter und Neuzeit. Städteforschung A 39 (Köln, Weimar, Wien 1996) 143-170.

Cilleßen 2017: W. Cilleßen, Die Altbauten: Das Saalhof-Ensemble. In: J. Gerchow / W. Cilleßen (eds), Frankfurt Museum – Führer durch das Historische Museum Frankfurt. Kunststücke des Historischen Museums Frankfurt 4 (Frankfurt am Main 2017) 35-40.

Codreanu-Windauer 2005: S. Codreanu-Windauer, Im Osten viel Neues! Neue Ergebnisse zur römischen Zivilbebauung in Regensburg (Oberpfalz). Das archäologische Jahr in Bayern 2004 (2005), 91-93.

Codreanu-Windauer/Dallmeier 2014: S. Codreanu-Windauer / L.-M. Dallmeier, Donaumarkt. Beginn der Ausgrabungen vor dem Museumsbau. Denkmalpflege in Regensburg 13, 2014, 318-323.

2015a: S. Codreanu-Windauer / L.-M. Dallmeier, Archäologie am Regensburger Donaumarkt. Eine erste Rückschau auf die Großgrabung 2012-2015. Denkmalpflege in Regensburg 14, 2015, 7-25.

2015b: S. Codreanu-Windauer / L.-M. Dallmeier, Neues zur Vorstadt der alten Metropolis – Endspurt der Großgrabung am Regensburger Donaumarkt. Das archäologische Jahr in Bayern 2014 (2015), 121-124.

Codreanu-Windauer/Herzig 2015: S. Codreanu-Windauer / F. Herzig, Vom Fluss umspült – Holzgebäude am Donaumarkt in Regensburg. Ein Vorbericht. In: H. May / G. Waldemer / A. Weidlich (eds), Neues aus der Hausforschung in Bayern. Schriften und Kataloge des Fränkischen Freilandmuseums in Bad Windsheim 75 = Quellen und Materialien zur Hausforschung in Bayern 16 (Bad Windsheim 2015) 293-304.

Codreanu-Windauer/Reuter 2008: S. Codreanu-Windauer / S. Reuter, Römer vor der Haustür – Die römische Zivilsiedlung im Osten Regensburgs (Oberpfalz). Das archäologische Jahr in Bayern 2007 (2008), 69-70.

Codreanu-Windauer/Wintergerst 2000: S. Codreanu-Windauer / E. Wintergerst, Regensburg – eine mittelalterliche Großstadt an der Donau. In: A. Wieczorek (ed.), Europas Mitte um 1000 [exhibition catalogue Budapest] (Stuttgart 2000) 179-183.

Codreanu-Windauer et al. 2000: S. Codreanu-Windauer / M. Hoernes / A. Rettner / K. Schnieringer / E. Wintergerst, Die städtebauliche Entwicklung Regensburgs von der Spätantike bis ins Hochmittelalter. In: P. Schmid (ed.), Geschichte der Stadt Regensburg 2 (Regensburg 2000) 1013-1053.

Dallmeier 1988: L.-M. Dallmeier, Archäologische Untersuchungen im Regensburger Salzstadel – Neues zum mittelalterlichen Schiffskanal. Verhandlungen des Historischen Vereins für Oberpfalz und Regensburg 128, 1988, 229-241.

2000: L.-M. Dallmeier, Fundort Regensburg. Archäologische Topographie der Stadt Regensburg. Vorgeschichte, römische Kaiserzeit und frühes Mittelalter innerhalb der zweiten Stadterweiterung. Regensburger Studien und Quellen zur Kulturgeschichte 10 (Regensburg 2000).

2009: L.-M. Dallmeier, Von Klöstern und Krautbauern. Archäologische Untersuchungen vor den Toren des hochmittelalterlichen Regensburg. Denkmalpflege in Regensburg 11, 2009, 32-40.

2011: L.-M. Dallmeier, Schwarzer Turm, Salzstadel und Hafenkanal. Archäologische Forschungen an den beiden Brückenköpfen der Steinernen Brücke in Regensburg. In: M. Prell (ed.), Archäologie der Brücken. Vorgeschichte. Antike. Mittelalter. Neuzeit (Regensburg 2011) 195-200.

Dallmeier/Hensch 2011: L.-M. Dallmeier / M. Hensch, Geheimnisse der Steinernen Brücke: neue archäologische Aufschlüsse zur mittelalterlichen Bebauung des südlichen Brückenkopfes. Denkmalpflege in Regensburg 12, 2011, 6-33.

Dallmeier/Kirpal 2011: L.-M. Dallmeier / U. Kirpal, Neue Forschungen am Regensburger Donauufer. Das archäologische Jahr in Bayern 2010 (2011), 132-134.

Dambeck 2005: R. Dambeck, Beiträge zur spät- und postglazialen Fluß- und Landschaftsgeschichte im nördlichen Oberrheingraben (Frankfurt am Main 2005).

Dietz et al. 1979: K. Dietz / U. Osterhaus / S. Rieckhoff / K. Spindler, Regensburg zur Römerzeit (Regensburg 1979).

Doll/Harthausen 1999: L. A. Doll / H. Harthausen, Ubi maxima vis regni esse noscitur. Ausgewählte Abhandlungen zur pfälzischen Geschichte. Quellen und Abhandlungen zur mittelrheinischen Kirchengeschichte 96 (Mainz 1999).

Dumitrache 1993: M. Dumitrache, Der Konstanzer Hafen im 12. und 14. Jahrhundert im Lichte der archäologischen Ausgrabungen auf der Marktstätte und in der Brotlaube. In: M. Gläser (ed.), Archäologie des Mittelalters und Bauforschung im Hanseraum. Eine Festschrift für Günter P. Fehring. Schriften des Kulturhistorischen Museums Rostock 1 (Rostock 1993) 331-340.

Ebeling 2005: H. Ebeling, Johann Gottfried Tulla und die Korrektion des Oberrheins. Zeitschrift des Historischen Vereins Mittelbaden 85, 2005, 495-514.

Ehlers 2013: C. Ehlers, Die Stadt der Staufer und der Fluss. In: J. Gerchow (ed.), Der staufische Hafen des Frankfurter Saalhofs (Frankfurt a. M. 2013) 10-18.

Eißing/Dittmar 2011: T. Eißing / C. Dittmar, Timber transport and dendro-provenancing in Thuringia and Bavaria. In: P. Fraiture (ed.), Tree rings, art, archaeology: proceedings of an international conference; Brussels, Royal Institute for Cultural Heritage, 10th-12th February 2010. Scientia Artis 7 (Brussels 2011) 137-150.

Ellmers 2004: Reallexikon der Germanischen Altertumskunde XXVII (2004) 32-50 s. v. Schiffbau (D. Ellmers).

Elmshäuser 1992: K. Elmshäuser, Kanalbau und technische Wasserführung im frühen Mittelalter. Technikgeschichte 59/1, 1992, 1-26.

H.-J. Engels 1989: H.-J. Engels, Ein neuentdeckter mittelalterlicher Hafen. In: H.-J. Engels (ed.), Unter dem Pflaster von Speyer. Archäologische Grabungen von 1987-1989 (Speyer 1989) 99-102.

R. Engels 1989a: R. Engels, Zur Topographie der Stadt Speyer vor 1689: Anmerkungen zu den Kartenbeilagen im zweiten Band der »Geschichte der Stadt Speyer« (Stuttgart 1989).

1989b: R. Engels, Überblick über die Stadtentwicklung Speyers vom 10.-18. Jahrhundert. In: H.-J. Engels (ed.), Unter dem Pflaster von Speyer. Archäologische Grabungen von 1987-1989 (Speyer 1989) 76-80.

2011: R. Engels, Speyer in der Salierzeit. In: L. Heeg (ed.), Die Salier. Macht im Wandel [exhibiton catalogue Speyer] (München 2011) 130-139.

Eschbach 1903: P. Eschbach, Zur Baugeschichte der Hohenstaufenpfalz Kaiserswerth. Beiträge zur Geschichte des Niederrheins 18, 1903, 156-164.

Escher/Hirschmann 2005: M. Escher / F. G. Hirschmann, Die urbanen Zentren des hohen und späteren Mittelalters: vergleichende Untersuchungen zu Städten und Städtelandschaften im Westen des Reiches und in Ostfrankreich. Trierer historische Forschungen 50 (Trier 2005).

Ettel/Wunschel 2014: P. Ettel / A. Wunschel, Regensburg – Metropole an der Donau. In: P. Ettel / F. Daim / S. Berg-Hobohm / L. Werther / Ch. Zielhofer (eds), Großbaustelle 793. Das Kanalprojekt Karls des Großen zwischen Rhein und Donau. Mosaiksteine. Forschungen am RGZM 11 (Mainz 2014) 79-80.

Fischer 1971: U. Fischer, Aus Frankfurts Vorgeschichte (Frankfurt am Main 1971).

Freund/Hardt/Weigel 2007: S. Freund / M. Hardt / P. Weigel (eds), Siedlungsforschung: Archäologie – Geschichte – Geographie. Flüsse und Flusstäler als Wirtschafts- und Kommunikationswege (Bonn 2007) 103-120.

Fried 1984: J. Fried, Die Wirtschaftspolitik Friedrich Barbarossas in Deutschland. Blätter für deutsche Landesgeschichte 120, 1984, 195-239.

Fuhrmann 2010: B. Fuhrmann, Wirtschaftlicher Ertrag der einzelnen Regionen – Monetarisierung Europas: Rohstoffe, Handel, Messen. In: In: B. Schneidmüller / S. Weinfurter / A. Wieczorek (eds), Verwandlungen des Stauferreichs. Drei Innovationsregionen im mittelalterlichen Europa (Darmstadt 2010) 378-398.

Gerlach/Meurers-Balke/Becker 2007: R. Gerlach / J. Meurers-Balke / T. Becker, Wo war der Rhein zur Römerzeit? Ein Beitrag zum Rhein-Limes-Projekt. Archäologie im Rheinland 2006 (2007), 9-17.

Gläser 2009: M. Gläser, Mittelalterliche Baulandgewinnung in Lübeck. Mitteilungen der Deutschen Gesellschaft für Archäologie des Mittelalters und der Neuzeit 21/1, 2009, 59-64.

Großmann 1983: G. U. Großmann, Der spätmittelalterliche Fachwerkbau in Hessen (Königstein im Taunus 1983).

Großmann/Michels 2002: G. U. Großmann / H. Michels, Fachwerk als historische Bauweise. Ein Materialleitfaden und Ratgeber (Suderburg-Hösseringen 2002).

Hammel-Kiesow 2001: R. Hammel-Kiesow, Der Lübecker Hafen von den Anfängen bis heute. In: R. Hammel-Kiesow (ed.), Seefahrt, Schiff und Schifferbrüder. 600 Jahre Schiffergesellschaft zu Lübeck 1401-2001 [exhibition catalogue] (Lübeck 2001) 75-81.

Hampel 2013a: A. Hampel, Die Kaimauer des staufischen Saalhofs in Frankfurt am Main. In: J. Gerchow (ed.), Der staufische Hafen des Frankfurter Saalhofs (Frankfurt a. M. 2013) 20-27.

2013b: A. Hampel, Eine staufische Kaimauer in der Frankfurter Altstadt. hessenArchäologie 2012 (2013), 164-167.

2016: A. Hampel, Neues zur Baugeschichte des staufischen Saalhofes in Frankfurt am Main. hessenArchäologie 2015 (2016), 126-129.

Hardt 2007: M. Hardt, Die Donau als Verkehrs- und Kommunikationsweg zwischen der ostfränkischen Residenz Regensburg und den Zentren an der mittleren Donau im 9. Jahrhundert. In: Freund/Hardt/Weigel 2007, 103-120.

Hausberger 1989: K. Hausberger, Geschichte des Bistums Regensburg. I: Mittelalter und frühe Neuzeit (Regensburg 1989).

Heilmeier 2008: H. Heilmeier, Der elektrische Schiffsdurchzug bei der Steinernen Brücke zu Regensburg – ein technisches Unikat. Donau-Schiffahrt 9, 2008, 80-108.

Heine 2008: K. Heine, Fluviale Sedimente und Formen – bedeutende Geoarchive für Umwelt- und Klimarekonstruktionen. Probleme der Interpretation am Beispiel der Donau bei Regensburg. In: T. Bosch (ed.), Festgabe 40 Jahre Lehrstuhl für Vor- und Frühgeschichte der Universität Regensburg. 1968-2008. Regensburger Beiträge zur prähistorischen Archäologie 20 (Regensburg 2008) 321-350.

Hensch 2018: M. Hensch, Erz, Feuer, Eisen: Eine kleine Geschichte des frühen Montanwesens in der mittleren Oberpfalz (Berlin 2018).

Herzig 2012: F. Herzig, Uferverbauung am Donaumarkt. Dendroarchäologische Untersuchung. Bayerisches Landesamt für Denkmalpflege. Praktische Denkmalpflege/Archäologische Denkmäler. Referat BV – Restaurierung, Archäologie und Dendrolabor [unpubl. report, Thierhaupten 17.1.2012].

Irsigler 1971: F. Irsigler, Die Frankfurter Messen und die Handelsbeziehungen zu Oberdeutschland im 15. Jh. In: E. Ennen / H. Stehkämper (eds), Köln, das Reich und Europa. Abhandlungen über weiträumige Verflechtungen der Stadt Köln in Politik, Recht und Wirtschaft im Mittelalter. Mitteilungen aus dem Stadtarchiv von Köln 60 (Köln 1971) 341-459.

1996: F. Irsigler, Jahrmärkte und Messesysteme im westlichen Reichsgebiet bis ca. 1250. In: P. Johanek / H. Stoob (eds), Europäische Messen und Märktesysteme in Mittelalter und Neuzeit. Städteforschung A 39 (Köln, Weimar, Wien 1996) 1-33.

Kalmring/Kröger/Kirchner 2017: L. Werther / L. Kröger / A. Kirchner, Fossata Magna – Kanäle des 1. Jahrtausends n. Chr. und ihr Erkenntnispotential für die Hafenforschung. In: S. Kalmring / L. Werther (eds), Häfen im 1. Millennium AD. RGZM –Tagungen 31 = Interdisziplinäre Forschungen zu den Häfen von der Römischen Kaiserzeit bis zum Mittelalter in Europa 4 (Mainz 2017) 61-80.

Kennecke 2014: H. Kennecke (ed.), Der Rhein als europäische Verkehrsachse. Die Römerzeit. Bonner Beiträge zur vor- und frühgeschichtlichen Archäologie 16 (Bonn 2014).

Knoll 2013: M. Knoll, Die Natur der menschlichen Welt. Siedlung, Territorium und Umwelt in der historisch-topographischen Literatur der Frühen Neuzeit. Histoire 42 (Bielefeld 2013).

Koch/Leininger 1993: R. Koch / G. Leininger (eds), Der Karlsgraben – Ergebnisse neuer Erkundungen (Bau intern Sonderdruck 1993).

König 2002: S. König, Die Ausgrabungen am St. Katharinenspital 1999-2000. Ein Beitrag zur Geschichte des Spitals juxa pontem Ratisponensis. Denkmalpflege in Regensburg 8, 2002, 69-80.

Kramer/Schlichtherle 1995a: W. Kramer / H. Schlichtherle (eds), Unterwasser-Archäologie in Deutschland. Archäologie unter Wasser. Forschungen und Berichte zur Unterwasserarchäologie zwischen Alpenrand und Nordmeer 1 (Mainz 1995).

1995b: W. Kramer / H. Schlichtherle, Unterwasser-Archäologie in Deutschland. Antike Welt 26/1, 1995, 3-16.

Kröger 2013: L. Kröger, Zwischen Main und Alpenrand. Ein Überblick zu den archäologischen Hinterlassenschaften von Wasserfahrzeugen in Süddeutschland. In: M. Chytrácek / H. Gruber / J. Michálek et al. (eds), 22. Treffen/Archäologische Arbeitsgemeinschaft Ostbayern, West- und Südböhmen, Oberösterreich. 20. bis 23. Juni 2012 in Attersee – Mondsee. Fines Transire, Jahrgang 22, 2013 (Rahden/Westf. 2013) 111-130.

2014: L. Kröger, Früh- und hochmittelalterliche Binnenschiffe in Mitteleuropa. Ein Überblick zum aktuellen Stand der Forschung. Přehled Výzkumů 55/2, 2014, 91-123.

2018: L. Kröger, Within the network of fluvial ports. In: L. Werther / H. Müller / M. Foucher (eds), European Harbour Data Repository, Vol. 01 (Jena 2018). DOI: 10.22032/dbt.35240 (pdf), 10.22032/dbt.35241 (csv), 10.22032/dbt.35242 (excel).

Kunow 2011: J. Kunow, Jahrestagung des Verbandes der Landesarchäologen in der Bundesrepublik Deutschland vom 9. bis 12. Mai 2010 in Schwerin, Mecklenburg-Vorpommern: wissenschaftliches Kolloquium am 11. Mai 2010 »Stand, Desiderate und Verbesserungsmöglichkeiten in der deutschen Unterwasserarchäologie im Vergleich zu den Nachbarstaaten«; Grußwort. Archäologisches Nachrichtenblatt 16/2, 2011, 111-113.

Lang et al. 2003: A. Lang / H.-R. Bork / R. Mäckel / N. Preston / J. Wunderlich / R. Dikau, Changes in sediment flux and storage within a fluvial system. Some examples from the Rhine catchment. Hydrological Processes 17/16, 2003, 3321-3334.

Lohrmann 1984: D. Lohrmann, Mühlenbau, Schiffahrt und Flußumleitungen im Süden der Grafschaft Flandern-Artois (10.-11. Jahrhundert). Francia 12, 1984, 149-192.

Luciano 2016: A. Luciano, The wooden medieval ports. In: B. Stanislawski / H. Öniz (eds), SOMA 2014. Proceedings of the 18th Symposium on Mediterranean Archaeology. Wroclaw – Poland, 24-26 April 2014 (Oxford 2016) 17-26.

Mai 2006: P. Mai, Regensburg und der Osten. In: E. Feistner (ed.), Das mittelalterliche Regensburg im Zentrum Europas. Forum Mittelalter Studien 1 (Regensburg 2006) 235-248.

Müller 1994: K. R. Müller, Die Mauern der Freien Reichsstadt Speyer als Rahmen der Stadtgeschichte. Beiträge zur Speyerer Stadtgeschichte 8 (Speyer 1994).

Müller 1982: R. Müller, Die Reichsstadt Speyer um 1525 (o.O. 1982).

Müller/Rösch/Schimmer 2014: U. Müller / F. Rösch / M. Schimmer, Von Haithabu nach Schleswig. Aktuelle Forschungen zur Gründung einer Metropole zwischen Wikinger- und Hansezeit. Mitteilungen der Deutschen Gesellschaft für Archäologie des Mittelalters und der Neuzeit 27, 2014, 25-36.

Neyses 1989: M. Neyses, Jahrringchronologische Untersuchungen an mittelalterlichen Holzfunden aus Speyer. In: H.-J. Engels (ed.), Unter dem Pflaster von Speyer. Archäologische Grabungen von 1987-1989 (Speyer 1989) 103-110.

Nießen/Wollenberg 2019: I. Nießen / D. Wollenberg, Der mittelalterliche Flusshafen in Regensburg. Uferentwicklung, Befestigung und Bebauung im Spiegel der Ausgrabungen Donaumarkt/Donaulände. In: P. Ettel / A. Th. Hack (eds), Flusstäler, Flussschifffahrt, Flusshäfen: Befunde aus Antike und Mittelalter. RGZM – Tagungen 39 = Interdisziplinäre Forschungen zu den Häfen von der Römischen Kaiserzeit bis zum Mittelalter in Europa 7 (Mainz 2019) 193-206.

Obladen-Kauder 2011: J. Obladen-Kauder, Kapazitäten in der deutschen Unterwasserarchäologie. Archäologisches Nachrichtenblatt 16, 2011, 114-120.

Orth 1994: E. Orth, Frankfurt am Main im Früh- und Hochmittelalter. In: Frankfurter Historische Kommission (ed.), Frankfurt am Main. Geschichte der Stadt in neuen Beiträgen (Sigmaringen 1994) 9-52.

Rothmann 1998: M. Rothmann, Die Frankfurter Messen im Mittelalter. Frankfurter historische Abhandlungen 40 (Stuttgart 1998).

Röber 2000: R. Röber, Konstanz und seine Häfen. Standort und Infrastruktur von der Antike bis in das 19. Jahrhundert. In: R. Röber (ed.), Einbaum, Lastensegler, Dampfschiff. Frühe Schifffahrt in Südwestdeutschland. ALManach 5/6 (Stuttgart 2000) 185-214.

Rösch 2016: F. Rösch, The Schleswig Waterfront – a place of major significance for the emergence of the town. In: S. Kalmring / L. Holmquist / C. Hedenstierna-Jonson (eds), New aspects on Viking-age urbanism c. AD 750-1100. Proceedings of the International Symposium at the Swedish History Museum, April 17-20th 2013. Theses and Papers in Archaeology B 12 (Stockholm 2016) 159-172.

Rössner 2013: C. Rössner, Archäobotanische Untersuchung der Bodenproben aus den Sondageschnitten von 2009 und 2010 am Donaumarkt in Regensburg [unpubl. report, Regensburg 18.12.2013].

Rückert 2004: P. Rückert, Pilgerfahrten auf dem Oberrhein im späten Mittelalter. In: R. Plötz / P. Rückert (eds), Jakobuskult im Rheinland. Jakobus-Studien 13 (Tübingen 2004) 15-32.

Schalies 1992: I. Schalies, Archäologische Untersuchungen zum Hafen Lübecks. Befunde und Funde der Grabung An der Untertrave/Kaimauer. In: Beiträge der Archäologie zum Lübecker Hafen. Lübecker Schriften zu Archäologie und Kulturgeschichte 18 (Bonn 1992) 305-344.

2009: I. Schalies, Wasserbaumaßnahmen im mittelalterlichen und neuzeitlichen Lübeck. Mitteilungen der Deutschen Gesellschaft für Archäologie des Mittelalters und der Neuzeit 21, 2009, 73-86.

2014: I. Schalies, Von Kaianlagen, Bohlwerken und Uferbefestigungen – archäologische Befunde zum Ausbau des stadtseitigen Trave-Ufers im 12.-20. Jahrhundert. In: A. Falk / U. Müller / M. Schneider (eds), Lübeck und der Hanseraum. Beiträge zu Archäologie und Kulturgeschichte. Festschrift für Manfred Gläser (Lübeck 2014) 161-172.

Schalles-Fischer 1969: M. Schalles-Fischer, Pfalz und Fiskus Frankfurt. Eine Untersuchung zur Verfassungsgeschichte des fränkisch-deutschen Königtums. Veröffentlichungen des Max-Planck-Instituts für Geschichte 20 (Göttingen 1969).

Schmetzer 1925: A. Schmetzer, Der Wiedfang bei der Steinernen Brücke zu Regensburg. Verhandlungen des Historischen Vereins für Oberpfalz und Regensburg 75, 1925, 75-88.

Schmid 2010: P. Schmid, »Regensburg liegt gar schön. Die Gegend musste eine Stadt herlocken.« In: F. Opll / C. Sonnlechner (eds), Europäische Städte im Mittelalter. Forschungen und Beiträge zur Wiener Stadtgeschichte 52 (Innsbruck 2010) 327-350.

Stamm 1967: O. Stamm, Der königliche Saalhof zu Frankfurt am Main: Mit einem Vorbericht des Museums für Vor- und Frühgeschichte 1958-1961 (Frankfurt a. M. 1967).

Untermann 2009: M. Untermann, Handbuch der mittelalterlichen Architektur (Darmstadt 2009).

Walbe 1979: H. Walbe, Das hessisch-fränkische Fachwerk (Giessen-Wieseck ²1979).

Wanderwitz 2006: H. Wanderwitz, Regensburg, ein früh- und hochmittelalterliches Handelszentrum. In: E. Feistner (ed.), Das mittelalterliche Regensburg im Zentrum Europas. Forum Mittelalter Studien 1 (Regensburg 2006) 46-50.

Wawrzinek 2014: Ch. Wawrzinek, In portum navigare. Römische Häfen an Flüssen und Seen (Berlin 2014).

Werther/Kröger 2017: L. Werther / L. Kröger, Medieval Inland Navigation and the Shifting Fluvial Landscape between Rhine and Danube. Post Classical Archaeologies 7, 2017, 65-96.

Werther/Wollenberg in prep.: L. Werther / D. Wollenberg, Der Frankfurter Hafen – Schauplatz herrschaftlicher Repräsentation im Früh- und Hochmittelalter? In: Th. Schmidts / M. Kocak / M. M. Vučetić (eds), Häfen als Orte der Repräsentation in Antike und Mittelalter. RGZM – Tagungen (in prep.).

Werther/Müller/Foucher 2018: L. Werther / H. Müller / M. Foucher (eds), European Harbour Data Repository. www.db-thueringen.de/receive/dbt_mods_00035239 (14.12.2018).

Werther et al. 2015: L. Werther / Ch. Zielhofer / F. Herzig / E. Leitholdt / M. Schneider / S. Linzen / S. Berg-Hobohm / P. Ettel / A. Kirchner / S. Dunkel, Häfen verbinden. Neue Befunde zu Verlauf, wasserbaulichem Konzept und Verlandung des Karlsgrabens. In: Th. Schmidts / M. M. Vučetić (eds), Häfen im 1. Millennium AD. Bauliche Konzepte, herrschaftliche und religiöse Einflüsse. RGZM – Tagungen 22 = Interdisziplinäre Forschungen zu den Häfen von der Römischen Kaiserzeit bis zum Mittelalter in Europa 1 (Mainz 2015) 151-185.

2018: L. Werther / L. Kröger / A. Kirchner / Ch. Zielhofer / E. Leitholdt / M. Schneider / S. Linzen / S. Berg-Hobohm / P. Ettel, Fossata Magna – a Canal Contribution to Harbour Construction in the 1st Millennium AD. In: C. von Carnap-Bornheim / F. Daim / P. Ettel / U. Warnke (eds), Harbours as Objects of Interdisciplinary Research – Archaeology + History + Geosciences. RGZM – Tagungen 34 = Interdisziplinäre Forschungen zu den Häfen von der Römischen Kaiserzeit bis zum Mittelalter in Europa 5 (Mainz 2018) 355-372.

Wintergerst 2002: M. Wintergerst, Hoch- und spätmittelalterliche Keramik aus der Altstadt Frankfurt am Main. Schriften des Archäologischen Museums Frankfurt 18 (Frankfurt am Main 2002).

Wolfsteiner 2006: A. Wolfsteiner, »Fluderer-Manner mit da langa Stanga«. Flößerei und Trift auf Regen und Naab. In: M. Berwing-Wittl (ed.), Burgen und Klöster – Stadt und Fluss. Festschrift zum 36. Bayerischen Nordgautag in Nittenau (Regensburg 2006) 85-94.

Wollenberg et al. 2019: D. Wollenberg / I. Nießen / L. Werther / A. Wunschel / P. Ettel, Forschungen zu den mittelalterlichen Binnenhäfen zwischen Rhein und Donau. In: C. Mielzarek / C. Zschieschang (eds), Usus Aquarum. Interdisziplinäre Studien zur Nutzung und Bedeutung von Gewässern im Mittelalter. Forschungen zur Geschichte und Kultur des östlichen Mitteleuropa 54 (Wien, Köln, Weimar 2019) 205-245.

Wunschel et al. 2015: A. Wunschel / P. Ettel / M. Hein / S. Linzen / Ch.-B. Roettig / M. Schneider / L. Werther, Hafen oder Landeplatz? – Untersuchungen zu Einrichtungen der früh- und hochmittelalterlichen Binnenschifffahrt ausgehend von den Fallbeispielen Karlburg und Salz in Unterfranken. In: Th. Schmidts / M. M. Vučetić (eds), Häfen im 1. Millennium AD. Bauliche Konzepte, herrschaftliche und religiöse Einflüsse. RGZM – Tagungen 22 = Interdisziplinäre Forschungen zu den Häfen von der Römischen Kaiserzeit bis zum Mittelalter in Europa 1 (Mainz 2015) 203-228.

2017: A. Wunschel / P. Ettel / M. Hein / V. Höfler / S. Linzen / M. Schneider / S. Dunkel / L. Werther, Entwicklung und Topographie des mittelalterlichen Siedlungskomplexes Karlburg am Ufer des Mains. In: S. Kalmring / L. Werther (eds), Häfen im 1. Millennium AD. Standortbedingungen, Entwicklungsmodelle und ökonomische Vernetzung. RGZM – Tagungen 31 = Interdisziplinäre Forschungen zu den Häfen von der Römischen Kaiserzeit bis zum Mittelalter in Europa 4 (Mainz 2017) 81-110.

2018: A. Wunschel / P. Ettel / M. Hein / S. Linzen / Ch.-B. Roettig / M. Schneider / L. Werther, The Waterfront of Karlburg and Salz in the Early and High Middle Ages – Interdisciplinary (Geo)Archaeological and Geophysical Studies. In: C. von Carnap-Bornheim / F. Daim / P. Ettel / U. Warnke (eds), Harbours as Objects of Interdisciplinary Research – Archaeology + History + Geosciences. RGZM – Tagungen 34 = Interdisziplinäre Forschungen zu den Häfen von der Römischen Kaiserzeit bis zum Mittelalter in Europa 5 (Mainz 2018) 373-402.

Zettler 2000: A. Zettler, Heilige, Mönche und Laien unterwegs. Bilder und Texte zur Schifffahrt auf dem Bodensee im frühen Mittelalter. In: R. Röber (ed.), Einbaum, Lastensegler, Dampfschiff. Frühe Schifffahrt in Südwestdeutschland. ALManach 5/6 (Stuttgart 2000) 109-120.

Zotz 2003: Lexikon des Mittelalters III (2003) 374-375 s.v. Curia regis (Th. Zotz).

Summary

This paper deals with the question how to identify inland harbours in archaeological records. Questions of terminology and methodology as well as suggestions for »harbour criteria« are discussed and exemplified with three case studies: the medieval towns of Regensburg on the Danube, Frankfurt on the Main and Speyer on the Rhine. The named sites are the object of the ongoing research project »Inland harbours – hubs of European communication networks« of the SPP. All three sites are founded on Roman preceding settlements and had superregional importance as royal, sacral or trading centres in the Middle Ages. Written sources prove their importance for inland navigation already in Roman times. The analysis of assumed harbour constructions in the archaeologic record, in contrast, does not always correspond with the historical tradition. As a main result it can be stated that water constructions mostly have been used multi-functionally for navigation, bank revetments, fortification, and water exploitation for crafts and land reclamation at the same time. The decision to spend time and effort on solid harbour constructions was therefore not related to navigation in the first place or to navigation only. In fact, it appears that bank revetments often seem to be linked to land reclamation processes of the growing urban centres in the High and Late Middle Ages. The determination of archaeological features as parts of harbour constructions clarifies if related to the landward topography and functional areas of the concurrent settlement, the landward harbour and trade-related infrastructure.

Zusammenfassung

Dieser Beitrag erörtert, wie aus archäologischen Befunden in mittelalterlichen urbanen Zentren Hafenstrukturen identifiziert werden können. Es werden dabei terminologische und methodologische Überlegungen angestellt und Kriterien für die Identifikation von Hafenbefunden am Beispiel der drei mittelalterlichen Städte Frankfurt am Main, Regensburg und Speyer zur Diskussion gestellt. Die genannten Fallbeispiele waren Gegenstand der Forschungen des von der Deutschen Forschungsgemeinschaft geförderten Projektes »Binnenhäfen in Zentraleuropa – Knotenpunkte europäischer Kommunikationsnetzwerke«, das Teil des Schwerpunktprogramms 1630 »Häfen von der Römischen Kaiserzeit bis zum Mittelalter« war. Schriftliche Quellen deuten darauf hin, dass diese Orte bereits in römischer Zeit eine wichtige Rolle für die Binnenschifffahrt spielten. Die materiellen Zeugnisse entsprechender Hafenanlagen spiegeln sich im archäologischen Befund allerdings nicht immer eindeutig wider.

Die Ergebnisse der Fallstudien zeigen, dass in mittelalterlichen Städten von einer multifunktionalen Nutzung von Wasserbauten auszugehen ist. Diese können gleichzeitig sowohl als Anlegestellen für Wasserfahrzeuge und als Uferbefestigung – insbesondere nach Landgewinnungsmaßnahmen – als auch für die Wasserversorgung verschiedener Gewerke dienen. Es zeigt sich, dass die Entscheidung, Zeit und Aufwand in die Errichtung fester Hafenstrukturen zu investieren, nicht primär und ausschließlich auf die Bedürfnisse der Binnenschifffahrt zurückzuführen ist. Die Identifikation archäologischer Befunde als Bestandteile von Hafen- oder Wasserbauten fällt leichter, wenn man die Stadttopographie und die verschiedenen Funktionsareale der Stadt, insbesondere die landseitige und mit dem Handel verbundene Hafeninfrastruktur berücksichtigt. Das Beispiel einer mutmaßlichen Kaimauer in Speyer zeigt aber auch, dass so mancher als »Hafen« deklarierte Befund einer Prüfung anhand der in diesem Beitrag vorgeschlagenen Kriterien nicht standhalten kann.

Steinerne Hafenbauten wie Kaimauern und Molen scheinen ein eher jüngeres Phänomen spätmittelalterlicher Städte zu sein, das mit der zunehmenden Verwendung von Stein als Baumaterial im Allgemeinen korrespondiert. Im Früh- und Hochmittelalter ist Holz das vorherrschende Baumaterial für Hafenbauten und Uferbefestigungen. Aufgrund der über die Jahrhunderte mitunter stark veränderten Flussbetten und Wasserpegel sind viele dieser Holzbefunde bereits vergangen. Im Falle von konstanten Uferlinien sind sie aufgrund moderner Wasserbauten und der intensiven modernen Binnenschifffahrt entweder partiell oder gänzlich zerstört, mindestens aber von Zerstörung akut bedroht. Denn Bauarbeiten unter Wasser oder im Bereich der amphibischen Zone wie etwa Fahrrinnenvertiefungen werden häufig ohne Beteiligung von Archäologen durchgeführt. Dies ist in erster Linie dem Umstand geschuldet, dass die Unterwasserarchäologie in Deutschland, anders als in Frankreich, kein inhärenter Bestandteil der Bodendenkmalpflege ist.

THOMAS LIEBERT

GROSSHÖBING AND ITS LANDING SITE DURING THE EARLY MIDDLE AGES – A RURAL ECONOMIC AREA NEXT TO THE EUROPEAN WATERSHED

A geological survey in the valley of the River Schwarzach in the vicinity of Greding (Middle Franconia) revealed first timber logs with tool marks in 1995. The finding of these well preserved timbers in the flood plain was quite unexpected. The survey preceded the planning and construction of the high-speed train line Nuremberg-Ingolstadt-Munich. This first site of discovery situated north-east of the village Großhöbing (Lkr. Roth/D) was soon followed by further sites (**fig. 1**). Until the end of the year 2001, a few thousand timber logs had been retrieved from different excavation sites throughout the flood plain of the river and the surrounding hillsides. They mostly date to Early and High Medieval periods. These more than 3,000 waterlogged timbers and wooden artefacts as well as the unearthed features, not only cast a new light on the many ways of intensive utilisation of flood plain areas but also offer a view on many different water related structures and their technical hydraulic constructions[1]. These structures have two facts in common: they are situated next to the River Schwarzach – which is the bio-geographical requirement for their operation – and they all add to the distinctive attributes of a central place[2].

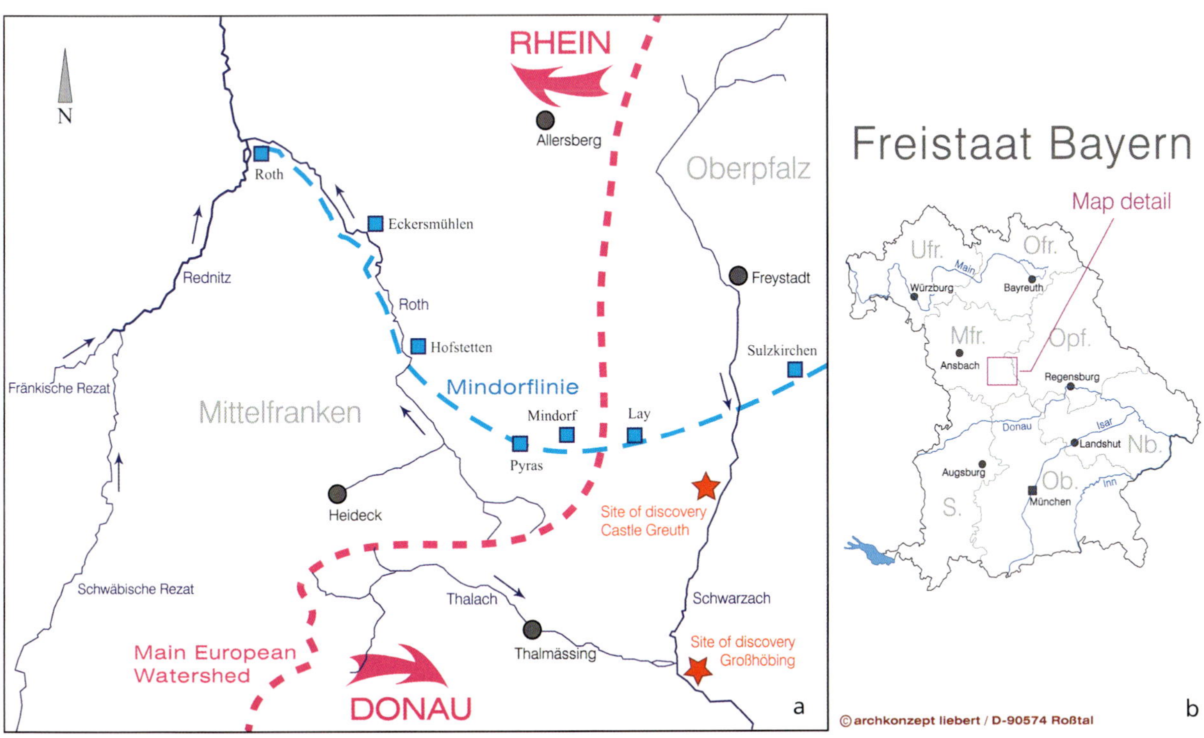

Fig. 1 The Free State of Bavaria with its administrative regions (**b**), the survey area with archaeological sites and the European Continental Watershed with the local catchments of Rhine and Danube (**a**). – (Graphic archkonzept liebert, 90574 Roßtal).

Fig. 2 Excavation photo: The two post rows of the landing sites of 819 AD and 854/855 AD and in the back the topmost layer of the thick lumber mesh. – (Photo Fa. FAUSTUS, 91186 Büchenbach).

To begin with, I will point out two important factors for the evaluation of the water related structures. Seen from the territorial perspective, the hydraulic constructions were situated in an early medieval border area between the contested political interests of the Frankish kings in the west and the Bavarian dukes in the east. Seen from the topographic perspective, the archaeological sites are located next to the main European watershed, separating the catchments of Danube and Rhine (**fig. 1**).

ARCHAEOLOGICAL EVIDENCE

What do the unearthed features look like and how could they be interpreted? The archaeological site north-east of Großhöbing revealed different structures and features of successive revetments of the riverbank, including boat landing places from the 9th century AD[3]. Their rows of posts were particularly striking. They consisted of different timber posts – round, half round and splitted. The oldest documented bank revetment was built in the year 769 AD. At this time, the wattle work still followed the natural riverbank. The more recent post rows of the 9th century AD bordered a new course of the River Schwarzach, which now ran in a regulated riverbed. It was straightened and flowed approximately in a north-south direction. Adjacent in the east to this new reinforcement, at the time of the construction phase from 819 until 854/855 AD (**fig. 2**) thick horizontal layers of lumber covered the river section of the 8th century AD. The effort to support the instable ground by this action is obvious. The river ran parallel west of the constructions of oak timbers. With these wooden structures we can record the eastern bank of a 6-7 m wide riverbed. The water may have been 70-80 cm deep[4]. The revetment built in 819 AD was constructed as a mixture of wattle work and planks between posts over a length of 17 m (**fig. 3**). In the southern part, a 4.5 m broad gap remained without any wooden structures. Here the riverbank sloped with a gradient of 15-20°. Later on, closely spaced half-posts from oak replaced the former bank revetment[5]. During this construction phase – dating to 854/855 AD – riverbed and bank, including the slope mentioned above, were revetted with a lining of local limestone. Moreover, the stone lining in this part also covered the top of the bank. In this area other posts and half-posts from oak were discovered. They stood at a distance of 2-3.6 m to each other. They certainly served as mooring poles for the vessels. The entire length of the construction of 855 AD measures 15.5 m. When combining all the features of both construction phases of the 9th century AD, the straightened riverbed, the parallel rows of posts as bank reinforcement, the sloped part of the embankment smoothly leading into the riverbed and also the efforts to stabilise the rearward parts of the bank by horizontal layers of lumber it is obvious that the site served as an inland harbour. The site at the River Schwarzach offered a quay as well as a landing place at the slope, which has been paved with limestones since 854/855 AD. It was possible

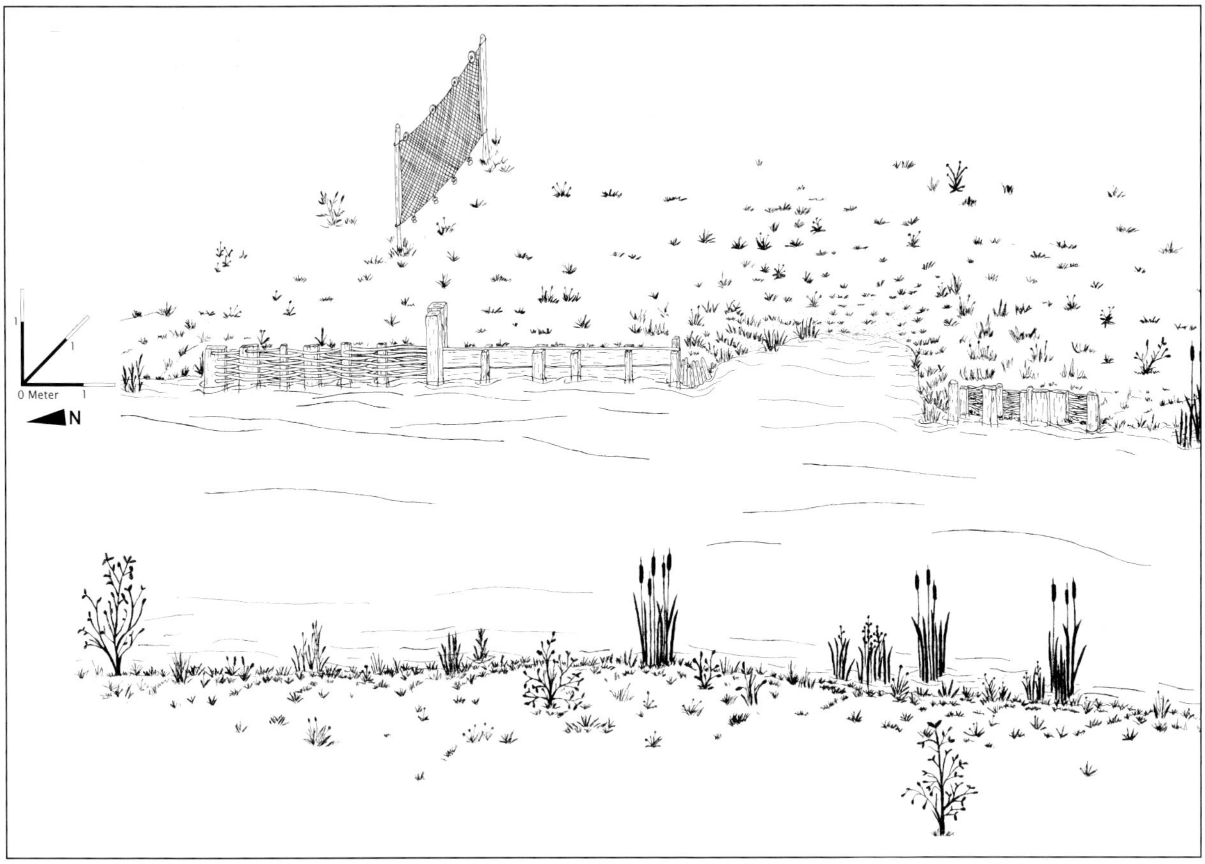

Fig. 3 Großhöbing (Lkr. Roth/D). Landing site (reconstruction drawing). – (Drawing Th. Liebert).

to pull boats ashore here, for example, to carry out maintenance work and to launch them again. Likewise, vessels could be moored afloat at the wooden quay for easy access and convenient loading and unloading. Subsequent construction phases at this site added minor changes. But nevertheless, they give evidence of continued use of the landing place and of the River Schwarzach as a navigable waterway during the second half of the 9th and maybe even the 10th century AD.

ANALYSING THE ARCHAEOLOGICAL FEATURES IN THE CONTEXT OF THE LOCAL, HISTORIC AND BIO-GEOGRAPHIC SURROUNDINGS

To what extent respectively in what mode were the Großhöbing landing sites at the River Schwarzach integrated into their environment?

Watermills and manorialism

The European world in medieval times, especially in the Early Middle Ages, was to a large extent an agrarian world. Depending on region and varying climatic conditions, the cultivation of different agricultural products characterized the landscape. Nevertheless, one mode of cultivation became the determinant throughout European landscape– the cultivation of grain. Due to the common diet of medieval society, cultivation of cereals was crucial. The erection of gristmills, which are indispensable for the processing of grain, was and still is closely linked to cereal cultivation. Already in 1935, Bloch pointed out the vital commercial and social importance of watermills in Europe[6]. Despite more and more archaeological discoveries of watermills all over Europe, the ongoing importance of quern-stones on which grain was ground by hand and treadmills powered by animals for vast parts of the medieval population should not be underestimated[7], though it may be difficult in the foreseeable future to estimate the actual emphasis between watermills and mills powered by human or animal movement[8]. Moreover, it must be kept in mind that the technical development of watermills already took place in Roman times[9]. Roman watermills in archaeological excavations in Europe and North Africa give prove of the high degree of technical evolution in late Antiquity[10]. Nevertheless, watermills in Roman times were not as widely used as in the Middle Ages and could not gain the same importance as later on. This is not the place to enlarge upon the various causes, which were already often discussed. But one important reason might be found in the agrarian economy of the manorial system, emerging in early medieval times[11].

Until the construction of the high speed train line, different watermills characterized the scenery in the Schwarzach Valley next to Großhöbing for more than 1,400 years. The remains of the oldest watermills at this site, successive constructions dating from the Early to the High Middle Ages, were excavated, documented and salvaged before and during the construction work of the train line. The oldest evidence dates to the end of the 6th century AD, but most of the archaeologically documented features belong to watermills erected in the 9th century AD[12]. These mills show the intensity of agricultural activity. The watermills were not located at the river, but a bit farther off. Just like in recent days, the mills were linked to the river by artificial canals. Every mill included hydraulic systems like mill channels, ponds, mill races and tail races[13]. These systems required permanent maintenance and were hard to uphold. It could have been too much effort for a single farmstead or even a small community. Manorial lords on the opposite may have been able to operate watermills and maintain their hydraulic systems[14]. Profitability of manors was many times higher and therefore also the gain of operating a mill, because it could be work to much better capacity. These reasons may be responsible for the increasing concentration of watermills on manorial territory[15]. Because of this the early medieval watermills in Großhöbing most likely have to be seen in relation to a feudal lord. With increasing power, the lords often were the sparking plug in the establishment of watermills[16]. In addition to intended economy of scales the growing influence of manorial lords on early medieval agricultural trade and the active part they began to hold in it was surely a motivation[17]. Peter Johanek described in his analysis of commerce in Carolingian times that agricultural products were the most important goods of internal trade in the Frankish kingdom[18]. In spite of the preponderance of manorial systems in the Early Middle Ages – at least in written sources – it should be kept in mind that singular mills were in possession of freemen. Yet, the construction and maintenance of mills required vast resources and mill operating had to be profitable for its feudal owners. Therefore, these facilities assumed two different tasks: On one hand the cereals for manorial use were ground here. On the other hand the peasants from the neighbourhood may have used the manorial mill for an interest[19]. Thus they did not have to maintain own mills, but had to pay for the service. Most likely even peasants, who did not belong to the manorial of the mill owner, would have brought their grain to be ground into flour. The »Mühlenbann« north of the Bavarian Alps is indeed not historical verifiable until the 14th century AD, though the actual living conditions may have differed from written law[20]. Koehne shows that already in Early Middle Ages the feudal lords were able to coerce their villeins to use only their mills[21]. Integrated to the feudal and agrarian framework of the time in such a manner, mills were preponderantly central sites.

The rise in cereal production and the expansion of area under cultivation at Carolingian times is doubtlessly owing to demographic increase[22]. This increase in turn promoted the spread of watermills and their rise in numbers[23], but at the same time was stimulated by the technological invention. After all, watermill technology made it possible to supply an increasing population with flour without rising effort of manpower.

Fig. 4 The River Schwarzach between Günzenhofen and Großhöbing (both Lkr. Roth/D), in the background Auer Berg (undated hillfort), to the left Großhöbing. – (Photo Th. Liebert).

Rivers as waterways and trading routes

Rivers were not only a source of energy for watermills, but also served a different but nevertheless significant function for medieval society. In the Early Middle Ages, when the excellent road network in the area of the former Roman Empire more and more decayed and the territories on the other side of the limes only had less developed simple paths, rivers became even more important as safe and efficient traffic arteries and ways of communication. In this way-system provided by nature small and smallest streams were also included, which do not seem navigable at all nowadays[24]. For example, the River Schwarzach at Großhöbing ranks at a scale of navigability at the lower end, but far from the bottom (**fig. 4**). How small a navigable waterway could be is documented by the Swabian Rezat, some 30 km to the west of Großhöbing. South of Weißenburg (Middle Franconia), it appears as a little brook. Even this rivulet could be turned into a waterway with a bit of construction work. It is the northern tributary to the *Fossa Carolina*, a canal which was constructed in 793 AD on the initiative of Charlemagne to bridge the main European watershed. Archival sources from the early 9th century AD give an account of the construction work and the remains of the canal are currently investigated by an interdisciplinary team employing historical, archaeological and geo-archaeological methods[25]. This edifice and its planning show the significance of waterways as means of travel and transport in the feudal society of the Early Middle Ages[26]. Restricting factors were that the routes were predetermined by nature and climate events like floods, low water and ice drift could obstruct navigation. Compared with terrestrial roads waterways offered many advantages. Travel speed downstream was much faster than overland transport and it was easier to move large quantities of commodities and travellers by boat. The examination of the itineraries of Charlemagne shows the preference of the sovereign for waterways as means of locomotion. Places at the Rhine or places at tributaries to the Rhine predominate this itineraries until the end of the 8th century AD[27]. In some cases, harbours and landing sites were also mentioned in written sources[28]. However, seen in the context of Europe-wide use of rivers as means of transport, the number of harbours and landing sites must have by far exceeded the few that are mentioned. This aspect is rarely reflected in written sources. They also lack additional details concerning the localisation, the ways of construction and purpose of the named harbour[29].

At least written sources give an idea of the significance and the purpose which rivers as waterways and harbours had for the manorial system[30]. The intensions of the Abbey of Lorsch (Kr. Bergstraße/D) are quite evident to attain as many landing sites and privileges for their vessels as possible at pivotal waterways[31]. The example of the Abbey of Lorsch might as well apply to many manorial lords. As important stakeholders in early medieval trade, their interest in waterways as transport corridors and in the connected infrastructure of landing places and harbours, as well as in gaining privileges for their vessels must, of course, have been quite strong.

The question if and to what extend ecclesiastical and noble manorial lords took part in trade during the 9th century AD was the subject of a fierce debate during last decades. The opinions range from almost non-existing manorial trade to revivification and increase of trade at his time[32]. One cause for the negative estimation of commercial activity during the 9th century AD lies in the agrarian structure of society. Some 20 years ago Johanek did research on Carolingian commerce[33]. He used written sources for his work and in his opinion, their number will not rise considerably[34]. In the context of his analysis he draws an entirely new picture of manorialism, which Dopsch already identified as an essential element of feudal society[35], and its function in trade. Johanek could prove the importance of agrarian products for inner Frankish traffic, an importance not only for times of extreme harvest failure but also for average crop years. For this he names two examples: Areas with good conditions for the cultivation of cereals like in Lower Frankonia next to the Main and the Alsace always transported and sold their surplus to regions where something else was produced, like livestock, also in times without harvest failure. And he quotes a source called »Einhards Wunderbericht« in which the permanent grain transport by ship on the River Main is described[36]. Apart from this balancing capacity, which resulted in wholesaling of foods over large distances, continuous retail trade with foods can also be documented[37]. It was obviously possible in this setting even for small agrarian units to generate financial profit[38]. Johanek argues that Carolingian statutes against exorbitant prices prove the participation by manorialism in trade because only they had the facilities to build up stocks on a larger scale[39]. Essential for the movement of goods is in the Early Middle Ages, due to Johanek, the access – at least of ecclesiastical manorial systems – to a network of communication, traffic, and shops based on their widespread properties and holdings. Adam stresses the influence, which ecclesiastical and monastic manorialism had as a determining factor on trade and market[40]. Thereby, the exchange took place not only in a few central market towns but also at harbours and in villages[41]. One example is the *portus* Zullestein (Kr. Bergstraße/D). It was in the property of one *comes* Werner before it was signed over to the Abbey Lorsch. Here the participation of noble lords in trade becomes evident[42]. The transfer of the *villa* Marolles situated at the border of two *pagi*, to the Abbey Saint-Germain-des-Prés (dép. Paris/F), in contrast, resulted in the erection of a small trans-shipment point at this site. Competition apparently prompted the Abbey to attach great importance even to a small market town with a limited catchment area[43]. This fact is also of interest with regard to Großhöbing. In the end Johanek concluded that manorialism played a most significant part in Carolingian commerce[44]. Adams shares this estimation. Within the boundaries of the Frankish Empire she distinguishes between the Roman *civitates* still occupying their function as economic centres in Early Middle Ages and regions in the north and east of the empire lacking these *civitates.* In the latter areas, the great manorial estates assumed the leading position in production and trade[45].

Fig. 5 The archaeological site of Castle Greuth (Lkr. Roth/D), aerial photo. – (Photo Karl-Heinz Richter, Greding).

Topography and watershed

The manorial lords were most likely the owner of the Großhöbing watermills. It may be assumed that the products were sold regional and supra-regional. The enormous importance of waterways and harbours for early medieval manorial trade and transport was already sufficiently illustrated in this context. We may, therefore, now cast a look at the local topography of traffic. The settlement is situated at the northern foothill of the Frankonian Jura. River Schwarzach runs next to Großhöbing through a long stretched valley which extends from the northern foothill to the south-eastern confluence with the River Altmühl. This north–south aligned natural traffic artery has always provided easy ascent to the north, crossing the Alb without any steep slope. Even today these convenient conditions were the reason to place the route of the Autobahn A9 and the high-speed train line Nuremberg-Ingolstadt through this valley. Historic research and in particular archaeological evidence of landing sites show that, at least during the 9th century AD, the River Schwarzach was a trading route. The development of a landing site at this spot of the stream surely had two geographical reasons. One is the location at a confluence of two river valleys. Directly to the north of the excavated landing place the brook Thalach flows from west into the Schwarzach Valley that stretches from north to south. The Thalach Valley offers a natural westbound traffic artery already used in the Early Middle Ages. The landing site in Großhöbing was located most convenient as a gateway from and to the west. Trading goods would have been transferred at this site from water shipment to overland passage and vice versa. Due to the confluence of its tributary Thalach the Schwarzach stream afterwards holds considerably more water and becomes more navigable. The author does not entirely want to exclude that already at an early point in time the border location between the early medieval sphere of interest of the Frankish kings in the west and the Bavarian dukes in the east may have promoted the erection of the site[46]. Later on, when the duchy Bavaria had become part of the Frankish Empire, it was still an inland border area to the district (German: Gau) Sualafeld[47].

At least as important was the route to the north. In a distance of 7 km upstream the River Schwarzach castle Greuth (Lkr. Kitzingen/D) is situated[48] (**figs 1. 5**). It was a lowland castle from the 8th to the 10th century AD, adjacent to the river. As far as current research showed, it could be reached by boat on the River Schwarzach under the assumption that water levels were high enough[49]. If the hydrographic conditions[50] at this time were too arid upstream from the confluence of the rivulet Thalach, the carried goods would have been transferred to overland transport at the site of Großhöbing. The positioning of the landing site at the left bank of the river could prove this assumption. Not far uphill archaeologists found part of an early medieval road which may have been an overland route to the north[51].

In this context it should be mentioned as well that on the River Schwarzach not only agrarian products could have been transported, but also bog iron ores or already smelted iron. On the plateau of the Jura south of Großhöbing bog iron ores can be found on the surface due to geological conditions[52]. Evidence of iron ore mining, processing and smelting in prehistoric[53] and early medieval times[54] was revealed at different archaeological sites throughout the Schwarzach Valley. One archaeological feature was excavated at a distance of just 180 m to the north-east of landing site. It is conveniently situated for conveyance between the road of the 8th/9th century AD and the contemporaneous *portus* Großhöbing.

Moreover, the latest research on castle Greuth has shown that transport of iron ore and its processing was of importance at this place, too[55]. Archival evidence for early medieval ore traffic by vessels, for example, is given by a letter from the year 851/859 AD Lupus de Ferrières addressed to Abbot Odo de Corbie[56]. Then as now, the shipment of bulk ore lumps by boat is most efficent.

The landing sites of Großhöbing were not only significant as transferring points for ore and its raw products as well as for agrarian products but also had importance as a trading place for the village and its vicinity. Regarding the above mentioned, the village Großhöbing seems to have served a valuable purpose as a distribution hub for its supposed manorial lord. This function was favoured by natural circumstances. In this context, the chronological overlapping of the landing site at Großhöbing and the castle Greuth during the 9th century AD is noteworthy.

Observed on a larger scale, the geographical features enhance the significance of the landing site in Großhöbing as well as castle Greuth even more[57]. This is the second reason why the landing site of Großhöbing was erected at this place. Most probably trading routes to the north used the River Schwarzach with its loading point at Greuth or, in case of low water, the named landing site to transcend the major European watershed, but not by the attempted constructing of a canal as done at the *Fossa Carolina*, situated a bit farther to the west near Treuchtlingen (Lkr. Weißenburg-Gunzenhausen/D)[58]. At castle Greuth the catchments of the Rhine and Danube come quite close which means the place offered an excellent possibility to transfer from vessels to overland passage (**fig. 6**). The link to the Main-Rhine region in the north was the River Roth. It rises next to the small village Stauf only a few kilometres west of the Schwarzach Valley, runs in north-western direction and flows into the River Rednitz next to the town Roth. The River Rednitz joins the River Pegnitz at Fürth (Middle Franconia) and, now named Regnitz, runs north as a tributary of the Main. By choosing the overland passage of just a few kilometres length, one would pass the present-day villages of Karm, Lay, Mindorf, Pyras and Hofstetten up to the Stephansmühle (all Lkr. Roth/D) or Lösmühle and it was possible to cross over from the Danube catchment into the Rhine catchment. There are no landing sites known at the River Roth nor the length of the navigable river section. It could have ranged to Eckersmühlen or a bit further upstream to the mentioned mills[59]. The navigability from Hofstetten seems unlikely. The distance between River Schwarzach at Greuth and the supposed navigable river section at River Roth is about 8-10 km overland. The difference in altitude, which the transported goods had to overcome to the highest point between Mindorf and Lay, amounts to 23 m. From Großhöbing, 7 km away from Greuth, the altitude is only 6 m more. The gradient at the River Roth is much steeper. At a distance of 8 km, between

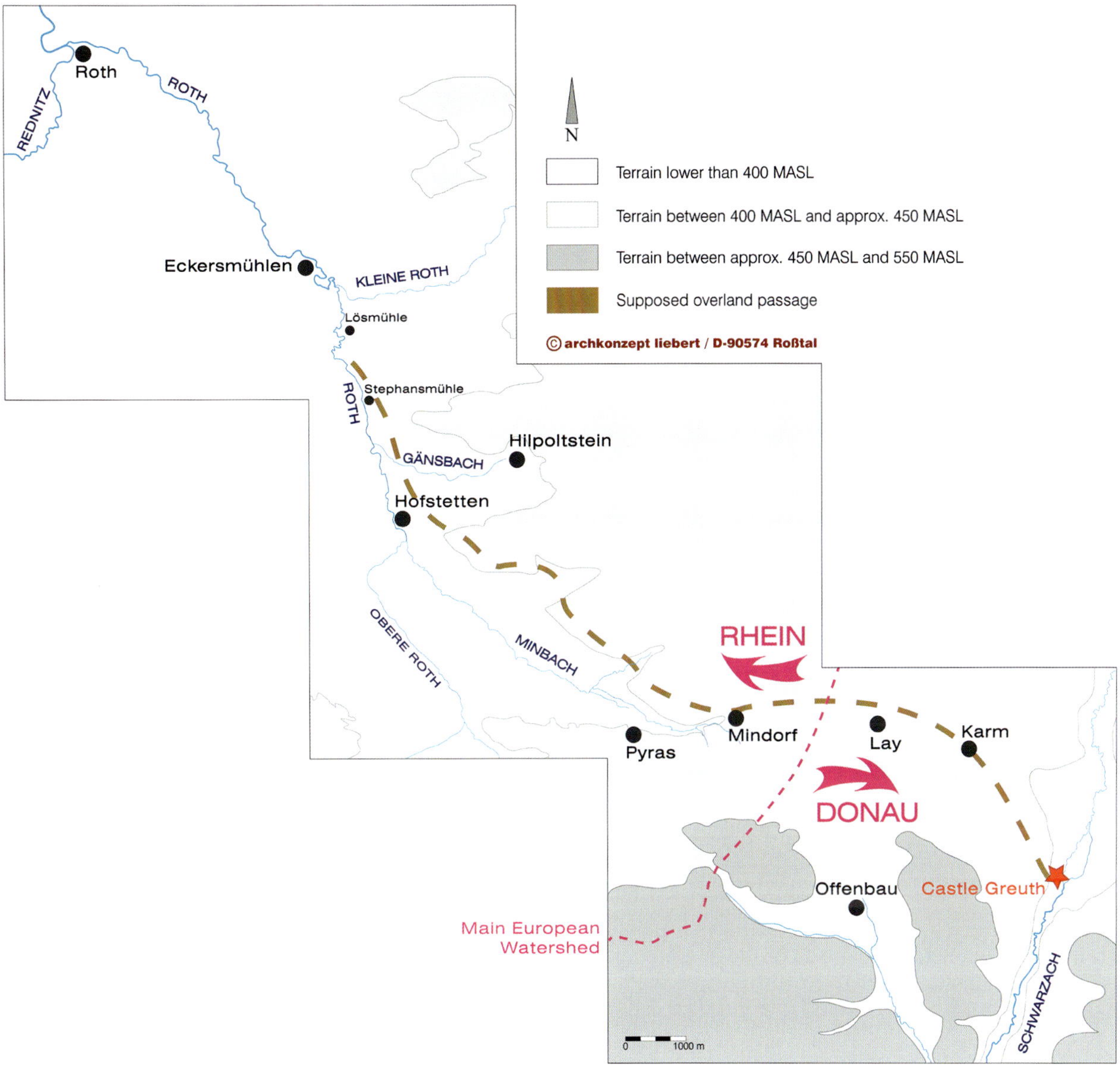

Fig. 6 Supposed overland passage transcending the watershed. – (Graphic archkonzept liebert, 90574 Roßtal).

Eckersmühlen (Lkr. Roth/D) and the town Roth, the difference in altitude adds up to 25 m. The riverbed is 6-9 m wide, the depth of the water 60 cm and more[60].

The suitability of the trading route mentioned above was proved by a construction scheme of the recent past: in the 1920s a new canal between Main and Danube was projected to replace the Ludwigskanal from the 19th century AD. One of the alternative routes was the so-called Mindorf-Linie. It was intended to run along the villages of Sulzkirchen, Lay, Mindorf, Pyras, Hofstetten, Eckersmühlen and the market town Roth[61] (**fig. 1**). Construction work began 1939 and ended in 1942 because of World War II. From the village Lay to the River Roth the line of the canal is identical with the supposed early medieval overland route.

CONCLUSIONS

The foregoing paper attempts to look at the archaeological features of early medieval watermills and landing sites not only from the perspective of archaeology. In fact, they should be integrated into manorial and agrarian contexts as far as the common and specific sources allow for this period of time. These contexts were studied with particular respect to the central function of Großhöbing, which this two facilities – landing sites and the watermills – fulfil for the economy of this rural area, taking into account the proximity of Großhöbing to the main European watershed. The author hopes to have achieved these aims for both, watermills and landing sites. The central function of the watermills arose from their significance as grain mills for peasants from the vicinity and as a facility to increase profits for manorialism. This may have been as a mill, to which peasants could come from their own will and pay an interest to get the grain ground, or as a mill with »Mühlenbann«, where the manorial lord would coerce his villains to use his facility. Watermills were, therefore, regularly frequented and of course, due to these visits, communication also occurred. So mills bestow a surplus of importance[62] on the place. In comparison to other central places, for example centres of power, this importance certainly ranges in a more humble context[63]. All in all, the significance of watermills for the European economy of the Early Middle Ages has to be assessed as very high. The particular status and the protection of mills in law records since the Early Middle Ages show that manorial lords attached an important central function to them.

In a similar way, the conclusions drawn above also apply to the Großhöbing landing sites. In the paper the general significance of waterways and harbours for trading, transport and communication in the Early Middle Ages was analysed, as well as the great attention of manorial lords to these facilities. Varying importance as central sites must be attached to landing sites and harbours as trans-shipment centres with distributional function for the inland traffic network. This varying amount of importance depends on the frequency of visits and the quantity of traded goods. Therefore, landing sites bestow a surplus of importance to the respective settlement. In case of the landing sites of Großhöbing, the surplus of importance was supra-regional, at least in times of low water, when castle Greuth could not be reached by vessels. The transgression of the main European watershed in the eastern part of the Frankish Empire was of great importance to the Carolingian kings. This becomes apparent at the *Fossa Carolina* near Treuchtlingen, some 30 km to the west of Großhöbing, one of the most important large-scale canal construction projects of the Early Middle Ages with the aim to bridge the watershed. The short overland passage across the main European watershed from the River Schwarzach to the River Roth was therefore a significant link between the catchments of Danube and Rhine and consequently part of the framework of inland navigation systems.

Notes

1) Liebert 2015.

2) Liebert 2013, 141-158.

3) Liebert 2004, 71-74; 2013, 150-151; 2015, 51-87.

4) Liebert 2015, 75-77. – The cross section of the canal fairway of the *Fossa Carolina* has similar proportions, Kröger/Werther 2017, 268.

5) Types of revetments at Großhöbing see also Liebert 2014, 99-102.

6) M. Bloch in: Hägermann 1997, 342-343. – Elmshäuser et al. 1993, col. 887. – Kuchenbuch 1978, 279.

7) Also Elmshäuser et al. 1993, col. 887. – Kuchenbuch 1978, 279.

8) Abel is cautious in his comment on the expansion of watermills in the Early Middle Ages. – Abel 1978, 47.

9) Cf. Baatz 1995, 5; see there also note 1, including the used translations and editions.

10) e.g. North Africa see Mills of Chemtou, Tunesia (Röder/Röder 1993, 95-102). – e.g. Europe see Barbegal near Arles (Schneider 1997, 309-310; Böhme 1999, 16ff.).

11) On the evolution of manorialism and its aspects see Rösener 1993a and Kuchenbuch 1991.

12) Liebert 2015, 87-137. 301-326; 2004, 69-71.

13) An exception is the oldest archaeologically documented watermill in Großhöbing. It was situated right on the bank of the dammed river; Liebert 2015, 88-93. 301-302. – Henning 1994, 10 refers in this context to the fact that the very same people could build and operate mills.

14) Similarly Bachmann (1988, 720): »denn nur die weltlichen und geistlichen Herren verfügten über das notwendige Kapital zur Errichtung der immer teurer werdenden Mühlen«.

15) The »urbar« of the monastery St. Emmeram (1031) counts 46 mills; Dollinger 1982, 385. 455-463. – The abbey Saint-Germain-des-Prés owned 85 watermills in the first third of the 9th century AD (Hägermann 1997, 343. 345. 368). – It would be interesting to know more about the reasons for the transfers, e.g. did the lord use forms of coercion, were there problems with the maintenance of the mills?

16) Hägermann 1997, 343. – Elmshäuser et al. 1993, col. 887.

17) For the Alemannic region and their neighbours east of the Rhine Rösener asserted, »dass insbesondere das 9. Jahrhundert im säkularen Konjunkturverlauf eine Phase des sichtbaren Wachstums der Agrarwirtschaft darstellte« (vgl. Rösener 1993b, 179).

18) Johanek 1987, 31. 41-44.

19) Kuchenbuch 1978, 280-281 with note 56; there you can find the reference to a double entry of *molina communis*, which the lord of the manor leased for a tenth of the revenues.

20) Dollinger 1982, 387-388. – »Mühlenbann« means the right of the feudal lord to coerce the villeins to use only his mill. – (The words and rights discussed in the following seem not to exist in English.) Im Gegensatz zu Dollinger differenziert Bachmann mehr zwischen dem Mühlenbann und dem Mahlzwang. Aus diesen beiden »Rechtstiteln« setzt sich ihm zufolge das Mühlenregal zusammen. Der Mahlzwang, der die Untertanen eines Grundherren nötigte nur die grundherrlichen Mühlen zu benutzen, wurde hierbei durch entsprechende Verbote gesichert, andere Mühlen in dem betroffenen Gebiet anzulegen. Das »sehr eingeschränkte Mühlenregal« entwickelte sich nach Bachmann in Bayern erst im späten 13. Jahrhundert n.Chr. (Bachmann 1988, 720-721).

21) Koehne 1904, 48.

22) Rösener 1993b, 177 with note 203.

23) Cf. Hägermann 1997, 343.

24) See also Eckoldt 1980. – Eckoldt 1986 with surprising results.

25) i.e. see Grewe 1998, 112-114, who argues that construction work at the *Fossa Carolina* was not finished. – On the contrary Koch 2002, 54-70. New research and results in: Ettel et al. 2014. – Kröger/Werther 2017, 268.

26) Johanek 1987, 19.

27) Hägermann 2002, 13-14.

28) As in the case of the court Zullestein, that had its own harbour in the mid of the 9th century AD (Elmshäuser 2002b, 39 with note 85), or in the district of *villa* Kamben, mentioned for the year 865, that was transferred to the monks of Abbey of Lorsch together with a harbour: *et ad fluvium Rheni portumque ad illorum naves in predicta parte Reni* (Elmshäuser 2002b, 41-42 with note 92).

29) See also Ellmers 1972, 123-124.

30) Canals as waterways on the other hand are rarely mentioned; Elmshäuser 1992, 15 with note 136.

31) Elmshäuser 2002b, 42. – Johanek 1987, 46-47. – Adam 1996, 180-181.

32) Johanek 1987, 8-11 with notes 3-13.

33) Johanek 1987, 7-68.

34) Johanek 1987, 8.

35) Johanek 1987, 10 with note 10; see there also bibliographic reference to Dopsch 1968.

36) Johanek 1987, 43: »Es ist auch bekannt, dass im Falle des Getreides Überflussregionen wie Mainfranken und das Elsaß anderen gegenüberstanden, in denen der Getreidebau gegenüber der Viehzucht zurücktrat. [...] Solche Gegenden waren auf Getreidezufuhr auch außerhalb von Notzeiten angewiesen, und Einhards Wunderbericht spricht ja von dem Getreidetransport auf dem Main als einer ständigen Einrichtung«.

37) Johanek 1987, 43. – Small scale trade (petty trade) is meant, which took place *per civitates et vicos atque per mercata;* loc. cit.

38) Johanek 1987, 41.

39) Johanek 1987, 31.

40) Adam 1996, 164-165.

41) Johanek 1987, 26: »nicht ausschließlich an wenigen großen und zentralen Plätzen [...], sondern auch in nichtstädtischen Siedlungen, sei es nun in Häfen [...] oder in unbedeutenden *villae* [...]«.

42) Johanek 1987, 54.

43) Johanek 1987, 50-51.

44) Johanek 1987, 67.

45) Adam 1996, 164.

46) The early medieval cemeteries of Thalmässing (Wießner 1978, 9) and Großhöbing (Weinlich/Nadler 2006, 42-43) exemplify this. The grave goods of Thalmässing are of Frankish origin. The authors of the publication on Großhöbing cemetery argue that this group of people and their settlement could have acted as a Bavarian »boarder post«.

47) The frontier ran some few kilometres west of Thalmässing from the north to the south; see von Guttenberg 1943, 1-17.

48) On the rediscovery of this castle see Wurdak 2002, 31-40.

49) Hermann 2008, 209-232.

50) Cf. Eckoldt 1980, 40-44.

51) Nadler/Weinlich 1998, 141 fig. 91; 142.

52) Schmidt-Kaler 1987, 42-43. – On the genesis see also Walter 1995, 368.

53) See also Nadler 2004, 31-32.

54) Nadler 2008, 15-16. 18-19 figs 12-15.

55) Werther 2011, 106.

56) Johanek 1987, 52.

57) See also Liebert 2013, 154.

58) Kröger/Werther 2017, 268 point out that new research suggest, »dass zumindest der nördliche Bauabschnitt sehr weit fortgeschritten war und partiell einen nutzbaren Ausbauzustand erreicht hatte«.

59) The estimation of the natural water level is not easy because the river is dammed for mills. Therefore, navigability becomes difficult to assess.

60) The measurement of water level was taken near the riverbank by the author at a survey carried out during the first week of July 2012, between Hofstetten (NW of Eckersmühlen) and Roth.

61) On the canal of the so-called Mindorf-Linie see Trögl 2002, 62 fig.; 64-65. The construction work began in 1939, had to be stopped in 1942 because of World War II; loc. cit. – An illustrative account with graphics can be seen at an information board north of the village Pyras (Lkr. Roth/D).

62) Vgl. Liebert 2013, 141-142. 155.

63) Nitz 1993, 420, on the other hand, observes that toponyms like Mühlhausen or Mühlheim seem to indicate that there were several mills in this location. The surplus of importance would have been correspondingly larger.

References

Abel 1978: W. Abel, Geschichte der deutschen Landwirtschaft vom frühen Mittelalter bis zum 19. Jahrhundert. Deutsche Agrargeschichte 2 (Stuttgart [3]1978).

Adam 1996: H. Adam, Das Zollwesen im Fränkischen Reich und das spätkarolingische Wirtschaftsleben. Ein Überblick über Zoll, Handel und Verkehr im 9. Jahrhundert. Vierteljahresschrift für Sozial- und Wirtschaftsgeschichte, Beiheft 126 (Stuttgart 1996).

Baatz 1995: D. Baatz, Die Wassermühle bei Vitruv X 5,2. Ein archäologischer Kommentar. Saalburg-Jahrbuch 48, 1995, 5-18.

Bachmann 1988: Ch. Bachmann, Zur Entwicklung des Mühlenrechts in Altbayern. Zeitschrift für bayerische Landesgeschichte 51, 1988, 719-765.

Bloch 1935: M. Bloch, Antritt und Siegeszug der Wassermühle. In: C. Honegger (ed.), Schrift und Materie der Geschichte. Vorschläge zur systematischen Aneignung historischer Prozesse. Edition Suhrkamp 814 (Frankfurt a.M. 1977) 171-197 (at first: Avènement et conquetes du moulin à eau. Annales d'Histoire Économique et Sociale 7, 1935, 538-563).

Böhme 1999: A. Böhme, Wassermühlen der Römerzeit. In: A. Böhme (ed.), Die Regnersche Mühle in Bretzenheim. Beiträge zur Geschichte der Wassermühle. Bretzenheimer Beiträge zur Geschichte 1 (Mainz 1999) 13-26.

Dollinger 1982: P. Dollinger, Der bayerische Bauernstand vom 9. bis zum 13. Jahrhundert (München 1982).

Dopsch 1968: A. Dopsch, Gesammelte Aufsätze. 2: Beiträge zur Sozial- und Wirtschaftsgeschichte (Wien 1938, reprint Aalen 1968).

Eckoldt 1980: M. Eckoldt, Schiffahrt auf kleinen Flüssen Mitteleuropas in Römerzeit und Mittelalter. Schriften des Deutschen Schiffahrtsmuseums 14 (Oldenburg, Hamburg, München 1980).

1986: M. Eckoldt, Die Schiffbarkeit kleiner Flüsse in alter Zeit. Notwendigkeit, Voraussetzungen und Entwicklung einer Rechenmethode. Archäologisches Korrespondenzblatt 16, 1986, 203-206.

Ellmers 1972: D. Ellmers, Frühmittelalterliche Handelsschiffahrt in Mittel- und Nordeuropa. Schriften des Deutschen Schiffahrtsmuseums 3 = Offa 28 (Neumünster 1972).

Elmshäuser 1992: K. Elmshäuser, Kanalbau und technische Wasserführung im frühen Mittelalter. Technikgeschichte 59, 1992, 1-26.

2002a: K. Elmshäuser (ed.), Häfen, Schiffe, Wasserwege. Zur Schifffahrt des Mittelalters. Schriften des Deutschen Schifffahrtsmuseums 58, Sonderdruck (Bremerhaven, Hamburg 2002).

2002b: K. Elmshäuser, Facit Navigium. Schiffahrt auf Seine, Marne, Mosel und Rhein in Quellen zur frühmittelalterlichen Grundherrschaft. In: Elmshäuser 2002a, 22-53.

Elmshäuser et al. 1993: Lexikon des Mittelalters 6 (1993) cols 885-891 s.v. Mühle, Müller (K. Elmshäuser / D. Hägermann / A. Hedwig / K.-H. Ludwig).

Ettel et al. 2014: P. Ettel / F. Daim / S. Berg-Hobohm / L. Werther / Ch. Zielhofer (eds), Großbaustelle 793. Das Kanalprojekt Karls des Großen zwischen Rhein und Donau. Mosaiksteine. Forschungen am RGZM 11 (Mainz 2014).

Grewe 1998: K. Grewe, Der Karlsgraben bei Weißenburg i. B. und der Fulbert-Stollen von Maria Laach. In: U. Lindgren (ed.), Europäische Technik im Mittelalter: 800 bis 1400. Tradition und Innovation; ein Handbuch (Berlin ³1998) 111-115.

von Guttenberg 1943: E. von Guttenberg, Stammesgrenzen und Volkstum im Gebiet der Rednitz und Altmühl. Jahrbuch für fränkische Landesforschung 8/9, 1943, 1-109.

Hägermann 1997: D. Hägermann, Technik im frühen Mittelalter zwischen 500 und 1000. In: D. Hägermann / H. Schneider, Landbau und Handwerk. 750 v. Chr. bis 1000 n. Chr. Propyläen Technikgeschichte 1 (Berlin 1997) 317-505.

2002: D. Hägermann, Karl der Große und die Schiffahrt. In: Elmshäuser 2002a, 11-21.

Henning 1994: J. Henning, Mühlentechnologie und Ökonomiewandel zwischen Römerzeit und Frühmittelalter. Saalburg-Jahrbuch 47, 1994, 5-18.

Herrmann 2008: V. Herrmann, Die frühmittelalterliche Burg »Greuth« in der Schwarzachaue bei Greding-Obermässing, Lkr. Roth. Beiträge zur Archäologie in Mittelfranken 8, 2008, 209-232.

Johanek 1987: P. Johanek, Der fränkische Handel der Karolingerzeit im Spiegel der Schriftquellen. In: K. Düwel / H. Jankuhn / H. Siems / D. Timpe (eds), Untersuchungen zu Handel und Verkehr der vor- und frühgeschichtlichen Zeit in Mittel- und Nordeuropa. 4: Der Handel der Karolinger- und Wikingerzeit. Akademie der Wissenschaften in Göttingen. Philosophisch-Historische Klasse: Abhandlungen 156 (Göttingen 1987) 7-68.

Koch 2002: R. Koch, Fossa Carolina. Neue Erkenntnisse zum Schiffahrtskanal Karls des Großen. In: Elmshäuser 2002a, 54-70.

Koehne 1904: C. Koehne, Das Recht der Mühlen bis zum Ende der Karolingerzeit. Untersuchungen zur Deutschen Staats- und Rechtsgeschichte 71 (Breslau 1904).

Kröger/Werther 2017: L. Kröger / L. Werther, Vom Rhein zur Donau – Überlegungen zur Binnenschifffahrt zwischen Römischer Kaiserzeit und Hochmittelalter. In: R. Atzbach / P. Cassitti / H. Kenzler / L. Löw (eds), Archäologie Mittelalter, Neuzeit, Zukunft. Festschrift für Ingolf Ericsson. Bamberger Schriften zur Archäologie des Mittelalters und der Neuzeit 6 (Bonn 2017) 249-282.

Kuchenbuch 1978: L. Kuchenbuch, Bäuerliche Gesellschaft und Klosterherrschaft im 9. Jahrhundert. Studien zur Sozialstruktur der familia der Abtei Prüm. Vierteljahresschrift zur Sozial- und Wirtschaftsgeschichte, Beiheft 66 (Wiesbaden 1978).

1991: L. Kuchenbuch, Grundherrschaft im früheren Mittelalter. Historisches Seminar N. F. 1 (Idstein 1991).

Liebert 2004: Th. Liebert, Neue Feuchtbodenbefunde im Schwarzachtal bei Großhöbing, Lkr. Roth – Ein Vorbericht. Beiträge zur Archäologie in Mittelfranken 7, 2003 (2004), 67-75.

2013: Th. Liebert, Siedlungskomplex Großhöbing: Mühlen und Bootsländen als Einrichtungen ländlicher Zentralorte. In: P. Ettel / L. Werther (eds), Zentrale Orte und zentrale Räume des Frühmittelalters in Süddeutschland. RGZM – Tagungen 18 (Mainz 2013) 141-158.

2014: Th. Liebert, Frühmittelalterliche Uferverbaue und Stauvorrichtungen im südlichen Mittelfranken. In: Ettel et al. 2014, 99-102.

2015: Th. Liebert, Frühmittelalterliche Wassermühlen und Wasserbauwerke im Schwarzachtal bei Großhöbing. Materialhefte zur Bayerischen Archäologie 101 (Kallmünz/Opf. 2015).

Nadler 2004: M. Nadler, Die Rettungsgrabungen entlang der ICE-Neubaustrecke Nürnberg-Ingolstadt (Abschnitt Mittelfranken) in den Jahren 1999-2002 (Teil 1). Beiträge zur Archäologie in Mittelfranken 7, 2003 (2004), 11-62.

2008: M. Nadler, Die Rettungsgrabungen entlang der ICE-Neubaustrecke Nürnberg-Ingolstadt (Abschnitt Mittelfranken) in den Jahren 1999-2002 (Teil 2) und Nachträge. Beiträge zur Archäologie in Mittelfranken 8, 2008, 9-40.

Nadler/Weinlich 1998: M. Nadler / E. Weinlich, Die Gräber der Herren von Höbing. Das Archäologische Jahr in Bayern 1997 (1998), 139-142.

2006: M. Nadler / E. Weinlich, Am Einfallstor nach Bayern – Der Herr von Höbing. In: Stadt Ingolstadt (ed.), Vom Werden einer Stadt – Ingolstadt 806 [exhibition catalogue] (Ingolstadt 2006) 42-45.

Nitz 1993: H.-J. Nitz, Siedlungsstrukturen der königlichen und adeligen Grundherrschaft der Karolingerzeit – der Beitrag der historisch-genetischen Siedlungsgeographie. In: W. Rösener (ed.), Strukturen der Grundherrschaft im frühen Mittelalter. Veröffentlichungen des Max-Planck-Instituts für Geschichte 92 (Göttingen ²1993) 411-482.

Röder/Röder 1993: G. Röder / J. Röder, Die antike Turbinenmühle in Chemtou. In: F. Rakob (ed.), Simitthus I. Die Steinbrüche und die antike Stadt (Mainz 1993) 95-102 pls 20-27. 86 suppl. 8.

Rösener 1993a: W. Rösener (ed.), Strukturen der Grundherrschaft im frühen Mittelalter. Veröffentlichungen des Max-Planck-Instituts für Geschichte 92 (Göttingen ²1993).

1993b: W. Rösener, Strukturformen der adeligen Grundherrschaft in der Karolingerzeit. In: Rösener 1993a, 126-180.

Schmidt-Kaler 1987: H. Schmidt-Kaler, Geologische Karte von Bayern 1:25 000. Erläuterungen zum Blatt 6933 Thalmässing (München 1987).

Schneider 1997: H. Schneider, Die Gaben des Prometheus. Technik im antiken Mittelmeerraum zwischen 750 v. Chr. und 500 n. Chr. In: D. Hägermann / H. Schneider, Landbau und Handwerk. 750 v. Chr. bis 1000 n. Chr. Propyläen Technikgeschichte 1 (Berlin 1997) 19-313.

Trögl 2002: H. Trögl, Die Geschichte einer Wasserstraße. Vom Karlsgraben zum Main-Donau-Kanal. Heimatkundliche Streifzüge. Schriftenreihe des Landkreises Roth 21, 2002, 45-73.

Walter 1995: R. Walter, Geologie von Mitteleuropa (Stuttgart 1995).

Werther 2011: L. Werther, Prospektionsarbeiten an der frühmittelalterlichen Niederungsburg Greuth im Schwarzachtal. Das Archäologische Jahr in Bayern 2010 (2011), 104-107.

Wießner 1978: W. Wießner, Hilpoltstein. Historischer Atlas von Bayern, Teil Franken (München 1978).

Wurdak 2002: E. Wurdak, Die Wasserburg bei Holzi. Versuch einer geschichtlichen Einordnung. Heimatkundliche Streifzüge. Schriftenreihe des Landkreises Roth 21, 2002, 31-40.

Summary

Großhöbing, situated in the south of Middle Franconia, most likely owes its existence to its ideal geographic location for transport. The settlement is not only situated on the northern edge of the Frankonian Jura but also next to the small River Schwarzach which rises at the northern foothill and joins the River Altmühl in the middle of the Franconian Jura. Therefore, the River Schwarzach is an important north-south link between the catchments of the Rivers Danube and Rhine. In the north of Großhöbing the brook Thalach flows from the west into the Schwarzach and offers a natural east-west traffic artery.
At least as important as its geographic location was the proximity to the summit of the European catchments. Just a few kilometres to the north of Großhöbing, it was possible to transcend the major European watershed by a short overland passage with only a slight slope. Depending on water levels, the landing sites of Großhöbing were the end or the beginning of the navigable river section of the Schwarzach during the Early Middle Ages.
Evidence of continuous use of the River Schwarzach as a navigable waterway during the second half of the 9th and maybe even the 10th century AD is given by the waterlogged features, excavated and analysed by archaeologists at the construction site of the high-speed train line during the years 1996-2001. Well preserved timbers from an archaeological site east of Großhöbing are parts of a landing place. It was situated at an artificial section of the River Schwarzach and was used and maintained during several construction phases, especially in Carolingian times. Embedded in a network of overland routes, the landing site was connected with the castle Greuth, situated upstream at the River Schwarzach. Numerous archaeological features of watermills from the 6th to the 12th century AD prove substantial farming in the immediate surroundings of Großhöbing. These mills and a large early medieval cemetery from the 6th and 7th century AD indicate the presence of some wealthy leading families. Surely these families would have particularly profited from the exploitation and the trade with bog iron ore. On the plateau of the Jura next to Großhöbing, due to geological conditions bog iron ore can be found on the surface and was mined, processed and smelted since prehistoric times.
It seems that since the 11th century AD the River Schwarzach was not used as waterway anymore. Climate changes might have caused this alteration. The Third Reich project to construct a channel at the so-called Mindorf-Linie as well as the contemporary Main-Donau-Canal shows the constant significance of the Großhöbing area for bridging the main European watershed.

Zusammenfassung

Großhöbing im südlichen Mittelfranken verdankt seine Existenz höchstwahrscheinlich seiner verkehrsgünstigen Lage. Es liegt nicht nur am Nordrand der Fränkischen Alb, sondern zugleich auch am kleinen Fluss Schwarzach, der im nördlichen Albvorland entspringt und inmitten der Fränkischen Alb in die Altmühl mündet. Somit stellt die Schwarzach eine wichtige Verbindung nach Süden zum Flusssystem der Donau dar. Durch das Tal der bei Großhöbing in die Schwarzach mündenden Thalach ergab sich eine ebenfalls naturbedingte Ost-West-Verbindung. Als mindestens ebenso wichtig dürfte sich darüber hinaus die Nähe zum Scheitelpunkt des europäischen Gewässersystems erwiesen haben. Nur wenige Kilometer nördlich von Großhöbing konnte die Europäische Hauptwasserscheide auf einem kurzen Landweg ohne große Steigungen bequem überwunden werden. Je nach Wasserstand war Großhöbing daher der End- bzw. Anfangspunkt der im frühen Mittelalter schiffbaren Schwarzach.
Dass die Schwarzach in jener Zeit tatsächlich als Wasserstraße genutzt wurde, zeigen die archäologischen Feuchtbodenbefunde, die in den Jahren 1996-2001 im Bereich der heutigen ICE-Trasse von Nürnberg nach Ingolstadt untersucht und geborgen wurden. Die an der Schwarzach östlich von Großhöbing dokumentierten Feuchthölzer stammen von einer Bootsanlegestelle, die an einem eigens dafür ausgebauten Abschnitt der Schwarzach angelegt worden ist. Sie wurde über mehrere Bauphasen hinweg insbesondere in karolingischer Zeit genutzt. Eingebunden in ein Landwegenetz stand die Anlegestelle zudem mit der schwarzachaufwärts gelegenen Burg Greuth in funktionaler Verbindung. Ein ausgedehntes, bei Großhöbing gelegenes frühmittelalterliches Gräberfeld des 6. und 7. Jahrhunderts n. Chr. sowie umfangreiche archäologische Befunde frühmittelalterlicher Mühlen des ausgehenden 6.-12. Jahrhunderts n. Chr. belegen die Anwesenheit einer wohlhabenden Führungsschicht sowie umfangreiche landwirtschaftliche Tätigkeit im direkten Umfeld Großhöbings. Vor allem die führende(n) Familie(n) des Ortes dürfte(n) von der Gewinnung und dem Handel mit Bohnerzen profitiert haben. Die unmittelbar oberhalb von Großhöbing anschließende Albhochfläche bietet natürliche Bohnerzvorkommen, die bereits in vor- und frühgeschichtlicher Zeit genutzt wurden.
Ab dem 11. Jahrhundert n. Chr. wurde die Schwarzach allem Anschein nach nicht mehr als Wasserstraße genutzt. Klimatische Veränderungen dürften hierfür den Ausschlag gegeben haben. Ein während des Dritten Reiches begonnenes Kanalbauprojekt wie auch der heutige Main-Donau Kanal belegen die aktuelle Bedeutung der Region um Großhöbing für die Überwindung der Hauptwasserscheide.

LUMÍR POLÁČEK

RIVER ARCHAEOLOGY AND THE SEARCH FOR A HARBOUR IN MIKULČICE

EARLY MEDIEVAL MIKULČICE

Early medieval Mikulčice in Moravia in the Czech Republic used to be a prominent centre in Great Moravia. This 9th century AD power-political structure of the western Slavs was situated north of the central part of the River Danube. The Mojmirid dynasty rulers adopted Christianity and achieved the establishing of the archbishopric of Moravia, led by Methodius. However, Great Moravia existed for less than a century because it was invaded by the Hungarians at the beginning of the 10th century AD and the main centres of power, including Mikulčice, were wiped out together with the state itself[1]. A typical characteristic of Great Moravia was the positioning of its main power centres in the floodplain of two great rivers, the Morava and the Thaya. The centres were island strongholds built on hillocks above the rivers or between their many distributaries[2].

The Mikulčice settlement agglomeration was located on both sides of the nowadays regulated border River Morava. Therefore, it is part of today's Mikulčice village in the Czech Republic and the Slovak village of Kopčany (okr. Skalica). The settlement areas were originally located on several river islands. The fortified core of the agglomeration was protected by a continuous ring of river distributaries, which are now silted up (**fig. 1**)[3]. In the backfill of these channels, below the level of ground water, wooden bridges, anti-erosion barriers, palisades, and other water constructions were excavated[4]. The wooden finds discovered during the excavations provide a wider picture of the material culture of the Great Moravian centre and are absolutely unique in this area[5].

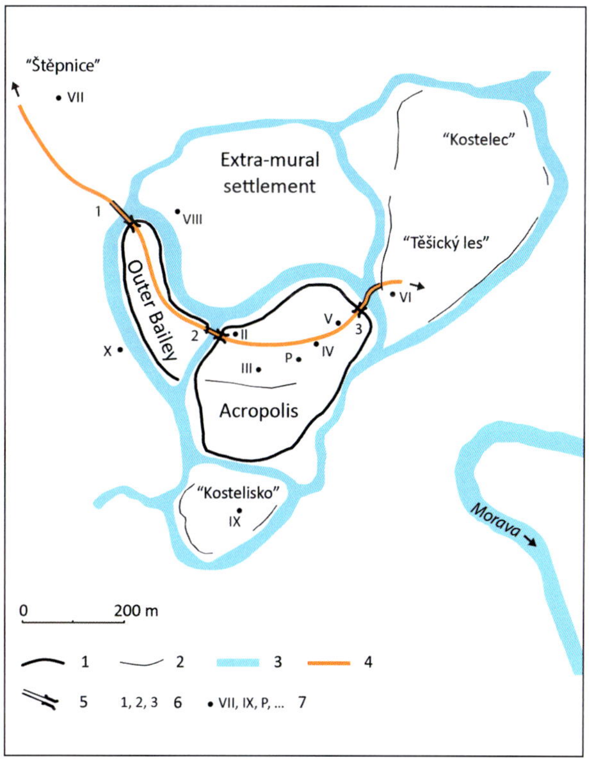

Fig. 1 The Mikulčice-Valy Stronghold. A schematic depiction of its topography including presumed locations of the main road and the three bridges. – **1** fortification of the acropolis and the outer bailey. – **2** terrain borders of elevated parts of the acropolis and the extra-mural settlement. – **3** presumed location of the river branches. – **4** the main road of the settlement agglomeration. – **5** wooden bridges and gates. – **6** numbers of bridges. – **7** officially accepted order of churches (**II, III, ...**) and the palace (**P**). – (Based on Poláček 2014b).

Mikulčice is the only archaeological site in the Czech Republic, where river archaeology has been systematically developed. Several large-scale excavations of riverbeds with a total area of 10,000 m² were conducted between the 1960s and the 1980s. Revisions and additional excavations of »riverbed 1« were conducted in 2012 and the results published in 2014[6].

However, a complex evaluation of the »old« large-scale excavations has now been conducted, 30-50 years later[7].

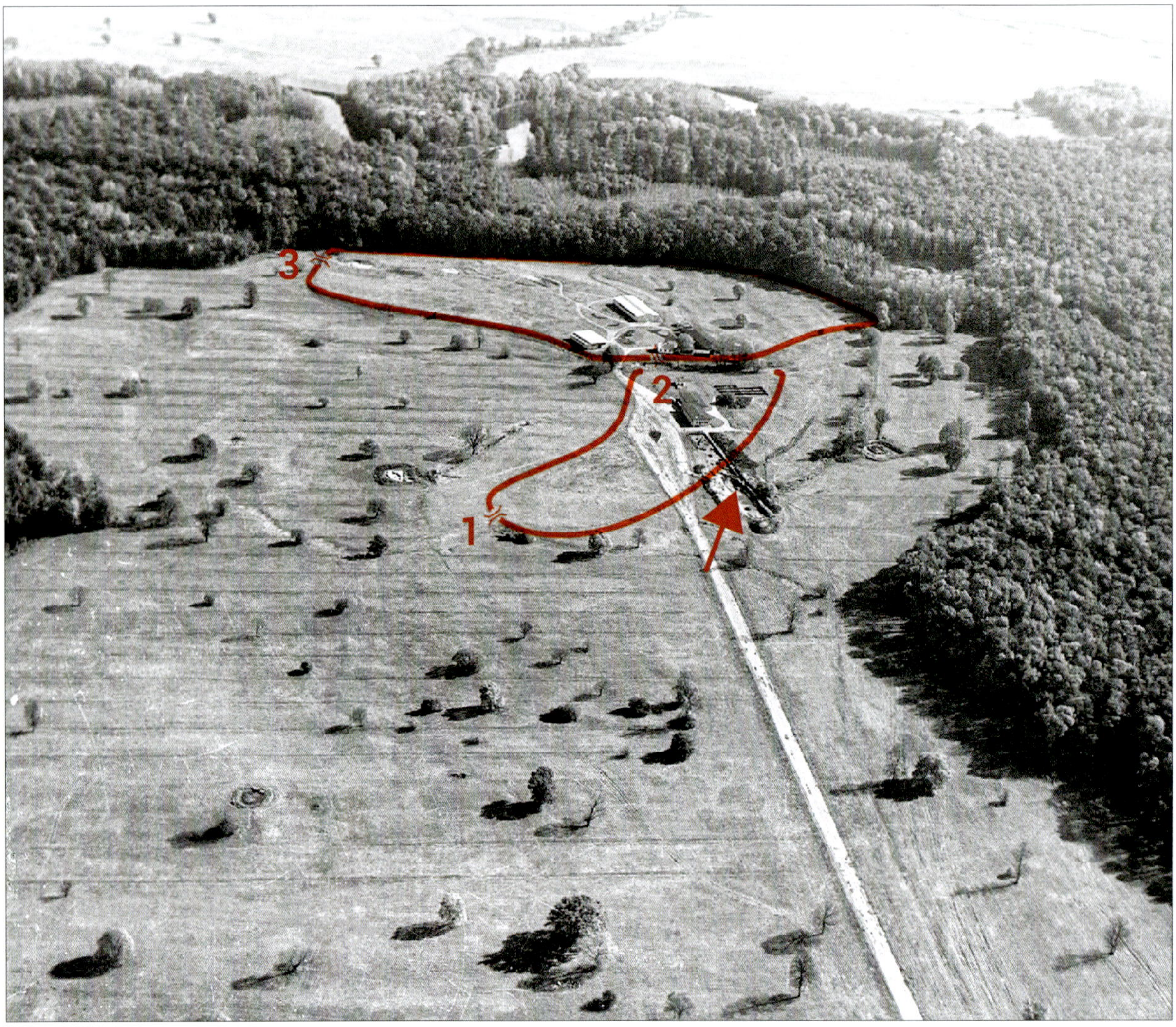

Fig. 2 The Mikulčice-Valy Stronghold. Aerial view of the site with the fortified centre: the early medieval agglomeration and the three gateways, each leading to a wooden bridge are marked. The arrow points to excavation area P 1963-64, where the silted riverbed was discovered for the first time in Mikulčice (outside the rampart). – **1** bridge no. 1 in front of the north-western gate of the bailey. – **2** bridge no. 2 in front of the western gate of the acropolis. – **3** bridge no. 3 in front of the north-eastern gate of the acropolis. – (Archive of the Czech Academy of Sciences, Institute of Archaeology, Brno).

THE STORY OF MIKULČICE RIVER ARCHAEOLOGY

The story begins in 1954 when the stronghold was discovered with great pomp[8]. This event was the beginning of a 40-year long era of large-scale excavations. The first ten years of field works focused on the most attractive objects: the palace, the ten churches, and the adjacent cemeteries, which were rich in finds[9]. In 1964, an extinct riverbed was discovered outside the rampart of the outer bailey (**fig. 2**)[10]. It was suggested that in the 9th century AD Mikulčice had been an island castle on the Morava River. To verify this hypothesis, the archaeologists conducted three large-scale excavations of the silted-up river channels around the fortified core of the settlement agglomeration (**figs 3-4**)[11].

A precondition for the realisation of these excavations was the artificial lowering of the groundwater level through a system of wells that were drilled around the excavation area and enabled systematic water extraction[12].

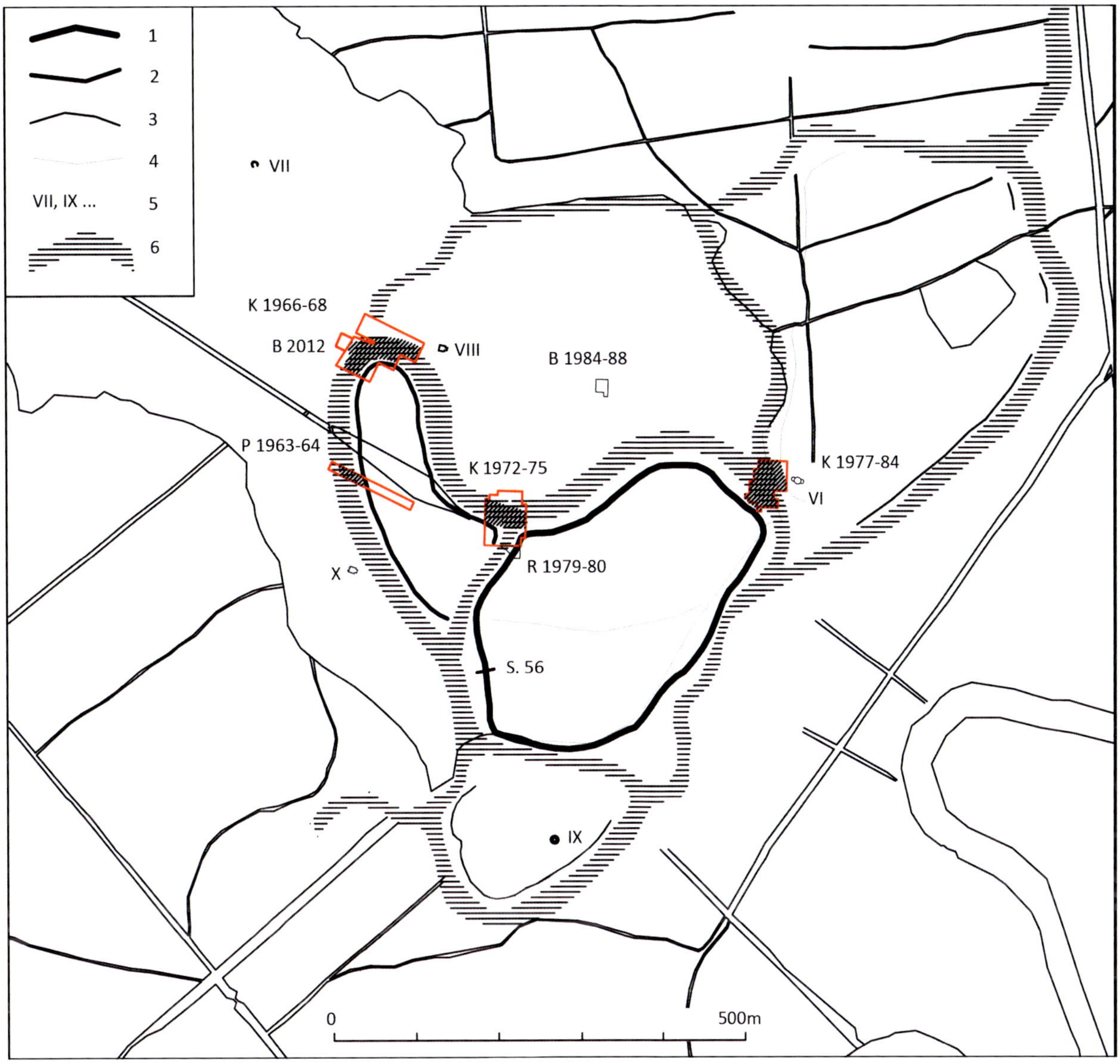

Fig. 3 The Mikulčice-Valy Stronghold. The topographic situation of the castle and the extra-mural settlement in the 9th century AD, including the presumed location of the river channels. Large-scale excavations of the riverbeds and other excavation sites, which partly uncovered the silted riverbeds. – **1** fortification of the acropolis. – **2** archaeologically proven fortification of the outer bailey. – **3** earthen dike on the perimeter of »Těšický les« (Těšice Forest) in the extra-mural settlement. – **4** terrain borders of elevated parts of the acropolis and the extra-mural settlement. – **5** locations of churches. – **6** presumed location of the river channels. – (Based on Poláček 1996).

Excavation area K 1966-1968, denoted as »riverbed 1«, contained the finds of the »first« wooden bridge connecting the outer bailey to the suburb. On the river bottom under the bridge, we discovered two ten-metre long logboats and a series of fishing baskets. The second area, K 1972-1975 (»riverbed 2«), situated at the northern mouth of the moat between the acropolis and the outer bailey, revealed the »second bridge« and a barrier separating the moat from the waterway. This barrier, constructed on the riverbed, consisted of wooden caissons filled with stones and reinforced trough pile structures. In the third area, K 1977-1984 (»riverbed 3«), the remains of the »third« bridge connecting the acropolis to the suburb was uncovered (**figs 3-4**)[13].

In 2012-2014, the post-excavation analyses of all »old« field work in the area of the silted river channels began as part of a research project called »9th century bridges in Mikulčice«. The project included a new revision and the additional excavation B 2012 in the area of the first bridge. A number of archaeological, historical, and environmental issues were identified on that occasion (**figs 4-5**)[14].

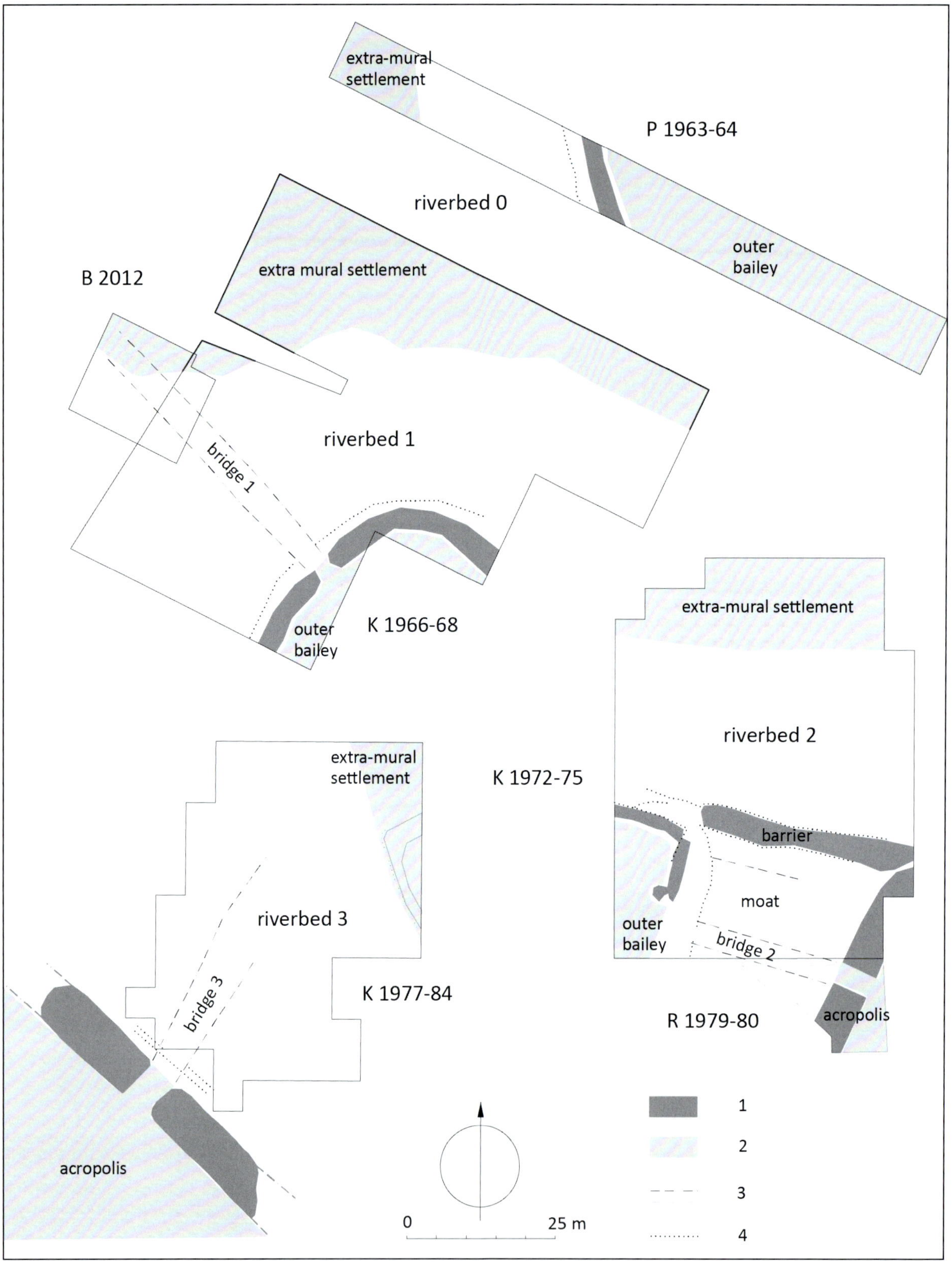

Fig. 4 The Mikulčice-Valy Stronghold. A scheme of large-area excavations of the silted-up river branches. – **1** rampart and barrier. – **2** riverbank. – **3** bridge. – **4** palisade (reinforced riverbank). – (Based on Poláček 2014).

Fig. 5 The Mikulčice-Valy Stronghold, excavation B 2012. Overall situation in the final phase of excavation of the river meander and bridge no. 1. – (Based on Poláček 2014b).

THE MIKULČICE RIVER SYSTEM

These are the main issues of today's river archaeology in Mikulčice[15]:
1. The reconstruction of the river network in the area of the 9th century AD settlement agglomeration.
2. The assessment of the water regime of the silted river distributaries surrounding the stronghold.
3. Paleoecological research into the development of the floodplain.
4. The determination of the design and dating of water constructions.
5. The location of the potential river harbour.

The reconstruction of the historical river network over the wider area of the castle surroundings is a complicated task. The results of a recent geophysical survey are unable to delineate the medieval river network with any great certainty. The most promising results are obtained through archaeological excavations, especially those that cover large areas. Only by using these methods, we have been able to ascertain the exact position of the river channel on the western and northern sides of the fortified area, where the channel used to meander. Other reconstructed locations of the original river network are more or less hypothetical (see **fig. 3**)[16].

Archaeobotanical research revealed that the water of the river channel having enclosed the castle had a low flow rate and was even stagnant at times[17]. Malacological findings support this conclusion[18], as do the fishing pots found on the bottom, which were designed to catch a specific kind of fish that lives in the muddy environment of slow or stagnant water[19]. The channels represented a natural (albeit sometimes rather symbolic) line of defence for the castle and its surroundings[20].

Paleoecological research into the development of the floodplain represents a number of issues, such as the interpretation and dating of river and flood sediments, the determination of the beginning of periodic floods, or more precisely, the siltation of the river distributaries[21].

The crucial question is why the channels around the castle silted relatively quickly by this massive layer of fluvial sands. Was it a natural evolution of a river system, or was it caused by humans? We have to realise that the filling of the channels caused the castle to lose a significant part of its natural strategic defences, and we should not rule out the possibility of human intervention in the river branches' water regime, particularly as it would have occurred at the same time as the violent fall of this power centre in the early 10th century AD. Connecting the active river channel with the meander ringing the castle would have been sufficient to achieve this goal, but at this point, we enter the realm of speculation and theories[22].

A further important issue is the dating of fluvial sand sedimentation and its end, as well as discovering when the sandy-clayey sediments (resembling flood loams) began to accumulate. Once again, we lack any direct chronological evidence, although we can revert to the argument of the castle wall and its »speedy« destruction. As we previously stated, its remnants fell into flood loams, so these sediments must have started to accumulate soon after the castle was destroyed. However, there are other ways to interpret these sediments: Is it evidence of the first early medieval floods, or the most recent phase of usual river sedimentation? The well-known floodplain work written by the archaeobotanist E. Opravil argues that periodic flooding and flood loam sedimentation only occurred in the 13th century AD[23]. The B 2012 excavation revealed new clues that might shed more light on the problem.

One of the main benefits of the interdisciplinary research into area B 2012 was at least a partial rendering of the development of the riverbed (**fig. 5**). The original »older meander« was gradually filled up with fluvial sands (point bar), during which it shifted and became shallower. The result was the »younger meander«, filled with fine sand-clay sediments characterised by flood-loam. This unit has been documented only in the northern profiles of the excavated area; the larger part, including the outer border, is to be searched for outside the examined area[24].

In spite of many arbitrary ambiguities and questions, a basic hypothesis can be formulated regarding the development of the river channel in the area of the north-western part of the first bridge. The area of interest is located in the north-west periphery of the meander between the outer bailey and the north-western extramural settlement (»riverbed 1«). At the time of the existence of the power centre, the riverbed was overlaid with a basal group of beds consisting of fine sands, loams or gravels interlaid with thin layers of organic material – mainly wood and plants remained. This material was deposited in the calmer areas of the channel, in particular, between the bridge piles. At a certain moment, the flow rate in the channel dramatically increased, which was probably caused by human activity rather than natural change. Coarser sands started to deposit relatively quickly, which gradually filled in the original meander. The channel became shallower and shallower and gradually shifted towards the north-west until it left the original meander and eroded away another »younger« meander. It cannot be ruled out that because of the need to bridge the younger meander, the bridge was extended towards the north-west. At this stage, there was a permanent disconnection from the channel; the cause of which should be looked for in a hydrographic change somewhere upstream[25].

Dendrochronological dating of 14 piles from area B 2012 (bridge no. 1) turned up only two dates: »after 875« (1ak) and 876/877 AD (Wk)[26]. Compared to the results from the dating of the originally excavated part of the bridge (approximately 40 dates from »after 828« to »after 871 AD«), this is the latest dendrochronological data acquired from bridge no. 1[27].

Fig. 6 The Mikulčice-Valy Stronghold. Excavation area K 1972-1975 (»riverbed 2«) with excavated wooden constructions and a transverse profile across the silted riverbank. – (Based on Poláček 2014a).

HYPOTHETICAL LOCATION OF THE HARBOUR

It is highly likely that a river harbour in the area of the power centre existed in the 9th century AD. From among the areas of the Mikulčice river channels excavated so far, »riverbed 2« can be considered a likely location (**figs 6-7**)[28]. The sluice gate and the adjoining protected area inside the stronghold do not rule out such an interpretation. The interpretation of this area as an access gate from the water is supported by the finds of axes at the bottom of the riverbed. A similar concentration of axes in Mikulčice was excavated in only two other places – always under the bridges in front of the gates. This is evidence for fighting around the main entrances to the castle[29].

To describe the find context: between the timber-framed wall that reinforced the riverbank in front of the rampart of the outer bailey and the barrier on the bottom of the river, there was a sluice, which was about 1 m wide and 10 m long (**fig. 7**). Theoretically, logboats were able to navigate through this sluice. The rows of posts perpendicular to the inner wall of the barrier could have been part of the construction of the landing stage. However, this interpretation is complicated because the whole structure was the result of a longer development; the timber-framed caissons of the barrier gradually deteriorated and were reinforced by posts

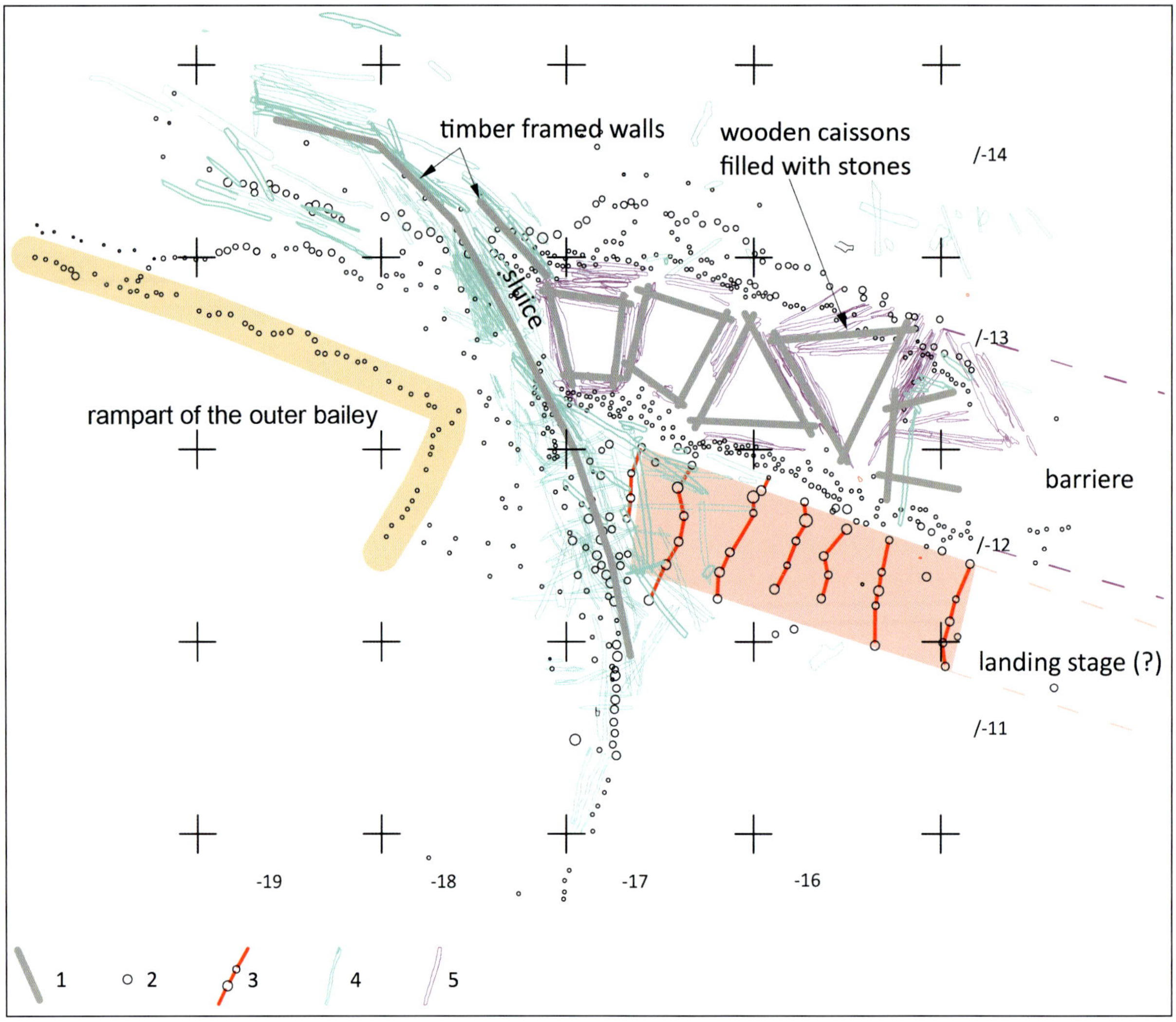

Fig. 7 The Mikulčice-Valy Stronghold. Find situation in the area of the hypothetical harbour (excavation area K 1972-1975; river branch no. 2). – **1** original log buildings (timber-framed walls and wooden caissons). – **2** wooden stakes. – **3** rows of stakes at the hypothetical landing stage. – **4** destructed construction of a timber framed wall. – **5** destructed wooden caissons. – (Reconstruction by L. Poláček; graphics P. Čáp).

driven into the riverbed. Unfortunately, this situation cannot currently be interpreted unambiguously; we are not able to date the posts because they do not allow dendrochronological analysis. The only hope is a complex post-excavation analysis of the field documentation and the whole find situation.

NAVIGATION ON THE RIVER MORAVA

As a tributary of the Danube, the River Morava was of significant geopolitical and economic importance for Great Moravia and the Mikulčice power centre. In the 9th century AD, the River Morava connected the main centres of Mojmirid Moravia with the Danube – an important European waterway that enabled trade and cultural contacts with the known »world«: In the west, it was the Carolingian Empire and in the east, it led to Bulgaria, Byzantium and further to the Asian continent via the Silk Road. The Morava stream and the adjacent part of the Danube also formed part of an important north-south trade route leading to the Adriatic area – Aquilea, Venice and Rome. The importance of river navigation and transport in the area of the Central Danube region and its left-bank tributaries, including the Morava, is evidenced indirectly by written sources: the Raffelstetten customs tariff (*Inquisitio de theloneis Raffelstettensis*) issued in 903/904 AD[30] mentions traders bringing Bavarian salt to the »market of the Moravians«[31]. Navigation on the River Morava in the 9th century AD is a matter of course; it is evidenced by archaeological finds from Mikulčice, such as boats/logboats and paddles[32].

Notes

1) Třeštík 2001. – Macháček 2009. – Štefan 2011. – Wihoda 2014.
2) Poláček 2001.
3) Poláček/Marek 2005, 12-17.
4) Poláček 2011; 2014b, 23.
5) Poláček/Marek/Skopal 2000.
6) Poláček 2014c.
7) Poláček 2014a.
8) Poulík 1975.
9) Poláček/Marek 1995; 2005. – Poláček 2008.
10) Klanica 1964, 50; 1965, 60.
11) Klanica 1967, 44-45; 1985.
12) Poláček 2014b, 23.
13) Poláček 2014a; 2014b, 20-23.
14) Poláček 2014c.
15) Poláček 2014a, 99-105.
16) Poláček 2014b, 16.
17) Opravil 1983, 23; 2000, 115. 133.
18) Horsák/Marek/Poláček 2003, 100.
19) Mazuch 2003, 366-374.
20) Opravil 1983, 23.
21) Havlíček/Poláček/Vachek 2003.
22) Poláček 2014b, 17-18.
23) Opravil 1983. – Poláček 2014b, 18.
24) Tarpin et al. 1999, 32-33 fig. 2.16.
25) Tarpin et al. 1999, 57 fig 2.16.
26) Tarpin et al. 1999, 41-42 fig. 2.11.
27) Compare Dvorská et al. 1999.
28) Poláček 2007a, 73.
29) Poláček/Marek/Skopal 2000, 199-202.
30) MMFH I 1966, 114.
31) Třeštík 1973, 874. – Poláček 2007b.
32) Poláček/Marek/Skopal 2000, 203-207.

References

Dvorská et al. 1999: J. Dvorská / K.-U. Heußner / L. Poláček / T. Westphal, Zum Stand der Dendrochronologie in Mikulčice (Mähren, Tschechien). In: L. Poláček / J. Dvorská (eds), Probleme der mitteleuropäischen Dendrochronologie und naturwissenschaftliche Beiträge zur Talaue der March. Internationale Tagungen in Mikulčice V = Spisy Archeologického Ústavu AV ČR v Brně 15 (Brno 1999) 69-78.

Havlíček/Poláček/Vachek 2003: P. Havlíček / L. Poláček / M. Vachek, Geologische Situation im Bereich des Burgwalls von Mikulčice. In: Poláček 2003, 11-38.

Horsák/Marek/Poláček 2003: M. Horsák / O. Marek / L. Poláček, Mollusken aus den archäologischen Grabungen in Mikulčice. In: Poláček 2003, 83-107.

Klanica 1964: Z. Klanica, Vorbericht über die Ergebnisse der Grabung des slawischen Burgwalles in Mikulčice für das Jahr 1963. Přehled Výzkumů 1963 (1964), 44-51.

1965: Z. Klanica, Vorbericht über die Grabungsergebnisse des altslawischen Burgwalles in Mikulčice für das Jahr 1964. Přehled Výzkumů 1964 (1965), 55-60.

1967: Z. Klanica, Předběžná zpráva o výzkumu slovanského hradiska v Mikulčicích za rok 1966, okres Hodonín (Vorbericht über die Grabung des slawischen Burgwalles in Mikulčice für das Jahr 1966, Bez. Hodonín). Přehled Výzkumů 1966 (1967), 41-51.

1985: Z. Klanica, Mikulčice, gegenwärtiger Stand und Perspektiven (Bez. Hodonín). Přehled Výzkumů 1983 (1985), 39-44.

Macháček 2009: J. Macháček, Disputes over Great Moravia: chiefdom or state? The Moravia or Tisza River. Early Medieval Europe 17/3, 2009, 248-267.

Mazuch 2003: M. Mazuch, Fischereigerät aus Mikulčice und die Frage des Fischanteils an der Ernährung der Bewohner des Burgwalls. In: Poláček 2003, 355-399.

MMFH I: Opera Universitas Purkynianae, Facultas Philosophica. 104. Magna fontes historici I (Brno 1966).

Opravil 1983: E. Opravil, Údolní niva v době hradištní. ČSSR – povodí Moravy a Poodří. Studie AÚ ČSAV v Brně XI, 2 (Praha 1983).

2000: E. Opravil, Zur Umwelt des Burgwalls von Mikulčice und zur pflanzlichen Ernährung seiner Bewohner. In: L. Poláček (ed.), Studien zum Burgwall von Mikulčice IV. Spisy Archeologického Ustavu AV ČR Brno 18 (Brno 2000) 9-169.

Poláček 1996: L. Poláček, Zum Stand der siedlungsarchäologischen Forschung in Mikulčice. In: Č. Staňa / L. Poláček (eds), Frühmittelalterliche Machtzentren in Mitteleuropa – Mehrjährige Grabungen und ihre Auswertung. Internationale Tagungen in Mikulčice III = Spisy Archeologického Ustavu AV ČR Brno 6 (Brno 1996) 213-260.

2001: L. Poláček, K poznání přírodního prostředí velkomoravských nížinných hradišť. In: L. Galuška / P. Kouřil / Z. Měřínský (eds), Velká Morava mezi východem a západem. Spisy Archeologického Ustavu AV ČR Brno 17 (Brno 2001) 315-325.

2003: L. Poláček (ed.), Studien zum Burgwall von Mikulčice V. Spisy Archeologického Ustavu AV ČR Brno 21 (Brno 2003).

2007a: L. Poláček, Die Rolle der südmährischen Flüsse in der Geschichte Großmährens. In: F. Biermann / T. Kersting (eds), Siedlung, Kommunikation und Wirtschaft im westslawischen Raum. Beiträge der Sektion zur slawischen Frühgeschichte des 5. Deutschen Archäologenkongresses in Frankfurt an der Oder, 4. bis 7. April 2005. Beiträge zur Ur- und Frühgeschichte Mitteleuropas 46 (Langenweissbach 2007) 67-78.

2007b: L. Poláček, Ninth-century Mikulčice: »the market of the Moravians«? The archaeological evidence of trade in Great Moravia. In: J. Henning (ed.), Post-Roman Towns, Trade and Settlement in Europe and Byzantium. 1: The Heirs of the Roman West. Millennium-Studien 5, 1 (Berlin, New York 2007) 499-523.

2008: L. Poláček, The Archaeology of Mikulčice. Mikulčice Guide, vol. 1 (Brno 2008).

2011: L. Poláček, Ninth Century Bridges of Mikulčice (Czech Republic). In: M. Prell (ed.), Archäologie der Brücken. Vorgeschichte. Antike. Mittelalter. Neuzeit (Regensburg 2011) 178-184.

2014a: L. Poláček, Grabungen im Bereich der ehemaligen Flussarme in Mikulčice. Flussarchäologie in Mikulčice I (Brno 2014).

2014b: L. Poláček, Notes on river archaeology in Mikulčice. In: Poláček 2014c, 11-25.

2014c: L. Poláček (ed.), Mikulčice River Archaeology. New Interdisciplinary Research into Bridge No. 1. Internationale Tagungen in Mikulčice X = Spisy Archeologického Ustavu AV ČR Brno 51 (Brno 2014).

Poláček/Hladík 2014: L. Poláček / M. Hladík, Archaeological excavation B 2012 of the filled up riverbed no. 1 in Mikulčice. In: Poláček 2014c, 27-59.

Poláček/Marek 1995: L. Poláček / O. Marek, Die Grabungen in Mikulčice 1954-1992. Geschichte, Grabungsmethoden und Dokumentation. In: F. Daim / L. Poláček (eds), Studien zum Burgwall von Mikulčice I. Spisy Archeologického Ustavu AV ČR Brno 2 (Brno 1995) 13-82.

2005: L. Poláček / O. Marek, Grundlagen der Topographie des Burgwalls von Mikulčice. Die Grabungsflächen 1954-1992. In: L. Poláček (ed.), Studien zum Burgwall von Mikulčice VII. Spisy Archeologického Ustavu AV ČR Brno 24 (Brno 2005) 9-358.

Poláček/Marek/Skopal 2000: L. Poláček / O. Marek / R. Skopal, Holzfunde aus Mikulčice. In: L. Poláček (ed.), Studien zum Burgwall von Mikulčice IV. Spisy Archeologického Ustavu AV ČR Brno 18 (Brno 2000) 177-302.

Poulík 1975: J. Poulík, Mikulčice. Sídlo a pevnost knížat velkomoravských (Praha 1975).

Štefan 2011: I. Štefan, Great Moravia, Statehood and Archaeology. The »Decline and Fall« of One Early Medieval Polity. In: J. Macháček / Š. Ungerman, Frühgeschichtliche Zentralorte in Mitteleuropa. Studien zur Archäologie Europas 14 (Bonn 2011) 333-354.

Třeštík 1973: D. Třeštík, »Trh Moravanů« – ústřední trh Staré Moravy. Československý Časopis Historický 21, 1973, 869-894.

2001: D. Třeštík, Vznik Velké Moravy. Moravané, Čechové a střední Evropa v letech 791-871 (Praha 2001).

Wihoda 2014: M. Wihoda, Großmähren und seine Stellung in der Geschichte. In: P. Sikora (ed.), Zentralisierungsprozesse und Herrschaftsbildung im frühmittelalterlichen Ostmitteleuropa. Studien zur Archäologie Europas 23 (Bonn 2014) 61-91.

Summary

Early medieval Mikulčice (Moravia, Czech Republic) used to be a prominent centre of Great Moravia. This 9th century AD power-political centre of the western Slavs was situated north of the central part of the River Danube. A typical characteristic of Great Moravia was the positioning of its main power centres in the floodplain of two great rivers, the Morava and Thaya. The centres were island strongholds built on hillocks above the rivers or between the many distributaries.

The Mikulčice settlement agglomeration was originally located on several river islands. The fortified core of the agglomeration was protected by a continuous ring of – nowadays silted up – river channels. In the backfill of these distributaries, under the level of underground water, wooden constructions, anti-erosion barriers, palisades, and other water constructions were excavated. The wooden finds discovered during the excavations of the riverbeds provide a wider picture of the material culture of the Great Moravian centre and are absolutely unique in this area.

Mikulčice is the only archaeological site in the Czech Republic where river archaeology has been employed systematically. Several large-scale excavations of riverbeds were conducted between 1964 and 1984. Revision and additional

excavations of »riverbed 1« were conducted in 2012. At present, the evaluation of older excavations is carried out.
As a tributary of the Danube, the River Morava was of significant geopolitical and economic importance to Great Moravia and the Mikulčice power centre. The importance of this transport and trade route is evidenced indirectly by written sources. The existence of navigation on the River Morava in the 9th century AD is a matter of course; it is evidenced by archaeological finds from Mikulčice, such as boats/logboats and paddles.
It is highly likely that a river harbour in the area of the power centre existed in the 9th century AD. From among the areas of the Mikulčice river distributaries excavated so far, »riverbed 2« can be considered a likely location. The sluice gate and the adjoining protected area inside the stronghold do not rule out such an interpretation. The verification of this hypothesis depends on a future complex post-excavation analysis of the »riverbed 2« excavation area.

Zusammenfassung

Das frühmittelalterliche Mikulčice (Tschechische Republik, Mähren) war ein wichtiges Zentrum des sogenannten Großmährischen Reiches. Das charakteristische Merkmal Großmährens war die Lage seiner Hauptzentren in der Talaue großer Flüsse – der March und der Thaya. Es handelte sich um Inselburgen, die auf mäßigen Anhöhen über dem Fluss oder zwischen seinen verzweigten Armen errichtet waren.
Die Siedlungsareale befanden sich ursprünglich auf mehreren Flussinseln. Der befestigte Kern der Agglomeration war durch einen zusammenhängenden Kranz von Altwässern geschützt. In der Verfüllung der ehemaligen Flussbetten erhielten sich unter dem Grundwasserspiegel hölzerne Brückenkonstruktionen, Uferbefestigungen und Palisaden sowie weitere Wasserbauten.
Mikulčice ist die einzige archäologische Fundstätte in Tschechien, an der langfristig Flussarchäologie betrieben wird. Von 1966 bis 1984 wurden dort mehrere großflächige Ausgrabungen in den ehemaligen Flussbetten vorgenommen. Die Revisionsgrabung im »Flussbett 1« fand im Jahre 2012 statt. Aktuell wird die Auswertung der Altgrabungen fortgesetzt.
Die March als Zufluss der Donau war für Großmähren sowie für sein Machtzentrum Mikulčice von enormer geopolitischer und wirtschaftlicher Bedeutung. Schriftliche Quellen belegen indirekt die Bedeutsamkeit dieser Verkehrs- und Handelsader. Die Existenz der Schifffahrt an der March im 9. Jahrhundert n. Chr. ist selbstverständlich, konkrete Nachweise bieten archäologische Funde aus Mikulčice wie Boote, Einbäume und Paddel.
Es ist sehr wahrscheinlich, dass es im Raum des Machtzentrums im 9. Jahrhundert n. Chr. einen Flusshafen gab. Im Rahmen der bisher untersuchten Fläche kommt der Raum von »Flussbett 2« infrage. Die dort gefundene Schleuse und der anliegende geschützte Raum innerhalb der Befestigung schließen eine solche Interpretation nicht aus.

MATHIAS BLOBEL

THE NORDIC PERSPECTIVE – RIVERINE HARBOURS IN VIKING AGE SCANDINAVIA

VIKING AGE HARBOUR ARCHAEOLOGY

The study of early medieval and medieval harbour structures in Scandinavia and the areas of Scandinavian influence has recently received a lot of (well-needed and well-deserved) attention, in large part due to the Priority Programme of the Deutsche Forschungsgemeinschaft (DFG) of which this conference publication is a part. However, while some harbour structures are relatively well understood by now (e. g. those of Hedeby [Kr. Schleswig-Flensburg/D][1]) or in the process of being intensely studied (e. g. Birka [Stockholms län/S][2]), there is a large amount of smaller sites in Scandinavia for which a harbour function is suspected, but not yet well understood. They have either been identified as harbour structures by their excavators or can be interpreted as such from published reports. It has to be surmised that the majority of boat and ship landing activity in the Viking Age would have been carried out at such small landing sites with or without formal harbour infrastructure. Any comprehensive synthesis of Viking Age harbour structures therefore has to be based on a corpus of sites that is very heterogeneous in terms of distribution and the quality of its source material. For historical reasons Viking Age settlement archaeology, and by extension the archaeology of harbours as well, has been focused for a long time on the larger proto-towns or *emporia*. These settlements are well known to have been part of a wide-ranging trade and exchange network[3]. In order to make them viable as exchange centres in a local landscape they were however also part of more local, denser networks of travel and exchange on a smaller scale. It is the harbour installations of these secondary networks, which must have relied mostly on river transport as well as on overland and coastal travel, in which this study is interested. In the following I intend to give an overview of some of these smaller harbour sites with a special focus on riverine locations. It is less intended as a comprehensive catalogue of sites than as a demonstration of the potential and the challenges of incorporating these less well-understood sites into a larger synthesis view.

IDENTIFYING VIKING AGE HARBOURS

Although prehistoric and medieval harbour archaeology has been practised for at least a century now and has attracted considerable attention lately it still has not quite established a unified terminology. Thus, it seems prudent to clarify a few terms used in the following. Following mainly Kalmring's and ultimately Ellmer's German terminology[4], I make a distinction between harbour structures that can only be used by grounding a boat or ship on the beach or riverbank and those that allow a vessel to dock while afloat (**fig. 1**). The former category can simply be called landing sites and can be further categorised into unreinforced sites and those with additional reinforcements. These reinforcements can either take the form of a consolidation of the sea or river bottom intended to protect the vessel from sinking in too deep upon grounding, or of jetties that allow dry and level access to a grounded vessel[5]. Harbour structures that allow floating docking can be grouped into jetties that only project into deeper water far enough that they can be used at their very end and jetties that can be used at their long sides as well. A third category are quay

Landing sites	Unreinforced landing sites
	Landing sites with consolidated ground
	Landing sites providing dry access
Docks	Jetties providing end access
	Jetties providing side and end access
	Quay walls

Fig. 1 Simplified classification of harbour types. – (M. Blobel).

walls without any projecting structures. Without knowing the exact water levels at the time of use it can be hard to distinguish between many of these types of harbour structures. For this reason, identifying past water levels through stratigraphy, microstratigraphy and soil micromorphology or other methods should be a primary concern of any excavation encountering waterfront structures, as should publishing the results of these methods. When it comes to maritime harbour structures all of the aforementioned types of port infrastructure can be found in Viking Age Scandinavia. While there is a general move from less complex to more complex harbour structures the chronological development of these types is not a straightforward evolutionary development[6].

IDENTIFYING RIVERINE HARBOURS

As explained below, riverine harbours of the Viking Age would have either catered both to maritime vessels and specialised rivercraft or exclusively to the latter. While Viking Age ships are a comparatively well-studied category of archaeological evidence there is little information available on smaller boats used for river travel. Some smaller Viking Age boats are known, such as the preserved 9th century AD vessels from boat graves in Årby (Uppsala län/S) and Tuna in Badelunda (Västmanlands län/S) and it is quite possible that these vessels are characteristic of the types of boats used for river travel, although different local boatbuilding traditions and transport needs, as well as change over time, mean considerable variation is likely across the Viking Age. The Tuna boat, an expanded logboat with an additional sewn- on plank has a (reconstructed) length of c. 7 m and a beam of c. 1.15 m[7]. The Årby boat, a clinker built plank boat, measures only c. 3.8 m × 1 m[8]. There is no indication that there was ever large-scale river transport in Viking Age Scandinavia in the kind of large flat-bottomed boats used for this purpose in the Carolingian empire at the same time[9]. The relatively small size of the boats used for river transport means that elaborate harbour structures might not have been necessary, even on rivers intensively used as transport routes. Such infrastructure would have been more necessary for oceangoing ships however. Therefore, when it comes to riverine harbours a distinction has to be made between true inland river harbours and coastal harbours set back into rivers for protection from the elements. These two categories of landing sites would have been visited by different types of vessels and would therefore have offered different infrastructure. Having to only provide access to true rivercraft, a harbour of the former category would need little to no infrastructure, making it hard to identify in the archaeological record; especially considering the fact that changes in the courses of rivers can displace these more ephemeral traces far from their expected location. Accordingly, only very few true inland river harbours have been identified (the closest example is probably the landing site at Grönån [Stockholms län/S][10], which does not, however, date to the Viking Age). However, such sites must have existed in large numbers in the Viking Age. There is direct and indirect evidence for rivers being an important part of early medieval and medieval transport networks. The wealth of the families furnishing the Iron Age and Viking Age boat grave cemeteries of Vendel and Valsgärde on the banks of the Fyris river system in Uppland/S, for example

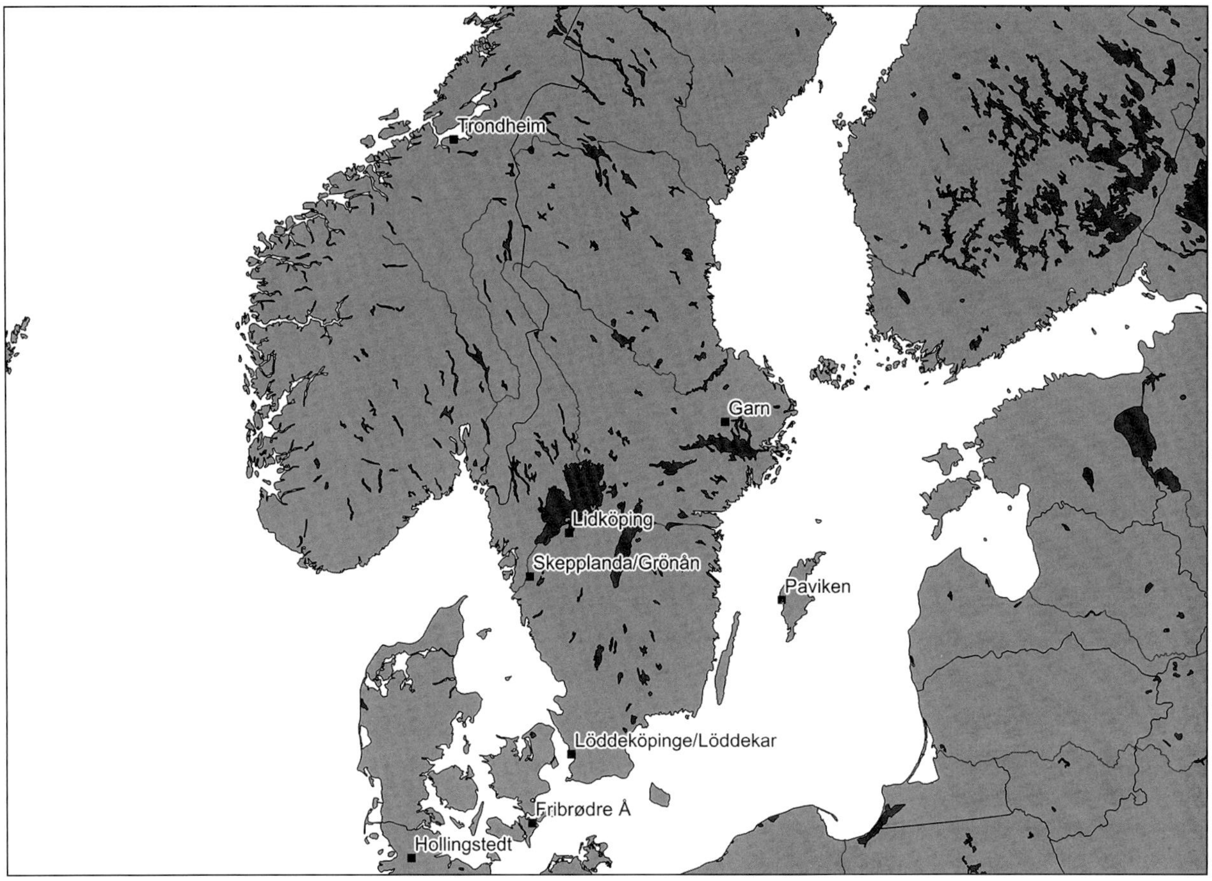

Fig. 2 River harbour sites mentioned in this article. – (Cartography M. Blobel).

have been interpreted as being derived from the river-based exploitation of the area's natural resources[11]. More direct evidence of river transport, albeit in the context of a maritime exchange network, is provided by the harbour facilities and cargo finds from Hollingstedt (Kr. Schleswig-Flensburg/D)[12].

Due to local geography it has to be expected that river travel would not have been used equally as a primary mode of transport in all of Scandinavia. More mountainous regions would have been more suited to coastal (and to a lesser degree land based) travel. This[13] is presumably one factor that explains why most of the examples used in this article are found in Denmark and South and Central Sweden (**fig. 2**).

Riverine harbours with maritime access

Viking Age examples of riverine harbours set back from the coast but ultimately intended as maritime harbours are more commonly found in the archaeological record than true inland harbours. A good example of this kind of harbour is the landing facilities of Trondheim (Sør-Trøndelag/N). The foundation of the town of Trondheim (then Níðarós) by King Óláfr Tryggvason is traditionally being dated to the year 996 AD[14]. While a preceding 10th-century AD settlement is known from excavations, its first expansion fits this date well[15]. The settlement lies on Trondheim Fjord, at the mouth of the River Nidelva. The nucleus of the Viking Age settlement, located on a spit of land between a small bay in the course of the river and the river mouth, has been excavated on the site of the people's library from 1973-1985[16]. From the beginning waterfront revetments facing the course of the river seem to have been part of the settlement. The excavators identified several phases of these structures, three of which are of interest here since they can be dated to the Viking Age. The first phase consisted of 14 postholes on the riverbank as well as several posts deeper in the river, one of which still had a bit of preserved cordage slung around it. While these posts cannot be reconstructed into a clear feature, the excavators interpreted them as the foundations of a jetty with outlying posts for tying down boats. Such an interpretation is certainly possible, however far from self-evident. The reconstructed (Mean High Water [MHW]) depth of the river in front of the hypothetical structure is c. 0.8 m. Unlike this first phase, the second phase of waterfront structures can be dated by dendrochronology to c. 980. It consisted of several metres of land reclamation created by dumping of sand and gravel and stabilised by a wattle revetment with stout rectangular posts. This facing was preserved to a height of up to 60 cm and would have provided a depth of c. 1.5 m for any docking operations. The third phase can be dated to the second half of the 11th century AD. It is a continuation of the land reclamation efforts with a revetment of vertical planks held by posts and probably featuring a covering of planks (some of which were recovered). This construction provided a MHW depth of 0.6-1.1 m. The quay wall seems to have been built by private landowners rather than centrally, as evidenced by the fact that parts of it jut further into the river, in line with the plot boundaries on land[17]. The excavators have also interpreted the waterfront revetments of the part of Viking Age Trondheim facing the above-mentioned river bay as a harbour area, however that seems rather unlikely. Water depths in front of the revetted platforms make it more likely that they are intended for land reclamation[18]. Due to its location on a river mouth, Viking Age Trondheim shows different harbour structures than comparable *emporia* such as Hedeby, Kaupang or Birka. Unlike those, which start out with simple landing sites, the river port of Trondheim seems to have been focused on providing floating berthing from the beginning.

Like Trondheim, the Viking Age settlement preceding modern Lidköping (Västra Götalands län/S) is situated on a river close to its mouth into a larger body of water. In the case of Lidköping this is not a fjord but the freshwater Lake Vänern. The bottom of the River Lidan preserves several archaeological features. Among these is a c. 300 m long and 15 m broad wall of drystone following the eastern bank. This stone feature has a number of wooden posts running along its riverward edge which can be dated to 1071 ± 35 and 1086 ± 35 AD. Unfortunately, these features are only known from a side scan sonar and diving survey. While it seems likely that they would have served as a quay wall, this cannot be proven by excavation or detailed studies of ancient water levels[19].

However, not all riverine harbours doubling as coastal harbours feature quay walls like Trondheim and Lidköping. Basic landing sites can be found as well. The complex series of harbour structures in Paviken (Västergarns socken, Gotland/S) includes at least two landing structures of this kind. The site of Paviken I proper refers to a settlement on Lake Paviken, which is connected by the River Västergarnsån to the Baltic Sea. The settlement lies on the gently sloping eastern shore of the lake and has been partially excavated in the years 1967-1973. It is dated by finds to the 8th-10th century AD and was probably given up around the year 1000 AD[20]. A semicircular rampart on the river's eastern bank a few hundred metres south of Paviken probably marks the settlement succeeding it. It has been shown at least to have been occupied in the second half of the 11th century AD[21]. The area around Västergarn and Paviken has yielded several harbour structures. The settlement of Paviken itself seems to have featured a simple unreinforced landing site described by the excavator only as two parallel hollows close to which a large amount of ship rivets had been found[22]. Unfortunately, the excavation is not published thoroughly enough to assess whether this really represents a landing site exclusively or whether it might be misinterpreted evidence that rather points to ship sheds of the hróf type. A much clearer example of a (reinforced) landing site is found further south on the western bank of the River Västergarnsån. A stone platform with a width of c. 3.5 m projects into the river at this point. From this platform protrudes a further jetty-like stone structure of c. 1.3 m width, which is accompanied on both sides by frames of thick logs. It is likely that this construction represents the remains of a reinforced landing site, that would have allowed boats to beach safely on the smooth log covering and to unload onto the stone jetty. The logs have been dated by dendrochronology as having been felled in the year 1008 AD[23]. There are further possible harbour structures in the Paviken-Västergarn area. These, however, are found in a (now dry) sound formed by the mainland and the island Kronholmen, and therefore are of no concern when it comes to riverine sites. It should be mentioned at this point however that one of the structures identified as the foundations of a quay wall is probably better explained as a defensive structure[24].

An unusual variation of the concept of the river harbour as a sheltered harbour with maritime access is provided by Löddeköpinge (Skåne län/S). Sitting further back from the river mouth than Trondheim and Lidköping, the Viking Age settlement of Löddeköpinge on the River Lödde Å has only yielded scant evidence of a harbour upon excavation (a few wooden structures have been interpreted as such)[25]. However, an island in the sea c. 1,000 m outside the river mouth seems to be connected to the harbour infrastructure of Löddeköpinge. The island, Lödde kar, presents itself today as a stone bar of c. 30 m length and 10 m width. Underwater however, the total length of the island is c. 160 m. It consists of a packing of stones in the form of a slight curve, the concave side of which faces the river mouth. The structure has been the subject of a diving survey in 1975, which produced evidence of a wooden substruction which could be dated to c. 1000 AD[26]. It seems the original structure was built as a series of caissons filled with loose stones. The reasons for this massive undertaking are not quite clear. It is too far away from the river mouth to have any defensive or protective function. One possible explanation is that it was used as a way to transship goods from larger ocean-going ships onto smaller rivercraft able to navigate the shallow river estuary. Since the water around the island is nowadays c. 4 m deep, it could well have been used as a quay. However, this interpretation is based on speculation and would have to be strengthened by further investigation.

The excavated harbour area of Hollingstedt does not date to the Viking Age by most definitions. The settlement is located on the banks of the River Treene, which cuts deep into the Jutish peninsula allowing access from the North Sea. It has long been established that it served as a transport hub for the Baltic Sea *emporium* Hedeby and its medieval successor Schleswig. This function of Hollingstedt is already mentioned in 12th century AD documents[27]. Ships travelling up the Treene would have transshipped goods for land transport to the two towns only c. 15 km away. The beginning of the settlement can be dated by loose finds to the 9th century AD but harbour structures are only known from the post-Viking Age period. They consist of two distinct phases of wooden post features. The older of the two overlapping structures consists of three parallel rows of posts covering an area of c. 6.8 m × 12.6 m with the outer two rows being interspersed with thinner posts which probably represent wattle side walls. The second structure of at least five rows of posts has not been completely excavated. Since the River Treene is a tidal river and the two structures have been shown by auger profiles not to have been standing in the water at all times, it seems most likely that they represent platforms used to unload ships landing on the riverbank at high tide. They can be dated to the 12th and 13th century AD, with the only available dendrochronological dating of one post indicating a felling date of 1161/1162 AD[28].

Inland harbours

As mentioned previously, inland riverine harbours of the Viking Age are less commonly found than those with maritime connections. What they could have looked like can be illustrated, however, by looking at a site from an earlier period.

A rescue excavation on the banks of the River Grönån near the appropriately named Skepplanda (Västra Götalands län/S) has yielded evidence of an area used for the repair and possible manufacture of carts and boats. It consisted of a thick layer of discarded wooden artefacts relating to these activities. Access to the area for boats was provided by a partially reinforced landing site which consisted of a series of four ditches of c. 5 m width leading from a common starting point on the former riverbed onto the northern bank. One of these features is longer than the others and leads up onto higher ground while the others end at the approximate former water level[29]. The longer groove ends in a shallow depression that has been interpreted as the negative of the keels and hulls of boats dragged onto land at this point[30]. The features are reinforced with driven posts in parallel with their outer edges and they filled up with clay and driftwood after use. The wooden material in the ditches provided the basis for a C^{14} dating which puts their date of use into a period of about 410-650 AD[31]. Seemingly the ditch features were dug into the glacial clay of the riverbank rather than having been formed naturally through landing activity alone. While it does not date to the Viking Age, this simple kind of almost unreinforced riverine landing site is presumably what a large amount of inland river harbours at that time would have looked like as well. Unfortunately, such features do not leave many recognisable archaeological traces, if they are not dug down into the soil like in Skepplanda. This can be illustrated by a Viking Age site very similar to the boat repair area on Grönån. On the banks of the River Fribrødre Å on Falster/DK a large amount of ship parts dating to the second half of the 11th century AD point towards a site where over several years a fleet of ships was repaired[32]. While a few posts and wattle structures have been found associated with this area, it seems unlikely they were part of any landing structures. Only a few of the larger posts have been interpreted as possibly belonging to a temporary jetty[33]. The unreinforced landing site that must have been used to beach the ships for repair and to relaunch them did not show up in the archaeological record.

Only little is known about another possible inland harbour near the farm of Garn in Uppsala län/S[34]. Today a small hill, in the Viking Age the site was on a peninsula in the River Örsundaån close to where it flows into Lake Alsta. Parallel to the riverbank a stone structure consisting of two rows of massive stones has been observed in an excavation. Blacksmithing debris connected to the site via a metalled access path dates to activity between the 8th and the 13th century AD. This waterfront feature has been interpreted by the excavators as the foundations of a harbour structure[35]. ^{14}C-dates suggest that while Viking Age landing activity has probably taken place at Garn, the more permanent stone structures date to the 16th century AD. However, a possible canal has been identified that might indicate 12th century AD waterfront consolidation work[36]. Thus, the site at Garn might represent a Viking Age riverine landing stage that either consisted of an unreinforced landing site or at least of harbour structures that were insubstantial enough to be covered entirely by later harbour structures. Yet, the existence of a canal dated to the Viking Age would show that considerable planning and labour was invested in riverine harbours, even if the landing facilities were basic. Before far reaching conclusions are drawn on the basis of this evidence however, the existence and dating of the canal should be confirmed by further excavation.

CONCLUSION

This short overview could only present a small sample of the wealth of river ports, that must have existed in the Scandinavian Viking Age. However, it is hoped that the diversity of sites in this sample can help to show both the need and potential of incorporating these smaller sites into a synthesis of Viking Age harbour studies. Especially at sites which also provided maritime access, the same types of harbours found in the maritime exchange networks of Viking Age Scandinavia in general can be shown to exist as riverine harbour structures as well. True inland harbours in the secondary transport networks – without direct connection to the sea – however are less commonly found and were probably mostly improvised unreinforced landing sites. In order to achieve the goal of being able to provide a synthesis of Viking Age river travel it is imperative that new harbour sites are not only identified, but also that those which have already been surveyed or excavated are published more extensively. Of the examples in this paper only one has been published reasonably exhaustively. The current paucity of evidence means that the sites above should not be seen as representative of Scandinavian Viking Age riverine harbour installations as a whole, but they offer a glimpse into what kinds of evidence can be found. It is hoped that further excavations together with the publication of existing evidence will be able to complete the picture to a point where more comprehensive conclusions can be drawn.

Notes

1) See Kalmring 2010 and subsequent publications.

2) See e.g. Kalmring/Holmquist 2016.

3) See e.g. Sindbæk 2015.

4) See e.g. Ellmers 1972, 123 ff. – Kalmring 2010, 375 ff.

5) Or both of these. For the purposes of this article, which is mainly concerned with river harbours, I am neglecting the further distinction that either of these types can be found in a tidal or non-tidal environment.

6) For an outline see Blobel 2013, 68 ff.

7) Nylén/Schönbäck 1994, 68.

8) Cederlund 1993.

9) See e.g. Bockius 2014.

10) See below.

11) Ambrosiani 1983, 22. In the same volume Schönbäck hypothesises that the vessels in Scandinavian boat burials in general would have been exclusively used for river transport (1983, 129). While this would massively expand the evidence for Viking Age river transport it seems rather unlikely, given the prevalence of boat burials in regions where coastal transport is more likely than river transport, such as Northern Scotland or Iceland.

12) See below.

13) Together with the higher density of archaeological excavations in more populous areas.

14) Christophersen 1998, 61 ff.

15) Christophersen 1998, 65-66.

16) Christophersen/Nordeide 1994.

17) For all of the above and site plans see Christophersen/Nordeide 1994, 84 ff.

18) For a more in-depth discussion see Blobel 2013, 26.

19) Peterson/Johansson 2008, 11. – Gainsford/Enqvist 2015, 9-10.

20) Lundström 1975; 1981.

21) Carlsson 2011, 93-94.

22) Lundström 1975, 89.

23) For site plan see Carlsson 2011, 150 ff., for discussion Blobel 2013, 31-32.

24) Carlsson 2011, 65. For discussion see Blobel 2013, 34.

25) Lindquist 1976, 21.

26) Ohlsson 1980, 70.

27) Brandt 1997/1998, 289.

28) Brandt 2002, 96-97.

29) Nordqvist 2011, 66 ff.

30) Nordqvist 2011, 80.

31) Nordqvist 2011, 73.

32) Skamby Madsen/Klassen 2010.

33) Skamby Madsen/Klassen 2010, 308. The types of wood used would not be suitable to a permanent waterfront structure.

34) Due to its location relatively close to Lake Mälaren, which would have been connected to the Baltic Sea in the Viking Age it could also be classified as a harbour with maritime connections.

35) Ilves 2011; 2012.

36) Ilves 2012, 16-17.

References

Ambrosiani 1983: B. Ambrosiani, Background to the boat-graves in the Mälaren valley. In: J. P. Lamm / H.-Å. Nordström (eds), Vendel Period Studies – Transactions of the boat-grave symposium in Stockholm, February 2-3, 1981. The Museum of National Antiquities, Stockholm: Studies 2 (Stockholm 1983) 17-22.

Blobel 2013: M. Blobel, Skandinavische Schiffslandeeinrichtungen und Hafenanlagen der Wikingerzeit – Ein Überblick. Zeitschrift für Archäologie des Mittelalters 41, 2013, 1-84.

Bockius 2014: R. Bockius, Binnenfahrzeuge im Karolingerreich. In: P. Ettel / F. Daim / S. Berg-Hobohm / L. Werther / Ch. Zielhofer (eds), Großbaustelle 793. Das Kanalprojekt Karls des Großen zwischen Rhein und Donau. Mosaiksteine. Forschungen am RGZM 11 (Mainz 2014) 81-86.

Brandt 1997/1998: K. Brandt, Neue Ausgrabungen in Hollingstedt, dem Nordseehafen von Haithabu und Schleswig. Ein Vorbericht. Offa 54/55, 1997/1998, 289-307.

2002: K. Brandt, Wikingerzeitliche und mittelalterliche Besiedlung am Ufer der Treene bei Hollingstedt (Kr. Schleswig-Flensburg) – Ein Flusshafen im Küstengebiet der Nordsee. In: K. Brandt / M. Müller-Wille / C. Radtke (eds), Haithabu und die frühe Stadtentwicklung im nördlichen Europa. Schriften des archäologischen Landesmuseums 8 (Neumünster 2002) 83-106.

Carlsson 2011: D. Carlsson, Vikingatidens Västergarn – En komplicerad historia. ArkeoDok Skrifter 3 (Stockholm 2011).

Cederlund 1993: C. O. Cederlund (ed.), The Årby boat. The Museum of National Antiquities, Stockholm: Monographs 2 (Stockholm 1993).

Christophersen 1998: A. Christophersen, Setja, efla or reisa kaupstad? A critical reading of the Sagas on the origins of Trondheim in the light of archaeological evidences. Hikuin 25, 1998, 61-78.

Christophersen/Nordeide 1994: A. Christophersen/S. W. Nordeide, Kaupangen ved Nidelva – 1000 års byhistorie belyst gjennom de arkeologiske undersøkelsene på Folkebibliotekstomten i Trondheim 1973-1985. Riksantikvarens Skrifter 7 (Oslo 1994).

Ellmers 1972: D. Ellmers, Frühmittelalterliche Handelsschiffahrt in Mittel- und Nordeuropa. Schriften des Deutschen Schiffahrtsmuseums 3 = Offa 28 (Neumünster 1972).

Gainsford/Enqvist 2015: M. Gainsford / D. Ní Chíobáin Enqvist, Marinarkeologi inför Hamnstaden. Bohusläns museum Rapport 2015/17 (Uddevalla 2015).

Ilves 2011: K. Ilves, Om landningsplatser inom arkeologin. Marinarkeologisk Tidskrift 34/3, 2011, 4-6.

2012: K. Ilves, Identifying Water-bound Strategies in the Archaeological Record. The Multi-Period Case of Garn, an Inland Lacustrine Site in Sweden. In: K. Ilves, Seaward Landward. Investigations on the archaeological source value of the landing site category in the Baltic Sea region. Aun 44 (Uppsala 2012) 1-20.

Kalmring 2010: S. Kalmring, Der Hafen von Haithabu. Die Ausgrabungen in Haithabu 14 (Neumünster 2010).

Kalmring/Holmquist 2016: S. Kalmring / L. Holmquist, The Dragonhead and the Wooden Jetty – Back in Birka's Black Earth Harbour. In: Zentrum für Baltische und Slawische Archäologie – Jahresbericht 2015 (Schleswig 2016) 58-61.

Lindquist 1976: P.-I. Lindquist, Marinarkeologi i Öresund. Ale. Tidskrift för Skåneland 197, 1976, 17-29.

Lundström 1975: P. Lundström, Paviken I bei Västergarn – Hafen, Handelsplatz und Werft. In: H. Jankuhn (ed.), Vor- und Frühformen der europäischen Stadt im Mittelalter II. Bericht über ein Symposium in Reinhausen bei Göttingen in der Zeit vom 18. bis 24. April 1972 (Göttingen 1975) 82-93.

1981: P. Lundström, De kommo vida – Vikingars hamn vid Paviken på Gotland (Uddevalla 1981).

Nordqvist 2011: B. Nordqvist, Våtmarksfynd från den forma årbädden vid Grönån. Träföremal, tillverkningsrester och båtrännor – ett omfattande och variationsrikt trämaterial från romersk järnalder till vendeltid. Västergötland, Skepplanda socken, Kattleberg 12:1 med flera, Skepplanda 226. UV Rapport 2011/124 (Göteborg 2011).

Nylén/Schönbäck 1994: E. Nylén / B. Schönbäck, Tuna i Badelunda – Guld, kvinnor, båtar. Västerås Kulturnämnds Skriftserie 27 (Västerås 1994).

Ohlson 1979/1980: T. Ohlson, The Löddeköpinge Investigations II – The northern part of the village area. Meddelanden från Lunds Universitets Historiska Museum 3, 1979/1980, 68-111.

Peterson/Johansson 2008: R. Peterson / L. G. Johansson, Innan Lidköping blev Lidköping – Marinarkeologisk undersökning av Lidån i centrala Lidköping (Lidköping 2008).

Schönbäck 1983: B. Schönbäck, The custom of burial in boats. In: J. P. Lamm / H.-Å. Nordström (eds), Vendel Period Studies – Transactions of the boat-grave symposium in Stockholm, February 2-3, 1981. The Museum of National Antiquities, Stockholm: Studies 2 (Stockholm 1983) 123-132.

Sindbæk 2015: S. Sindbæk, Northern Emporia and Maritime Networks – Modelling Past Communication Using Archaeological Network Analysis. In: J. Preiser-Kapeller / F. Daim (eds), Harbours and Maritime Networks as Complex Adaptive Systems. RGZM – Tagungen 23 = Interdisziplinäre Forschungen zu den Häfen von der Römischen Kaiserzeit bis zum Mittelalter in Europa 2 (Mainz 2015) 105-118.

Skamby Madsen/Klassen 2010: J. Skamby Madsen / L. Klassen, Fribrødre Å – A late 11th century ship-handling site on Falster. Jutland Archaeological Society Publications 69 (Højbjerg, Århus 2010).

Summary

This study attempts to give an overview of the kinds of sites providing evidence for riverine harbours in Viking Age Scandinavia. While harbours in a maritime context have been the subject of considerable attention in this region, little is known about riverine harbours, which must have existed as a backbone of transport. A distinction has to be made between those harbours, which are set back into river mouths to provide shelter from coastal weather conditions, but which are ultimately maritime harbours, and those that are true inland harbours. Almost no evidence exists for the latter in the Scandinavian Viking Age and thus, conclusions must be drawn from earlier sites. A range of examples is given to demonstrate the kinds of sites riverine harbours can produce.

Zusammenfassung

Während die wikingerzeitliche Hafenarchäologie in Skandinavien in den letzten Jahrzehnten durch einige vorbildliche Grabungs- und Publikationsprojekte vor allem von Fernhandelsplätzen (z.B. Haithabu, Birka) vorangetrieben wurde, ist nur relativ wenig über Flusshäfen der gleichen Zeitstellung bekannt. Gleichzeitig müssen solche Häfen bestanden haben, Flüsse bilden nämlich als Transportrouten zusammen mit Land- und Küstentransport das sekundäre Transportnetzwerk, das den Fernhandel erst möglich macht. Deshalb erscheint es angebracht an dieser Stelle einen Überblick über bisher ergrabene Flusshäfen dieser Zeitstellung und Region zu geben.

Wie die Seehäfen lassen sich Flusshäfen in verschiedene Typen einteilen, je nachdem ob sie schwimmendes Anlegen erlaubten oder ein Aufgrundlaufen des anlandenden Schiffes oder Bootes nötig war. Eine archäologische Unterscheidung zwischen den verschiedenen Typen ist oft nur möglich, wenn parallel zur Ausgrabung Studien zu den historischen Wasserständen durchgeführt wurden. Über die Arten von Booten, die im wikingerzeitlichen Flusstransport verwendet wurden, ist nur wenig bekannt. Einige wenige erhaltene Exemplare, wie die Boote von Årby und Tuna in Badelunda, deuten auf kleinere Fahrzeuge hin. Es gibt keinen Hinweis auf die Verwendung größerer Flachbodenschiffe, wie dies zur gleichen Zeit im Karolingerreich der Fall war.

Grundsätzlich muss zwischen zwei Arten von Flusshäfen unterschieden werden: Häfen, die in den Mündungsgebieten von Flüssen lagen, um sie vor den Unbilden des Wetters zu schützen, und die damit auch Seeschiffen das Anlegen erlaubten, und echten Binnenhäfen, die im Landesinneren an Flüssen lagen und speziell auf Flussboote ausgelegt waren.

Zur ersten Kategorie gehören die verschiedenen wikingerzeitlichen Hafenphasen von Trondheim. Im 10. und 11. Jahrhundert n.Chr. finden sich hier im Mündungsgebiet des Nidelva drei Phasen eines Flusshafens. Die erste Phase kann nicht sicher als Hafen interpretiert werden, aber die darauffolgenden Konstruktionen zeigen sich als Kaimauern, die ein schwimmendes Anlegen erlaubten. In einer ähnlichen Flussmündungslage liegt Lidköping am Vänernsee. Auch hier lässt sich eine Kaianlage am Flussufer nachweisen. Sie datiert wohl in das 11. Jahrhundert n.Chr. und besteht aus einer steinernen Trockenmauer. Das komplexe Siedlungsgebiet von Paviken und Västergarn auf Gotland enthält mehrere Flusshäfen, darunter eine unbefestigte Schiffslände in der Siedlung Paviken I und eine befestigte Schiffslände der ersten Jahrtausendwende. Eine enigmatische Struktur aus Löddeköpinge könnte mit einer Flusshafenfunktion der Siedlung zusammenhängen. Es handelt sich um eine um das Jahr 1000 n.Chr. künstlich angelegte Insel im Meer ca. 1000m außerhalb der Mündung des Lödde Å. Sie wurde als ein Umschlagplatz für den Transport in das flache Mündungsgebiet und den Fluss interpretiert. Aus Hollingstedt sind postwikingerzeitliche Hafenanlagen bekannt, die den Ort zum (auch schriftlich belegten) »Nordseehafen« Haithabus und Schleswigs machten. Echte Binnenhäfen sind aus der Wikingerzeit in Skandinavien bisher noch nicht sicher nachgewiesen. Als Vergleich lohnt sich ein Blick auf eine Fundstelle früherer Zeitstellung. Am Grönån wurde ein Areal des Baus und der Reparatur von Booten und Wägen ergraben, das in die römische Eisenzeit und die Vendelzeit datiert. Teil der Anlage waren vier Gräben, die vermutlich dafür benutzt wurden, Boote an Land zu ziehen. Unbefestigte Schiffsländen der Wikingerzeit müssen ähnlich ausgesehen haben. Ein vergleichbares Areal der Wikingerzeit in Fribrødre Å wies allerdings keine deutlichen Hinweise auf eine solche Anlage auf. Ein möglicher Flusshafen ist aus Garn bekannt, wo spätere massive Steinmauern wohl eine wikingerzeitliche Hafenanlage verdecken, die möglicherweise durch einen Kanal zugänglich war.

Insgesamt kann dieser kurze Überblick nur Denkanstöße geben, wie vielfältig Flusshäfen der Wikingerzeit in Skandinavien zu sein scheinen. Es bleibt zu hoffen, dass weitere Ausgrabungen und Publikationen existierender Daten das Bild weiter vervollständigen können.

SASCHA BÜTOW

A »LONGUE DURÉE« OF USING WATERWAYS

INLAND NAVIGATION AND ITS INFRASTRUCTURE IN MEDIEVAL AND EARLY MODERN BRANDENBURG ELECTORATE

FROM BAUTIER TO MOLKENTHIN – A SHORT INTRODUCTION TO RESEARCH ON MEDIEVAL WATERWAYS

The aim of this article is a short overview of waterway-using in Brandenburg Electorate from the 15th to the 16th century AD. A review of research in the history of roads and inland waterways shows that these topics play a prominent role even for archaeologists, historians and engineers[1], as Reiner Christoph Schwinges mentioned several years ago. The publication at hand is an example of this development. According to Schwinges, inland navigation and water routes formed the backbone of medieval trade and traffic[2]. Perspectives like these reflect the high importance of waterways in the Middle Ages[3].

Nevertheless, many aspects of medieval waterway-using are still unknown, as Uwe Schnall pointed out[4] – and methodologies of medieval inland navigation research are developed rudimentary. Basically, there are two assumptions concerning the high importance of waterways during the Middle Ages. Here is not the place to thoroughly review these theories[5], a short overview may be sufficient. On the one hand, research demonstrated that waterways were the dominant routes in medieval time. In accordance with this position, it is useful to consider the arguments connected with this point of view. First: rivers were navigable by nature; therefore, no huge anthropogenic modifications were necessary. Furthermore, waterways were more comfortable than terrestrial routes, which were very often characterized by bad condition. According to many historians, water transport was cheaper than land transport, which is associated with a higher transport quantity. Last but not least the traffic downstream was very often faster than the transport by land, as several studies pointed out. Taking all these facts into account, we believe that waterways played a significant role in medieval traffic and trade. To give an example: regarding France, Robert-Henri Bautier postulates that medieval traffic preferred rivers as transport roads. In his words, they had the same significance as the railroads in the 19th and 20th century AD[6].

The plausibility of these general assumptions was doubted by Ralf Molkenthin in 2006[7]. He refutes the idea that waterways were the dominant routes in medieval time. In fact, Molkenthin has no doubts about the importance of waterways, but he negates that they are the main traffic routes during the Middle Ages. In his opinion, this very popular thesis could only be evidenced by quantitative studies and numeric comparisons between land and water transport and traffic. If we concentrate on this outcome, we have to admit that there are not enough significant sources for such quantitative studies. Therefore, as historians, we have to find other methods to evaluate the importance of medieval waterways.

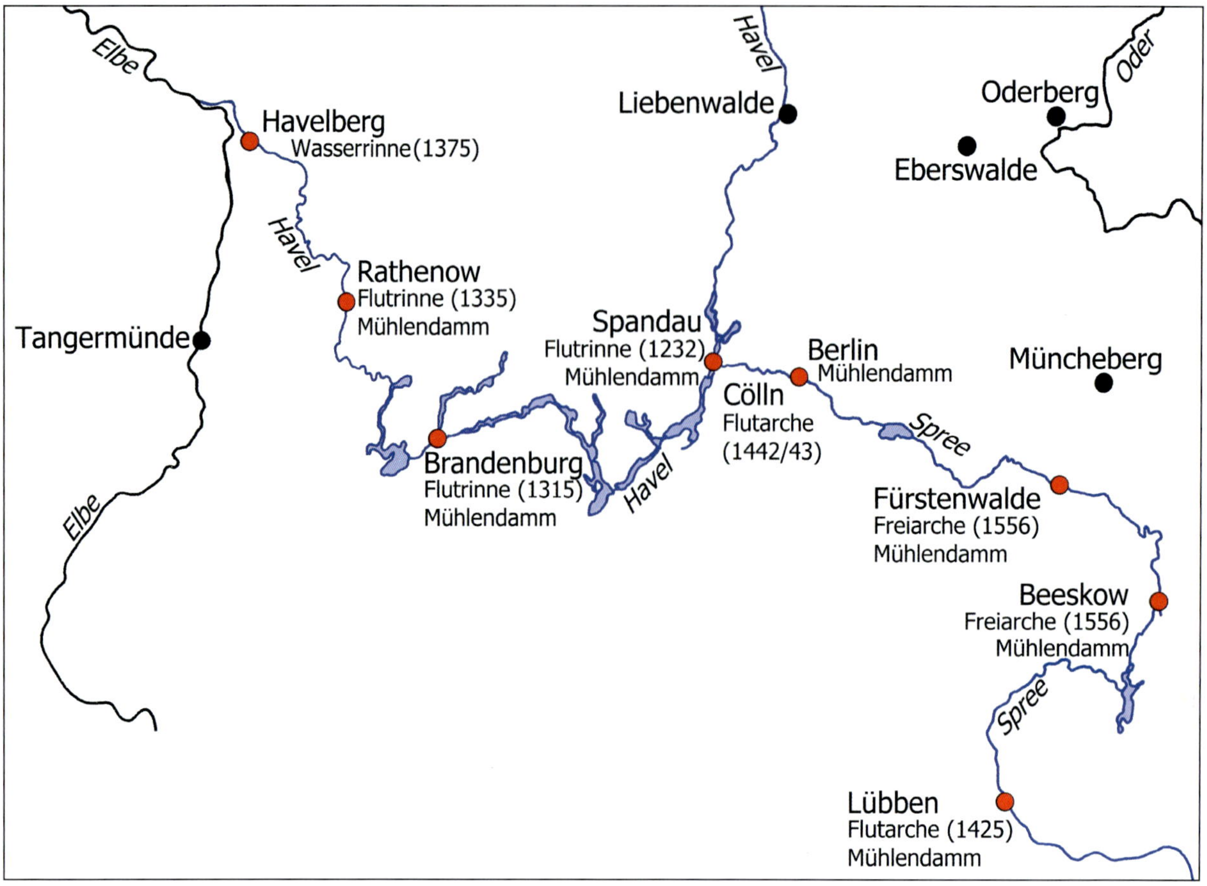

Fig. 1 Locks (»Flutrinne«, »Flutarche«, »Wasserrinne«) and mill-dams along the Rivers Spree and Havel with the dates of their first mention. – (Cartography and data collection S. Bütow).

NEW METHODS

In order to solve this problem, we have to admit that the importance of a route depends on the traffic, which uses this route. Basically, there is a flow of traffic between point A and another point B; on the ground, on the water or in the air. This, in turn, depends on natural conditions, for instance: climate, soils, topography. In addition, there is a human factor in traffic, because there are no natural traffic routes. In contrast, people build roads and bridges, they change the course of routes, they plan traffic and its infrastructure. The more people practice this, the more the importance of routes will become visible. This human intervention can be classified with the help of several criteria[8]. They will help to evaluate the significance of roads, ways and streets. It seems useful to summarize these five criteria. First, there are several facilities or buildings along the routes, which are important for traffic, such as hospitals, guideposts, custom offices, milestones, harbors and so on. Second, initiations of road-building and improvement of routes managed by rulers, the church and citizen can be found in numerous medieval documents. Third, the control and direction of traffic and its routes, which is associated with the jurisdiction over traffic, trade and streets. Fourth, we need to consider social aspects, for instance merchants, who took care of roads and bridges by will[9]. Another example is communities of mariners, which donated several altars dedicated to St. Nicholas, the patron of sailors, whose aid is invoked in storms and tempests. The fifth and last criterion reflects the limited use of routes influenced by human intervention, economic change or weather and nature.

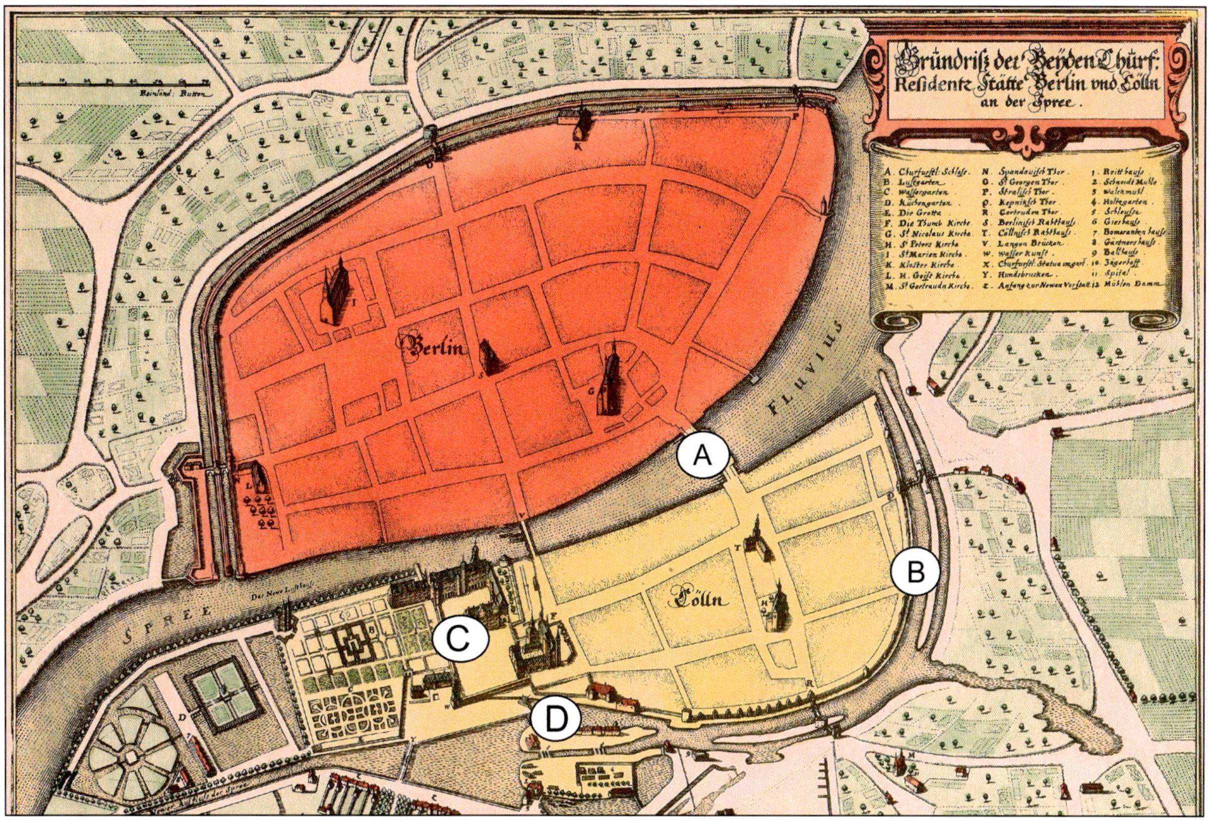

Fig. 2 Plan of Berlin by Johann Gregor Memhardt (1652, colored 1888). – **A** mill-dam. – **B** »moat of Colonia«. – **C** Berlin castle. – **D** watergate. – (Source Zentral- und Landesbibliothek Berlin; notes and descriptions S. Bütow).

Focusing Brandenburg Electorate – research results

Based on these criteria we can look at the inland navigation in Brandenburg Electorate in a different way. Until now, the use of waterways in this territory during the Middle Ages is generally considered in a bad light. For instance, in 1934 Willy Bertz mentioned that the medieval rivers in Brandenburg were in a primitive state[10]. Nearly at the same time, Wilhelm Groth pointed out an imperfection of waterways and means of transport in Brandenburg[11]. To quote one last example, the chronology of waterway engineering published by Hans-Joachim Uhlemann starts not before 1586 AD[12].

In spite of this, the five criteria can lead to another conclusion. Therefore, the period from the 13th to the 16th century AD was characterized by a many-sided waterway development (**fig. 1**). Following the streams of the Rivers Spree and Havel, several medieval locks called »Flutrinne«, »Wasserrinne« or »Freiarche« can be identified in medieval documents of Brandenburg territory. These infrastructural buildings seem to be arranged in a systematic way; grouped in every town or community along the waterways as shown in **figure 1**. Furthermore, these locks were also equipped with bypass canals, which allowed the release of excess water. This system was only possible due to expensive dams, which were primarily constructed as mill-dams (»Mühlendamm«). In the catchment area of the mills, bypass canals were erected to allow of uncomplicated navigation around their mill-dams. Thus the bypass canals served as navigation canals. This shall be illustrated with the help of a historical map of Berlin made by Johann Gregor Memhardt in 1652 AD (**fig. 2**): the mill-dam across the Spree River is situated almost in the middle of the map. In this area, the water accumulated behind the Berlin mill-dam. A drain led the water from the upper to the lower Spree River. This was enabled by a small bend of the river, which was the so-called moat of Colonia (referring to

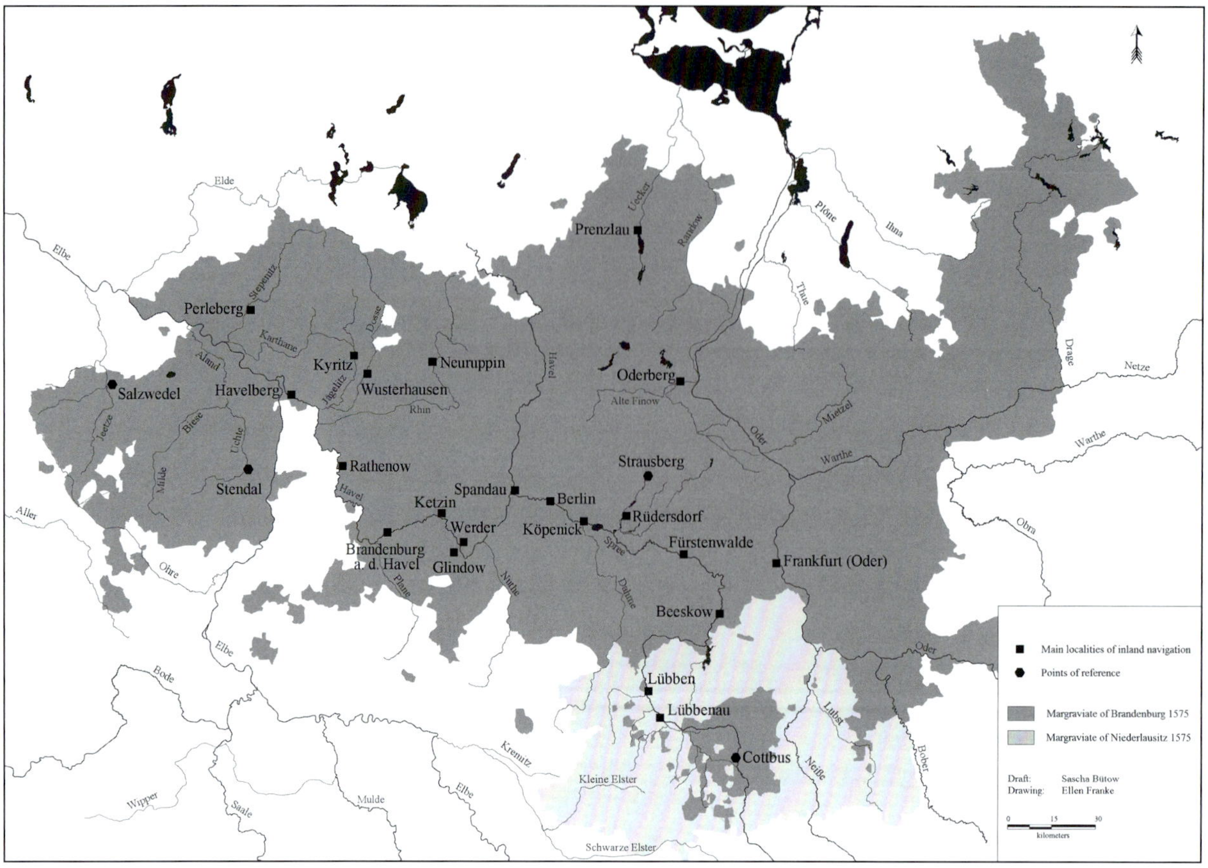

Fig. 3 Main localities of inland navigation in medieval Brandenburg Electorate. – (Draft S. Bütow; drawing Ellen Franke, Berlin).

Cologne – the twin town of Berlin). This moat was also used as a navigable canal for passing the mills of Berlin. In the area of the later Berlin castle, a lock constructed for water regulation and transferring vessels and rafts can be found on the map[13]. This situation illustrated by the examples of Berlin and Colonia is also typical for the other towns along the Rivers Spree and Havel as can be seen in **figure 1**.

The triad of watermill, mill-dam and bypass canal was created in a regular way during the 13th and 14th century AD in all these communities. This system was indispensable for the use of waterways in medieval Brandenburg. The towns became important interfaces between land and water transport. Moreover, the watermills and their dams generated several sections of navigation on the Rivers Spree and Havel. These sections result from several rights connected with these infrastructural buildings. This affects, for example, the authority to regulate trade by arranging repositories, customs and charges, which also applies to smaller rivers like the Stepenitz, the Dosse or the Rhine (**fig. 3**)[14].

This definitely represents a unique feature in medieval Brandenburg. In comparison to this, a former researcher like Hans-Joachim Uhlemann set priorities on the family of Hohenzollern as the ruling dynasty. According to his point of view, Frederic II was the first ruler, who provided the basis for a network of waterways in Brandenburg and Prussia during Early Modern Times[15]. This is a common view shared by many historians and researchers, which focuses on the central role of the electors and kings in Brandenburg and Prussia as the only guarantors for building effective waterways[16]. This leads to the problem of a so-called fiscal state perspective, which is inapplicable for medieval Brandenburg[17]. Another illustration may prove this.

The following map (**fig. 4**) is based on information collected from the fragmentary town book of Colonia written in 1442 AD[18]. This valuable document contains information about the town council of Colonia as

Fig. 4 Lease costs of Colonian pram-leaders (1442 AD). – (Cartography and data collection S. Bütow).

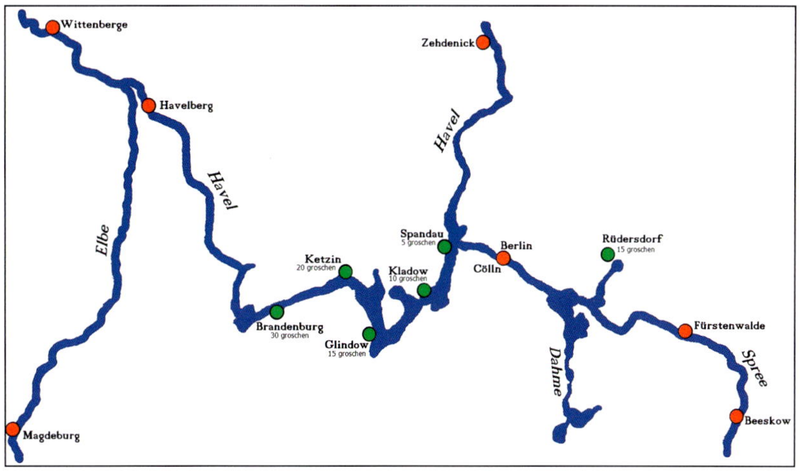

Fig. 5 Network of slaking, finishing and selling limestone created by Johann Blankenfelde (1571 AD). – (Cartography and data collection S. Bütow).

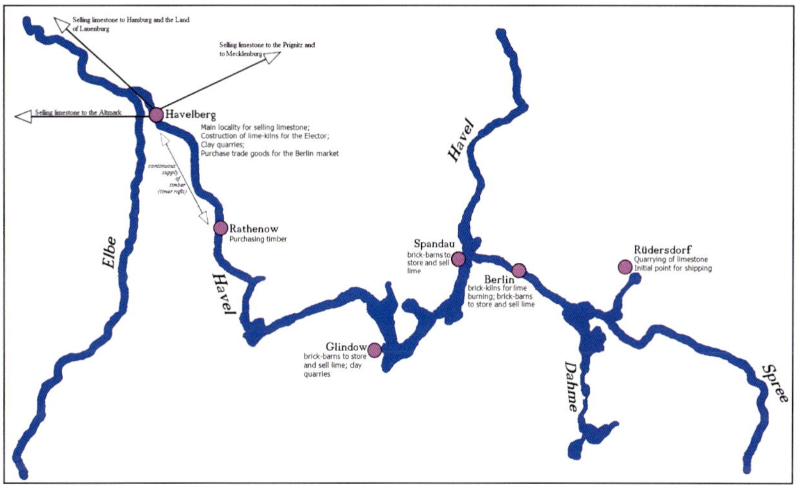

an important owner of prams and other vessels. Therefore, it is possible to state that the councilmen engaged a number of pram-leaders, which rented these ships. In this role, the pram-leaders were responsible for supplying the town of Colonia with several resources and building materials. For example, they shipped clay and brick earth from Brandenburg, Kladow or Glindow to Colonia. On the other side of the River Spree, they transported limestone from Rüdersdorf and limber from Woltersdorf. Depending on the distance, they had to pay different rentals to the town council as shown in **figure 4**. A journey to Ketzin, for instance, costs ten Groschen, while a ride to Spandau costs five Groschen. It is obvious that such a pram-leader was a kind of businessman, who earned a lot of money by satisfying someone's needs. Consequently, he not only provided the town and the town council but individuals and communities like monasteries, chapters and villagers as well.

Colonia is not a single case. The town councils of Berlin, Spandau, Brandenburg and Rathenow also had their own pram-leaders with the same duties and responsibilities as shown for Colonia. These forms of using the water transport system document the efficiency of the medieval waterway network in Brandenburg. This network was founded long before the 18th century AD.

This leads back to the Middle Ages when very often towns and communities were in charge of building and maintaining roads, canals, landing sites, locks and other infrastructural buildings. This situation did not change much with the construction of the tide lock within the whole territory of Brandenburg in the middle of the 16th century AD, which represents a tremendous change in the history of inland navigation in the eyes of many researchers[19]. Thus, following Friedrich Engelhard, the tide lock had clearly brought about an improvement in the efficiency of navigation[20]. In this context, also the water engineer Ernst Klehmet spoke about a great new era of projects referring to navigation[21]. But is there really such a big change between the Middle Ages and the Early Modern Times regarding the use of waterways, the responsibilities of maintaining water infrastructures and organizing the water transport? There are good reasons to doubt this, which could be underlined by a map (**fig. 5**), which is based on a memorandum of the former mayor of Berlin, Johann Blankenfelde[22]. In 1571 AD he sent this document to the elector of Brandenburg, Johann Georg. In the memorandum, Johann Blankenfelde demonstrated ways, by which the sale of limestone from Rüdersdorf in the east of Berlin could be made more efficient. In his own words, this should be an important way to increase the elector's earnings. As the map illustrates, Johann Blankenfelde did put several locations into a network by arranging them. Every location plays a significant role in the process of cement production. For instance: first transported from Rüdersdorf to Berlin, the limestone should be burned in the town's brick-kiln. In Blankenfelde's eyes, Berlin was also a profitable marketplace for selling the limestone. However, he mentioned that Havelberg, where the River Havel joints the River Elbe, was more attractive for slaking and selling limestone. Therefore, he planned constructing a number of kilns in Havelberg close to the river. The required firewood should be transported by rafting from a heathland near Rathenow. This way, Havelberg should become a central place for selling/distributing the limestone from Rüdersdorf. In Blankenfelde's planning Hamburg, Lauenburg, the Altmark, Mecklenburg and Pomerania should become important key markets for the limestone. Regarding this whole concept of producing and selling limestone, it can be asserted that Blankenfelde has created nothing new. He assumed habits and forms of organization, which were familiar to the pram-leaders as mentioned above. Moreover, his concept refers to the infrastructure, which was founded centuries before, like the brick-kilns and the reloading points like Berlin, Brandenburg or Havelberg. Furthermore, he advised his lord to use the brick areas in Glindow, which were used since the Middle Ages. His major plan was to integrate the cycle of brick burning into the process of the limestone production based on the use of waterways as practiced since the 13th century AD. In the middle of the 16th century AD, Blankenfelde himself supported the construction of new tide locks by organizing their funding. These new constructions were added to the old structure of waterways in Brandenburg. In this point of view, the 16th century AD marks no significant change. This means that the system of waterways and traffic infrastructure founded during medieval times, was proceeded by later generations in accordance with their needs. Some new waterways completed this system and other medieval waterways like the Ucker between the town of Prenzlau and the Stettiner Haff lost their importance during Early Modern Times[23].

However, this does not show the superiority of one historical period over another. In fact, this is a proof for the limited use of ways and expression for various needs and requirements characterizing different times. Thus, it appears that Brandenburg is characterized by a longue durée of using waterways. There is no doubt that this could be applied to other territories and countries. Research has to go on!

Notes

1) www.dwhg-ev.com (8.9.2017).

2) Schwinges 2007, 12-13.

3) Bautier 1989, 33. 35-36.

4) Schnall 2002, 197.

5) To deepen see Bütow 2015, 23-39.

6) Bautier 1989, 36.

7) Molkenthin 2006, 126.

8) For terrestrial routes/roads see Denecke 1969 and 2003, for waterways see Bütow 2015, 40-61.

9) Denecke 1986, 208. – Spufford 2002, 192.

10) Bertz 1934, 5-6.

11) Groth 1938, 6.

12) Uhlemann 1993, 13.

13) Ribbe 1998, 77.

14) For a more detailed insight in examples of navigation on small rivers in medieval Brandenburg see Bütow 2011.

15) Uhlemann 2005.

16) Groth 1938, 6. – Calvert 1975, 131-132. – Natzschka 1971, 22.

17) Bütow 2019.

18) Clauswitz 1921.

19) Suppán 1902, 114-115. – Mattern 1922, 8. – Bertz 1934, 5-6. – Uhlemann 2002, 83: in his point of view the tide lock was a great feat in human history.

20) Engelhard 1921, 4.

21) Klehmet 1908, 195.

22) For details about Blanckenfelde and his memorandum see Bütow 2015, 267-272.

23) Bütow 2014, 157-161.

References

Bautier 1989: R.-H. Bautier, La Circulation fluviale dans la France médiévale. In: Recherches sur l'economie de la France médiévale. Les voies fluviales – la draperie. Congrès National des Sociétés Savantes, Lyon, 1987 (Paris 1989) 7-36.

Bertz 1934: W. Bertz, Geographie der Märkischen Wasserstraßen zwischen Berlin und der Elbe (Eisfeld i. Thür. 1934).

Bütow 2011: S. Bütow, Die brandenburgische Binnenschifffahrt auf Klein- und Nebenflüssen im 13. und 14. Jahrhundert. Mitteilungen des Vereins für Geschichte der Prignitz 11, 2011, 5-92.

2014: S. Bütow, Zwischen Brandenburg, Pommern und Dänemark – Mittelalterliche Wasserwege- und Infrastrukturplanung am Beispiel der uckermärkischen Stadt Prenzlau. In: M. Bauch / B. Förster (eds), Wasserinfrastrukturen und Macht: Politisch-soziale Dimensionen technischer Systeme von der Antike bis zur Gegenwart. Historische Zeitschrift, Beiheft 63 (München 2014) 142-164.

2015: S. Bütow, Straßen im Fluss: Schifffahrt, Flussnutzung und der lange Wandel der Verkehrsinfrastruktur in der Mark Brandenburg und der Niederlausitz vom 13. bis zum 16. Jahrhundert. Studien zur brandenburgischen und vergleichenden Landesgeschichte 18 (Berlin 2015).

2019: S. Bütow, Provided for Public Welfare: Traffic Infrastructure and »The Bonum Commune Topos« with Examples from Fifteenth- and Sixteenth-Century Brandenburg Electorate. In: M. Tanimoto / R. Bin Wong (eds), Public Goods Provision in the Early Modern Economy. Comparative Perspectives from Japan, China, and Europe (Oakland CA 2019) 216-234.

Calvert 1975: R. Calvert, Inland Waterways in Europe (Hassocks ²1975).

Clauswitz 1921: P. Clauswitz (ed.), Das Stadtbuch des alten Köln an der Spree aus dem Jahr 1442. Schriften des Vereins für die Geschichte Berlins 52 (Berlin 1921).

Denecke 1969: D. Denecke, Methodische Untersuchungen zur historisch-geographischen Wegeforschung im Raum zwischen Solling und Harz. Ein Beitrag zur Rekonstruktion der mittelalterlichen Kulturlandschaft. Göttinger geographische Abhandlungen 54 (Göttingen 1969).

1986: D. Denecke, Straße und Weg im Mittelalter als Lebensraum und Vermittler zwischen entfernten Orten. In: B. Herrmann (ed.), Mensch und Umwelt im Mittelalter (Stuttgart 1986) 203-219.

2003: D. Denecke, Altwegerelikte: Methoden und Probleme ihrer Inventarisation und Interpretation: Ein systematischer Überblick. In: B. Knoche (ed.), Wege als Ziel. Kolloquium zur Wegeforschung in Münster 2002. Veröffentlichungen der Altertumskommission für Westfalen 13 (Münster 2003) 1-16.

Engelhard 1921: F. Engelhard, Kanal- und Schleusenbau. Handbibliothek für Bauingenieure III. Wasserbau 4 (Berlin 1921).

Groth 1938: W. Groth, Rückblick auf die geschichtliche Entwicklung der märkischen Schiffahrt. Schriftenreihe des Zentral-Vereins für Deutsche Binnenschiffahrt 39 (Berlin 1938).

Klehmet 1908: E. Klehmet, Beiträge zur Geschichte der märkischen Wasserstraßen bis zum Jahre 1600. Wochenschrift des Architekten-Vereins zu Berlin 3/35, 1908, 177-181; 3/37, 1908, 191-195.

Mattern 1922: E. Mattern, Die Wasserstrassen, Häfen und Landeskulturarbeiten in Wirtschaft und Verkehr (Leipzig 1922).

Molkenthin 2006: R. Molkenthin, Straßen aus Wasser: Technische, wirtschaftliche und militärische Aspekte der Binnenschifffahrt im Westeuropa des frühen und hohen Mittelalters (Berlin 2006).

Natzschka 1971: W. Natzschka, Berlin und seine Wasserstraßen (Berlin 1971).

Ribbe 1998: W. Ribbe, Cölln bei Berlin: Die topographische und stadtgeschichtliche Entwicklung der Spree-Insel im Mittelalter und in der frühen Neuzeit. In: H. Engel (ed.), Geschichtswerkstatt Spree-Insel: Historische Topographie – Stadtarchäologie – Stadtentwicklung (Potsdam 1998) 73-86.

Schnall 2002: Lexikon des Mittelalters 2 (2002) 197-199 s. v. Binnenschiffahrt (U. Schnall).

Schwinges 2007: R. C. Schwinges, Straßen- und Verkehrswesen im hohen und späten Mittelalter. Eine Einführung. In: R. C. Schwinges (ed.), Straßen- und Verkehrswesen im hohen und späten Mittelalter. Vorträge und Forschungen des Konstanzer Arbeitskreises für Mittelalterliche Geschichte 66 (Ostfildern 2007) 161-183.

Spufford 2002: P. Spufford, Power and Profit: The Merchant in Medieval Europe (New York 2002).

Suppán 1902: K. V. Suppán, Wasserstrassen und Binnenschiffahrt (Berlin 1902).

Uhlemann 1993: H.-J. Uhlemann, Wasserstraßenentwicklung in der Mark Brandenburg. In: H.-J. Rook (ed.), Segler und Dampfer auf Havel und Spree: Streiflichter zur Potsdamer Schifffahrtsgeschichte (Berlin 1993) 7-13.

2005: H.-J. Uhlemann, Kurfürst, König, Kaiser: Eine kurz gefasste Geschichte des Wasserstraßenbaus der Hohenzollern. Navalis 2, 2005, 4-15.

2002: H.-J. Uhlemann, Schleusen und Wehre: Technik und Geschichte (Hamburg 2002).

Summary

The traditional historical research of traffic and inland navigation considers the waterways between the Rivers Elbe and Oder only in a marginal way. Regarding medieval times, inland navigation in this area often seems to be underdeveloped and unimportant for research. Therefore, successful water engineering is first achieved by the electors of Brandenburg since the 17th century AD. In contrast, inland navigation in medieval Brandenburg was very multifaceted and systematically organized, not primarily by the electors, but the three church orders. Especially towns became important centers for maintaining waterways, inland navigation and traffic infrastructure. This civic planning of traffic and its infrastructure was not less successful and effective than in later times under the rulers of the House of Hohenzollern. Moreover, in this period a »Longue Durée« of using waterways was initiated which lasted several centuries. For that reason, we can speak about a period of continuity from the 13th to the 16th century AD.

Zusammenfassung

Die historische Forschung hat der Verkehrs- und Binnenschifffahrtsgeschichte im Raum zwischen Elbe und Oder bisher nur geringe Aufmerksamkeit gewidmet. Insbesondere die mittelalterliche Binnenschifffahrt in diesem Gebiet galt lange Zeit als unterentwickelt und unbedeutend. Die Umsetzung erfolgreicher wasserbaulicher Maßnahmen wurde allenfalls den regierenden brandenburgischen Kurfürsten seit dem 17. Jahrhundert n. Chr. zuerkannt. Im Gegensatz zu dieser Sichweise war die mittelalterliche Binnenschifffahrt in der Mark Brandenburg vielseitig und systematisch organisiert, vorrangig nicht durch die Kurfürsten, sondern durch die märkischen Landstände. Insbesondere die Städte traten hierbei hervor, indem sie Wasserwege anlegten, Binnenschifffahrt betrieben und Verkehrstinfrastruktur unterhielten. Diese gleichsam »nicht staatlichen« Planungen von Verkehr und Infrastruktur waren nicht weniger effektiv und erfolgreich als diejenigen, die später durch die Herrscher aus dem Haus der Hohenzollern verantwortet werden sollten. Darüber hinaus entstand während dieser Periode eine »Longue Durée« der Wasserwegenutzung, die mehrere Jahrhunderte andauerte. Aus eben diesem Grund kann für das 13.-16. Jahrhundert n. Chr. von einem Zeitraum der Kontinuitäten ausgegangen werden.

JAN TRACHET

MONNIKEREDE AND HOEKE: A TOPOGRAPHIC ANALYSIS OF TWO DESERTED LATE MEDIEVAL HARBOURS IN BELGIUM

Since the middle of the 13th century AD, the small outports of Monnikerede and Hoeke (prov. West-Vlaanderen/B) were part of the portuary system of the late medieval international market of Bruges, which used the Zwin tidal inlet as its gateway to overseas markets (**fig. 1**). Originating as small communities of fishermen and skippers, these small landing sites soon developed into harbours with urban rights and specific staple privileges. During the 16th century AD, political, economic and environmental conditions in the Zwin area deteriorated, slowly transforming the outports into depopulated ghost towns. Whereas Monnikerede eventually disappeared from the landscape, Hoeke shrank into a small hamlet refocussing around its church. In order to analyze the morphology and functionality of these deserted late medieval harbours, an interdisciplinary research scheme was initiated and aimed at integrating historical, cartographic, archaeological and geophysical data. Through a GIS-based methodology, this integration of complementary sources enabled a topographical reconstruction up to the level of individual parcels and allowed for the discernment of a socio-economic topography. This paper accumulates and integrates the results from various research articles into a summarizing interpretation of both harbour sites and sets them in an international framework of the late medieval harbours of the North Sea area (**fig. 1**).

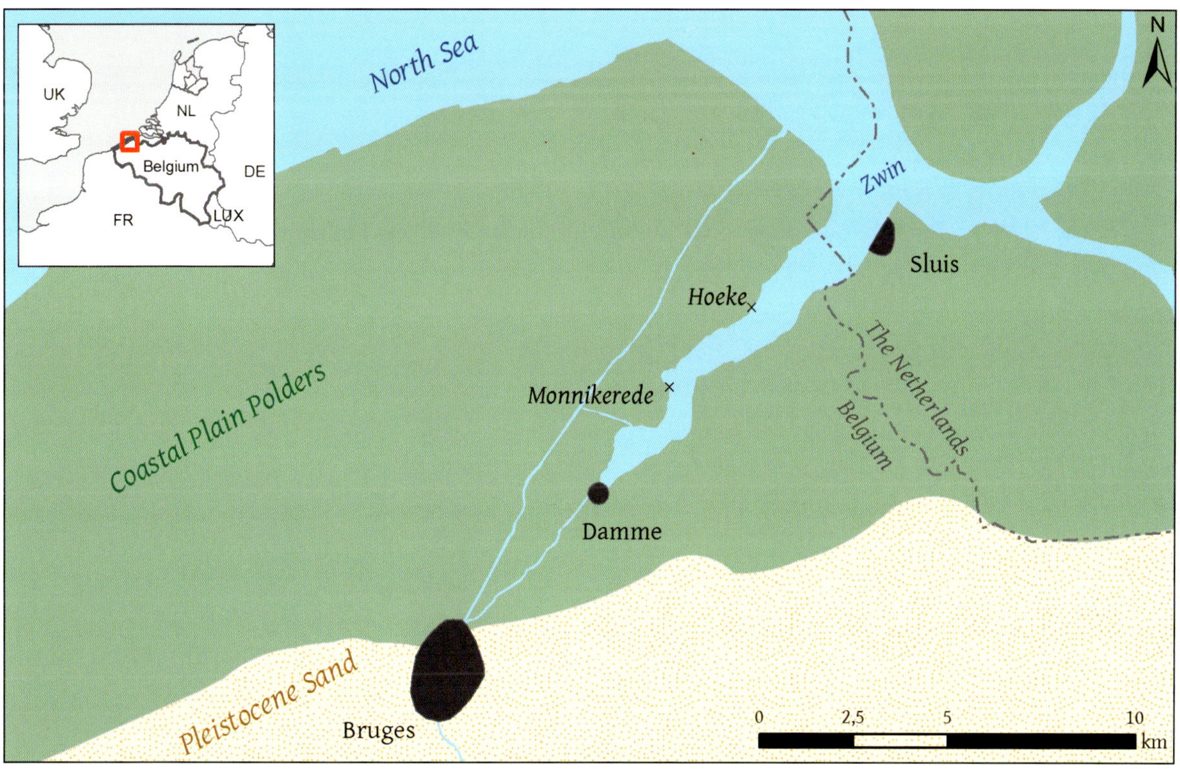

Fig. 1 Schematic reconstruction map of the Zwin area around 1300 AD. – (J. Trachet).

MONNIKEREDE

Our research in Monnikerede started with the revision and further processing of earlier datasets. Bieke Hillewaert's cartographic and land register research, as well as her field-walking and microtopographic survey, are undeniably the foundations upon which this research could build. By processing these 30-year-old datasets, it became clear that the application of renewed landscape-archaeological technologies and methodologies on the richly available source material could considerably advance the knowledge of medieval Monnikerede.

The basis of the previous topographic research in Monnikerede is a set of micro-scale early modern cadastral maps. Although analog analysis had already rendered the reconstruction of the medieval road system, GIS-integration now allowed more detailed and geographically correct localization and parcel-level vectorization of the maps. LiDAR-data clearly depicted the remnants of the left outer dike of the Zwin tidal inlet, along which microtopographic anomalies insinuated remains of habitation. Although these topographic differences had already been surveyed by Hillewaert [1], their outline was better defined through the LiDAR-visualisation. The study of aerial photographs of the Monnikerede area had no outcomes worth mentioning. Only a series of oblique aerial photographs, taken in the aftermath of Hillewaert's microtopographic survey, showed shadow marks coming from the same dike segment and elevated platforms. To step up the visualisation of these promising microtopographic variations, more than 2,000 aerial photographs of a camera-mounted UAV-survey were processed into a highly detailed 2.5D digital surface model with enhanced orthophoto-texturing. As a result, already detected features, such as the small fortification, could be delineated more accurately, and previously unknown features, such as the network of ditches, were mapped for the first time [2].

Moreover, the new set of accurate aerial photographs of the site uncovered the extent of a phenomenon which at first sight might not directly be related to archaeology, yet obviously affected its subsoil conservation: mole activity. More than 5,000 artefact-dotted molehills demonstrated the intensive burrowing activities taking place at the field that teemed with (unploughed) archaeological remains. Determination of the ceramics sieved from more than 700 of these molehills proved that the material culture represented in the mounds corresponds with the field-walking surveys on the adjoining fields. Moreover, comparison of the different material categories and the molehill distribution with the geophysical-sensed electromagnetic anomalies allowed to fingerprint the road section and building areas as distinct features [3].

The geophysical survey chiefly consisted of an electromagnetic (EMI) survey, covering c. 11 ha, and was supplemented by two magnetometer surveys providing for another 2 ha. In general, the geophysical surveys enabled the precise delineation of ditches, housing areas and streets that configured the topography of the medieval settlement. A chronological and typological layer of interpretation could be added through the precise registration of surface artefacts. Supplemental to the processing of Hillewaert's 10 m × 10 m grid survey, which covered 3.25 ha near the centre of the site, we deployed an artefact-accurate line-walking survey which covered 5.2 ha and also integrated the fields stretching west, away from the centre. After determination of the more than 8,000 finds spatial analysis of artefact distribution allowed to discern zones of high density aligned to a linear zone of lower density, which generally corresponded with a pattern of high and low magnetic responses from the geophysical surveys. Moreover, by plotting the ceramics per century, we observed a lateral expansion from 13th-century AD concentration near the presumed harbour area, towards the east and west in the 14th and 15th century AD. Whereas the eastward expansion could be linked to the occupation of the silted-up tidal area, the westward expansion could be framed in an eventual reorientation towards nearby Oostkerke (prov. West-Vlaanderen/B) [4]. The objects uncovered through metal detecting confirmed this pattern, as late medieval artefacts seem to cluster around the centre, whereas the post-medieval objects have more widespread and eastbound distributions.

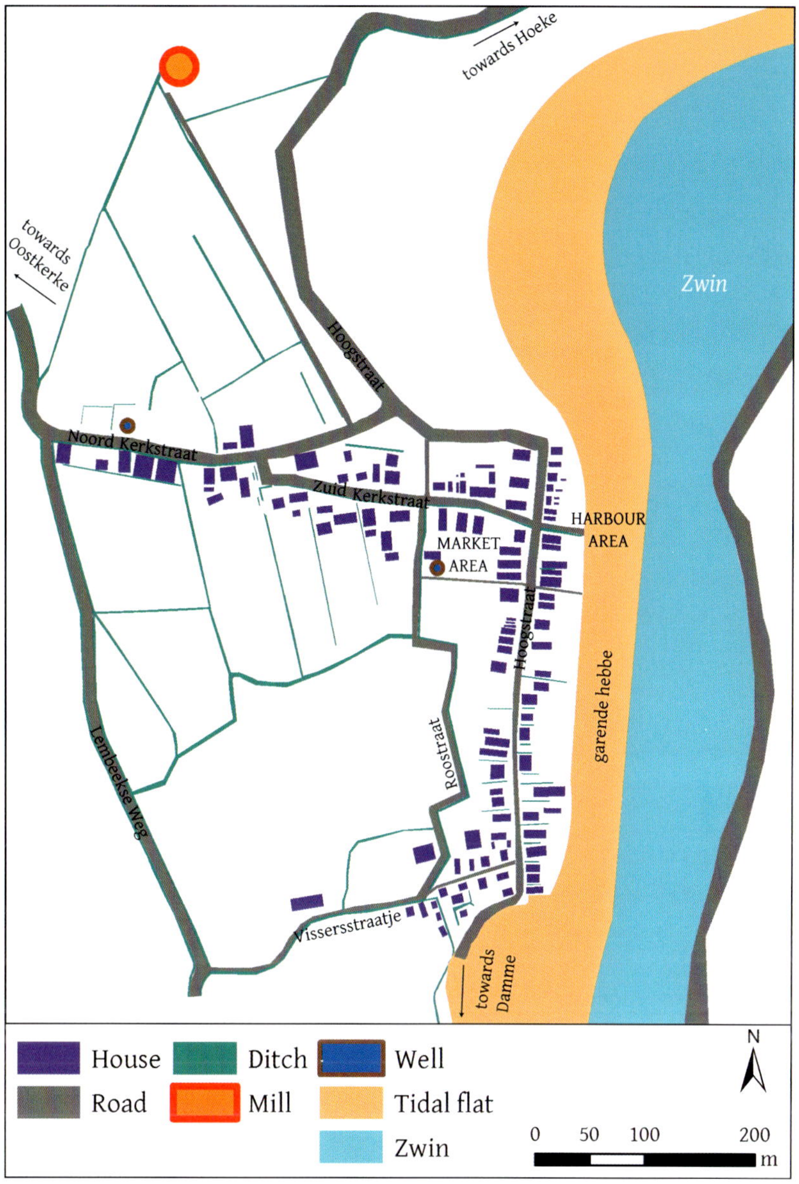

Fig. 2 Reconstruction of Monnikerede around 1400 AD. – (J. Trachet).

The renewed historical research in the Monnikerede case-study especially focussed on the topographic reconstruction of the site and managed to link the spatial descriptions of various land- and rent registers to the above mentioned historical maps, resulting in seven site-covering, parcel-level time-frames reconstructing the site between 1449 and 1854 AD. Specific parcels that were annually mentioned in the urban accounts even opened windows of information dating back into the late 14th century AD. Both the delineation of plots and streets, as well as the degeneration of the urban fabric and reorientation of towards Oostkerke were also observed from the analysis of these reconstructions, demonstrating the congruence and complementarity of the archaeological and historical sources[5]. A final topographic integration of all the above source categories allowed to put forward a reconstruction of Monnikerede's topography around 1400 AD, discerning 59 inhabited parcels, occupied by 117 houses or structures (**fig. 2**).

In a summarizing topographical interpretation of the settlement, we discern two main axes along which the habitation was situated. The »Hoogstraat« lay on top of the left outer dike of the tidal inlet and thus ran parallel to it. The »Kerkstraat« lay perpendicular to the »Hoogstraat« and ran in a western direction towards the church of Oostkerke. The intersection of both streets constituted the political and economic centre and connected a central open square in front of the city hall with the banks of the Zwin where ships could moor, hence forming the place of transshipment between land- and water transport. Trade-related buildings and activities, such as the meat house, the fish market and the scales were also located in the vicinity of these crossroads. More prominent elite residences were clustered in the quarters just north of the centre. A remarkable observation was that the land outside the dikes – the so-called garende hebbe – was transformed into a building area at least from the early 15th century AD onwards. Moreover, comparative research shows that the gradual reclamation of accreted tidal mudflats and its transformation into buildable land was far from unusual in harbour towns. Combined historical and archaeological research on the medieval harbour of King's Lynn (Norfolk/GB), for example, demonstrated that accreted tidal lands soon developed from simple beaching wharves to the place, where merchants had their dwellings, warehouses and private quays[6]. Similar research in Dublin archaeologically confirmed historical attestations of citizens building houses outside the dike, »in sand and mudbanks«[7]. Furthermore, the observed accumulation of small riverside plots into larger parcels once the harbour function diminished, has equally been recorded in New Winchelsea (East Sussex/GB)[8]. In fact, the gradual extension of the waterfront in the direction of a tidal river is a process that has been frequently observed in harbours all over the medieval North Sea area (e.g. Hull, London, Schleswig, or Bergen)[9].

A second topographic feature in Monnikerede complying with more general topographic characteristics of harbour morphologies is the specific layout of the street pattern. In the harbours of medieval Denmark, Jan Bill discerned a general pattern consisting of two main axes: one running parallel to the waterline, while another short street ran perpendicular to it and closely connected a central square with the mooring point on the one end, and linked up to the wider road system at the other end[10], which is exactly what we observe in Monnikerede. Whereas the strategical position of the »Hoogstraat« on top of the outer dike is straightforward, the exact function, importance and connection with the wider road system of the »Kerkstraat« is less obvious. On a local scale, it is clear that the »Kerkstraat« ran from the church of Oostkerke (hence the name) over the market of Monnikerede, towards the presumed harbour area. However, considering the frequently mentioned ferry services, the »Kerkstraat« probably also had a functional continuation at the other side of the inlet, as suggested by the habitation and streets on 16th century AD maps. Even more, as we assume the Zwin inlet scoured its way through an occupied and organised pre-12th-century AD landscape, such a road continuation might even date back from before that period. Another peculiarity of the »Kerkstraat«, that has remained unexplained, is its borderline function between the water boards of the »Kerkwatering« to the west and »Heer Baselishoek« to the east. Because the onset and institutionalisation of the water boards can only be roughly dated to the 13th century AD[11], we cannot use it as a proper terminus. Yet again, liminality and connectivity as typical characteristics of a harbour, also come to the front as elements in Monnikerede.

Although the landward part of Monnikerede could be uncovered in detail, the exact layout and elements of the seaward part of the harbour remains a matter of debate. The absence of written or archaeological sources indicating mooring facilities has always supported the assumption that the harbour of Monnikerede only offered a tidal flat on which ships could strand. Although the newly found attestation of a jetty, stairs and a jetty door could still be translated and interpreted differently, we advocate adjusting this view and propose at least the presence of some mooring facilities in addition to the shelving beaches. Indeed, McGrail argues that 13th-century AD cogs, which are mentioned as the ships that were used by Monnikerede's traders, could be beached on a simple mudflat, coming alongside a built-up waterfront with sufficient depth was probably preferred[12]. Moreover, tidal areas like the Zwin gateway pose specific problems to waterfront organisation, which might have been remedied by the construction of jetties and stairs, allowing a more flexible use of the tidal flats[13]. Wooden quay stairs as referred to in Monnikerede, are specifically mentioned

Fig. 3 Late 19th and early 20th-century AD images of Rownham Ferry, crossing the tidal Avon River near Bristol at low tide (**a**) and high tide (**b**). Mind the steep mudflats and the mooring infrastructure at the right side. – (a photo retrieved from Paul Townsend Flickr page www.flickr.com/photos/brizzlebornandbred/8235686762 [15.9.2018]); b photo retrieved from www.bowerashton.co.uk/rownham-ferry.php#1873 [15.9.2018]).

at the tidal harbour of Poole (Dorset/GB) in 1551 AD[14]. Other examples from Greenwich and Winchelsea then again show that ships of considerable size were still being beached on mudflats as late as the 15th century AD[15] and remind us of the diversity of mooring possibilities in medieval harbours. Tidal range, rate of flow, level of sedimentation, draught of ships, type of commodities and sort of activities must all have been decisive factors in the construction of mooring facilities (**fig. 3**)[16].

Moreover, the fact that these factors are susceptible to change, implies that harbour facilities themselves regularly changed over time.

The only excavated reference site for coastal Flanders is the medieval coastal settlement of Raversyde (prov. West-Vlaanderen/B), yet a comparison between both settlements falls short. On the one hand there are some similarities, such as an estimated population of c. 500 inhabitants living closely spaced in a limited area, the occasional occurrence of exotic ballast stones as a secondary construction element, or the fact that the settlement did not develop into an independent parish and only had a chapel at their disposal. On the other hand, there are marked differences, such as the layout of the street pattern, the absence of a market infrastructure or the lower quantities of imported ceramics[17]. Although other factors also played their part, the specific economic trading and transhipment activities in Monnikerede are presumably key to explain these dissimilarities. In summary, the research in Monnikerede surpassed the expectations, as the largest part of the inhabited area could be reconstructed at the level of individual parcels. Moreover, research into the written sources enabled us to link the socio-economic evolution to the topographic development of the settlement. Harbour-related facilities could not be archaeologically substantiated through the non-invasive methods, yet the topographical reconstruction and scarce attestations in written sources suggest that at least a crucial part of it is situated near the end of »Kerkstraat« and that at least some part consisted of wooden revetments. From an archaeological perspective, many of the attested subsoil anomalies and artefact concentrations would be worth to consider further invasive prospection. Yet, the detection of the more specifically harbour-related infrastructure remains one of the lacuna in the knowledge of this site and would prosper the most from invasive research. Unfortunately, much of the central harbour area is probably affected by the construction of two post-medieval canals, leaving only a relatively small triangle of arable land available for survey. Considering the survey-problems related to these post-medieval interferences and its small surface area, it is unsure whether further invasive research in this area could sufficiently elucidate the development of harbour infrastructures. More to the southeast the enigmatic pattern of ditches outlined through various survey techniques could not be clarified through coring and would be a good candidate for further invasive research.

HOEKE

In comparison with Monnikerede, archaeological and historical research in Hoeke was quasi non-existent before our project had started. A single but firm base of knowledge could be found in the chance-find collection and expertise of a local farmer, who already ventured into the available historical and archaeological sources since childhood. The sparse historical research in which Hoeke has been involved, specifically concerned its role in the mid-13th century AD negotiations between Hanse merchants and the countess of Flanders. Similar to the research in Monnikerede, analyses of remote sensing data had little result.

The cartographic research in Monnikerede could rely on two important historical maps. First, the Pourbus map depicts Hoeke in 1571 AD, just before it abandoned its urban rights and draws it as a dispersed settlement near the Reighaertsvliet side-branch of the Zwin inlet. It specifically denotes the place of the city hall, clustering with another 13 houses, remarkably detached from the church in the west. The second, more micro scale map only dates back to 1774 AD and depicts the eastern area of Hoeke on a parcel level. Although almost no houses were left in this zone at this moment, digitalisation, georectification and vectorisation of the map enabled us to capture the late 18th century AD parcel- and road system, which could serve as the spatial framework for further research. Thanks to the relative small time interval and limited topographical alterations, Hoeke's land register from 1554 AD was successfully linked to the vectorised historical map. Unfortunately, as no older usable land register documents are preserved, further land register-based reconstructions of the late medieval occupation phase of Hoeke, similar to those of Monnikerede, were impossible.

Nevertheless, the mid-16th century AD reconstructed topography offered some spatial reference points, such as the city hall or the chapel, to which anecdotal spatial information from the urban accounts could be linked. Although most of this additional information centered around the city hall, the chapel, city well, and quays were also sporadically mentioned. Similar to the historical research in Monnikerede, a demographical curve for Hoeke was estimated for the 15th and 16th century AD. Also, here the population fluctuated around 500 persons at the onset of the 15th century AD and plunged from the 1430s AD onwards. Whereas the spatial and chronological information from the written and cartographic sources was rather limited, the non-invasive archaeological prospections provided further information on both matters.

The geophysical survey solely consisted of electromagnetic induction and covered c. 13 ha. First, the magnetic response enabled to delineate specific zones of high activity dotted along the »Hoogstraat« dike. Whereas the southern survey area showed high anomalies at both sides of the dike, the northern zone only had anomalies at its landward side. In this northern part, the leveled dike was characterized as a linear low magnetic feature, as was also the case in Monnikerede. Next, the electrical response allowed to discern zones with different levels of conductivity. At the north-western corner of the site, drier and sandier conditions prevailed, especially at the landward side, but also c. 30 m in the area outside the dike. East from there, more clayey and wet soils characterize the former course of probably a side branch of the Zwin inlet. Slightly deviant from this general pattern is the more conductive zone centrally located at the landward side. When both the magnetic and conductive measurements are superimposed, it appears that the zones interpreted as high activity zones are clearly situated on the drier areas, whereas the more wet areas seem to have been devoid of occupation.

The artefact-accurate field-walking survey covered 10.75 ha and nearly overlapped the entire area that was surveyed with the EMI-sensor. Spatial analysis of the c. 3,850 artefacts allowed to discern a pattern of clusters of high densities and empty zones. In line with the observation in Monnikerede, these high density zones spatially correspond with the high magnetic zones and vice versa. When the 13th-century AD fragments and the 14th- and 15th-century AD fragments were processed separately, the earlier cluster could be linked to the more dry south-western landward area, whereas the later ceramics are more spread to the northern edge on the one hand, and east over the dike on the other[18]. For what is worth a quantification of the ceramics (it is based on the sum of the rim, handle and base fragments of survey material), there seems to be a marked presence of imported German stoneware (21 % in Hoeke cfr. 15 % in Monnikerede). Furthermore, imported ceramics from France (Normandy and Saintonge) and England (Scarborough) were also found in smaller but meaningful quantities. Without specific metal detection survey, the field-walking also yielded Scottish and German coins, dozens of forged iron nails and specific concentrations of metal slags. Remarkably, large metal slags were found above highly anomalous electromagnetic values, which prompted the interpretation of these locations as furnaces. A series of cores transecting the anomalies affirmed this interpretation as the samples contained fragments of metal slag and coal before a layer of brick obstructed further coring.

A final find category, not only picked-up during field-walking survey, but also found in considerable quantities in nearby pathways and buildings, were natural stones of exotic origin[19]. Geological determination appointed a first group of those stones to southern Scandinavia as their prime region of origin, yet subsequent glacial transport deposited them on the south-western Baltic shores. A second group of stones could be assigned to the east coast of the UK, and more specifically to the region of Berwick-upon-Tweed. Both the Baltic shores and the east coast of the UK are known for their industrious late medieval oversea trade activities, specifically with Flanders and Bruges. In all probability, ships departing from these ports ballasted their cargoes with local stones and subsequently disembarked those stones upon arrival in Hoeke. In fact, further historical research revealed several good reasons why this would happen in Hoeke: (1) Its location near the deeper water of the Zwin mouth made Hoeke a place of transhipment where larger seagoing ships transferred their cargo into smaller vessels, that then headed towards Bruges in the shallower water of the Zwin channel; (2) ballast would have been essential to stabilize ships importing the relative low mass density commodities of Scottish wool and Scandinavian stockfish; (3) typical exported freight, such as wine or cloth, are more heavy and would need less counterweight; (4) the harbour of Hoeke was known as the place for ships to be repaired and to hibernate on the mudflats, which required an empty hold; and (5) Hanseatic ships leaving the Zwin harbour were appointed specific places near Hoeke to re-ballast with sand. Possibly, this ballasted sand that was reshipped to the Baltic harbours where it was used as construction material, as could be attested in the harbour of Wismar (Lkr. Nordwestmecklenburg/D)[20].

Although the study of material culture such as ballast or ceramics conceal many complexities when interpreted as indicators of international mobility, exchange, trade and identity[21]; we believe that the cross-disciplinary study has shown that the site of Hoeke is characterised by marine activities in which, at least at a certain moment, The Hanseatic League played an important role. Marine trade activities can be deduced from the occurrence of ballast stones, caulking material, and the unusual high presence of imported ceramics. The Hanseatic blueprint stems from written negotiations in 1250s AD, the attestation of German settlers, financial donations and maritime laws in the 1290s AD, the Scando-Baltic origin of the ballast- and whetstones and the high representation of German stoneware. Whereas the presence of Easterlings is ascertained in the second half of the 13th century AD, their interest in Hoeke probably diminished in the run of the 14th century AD. On the one hand the German traders moved their consular court for internal business affairs and staple to Bruges itself, where they became officially organised as a »Kontor« (»comptoir«) in the middle of the 14th century AD, and on the other hand, transhipment of commodities increasingly took place at the more easily accessible harbour of Sluis (prov. Zeeland/NL), founded only at the end of the 13th century AD, but quickly overtaking the other outports. Although the settlement maintained its urban status and economic privileges and continued to function as an outport in Bruges' metropolitan portuary system, it gradually lost significance by the end of the 15th century AD. Although renewed detailed socio-economic

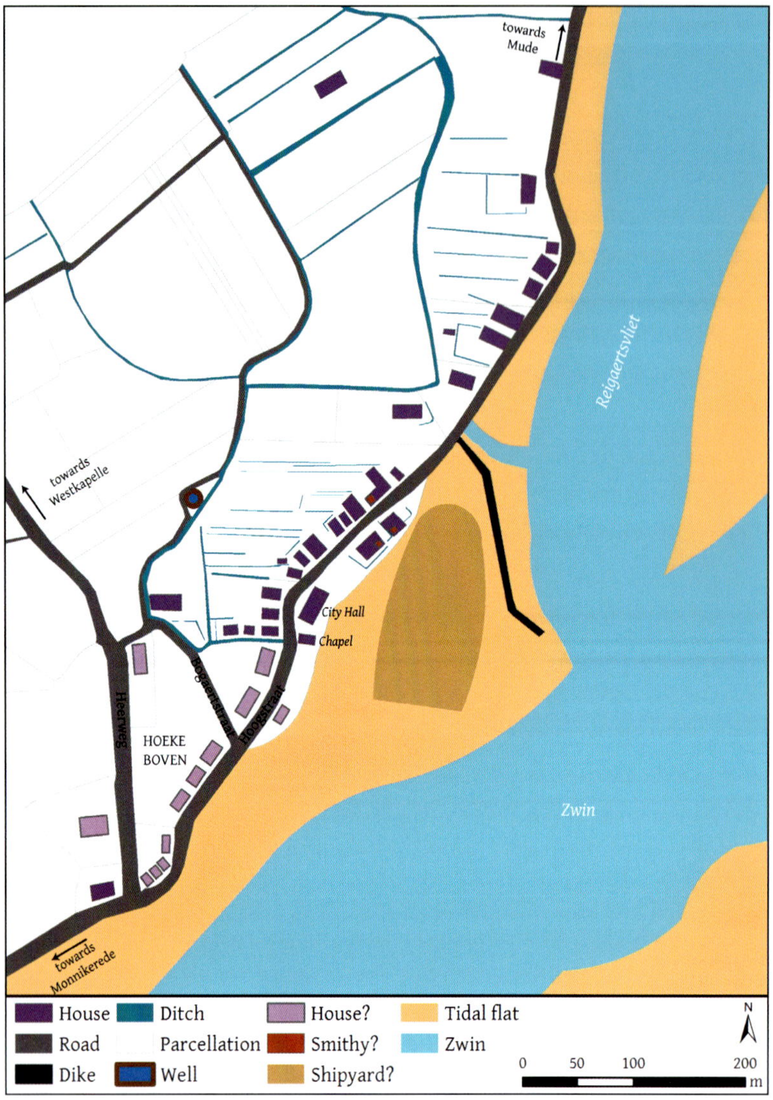

Fig. 4 Reconstruction of Hoeke around 1450 AD. – (J. Trachet).

analysis of the urban accounts was not executed in Hoeke (yet), we can assume that factors similar to that of Monnikerede attributed to the decline in its twin town.

The internal topographical analysis of Hoeke was hampered by the limited availability of land registers and historical maps. Moreover, due to its vaster extent (nearly the double of Monnikerede), the topographical study mainly focussed on the abandoned harbour area (**fig. 4**).

The main axis of the settlement was the »Hoogstraat«, which originally functioned as the left outer dike of the Zwin inlet. A road coming from »Westkapelle« in the north passes the windmill and splits up in two smaller streets near the dike. The largest part and the western branch of this road is mentioned as »Heerweg«, whereas the most eastern branch is called »Bogaertstraat«. The area surrounding these streets is named Hoeke-Boven. Similar to Monnikerede, where the suffix »Boven« indicated the political and economic centre, this would be the place to look for harbour-related topographic elements. Like in Monnikerede, early-15th-century AD urban accounts mention the repairs of a »stegher« (quay). Yet, whereas the interpretational context of this attestation was unsure in Monnikerede, the »stegher« mentioned in Hoeke should undoubtedly be interpreted as quay for embarking ships. In 1410 AD the city decided to build a new quay at the far end of the city. Moreover, the accounts mention how it was constructed: twelve square wooden beams were driven into the ground and nailed with planks. Next, seven boats of grit and six boats of stones, which were partly collected in front of the old »stegher«, were thrown on and next to the new construction. This description bears close resemblance to the way medieval timber revetments were constructed according to Unger[22] and as was excavated in the late medieval harbours of for example Køge (Sjælland/DK), London or Dublin (**fig. 5**)[23].

Nearly 100 years after the last attestation of the »stegher«, the accounts of the 1540s AD mention a »hooft« as the place where stones were transhipped from boat to cart. However, it is unclear whether both attestations concern one place, that is named differently, or two separate places. Neither the accounts, nor the land registers offer exact topographic indications of where the old and new »steegher« or the »hooft« were situated. However, taking into account the fact that the new »steegher« should be looked for »at the far end of the city«, a closer look to the mid-16th century AD Pourbus map might give more indications (**fig. 6**).

Indeed, at the eastern border of Hoeke, Pourbus depicted a small creek, branching of westward from the Zwin inlet into the direction of the »Hoogstraat« dike (**fig. 6a**). Not far from there, and roughly with the same orientation, we find the small dike in the reconstructed land registers of 1554 AD (**fig. 6b**). The combination of both these features, perpendicular to dike and waterway, could hint at the presence of the mentioned new quay. The closer position to the deeper waters of the outside curve of the tidal inlet could explain the choice for this remote location. Unfortunately, neither of both features could be detected in the geophysical survey. The position of the small dike as such, perpendicular to the »Hoogstraat«, is another remarkable topographic feature. After all, it seemingly blocked the inlet in its course towards Hoeke-Boven. At the same time, it protected the area southwest of it, where the building of houses already occurred outside the dike from at least 1435 AD onwards. Moreover, the area shielded by the dike would have formed an ideal harboured zone designated for ship repairs and hibernation. Examples from Small Hythe

Fig. 5 Excavated examples matching the description of the revetted quay as mentioned in Hoeke. – **a** a 15th-century AD revetment of vertical wooden beams and nailed with planks in the harbour of Køge. – **b** a 13th-century AD revetment in at Wood Quay, Dublin. – (a Rasmussen 1999, 249 fig. 13; b Wallace 1981, 114 fig. 110).

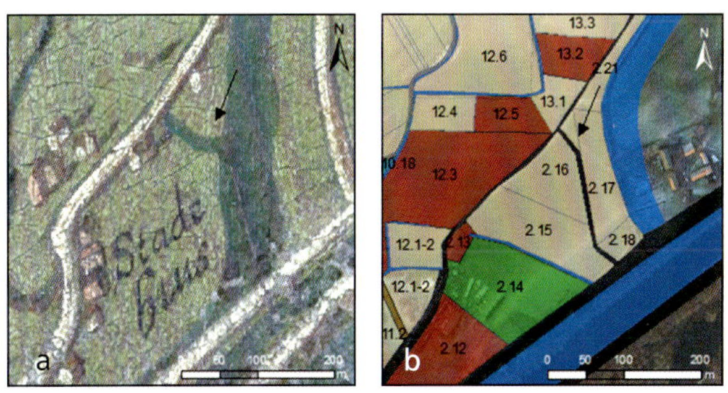

Fig. 6 Arrows indicating the possible location of the younger quay, alongside the small side-branch on the Pourbus map (**a**) and the reconstructed perpendicular dike (**b**). – (J. Trachet).

(Kent/GB), Stralsund (Lkr. Vorpommern-Rügen/D), Bergen (fylke Hordaland/N) and Hamburg show that the locations for boat-building and -repairs are often situated outside the city centre on sloping mudflats or river beaches[24]. Also, the presumed smithies for ship-related metal-processing are detected near the safe side of the small perpendicular dike. As with other manufacturing activities that involve firing and cause polluted air and soil, the location of such a smithy would be outside the city centre, near the proximity of water, and near to the place where ships could beach. Although the latter two premises for location of the smithy in Hoeke are fulfilled, the spatial relation to a well-defined city centre is unclear. After all, the city hall is located more than 500 m away from the church, and no specific market area or something similar could be discerned. If we assume that Hoeke-Boven was the most important nucleus, then the smithy was located only 250 m away. Topographic features for which we are better informed through written sources are the city hall and the St. Jacob chapel. Remarkably, both buildings are located outside the dike, on the former mudflats of the Zwin. Their relatively late construction date (the city hall in 1435 AD and the chapel in 1470 AD) can explain this audacity. Strikingly, yet probably not coincidentally, is that the chapel of Monnikerede was constructed only one year earlier in 1469 AD and that its location – near the city hall, on a parcel outside the dike, yet closely bound to the »Hoogstraat« – is very similar to that of Hoeke.

In summary, the research in Hoeke managed to reconstruct the deserted eastern sector of medieval Hoeke. Although the results do not come near those of Monnikerede, the lesser preservation of written sources and archaeological remains, and the extent of the site can be invoked as limiting factors. Nevertheless, the interdisciplinary integration of written and archaeological sources enabled us to assign specific harbour-related features and a Hanseatic hand in the harbour area of Hoeke. From a topographic perspective, the non-invasive research could only focus on the eastern side of the settlement and partially missed the (economic) centre of Hoeke. If we assume this centre was situated more to the west near Hoeke-Boven, than it partially sits under a present-day farm on the one hand, and partially under the north-south oriented motorway on the other hand.

Notes

1) Hillewaert 1986, 24.

2) De Reu et al. 2016 discusses the methodological and topographical results from this survey.

3) Trachet et al. 2017b discusses the methodological and topographical results from this survey.

4) Trachet et al. 2017a discusses both the geophysical and surface artefact survey in Monnikerede.

5) Trachet et al. 2018 describes in detail how these proto-cadastral sources were mapped and gives a clear overview of the reconstructions and time-frames.

6) Clarke 1981, 135.

7) Wallace 1981, 113-114.

8) Martin/Martin 2004, 36-37.

9) Christophersen 1999, 164. – Milne 1981, 32. – Unger 2006, 322-323.

10) Bill 1999, 257-258.

11) Soens 2009, 17-27.

12) McGrail 1981, 22.

13) McGrail 1981, 23.

14) Horsey 1991, 51.

15) McGrail 1987, 269.

16) Hobley 1981, 8. – Milne 1999, 146.

17) Pieters et al. 2013. – Pieters/Verhaeghe 2009. – Tys 1997. – Tys/Pieters 2009.

18) Trachet et al. 2017a discusses the geophysical and surface artefact surveys of Hoeke in detail.

19) De Clercq et al. 2017.

20) Ansorge/Frenzel/Thomas 2011.

21) Buckland/Sadler 1990. – Gaimster 2014. – Mehler 2009. – Verhaeghe 1992.

22) Unger 2006, 322.

23) Egan 1991. – Rasmussen 1999. – Wallace 1981.

24) Clarke/Milne 2002. – Kulessa 1999. – McGrail 1981, 22. – Mehler 2015, 363-364.

References

Ansorge/Frenzel/Thomas 2011: J. Ansorge / P. Frenzel / M. Thomas, Cogs, sand and beer – a palaeontological analysis of medieval ballast sand in the harbour of Wismar (Southwestern Baltic Sea Coast, Germany). In: H. R. Bork / H. Meller / R. Gerlach (eds), Umweltarchäologie – Naturkatastrophen und Umweltwandel im archäologischen Befund. 3. Mitteldeutscher Archäologentag vom 07. bis 09. Oktober 2010. Tagungen des Landesmuseums für Vorgeschichte Halle (Saale) 6 (Halle [Saale] 2011) 161-173.

Bill 1999: J. Bill, Port topography in medieval Denmark. In: Bill/Clausen 1999, 251-261.

Bill/Clausen 1999: J. Bill / B. L. Clausen (eds), Maritime Topography and the Medieval Town. Papers from the 5th International Conference on Waterfront Archaeology in Copenhagen, 14-16 May 1998. Publications from the National Museum. Studies in Archaeology & History 4 (Copenhagen 1999).

Buckland/Sadler 1990: P. C. Buckland / J. Sadler, Ballast and Building Stone: a Discussion. In: D. Parsons (ed.), Stone: Quarrying and Building in England, AD 43-1525 (Chichester 1990) 114-125.

Christophersen 1999: A. Christophersen, The waterfront and beyond. Commercial activity and the making of townscapes. In: Bill/Clausen 1999, 161-168.

Clarke 1981: H. Clarke, The medieval waterfront of King's Lynn. In: G. Milne / B. Hobley (eds), Waterfront Archaeology in Britain and Northern Europe (London 1981) 132-135.

Clarke/Milne 2002: H. Clarcke / G. Milne, A Medieval Shipyard at Smallhythe. The Romney Marsh Irregular 20, 2002, 12-22.

De Clercq et al. 2017: W. De Clercq / R. Dreesen / J. Dumolyn / W. Leloup / J. Trachet, Ballasting the Hanse. Baltoscandian erratic ciobbles in the later medieval port landscape of Bruges. European Journal of Archaeology 20/4, 2017, 710-736.

De Reu et al. 2016: J. De Reu / J. Trachet / P. Laloo / W. De Clercq, From low-cost UAV survey to high-resolution topographic data: developing our understanding of a Medieval outport of Bruges. Archaeological Prospection 23/4, 2016, 335-346.

Egan 1991: G. Egan, Industry and economics on the medieval and later London waterfront. In: G. L. Good / R. H. Jones / M. W. Ponsford (eds), Waterfront Archaeology. Proceedings of the third International Conference on Waterfront Archaeology held at Bristol 23-26 september 1988. Council for British Archaeology: Research Report 74 (London 1991) 9-18.

Gaimster 2014: D. Gaimster, The Hanseatic Cultural Signature: Exploring Globalization on the Micro-Scale in Late Medieval Northern Europe. European Journal of Archaeology 17/1, 2014, 60-81.

Hillewaert 1986: B. Hillewaert, La petite ville de Monnikerede: analyse du reliëf et étude microtopographique. Scholae Archaeologicae 4, 1986, 5-48.

Hobley 1981: B. Hobley, The London waterfront. The exception or the rule? In: G. Milne / B. Hobley (eds), Waterfront Archaeology in Britain and Northern Europe (London 1981) 1-16.

Horsey 1991: I. P. Horsey, Poole: the medieval waterfront and its usage. In: G. L. Good / R. H. Jones / M. W. Ponsford (eds), Waterfront Archaeology. Proceedings of the third International Conference on Waterfront Archaeology held at Bristol 23-26 september 1988. Council for British Archaeology: Research Report 74 (London 1991) 51-53.

Kulessa 1999: B. Kulessa, The harbour suburb and its significance for the urban development of Stralsund. In: Bill/Clausen 1999, 71-77.

Martin/Martin 2004: D. Martin / B. Martin, New Winchelsea Sussex. A Medieval Port Town. Field Archaeology Unit Monograph (King's Lynn 2004).

McGrail 1981: S. McGrail, Medieval boats, ships, and landing places. In: G. Milne / B. Hobley (eds), Waterfront Archaeology in Britain and Northern Europe (London 1981) 17-23.

1987: S. McGrail, Ancient boats in North-West Europe: the archaeology of water transport to AD 1500 (London, New York 1987).

Mehler 2009: N. Mehler, The Perception and Interpretation of Hanseatic Material Culture in the North Atlantic: Problems and Suggestions. Journal of the North Atlantic Special Volume 1: Archaeologies of the Early Modern North Atlantic, 2009, 89-108.

2015: N. Mehler, Marine trade and transport-related crafts and their actors – people without archaeology? In G. Hansen / S. Ashby / I. Baug (eds), Everyday Products in the Middle Ages. Crafts, Consumption and the Individual in Northern Europe, c. AD 800-1600 (Oxford 2015) 360-374.

Milne 1981: G. Milne, Medieval riverfront reclamation in London. In: G. Milne / B. Hobley (eds), Waterfront Archaeology in Britain and Northern Europe (London 1981) 32-38.

1999: G. Milne, Marine topography & Medieval London. In: Bill/Clausen 1999, 145-152.

Pieters/Verhaeghe 2009: M. Pieters / F. Verhaeghe, Medieval fishing communities in coastal Flanders, Belgium, and western Mediterranean commodities. Medieval Ceramics 30, 2009, 103-118.

Pieters et al. 2013: M. Pieters / C. Baeteman / J. Bastiaens et al., Het archeologisch onderzoek in Raversijde (Oostende) in de periode 1992-2005. Relicta Monografieën 8 (Brussels 2013).

Rasmussen 1999: U. F. Rasmussen, Koge – the topography of a planned harbour town. In: Bill/Clausen 1999, 237-249.

Soens 2009: T. Soens, De spade in de dijk?: waterbeheer en rurale samenleving in de Vlaamse kustvlakte (1280-1580) Historische Economie en Ecologie (Gent 2009).

Trachet et al. 2017a: J. Trachet / S. Delefortrie / M. Van Meirvenne / B. Hillewaert / W. De Clercq, Reassessing surface artefact scatters. The integration of artefact-accurate fieldwalking with geophysical data at Medieval harbour sites near Bruges (Belgium). Archaeological Prospection 24/2, 2017, 101-117.

2017b: J. Trachet / M. Poulain / S. Delefortrie / M. Van Meirvenne / W. De Clercq, Making a mountain out of a molehill? A low-cost and time-efficient molehill survey on the lost medieval harbour site of Monnikerede (Belgium). Journal of Field Archaeology 42/4, 2017, 503-513.

2018: J. Trachet / W. Leloup / K. Dombrecht / S. Delefortrie / J. Dumolyn / E. Thoen / M. Van Meirvenne / W. De Clercq, Modelling Monnikerede. The topographical reconstruction of a deserted medieval outport near Bruges. The Medieval Low Countries. An Annual Review 4, 2018, 91-130.

Tys 1997: D. Tys, Landscape and settlement: the development of a medieval village along the Flemish coast. In: G. V. De Boe / F. Verhaeghe (eds), Rural settlements in Medieval Europe. Papers of the »Medieval Europe Brugge 1997« conference. Instituut voor het Archeologisch Patrimonium: Rapporten 6 (Zellik 1997) 157-167.

Tys/Pieters 2009: D. Tys / M. Pieters, Understanding a Medieval Fishing Settlement along the Southern North Sea: Walraversijde, c. 1200-1630. In: L. Sicking / D. Abreu-Ferreira (eds), Beyond the Catch. Fisheries of the North Atlantic, the North Sea and the

Baltic, 900-1850. The Northern World 41 (Leiden, Boston 2009) 91-122.

Unger 2006: R. W. Unger, Investment and Risk: Ship Design & Investment in Port Infrastructure, 1200-1800. In: S. Cavaciocchi (ed.), Richezza del mare, ricchezza dal mare. Secc. XIII-XVIII. Atti della »Trentasettisima di Studi«, 11-15 aprile 2005. Atti delle »Settimane di Studi« e altri Convegni 37 (Firenze 2006) 317-342.

Verhaeghe 1992: F. Verhaeghe, Ceramiekverspreiding en handel in de middeleeuwen: interpretatie en problemen. In: A. Carmiggelt (ed.), Rotterdam Papers VII. Handel, handelsplaatsen en handelswaar vanaf de Vroege Middeleeuwen in de Lage Landen (Rotterdam 1992) 85-116.

Wallace 1981: P. F. Wallace, Dublin's waterfront at Wood Quay. In: G. Milne / B. Hobley (eds), Waterfront Archaeology in Britain and Northern Europe (London 1981) 109-118.

Summary

The main objective of the research project in »Medieval Bruges and its outports. A landscape-archaeological contribution to the Zwin-debate« was to detect the location, morphology, and state of preservation of deserted harbour sites of Bruges' medieval outport network. Methodologically, this research aimed at the optimal integration of non-invasive archaeological data with written sources. This paper summarizes the results for two late medieval harbour sites: Monnikerede and Hoeke. At the site of Monnikerede, the affluent and corresponding archaeological and written sources allowed the detailed topographic reconstruction of the late medieval town, to the level of individual parcels. Moreover, both a social topography and topographical elements typical for medieval harbours could be discerned. In Hoeke, the available sources only allowed to reconstruct the mid-16th-century AD deurbanized townscape. Nevertheless, the interdisciplinary integration of written and archaeological sources enabled the assignment of specific harbour-related features and a marked Hanseatic presence in Hoeke's harbour area.

Samenvatting

De brede getijdegeul van het Zwin maakte niet enkel van Brugge een economische en culturele middeleeuwse metropool, maar zorgde op zijn oevers ook voor een ketting bloeiende voorhavens. Na 1500 waren de economische hoogdagen van Brugge en zijn voorhavens voorbij, verlandde het middeleeuwse havencomplex en verdwenen de stadjes. Door de integratie en confrontatie van traditionele bronnen en technieken met innovatief interdisciplinair landschaps-archeologisch onderzoek, is dit project tot een beter historisch begrip gekomen van één van Europa's belangrijkste, maar weinig gekende, middeleeuwse havennetwerken. Dit artikel focust op de topografie, morfologie en bewaringstoestand van twee laatmiddeleeuwse voorhavens van Brugge. De site van Monnikerede bleek een goudmijn aan archeologische en historische data. Quasi de hele site kon geofysisch onderzocht worden door een combinatie van elektromagnetische inductie en magnetometrie. Op de velden die regelmatig geploegd worden voor akkerbouw vonden we duidelijk geconcentreerde clusters middeleeuws aardewerk. Ongeploegd weiland kon dan weer onderzocht worden door middel van drones en molshopen. Goed bewaarde proto-kadastrale documenten en stadsrekeningen lieten zich bovendien makkelijk integreren met deze archeologische data, hetgeen resulteerde in gedetailleerde topografische reconstructie van het middeleeuwse stadje. Morfologisch bestond het stadje uit twee kruisende hoofdassen waarlangs het gros van de bewoning zich situeert. De kruising van beide wegen vormde het centrum van het stadje alles wijst erop dat ook de havenfaciliteiten in de onmiddellijke omgeving gezocht moeten worden. In de vier kwartieren die het kruispunt maakt, vinden we niet enkel de grootste economische bedrijvigheid, maar ook de belangrijkste administratieve en religieuze gebouwen, én »Monnikerede Boven«: de plaats waar de huizennamen laten vermoeden dat hier de meest welgestelden woonden. Hoeke was voorheen de minst onderzochte site binnen dit project, maar bleek eveneens over een schat aan archeologische en historische data te beschikken. Vooral de gecombineerde veldprospectie en geofysische survey leverde waardevolle topografische informatie op. Aangezien de cartografische en proto-kadastrale bronnen slechts bewaard waren tot het midden van de 16e eeuw, kon er op basis van deze bronnen slechts een reconstructie gemaakt worden van het reeds deels ontvolkte stads-en havenlandschap. Niettemin is de interdisciplinaire integratie van kaartmateriaal, geschreven bronnen en archeologische indicatoren erin geslaagd om enkele specifieke haven-gerelateerde kenmerken vast te stellen. Zo ontdekten we in de stadsrekeningen dat er in Hoeke op zijn minst twee scheepskades moeten geweest zijn. De beschrijving van de opbouw van deze kades doet bovendien erg denken aan steigers die archeologisch werden opgegraven in bekende middeleeuwse havensteden als Dublin en Londen. Naast deze steigers beschikte de haven van Hoeke waarschijnlijk ook over een beschutte havenkom die beschermd werd door een dijk, en waar schepen op de oever konden worden getrokken voor herstelling of overwintering. Binnendijks, net tegenover deze zone, wijst de gecombineerde vondst van grote metaalslakken aan het oppervlak, boven geofysisch gedetecteerde anomalieën en aangeboorde baksteenvloertjes, mogelijk op de aanwezigheid van metaalverwerkende oventjes. Ook een dergelijke topografische configuratie wordt dikwijls teruggevonden bij middeleeuwse havens in Noordwest-Europa.

PHILIPPE MOYAT

PORT D'ENVAUX-LE PRIOUTÉ: DISCOVERY OF THREE MEROVINGIAN VESSELS IN THE CHARENTE RIVER

The site of Le Prioué is located at the Charente River, in the district of Port d'Envaux (dép. Charente-Maritime/F), 7 km downstream from Saintes (a major ancient population centre), 4 km upstream from the early medieval port zone of Taillebourg-Port d'Envaux[1], and around 30 km upstream from Rochefort (dép. Charente-Maritime/F) and the Atlantic coast (**fig. 1**).

At this level, the Charente River forms a meander bordered on its right bank by a floodplain, and on its left bank by a steep landscape overlooking the river where no archaeological site is known. No historical map has provided any information on the site of Le Prioué. The Cassini map (18th century AD) shows two hamlets without a church (Saint-Thomas and La Pommeraie Haute). Claude Masse's map dating back to 1652 AD does not show any building, port facility or tracks. The closest ports are la Grande Porte and Saint-Thomas. In the current stage of research, no early medieval site is known on the banks.

The immersed site of Le Prioué, discovered at the beginning of the 1980s had at the time revealed a few objects datable to the Early Middle Ages. New excavations have identified a first assembled wreck as well as a dugout canoe, ^{14}C-dated to a period between the late 8th and the late 10th century AD. A bathymetric survey of the bottom of the river shows two anomalies in this zone on the left bank (**fig. 2**): the first anomaly is in the same location as the dugout canoe and the EP1 wreck; it may correspond to an old quay or a bank reinforcement totally dismantled nowadays and evidenced by a stone build-up. The second anomaly is situated upstream; it is a quadrangular shoal occupying nearly half of the channel width. On the right bank,

Fig. 1 Location of the site. – (CAD Ph. Moyat).

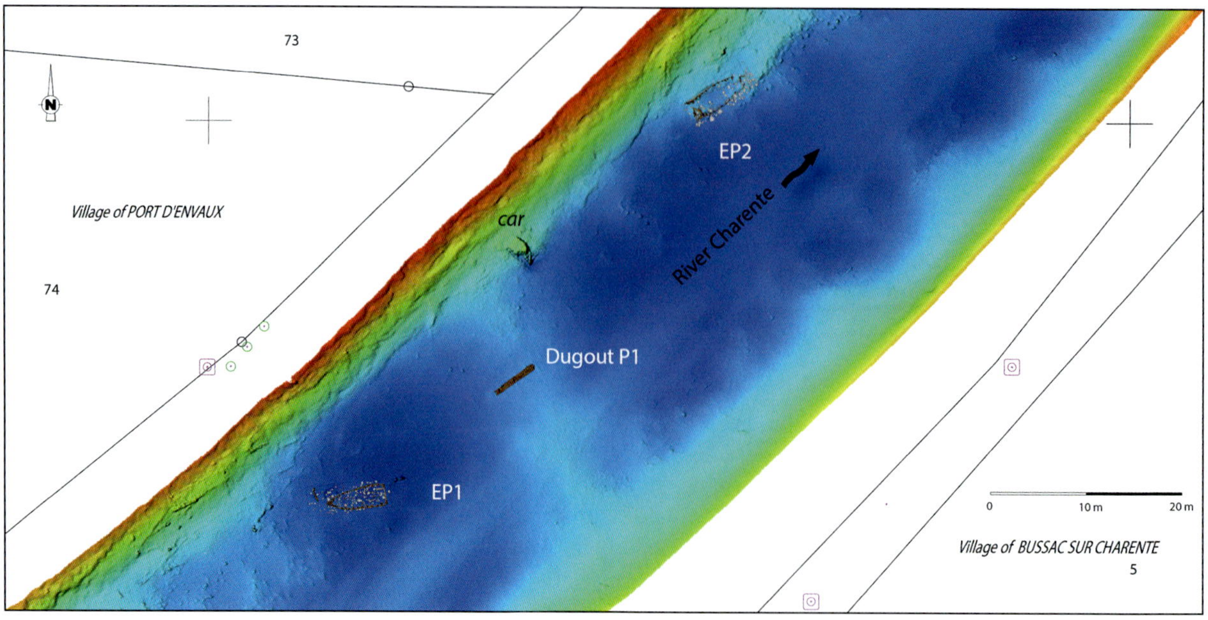

Fig. 2 Boundary survey of the site and the vestiges readjusted on the cadastre and the river bathymetry (Mesuris 2013). – (Records S. Marchylie, société Mesuris; CAD Ph. Moyat).

opposite this shoal that may have been developed, is the place called »Le Prioutè« possibly reminding the presence of a medieval religious establishment (a priory).

The investigation of this site has not yet been completed and two assembled wrecks, which were excavated between 2011 and 2015, have been the object of a comprehensive study. The unfavourable climatic conditions have prevented diving in the Charente River in 2016 and 2017. The third wreck will be excavated and studied in 2018 and 2019.

STATE OF PRESERVATION AND DATING OF THE WRECKS

The first observations have clearly indicated that the whole site is subjected to significant erosion: The EP1 wreck (**fig. 3**), the most endangered due to the current partly clearing the sediment, was excavated first. At the same time, a systematic prospection of the river in this area resulted in the discovery of two more wrecks.

The EP1 wreck, oriented east/west, essentially lays in a horizontal position, facing the current, in an eight-metre-deep pit. At the time of its discovery, the upper parts of the cross-members, a few eroded side planks, the stem and the upper part of the stern emerged from the clay[2].

Two radiocarbon analyses provided a construction date of the EP1 wreck between the middle of the 7th and the end of the 9th century AD: one analysis was done on a cross-member (680-874 AD in calibrated age), the other on a plank closing the aft (643-717 AD in calibrated age). Taking the second dating into consideration, with a tighter range, this vessel can then be linked to a period situated between the middle of the 7th and the early 8th century AD.

The EP2 wreck, located only 50 m downstream from EP1, is oriented north-east/south-west (**fig. 3**). It is buried upside down, hull up and stern facing the current. The floor of the boat has mostly disappeared due to its exposure to erosion. The sides have been preserved in a layer of compact clay. The left side has been preserved better than the right side, which is poorly preserved. The charts show a rather significant distor-

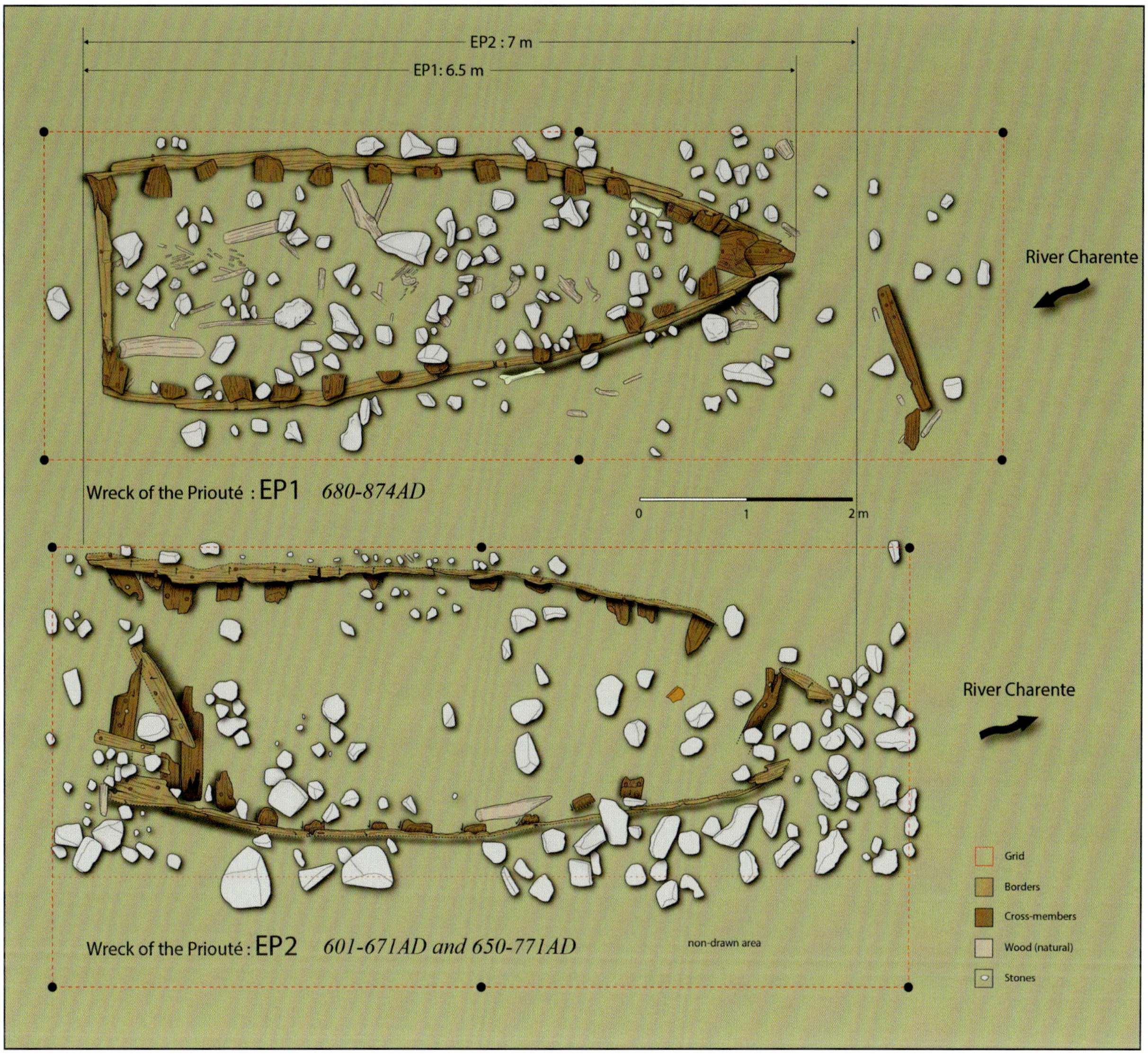

Fig. 3 *In situ* drawings of EP1 and EP2 (same scale). – (Drawings and CAD Ph. Moyat).

tion of the sides whose angles do not definitely match the originals. The bow has also partially disappeared: only two fragments are left and the test pits undertaken in 2014 have confirmed the absence of the stem, undoubtedly destroyed by erosion. The stern, which was probably closed up with planks, has almost entirely disappeared as well; the only elements that are still visible are much degraded. The vestiges were initially observed *in situ*, then the parts were dismantled and lifted out of the water for a detailed study, and sample taking for the dendrochronological analysis (ongoing study).

Two ^{14}C-samples of the EP2 wreck have been dated. The first dating on a brace, stern side, obtained a range between 601 and 671 AD[3] in calibrated age. The second was performed on another brace, bow side, and obtained a range between 650 and 771 AD[4] in calibrated age. The vessel was thus built between the middle of the 7th and the late 8th century AD and is likely to be contemporaneous with EP1.

In 2014, the exploration led to the discovery of a third wreck called EP3. A ^{14}C-dating was performed on a brace, and resulted in a range from 662 to 770 AD[5] in calibrated age. Thus, the vessel was built between the middle of the 7th and the late 8th century AD, making it chronologically very close, if not contemporane-

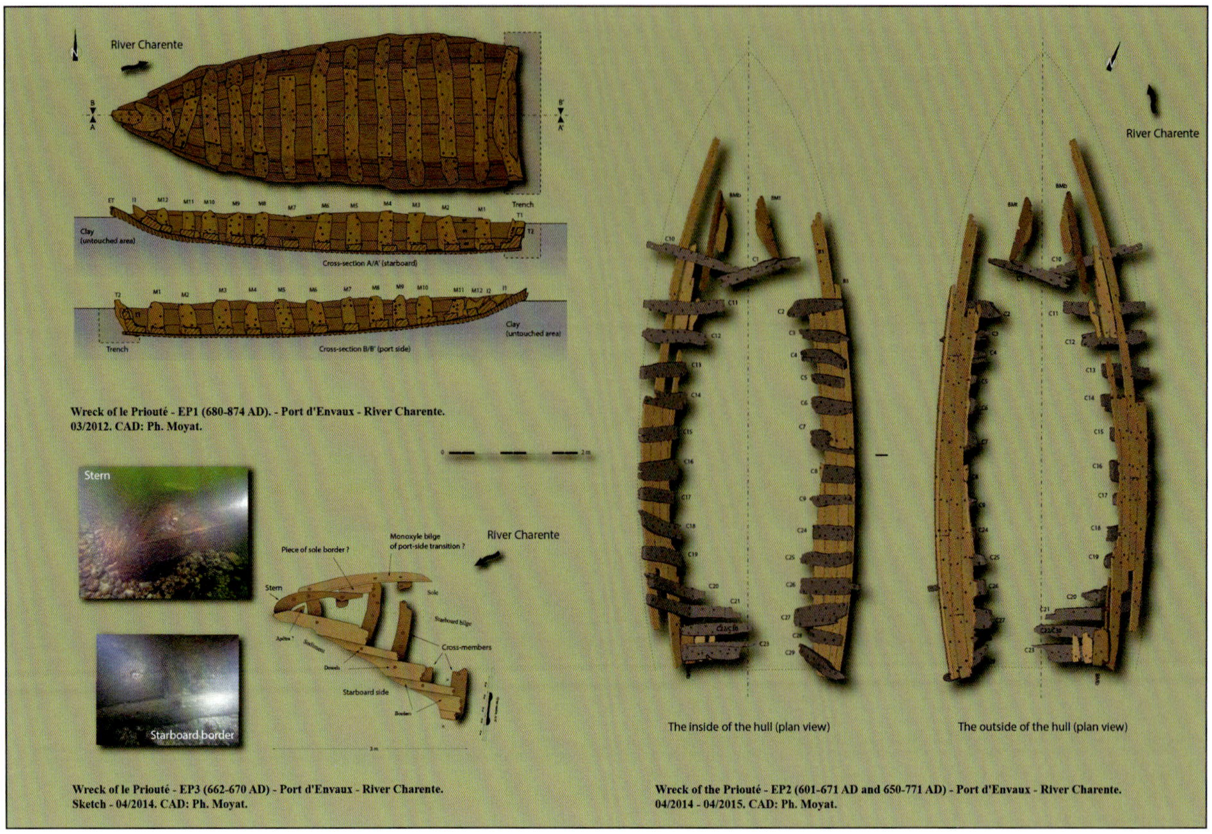

Fig. 4 Plan and sectional view of EP1 and EP2, field sketch of EP3. – (CAD Ph. Moyat).

ous with the wrecks EP1 and EP2. At first sight, the few visible remains of its architecture and shape seem also to confirm a similarity of construction with the wrecks EP1 and EP2.

The clearing, the excavation and the charting were performed in poor visibility conditions. EP1 was studied entirely at the bottom of the river, no component having been lifted to the surface or dismantled. EP2 was partly dismantled at the bottom, and some components were lifted out of the water to be studied and photographed. The data for the two wrecks have been integrated into the Sketchup software in order to produce a three-dimensional view. A mosaic of the wrecks' photographs provides a two-dimensional vision of the immersed remains.

ARCHITECTURAL STUDY OF LE PRIOUTÉ VESSELS EP1 AND EP2

The three wrecks should be classified as small crafts: 6.60 m in length and 2.40 m in width for EP1, 9.10 m in length and roughly 3.00 m in width for EP2, and 3.00 m in length visible for EP3 (**fig. 4**).

Despite shortcomings due to the poor state of preservation, the architecture of both EP1 and EP2 displays similarities. Their overall shape is related to the ogival shape defined by B. Arnold[6], the front being shaped as a lancet, the back truncated by an assembly of planks (**fig. 5**). The two vessels are made of oak, with single-piece bilges and a flat floor; the assemblies of planks are held together with dowels and a few nails. The cross-members are made of squared timber planks assembled two by two in a symmetric fashion. The sides were initially made of five rows of planks fastened to the transition single-piece bilge.

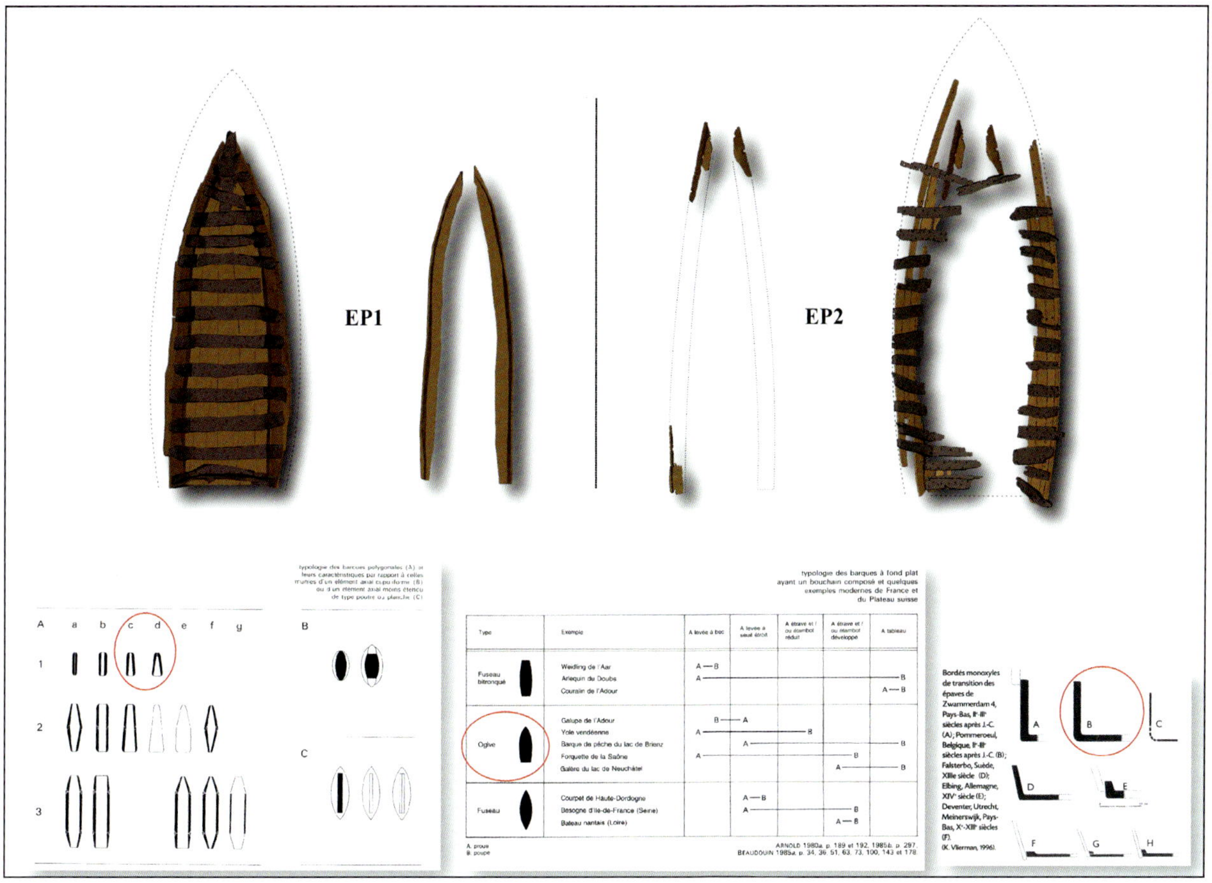

Fig. 5 Comparisons and typologies of vessels according to B. Arnold and of monoxyle hulls according to K. Vlierman with the wrecks of Le Prioutė. – (CAD Ph. Moyat).

Bilges

Bilges are two single-piece parts made of oak placed on each side of the vessel. They give the vessel its symmetric ogival profile (**fig. 5**) and are categorised as transition bilges since they form part of the bottom and sides of the boat. Each of them is made of an L-shaped single piece of wood, reaching from the stern to the bow, with an average angle of 120° for EP1 and 90° for EP2 (measurements taken from the centre of the wreck). On each side of EP1, their largest surface makes up the bottom and measures 25 cm on the right and 18 cm on the left. The parts making up the border are nearly identical in dimensions: 16 cm on the right side and 15 cm on the left. Due to the erosion level, the full dimensions of EP2 bilges are difficult to determine exactly. Their assembly with the aft of the boat and the cross-members is solely secured with dowels; besides dowels, nails have been used on EP1 for the connection to the stem and to the part closing up the back. These nails were probably used to strengthen the assemblies at either end of the vessel.

The floor of the vessels

The floor of the EP2 wreck has practically disappeared. What is left, at the stern, are two small and much eroded fragments measuring respectively 48 cm × 17 cm, and 46 cm × 12 cm, with a preserved thickness of 3 cm (**fig. 4**).

Much better preserved, the floor of EP1 is made up of six oak planks installed at freeboard. The central plank measuring 4.87 m in length and 40 cm in width makes up the main longitudinal component of the vessel. It is placed at the centre of the boat and is connected to the stem under a cross-member.
On the right side, two planks placed one after the other make the link between the central plank and the bilge. The planks are 31 cm wide in the centre of the wreck and have a total length of 5.50 m. Their shape is curved in order to fit the curvature of the bilge. The joint is located under cross-member no. 5 where an additional small piece of wood can be seen.
On the left side, the constructors' solution is more complex since the bottom of the boat is formed, not with one single plank, but three, between the central plank and the bilge. At the back, between the transom and cross-member no. 4, two 2.10 m long parts have been placed side by side, extended beyond the cross-member to the stem by a 3.10 m long plank. Their cumulated width at a joint level under cross-member no. 4 is 37 cm. The thickness of the EP1 bottom planks could only be measured at the back. It varies between 4 and 6 cm (**fig. 4**).

Cross-members

There are twelve cross-members on EP1 and 17 on EP2 (**fig. 4**). The cross-members are made of squared oak timber symmetrically assembled by twos. This alternate assembly solution allows to distribute the potential weaknesses on both sides of the vessel. On EP1, the L-shaped part is alternating from the left to the right, from the stern to the bow.
The first L-shaped part covers the bottom and some of the side. The second part, I-shaped, lays as an extension to the first. The whole produces a wide opened U with a 50° angle on each side. The placement of these components cannot be known with precision on EP2 due to its erosion. It can be noted that the last four cross-members on the stern do not appear to have been alternately placed.
The spaces between each cross-member vary from 16 cm at the bow to 32 cm at the stern on EP1. On EP2, these spaces are not regular.
On EP1, the twelve cross-members are assembled with dowels driven into the floor and the sides. Their shape hugs the shape of the two bilges and sides despite the angle difference noted, the sides being more widely opened by 21° compared with the bilges. It is noted that nails have been driven into the outer hull on one EP2 cross-member. Another particular disposition was noted: a piece of timber with a 3 cm diameter hole protrudes from the side. Traces of wear, which are still visible, suggest that ropes used to be fastened to it. This component may have served as a mooring cleat at the back of the boat or a bracing system (guy rope) or more likely as a fastening system for the rudder outside the hull. For this type of vessel, outside rudders are generally fixed by twos to the sides at stern level. In the case of EP2, it is no longer possible to verify its presence on the other side as it has not been preserved.
The cross-members are never perfectly sealed and it is assumed that the space between them and the bilges could have been used as a drain allowing water to flow inside the boat. There is indeed no other visible space that could have served this purpose.

The sides

Eight oak planks belonging to EP1 sides have been preserved (**fig. 4**). In order to secure the connection with the bilge, two 30 cm wide planks with a length of 6.40 m on the left and 6.50 m on the right, are noted on

both sides at floor level. The evenly shaped planks fit the curvature along the whole length of the vessel, and are maintained by two or three dowels on each cross-member. Above the planks and on each of the two sides three planks are placed end to end covering the entire length of the vessel. Their thickness varies from 4 to 6 cm. All joints between the planks are systematically placed under braces, which consequently serve the twin purpose of cross-member and assembly part between the components of the sides. The observation of a partially dismantled assembly due to erosion has revealed a jointed-side assembly.
The better-preserved components of the EP2 wreck are the sides (**fig. 4**). They were made of five rows of planks on top of the monoxyle bilge which ensured jointing with the bottom of the boat. The right side still has four rows of planks and the joints are always placed under the cross-members. The first row from the top of the side, 13 cm wide and 7 cm in average thickness, has a flat profile inside the hull and nearly semi-circular outside. It is distinctive from the other rows as no joint is visible, indicating that it was most certainly made out of one single piece of timber curved along the whole length of the vessel. Additionally, it is the only component of the boat that is made of chestnut wood, a species probably used for its flexibility. 6 m have been preserved beginning from the stern; the part near the bow has disappeared. It is fixed to each cross-member by a dowel. The following three rows of planks are made of oak with an average width of 24.5 cm for a thickness of 4 cm; the fifth row has totally disappeared. The left side, which is more degraded, also has four preserved rows of planks placed identically to the opposite side. The first row has totally disappeared and the following four rows, although much eroded, have similar dimensions to those on the right side.

The stern

The mechanism closing up the back of EP1 is made of two overlapping components assembled by rebates and held by two vertical dowels (**fig. 4**). The bottom part, with a much bigger size as the top part, assumes the shape and purpose of a brace. It closes up the aft, and has a semi-circular shape that fits the curvature of the bilge at the bottom in order to ensure its waterproofness and increase its resistance. The side planks are directly assembled above with dowels (two per plank). On the outside, the fact that these dowels protrude by 1.5-3 cm from the planks could indicate the disappearance of one or more components due to erosion. Only one timber part measuring 140 cm in length, 12 cm in width and 17 cm in thickness, remains from the top part of the back mechanism. Another component that was swept away by the current after the vessel was discovered, was fitted above. Consequently, it is impossible to restore the back of the vessel in its totality. An iron nail was noted, probably a repair around the joint between a bottom plank and the back mechanism.
Less well preserved (**fig. 4**), the stern on EP2 was probably closed up by a similar mechanism as EP1 made of components overlapping horizontally, assembled by rebates and held together with dowels. The floor part has totally disappeared.

The bow

The bow of EP1 is made out of two components. The first one, the stem, has been preserved on a length of 170 cm, a maximum width of 24 cm and a thickness of 20 cm (**fig. 5**). Its curved shape reminds one of the natural curvature of the branch out of which it was carved. Its thickness being superior to that of the bottom planks, it extends by 4 cm outside the boat. As this difference was not rectified, it could suggest that

the boat had not been completed when it sank. The second component, shaped like a U, was designed to close up the bow of the boat by ensuring the joint between all parts of the floor and sides and by serving as the ultimate cross-member. It was clearly carved in the natural fork of a branch.
The two components were assembled with a large 5 cm diameter dowel, and fastened to the sides by two dowels with wedges on each plank. A test pit has also revealed the presence of three nails on the outside of the hull, strengthening the dowels. They are distributed as follows: one at the end of the right bilge (the only one that was entirely accessible by test pit), one at the end of the preserved side plank, and one on the left side at the top of the stem which is very eroded at that place; the third nail is probably the only vestige of the assembly of a top side plank with the stem. The EP2 bow was not preserved but the shape and dimension of the boat indicate that it was also completed by a stem.

Dowels, nails and caulking

All EP1 components have been assembled with dowels, strengthened by at least four iron nails placed strategically (three at stem level, one under the floor at aft closing level). Others would probably become visible if the outside of the hull was cleared, excavation option which has been dismissed in order to protect the wreck.
The 252 dowels, clearly all made of oak, have a diameter substantially similar over the whole EP1 wreck (from 2.8 to 3.2 cm), many of them with wedges. The holes have most certainly been made using a 3 cm diameter auger, except for one 5 cm diameter dowel used probably to strengthen the assembly with the stem.
Several punctual test pits performed on the outer hull of the EP1 wreck have shown that the dowels protrude by 1.5-3 cm from the external planks beyond the ends of the hull and probably over its whole surface. This could indicate the existence of a timber lining of the hull or braces, which are missing today. However, one may question whether this might be an additional clue suggesting that this vessel was never entirely completed. It can be assumed that the supports used in the construction of this vessel on the building site had removed access to these dowels so their length could not be rectified before the boat launch; the builders would have left them protruding from the external face of the hull.
On wreck EP2, the dowels are placed by twos on the braces for the side plank assemblies. They present a substantially similar diameter on the whole wreck (from 2.8 to 3.2 cm) with wedges on many of them inside the vessel. As for EP1, the holes have certainly been drilled with a 3 cm diameter auger. Despite the important degree of erosion of the wreck, it is noted that some dowels fitted from the outside of the hull towards the inside still protrude by 2-3 cm on the external face; these dowels are cylindrical, except on the wider external part where they are conical and quadrangular. This type of assembly produces a firm joint. They may have been installed in order to consolidate the assemblies during the boat construction. Navigation on a vessel that includes protruding dowels may seem inappropriate and even dangerous for the assemblies. It can be assumed that they facilitated the securing of components which were once latched onto the outside of the boat but have not been preserved.
The EP2 wreck has delivered more nails than EP1. Two nails have been found at the juncture of planks on the right side where the placement of dowels was impossible. On the left side, three nails are visible and six more nails have also been found in the clay at the beginning of the excavation, at the bow and stern levels, having probably come loose from eroded timber components. A nail most likely from another perished assembly was found at the bottom of a test pit.

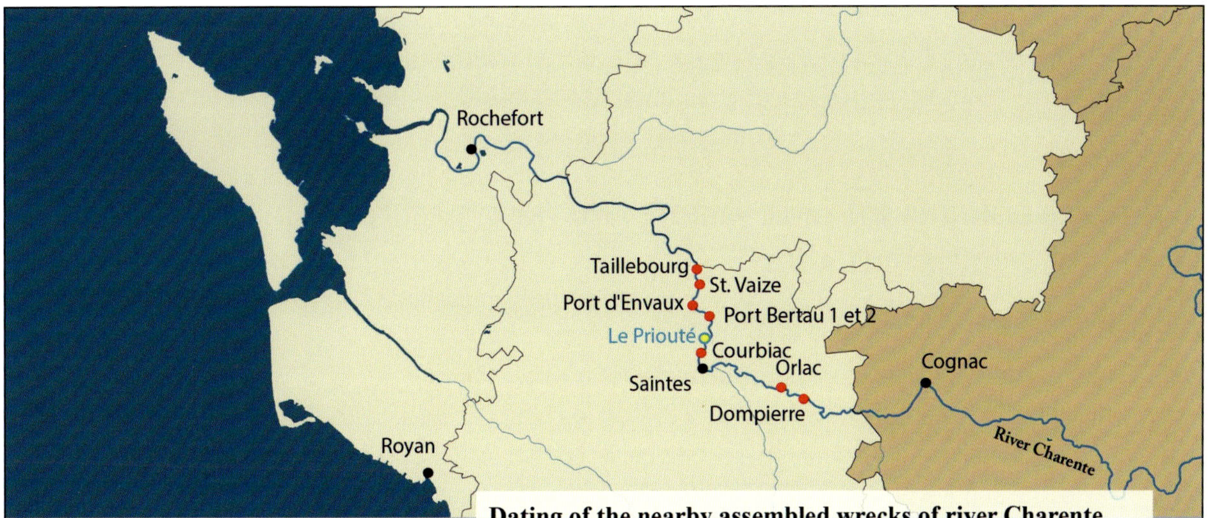

Dating of the nearby assembled wrecks of river Charente

Orlac : 1021-1042 (dendrochronology)
Courbiac : 230-390 AD
Port Berteau : 599 (tree cut - Dendrochronology)
EP1 Taillebourg : 145-420 AD
Saint-Vaize : 663 and 775 AD

Le Prioutè EP1 : bulkhead: 680-874 AD, and transom: 643-717 AD
Le Prioutè EP2 : cross-member: 601-671 AD, and bulkhead: 650-771 AD,
Le Prioutè EP3 : cross-member: 662-670 AD

All the wrecks of the Prioutè are dating between the beginning of the 7th en the end of the 8th c.

Comparisons of load capacity between wrecks found in the river Charente

	Type of vessels	Lenght (m)	Width max (m)	Deep (m)	Weight (T)	Load max (T)	Weight / load relation
Mortefon 2	Monoxyle dugout	9.060	0.6/0.7	0.462	0.649	1.800	2.77
Mortefon 2 *	Monoxyle dugout	9.060	0.6/0.7	0.462	0.671	1.303	1.94
Port berteau II	Fluvio-maritime coaster wreck	14.290	4.800	1.20	6.800	19.350	2.84
Orlac	Assembled monoxyle vessel	15.500	2.100	0.41	4.000	8.200	2.05
Taillebourg pg7	Monoxyle dugout	11.000	0.750	0.50	0.976	1.672	1.70
Taillebourg pg9	Monoxyle dugout	4.250	0.500	0.40	0.256	0.237	0.90
Prioutè EP 1	Assembled wreck	6.520	2.360	0.80	1.263	4.946	3.9
Prioutè EP 2	Assembled wreck	9.130	3.696	1.0	2.526	16.405	6.4

Fig. 6 Comparisons of load capacity (J.-F. Mariotti) and dating of the Charente wrecks. – (CAD Ph. Moyat).

Remains of caulking (sealant that ensured the waterproofness of vessels) have been noted on EP1. A sample taken between two-floor planks has enabled the identification of the substance as hemp (*Cannabis sativa* – identification by Julian Wiethold, Inrap). The complete dismantlement of the wreck would have been necessary to study the caulk distribution in the assembly of the various floor and sides components. On the internal face, there was no trace of vegetal strips, or metallic staples, which could have been used to block this plant matter in the wood crevices.

The EP2 wreck was partially dismantled which made it possible to note that the plank assemblies were joined side by side. On the less eroded external parts of the sides, a gash allowing to insert the caulk was noted. However, the plant matter was not identified due to insufficient quantity.

DISCUSSION: THE SITE OF LE PRIOUTÉ AND THE CHARENTE RIVER IN THE EARLY MIDDLE AGES

After five campaigns of exploration and underwater excavation, the river site of Le Prioutè counts four vessels among which is one dugout canoe, dating back to a period between the late 8th and the mid-10th century AD, and three assembled boats, ^{14}C-dated to a period between the mid-7th and late 8th century AD (**fig. 6**). Hopefully, the ongoing dendrochronological analyses will make it possible to define these dates more precisely. The findings can be compared to other discoveries made in the Charente River (**fig. 6**). The wrecks of Le Prioutè are more ancient than the assembled monoxyle wreck of Orlac (dép. Charente-Maritime/F), dendrochronologically dated to 1021-1042 AD[7], and probably more recent than the fluvio-maritime coaster wreck of Port Berteau II (dép. Charente-Maritime/F) that ^{14}C-dating has situated in the range 5th-7th century AD and dendrochronology to the early 7th century AD[8]. Equally, the EP1 wreck of Taillebourg seems to have been built before, however, available dating offers a wide range between 145 and 420 AD. The Saint-Vaize (dép. Charente-Maritime/F) wreck is the closest in time with a date between 663 and 775 AD in calibrated age[9].
Furthermore, this period is well represented in the port zone of Taillebourg-Port d'Envaux, where crafted wood and canoes bear witness to substantial activity associated with the river in the 7th and 8th century AD[10]. Finally, the dugout canoe discovered near the assembled wrecks of Le Prioutè has been dated to a period between the late 8th and the mid-10th century AD. The wrecks of Le Prioutè were found in an already discovery-rich context and confirmed that traffic along the Charente River was significant in Merovingian times.
For the time being, no direct typological comparisons with any contemporaneous vessel with similar technical characteristics have been found. Its overall shape belongs to the so-called category »en ogive« defined by B. Arnold[11], the front end shaped like a lancet, the aft closed up by an assembly of several components. The EP1 wreck of Le Prioutè, with its 6.60 m in length and its 2.40 m in width is half the size of the fluvio-maritime coaster of Port Berteau (14.60 m × 4.80 m). EP2 and EP3 are a lot smaller than this vessel as well. The width of EP1 (2.40 m) is nearly identical to the assembled monoxyle of Orlac (2.10 m), but the comparison ends there since that boat is 15.50 m long. Once more, the closest dimensions for the Charente belong to the wreck of Saint-Vaize. In its current state, it measures 4 m in length and 1.3 m in width, but its original dimensions before erosion were slightly bigger. However, this vessel was not constructed at all according to the same architectural design. Indeed, although it is much degraded, it is made of a fragment of monoxyle extended by an assembled section. This section is made of a sole formed by eight planks strengthened by cross-members. The only preserved side on this section appears to also be monoxyle, but in consideration of the degree of erosion of the vessel, it is rather difficult to ascertain on which side the stem was.
The wrecks of Le Prioutè belong to the class of flat-bottomed vessels whose longitudinal rigidity is assured by bilges. Wrecks presenting monoxyle bilges exist in various river basins, but they are not contemporaneous, or they may present other technical solutions for the hull (for example, the EP1 wreck from Saint-Georges' parking, 18th century AD[12]). Additionally, on some vessels with monoxyle bilges, these components are the result of a monoxyle split in halves, and whose parts have been entirely preserved, moved apart and connected by a number of plating planks. At Le Prioutè, these bilges form only a small part of a log.

B. Arnold also reminds us that the constraints linked to the raw material timber, must have guided the transition of the monoxyle to the assembled wreck because, on the one hand, there no longer were sufficiently tall oaks and, on the other hand, because the aim was to achieve a superior payload. In the context of this evolution, the wrecks of Le Prioutè belong to an intermediary phase when bilges were not yet compound (formed by two planks with a sharp-edged joint). Bilges remained components that were carved in one block (monoxyles), however with a limited spread.

The means of propulsion remain unknown. Indeed, the absence of a mast foot, rudder and daggerboard does not allow to settle between hauling and propulsion by means of a pole or oars. It may be simply recalled that these vessels could be used to navigate the ebb and flow of the tide currents, still quite significant at this point along the river. The study of the third vessel will undoubtedly bring additional information to understand the other two.

One of the particularities of Le Prioutè vessels is the presence of a stem and a closing system at the aft of the boat. A stem can be found on the wreck of Port Berteau, a boat whose dimensions and typology are different from the vessels of Le Prioutè.

According to the current state of research, there does not exist any medieval vessel with a similar stern in the Charente basin. On other waterways, the aft of vessels was finished in this manner but they date to the modern era. Indeed, the contemporary ethnographic directory provides a number of specimens such as the galupe of Adour, the yole of Vendée, the forquette of the Saône and the galley of Neufchâtel[13]. At regional level, we can add the lasses of Oléron and the plate or yole of the bay of Aiguillon[14]. These vessels could navigate in the strait of Charente and in the estuary of the Gironde[15]. They present a profile »en ogive«, a stem to break through the waves, and a bottom allowing navigation with a low draught.

The vessels discovered on the site of Le Prioutè were not exclusively intended for river navigation, and they were probably designed to also navigate in the estuary and even along the Atlantic coast. The calculations of load capacity performed at the end of the excavations of EP1 and EP2, based on the restoration of the hulls, allow an evaluation of the maximal weight of goods that could be carried to 5 tons for EP1 and 16 tons for EP2 (**fig. 6**).

It is likely that the target of their purpose was not solely to carry goods. Their shallow draught and the existence of a stem enable river and marsh navigation (marshland was indeed widespread in the Saintonge region in the Early Middle Ages) and perhaps also coastal navigation. Fishing, shellfish aquaculture or salt extraction were the many contexts this type of boat would have suited.

Within the immediate surroundings of the wreck of Le Prioutè, the existence of contemporaneous weapons and a canoe could suggest the presence of a port area very near the port zone of Taillebourg-Port d'Envaux. If this data should be confirmed by further research, a gradual image of a river punctuated downstream by ports of varying importance in the Early Middle Ages would appear. The term »port« is used here as a translation of the word *portus* which, in Medieval Latin has many meanings and may describe a quay along a river, a ferry crossing point or more generally a transit toll[16]. In the case of Le Prioutè, the toponym may recall the existence of a priory which could have been the origin of the development of the Charente riverbank, and the creation of a transhipment point in this location. One must remember that a medieval port does not necessarily imply the setting up of significant structures: it may have only been a beach or a bank with easy access with a timber support, which does not always leave traces and when buried under the bank, is undetectable. As highlighted by C. Treffort, the economic actors are unfortunately not well known for this region, and sources mainly concern the clerical world, but in the current state of research no available text mentions the existence of a priory in this location[17]. As it is the case in Taillebourg-Port d'Envaux, the uniqueness of the vestiges preserved underwater in today's active channel, as well as their date, is in sharp contrast with the absence of writings and the lack of knowledge regarding the populations established on the banks. Because this area hardly touched by major developments, no preventive archaeology has been undertaken here. This explains in part the relative poverty of the banks archaeological map. The present research provides new data for a period about which the archives and terrestrial archaeology deliver very little information. The richness of the discoveries (at Le Prioutè, three boats and one canoe) highlights the key role played by the river on the dynamics of the Early Middle Ages in Saintonge.

Notes

1) Mariotti/Dumont/Zelie 2010. – Dumont/Mariotti 2013.

2) Moyat et al. 2016.

3) Ly-16230: 1395±30 BP.

4) Ly-16231: 1325±30 BP.

5) Poz-64857: 1295±30 BP.

6) Arnold 1992, 75.

7) Chapelot/Rieth 1995.

8) Rieth/Carriere-Desbois/Serna 2001.

9) Dumont/Mariotti 2013.

10) Dumont/Mariotti 2013.

11) Arnold 1992, 75.

12) Rieth 2010.

13) Arnold 1992. – Beaudoin 1985. – Bonnamour 1998.

14) Beaudouin 1975.

15) Gaubert 2005, 48.

16) Niermeyer/Van de Kieft 1976. – Blaise 1975.

17) C. Treffort in: Dumont/Mariotti 2013, 264.

References

Arnold 1992: B. Arnold, Batellerie gallo-romaine sur le lac de Neuchâtel 1-2. Archéologie Neuchâteloise 12-13 (Sainte-Blaise 1992).

Beaudouin 1975: F. Beaudouin, Bateaux des côtes de France (Grenoble 1975).

1985: F. Beaudouin, Bateaux des Fleuves de France (Douarnenez 1985).

Blaise 1975: A. Blaise, Dictionnaire latin-français des auteurs du Moyen Âge (Turnholti, Brepols 1975).

Bonnamour 1998: L. Bonnamour, Bateaux de Saône, 3000 ans d'évolution. Archaeonautica 14, 1998, 13-21.

Chapelot/Rieth 1995: J. Chapelot / E. Rieth, Navigation et milieu fluvial au XIe s.: l'épave d'Orlac (Charente-Maritime). Documents d'Archéologie Française 48 (Paris 1995).

Dumont/Mariotti 2013: A. Dumont / J.-F. Mariotti (eds), Archéologie et histoire du fleuve Charente. Taillebourg – Port d'Envaux: une zone portuaire du haut Moyen Âge sur le fleuve Charente (Dijon 2013).

Gaubert 2005: Y. Gaubert (ed.), Voiles atlantiques (Douarnenez 2005).

Mariotti/Dumont/Zelie 2010: J.-F. Mariotti / A. Dumont / B. Zelie, Un port fluvial et un pont du Haut Moyen Âge sur la Charente à Taillebourg – Port d'Envaux (Charente-Maritime). In: Actes des XXVIIe Journées internationales d'archéologie mérovingienne, Autour de la bataille de Vouillé: Francs et Wisigoths (507-2007). Recherches récentes sur le haut Moyen Âge dans le Centre-Ouest de la France, Vouillé-Poitiers 2007 (Saint-Germain-en-Laye 2010) 279-299.

Moyat et al. 2016: Ph. Moyat / A. Dumont / J.-F. Mariotti / J. Wiethold, Une nouvelle épave mérovingienne découverte dans la Charente à Port d'Envaux (17). In: E. Peytremann (ed.), Des fleuves et des hommes à l'époque mérovingienne: territoire fluvial et société au premier Moyen Âge (V[e]-XIIe siècle). Actes des 33e Journées Internationales d'Archéologie mérovingienne, Strasbourg 2012. Mémoires de l'Association Française d'Archéologie Mérovingienne 32 = Revue Archéologique de l'Est, Supplément 42 (Dijon 2016) 105-118.

Niermeyer/Van de Kieft 1976: J.-F. Niermeyer / C. Van de Kieft, Mediae latinitatis lexicon minus. Lexique latin médiéval – français/anglais (Leiden 1976).

Rieth 2010: E. Rieth (ed.), Les épaves de Saint-Georges. Lyon – Ier-XVIIIe siècles. Analyse architecturale et études complémentaires. Archaeonautica 16 (Paris 2010).

Rieth/Carrierre-Debois/Serna 2001: E. Rieth / C. Carrierre-Debois / V. Serna, L'épave de Port Berteau II (Charente-Maritime). Documents d'Archéologie Française 86 (Paris 2001).

Summary

The immersed site of Le Prioutė is located at the Charente River, in the district of Port d'Envaux, barely 4km upstream from the medieval port area of Taillebourg-Port d'Envaux. Underwater surveys have resulted in the discovery of three assembled wrecks (EP1, EP2, EP3) and one dugout canoe, all dating to the Early Middle Ages. The charting of the discoveries and the study of the main technical characteristics of two wrecks (EP1 and EP2) were performed during three underwater excavation campaigns. The excavation of EP3 has not yet been completed.
The vessels of Le Prioutė were found in an already discovery-rich context and confirmed that the traffic along the Charente River was significant in Merovingian times. Both EP1 and EP2 wrecks are modest in size, but some of their structural elements suggest that the boats were not solely intended for river navigation. They may have also been designed for estuary navigation and even for sailing along the Atlantic coast.

Résumé

Le site immergé du Prioutė se trouve dans le fleuve Charente, sur la commune de Port d'Envaux, à seulement 4km en amont de la zone portuaire médiévale de Taillebourg – Port d'Envaux. Les prospections subaquatiques ont permis de découvrir trois épaves assemblées (EP1, EP2, EP3) et une pirogue monoxyle, toutes datées du haut Moyen Âge. Trois campagnes de fouilles subaquatiques ont permis de faire le relevé et d'étudier des principales caractéristiques techniques de deux épaves (EP1 et EP2). La fouille d'EP3 n'est pas terminée.
Les bateaux du Prioutė s'inscrivent dans un contexte déjà riche en découvertes, et confirment que le fleuve Charente connaissait, à l'époque mérovingienne, une navigation relativement importante. Les dimensions des épaves EP1 et EP2 restent modestes, mais certains éléments de leur structure laissent penser qu'elles n'étaient pas uniquement destinées à naviguer sur le fleuve, et qu'elle pouvait également avoir été conçue pour naviguer dans l'estuaire, voire pour longer la côte Atlantique.

SYLVAIN AUMARD*

PORTS AND THE TIMBER TRADE IN THE YONNE VALLEY IN THE MIDDLE AGES AND THE MODERN PERIOD

A STUDY FROM BUILDING ARCHAEOLOGY

Ports play a decisive role in the economy of construction and contribute significantly to shaping the landscape of a city and its monuments. To a great extent, they enable the supply of materials to permanent urban worksites. Compared to carriage by road, river-based transport of heavy cargo is both easier and cheaper[1].

In northern Burgundy, substantial material resources have been exploited for the construction of buildings. The archives mention intensive exploitation of forest areas and limestone deposits, but the modes of transport are not always well described, leaving several questions unanswered about how timber was transported[2]. Unlike stone, timber can be transported in different ways, by boat or by being floated downstream. It can also be transported in different forms, particularly either as logs or as squared baulks.

In the Yonne Valley, the methods chosen are not represented either in the literature or in current research[3]. Such studies mainly focus on wood for fuel and the socio-economic issues involved[4]. The transport of timber by water coexisted with the trade in firewood, however, as is evidenced from construction contracts and commercial codes[5]. The data should therefore be re-examined to highlight this topic, by associating the analysis of records with the evidence of archaeology. Despite the scarcity of such evidence, it provides concrete insights into methods of transport, as well as chronological markers when written sources are scarce or non-existent.

For the city of Auxerre (dép. Yonne/F), the archives contain a number of carpentry agreements for the construction of structures, such as houses, mills, and presses. The texts are not, however, very explicit about the types of materials transported on the river or received at the ports and building sites[6]. A systematic in-depth approach to this corpus of texts is greatly needed, particularly with regard to the technical vocabulary, where approximations are inevitable. Several transactions seem to concern logs and squared timbers, but they contain no precise information concerning the mode of transport. The earliest written testimony so far identified that explicitly mentions floating timber down the Yonne, dates to 1550 AD[7].

This lack of information is not specific to the Yonne Valley, rather reflecting the general state of knowledge of a subject that is rarely addressed in current research[8]. Some clues are nevertheless emerging almost everywhere both in France and elsewhere in Europe, as each city had its own port for materials or timber. One of the best documented towns is probably Liège (prov. Liège/B). Here, a mid-16th century AD sketch, gives realistic details of wood management: from landing at the port, to storage and squaring in small workshops, before transport to the centre of the city (**fig. 1**)[9].

Full-scale investigation and data collation still needs to be undertaken for the Yonne Valley. This contribution simply seeks to draw attention to archaeological evidence that is, as yet, rarely exploited in France, which is likely to shed light on the role of ports in the organisation of the timber trade. This first stage of enquiry is based on a survey limited to a few monuments in the Yonne Valley, for which the collected data are the most complete. The ideas outlined here are based on a limited corpus that should be complemented by more extensive research.

Fig. 1 Liège, the port for timber, c. 1550 AD. – (Archives de l'État à Liège, Tribunal de la Chambre impériale, no. 1441; photo by AEL).

INTERPRETING ARCHAEOLOGICAL DATA

Four sites in the Yonne Valley were selected, providing five contexts (**fig. 2**):

- Vermenton (dép. Yonne/F), the church of Notre-Dame, roof framework of the nave, erected around the middle of the 14th century AD[10];
- Auxerre, Cathedral of St. Etienne, roof framework of the south transept, erected between about 1335 and 1340 AD[11];
- Auxerre, Cathedral of St. Etienne, the western part of the roof framework of the nave, erected around 1515 AD[12];
- Auxerre, a house called »Coche d'eau«, timbering and roof framework erected between 1500 and 1550 AD[13];
- Saint-Julien-du-Sault (dép. Yonne/F), a house called »de l'Officialité«, roof framework erected between 1265 and 1270 AD[14].

The locations of these buildings indicate a special link with the Yonne, a major economic axis since Antiquity[15]. Although no thorough archaeological study has been carried out, the examination of assembly methods and carpenters' marks, before sampling for dendrochronological analysis, shows that they are indeed coherent structures that have been little modified since their erection.

Each of these buildings presents some unexpected evidence, unrelated to the shaping of the beams or the erection of the structure. Even without systematic examination, such factors can easily be recognised and characterised. They comprise oblique perforations drilled into the corners of the timbers often associated in pairs, and at some distance from the carpenters' joints and markings (**figs 3-4**). These holes are rarely found

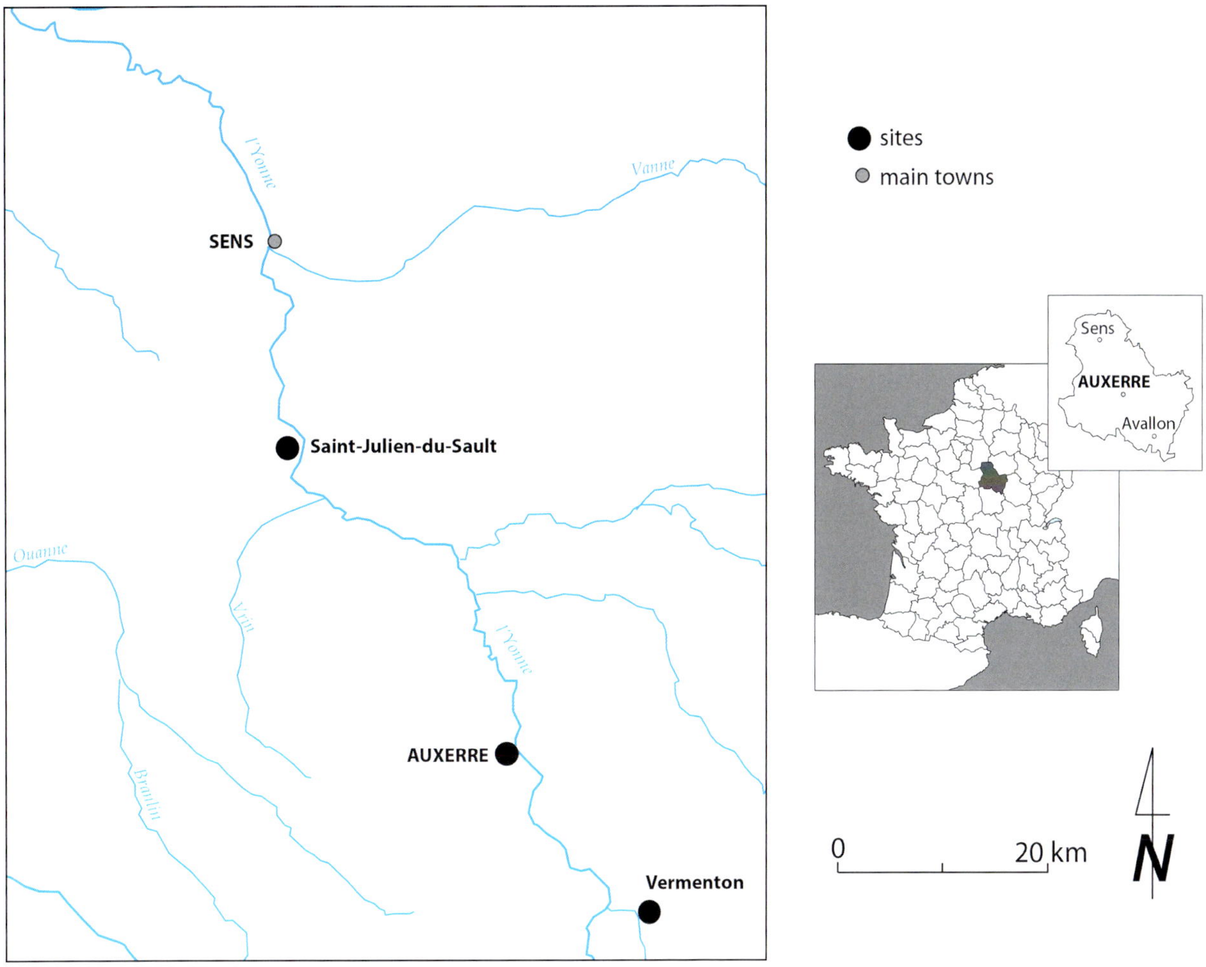

Fig. 2 Map of the studied sites. – (CAD by CEM, Auxerre).

in the middle of the beams[16], and are in most cases a little less than one metre from the ends of the beams, rarely is there more than one pair of holes. It also seems clear that these perforations are never made in all four corners, so that they are always found on two edges of the same face. The choice of the direction these holes seems to follow a complex logic, because they not only penetrate through the corners, but also deviate slightly in the direction of the wood fibre along the length of the beam.

They were made with an auger of about 20 mm and are of surprising quality in execution: providing a surface, with no tearing of the wood fibre. In the same way, their position, very close to or even on the edges of the beam, is unexpected, because clear traces of splintering would be expected, which is not the case. These clues indicate that the holes were drilled before the timbers were converted from logs to beams, when the wood was so thick that it could not crack under the cutting force of the auger. When the timber was squared, these holes would be cut back to varying degrees, thus explaining the great variability of their distance from the edges of the beam, and even their almost complete disappearance. Many of these perforations are indeed barely noticeable and often incomplete, as a result of the more or less extensive squaring of the logs, according to the section of the beam to be produceed. Therefore, it can be postulated that, in some cases, these clues have completely disappeared, as have the preparatory holes made by the chisel, which are necessary to allow the auger to drill at a specific point without slipping (**fig. 5**).

As it was the logs and not the beams that were drilled, and as the resulting perforations played no role in the construction process, they presumably played a role in transport, in particular in the assembly of timber

Fig. 3 Oblique perforations: **a** Saint-Julien-du-Sault, »maison de l'Officialité«. – **b** church of Vermenton. – (Photos S. Aumard).

rafts. Some of the holes contain fragments of wood, at Vermenton in particular. These probably represent the remains of pegs, suggesting a method of tying the logs together (**fig. 3b**)[17]. In addition, the distance between pairs of holes (usually 90 cm?)[18] could identify the location of transverse members used to reinforce the cohesion of the timber rafts (**fig. 4**). It can be deduced from these structures, built between the 13th and the 16th centuries AD, that wood would not have been transported in the form of beams but rather as logs, which would be squared once the final destination was reached (**fig. 6**).

At this stage of the research it is not possible to be certain of raft design, which would require a more systematic exploration of all the evidence. If, by its very nature, the approach proposed here is somewhat limited, comparable observations in Orleans (dép. Loiret/F) or in the regions of northern and eastern France generally support our hypotheses[19]. Despite the vestigial nature of these clues, evidence for this stage in the preparation of timber for rafting has been identified in Belgium, at Furnes (prov. West-Vlaanderen/B) (**fig. 5**), in Germany, in the region of Tübingen (Baden-Württemberg/D), and in Switzerland, in Basel (Kt. Basel-Stadt/CH), where the constraints of the wood and a similar arrangement of holes in the corners of the log indicate such devices[20].

PORTS AND TIMBER

Beyond their appearance, these data bring new knowledge about how timber was transported and, potentially, about the design of timber rafts. They also provide information about how timber ports were managed: logs did not only pass through the ports, timber squaring also occurred there. Previously, the commonly held opinion was that squaring only took place on construction sites. Yet, as suggested by the sketch of the port of Liège, the timber squaring activity was probably not merely a side-line at the ports, nor the result of large orders or a boom in the construction economy. Several factors even suggest that this preliminary transformation of logs was probably intrinsic to port areas given over to the timber trade. Squaring must have been part of the wood management process, together with other commercial activities, such as the reception, checking, and dismantling of timber rafts. Finished products would present the advantage of being less heavy to transport, while also conserving the limited space available at building sites, so that timber squaring must often have been relegated to other places, such as cloisters or cemeteries[21]. It is important to keep in mind the limited dimensions of the building site, whether for a house or a major building, and there must have been considerable congestion in the rough-hewing zones, where the wood was shaped piece by piece into the structural elements of a roof framework.

Fig. 4 Twinned perforations, at various distances: **a** Coche d'Eau house in Auxerre (3 place du Coche d'Eau). – **b** church of Vermenton. – (Photos S. Aumard).

Fig. 5 Furnes (Belgium), choir of St. Walburg's Church: marking and oblique perforation. – (Photo P. Hoffsummer, University of Liège).

If the timber squaring operations at ports is difficult to prove from documentary evidence, it can easily be deduced from archaeology. Other evidence can also be found, such as the enigmatic marks on the beams of the southern transept of the Cathedral in Auxerre, which seem to represent symbolically a boat in the form of a half moon and a double mast (**fig. 7**)[22]. Such signs can be seen on most beams, and seem to belong to a process different from that of the carpenter preparing to raise of the trusses. In association with the

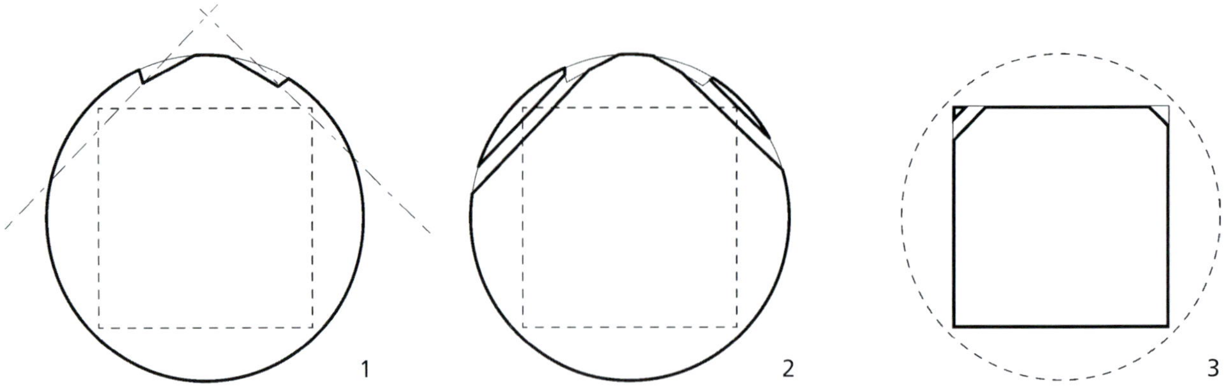

Fig. 6 From the floated log to the squared beam, proposed reconstruction of the wood management chain: **1** at the port of departure, marking with a chisel to prepare for drilling. – **2** making auger holes through the marks, then binding the logs together. – **3** at the port of arrival, releasing the logs, then squaring them into beams, with traces of oblique perforations. – (Drawing S. Aumard).

oblique perforations, they should identify the pieces of wood prepared at the port before their transport to the construction site.

If ports did not face the same constraints of space as those of intramural construction sites, their space was nevertheless limited by buildings and the river, which was also subject to seasonal variation. In Liège, as in Auxerre, despite the limitations of iconography, pictorial evidence does indeed suggest large areas mainly occupied by the timber trade, probably organised around the arrival and dismantling of the timber rafts, and then the storage of the logs, the preparation of beams, and their transport (**fig. 8**). The timber-squaring workshops would also occupy a substantial area. But their role must have been indispensable, allowing timber to be converted before its removal. It is even possible that this preliminary conversion, far from being incidental, is an essential component of these zones, facilitating the turnover of timber, from reception to departing.

In any case, this profusion of activities implies careful management of the space available on the banks, especially since it also had to be shared with the firewood trade, which would inevitably lead to conflicts. An in-depth study of written records would almost certainly identify interesting evidence about this issue, as already suggested by several regulations favourable to the professions involved (to facilitate landing, storage, and transit)[23]. The sketch of the port of Liège, produced during a trial between mairniers (sic) and haleurs (boatmen and hauliers),

Fig. 7 Auxerre, southern transept of the Cathedral of St. Etienne: mark symbolising a boat, probably made after squaring the beam at the port. – (Photo G. Puech).

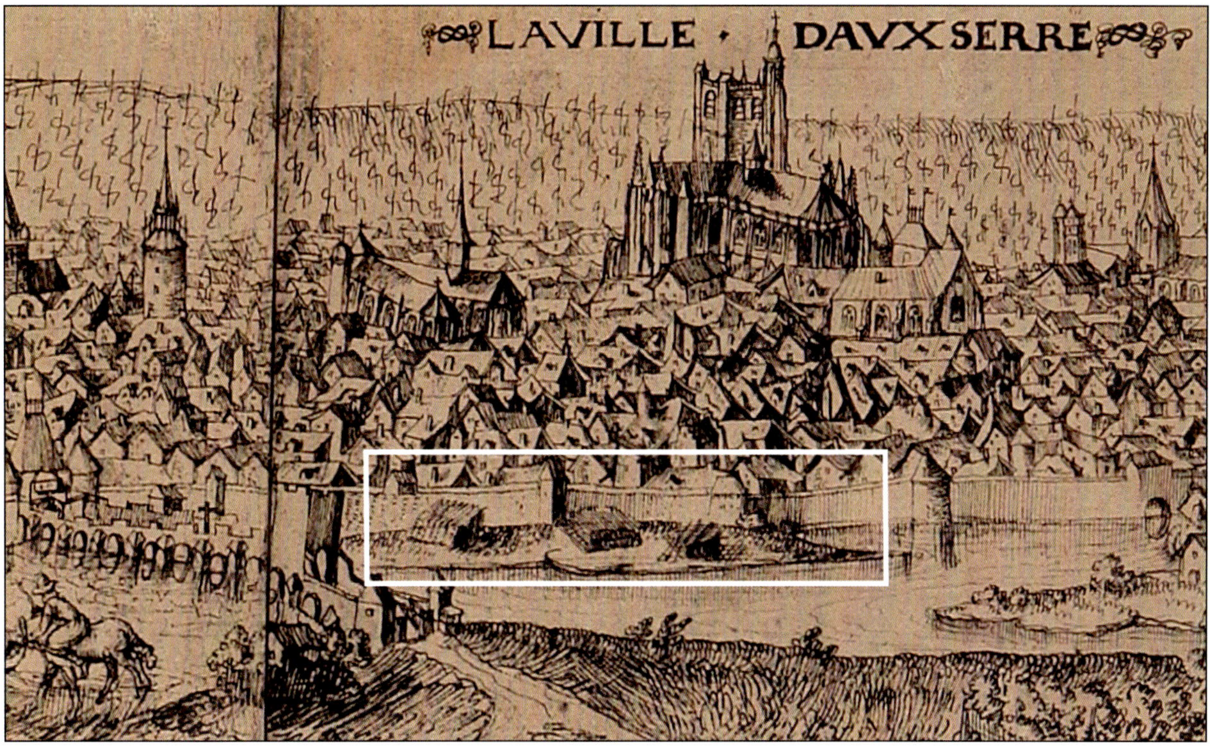

Fig. 8 The timber port in Auxerre. – (Joachim Duviert, 1609, Auxerre Municipal Library).

who were unable to use the riverbank congested by logs, fully illustrates the problem of managing and sharing space along the riverbanks.

DISCUSSION

The approach proposed here addresses new aspects concerning the organisation of timber ports and supply, based on archaeological evidence, which is, as yet, rarely explored. These findings provide evidence of wood management, conversion from logs to beams, and also some insight into the organisation of port activities. Through the study of wooden roof structures, dated by dendrochronology, it is possible to retrace the reality of this trade at least back to the 13th century AD, a period lacking much written evidence on this topic. However, there is every reason to believe that the timber trade was already part of a long tradition, and that the wood of Saint-Julien-du-Sault dating from c. 1260 AD is not the oldest to have been floated down the Yonne. Even from the middle of the 12th century AD, builders working in the Île-de-France seem to have been in the habit of looking to land around the Yonne to solve their supply problems. This is the case for Abbot Suger, who left a famous testimony: requiring a great deal of wood for the Basilica of St. Denis (probably tie-beams), he was advised to seek wood from the region of Auxerre, because of the scarcity of forests in the region of Paris[24]. Archaeological evidence seems to prove the continuity of this timber trade, although documentary evidence does not go back so far. It is also supported by Abbot Suger's testimony.
The observed archaeological evidence shows the importance of ports in the local economy of wood construction, not only for supply and for trade, but also as a sort of antechamber for the building site where the wood underwent a preliminary processing. The absence of such evidence from most buildings structures is, however, generally the case. In Auxerre, for example, it demonstrate that the river was probably not the only way to meet the needs of construction works. It is true that identifying perforations is subject to many

uncertainties, with respect to research, data conservation, and the timber squaring process. However, in the case of the great roof space in the Cathedral of St. Etienne, erected between the beginning of the 13th century AD and the beginning of the 16th century AD, the overwhelming majority of the wooden elements do not show any evidence for rafting process. If transport by road should also be taken into account, the limits of the method allow us to consider other techniques of floating timber, without raft for example. This second floating process would have left only few traces, and may have been used for transportation over short distances, or transportation of great beams[25].

In addition, this new research significantly alters the current view on timber floating on the Yonne, which has been considered to be essentially focussed on firewood by the majority of previous historical studies. Without denying the great importance of this sector of the economy, it appears that the timber trade and transport was of importance throughout the Middle Ages and the Modern period. It benefitted from the same infrastructures, and was presumably governed by the same forms of control and regulation[26]. Far from negligible, the importance of this economy is commensurate with forest resources and opportunities. Great architectural innovations, such as the Gothic style around Paris, were obviously linked to the development of wood construction activities. Reciprocally, it is evident that stone architecture cannot emerge without a major contribution from wood for building site installations (scaffolding, centring, shoring, temporary structures, lifting equipment, etc.)[27]. The seemingly decisive implication of Paris carpenters in the organisation of firewood floating, around 1545-1550 AD, illustrates how well the lines of communication were mastered and put to good use for the construction sector. This, to the point where the profession could access new opportunities and resources[28]. Timber trade on the Yonne, as other goods trades, clearly seems to have enhanced the role of ports as genuine exchange networks.

This survey has laid the foundation for an original archaeological approach to the timber trade at ports in the Yonne Valley. Even though it will necessarily be enriched by new data in the future, it must still be supplemented by further study of written records, which have mainly been explored until now for firewood references. This approach will allow the timber process to be better known, from tree to beam, from felling to erecting, through timber squaring, and from forest to building site, using the river and the ports.

Notes

*) Translation by C. Chateau Smith and M. Foucher. Many thanks to Pr. Nathaniel Alcock (University of Warwick), particularly for his suggestions and translating of specific vocabulary.

1) Dubois 1980, 80-82. – Bernardi 1995, 133.

2) Chapelot 1975.

3) See current research by Dimitri Langoureau (2015); also his ongoing research in the Vosges Mountains, for example (in prep.).

4) This point of view is also shared by Dimitri Langoureau (pers. comm.), to whom the author expresses his gratitude.

5) Moreau 1840.

6) See, for example: Forestier 1942. – Drot 1902. – Aumard/Rymarczyk/Muller 2006.

7) Moreau 1843, 92-95: Letters patent from the King, granting Guillaume Sallonnier the right for floating firewood and timber downstream on the Yonne in 1550.

8) See, for example: Bernardi 2007. – Angeli 2008. – Bouticourt 2016, 55-69.

9) Archives of the State of Liège, c. 1553, in Hoffsummer 1999, 61.

10) Felled between 1318 and 1349 (Blain/Hoffsummer 2014).

11) Felled in autumn/winter 1328-1329 (Locatelli/Pousset/Lavier 2011, 179).

12) Felled in autumn/winter 1512-1513 (Locatelli/Pousset/Lavier 2011, 178).

13) According to Lambert/Lavier 1992, 147.

14) Felled in autumn/winter 1265-1266, according to C. Locatelli in: Hoffsummer 2002, 189.

15) Delor 2002.

16) Situation observed on the longest beams, e.g. the roof posts in Vermenton.

17) The xylological determination of these wooden remains, known as »hards« or »harts«, has yet to be established. In the south of France, most of the remains so far identified are of alder wood (Bouticourt 2016, 58-59).

18) Measurements from two ceiling joists, on the second floor of the Coche d'Eau house, in Auxerre. These values are very similar to most of the measurements observed between the end of the beam and the isolated twinned holes, as if the second pair was embedded in the existing structure, or had disappeared when the length of wood was cut. In the roof space of the church in Vermenton, this distance seems to be smaller (not recorded due to inaccessibility).

19) Alix 2013, 224. Most of these observations date from the 15th-16th century AD, but C. Alix (to whom the author expresses his gratitude) has pointed out similar traces dating back to the 13th century AD.

20) Respectively: Hoffsummer 2002, 54. – Marstaller 2012, 64. – Lutz 2005, 121. 125. Most of these examples date from the 15th-16th century AD.

21) Épaud 2007, 45 (cemeteries of Rouen in 1469 and 1478). – Quantin 1870, 74 (cloister of the Cordeliers in Auxerre in 1425). – Hoffsummer 1999, 61-63 (Liège timber port in 1553).

22) King 2011, 189. I thank Stephen King for pointing out the particularity of this roof, during the survey work undertaken in winter of 2002-2003 under his direction and that of Heike Hansen, as part of the Institut für Architekturgeschichte of the University of Stuttgart, with the funding of the Deutsche Forschungsgemeinschaft. Since then, the corpus of oblique perforations has grown steadily and has given rise to the ideas being presented in this paper.

23) Moreau 1840, 41. 49. 68-70. 86. 91. 151. 162.

24) *De Consecratione Ecclesiae Sancti Dionysii*, Gasparri 1996, 19 (§ 5).

25) Again, these points deserve to be analysed by more detailed archival research, but both cases are described in Moreau 1840, 24. 38. 40. 71.

26) In Germany, the question of floating has been discussed on the basis of archaeological features dating back to the Bronze Age, according to Ellmers 1985, 12-33. On the River Regen, this mode of transport is mentioned as early as 990 AD, according to Wolfsteiner 2006 (information L. Werther, to whom the author expresses his gratitude).

27) Bernardi 2011.

28) Moreau 1843, 41-45. The author explicitly mentions a series of original documents evoking the first rafting of firewood to Paris, in April 1547 AD, by the carpenter Charles Le Conte. But none of these documents seems to have been the subject of a critical study (Moreau 1843, 84 onward).

References

Alix 2013: C. Alix, Les maisons en pan de bois d'Orléans du XIVe au début du XVIIe siècle: bilan de treize années de recherche. In: C. Alix / F. Épaud (eds), La construction en pan de bois au Moyen Âge et à la Renaissance (Tours, Rennes 2013) 221-270.

Angeli 2008: C. Angeli, L'approvisionnement de Strasbourg en bois de construction (1262-1681). Cahiers Alsaciens d'Archéologie, d'Art et d'Histoire 51, 2008, 57-71.

Aumard/Rymarczyk/Muller 2006: S. Aumard / S. Rymarczyk / W. Muller, Travaux du laboratoire d'archéologie du bâti: morphologie des tuiles anciennes et marchés d'ouvrages. Bulletin du Centre d'Études Médiévales d'Auxerre 10, 2006, 67-72.

Bernardi 1995: P. Bernardi, Métiers du bâtiment et techniques de construction à Aix-en-Provence, à la fin de l'époque gothique (1400-1550) (Aix-en-Provence 1995).

2007: P. Bernardi (ed.), Forêts alpines & charpentes de Méditerranée [exhibition catalogue Gap] (L'Argentière-la-Bessée 2007).

2011: P. Bernardi, Bâtir au Moyen Age, XIIIe-milieu XVIe siècle (Paris 2011).

Blain/Hoffsummer 2014: S. Blain / P. Hoffsummer, Rapport d'analyse dendrochronologique: Vermenton (89, Yonne, France) [Univ. Liège 2014].

Bouticourt 2016: E. Bouticourt, Charpentes méridionales. Construire autrement: le Midi rhodanien à la fin du Moyen Âge (Arles 2016).

Chapelot 1975: O. Chapelot, La construction sous les ducs de Bourgogne Valois: l'infrastructure (moyens de transport, matériaux de construction) [diss. Univ. Paris 1, 1975].

Delor 2002: J.-P. Delor (ed.), Carte archéologique de la Gaule. 89, 1-2: l'Yonne (Paris 2002).

Drot 1902: E. Drot, Recueil de documents tirés des anciennes minutes de notaires déposées aux archives départementales de l'Yonne. Bulletin de la Société des Sciences Historiques et Naturelles de l'Yonne 56, 1902, 97-121.

Dubois 1980: H. Dubois, Techniques et coût des transports terrestres dans l'espace bourguignon aux XIVe et XVe siècles. Annales de Bourgogne 52, 1980, 65-82.

Ellmers 1985: D. Ellmers, Flösserei in Vorgeschichte, Römerzeit und Mittelalter. In: H.-W. Keweloh (ed.), Flösserei in Deutschland (Stuttgart 1985) 12-33.

Épaud 2007: F. Épaud, De la charpente romane à la charpente gothique en Normandie. Évolution des techniques et des structures de charpenterie aux XIIe-XIIIe siècles (Caen 2007).

Forestier 1942: H. Forestier, Archives du département de l'Yonne. Documents et inventaires complémentaires. Répertoires et inventaires de fonds déposés par les notaires de l'Yonne. Études de Me Rolland Sampic, notaire à Seignelay, et de Me Louis Jouvin, notaire à Auxerre (Auxerre 1942).

Gasparri 1996: F. Gasparri (ed.), Suger. Œuvres. I: Écrit sur la consécration de Saint-Denis. L'Œuvre administrative. Histoire de Louis VII. Les Classiques de l'Histoire de France au Moyen Age 37 (Paris 1996).

Hoffsummer 1999: P. Hoffsummer, Les charpentes de toitures en Wallonie: typologie et dendrochronologie (XIe-XIXe siècle). Division du Patrimoine. Série Monuments et Sites: Études et Documents 1 (Namur 21999).

2002: P. Hoffsummer, Du bois à la charpente. In: P. Hoffsummer (ed.), Les charpentes du XIe au XIXe siècle. Typologie et évolution en France du Nord et en Belgique. Cahiers du Patrimoine 62 (Paris 2002) 53-71.

King 2011: S. King, Les charpentes des principaux vaisseaux. In: C. Sapin (ed.), Saint-Étienne d'Auxerre: la seconde vie d'une cathédrale. 7 ans de recherches pluridisciplinaires et internationales (Paris 2011) 183-207.

Lambert/Lavier 1992: G.-N. Lambert / C. Lavier, L'étalon de datation dendrochronologique Bourgogne 29. In: G.-N. Lambert / B. Maurice (eds), Les Veines du temps. Lectures de bois en Bourgogne [exhibition catalogue] (Autun 1992) 123-156.

Langoureau 2015: D. Langoureau, Flottage et Flotteurs sur l'Yonne XVIIIe siècle - 1923 (Auxerre 2015).

Locatelli/Pousset/Lavier 2011: C. Locatelli / D. Pousset / C. Lavier, Synopsis des chantiers de bois depuis 1235. In: C. Sapin (ed.), Saint-Étienne d'Auxerre: la seconde vie d'une cathédrale. 7 ans de recherches pluridisciplinaires et internationales (Paris 2011) 177-181.

Lutz 2005: Th. Lutz, Das Bauholz: Flösserei, Provenienz, Handelsformen, Kennzeichnung. In: T. Lutz / G. Wesselkamp (eds), Dächer der Stadt Basel (Basel 2005) 115-137.

Marstaller 2012: T. Marstaller, Zu Lande und zu Wasser. Bauholzimporte des 12.-17. Jahrhunderts im mittleren Neckarraum. In: A. Diener / M. Untermann (eds), Holzbau in Mittelalter und Neuzeit. Mitteilungen der Deutschen Gesellschaft für Archäologie des Mittelalters und der Neuzeit 24 (Paderborn 2012) 61-70.

Moreau 1840: F. Moreau, Code du commerce des bois carrés: charpente, sciage et charronnage réunis, pour l'approvisionnement de Paris (Paris 1840).

1843: F. Moreau, Histoire du flottage en trains. Jean Rouvet et les principaux flotteurs anciens et modernes (Paris 1843).

Quantin 1870: M. Quantin, Histoire anecdotique des rue d'Auxerre, avec plan de la ville ancienne et moderne (Auxerre 1870).

Wolfsteiner 2006: A. Wolfsteiner, »Fluderer-Manner mit da langa Stanga«. Flößerei und Trift auf Regen und Naab. In: M. Berwing-Wittl (ed.), Burgen und Klöster – Stadt und Fluss. Festschrift zum 36. Bayerischen Nordgautag in Nittenau (Regensburg 2006) 85-94.

Summary

The historical literature about trade on the Yonne River often refers to firewood for the market in Paris, from the 16th century AD onwards, while timber used for building is rarely mentioned. Through the study of timber-framed buildings and roofs, building archaeology provides new data from as early as the 13th century AD, identifying wooden elements that were transported by floating. The available archaeological data are limited, but very informative about the little-known aspect of timber trade and about medieval construction sites that were supplied by water transport.

By combining archaeology with the analysis of the few accessible written records, the history of wooden elements can be traced from preparing rafts to hewing beams. Timber may have reached the ports in the form of logs or as squared timber, resulting in different types of activity on the banks or at the wharves. Regarding timber, it seems that medieval ports were not only intended for the temporary storage and transhipment of goods. The preliminary transformation of logs could also have been carried out in areas set aside for hewing and squaring.

Résumé

L'historiographie du commerce sur l'Yonne fait la part belle au bois de chauffage alimentant le marché parisien depuis le 16e siècle apr. J.-C. Qu'en est-il du bois d'œuvre utilisé notamment en charpente? L'archéologie du bâti, par la lecture des ouvrages en pans de bois et des combles apporte depuis une décennie de nouveaux éléments de réponse, en mettant en évidence des pièces transportées par flottage depuis au moins le 13e siècle apr. J.-C. Loin de prétendre à une synthèse exhaustive, cette contribution est l'occasion de faire le point sur les données archéologiques, peu nombreuses, mais très évocatrices de cet aspect méconnu du commerce et de l'approvisionnement des chantiers de construction médiévaux.

En associant l'analyse des rares témoignages écrits, on évoquera autant que possible le parcours des bois depuis la préparation des trains de flottage à la mise en œuvre/forme des poutres. Ce sera l'occasion de s'interroger sur les modalités de réception des bois dans les ports, sous forme de grumes ou de pièces équarries et, par conséquent sur les activités déployées sur les berges ou les quais. Dans le domaine du bois d'œuvre, il semble en effet, que les ports médiévaux ne soient pas seulement dévolus au stockage provisoire et au transbordement des marchandises, mais ils paraissent également le lieu d'une première transformation des grumes avec la présence d'ateliers d'équarrissage.

ARJAN CONIJN · JANINE LANGE · CARSTEN ZUBE · BERTIL MÄCHTLE · THOMAS MEIER

EARLY FLOODS AND EARLY DIKES: RESEARCH STRATEGY IN COMBINING GEOARCHAEOLOGICAL AND HISTORICAL SOURCES IN THE UPPER RHINE VALLEY

Despite the presence of kilometres-long dikes bounding the River Rhine, flooding is still regarded as a risk. Many flood prevention measures are still being studied at universities, debated in local forums, and executed along the rivers. Flooding is currently a matter of particular interest because of climate change, but it has been a threat to humankind ever since people first started to settle along rivers, which they have done for many millennia.

In this paper, a flood is considered as high water causing inundation of land that is normally free of water. It can be debated which factors are the causes of flooding, whether natural or human; also, variations in the perception of floods can be discussed. However, it can be stated that for centuries humans have made efforts to reduce the catastrophic effects of flooding by building flood defences. Although in this study mainly dikes are considered, dams, water storage, drainage, sluices and pumping stations, among others, are not left aside. Most likely, defence against high water was, or is, not the only purpose of these landscape elements, but the malfunction of the water defensive aspect can result in flooding[1]. It should also be taken into account that dike-building and water drainage have been done on an individual scale from pre-Roman times onward, but, during the medieval period, cooperatives started to build dikes that protected larger areas. This might be considered to represent the start of dike-building as we now know it. Today dike-building is ordered to execute by states (or countries) following on national and European directives.

As a regional study, this paper will introduce the interdisciplinary approach of the project »Land unter?« by discussing its research questions, its hypotheses and starting point, some preliminary findings after the first year of research and its future research strategy. A critique of the first year of this project may provide a perfect starting point for further improved interdisciplinary research in historical geoarchaeology.

WHAT DO WE WANT TO KNOW?

The Holocene history of the Upper Rhine Valley was heavily influenced by its main river, not the least by creating a broad alluvial plain with continuously developing, changing and disappearing water courses resulting in a vast hybrid area between land and water. Early records of Roman and early medieval settlements surprisingly point out locations within this low-lying alluvial plain (**fig. 1**)[2], an area that is nowadays protected against flooding by many kilometres of connected dikes.

The fact that these villages were located for centuries within areas at risk of flooding is interesting, since (cooperative) dike-building in Western Europe has not been recorded prior to the 10th or 11th century AD. A case study at the Loire shows a late 11th century AD dike of about 30 km in length, which is too extensive for a single village and, therefore, must have protected the agricultural lands of multiple settlements[3]. Similar case studies are available along the Dutch Rhine[4] and a 12th century AD flood defence system was recorded along the Rhône[5]. This leaves us with the impression that around the 11th century AD the need for such

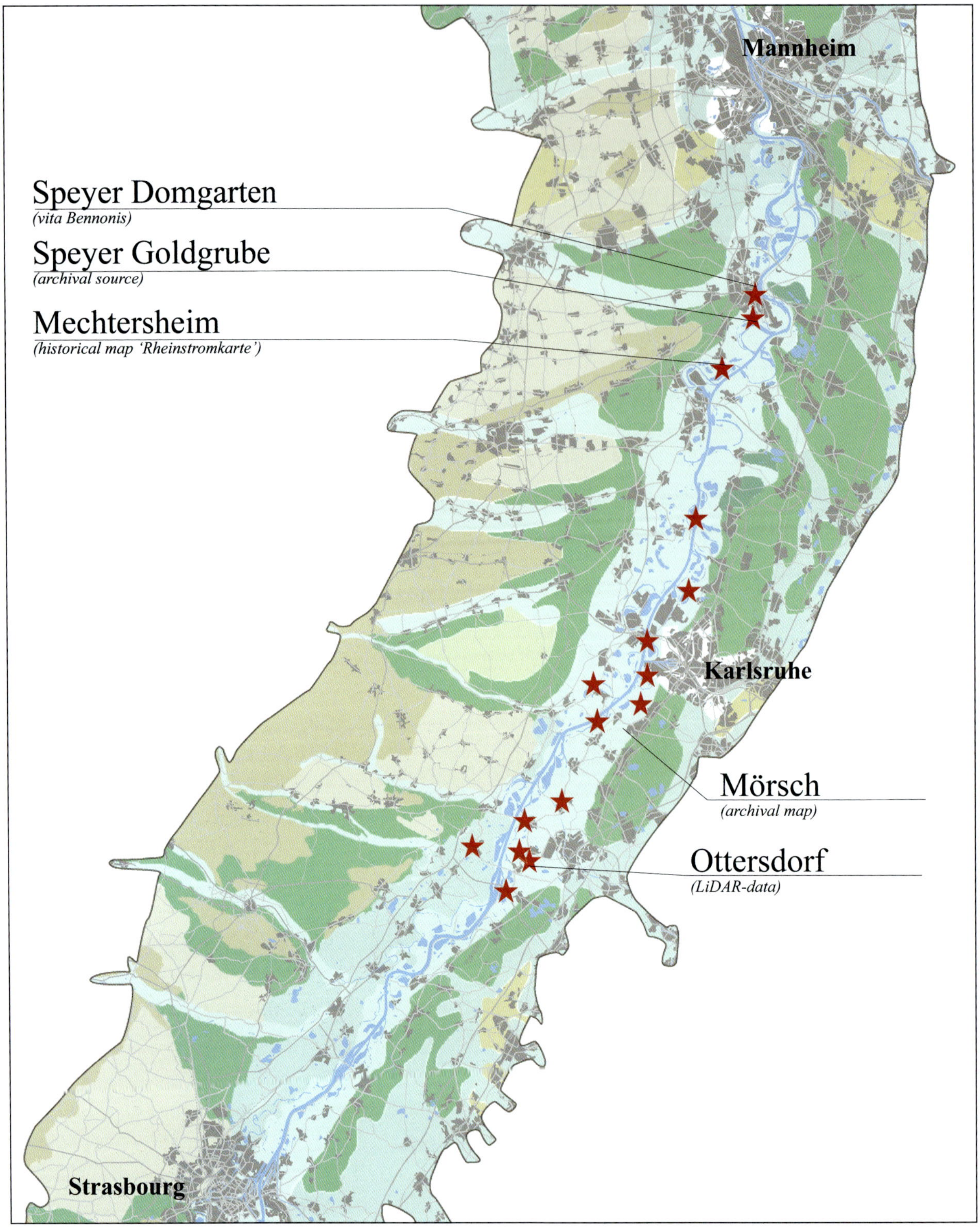

Fig. 1 Upper Rhine Valley section from Strasbourg to Mannheim, with case studies in Speyer and Ottersdorf, amongst others. – (© Arjan Conijn, based on Google Maps through snazzy maps [villages] and Bodenatlas Deutschland / Carte des petits domaines morphologiques de la carte des sols d'Alsace. ARRA [soils]).

large-scale flood protection increased. Three hypotheses on the cause of this sudden emergence of flood protective building projects are the take-off point for the present project's research strategy:

1. Did the frequency and magnitude of floods increase around the 11th century AD? A case study in the lower Rhône Valley shows a phase of stable fluvial dynamics with undisturbed development of soils in the alluvial plains from the 8th century AD throughout the early and high medieval period, followed by a period of severe erosion and, thus, high-dynamic fluvial activity during the 13th century AD[6]. A similar study on the Danube close to Ingolstadt shows an increase of river dynamics from the 14th century AD onward[7]. Correlation between these two case studies could be expected, but further research on other major rivers in Western and Central Europe is lacking. It is, therefore, hardly possible to say if these rough correlations are coincidental or if they prove a general change in environmental dynamics. In conducting such a study for the Upper Rhine alluvial plain, both climatological influences and the effects of changing human behaviour are taken into consideration.
2. Was the sudden emergence of dike-building caused by a change in the cultural perception of floods, a shift from seeing flooding as a natural event towards perceiving floods as catastrophes[8]? If flooding of agricultural lands and settlements happened before the 11th century AD as well, it might not have been perceived as such a problem in the manner that it is nowadays. Being inconvenienced by flooding may have been accepted as simply part of living alongside a river. In Western Europe, this proposed 11th century AD change of perception coincides with the intensification of agriculture (»Vergetreidung«), meeting the demands of newly founded towns[9]. Therefore, the losses in yield resulting from a flood might have endangered the provisioning of these towns and augmented the willingness of landlords and/or the rural population to act.
3. Was flooding no longer considered to be an act of divine will and people became open to adapt, form and control their natural environment[10]? The perception of what a flood was, what its causes were and what it meant shifted over the centuries. While, in Antiquity, a river might have been considered an entity in and of itself, deciding of its own volition when to flood, during the early middle ages, floods came to be understood as a signal of important happenings, or as a sign of bad moral behaviour. Later, people started to understand their relationship to rivers differently, and, using technical solutions, they tried to tame them. Such shifting perspectives existed in parallel, since many different groups of people each found themselves experiencing flooding issues. But also, an individual could contribute by building dikes one day and join a procession against flooding the next day. The various concepts people have with regards to flooding influence the way they deal with this problem[11].

The present project covers topics, which have yet to be thoroughly explored in the Rhine area. Various river landscapes in Western Europe have more extensive and earlier records and relicts of dike-building than the Upper Rhine Valley. The first hard evidence of dike-building in the Netherlands comes from the diocese of Utrecht. The »Lekdijk Bovendams« was an early 12th century AD dike built in order to enable land reclamation in the frequently flooded area between Utrecht and the Utrechtse Heuvelrug. Reclamations and their associated canal and dam building were already common practice in this area at that time[12]. The levees along the Loire, on the other hand, are one of the first parallel dikes in France. According to Dion, the oldest parts can be dated back at least to the 12th century AD[13]. Our research aims to provide a body of data to enable comparisons with other big rivers in Western Europe. This will shed new light on the spread of ideas and techniques relating to water management and dealing with flooding. Far more than a local historical overview of the Upper Rhine Valley and its flood dynamics, this research aims to contribute to a western European understanding of flooding and the medieval response to it.

WHAT DO WE ALREADY KNOW?

The Rhine we know today is not like the Rhine during the medieval period. Before the Tulla rectification in the 19th century AD, the Rhine was not completely diked, which gave the river far more space to extend its braids and meanders, change its course and create or engulf islands. The more »natural« landscape of swampy grasslands and closed off river arms had a bigger influence on fluvial dynamics and the lack of dikes resulted in a higher risk of flooding. Nevertheless, settlements and agriculture have been recorded within this flood plain for many centuries[14].

For the Rhine section between Strasbourg (dép. Bas-Rhin/F) and Mannheim (Baden-Württemberg/D), the earliest records of flood protection found in written sources suggest an early flood protection to have been built near the medieval bishop's see of Speyer (Rhineland-Palatinate/D). According to his vita, Bishop Benno II of Osnabrück (Lower Saxony/D), the architect of phase II of the cathedral of Speyer, is said to have protected this cathedral against the oncoming river as early as the 1080s AD with a huge mass of boulders[15]. The next sources mentioning a flood defence in the Upper Rhine Valley date to 1294 AD, thus, more than two centuries later: The villagers of Eggenstein (Lkr. Karlsruhe/D) obtained help from the Cistercian monks of Maulbronn (Enzkreis/D) in order to clean the rim of the river terrace. But we should bear in mind that these works refer not to a dam, but rather to the »natural« riverbank, and that the sources do not clearly indicate that this measure was regarded as a defence against flooding or, at least, against erosion – although this is highly probable[16]. While the case of Speyer roughly meets the age of the Dutch and French examples, the subsequent lack of any remarks on dike-building in the Upper Rhine Valley for more than 200 years is striking and increases our curiosity as to the lack of such evidence.

One of the preconditions of diking in the Upper Rhine Valley, as elsewhere, is the technical ability to dike. Several examples of technical water management are known from the Carolingian era onwards. On the Danish Island of Samsø, 8th century AD Vikings built a canal for navel defensive purposes and to shortcut the shipping route around the island[17]. In today's Germany, a canal was built as early as 793 AD, not only to shorten a shipping route, but to cross the European main watershed between the Danube (flowing to the Black Sea) and the Main (draining into the North Sea). This so-called Karlsgraben shows a developed understanding of nature and the technical ability to deal with water management issues[18]. Centuries later, and even closer to the Upper Rhine Valley, the monks of Maulbronn demonstrated confidence in their own technical expertise by living in their monastery beneath the 10m high dam they had built to contain their provisioning lake[19]. Building this dam and trusting it to last clearly demonstrates the capability of mid-12th century AD Cistercian Monks[20]. The influence of the monastery of Maulbronn within the Upper Rhine Valley is recorded multiple times and it may therefore be assumed that their technical knowledge spread over the Upper Rhine Valley during the late 12th and 13th century AD. Another indication of the technical ability of medieval water managers is derived from the 13th century AD manuscript of the Sachsenspiegel, which also refers to dike building. Although the various copies of the Sachsenspiegel claim to be of Carolingian age, they are considered as a fraudulent production of the 13th century AD. It can, however, yet be stated based on this text that dike building was known along the Elbe and its tributaries at least from the 13th century AD onward[21].

Various authors have studied records of flooding in written sources over the centuries. Among others, Weikinn, Gottschalk and, more recently, the website Tambora.org have gathered and organized the records from historical and archival sources that mention floods during the medieval period[22]. Over 25 of these records include floods that were recorded specifically for the Upper Rhine Valley, and which are listed in **table 1**. It should be kept in mind, however, that, during the medieval period, the intensity of writing increased as did the details of the records. Therefore, we may assume that during the early and high medieval

year	month	country	location	source
711		Germany	Rhine	Weikinn 1958
815		Germany	Rhine	Gottschalk 1974
850		West-Germany	Rhine	Gottschalk 1974
857		South-Germany		Weikinn 1958
868		West-Germany	Rhine	Gottschalk 1974
886		Germany	Rhine	Gottschalk 1974
987		Germany	Rhine	Weikinn 1958
1012		Germany	Rhine	Weikinn 1958
1086	January	Germany	All rivers	Weikinn 1958
1097		West-Germany	South-, West- and North-Germany	Gottschalk 1974
1124		Germany	Rhine	Weikinn 1958
1150		West-Germany	Strasbourg	Gottschalk 1974
1152	January	West-Germany	Strasbourg	Gottschalk 1974/tambora.org
1170	September	Germany	South	Weikinn 1958
1174		Germany	Rhine	Weikinn 1958
1184	November	France	Strasbourg	Alexandre 1987
1198	January	France	Strasbourg	tambora.org
1206	December	Germany/France	Rhine	Weikinn 1958
1246		Germany	Rhine	Weikinn 1958
1258	March	Germany	Worms	tambora.org
1260		Germany	Rhine	Weikinn 1958
1269	January	Germany	Black Forest	tambora.org
1270		France	Alsace and Basel	Gottschalk 1974
1280		France	Alsace	Weikinn 1958
1281	February	France	Alsace	tambora.org
1286		Germany	Rhine	Weikinn 1958
1290		France	Rhine	Weikinn 1958
1295		Germany	Upper Rhine	Weikinn 1958

Tab. 1 Records of Upper Rhine floods on the section from Strasbourg to Mannheim, between 700 and 1300 AD.

period only catastrophic floods with a high impact, causing much damage and many casualties, were recorded at the best and it is possible that more and even disastrous floods occurred, but were not recorded. Based on only the written records of medieval flooding in the Upper Rhine Valley, it could be inferred that the Rhine did not experience less flooding during the medieval period, as did the Rhône. However, our project aims to contrast this assumption with geophysical data to control for the difference from the Rhône Valley and to verify the reliability of historical sources.

After the Rhine found its current flood plain thousands of years ago during the early Pleistocene, both drainage of rainwaters and melting waters flowed through the Upper Rhine Valley, depositing fluvial sediments in various layers over the alluvial plain. The decay of the river influences its character; south of Strasbourg, the Rhine is a braided river, while north of Strasbourg it gradually becomes a more meandering river. Resulting from a dynamic alternation between periods of erosion and sedimentation, the braiding part is characterized by the rise and engulfing of small islands caused by flooding. Bypasses and changes of riverbeds during flooding, responsible for the creation of multiple former arms of the Rhine, characterize the meandering section of the river[23]. The multitude of islands and former Rhine arms indicate a long history of flooding in which the Rhine was the main driving force of the Upper Rhine Valley landscape. In order to reconstruct a high resolution flooding history for the Upper Rhine section from Strasbourg to Mannheim, it would be necessary to combine an enormous number of soil samples with extended LiDAR and aerial photograph analysis. This, however, goes beyond the scope of our current research. Nevertheless, small-scale explorations will be executed within the specified case study areas.

It has been widely debated that the alternating periods of erosion and sedimentation might have been caused by climatological fluctuations. Is it possible that, after the cooling during the early middle ages (6th-9th century AD), temperatures rose again in the 10th century AD[24]? That would correspond quite well with the aforementioned period of increasing erosion in the Rhône Valley and the period of dike-building in the Netherlands. And if it is true that temperatures went down again during the 14th century's AD medieval Little Ice Age, questions may be asked as to whether flooding increased during warm or cold periods and, therefore, if irregularities in flooding were indeed caused by climatological conditions or depended much more on cultural factors[25].

Therefore, besides geophysical and climatological arguments for flooding, it should be taken into account that human factors may contribute to flooding as well. For example, deforestation causes a higher overland water discharge; less water is absorbed by trees and plants and, on top of that, an absence of trees can lead to an increase of erosion. This especially counts for areas with loess soils, like many parts of the Upper Rhine Valley. It should be more thoroughly studied as to whether an increase of erosion bringing more sediments into rivers results in higher river bottoms and increasing flooding[26]. Also, the effects of early dike-building upon a river's sedimentation and erosion ought to be examined, and indeed an exploration of this is taken into account in the context of the case studies during this research[27]. Therefore, sedimentological and geochemical studies in the context of dikes have to be applied, as they may record climate and/or human influence of river dynamics. During the last millennium, the sediments point to a shift from slow and constant sedimentation towards more discontinuous and more rapid sedimentation at the transition to the Little Ice Age[28]. This includes Alpine sediments, but also alluvial loam which consists of loess-derived material from the lowermost slopes of the Black Forest as well as the foreland (»Weinstraße«) of the Palatinate forest[29].

Within this project, we not only question the causes of flooding, but also aim to gain some understanding of various local perceptions of flooding (second and third hypothesis): Has flooding always been perceived as a problem? How did various actors perceive flooding over the centuries?

Since high water often does not occur as suddenly as, for example, an earthquake, it leaves people with enough time to evacuate their valuables. In the medieval period, people owned far less than we do nowadays and some of their most valuable belongings, their cattle, could have either walked to higher ground or been transported out by boat[30]. Since this was certainly not the case for cereals and other crops, more reflection is necessary on what were valuables endangered by and protected from flooding. The wattle and daub houses of Central Europe that people lived in during the early and high medieval period probably sustained hardly any damage from the waters of a flood (but may have been threatened by driftwood), and if valuables were stored on higher levels under the roof, an inundation will have hardly affected these possessions. It might be argued that, to medieval people, a flood was not so different from heavy snowfall: it is inconvenient for a number of days, but afterwards, the people move on with their daily lives. As long as flooding did not threaten human valuables, causing damage and death among society, it was probably perceived as merely a natural event of little interest and not as a disaster at all[31]. One contributor to an increasing perception of flooding as a disaster could be the population growth of the 12th and 13th centuries AD. Whereas small farmsteads could previously produce all the food they needed on the river levee, a growing population demanded more efficiency and proper drainage of adjacent wetlands[32]. In this argument, flood-

ing first becomes perceived as a problem, when lands threatened by inundation become indispensable for society. As stated, the inconveniences of flooding might, until that time, have simply been considered a part of living alongside a river.
Another change in perception is based in a shifting worldview among various actors, for example, caused by the growing importance of monasteries and the emergence of the Cistercian order during the 11th and 12th century AD and the growth of towns with markets and an early capitalist rationality. It is argued that Cistercians were the first monastic order that aimed to finish God's work on earth and cultivate the wilderness to turn it into paradise[33]. This perspective enabled Cistercians to manipulate their environment in accord with the divine creation of nature, god's will and the bible – and this was a high contrast to previous perceptions regarding the manipulation of nature as disobedience to the divine providence. Changing the worldview in the Cistercian way might have greatly contributed to flooding no longer being perceived as subject to divine will, and towards a developing confidence in one's ability to control the natural event of flooding in accordance with this divine will. When studying such arguments, it should be considered that medieval sources often reproduce the knowledge and worldviews of a literate elite of the church. Since we cannot take for granted that they were the ones who built flood protections, other medieval perspectives should also be taken into account. In order to find out what interest the most important actors had in dike-building, archival sources, toponyms and contextual literature are being studied. In addition, the influential position of various groups of actors is taken into account. Extending this study to consider the interests and influences of various stakeholders allows us to form an idea of the perception of flooding among such actors in medieval times.
The Church: The church elite assembled the most literate people of medieval times and the church could be considered the transferor of medieval knowledge to us, although often from a perspective that contributed to existing power relations. The church's primary interest in dike-building is assumed to have lain in extending their tax incomes[34], but, as stated above, religious reasons may have been the driving force behind expanded cultivation of the land[35]. In accord with most historians we assume that the influence of the church was outstanding. The extended network of churches, chapels and monasteries made it easy to spread their ideas. Because the church possessed many servants and widely owned land, it was able to conduct large-scale infrastructure projects like the Maulbronn dam. In a greatly simplified sketch of the medieval church, it could be expected that, around the 12th century AD, it perceived flooding as a punishment from God meant to motivate its followers towards good moral behaviour and respect of his power and that of the church[36].
Servants and peasants: Since peasants or servants (unfree) and other kinds of agricultural workers were by far the largest group in the rural medieval Upper Rhine Valley, they should be taken into account. But studying their ideas and worldviews is quite difficult, since they were hardly literate. The best idea of how peasants lived and what they believed can be gained from archaeological research supplemented with tax books, toponyms and a few medieval manuscripts and illustrations[37]. An interest in dike-building for peasants is undeniable. Peasants live off the land; their crops, husbandry and houses would be under threat of damage during flooding. However, their influence on building dikes at this point of research is unclear. On the one hand, they depended on landowners and, on the other hand, they could have formed a cooperative together[38]. It can be expected that peasants would have benefited from controlling the river, but their complex interconnectedness with the church makes the possibility of their sharing a perception of flooding as a punishment from God feasible as well[39].
Landlords: Secular as well as ecclesiastical landlords owned huge areas of land in the Upper Rhine Valley and some medieval tax records provide insight into their perception of the land. The high medieval landlords were engaged mainly in increasing economic profit, and therefore, their interest in dike-building

would have been acute. In the Netherlands and France, there are also some examples of dikes having been built in order to inundate lands for military purposes[40]. Besides their economic interest in dike-building as landowners, wealthy landlords would have been in a position to gather the manpower necessary to conduct such large-scale building projects and would have had sufficient influence to do so. Thus, it could be expected that landlords perceived flooding as a danger to their economic profits and power and, therefore, wished to exert control upon the river, although, again, the influence of the church leaves open other possible perceptions, which might lead to moral conflicts especially in the case of ecclesiastical landowners[41].

In our research, we are looking for clues to who started building dikes and what their social impact was; beyond simplified and roughly cut models of the medieval society and its groups. We take into account complex, ill-defined and changing forms of cooperation between the groups specified above, and beyond their limits. Especially the location of dikes can provide enlightening clues – e. g. whether medieval people aimed to protect their houses and settlements, or their fields and harvests, or their meadows. Such hypotheses leave us with many and various questions, to be answered by an interdisciplinary approach combining both natural scientific methods and archaeological and historical sources.

WHICH SOURCES DO WE USE?

For the purpose of this project, we regard flood defences like dikes as interactions between man and nature. The landscape element »dike«, often built from natural materials, aims to protect human culture against »natural« events like flooding, which in themselves are partly induced by nature, partly by cultural behaviour. Knowledge of river systems is essential (geomorphology, hydrology and geology), but cultural factors also become evident on a dike (construction techniques, social cooperation, maintenance). Dikes do not occur naturally; they are always man-made cultural expressions. Locations and technical construction are as heavily influenced by cultural factors, as they are by natural environmental factors. Dikes, being exactly on the crossing point between nature and culture, ask for an integral and interdisciplinary approach[42].

Therefore, an interdisciplinary approach is necessary for this project. Geophysical measurements require a more specific study area and provide only scientific data. Historical and archaeological research can add a narrative to the case study and provide a broader understanding of the dike-building history in the context of the Upper Rhine Valley. At the same time, archival sources and toponyms provide a multitude of assumptions, which can be supported by providing data gathered through natural scientific methods.

The natural aspects of a dike, its location in relation to the river and to soils, can best be studied through scientific methods. GIS analysis on LiDAR-data, soil data and hydrological maps are essential as an explorative step. Especially the LiDAR-data and aerial photographs contribute to the selection of potential former dike lines. Although special attention is given to unnatural linear structures on the maps, former river arms are also studied more specifically. On aerial photographs, land-use is taken into account in order to gather an understanding of the underlying landscape as formed by rivers.

Once a spot is selected, we conduct geoelectric resistivity measurements. Geoelectric tomography is a non-destructive geophysical method used to determine apparent electrical resistivity (unit Ωm) by feeding direct current into the subsurface. A Geotom 200/100 RES/IP multi-electrode system from GEOLOG2000 is used. This system automatically switches 100 electrodes in a four-point arrangement in series and produces a vertical 2D pseudo-section of the subsurface. Whenever the geoelectric resistivity measurements provided promising results, and in order to calibrate the geophysical data by comparing them to the sedimentology, supplementary cores are taken.

In percussion drilling, a core is hammered into the ground providing undisturbed soil samples within in liner tube of 5 cm diameter. Corings are done in sections of 1 m, but can go as deep as six or more metres. On each of our geoelectric lines, three corings are performed, one on both sides of the potential dike and one in the middle of the dike. In the laboratories, the pipes are opened up for more detailed research. Besides a detailed sketch of each coring, organic materials are collected for ^{14}C-dating to infer on the age of the sediments and – probably – of the dike. The corings on both sides of the dike should show several variations in soil material, since, on the river side, fluvial sediments like gravel and sand continued to be accumulated, while, inside the diked area, an anthropogenic or humus layer could be expected on the surface, depending on the land use. By lining up the soil profiles along the geoelectric line (corrected in topographic height) it provides a detailed stratigraphy without heavily disturbing the soil. Additionally, grain-size, colour and mineral studies can be carried out to collect more information on the origin of the sediments.

In order to understand the cultural aspects of a dike, multiple and varied methods are required. Archaeological analysis on the technical construction of the dike provides information on human possibilities, the transfer and appropriation of knowledge, and the network of the builders. It might, by contextualisation, also provide a clue towards dating the dike by ^{14}C- or OSL-methods. In addition, in studying these technical aspects, various archival sources might provide a broader understanding of the local society during the building of a dike. It costs a lot of time to build a dike, and it will not function if it is not connected to adjacent dikes. It is therefore hardly imaginable that a dike would not be built by a cooperative of various stakeholders. The building process of a dike could, thus, contain information on contemporary societies, power relationships, societal hierarchy, but also on local rural agency. The administration of these building activities can provide valuable insights into the construction process, although such archival sources are rare in early and high medieval times.

Understanding the location of a dike can – alongside the scientific approach – be studied through historical maps as well. These maps might show important settlements nearby, trade routes, river crossings or areas relevant for military purposes that might have influenced the location of a dike. In the Upper Rhine region, historical maps go back to the 16th century AD and should be carefully taken into account, since mapmakers often developed their maps with certain purposes in mind, which means a map is hardly ever objective[43].

Toponyms could provide additional information on an area leading back further in history. Besides the functions of fields and grassland, toponyms provide insights into former values and the meaning of a landscape. However, field names and toponyms might have changed their places and/or meaning over the centuries and their origin might not always be clear and unambiguous; they, nevertheless, provide valuable insight into the environmental perception of former societies.

Elaborating on these natural and historical methods, a spatial study on a landscape cannot be executed without personally standing in the field, as suggested by Matthew Johnson, who supports his recommendation based on iconic landscape researchers W. G. Hoskins and George Muir[44]. Several field surveys of the study area can provide a depth of knowledge which cannot be gathered from behind the desk. Ecological data tell the story of a landscape, but also an understanding of distances, viewsheds e. g. towards the church tower and height differences of a few centimetres are important aspects to be ascertained while standing within a landscape and may lead to new insights. This additional type of knowledge about our study area narrowed down our selection of potential flood defences substantially. Areas that have been heavily disturbed in contemporary building projects or potential dams that still carry out a protective function, were eliminated. The most accessible and promising dikes were considered for a more detailed and thorough study in the archives, via a field name survey and by means of geo-electric measurements and corings. But still a further selection of potential historical dike lines had to be made on basis of an interdisciplinary set of resources: The northern part of the Upper Rhine Valley from Strasbourg to Mannheim was analysed geomorphologically and a relief was produced using available LiDAR-data. The first cadastral records of

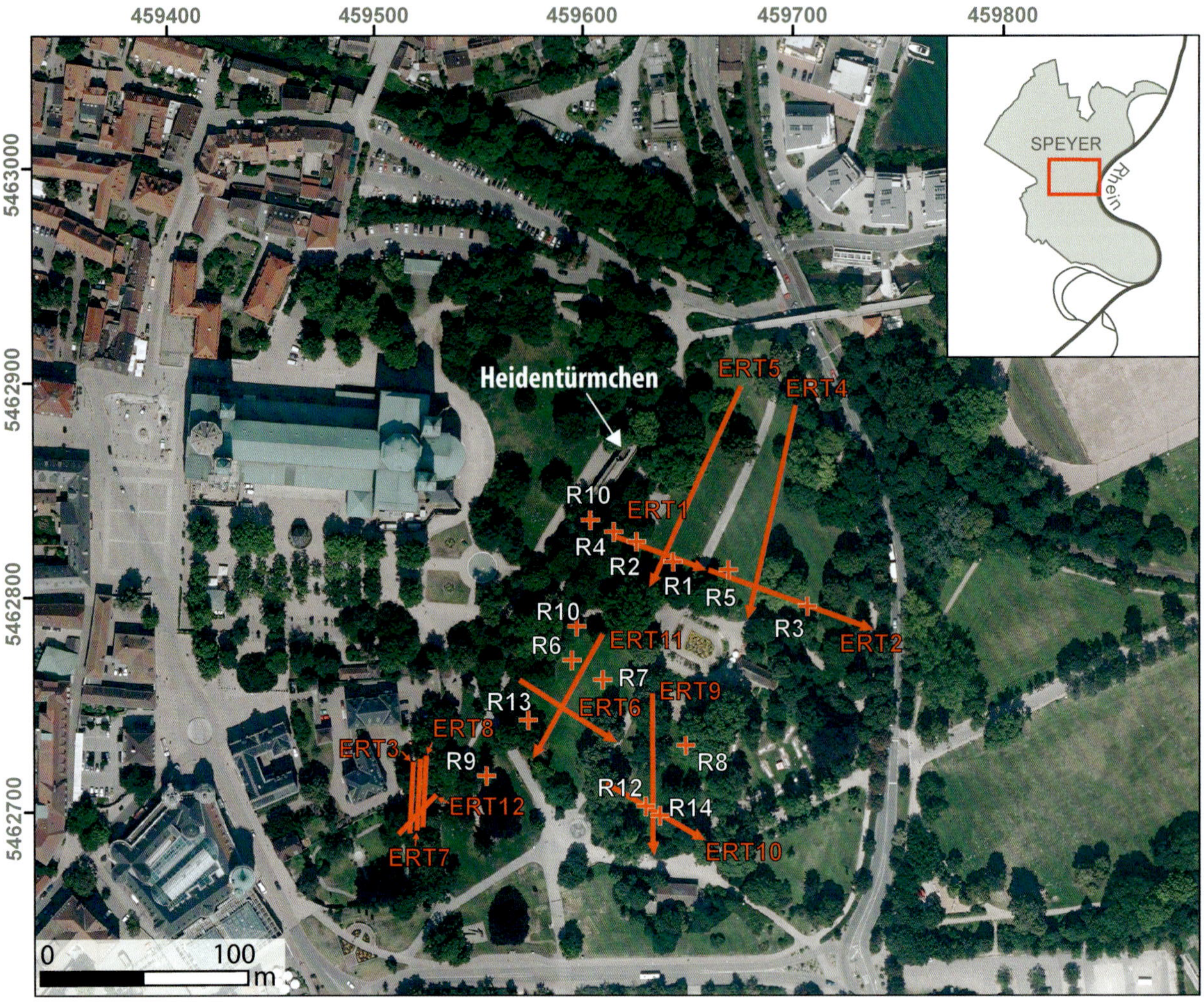

Fig. 2 Speyer-Domgarten locations of corings and geoelectric resistivity measurements. – (© Carsten Zube, based on GeoBasis-DE/LVermGeoRP2015-02-18).

villages were inventoried and mapped in GIS. Not only these first records, but also settlement names that are known to be pre-medieval or medieval, such as those ending in -heim, -ingen or -dorf, were selected[45] as they are – quite frequently – indicating settlements within the alluvial plain at least from the 8th century AD onward.

Employing the variety of methods described in the previous chapter has led to several case studies being undertaken, spread over the northern Upper Rhine Valley. Archival texts led us to case studies in the Domgarten of Speyer and at Daxlanden (Lkr. Karslruhe/D). Historical maps revealed dike lines at Au am Rhein, Iffezheim, Plittersdorf (all Lkr. Rastatt/D) and Mörsch (Lkr. Karlsruhe/D). Wilhelm Besserers 16th century AD »Kurpfälzische Rheinstromkarte« clearly shows various dikes along the Rhine, which provided us with the case studies of Beinheim (dép. Bas-Rhin/F), Neuburg (Lkr. Germersheim/D), Knielingen, Linkenheim (both Lkr. Karlsruhe/D) and Mechtersheim (Lkr. Rhein-Pfalz/D). Lastly, LiDAR-data clearly revealed a dike at Ottersdorf (Lkr. Rastatt/D), which could later be confirmed through archival sources. Since case studies for only a few of these potential dikes can be executed in more detail within the scope of this project, the most promising cases have been selected based on the oldest known records and the current accessibility of the site. In this paper, the case of the Domgarten in Speyer is discussed and some brief remarks are made in regards to our ongoing research at Ottersdorf.

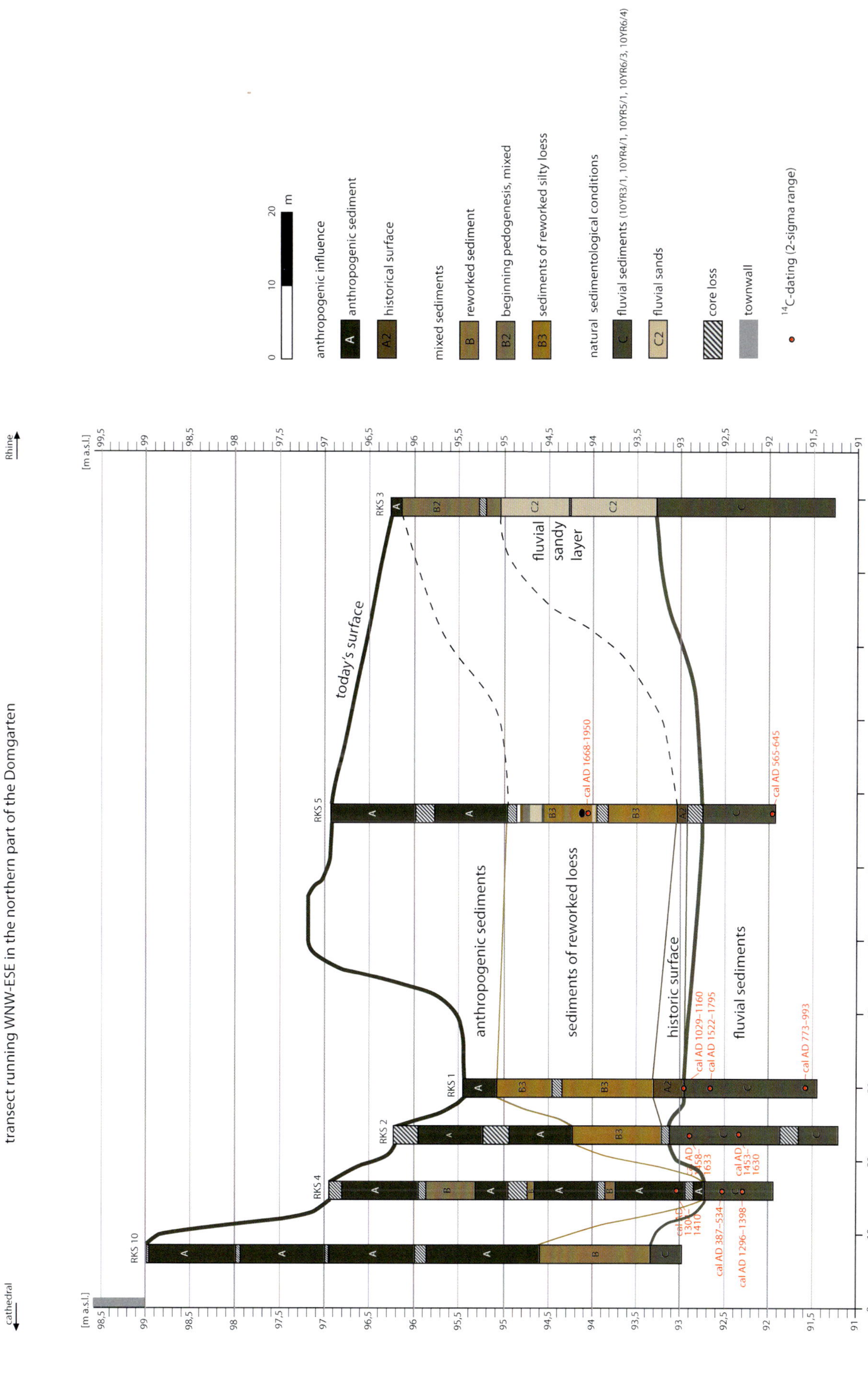

Fig. 3 Speyer-Domgarten corings section. – (© Carsten Zube).

Speyer-Domgarten

In 1080 AD, emperor Heinrich IV, ordered Benno II, bishop of Osnabrück, to refurbish the cathedral of Speyer (Speyer II), which was only a few decades old. A few years after Benno's death, Norbert, abbot of Iburg (Kr. Höxter/D), wrote Benno's biography, hoping to foster his former promoter's canonisation. Norbert briefly touches on Benno's building activities in Speyer, mentioning that the cathedral, due to its size, uncarefully stretched towards the bank of the Rhine and that Benno, among other innovations, constructed an immense mass of stone (»*immensas saxorum moles [obstruxit]*«), so that the cathedral would not be subverted by the rush of the river (»*ne fluminis illisione subverteretur*«)[46]. So far, it has been interpreted based on this that Benno built a dike or some other kind of flood protection at the foot of the offset on which Speyer cathedral is placed[47]. Since no evidence for this construction has ever been found, our research started from nothing in an effort to locate this alleged medieval flood protection[48].

The town of Speyer, which emerged in pre-Roman times, is located on the Western bank of the Upper Rhine in the country of Rhineland-Palatinate. Most parts of the town were located within the lower terrace. On the tip of the lower terrace, the cathedral of Speyer was built as an iconic landmark, visible from all surrounding directions, including from the river Rhine. It is known that Speyer had a harbour and it is therefore assumed that the town was originally located directly on the Rhine. Nowadays, the cathedral is situated about 500 m from the Rhine, because the river changed its course over the years and was straightened and diked by Tulla during the 19th century AD[49]. The cathedral on the land tongue is elevated about 7 m above the so-called Domgarten park, which is located within the alluvial plain and partially on the former riverbed. As a result of many centuries of human interference, the former course of the Rhine is not completely ascertainable. For this reason, it is also not easy to locate former flood defences. Since a former arm of the Rhine most probably crossed the Domgarten from south-west to north, geoelectric sections were laid out from west to east to capture the most interesting part with height differences and possible flood protections (**fig. 2**). Corings were taken along these lines in order to provide more detailed information. Additional north-south geoelectrics connected the east-west lines to provide a full picture of the subsurface.

Corings taken along the northernmost line show a variety of anthropogenic sediments on top, varying in thickness from 0.5 to 5 m, filling an old channel (**fig. 3**). The fact that these sediments are mixed could indicate fluvial activity, but this could also be caused by human disruption. Unfortunately, these mixed soils make it hard to decide, if a river once ran through the area. As a flowing river would have disturbed the sediments, it could be expected that the whole research area would consist of mixed layers. Since this is not the case, we assume that the thicker mixed areas (corings RKS2 & RKS4) are former channels of the Rhine, as is correspondingly derived from an 18th century AD map (**fig. 4**)[50]. The organic materials in a layer of fluvial sediments underneath, which date back from the 10th to the 16th century AD, also support this idea. All in all, the data indicates that this area was part of the riverbed during the 18th century AD and that, later, the channel was filled up with anthropogenic sediments and reworked organic material.

Coring RKS3 contains a fluvial sandy layer, which indicates a former river arm, corresponding with the geoelectric resistivity. At coring RKS5, no sandy sediment was found underneath the anthropogenic deposits, which are about 2 m thick at this point. Instead a 2 m layer of reworked loess can be recognized. Aeolic loess is widespread in the region, but makes little sense as a material used in anthropogenic flood protection, e. g. as an earthen wall, because loess is easily carried away by water. Instead, we assume that this material was deposited as result of increased erosion during the second half of the Little Ice Age in the surroundings and filled an old flood channel of the Rhine River. This would be consistent with ^{14}C-dating of organic materials. When combining these corings and geoelectric readings with the ^{14}C-dating of organic materials, it is expected that the Rhine, or an arm of the river, did indeed flow through the Domgarten around RKS5, already

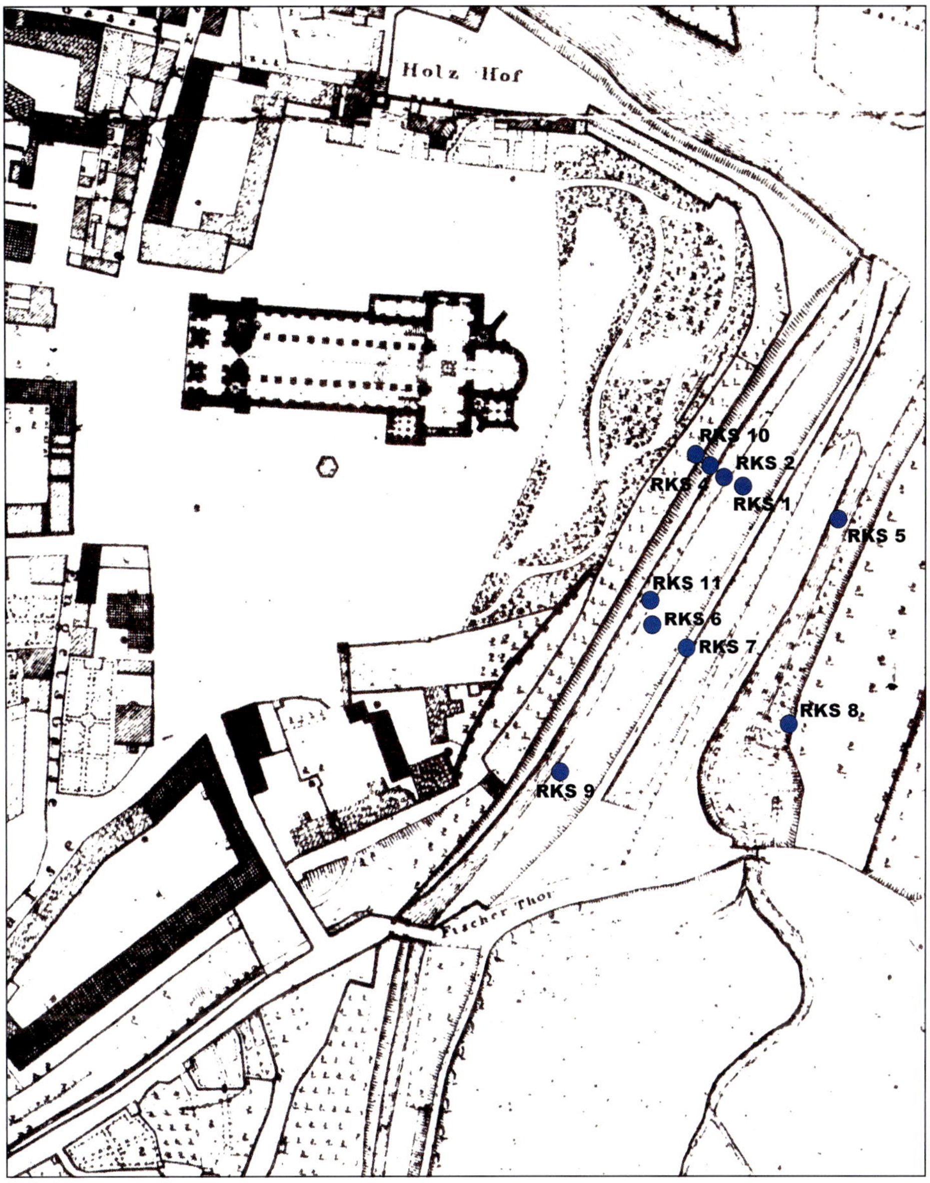

Fig. 4 Detail of Gabriel Bodenehr's map of Speyer (18th c.) showing the area of the cathedral and today's Domgarten; indicated are the spots of core drillings (based on a copper engraving by Gabriel Bodenehr, Stadtarchiv Speyer: 234_III-41).

before the 16th century AD (**fig. 3**). At the base, an old soil layer and material from the High Middle Ages may indicate the top of an older flood channel, active before the onset of the construction of the cathedral or at least filled up with organic material from the 7th and 9th century AD. Likely, this channel was reactivated during the time of bishop Benno.

To conclude, our tomographies and corings did not give any hint of a massive medieval flood protection, but they did indicate a former Rhine arm and, potentially, a later harbour channel, which is also indicated by early modern maps. Considering the narrow net of our geoelectric survey, hardly space is left for the alleged massive boulders of bishop Benno. Either they never existed as a flood protection at the foot of the terrace below the cathedral, or they were rather ineffective and the river has already transported them away in the course of numerous floods over the past centuries.

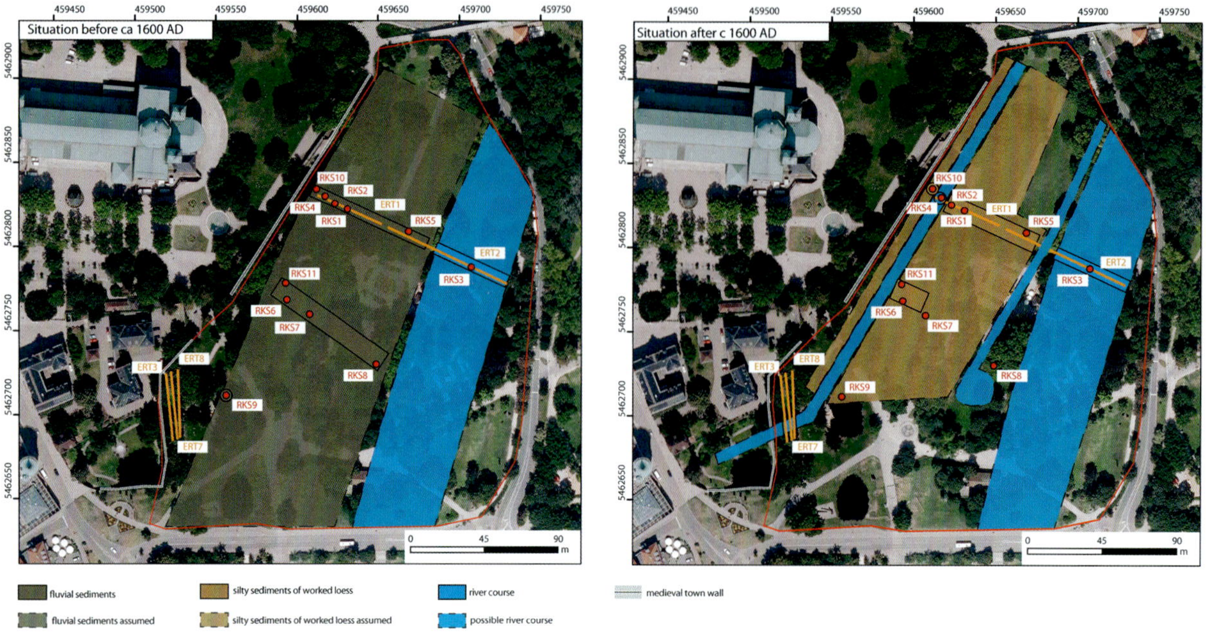

Fig. 5 Speyer-Domgarten plan sketch before and after about 1600 AD. – (© Carsten Zube, based on GeoBasis-DE/LVermGeoRP 2015-02-18).

Ottersdorf

Careful scanning of the LiDAR-data on unnatural looking linear elements, if possible parallel with a current or former river arm, provided us with the Ottersdorf dikes (**fig. 6**). Since the LiDAR-data show a clear line, it could be expected that this dike would also be visible in the field. A field visit confirmed our expectations and the west – east dike (**fig. 6, I-a-c**) was clearly visible in the forest. On analogy to modern dikes, we expected that a medieval dike would also be a linear element in the landscape, but, as visible on the LiDAR-image, several irregularities can be identified along the dike element. This is a clue indicating that the constructing of the dike, as can be seen nowadays, was done in several phases. These phases can be relatively dated, when looking at the dike's connections. A younger dike most probably connects to an earlier one in order to extend or adapt the protective system and reduce the chances of flooding. It is expected that the eastern and quite straight section of the west-east dike (**fig. 6, I-a**) is the oldest, followed by the middle section (**fig. 6, I-b**), while the western section (**fig. 6, I-c**) is expected to be the youngest. These suspicions are confirmed by the known regularity that a river meander always moves to its outside turn; therefore, it makes sense that the most recent breakthroughs or dike improvements would have occurred in this outer corner, as is the case at the Ottersdorf dike. The north – south dike (**fig. 6, II**) located east of the other one is assumed to be even older than the aforementioned dike I, since the parallel oriented elevations, indicating a large flood, are cut off by the old Rhine arm. This suggests that the north – south dike was already there during the flood that relocated the Rhine arm. Further field measurements should confirm these thoughts. An explanation for this hundreds of metres long dike along a now nearly dried out stream might be found in local historical accounts. According to historian Franz Ruf, the small stream used to be a former arm of the Rhine. Archives of the Wissembourg monastery show that the villages of Plittersdorf, Ottersdorf and Wintersdorf (all Lkr. Rastatt/D) used to be on the Alsacian side, i.e. the western bank of the Rhine, until the river chose a new path, probably during the 1306 AD flood, which demolished the Selz monastery (dép. Bas-Rhin/F)[51]. Other archival sources note that the former Rhine arm along our dike fell out of use for shipping around 1472 AD, when it was blocked for ships. It is, therefore, expected that the Ottersdorf dike

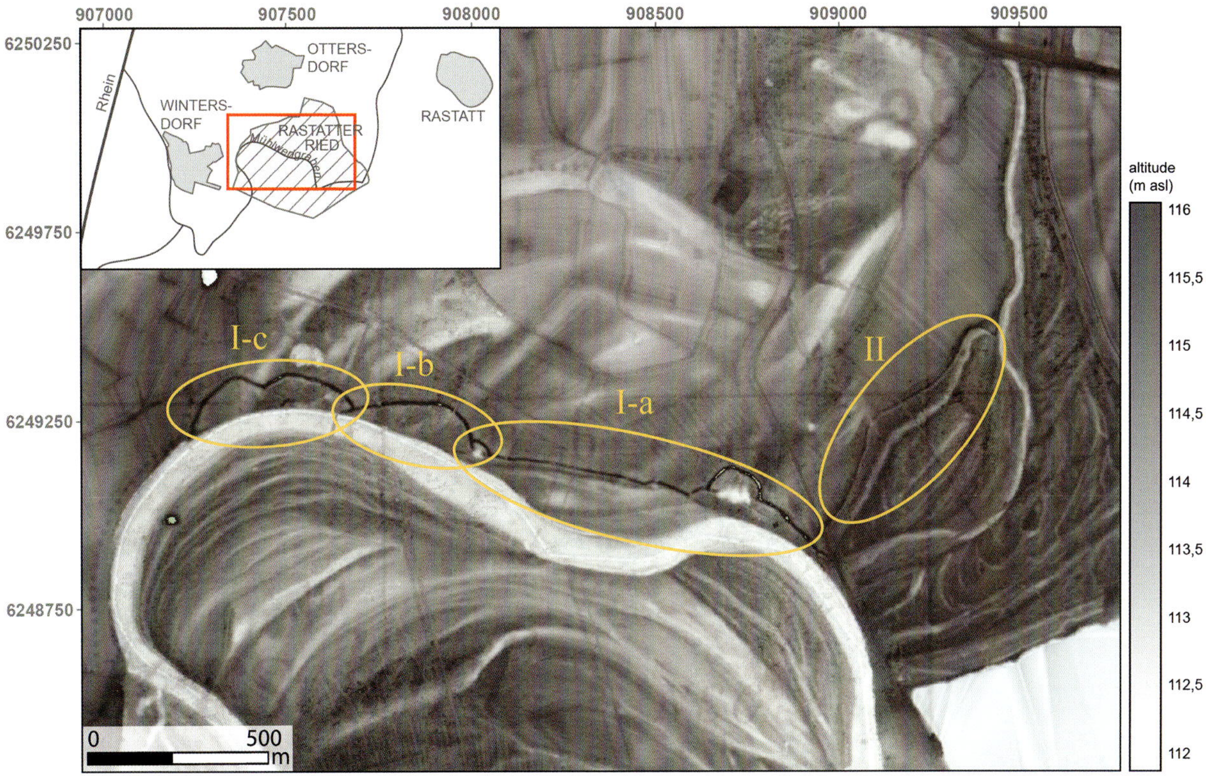

Fig. 6 Ottersdorf, various dike lines on LiDAR-data. – (Overlay of LiDAR-data [© Landesamt für Geoinformation und Landentwicklung Baden-Württemberg, www.lgl-bw.de] and TK50 Rastatt 2007, sheet L7114).

can be dated at least before 1472 AD and probably even before 1306 AD, which places it in a timeframe among the oldest known flood prevention measures in the region[52].

Exact dating of the dike is expected from geoarchaeological investigations like coring, geoelectric measurements and profile cuts through the dike during an archaeological campaign.

The context in which the dike was built will be reconstructed by extended archival studies on the tax books of the 15th century AD and interpretation of the landscape via soil data, hydrology, aerial photographs and LiDAR-data, and will be supported by historical maps and the local history from the Late Middle Ages. Additionally, actor-analysis and toponymical research will provide insights into the local perception of the medieval landscape and, therefore, contribute to our understanding of the environmental changes occurring there and the shifting relations between man and river.

(NO) CONCLUSIONS

Since this article aims only to set the scope of our research, we will not go into preliminary conclusions. Besides the case study selection and some brief results in Speyer and Ottersdorf, much more research is to be done. Archaeological excavations are still to be started and, in the end, the plurality of sources will be brought together. It is the aim of this research to develop a historical overview of flooding and flood protection in the northern Upper Rhine Valley from Strasbourg to Mannheim in order for this Rhine area to be compared to other European rivers like the Danube, the Loire and the Lower Rhine in the Netherlands. A comparison of these results can give us some insight into the medieval reaction to flooding and will provide us with ideas for future development on flooding.

Acknowledgements

We are cordially thankful to the Fritz Thyssen Foundation. Without the generous financial support of the foundation this study would not have been possible. Moreover, we want to thank the participants of the Dijon-meeting for their valuable questions and comments, from which this paper has benefited a lot. Nicolas Jansens has kindly corrected and much improved the language of our paper – but we insist that all faults and mistakes remain our own.

Notes

1) van de Ven 2004.
2) Musall 1969, 43. – Meier 2017, 24-25.
3) Dion 1961. – Zadora-Rio 2004.
4) Cf. van de Ven 2004.
5) Stouff 1993.
6) Berger/Brochier 2006.
7) Jerz/Peters 2002.
8) Groh/Kempe/Mauelshagen 2003, 11-33. – Meier 2005.
9) Rösener 1997. – Burnouf/Carcaud/Garcin 2002.
10) Meier 2005.
11) Haas/Stork 2016.
12) van de Ven 2004, 72.
13) Dion 1961. – Zadora-Rio 2004.
14) Blackbourn 2006, 2. – Faustmann 2007, 304 diagr. 30-31.
15) Vita Bennonis II, cap. 21.
16) Rückert 2005. – GLA 38/1379.
17) Nørgård Jørgensen 1998.
18) Ettel et al. 2014, IX-X.
19) Seidenspinner 1997.
20) Grewe 1991, 45.
21) Koschorreck 1989.
22) Weikinn 1958. – Gottschalk 1971. – Alexandre 1987. – Tambora.org (30.10.2017).
23) Jongmans et al. 2013, 379.
24) Abert, 2015, 49.
25) Hoffmann 2014, 75.
26) Bork et al. 1998, 221.
27) van de Ven et al. 1995, 50. – Jongmans et al. 2013, 464. – Cohen et al. 2009, 69.
28) Holzhauer et al. 2017.
29) Berner et al. 2012. – Hagedorn 2004.
30) van Dam 2012.
31) Meier 2005.
32) van de Ven et al. 1995, 24.
33) Duby 1989, 15. – Schouten 2005, 112.
34) Mol 1992.
35) Schouten 2005.
36) Haas/Stork 2016.
37) Epperlein 2003.
38) Stouff 1993. – Zadora-Rio 2004.
39) Haas/Stork 2016.
40) van de Ven 2004, 174.
41) Haas/Stork 2016.
42) Huijbens/Palsson 2015. – Kolen 2015.
43) Sabala 1997, 5.
44) Johnson 2007.
45) Musall 1969.
46) Vita Bennonis II, cap. 21.
47) Doll 1964, 478. – Klimm 1953, 16-17.
48 The rest of this chapter mainly follows Zube 2016.
49) Müller 1994, 90.
50) Bodenehr 18th century.
51) Glöckner/Doll 1979.
52) Ruf 1995.

Sources

Bodenehr 18th century: Kupferstich von Gabriel Bodenehr, Stadtarchiv Speyer: 234_III-41

GLA: Generallandesarchiv Karlsruhe, 38/1379.

Glöckner/Doll 1979: K. Glöckner / L. A. Doll, Traditiones Wizenburgenses – die Urkunden des Klosters Weissenburg 661-864 (Darmstadt 1979).

Vita Bennonis II: H. Bresslau (ed.), Vita Bennonis II. episcopi Osnabrugensis auctore Nortberto abbate Iburgensi. Monumenta Germaniae Historica. Scriptores rerum Germanicarum in usum scholarum ex Monumentis Germaniae historicis separatim editi 56 (Hannoverae, Lipsiae 1902).

References

Aberth 2015: J. Aberth, An Environmental History of the Middle Ages – The Crucible of Nature (New York 2015).

Alexandre 1987: P. Alexandre, Le Climat en Europe au Moyen Âge. Contribution à l'histoire des variations climatiques de 1000 à 1425, d'après les sources narratives de l'Europe occidentale. Recherches d'Histoire et de Sciences Sociales 24 (Paris 1987).

Berner et al. 2012: Z. A. Berner / S. Bleeck-Schmidt / D. Stüben / T. Neumann / M. Fuchs / M. Lehmann, Floodplain deposits: A geochemical archive of flood history – A case study on the River Rhine, Germany. Applied Geochemistry 27/3, 2012, 543-561.

Berger/Brochier 2006: J. F. Berger / J. L. Brochier, Paysages et climats en moyenne vallée du Rhône apports de la géo-archéologie. In: O. Maufras (ed.), Habitats, nécropoles et paysages dans la moyenne et la basse vallée de Rhône (VIIe-XVe Siècle). Contribution des travaux du TGV-Méditerranée à l'étude des sociétés rurales médiévales. Documents d'Archéologie Française 98 (Paris 2006) 163-208.

Blackbourn 2006: D. Blackbourn, The conquest of Nature (London 2006).

Bork et al. 1998: H. R. Bork / H. Bork / C. Dalchow / H. P. Piorr / Th. Schatz / B. Faust, Landschaftsentwicklung in Mitteleuropa. Wirkungen des Menschen auf Landschaften (Stuttgart 1998).

Burnouf/Carcaud/Garcin 2002: J. Burnouf / N. Carcaud / M. Garcin, Alea et risque dans la vallee de la Loire au Moyen Age: la question des »levees« (le cas de la »Loire océanique entre Tours et Angers«). In: G. Helmig / B. Scholkmann / M. Untermann (eds), Centre, region, periphery, Medieval Europe Basel 2002. Preprinted papers. 3rd International Conference of Medieval and Later Archeology, Basel (Switzerland) 10.-15. September 2002 (Basel 2002) 44-49.

Cohen et al. 2009: K. M. Cohen et al., Sand-depth maps of the central and upper Rhine-Meuse delta, including the IJssel valley (Arnhem 2009).

van Dam 2012: P. J. E. M. van Dam, De amfibische cultuur: Een visie op watersnoodrampen (Amsterdam 2012).

Doll 1964: A. Doll, Stadtpläne aus dem Anfang des 19. Jahrhunderts I. Speyer 1820. In: W. Alter (ed.), Pfalzatlas. Textband I (Speyer 1964) 478-486.

Dion 1961: R. Dion, Histoire des levées de la Loire. Annales de Bretagne 68/3, 1961, 491-494.

Duby 1989: G. Duby, L'art Cistercien, Flammarion (Paris 1989).

Epperlein 2003: S. Epperlein, Bäuerliches Leben im Mittelalter. Schriftquellen und Bildzeugnisse (Köln, Weimar, Wien 2003).

Ettel et al. 2014: P. Ettel / F. Daim / S. Berg-Hobohm / L. Werther / Ch. Zielhofer (eds), Großbaustelle 793. Das Kanalprojekt Karls des Großen zwischen Rhein und Donau. Mosaiksteine. Forschungen am RGZM 11 (Mainz 2014).

Faustmann 2007: A. C. Faustmann, Besiedlungswandel im südlichen Oberrheingebiet von der Römerzeit bis zum Mittelalter. Freiburger Beiträge zur Archäologie und Geschichte des ersten Jahrtausends 10 (Rahden/Westf. 2007).

Gottschalk 1971: M. K. E. Gottschalk, Stormvloeden en rivieroverstromingen in Nederland. I: De Periode voor 1400. Sociaal-Geografische Studies 10 (Assen 1971).

Grewe 1991: K. Grewe, Wasserversorgung und -entsorgung im Mittelalter. Ein technikgeschichtlicher Überblick. In: Frontinus-Gesellschaft e. V. (ed.), Die Wasserversorgung im Mittelalter. Geschichte der Wasserversorgung 4 (Mainz 1991) 9-86.

Groh/Kempe/Mauelshagen 2003: D. Groh / M. Kempe / F. Mauelshagen, Naturkatastrophen. Beiträge zu ihrer Deutung, Wahrnehmung und Darstellung in Text und Bild von der Antike bis ins 20. Jahrhundert. Literatur und Anthropologie 13 (Tübingen 2003).

Haas/Stork 2016: Th. Haas / K. Stork, Hochwasser, Schutz, Konflikte. Eine transdisziplinäre Perspektive. Akademie-Konferenzen 22 (Heidelberg 2016) 9-32.

Hagedorn 2004: E. M. Hagedorn, Sedimentpetrographie und Lithofazies der jungtertiären und quartären Sedimente im Oberrheingebiet (Köln 2004).

Hoffmann 2014: R. C. Hoffmann, An Environmental History of Medieval Europe (Cambridge 2014).

Holzhauer et al. 2017: I. Holzhauer / A. Kadereit / G. Schukraft / B. Kromer / O. Bubenzer, Spatially heterogeneous relief changes, soil formation and floodplain aggradation under human impact – geomorphological results from the Upper Rhine Graben (SW Germany). Zeitschrift für Geomorphologie, Supplementary Issues 61/1, 2017, 121-158.

Huijbens/Palsson 2015: E. Huijbens / G. Palsson, The Marsh of Modernity. In: J. Kolen / H. Renes / R. Hermans (eds), Landscape Biographies. Geographical, historical and archaeological perspectives on the production and transmission of landscapes (Amsterdam 2015) 49-70.

Jerz/Peters 2002: H. Jerz / M. Peters, Flussdynamik der Donau bei Ingolstadt in vorgeschichtlicher, geschichtlicher und heutiger Zeit, mit Ergebnissen zur Landschafts- und Vegetationsentwicklung. Katastrophe oder Chance? Hochwasser und Ökologie. In: Rundgespräche der Kommission für Ökologie 24 (München 2002) 95-108.

Johnson 2007: M. Johnson, Ideas of Landscape (Oxford 2007).

Jongmans et al. 2013: A. G. Jongmans / M. W. van den Berg / M. P. W. Sonneveld / G. J. W. C. Peek / R. M. van den Berg van Saparoea, Landschappen van Nederland. Geologie, bodem en landgebruik (Wageningen 2013).

Klimm 1953: F. Klimm, Der Kaiserdom zu Speyer (Speyer 1953).

Kolen 2015: J. Kolen, Biographies of Biotopes. In: J. Kolen / H. Renes / R. Hermans (eds), Landscape Biographies. Geographical, historical and archaeological perspectives on the production and transmission of landscapes (Amsterdam 2015) 71-98.

Koschorreck 1989: W. Koschorreck, Der Sachsenspiegel (Frankfurt am Main 1989).

Meier 2005: Th. Meier, Archäologie und Naturereignis. Siedlungsforschung. Archäologie – Geschichte – Geographie 23, 2005, 253-290.

2017: Th. Meier, Potentiale und Risiken der Umweltarchäologie. In: S. Brather / J. Dendorfer (eds), Grenzen, Räume und Identitäten. Der Oberrhein und seine Nachbarregionen von der Antike bis zum Hochmittelalter. Archäologie und Geschichte – Freiburger Forschungen zum ersten Jahrtausend in Südwestdeutschland 22 (Ostfildern 2017) 13-53.

Mol 1992: J. A. Mol, Middeleeuwse kloosters en dijkbouw in Friesland. In: J. J. J. M. Beenakker / H. S. Danner (eds), Strijd tegen het water. Het beheer van land en water in het Zuiderzeegebied (Zutphen 1992) 21-34.

Müller 1994: K. R. Müller, Die Mauern der Freien Reichsstadt Speyer (Speyer 1994).

Musall 1969: H. Musall, Die Entwicklung der Kulturlandschaft der Rheinniederung zwischen Karlsruhe und Speyer am Ende des 16. Jahrhunderts bis Ende des 19. Jahrhunderts. Geographische Arbeiten 22 (Heidelberg 1969).

Nørgård Jørgensen 1998: A. Nørgård Jørgensen, The Kanhave Canal on Samsø – New investigations, In: Chateau Gaillard. Études de Castellologie médiévale XVIII (Caen 1998) 153-157.

Rösener 1997: W. Rösener, Einführung in die Agrargeschichte (Darmstadt 1997).

Rückert 2005: P. Rückert, Hochwasser und Flussbau – Zur anthropogenen Gestaltung der Flusslandschaft am Oberrhein im späteren Mittelalter. Siedlungsforschung. Archäologie – Geschichte – Geographie 23, 2005, 113-130.

Ruf 1995: F. Ruf, Ortschronik Ottersdorf (Rastatt 1995).

Sabala 1997: M. Sabala, Kulturlandschaften am Oberrhein in alten und neuen Karten [exhibition catalogue] (Karlsruhe 1997).

Schouten 2005: M. Schouten, Spiegel der Natur (Utrecht 2005).

Seidenspinner 1997: W. Seidenspinner, Kloster und Landschaft – Zum Problem einer Morphologie der Kulturlandschaft aus denkmalpflegerischer Perspektive am Beispiel der historischen Funktionseinheit Kloster Maulbronn. In: Landesdenkmalamt Baden-Württemberg (ed.), Maulbronn – zur 850-jährigen Geschichte des Zisterzienserklosters. Forschungen und Berichte der Bau- und Kunstdenkmalpflege in Baden-Württemberg 7 (Stuttgart 1997) 555-574.

Stouff 1993: L. Stouff, La lutte contre les eaux dans les pays du bas Rhône (XIIe-XVe s.). L'exemple du pays d'Arles. Méditerranée 78/3-4, 1993, 57-68.

van de Ven 2004: G. P. van de Ven, Man-made Lowlands. History of water management and land reclamation in the Netherlands (Utrecht 2004).

van de Ven et al. 1995: G. P. van de Ven / A. M. A. J. Driessen / W. Wolters / J. Wasser, Niets is bestendig – de geschiedenis van rivieroverstromingen in Nederland (Utrecht 1995).

Weikinn 1958: C. Weikinn, Quellentexte zur Witterungsgeschichte Europas von der Zeitwende bis zum Jahre 1850. I: Hydrographie 1. Quellensammlung zur Hydrographie und Meteorologie 1, 1 (Berlin 1958).

Zadora-Rio 2004: E. Zadora-Rio, Aménagements hydrauliques et inférences socio-politiques: Études de cas au moyen age. In: J. Burnouf / P. Leveau (eds), Fleuves et marais, une histoire au croisement de la nature et de la culture. Sociétés pre-industriélles et milieu fluviaux. Lacustres et palustres: Pratiques sociales et hydrosystèmes. Archéologie et Histoire de l'Art 19 (Paris 2004) 387-393.

Zube 2016: C. Zube, Fluviale Dynamik im Bereich des Speyerer Domgartens [unpubl. B.A. thesis, Univ. Heidelberg 2016].

Summary

»Land unter? – Hochwasser und Hochwasserschutz am Oberrhein während des frühen und hohen Mittelalters«, an interdisciplinary research project at the University of Heidelberg, funded by the Fritz Thyssen Foundation, aims at developing a regional history of floods and flood prevention measures based on archaeological and geomorphological studies on the Upper Rhine between Strasbourg and Mannheim.

While it appears to us today that floods must always have been perceived as a problem because of the great damage they can cause, it is not, in fact, self-evident that this was the case in the past. On the one hand, the cultural perception may have changed: Floods have probably come to be a real problem/disaster only as more and more valuables (e.g. cornfields, houses and facilities) have accumulated in the floodplains. In this project, we take the presence of dikes to be an indicator of a cultural perception of floods as a hazard, because dikes are labour- and cost-intensive projects that only provide a return on investment if immediate danger is expected. On the other hand, as the frequency and magnitude of floods depend on the regional climate and the intensity of agricultural activity, we cannot therefore proceed from our understanding of present environmental conditions, but must reconstruct from geoarchaeological sources a chronology of regional flood dynamics.

The project's main focus is to establish just such a history of flooding on the Upper Rhine in the Middle Ages and to identify the lines of early dikes in the field. Taking a multi-methodological approach, our team aims not only to clarify the construction and dating of dikes, but also to reconstruct the contexts of their origination and their effectiveness in connection with flood sediments. The combined analysis of historical, geomorphological and topographic data allows potential courses of dikes to be identified and studied using geo-archaeological and historical methods.
One of our test sites is located close to the cathedral of Speyer (Palatinate), where written sources record a massive late 11th century AD intervention to protect the cathedral against the water of the Rhine. Corings and geoelectric measurements have been performed to determine the exact location of the flood protection measures taken. A combination of LiDAR-data, archival sources and soil samples has helped to date sediments in the area and provide a deeper understanding of the river's dynamics and its relation to the city of Speyer. The results of our fieldwork, however, do not point to massive flood prevention measures. Instead they suggest that some protection of the cathedral may have been provided by a fluvial channel. The ground of this channel was filled with rubble to slow the flow of water during flooding and thereby diminish the Rhine's erosive force.

Zusammenfassung

Das von der Fritz-Thyssen-Stiftung geförderte interdisziplinäre Forschungsprojekt »Land unter? – Hochwasser und Hochwasserschutz am Oberrhein während des frühen und hohen Mittelalters« hat zum Ziel, auf Grundlage archäologischer, historischer und geomorphologischer Untersuchungen für den Oberrhein zwischen Strasbourg und Mannheim eine regionale Geschichte der Hochwasser und Hochwasserschutzmaßnahmen zu erarbeiten.
Zwar erscheint es uns heute aufgrund der großen Schäden und Gefahren als selbstverständlich, dass Hochwasser schon immer als Problem wahrgenommen wurden – aber war das wirklich so? Auch die kulturelle Wahrnehmung könnte sich geändert haben: Wurde Hochwasser etwa erst zum Problem, als man immer mehr Kapital (z. B. Getreidefelder, Gebäude und andere [kritische] Infrastrukturen) in den Flussauen akkumulierte? Der im Lauf des Hochmittelalters einsetzende Hochwasserschutz wäre dann Ausdruck eines Mentalitätswandels, durch den Hochwasser erst vom Ereignis zum Problem wurden. Zugleich kann der einsetzende Hochwasserschutz auf konzeptionelle Veränderungen im Mensch-Natur-Verhältnis verweisen, indem Naturereignisse nun nicht mehr etwa als Ausdruck göttlichen Willens schlicht hinzunehmen waren, sondern es dem Menschen offenstand, die Natur zu formen und zu kontrollieren.
In diesem Projekt untersuchen wir den Bau von Deichlinien als Indikator für eine Veränderung der kulturellen Wahrnehmung von Hochwasser, die den Aufwand sowohl bei der Planung und Errichtung solcher Großbauprojekte, als auch ihres folgenden Managements rechtfertigte und erforderte. Da die Frequenz und Magnitude von Hochwassern vom regionalen Klima und der Intensität der landwirtschaftlichen Nutzung abhängig sind, treten auch in der Intensität der Hochwasser erhebliche regionale Unterschiede auf. Wir können daher nicht von heutigen Verhältnissen ausgehen, sondern müssen eine Chronologie der regionalen Hochwasserdynamiken anhand geoarchäologischer Untersuchungen rekonstruieren.
Dies sowie die Identifikation früher Deichlinien im Gelände stehen im Mittelpunkt des Projektes. In einem multimethodischen Ansatz möchte das Team nicht nur Aufbau und Datierung dieser Deiche klären, sondern auch Entstehungszusammenhänge und Wirkungsweisen im Kontext mit Hochwassersedimenten rekonstruieren. Verdachtslinien werden zunächst durch die kombinierte Auswertung historischer, geomorphologischer und topographischer Karten identifiziert und anschließend mit geoarchäologischen und historischen Methoden untersucht.
Eines unserer Untersuchungsgebiete befindet sich im Speyerer Domgarten, östlich des Speyerer Doms (Rheinland-Pfalz), wo im späten 11. Jahrhundert n. Chr. gewaltige Steinblöcke errichtet worden sein sollen, um den Dom gegen Rheinhochwasser zu schützen. Zur Lokalisierung dieser mutmaßlichen Hochwasserschutzmaßnahme wurden Rammkernsondierungen und geoelektrische Widerstandstomographien durchgeführt. Darüber hinaus soll die kombinierte Auswertung aus LiDAR-Daten, archivalischen Quellen und Altersdatierungen (^{14}C-Datierungen) organischen Materials aus den Sedimentproben ein tieferes Verständnis der fluvialen Dynamik im Gebiet des Speyerer Domgartens liefern.
Allerdings erbrachten die durchgeführten Geländearbeiten keinen Hinweis auf einen massiven Hochwasserschutz, sondern die Verfüllung einer im Domgarten detektierten fluvialen Rinne mit Bauschutt könnte bei Hochwasser die Fließgeschwindigkeit und damit die Erosionskraft des Rheins an dieser Stelle möglicherweise wirksam herabgesetzt und zum Schutz des Doms beigetragen haben.

LIST OF CONTRIBUTORS

Éric Armynot du Châtelet
LOG-UMR 8187
Maître de conférences – Université de Lille 1
Bâtiment SN5
F - 59655 Villeneuve d'Asq Cedex
eric.armynot@univ-lille1.fr

Rémy Arthuis
LARA-UMR 6566 CReAAH
Inrap Grand-Ouest
4 rue du Tertre
F - 44477 Carquefou Cedex
remy.arthuis@inrap.fr

Sylvain Aumard
Centre d'Études Médiévales
3 place du Coche d'Eau
F - 89000 Auxerre
sylvain.aumard@cem-auxerre.fr

Mathias Blobel
D - 91625 Schnelldorf
mathiasblobel@gmx.de

Guillaume Bruniaux
Université de la Rochelle
UMR 7266 LIENSs, CNRS
2 rue Olympe-de-Gouges
F - 17000 La Rochelle
guillaume.bruniaux@univ-lr.fr

Sascha Bütow
Zentrum für Mittelalterausstellungen
Otto-von-Guericke-Str. 68-73
D - 39104 Magdeburg
buetow@mittelalterausstellungen.de

Adrien Camus
Université de la Rochelle
AGPhy vaLoR – ADERA
UMR 7266 LIENSs, CNRS
2 rue Olympe-de-Gouges
F - 17000 La Rochelle
adrien.camus@univ-lr.fr

Julien Cavero
Labex TransferS, École normale supérieure
29 rue d'Ulm
F - 75230 Paris Cedex 05
juliencavero@lgp.cnrs.fr

Morgane Cayre
EVEHA Poitiers
Route de Larnay
La Tardiverie
F - 86580 Biard
morgane.cayre@eveha.fr

Arjan Conijn
Ruprecht-Karls-Universität Heidelberg
Institut für Ur- und Frühgeschichte und Vorderasiatische Archäologie
Sandgasse 7
D - 69117 Heidelberg
arjan.conijn@gmail.com

Annie Dumont
Ministère de la Culture
DRASSM and ARTEHIS UMR 6298
6 boulevard Gabriel
F - 21000 Dijon
annie.dumont@u-bourgogne.fr

Peter Ettel
Friedrich-Schiller-Universität Jena
Philosophische Fakultät
Institut für Orientalistik, Indogermanistik und Ur- und Frühgeschichtliche Archäologie
Löbdergraben 24a
D - 07743 Jena
p.ettel@uni-jena.de

Camille Faisse
UMR 5140, CNRS, MCC
Université Paul-Valéry Montpellier
Route de Mende
F - 34000 Montpellier
fcamille@live.fr

Clément Flaux
UMR 5140, CNRS, MCC
Université Paul-Valéry Montpellier
Route de Mende
F - 34000 Montpellier
flaux.clement@gmail.com

Marion Foucher
Université de Bourgogne Franche-Comté
ARTEHIS UMR 6298
6 boulevard Gabriel
F - 21000 Dijon
marion.foucher@u-bourgogne.fr

Axelle Ganne
UMR 6566 CReAAH
Université de Rennes 1
2 rue du Thabor
F - 35000 Rennes

Evelyne Goubert
Laboratoire Geosciences-Océan – UMR 6538
Maître de conférences – Université de Bretagne Sud
Campus de Tohannic
Rue André Lwoff BP 573
F - 56017 Vannes Cedex
evelyne.goubert@univ-ubs.fr

David Gucker
Inrap
28 rue Fulton
F - 51100 Reims
david.gucker@inrap.fr

Romain Guichon
Archeodunum SA / UMR 5138
En Crausaz 10
CH - 1124 Gollion
r.guichon@archeodunum.ch

David Guitton
Inrap
HeRMA EA 3811
122 rue de la Bugellerie
Zone République III
F - 86000 Poitiers
david.guitton@inrap.fr

Marc Guyon
Inrap Auvergne – Rhône-Alpes
UMR 7299 – Centre Camille Jullian – CNRS
12 rue Louis Maggiorini
F - 69500 Bron
marc.guyon@inrap.fr

Marie-Pierre Jézégou
DRASSM
147 plage de l'Estaque
F - 13016 Marseille
marie-pierre.jezegou@culture.gouv.fr

Émilie Jouhet
Inrap
28 rue Fulton
F - 51100 Reims
emilie.jouhet@inrap.fr

Lars Kröger
Deutsches Schifffahrtsmuseum
Leibniz-Institut für Maritime Geschichte
Hans-Scharoun-Platz 1
D - 27568 Bremerhaven
kroeger@dsm.museum

Janine Lange
Ruprecht-Karls-Universität Heidelberg
Geographisches Institut
Im Neuenheimer Feld 348
D - 69120 Heidelberg
janine.lange@uni-heidelberg.de

Thomas Liebert
Schwalbenhof 4
D - 90574 Roßtal
thomas.liebert@archkonzept.com

Bertil Mächtle
Ruprecht-Karls-Universität Heidelberg
Heidelberg Center for the Environment und
Geographisches Institut
Im Neuenheimer Feld 348
D - 69120 Heidelberg
bertil.maechtle@uni-heidelberg.de

Vivien Mathé
Université de la Rochelle
UMR 7266 LIENSs, CNRS
2 rue Olympe-de-Gouges
F - 17000 La Rochelle
vivien.mathe@univ-lr.fr

Thomas Meier
Ruprecht-Karls-Universität Heidelberg
Heidelberg Center for the Environment und
Institut für Ur- und Frühgeschichte und Vorderasiatische Archäologie
Sandgasse 7
D - 69117 Heidelberg
thomas.meier@zaw.uni-heidelberg.de

Frédéric Mercier
Pôle de recherche archéologique
114 boulevard Michelet
F - 44000 Nantes
frederic.mercier@nantesmetropole.fr

Laure Meunier
ARC-Nucléart, CEA
17 rue des Martyrs
F - 38054 Grenoble Cedex 9
laure.meunier@cea.fr

Jimmy Mouchard
Université de Nantes
UMR 6566 CReAAH – LARA
Bâtiment Tertre – Aile B2 – RDJ – Bureau 919
Chemin de la Censive du Tertre BP 81227
F - 44312 Nantes Cedex 3
jimmy.mouchard@univ-nantes.fr

Philippe Moyat
ETSMC & UMR 6298 ARTEHIS
6 boulevard Gabriel
F - 21000 Dijon
philippe.moyat@wanadoo.fr

Hartmut Müller
i3mainz – Institute for Spatial Information and Surveying Technology
Hochschule Mainz – University of Applied Sciences
Lucy-Hillebrand-Str. 2
D - 55128 Mainz
hartmut.mueller@hs-mainz.de

Sébastien Nieloud-Muller
Sorbonne Université
Faculté des Lettres
UMR 8167 – Orient & Méditerranée
7 rue Michelet
F - 75006 Paris
sebastien.nieloud-muller@sorbonne-universite.fr

Iris Nießen
Karolinenstr. 18
D - 96049 Bamberg
niessen.iris@web.de

Lumír Poláček
The Czech Academy of Sciences
Institute of Archaeology
Čechyňská 363/19
CZ - 602 00 Brno
polacek@arub.cz

Philippe Rollet
Inrap
28 rue Fulton
F - 51100 Reims
phirollet51@gmail.com

Corinne Sanchez
CNRS, ASM, Archéologie des Sociétés Méditerranéennes
UMR 5140, CNRS, MCC
Université Paul-Valéry Montpellier
Route de Mende
F - 34000 Montpellier
corinne.sanchez@cnrs.fr

Jan Trachet
Universiteit Gent
Sint-Pieternieuwstraat 35
B - 9000 Ghent
jan.trachet@ugent.be

Lukas Werther
Eberhard Karls Universität Tübingen
Abteilung für Archäologie des Mittelalters
Schloss Hohentübingen
D - 72070 Tübingen
lukas.werther@uni-tuebingen.de

Doris Wollenberg
Friedrich-Schiller-Universität Jena
Philosophische Fakultät
Institut für Orientalistik, Indogermanistik und Ur- und Frühgeschichtliche Archäologie
Löbdergraben 24a
D - 07743 Jena
doris.wollenberg@uni-jena.de / doriswollenberg@gmx.de

Carsten Zube
Ruprecht-Karls-Universität Heidelberg
Geographisches Institut
Im Neuenheimer Feld 348
D - 69120 Heidelberg
carsten.zube@gmx.de